BRIEF CONTENTS

DETAILED CONTENTS

PART II   **Studying Everyday Conversations   169**

CHAPTER 4
Identifying Communities   171

CHAPTER 5
Analyzing Everyday Conversations   200

CHAPTER 6
Writing in Ethnographic Genres   240

Additional Readings   285

What are the sources of our strengths as writers? Where do we begin to learn to use language in interesting and powerful ways? Some of us might point to a specific moment of classroom instruction in writing, others to the reading we've done. But for all of us, it's the conversations we've been in, the talk that has gone on in our most comfortable and familiar settings, that has contributed the most to what we know about how to communicate effectively within a particular setting.

Exploring Literacy presents a model of literacy situated in the ongoing practices of communities and the experiences of readers and writers within them. College writers, especially at the beginning of their studies, are in the process of developing new social identities both outside and inside the classroom—through the friendships they form, the activities they engage in, the courses they choose, and the majors they'll pursue. In the process, they are acquiring a variety of new literacy practices associated with each of these worlds. Here they are invited to explore their own experience of some of these communities, identities, and practices while acquiring and using the ways of reading and writing that have been shaped by the needs and concerns of the academic communities they are entering.

While the thematic focus of *Exploring Literacy* is on conversations and discourse communities, the pedagogical focus is on inquiry. If we want our students to discover and to be excited about the very sorts of things that we've discovered in the field of composition, we need to invite them to make their own inquiries into the linguistic worlds they inhabit. *Exploring Literacy* provides an inquiry-based approach to the study of how communication goes on effectively within communities—private and public, informal and formal, nonacademic and academic. In each chapter, a topic is explored through three types of inquiry: reading, observation, and reflection. The three parts of the book guide students through extended explorations that are based in reading and reflection, in the observation and data gathering of ethnographic field research, and in the extension of field research through library research.

Exploring Literacy combines elements of a reader, a rhetoric, a guide to field and library research, and a handbook. As a reader, it offers selections of memoirs, ethnographic writings, and studies of academic settings by both student and professional writers and researchers—readings that you can select and organize your course around, much as you would with any other reader. As a rhetoric it offers guidance to readers and writers about the ways in which they might proceed and an introduction to some of the shapes and forms—the genres—they might encounter as readers and work in as writers. As a research guide, it highlights the role of inquiry in all reading, writing, and learning, while introducing common approaches to field research and library research. As a handbook, it provides the guidelines for editing, using quotations, and documenting sources that are needed by writers who are doing the sort of work outlined here.

The organization of the book offers three related but different extended units of work that can be used together or spread across a two-semester sequence. Each part builds on a sequence of informal, exploratory writings based on reading, observation and analysis, and reflection toward the shaping of a larger more formal piece of writing within a defined genre. In addition, each chapter offers prompts for writing in other relevant essay genres.

Part I, Writing About Personal Discourse Communities, invites student writers to work in the genre of the memoir, the genre most commonly used for recalling the past and reflecting on its significance in the present, and to read the memoirs of other writers about language and literacy experiences within particular discourse communities while writing their own. While more confident and accomplished writers have found it valuable to move through this work somewhat quickly, Part 1 has been used effectively as a semester-long curriculum for writers who are still developing more basic skills.

In Part II, Studying Everyday Conversations, chapters, readings, and prompts guide students through the study of familiar discourse communities of their choice outside of the formal academic context, as they read ethnographic studies of communication in several different settings and write their own ethnographic reports. Students observe speech acts and speech genres, literacy acts and literacy genres in the setting they choose; they tape and transcribe conversations among friends, family members, roommates, or team-members, in their apartments, their workplaces or churches, or they make a permanent copy of on-line instant-messaging conversations or chat-room discussions or game exchanges.

Part III, Participating in Academic Conversations, explores the ways in which the classroom communities of introductory courses invite students into the shared understandings, interests, and questions of disciplinary communities (or of technical or professional communities). It guides students to apply methods of field inquiry to studying the discourse community created in one of their courses across the disciplines, and to exploring the ways in which that immediate community is connected to the wider culture of the field as represented in examples of its published scholarship (or public writing). It presents two options for development of this field and library research into a final report: an ethnographic report supported by insights about the larger academic discourse community from library research, or a library research report that follows a question that has arisen for the researcher through the conversations of the classroom community.

Finally, Part IV, Strategies for Reading, Writing, and Research, presents a range of strategies for students to draw on as participants in the conversations invited by this book and within their classroom communities. It includes specific suggestions for developing effective reading, writing, editing, and research processes in academic settings, ones that we introduce as we move through the chapters of Part I, II, and III. A section on documenting sources provides a brief guide to MLA and APA documentation styles.

The voices of student writers are present throughout the book, in sample responses to prompts within each chapter, in the essays and reports that are included in the readings for Part I, II, and III and in the examples for the strategies of Part IV. They show how students, through their own writing and research, can contribute to the larger conversation that takes place in an academic community. We hope that students will come to understand that, in new academic settings, as in new workplace or social settings, they are always going to be in the process of becoming insiders—that their academic success depends less on an innate ability in one area or another than on their patience with this process, the seriousness yet flexibility with which they engage in it, and the strategies they bring to the talk and writing, the listening and learning—the conversations—that go on there.

A MANUAL FOR TEACHERS

Accompanying *Exploring Literacy* is an Instructor's Manual that draws from the experience of a number of composition instructors who have used these materials with diverse college students at different types of institutions. Cowritten by Eleanor Kutz and Denise McLaughlin, a young composition instructor who began her own teaching using these materials as a graduate student, it is intended particularly to meet the needs of beginning teachers. The Instructor's Manual introduces the theoretical underpinnings for this book in the field of composition and literacy studies and presents some of the practices for teaching reading, writing, and research that have proved effective in composition classrooms. It provides a guide to each chapter of the text, moving through the various inquiries that can provide the structure for the work of a composition course. In the discussion of each chapter, it suggests the key understandings that instructors will want students to develop, the prompts in the text that guide students' work and the purposes these prompts serve, the ways in which other instructors have introduced those prompts and drawn on them in the classroom, and the ways in which they've responded to the writing students have done in response to them. It also suggests additional activities that classes may want to try.

ACKNOWLEDGMENTS

Many colleagues and students have contributed, over the years, to the understandings represented in this book. In particular, I'd like to thank Shirley Brice Heath, who first encouraged us at UMass/Boston to engage our students in the study of the "ways with words" of their own communities (providing the first tape-recorders that we used in that work), and who continues to inspire and support thoughtful and respectful approaches to enhancing the literacies of diverse learners. I'd like to thank Peter Elbow, who served as my first mentor as I turned my own work to the field of composition and who has responded generously to parts of this manuscript, seeing its socially-situated perspective as contributing to his own enterprise of helping student writers draw on the diverse languages and voices they bring to the classroom. I'd also like to thank Jim Gee and other literacy researchers who shared what they were learning about the literacy practices of different communities and worked to theorize the relationships of language, literacy, discourses and social context in many working discussions at the Literacies Institute and UMass/Boston. In addition, Mary Ann Crawford and other members of the College Composition and Communication Language Caucus have offered interest, encouragement, and helpful feedback for this work.

At UMass/Boston, I've been most fortunate to have had as close friends and colleagues, scholars whose understandings in these areas have greatly enhanced my own. These include Vivian Zamel, whose research in ESL composition reinforces the importance of providing the opportunity for second language learners to engage in meaningful ways in the authentic work of the communities they enter, and who has tested parts of this curriculum with her own ESL students as they explore their experiences in writing across the curriculum; Elsa Auerbach, whose research into the literacy practices of families and communities has helped me to further appreciate the richness of the knowledge that all students bring to their classrooms; and Judy Goleman, whose focus on critical reading within the freshman writing curriculum has pushed me to think in much more complex ways about how we invite students into the ways of reading in academic settings. Still other colleagues at UMass and other colleges have taught with and helped shape this curriculum: Ruth Spack, from her own teaching of Part III, has offered valuable refinements of the research prompts and suggested the research memo as a genre of informal writing; Jackie Cornog, who first came to this curriculum as a graduate coteacher for my freshman writing classroom, has continued to think with me, through her teaching at UMass and beyond, about all of its workings in ways that continually enrich my own perceptions. Above all, Denise Paster, a gifted young teacher who has coauthored the instructor's manual that accompanies this text while adapting the curriculum to her own teaching in a two-year technical college, has taught me much about how to put my own pedagogical ideas into practice.

At UMass, I've been even more fortunate to have worked with many enormously talented graduate students and teaching interns, and the following have made particular contributions as we've refined this curriculum and developed its pedagogical approaches: Ava Chan, Brenda D'Alotto, Maura Giles, Keith Halladay, Lisa Kim, Linda Lawrence, Katie Los, Kevin Morrissette, Joe Piazza, Sean O'Connell, Abigail Richardson, Debbie Scaggs, Ryan Schiff, and Asha Tall, as well as Elaine Hays whose classroom conversation appears in Chapter 2.

Our freshman writers have contributed generously as well, helping us to see and understand the rich and complex discourse practices of their own communities, reflecting in open and valuable ways on this curriculum and how it has worked for them, and contributing their own writing and research to the book itself, and I'd like to thank those whose insights, observations, and writings appear here: Leon Babakian, Charles Bazile, Lawrence Bereweiso, Robert Calden, Salina Chan, Lorraine Cecere, Richard Corrente, April Corso, Matt Darois, Dann De Gennaro, Kristen Farmer, Jayme Galiguis, Bryan Gangemi, Erin Gillis, Janna Goldstein, Juliette Houlne, James Jean, Dana Joly, Sophia Kang, Joan Kingsbury, Shayna Krochmal, Mike LeVert, Denise Linane, Abby Lugo, Laysian McDonald, James McDonough, Melissa Marroto, Melissa Mulloy, Matt O'Brien, Obioma Okafor, Vanessa Ortega, Laura Overton-Gersch, John Pappas, Agnes Portaleska, Deni Rico, Reena Schafer, Blanca Shahane, Jessica Smith, Sean Smith, Matt Snow, Karen Thorton, Dina Tsirelson, Jonathon Upton, Pebely Vargas, Jake Wark, and Tom Wimer. And a special thank you to Karen, Melanie, and Shanna for their patience in allowing me to tape and study so many of their childhood conversations.

Many readers have contributed to the shape of the final manuscript through their careful and sustained comments on the project at various stages. I'm grateful for their time and commitment to the book. Thanks to: Ellen Barton, Wayne State University; Anne Beaufort, SUNY-Stony Brook; Cynthia Cox, Belmont University; Mary Ann Crawford, Central Michigan University; Susan DeRosa, Eastern Connecticut State University; Janet Eldred, University of Kentucky; Chris Gallagher, University of Nebraska; Robin Cartwright Gallagher, Ohio University; Susan Hanson, Ohio State University; Amy Hawkins, Columbia College; Georgina Hill, Western Michigan University; Glenn Hutchinson, UNC-Charlotte; Carrie Leverenz, Texas Christian University; Laurence Musgrave, Saint Xavier University; Priscilla Perkins, Roosevelt University; Stephen Price, Mississippi College; David Seitz, Wright State University; Mark Shadle, Eastern Oregon University; and Terry Myers Zawacki, George Mason University.

I want particularly to thank my editors, Lynn Huddon, whose sustained support of this project made it possible, and Michael Greer, whose rich understanding of the project made him a great person to think with through the final development of the manuscript.

Finally, thank you to my family and friends, and especially to my husband Ron Thornton, for their patience with and continuing support for my endeavors.

ELEANOR KUTZ
University of Massachusetts–Boston

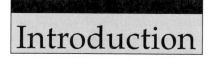

Introduction

Writers, Conversations, and Contexts

Exploring Literacy begins by introducing you to a new way of thinking about writing—as a kind of conversation. The idea that writing is a conversation forms the groundwork for the book and shapes the way it is organized. The reading and writing strategies presented in Parts 1, 2, and 3 all build from this starting point.

Perhaps you have come to view writing as a solitary process. Certainly writing can be lonely and difficult, especially when you imagine what it feels like to be staring at a blank page or screen trying to come up with things to say. This book asks you to think about writing differently, as a conversation. Conversations are social exchanges, a give-and-take process in which participants shift from talking to listening and back many times. What if we think of writing as a similar kind of exchange?

This question leads to a series of inquiries that guide our approach in this book. An *inquiry* is an ongoing investigation, an exploration that shapes how we look at and think about a set of issues or problems—in this case, how to develop and improve as writers. Our key question— *What happens when we view writing as a conversation?*—leads to several others; these questions make up what we'll call the *inquiry strands* that tie each part of this book together. Our main inquiry suggests several other questions that we'll explore in this introduction:

- How are conversations shaped by the settings in which they take place?

- How might exploring conversations and their contexts help us as writers to draw on our rich experience with communication in a variety of settings?

- What might be some of the ways in which we, as writers, are influenced by the voices we've heard and the conversations we've taken part in?

We'll start by reading an author who explores questions like these, prompting you to consider some of the ways you'll be participating as a writer and a reader in the conversations invited by this book. Then we'll look ahead, with an overview of the book and the types of reading and writing we'll engage in. Finally, we'll look at an excerpt from a spoken conversation, in order to identify some key concepts that we can apply to both written and spoken conversations.

Think of who you are, at this moment, as a writer. Each time you enter a new setting, you bring with you a unique history that includes all of the voices you have heard and used as a speaker and a listener, a reader and a writer. When you enter a conversation or a situation that is new, like a college writing class, you bring to it bits and pieces from all of the other conversations you have participated in before, especially those where you have felt most comfortable and at home. Those past conversations are an important resource for all writers as they move from one setting to another.

READING ABOUT CONVERSATIONS AND WRITERS

As a young writer in college, I was aware I had to find my voice, but how was I to know it would be the voice I used at home, the one I acquired as a result of one English-speaking mother and one Spanish-speaking father? —**Sandra Cisneros, author of *The House on Mango Street***

Well-known writers are often asked how they became writers—what they had to learn and how they learned it. Many times their responses are much like the one Sandra Cisneros offers: they had to read and write a lot, but in addition, to their surprise, they had to appreciate and draw on the voices they had been hearing around them throughout their lives.

When you think about yourself as a writer, what comes to mind first? Do you recall the writing you've done for English classes, and the comments you've received? Do you think first of "rules"—for how to organize a paper or punctuate a sentence? Or do you think, as Cisneros gradually learned to do, about the ways in which you see and talk about the world, and how those ways have been influenced by the voices of your home, church, or friends? Do you remember moments in which what you wrote or read reflected real conversations, real instances of communication, whether in school or out?

In school, writing has generally been treated as a separate category of activity from other communication, requiring specialized knowledge about forms and structures without much sense of how these "rules" of writing might contribute to a real written conversation. As a result, to gain confidence in the power of their writing to communicate, many writers, like Cisneros, have had to rediscover what they already knew from the world outside of school—from the many different communities where they are already effective participants in the conversation, whether those conversations go on in speaking or in writing.

Reading as Conversation

Although we don't tend to think of reading as conversation, it is like our spoken conversations in that an exchange takes place (even though it is in the reader's head) between what the writer has written and the ways that the reader responds and reacts. (At the same time, the writer has tried to anticipate a reader's reactions and responses—to say things that readers will think about and be able to connect with.) As a reader, you typically step into such conversations with questions—wondering what the writer will have to say to you, whether you'll be interested, and whether you know anything that might connect to what the writer is saying. Such questioning—such inquiry—makes you an active participant in the conversation, not just a passive receiver of some information a writer has passed on. To highlight that active role, read what Cisneros writes in the following brief excerpt from "Ghosts and Voices." In that memoir, she describes her poor and "solitary" childhood. Living with her parents and six brothers in "a cramped apartment," she turned to books for companionship; later, as a writer, she turned away at first from the world in which she grew up. As a beginning college writer, she didn't know that she could draw on the voice she'd used at home, a voice she had acquired from her English-speaking mother and Spanish-speaking father.

> My mother's English was learned in the Mexican/Italian neighborhood she grew up in on Chicago's near south side, an English learned from playmates and school, since her own parents spoke Spanish exclusively. My father, on the other hand, spoke to us in a Spanish of grandmothers and children, a language embroidered with the diminutive. . . .
>
> These two voices at odds with each other—my mother's punch-you-in-the-nose English and my father's powdered-sugar Spanish—curiously are the voices that surface in my writing. . . .
>
> It wasn't until Iowa University and the Writer's Workshop that I began writing in the voice I now write in, and, perhaps if it hadn't been for Iowa I wouldn't have made the conscious decision to write this way, . . . What did I know except third-floor flats? Surely my classmates knew nothing about that. That's precisely what I chose to write: about third floor flats, and fear of rats, and drunk husbands sending rocks through windows, anything as far from the poetic as possible. And this is when I discovered the voice I'd been suppressing all along without realizing it.

Drawing on the passage above, think about the following questions:

READING RESPONSE

According to Cisneros, how has her experience growing up influenced what she writes about and the voice she writes in?

What questions come to mind as you read her comments about finding her voice as a writer?

Are there any ways in which her experience with talking and writing connects with or seems different from your own?

Write a brief, informal response about what you've discovered from reading this passage: the details that struck you and contributed to your understanding of Cisneros's perspective, the questions and ideas that this passage stimulated, and/or the connections and differences that you found between Cisneros's experiences and your own.

Writing as Conversation

Most often our conversations with what we read go on in our heads, and earlier in her memoir, Cisneros suggests that she had many such conversations with the books she read growing up. But our focus is on writing and writers as well as reading and readers, and one way in which writers come to think of themselves as writers is, simply enough, by writing—by putting some of those comments and ideas that would otherwise stay in their heads onto paper. Much of the time they do this in a very informal and exploratory way, often in a diary or private journal that they keep for themselves. But a private journal doesn't bring writing back into a larger conversation until the writer chooses to make it public (maybe not for a whole lifetime). In order for writing to be part of an ongoing conversation within a community of readers and writers, it needs to be shared with others, so that you're most often writing for real readers.

This book follows two guiding principles:

- Much of what we need to know as writers is an extension of what we already know as speakers. Our fundamental competence in using language to communicate is being developed continually through all of our interactions, in talk as well as in writing.
- When we write something that other people will read, we are indeed carrying on written conversations that are both similar to and different from the conversations we've been having all our lives.

LOOKING AHEAD

The Organization of This Book

This book is organized to take advantage of what you already know from all of the worlds in which you've been communicating most comfortably. Although its goal is to help you write effectively in college, for academic purposes, it doesn't begin with the "rules" for writing papers for college classes (because there isn't a simple set of rules to use). Instead, it is designed to do two things: to help you discover or rediscover the resources you bring to any new writing situation from all of your other experiences with communication and conversation in many different settings; and to help you see how to use these resources to become an effective writer for new situations you enter—particularly the academic settings represented by different college classes. It invites you to explore all of the underpinnings of your own *literacy*—all of the complex activities of speaking, listening, reading, and writing that you draw on in different settings—and to explore the ways that these activities are drawn together in the particular forms of *academic literacy* practiced in different college courses.

The book is organized in three parts, moving from explorations that focus on your past experience talking and writing in communities, to your current experience as an insider to the conversations of informal, nonacademic communities, and then to your developing "insiderness" in the academic communities formed by your introductory courses. Each part is designed to guide you into a particular area of inquiry, and each will include a set of chapters that build on each other to guide you through one writing project.

Part 1 invites you to reflect on your experience in the communities of your past. In it, your inquiry will focus on the theme of language and social identity and the ways in which your experience with talk and writing in different settings has shaped who you are, at this moment, as a writer and a learner. You'll remember and reflect on some of your own familiar settings and the conversations that have taken place in them. You'll read and respond to memoirs that others have written about their own past experience in particular settings and how those experiences have influenced them in the present. You'll also work toward writing a memoir of your own.

Part 2 invites you to explore an informal, familiar community. Here, you'll focus on a setting—with friends or family, in a gym, a workplace, or a dorm, for example—where you're currently an insider, to learn more about what insider communication looks like in a specific context. You'll look at the conversations and the various types of exchanges that go on in the setting you've chosen, and you'll see what you can discover about the shared knowledge, purposes and ways of the participants. You'll read ethnographic reports written by researchers who have studied other settings and communities, as well as other examples of writing about such communities, and you'll work toward writing your own ethnographic report of your field research.

Part 3 invites you to focus on one of your other courses, looking at classroom conversations and at other elements of the course, and seeing how the course works to introduce you to the conversations of the field it represents. You'll read other studies of such communities, and you'll also do library research, discovering something about what insiders to the field study and write about. You'll work toward writing a final report for this unit that will draw on either field research or library research, or both.

Within each part, chapters will include several common elements:

- guiding questions about an area of inquiry related to the relationship between reading, writing, and the experience of spoken and written conversations in different settings;
- a reading or readings that contribute to the area of inquiry;
- a related observational inquiry into the ways in which a spoken or written conversation or your role in such conversations is carried out;
- a reflective inquiry that guides you to step back and consider larger patterns over multiple examples and experiences;
- a background discussion of the concepts and ideas that are useful in exploring these questions, the issues they raise, and ways of approaching these inquiries;

■ some examples from other students' inquiry into the question, to give you a picture of what other college writers have discovered through these activities;

■ end-of-chapter suggestions for exploratory essays that will guide you in giving more coherent shape to your ideas and in thinking about the genres of academic writing and the expectations of readers in academic settings.

In addition, the chapters will point to some specific *strategies* that will be useful to you as a reader, writer, or researcher. Because these strategies are ones that you may draw on repeatedly in your work for this and other courses, they appear in a separate "Strategies" section (Part 4). You may want to look quickly through that section before you begin to work with this book. Then you can more easily return to it and make use of its suggestions in future reading, writing, and research assignments.

Much of the writing suggested in each chapter will consist of informal responses of the sort that you wrote after reading about Cisneros's early experience—responses that allow you to follow out your thinking in an exploratory way. These informal written responses are divided into three types. Sometimes the suggestions for these responses will focus on connections you might make between something you've read and an aspect of your own experience; in that case they'll be identified with the label *reading response*. Sometimes they'll ask you to observe the conversations and other aspects of the world around you directly; they'll be named *observation account* (or in Part 2 and 3, *research memo*). Sometimes they'll ask you to step back and reflect on the patterns you're finding across a number of readings, observations, or experiences with the spoken or written conversations of different communities; informal writing of this type will be labeled *reflective inquiry*. The suggestions for these types of informal writing will typically ask you to engage directly with the texts you read or the details you observe or remember. They'll suggest bringing some of the words of the text or the details of the observation or memory into the response you write and into the conversation you'll be having with your readers, so that those readers can see both what you're thinking about and how you're thinking about it. But they won't focus on a particular structure or format (as the book's suggestions for formal essays and reports may do). Rather, your informal writing responses will be a place to follow out your ideas freely, in an extended way, to work through an analysis, or to report in a preliminary way on what you're finding, before you begin to worry about the final organization and presentation of those ideas for a particular audience.

The Classroom Community

As you engage in the ongoing work of the classroom—asking and answering questions, reading and writing, and sharing your perspectives and discoveries with the other student writers in your classroom—you'll create a common and shared (and continually developing and changing) backdrop of understandings from which each new phase of inquiry will begin.

Discussions in the classroom—in groups or as a whole class—can help to support the understandings that can guide your work as a reader, writer, and researcher because they allow you to compare responses and to discover what they have in common. They allow you to see what everyone's assumptions are as you undertake a particular task, to see how different writers have approached particular activities of reading and writing, or to see what common elements appear across the varied experiences these writers have had and are having in different communities. Your informal writing will allow you to generate ideas to bring back to your classroom community. As you share that writing, you'll be contributing to an ongoing classroom conversation about what can be learned from the range of your experiences and responses as writers, readers, and participants in different communities. You'll also be creating a community of writers.

To connect your classroom community to a larger world of college writers, this book also includes some responses to these inquiries that other writers from other classrooms have already shared. Much writing done in academic settings depends on such sharing among peers—among those who are reading, writing, and carrying out research on similar topics in similar ways, and who read and critique each other's work as equal participants in the same enterprise. Shared *student voices*, both those included in this book and those of other writers in your classroom, will give you a chance to see the connections that others make and the ways they draw from their own observations and experiences.

In the Student Voices box are some points of contact that other writers who've read and written about Cisneros's experience have discovered. Their responses may help you make further connections of your own.

STUDENT VOICES

As you read the responses of other writers, what connections do you find between their responses and your own? To what extent did you pick up on similar aspects of Cisneros's experience? On different aspects?

Finding out who I am has shown to be the one thing I cannot do. Over the past two years I have struggled for an identity. I compare myself to my six closest friends who all seemed to know who they are. As my closest friend joined the Armed Forces and another moved halfway across the world, I wondered why haven't I found who I am and what I am going to do.

Cisneros's life seems similar as she searched for her voice. She struggled with it for a long time, and didn't find it until a writers' workshop at Iowa University. The thing that really interests me is her voice makes so much sense. How could she possibly write in a voice of prestigious private schools or big houses? She couldn't! All it took for her to find her voice and how she wanted to express herself is to realize the life she had lived in the past.

(continued)

(continued)

I have yet to find my voice and how I want to express myself and that is the other component of this essay that grabbed me as I read it. I am not sure if my answer lies in my past, present or future. **(Tom)**

Sandra Cisneros struggled growing up. She lived in poverty and fear, things she thought were not worth writing about. What she didn't realize until college was that there were other aspects of her life and experiences that were worth writing about because they were unique and interesting. Growing up in Newton, Massachusetts which has a strong Jewish community, I did not feel unique when I had to miss school on the high holidays or when my grandmother spoke to me in Yiddish in front of all my friends. I also did not think it was worth talking about my most sacred day, Yom Kippur, because it is a gloomy day with fasting and praying and repenting. However, now after experimenting with other religions and ethnicities and rebelling on my high holidays, I realize my culture and my sacred day are unique and worthy. Just like Cisneros did not think tiny, dirty apartments were worth writing about, I did not think Yom Kippur was worth writing about. But it is different for my family and I than most. My father is the cantor on high holidays so we go and sit in the front row at temple and everyone knows us and my dad is in the spotlight. I do not mind fasting and praying all day because it is cleansing me of my sins and bringing me closer to G-d. I am lucky I have that day. I love that my Bubby teaches me Yiddish and tells me stories of Poland. I feel proud to be in my family and related to such courage as my great aunts and uncles displayed giving their lives in the Holocaust. Cisneros is correct, our stories are worth sharing not just because they are interesting but because they help us all to learn things we did not know before. Although Sandra Cisneros will never understand the feelings of being middle class and Jewish, she can still gain insight and knowledge about that. I will never know the life of a Mexican-American with six brothers and tiny apartments but after reading her story, I do feel the pain she went through and have gained insight into her loneliness. One's life and more importantly one's feelings are always unique and worth writing about. **(Janna)**

The Course and the Syllabus

While this book will provide a useful guide to the work you'll do in your writing course, that work will be supported by everything that is present in your college writing class: your teacher, the other students, the syllabus, and any other materials that are brought into the course, including whatever you and your classmates contribute and produce. Although the inquiry process—the reading, writing, and research you'll engage in—will take place within some structured guidelines and directions, the context in which you will be carrying it out will continually be reshaped by what you're learning from those very activities.

The expected workings of a course are typically spelled out in a *syllabus*. A syllabus is a formal institutional genre—a contract of sorts between you and your teacher. Most syllabi offer a sense of the underlying philosophy or orientation of the course, the goals of the course, and the place of particular kinds of work in meeting those goals, as well as information about evaluation—about how the teacher will determine whether the student has met the learning goals that are spelled out. A syllabus also typically includes attendance policies, information on texts and readings, assignment due dates, information about the instructor's office hours, and other details relevant to the smooth working of the course. It may also include a statement supporting access for students with disabilities, with information about where and how support is provided at that institution. Sharing your understandings of what you've learned from looking through the book and the syllabus is a good way to start the conversations of your classroom community.

Quickly scan this book, looking at:

    the table of contents;

    the setup of chapters;

    the sorts of headings that appear;

    additional features like an index.

OBSERVATION ACCOUNT

You'll not only be a reader of this book, but you're likely to move around in it, to refer back to concepts and explanations that have gone before or to look ahead to plan for work you'll be doing. From scanning the book, how would you describe how it's set up and structured? What questions do you have about how it's set up and how you'll use it? From reading this introduction so far, what questions do you have about the work that's been described?

Then look at the syllabus or course overview from your writing course. What does it tell you about the goals of the course, work you'll be doing, how the course will be structured, and how your work will be assessed? What other information does it give you? What questions do you have about the course after a careful reading of the syllabus? Are there any terms or is there any other information that you don't understand or are uncertain about?

After examining these two texts, what questions do you want to bring back to your classroom community about the work you'll be doing this semester?

BRINGING PRIOR EXPERIENCE TO YOUR PRESENT COMMUNITY

In her memoir, Cisneros reflects on her prior experience in the community she grew up in. She has also drawn on that experience and represented it in fictional form in many of the novels and short stories she has written. "My Name," from *The House on Mango Street*, about a fictional girl with a fictional name, is strongly rooted in the real conversations and experiences from Cisneros's own childhood. Names say a lot about how different communities have contributed to aspects of your present identity. One way to begin an exploration of what you've drawn from your past experiences in different communities is by reflecting on how you were named and what you've been called and have called yourself in different places and at different times.

My Name

Sandra Cisneros

1   In English my name means hope. In Spanish it means too many letters. It means sadness, it means waiting. It is like the number nine. A muddy color. It is the Mexican records my father plays on Sunday mornings when he is shaving, songs like sobbing.

It was my great-grandmother's name and now it is mine. She was a horse woman too, born like me in the Chinese year of the horse—which is supposed to be bad luck if you're born female—but I think this is a Chinese lie because the Chinese, like the Mexicans, don't like their women strong.

My great-grandmother, I would've liked to have known her, a wild horse of a woman, so wild she wouldn't marry. Until my great-grandfather threw a sack over her head and carried her off. Just like that, as if she were a fancy chandelier. That's the way he did it.

And the story goes she never forgave him. She looked out the window her whole life, the way so many women sit their sadness on an elbow. I wonder if she made the best with what she got or was she sorry because she couldn't be all the things she wanted to be. Esperanza. I have inherited her name, but I don't want to inherit her place by the window.

5   At school they say my name funny as if the syllables were made out of tin and hurt the roof of your mouth. But in Spanish my name is made out of a softer something, like silver, not quite as thick as sister's name—Magdalena—which is uglier than mine. Magdalena who at least can come home and become Nenny. But I am always Esperanza.

I would like to baptize myself under a new name, a name more like the real me, the one nobody sees. Esperanza as Lisandra or Maritza or Zeze the X. Yes. Something like Zeze the X will do.

REFLECTIVE INQUIRY   After reading, "My Name," by Sandra Cisneros, think back over your own experience with your name, and what you'd be willing to share with others in your class about that experience.

Is there a story you might tell about your given name, or about any aspect of naming in your life (perhaps a family history of the name you were given, or an experience that led you to more often use another name if not your given name)?

Are you sometimes in a setting where you're called by a different name (a more formal name, a more informal nickname or pet name) from the one you use in school settings? If so, what is the setting and why is what you're called there appropriate to that setting but different from how you're known (or want to be known) in the classroom?

Sharing your responses with a partner and then your class is a good way to get to know each others' names and begin to create a new community in the classroom.

Reflection on prior experience can play an important role as you enter new settings. One way to become a more effective writer or speaker in any community is to just hang around that community long enough so that you gradually acquire its ways. But that takes a long time—longer than most people have to spare. It's possible to push the process, to make it go faster, by relying on the very thing that education is good at—using the opportunity to step out of a situation, to study it, to see what makes it work, and to apply what you learn in a systematic way. It's a matter of not only knowing things, but knowing <u>that</u> you know them and <u>how</u> you know them—something that you can begin to see as you make connections between what you know and do in one situation and what you know and do in another.

Here's a brief example, a reflection from a student writer after she had completed the inquiries set forth in this book.

> I found that as a writer I have several different personalities. Being a part of several discourse communities (Home—African-American, urban setting, School—psychology major, Work—Human Resources, Mission Hill Summer Program) has given me the ability to see things from different perspectives. When you are a part of different discourse communities, which most people are, you learn a lot about yourself and your life. I also found that I could write in different ways for different settings. And when I listened to and read the transcription from a conversation I saw how versatile I was. **(Kristen)**

With the term "versatile," this writer has found her own powerful concept to name what she has learned about herself through the work of her freshman writing course. In recognizing the value of *versatility*—the ability to adapt her ways of talking and ways of writing so that she can participate effectively in different settings—she has generated for herself a larger understanding about an important aspect of the competence that she brings to and continues to develop through her participation in each new setting.

Understandings like these connect two processes: *inquiry* and *reflection*. *Inquiry* most often involves trying to find out about something that interests you: asking questions and engaging in activities that can help you to find possible answers, such as reading or observation. As a student engaging in a process of inquiry, Kristen tried to learn more about what let her be an insider to several communities. She did this by observing what went on in those communities and discovering the sorts of implicit understandings she had gained by being part of them. *Reflective inquiry* on the other hand, involves stepping back from the activities you've been involved in and trying to think about why they're important and what you can learn from them. It's when she steps back to reflect on what she's discovered that Kristen is able to name a new understanding she's gained about herself in each of these settings. Likewise, Cisneros has stepped back from her usual writing of novels to ask herself, implicitly, "What is it that shaped me as a writer?" and she has tried to answer that question by reflecting on her past experiences.

Understandings like the one Kristen has come to, because they come from stepping out of the level of daily activity and immediate situations and looking at multiple examples of those activities and situations from a higher level, are sometimes referred to as *meta-level understandings*. Imagine, for instance, that you observed someone guiding a soccer team, someone helping a high school student prepare for SATs, and someone working with a singer who wanted to develop a new repertoire. While you might apply the term "coaching" to each of these activities, it's only after stepping back (or stepping up a level) and thinking of all three activities at once that you can perceive the elements of all three activities that allow one common concept to represent them all.

Meta-level understandings and concepts apply across situations. They're typically gained through a combination of activity and reflection—through first stepping into a situation to participate in whatever ways are appropriate to it, and then stepping back out of the situation to think about what it was like, what you and others did while you were in the situation, and why you did what you did—and to see what different actions in different situations might have in common.

REFLECTIVE INQUIRY

Consider what understandings you bring to your work as a writer from your experience in prior conversations, both spoken and written, in various settings.

What are some of the settings for conversations that you think played a significant role in your life over the years? In which did you feel most fluent, most able to engage in the conversation (in speaking or in writing) in a comfortable way? Who were the participants in these conversations? What roles did they (and you) play? What sorts of things were typically talked about? What do you remember of those conversations, and what do you think you bring from them into your present life and into your present writing?

Write a reflective response in which you explore your experiences with conversations, whether spoken or written. What can you bring to the new conversation of your writing class from your past experiences and what are your hopes and expectations for the new experiences the class might offer?

OBSERVING SPOKEN CONVERSATIONS

To begin to build the larger, meta-level understandings about spoken and written conversations that can help guide your work as a writer, it's useful to develop some working concepts that can help guide your exploration. *Working concepts* are tools for thinking. They help you think about a question or a topic by drawing on some key understandings others who have explored that topic have come to. Working concepts capture these understandings with terms that you can apply to new situations and examples. *Conversation*, for example, is a working concept that we'll apply to all of the ways in which people carry out an extended interaction in words, whether spoken or written. Bringing many sorts of interactions under one concept lets us think about what's common to all of them.

Working concepts are created, not by memorizing definitions but by trying to use the concept—applying it to a situation and seeing how it fits and how it might be adjusted. Not everyone agrees on exactly what constitutes a conversation, for example, and people who find the concept useful may nevertheless have slightly different definitions. All of the new terms introduced in this book will be treated as working concepts—as concepts to test and try out, developing a shared understanding with others who are trying to use and apply the concepts in the same ways. You'll want to use these working concepts as intellectual tools that can help you think about particular aspects of the world and of your experience in it.

We can begin this development of working concepts that are useful for writers by considering what might be involved in *conversation*. You may have commented on the quality of the different communicative events you've participated in, saying "We had a great conversation," or "The class was good today," or "I got a really nice letter from Aunt Emma," or "I loved that book. I couldn't put it down." What distinguishes these events from the moments where the conversation is strained, the class is boring, the letter is weird, the book is one that's put down and never finished? Are there common elements to all of these successful "conversations"? We can discover more about conversations by taking a look at a short excerpt from a spoken one—the sort of informal exchange that might have gone on in Cisneros's kitchen when she was younger, or that might have gone on in your own—the conversation of adolescent girls who are sitting around a kitchen table eating pizza. (Later, we'll see the ways in which conversations like this one influenced one of the participants as a freshman writer.)

As you read the transcript of this tape-recorded conversation, you'll probably find it hard to understand what's going on at first. That's in part because we're not generally used to reading transcribed speech—it's not a common genre of writing, and we don't have a familiar template for it that lets us process it easily, the way we would a story or a textbook chapter. We also miss the intonations that convey a lot of the meaning when something is spoken. And we're outsiders to a conversation that takes place among people who know each other well. But even noting what's hard to understand will help you understand how such conversations work.

This conversation took place among three young girls, ages twelve and thirteen, sitting at the kitchen table.

MELANIE: My favorite place to shop . . . is *downtown* Boston.

KAREN: Downtown

MELANIE: They have High Gear down there . . . Fresh stuff . . . They have these shoe boots I want. Combat boot shoes?

KAREN: Oh, those? What do you want?

MELANIE: The low tops.

KAREN: Doc Martens?

SHANNA: Do they call them that?

MELANIE: I don't call them that.

KAREN: Doc Martens is what they call them.

MELANIE: Yeah, I know that's what they call them. I just call them combat boots.

KAREN: My friend has 24 holes, up to here.

SHANNA: She has what?

KAREN: 24 holes.

MELANIE: Holes of what? Shoelace holes?

KAREN: Mmmm. They're called 24's, cause up to here is 24 holes—(gesturing) 16, 9, and 6.

MELANIE: Mine are gonna be to here, for sure.

KAREN: What color, red or black?

MELANIE: Red, black, and orange.

Pause here for a moment and make a few notes for yourself in response to the following questions:

- <u>What</u> are the girls talking about?
- <u>Why</u> do you think they're talking about it?
- What do you notice about how they talk about it—about <u>how</u> the conversation moves from one point to another?
- Is there more you'd like to know about this <u>situation</u>, to help you make better sense of what's going on?

Shared Knowledge, Purpose, and Ways

It's probably clear to you that the girls are talking about where they like to shop and what they want to buy, focusing on a particular style of shoes that they give various names to. But the conversation is not just about the topics they introduce and what they know and can say about those topics. It's also about asserting and shaping their own identities, building and defining their relationship with each other, and doing all of that in a way that makes sense as the conversation evolves—as a text that they're creating together.

In any conversation (spoken or written), in order for successful communication to take place, not only does there have to be a <u>what</u> (something that's talked about), a <u>why</u> (a reason or purpose for talking about it), and a <u>how</u> (a way that the conversation is structured, with one contribution building on another), but each of these elements has to be shared by the participants. We can see how these elements work by looking back at the girls' conversation.

Shared Knowledge (What)

It's impossible to have a conversation unless all of the participants have a reasonable level of shared understanding of what it's about. When people know each other well, they can anticipate what others know or don't know. In face-to-face conversation, they can fill in with more background information if everyone doesn't understand, and they can ask questions if a speaker hasn't told them enough. We can see that the initial lack of shared knowledge is one of the problems in the girls' conversation. Melanie, who is a little older than the other two girls, may be intending to show off her greater knowledge about what's in style, and even that she knows what's in the stores "downtown" where the other girls aren't likely to have shopped. But once the topic of "combat shoe boots" has been introduced, the conversation on that topic can go on only if everyone knows what they are. Much of this conversation is about defining the terms that Melanie has introduced and Karen has added to, until everyone's on the same wave length.

Shared Purpose (_Why_)

In order for each conversation to be successful, there has to be some general agreement among the participants about its purpose. The primary purpose of conversations like this is most often an interpersonal one. For the girls, the most important purpose is just to keep on hanging out together, as friends, and more specifically, in this segment, it's to show what they know and to learn what they need to know about what's in style and how to talk about it as they begin to move into a new identity as teens.

The girls manage the larger _shared purpose_ of maintaining their friendship by sharing what they've learned in other settings with other friends, and bringing those new understandings back to each other— placing them "on the table," in a sense, for everyone to examine. Keeping a friendship going requires some degree of shared understanding about the world, and the girls keep creating this shared understanding in their conversations, but it doesn't really matter what topic they're discussing at any moment, just that they're sitting around together discussing it. Keeping that connection going is the most important purpose here, no matter what the conversation is about.

Shared Process and Ways (_How_)

For conversations to be successful, the participants need to have some sort of shared understanding about how to carry out a conversation in this setting. The biggest issues are how to get a turn to speak and how long a turn you can take, and some of that is determined by pre-existing roles. Among the girls, Melanie, the oldest, is almost always the leader. We can see in the girls' conversation that once a topic has been introduced by Melanie, the other girls stay on that topic, linking their comments to whatever has been said last. No one questions their right to have a turn as long as whatever they say is clearly connected to what has gone before, although when Karen says "24 holes" and neither Shanna nor Melanie knows what she's talking about, she has to explain what she means to both of them, showing them that it's relevant before the conversation continues. Nevertheless, this is a three-way conversation, and everyone gets to jump in and respond to anyone else.

This act of communication is, in the end, successful in several ways: by the end of this segment, all of its participants have a reasonable amount of shared knowledge about the topic they're discussing, they all continue to have a place in a relationship that's maintained through such conversation, and they have once again used what they know about carrying on conversations (taking turns, asking and answering questions) to share that knowledge and maintain that relationship. They still don't necessarily agree about how to name the shoes they're talking about; participants in communities often disagree about such things. But knowing how to participate effectively in a conversation, even to voice disagreements, is a sign of being a competent communicator, and the girls display their *competence* as they carry out this conversation.

Participants in a conversation like this have to pay attention to several things at once. They have to keep track of their own ideas while taking into account what the other participants are likely to know. They have to contribute in ways that will keep the conversation going, even while they try to maintain their own position in this relationship. And they have to do all of this very quickly, in a conversation that's changing all of the time with each new contribution. The girls don't have time to think, consciously, about any of this. Rather, they draw on the implicit knowledge about how to carry on conversations (how to take turns, how to pick up on what someone else has said) that they've gained from all of the conversations they've heard and taken part in for their whole lives. In addition, because they've been friends for years, they also have a great deal of implicit knowledge from their own conversations with each other about each person's likely knowledge, interests, and intentions. They are insiders to this small community, and like any insiders, they know how insiders talk and act without having to think much about it. We'll see that writers, too, need to know how to build shared knowledge and shared purposes with their readers in ways that reflect the shared expectations of participants in the communities they write for.

OBSERVATION ACCOUNT

Try applying these concepts to a conversation that you hear in one setting where you regularly spend time.

While a conversation is going on, try to write down exactly what you hear for five minutes or so. Then ask yourself the following questions:

- What are people talking about in this conversation? (What knowledge do they seem to share and what shared knowledge do they have to create?)

- Why do they seem to be talking about it? (Do they seem to share the same purposes or do they have some different intentions that have to be negotiated?)

- What do you notice about how they talk about it? (Does everyone talk equally? Do they all contribute in the same ways—introducing topics, asking questions, giving details—and in the same style?)

(continued)

> - Do the participants seem to have sufficient shared knowledge, shared purposes, and shared ways of carrying out a conversation for the conversation to be successful and smooth-flowing?
>
> Write an informal account of your observations in which you share the conversation you observed and what you discovered as you applied these concepts to it. If you were a participant in the conversation, comment also on your own role and the ways in which you participated.

The Concept of Discourse

As someone who wanted to become a strong writer, Sandra Cisneros initially thought that the conversations she'd learned to take part in at home were so different from the ways she needed to write that she had to leave the voices of home entirely behind. What she didn't realize, until much later, was that the things she'd learned in all of those prior conversations could also help her move between settings and find her voice as a writer. While she captures the sounds of the early conversations of her home and neighborhood in many of the stories she writes, she is also part of a community of writers who write to each other, about writing, in a different sort of language. It's her ability to make her writing, like her talk, fit with different settings and purposes, that makes her work powerful for readers. And that knowledge of how to make language fit the context of the conversation is something she has learned from all of her conversations, in every setting. The concepts of *discourse* and of a *discourse community* can help us to understand more about the knowledge that we all have as language users and that we need to draw on as writers.

The term *discourse* refers to language as it is actually used by people to communicate their meanings in real situations (as opposed to the made-up clauses and sentences in grammar books). *Discourse* suggests the language-in-use of talking, writing, reading—language that flows along, connecting to what has gone before and what is to come—the language of spoken and written conversations.

Both spoken and written conversations are shaped very much by where they take place, who the participants are, and what their purposes are for being involved in this activity. When you get together regularly with any group of people, when you have a sense of belonging to a group of friends, a family, a church, a workplace, or even a classroom, where people share some connections and also share certain ways of thinking and talking about them, you are part of a community. Because all of you express your shared values, interests, and ideas in typical ways that you're all likely to understand, you share the same language-in-use: the same discourse. Thus you belong not only to the same community but to the same *discourse community*. A *discourse community* can be defined as a group of people who share not only some of the same knowledge, beliefs, and values in a certain area of interest, but also similar ways of talking or writing about these things. Because the adolescent girls at the kitchen table are long-term friends who share not only the same interests and values, but also similar ways of talking that have evolved through their many conversations, they can be said to form a small discourse community.

People can identify themselves as belonging to a group of like-minded people in many ways—by the style of clothes they wear, by the cars they drive, by the food they eat, or the music they listen to. At twelve and thir-teen, Karen, Melanie, and Shanna show which junior high school groups they want to be part of by the shoe styles they choose. Such markers help to indicate not only who's an insider, but also who's an outsider to a group. But it's language that often provides the strongest indicator of insider or out-sider status for particular groups of people, distinguishing one discourse community from another even if the different groups are in the same physi-cal location. Bring Karen's and Melanie's older brothers together at the same kitchen table, and both what they talk about and how they talk about it will be very different.

Not only do the girls have many shared interests (including what styles are in fashion for girls their age), they share ways of naming and talking about these things—or when they don't, they learn quickly what terms the others use. At the same time, the girls are also participants in other discourse communities (they attend different schools and different churches, for exam-ple) and they sometimes bring different expectations from those communi-ties that they have to negotiate. In contemporary society, people rarely par-ticipate in only one close-knit community; more commonly, they move among different settings with different participants and purposes, and thus different conversational styles. They need to be able to draw on the commu-nicative strategies they've gained across various settings so that they can participate reasonably well in new ones, and such adaptability is an impor-tant aspect of *discourse competence*—of the competence with using language appropriately that speakers and writers share when they're insiders to a community.

When you're a member of a discourse community, communication with other members is easy because you know what others are likely to know, what they're likely to understand, and how they'll expect something to be said. But all of this shared understanding is implicit. If you want to develop your ability to communicate in both speaking and writing as you move across settings, it's useful to begin to talk and think explicitly about what some of the elements are of this easy, insider communication within a discourse community—to ap-ply some of the things you know how to do when you talk as an insider in one setting to the talking and writing you'll do in new settings, including aca-demic ones.

OBSERVATION ACCOUNT

Look back at the conversation you observed and try to name the discourse community in which it took place. What are some of the other discourse communities that the participants in that conversation spend time in?

Drawing from this example, what do you understand the term discourse community to mean? What characterizes one or more of these communities, and what are the elements that make you think it might be a good example of a discourse community? Are there questions about discourse communities that you have, at this point, from thinking about these examples?

STUDENT VOICES

Here are some working definitions of discourse communities and some examples that other students have generated. Note that each response is slightly different, but that each contributes to a general understanding and represents that understanding in the writer's own words, while the examples help to test that understanding (so that some may be rejected and others added as the inquiry goes on). See whether these working definitions and examples suggest further questions or additional examples to add to your own list.

> From the reading, my take on discourse community is a social structure that you interact in and live with. I am part of school discourses, work discourses, and also a social group of friends that works as a discourse, and my church community is a discourse community. **(Matt O.)**

> Any setting of conversation that has distinct and recognizable characteristics. What makes that particular conversation recognizable is that all participants know how the conversation will proceed. Each person has a place in adding their own knowledge into the equation and they know how and when to add it. **(Matt S)**

> A discourse community is a group of people having relatively the same background. A group of people who come from the same area, that speak a certain way, act a certain way. **(Christine)**

> That word discourse community to me says that you're comfortable to talk or act any way you would like around someone without having to worry about what they think. **(Matt D)**

> Discourse community is a somewhat difficult term to explain. I guess it's a common language found between two or more people. And maybe even some common interests or activities. For example, if you and I both liked reading Sidney Sheldon and we both liked the New England Patriots and hung around together and talked about the same things we would have the same discourse community. **(Leon)**

Examples of possible discourse communities: friends in a carpool; senior class; information technology community; sports teams; family; a hikers' club; football fans; boaters; friends who share military experience; this class.

Situation, Context, and Genre

When all of the participants in a conversation belong to a common discourse community and share the <u>what</u>, the <u>why</u>, and the <u>how</u> (the common knowledge needed to build on in the conversation, a common purpose in having the conversation, and a common understanding of how to proceed) their conversation can continue. Of course, not all of this knowledge is shared before a conversation begins; in that case, there wouldn't be any need for anyone to say anything. But there needs to be enough of a common base in some of these areas for the participants to build on. Two strangers waiting at a campus bus stop on the first day of the semester, for example, might start up a conversation. But they have to know appropriate ways to do that. They need to share a purpose, even if it's just to pass the time, and they need to find some interest that they share, such as what time the bus arrived yesterday or what the weather is likely to be this afternoon. If those opening exchanges go well, they may go on gradually to ask for more personal information: "Are you a student here?" "What's your major?" "What are you taking this semester?"—information that might typically be shared by acquaintances. But if one asks the other, "How much money did you earn last year?" that question is likely to be seen as inappropriate, as asking for information that's too personal for such a setting, as having no place when the purpose of the conversation is just to pass the time. What goes on next is likely to be an avoidance of the conversation, rather than its continuation. At the financial aid office though, the clerk behind the desk, equally a stranger (or maybe even the same stranger who was at the bus stop), might ask the very same person the same question, and this time receive not only an answer, but the detailed explanation that extends the exchange and allows it to continue. This time the question is seen as relevant to the purpose of the conversation.

As you can see from these examples, the *situation* in which any conversation takes place determines what purposes are appropriate to it and what information is relevant and necessary, as well as how the exchange will proceed. *Situation* is an important concept in the study of discourse. It means not only the setting—<u>where</u> the conversation takes place, whether at a bus stop or a financial aid office—but also <u>who</u> the participants are, what their roles are, and even <u>when</u> a particular exchange takes place in relation to other conversations with the same people in the same setting. By the second morning at the bus stop, the same two people are becoming acquaintances, not strangers, and their second conversation will build on the knowledge acquired in the first. Likewise, a second visit to the financial aid office should not require that the visitor provide again all of the information that has already been provided the first time. If she's asked the same questions a second time, she may rightly wonder whether the larger purpose of such an exchange is to provide assistance, or whether it's to deter her from seeking the help she needs.

So the <u>what</u>, <u>why</u>, and <u>how</u> that shape the immediate conversational text that's being created are in turn determined by the <u>where</u>, <u>when</u>, and <u>who</u> of the larger situation in which the conversation is taking place. And it's the situation that helps participants determine what's significant—what's meaningful and important enough for the conversation to build on, and what's not so significant. It's the situation of three young adolescent girls having another of their many conversations about shopping and styles that makes the subject of combat boot shoes engaging rather than trivial to the participants.

The context for a conversation includes the immediate situation but also a larger *social and cultural context*, where similar exchanges have gone on over and over again, and patterns have developed that provide the background for what is happening in any particular moment. The exchanges in many English classes, where students read texts, discuss them, and write papers about them, will be a lot like the one we'll look at in Chapter 1. If you step into any financial aid office in any college in the United States, you're likely to hear very similar patterns of questions and answers. And even if you eavesdrop on a group of young adolescent girls in any kitchen in the country, it's not likely to be too long before the topics of shopping and clothing styles come up, as they begin to define who they are by what they want—in the terms that a consumer society, with advertising and brand names, offers them—as Melanie does here.

Return to the conversation you've observed and describe the situation in which it took place, the <u>who</u>, <u>when</u>, and <u>where</u>. In what ways do you see these elements of situation as contributing to what was said there and why and how it was said? **OBSERVATION ACCOUNT**

When similar conversations go on frequently, the repetition gives rise to *genres* that may become formalized (the financial aid interview, the joke or the put-down in friends' conversations, or the discussion vs. lecture format in a classroom). Genres arise when people repeatedly talk or write in similar ways for similar purposes and use similar forms each time. Waitpersons in restaurants are likely to start each exchange with customers with "Good evening! My name is X. May I tell you what our specials are this evening?" Resumes often start out by naming the sort of position the person is seeking, then give educational background, and finally add work experience. These forms change over time, but only slowly. The *memoir* is an example of a common written genre—a writer's reflection on some aspect of her or his past experience from the perspective of the present. We'll read other examples of that genre in later chapters, and you will work toward writing your own.

WRITING IN ACADEMIC GENRES: INFORMAL GENRES

Genre is a term that's used not only for identifying major categories of literature—fiction, poetry, drama—but for naming any form that's used repeatedly within a community. As we'll discover, genres are created because people in the community find they need to do that sort of thing, in that sort of form, over and over again. Pretty soon they give a name to the form they've created: shopping list, movie review, email message. In college writing communities, there's a need not only for the formal genres of essays and reports of various types, but for informal genres of writing that let people participate in the ongoing work of the writing classroom in similar ways. People within the community develop, over time, their own shared assumptions for what these genres should look like and what they should do. For each of the informal genres of writing that are suggested in this book, there are some common assumptions that are held by many writers in such settings—that they won't require a specific formal shape, for example, but that generally they'll include specifics—quotations in reading responses, details of what was observed in observation accounts, examples in reflective inquiries. The peer responses that writers give to each others' work are usually guided by these shared assumptions.

As you work with both informal and formal genres of academic writing, you'll want to generate your own shared assumptions as a classroom writing community. What purposes do you think that type of writing will serve in your community? What elements should be included to help it serve those purposes? Is there a typical length that will generally work well for those purposes? If you generate, together, your own shared assumptions about any type of writing, and then test out those assumptions against what you actually do when you try to use that type for a particular task, you'll soon be able to identify what really matters and what doesn't for the purposes you've set. The following chapters will invite you to try out and discuss a variety of genres as you explore the ways of academic communities.

OBSERVE AN INFORMAL RESPONSE

Informal writing experiences make space for you to engage in exploratory thinking by doing the following:

- *Connecting*—finding connections among readings, experiences, and observations (your own and your classmates') and making connections between those readings and experiences and the concepts that the book presents

- *Elaborating*—following out details and examples to see what they tell you about the ideas you're exploring

- *Questioning*—asking questions about what you observe, read, and experience, and finding questions that can guide new stages of your own inquiry into the ways in which participating in various discourse communities can inform your work as a writer

- *Speculating*—imagining possible answers to some of your questions by asking "What if?" and exploring potential connections and relationships

Look back at your first informal response to see if you find any examples of just such exploratory thinking or to see new ways to expand your initial ideas.

Exploring the Writer's World

In Part I, you'll explore some significant moments in your past experience, focusing on how language has been used and on the conversations that have taken place in communities you've been part of. You'll examine how those conversations have helped to shape your social identity and your sense of who you are now as you participate in the new conversations of an academic setting. The readings in Part I include memoirs by other writers who have explored their past experience from the perspective of the present. These memoirs will help you explore three interrelated strands of your larger inquiry, focusing on yourself as a reader, as a writer, and as someone looking at the past to see how it contributes to your current participation in a new community of learners.

The work you do in Chapters 1, 2, and 3 will lead you to write your own formal memoir. As you think about your own response to the memoir of Richard Rodriguez in Chapter 1, you'll be starting to work with the form of the memoir in ways that will help as you create your own. This work will continue in Chapter 2, when you'll look at another memoir from a writer's perspective and inquire into spoken and written stories. More specifically, you'll analyze how stories work to meet their audiences' expectations. This work will be completed in Chapter 3, when you'll read a number of other memoirs while drafting and revising your own.

As you work toward writing your own memoir, you'll draw on the informal writing you'll produce as you explore the questions posed in these chapters: How does your experience in past communities shape your view of yourself in a new academic setting? How can you build on your prior conversations as a foundation for writing and speaking in this new setting? What are some of the common expectations for conversations, both spoken and written, in academic settings? How might taking on the identity of a college learner both draw from and challenge the identities you've shaped in other discourse communities? Each of the inquiries in Part I is designed to give you a different angle on these questions, so that you gradually develop a complex understanding of what you bring to your current work and the strategies that will help you proceed.

LEARNING GOALS

- To discover the competence you have gained as a participant in various discourse communities and how it contributes to the competence you'll draw on as a reader, writer, and learner in academic settings

- To gain new ways of participating in conversations as a reader and writer and member of a classroom community

- To analyze the different ways other writers have explored their past experiences from present perspectives and explore possibilities to try out as a writer

- To write a formal memoir that offers a present perspective on your own experience, shows what you have learned about that experience, and demonstrates your understanding of the conventions of written memoirs

CHAPTER

1

Reading as Conversation

Chapter 1 explores how writers and readers are influenced by their experiences in discourse communities. We'll read about one writer's childhood experience moving between home and school. Richard Rodriguez's memoir, "Aria," will allow us to consider the ways readers can participate in a written conversation, as well as the ways writers work to invite their readers into their written conversations.

Because you will be reading Rodriguez's memoir in a specific context (the classroom setting in which you're using this book), we'll also consider how that context and the discussions that go on there shape your purposes as a reader, looking at a conversation about "Aria" that takes place in one college writing classroom. We'll then return to reflect on how our purposes as readers and the contexts for which we are reading might shape our participation in written conversations with others' texts in particular ways.

Chapter 1 explores three related questions:

- What does our reading tell us about the ways we participate as readers in written conversations?

- How do the conversations that take place in academic settings compare to those in informal contexts, and how do they shape our purposes as writers and readers?

- What can we learn by reflecting on how new purposes and situations shape our reading?

These questions can be explored with any reading, and you may want to turn next to another memoir (from the collection at the end of Part I) to read about a different sort of experience.

Chapter 1 concludes with suggestions for following up on what you've discovered as a reader in a more formal academic essay.

EXPLORING THE READER'S ROLE

The Reader as a Participant

A written conversation begins any time a writer writes something down for an imagined reader and continues when an actual reader picks up the written text and reads what's there. As a reader, you step into a written text much as if you're entering a room where a conversation is about to begin (or sometimes, as with some modern fiction, as if the conversation is already going on when you get there). Like the girls in the Introduction, you bring your experience and interests from other worlds to this new conversation, and those frames of reference will shape what you make of it. But, as a reader, you can't alter the course of the conversation in any direct way; you can't generally ask questions of the writer and get responses while you are reading. Rather, your participation as a reader goes on through the engagement of your own mind.

A writer has to imagine the reader and how to keep that reader involved in the conversation—taking into account the reader's purposes for reading and the shared knowledge the reader might bring to the conversation. A writer is taking a very long turn in a conversation where the other participants can't interrupt (except in their heads), although they can stop reading altogether. So the writer also has to imagine the reader saying, "So what?" and respond to that question in some way—either explicitly, by linking what he or she is writing to some issue an audience of readers is likely to be concerned about, or implicitly, by drawing readers in through a powerful opening scene or arresting language and imagery.

A good place to look at how this works is with a memoir, one that's included in a collection of autobiographical essays by the writer Richard Rodriguez, titled *Hunger of Memory*. In this collection, Rodriguez chronicles his educational experiences as a child in a working-class Hispanic family, from the time he began school through his graduate study in English. The essay included here, "Aria: A Memoir of a Bilingual Childhood," appears early in the book.

Writing for a public audience, Rodriguez has to create a conversation with readers he doesn't know but can only imagine—a conversation to which he brings a particular purpose or purposes and some things he wants to say. But he has to do so in a way that brings all of those unknown readers along and keeps them interested, that justifies his demanding their time and attention. And, to the conversation he has started, each of us, as an active, engaged reader, brings ideas, experiences, and associations that are awakened in the process of reading. Rodriguez writes about his specific childhood experience moving between languages as he went from home to school. But even if you haven't had such an experience, this written conversation will evoke a rich base of shared knowledge about families, school, and the tensions between them, and about the concerns and fears of children taking their first steps into the larger world. What we don't already know, Rodriguez will tell us explicitly, creating the shared knowledge we need.

The way you read "Aria" will be shaped in part by the context in which you're reading, including the conversations in your classroom that have preceded this reading. You might, in the context of this book, find yourself thinking about the sorts of conversations the young Rodriguez has with his family, and the ways in which those are changed once he goes to school (in his case moving from one language to another). You might be reminded of something in your own early school experience. Or you might find yourself focusing on the purpose Rodriguez himself names, seeing how his personal experience affects his ideas about bilingual education. Any of these ways of engaging with the ideas and experiences Rodriguez presents may be called a *participatory reading*—one that brings you into a conversation with the text and its writer and allows you to make as many connections as possible with the experiences and understandings represented there.

Before you begin your participatory reading of "Aria," ask yourself:

■ What expectations do I bring to this memoir from any memoirs (or essays of personal experience) I've read in the past? What do I already know about this memoir, and what do I expect to find here?

As you read the memoir, keep the following questions in mind:

■ What does the writer say to me through this text?

■ How does it contribute to what I know and have thought about? Does it connect with other things I've read or heard or to aspects of my own experience? If not, what can I learn from encountering a very different experience?

■ Are there points where it clashes with what I know, or where I want to argue with it?

■ What might I want to take away from it to think about later?

This is a good moment to turn to the essay and begin your own participatory reading. Keep track of the conversation you have with Rodriguez by marking the text to show where you've been struck by what he says, where you find connections to your own experience or to other things you've read, where you'd ask him a question or disagree with him if he were present in the room. Such interactive reading and marking of a text is often referred to as *glossing*. Although your conversations with writers will go on in your head any time you read, it's important for your work as a writer that you leave traces of those conversations. When you annotate your text as you read, you can see what you made of the things the writer had to say, and go back to your own understandings, ideas, and responses. For all of your reading in this book, you'll be encouraged to *gloss* the text while you are reading. Make notes in the margin; comment on the things that interest you; and actively keep track of the ways in which your own thinking moves in relationship to what you're reading.

Try your hand at glossing the text as you read "Aria," following the suggestions that appear in the Strategies section (p. 499). (You'll find a sample glossed page there as well.)

After you've finished reading and glossing the first two pages of "Aria," write an informal journal entry in which you draw on your own glossing of the text to explore some aspect of your response as a reader to the the conversation Rodriguez has begun.

Aria

Richard Rodriguez

I

1   I remember to start with that day in Sacramento—a California now nearly thirty years past—when I first entered a classroom, able to understand some fifty stray English words.

The third of four children, I had been preceded to a neighborhood Roman Catholic school by an older brother and sister. But neither of them had revealed very much about their classroom experiences. Each afternoon they returned, as they left in the morning, always together, speaking in Spanish as they climbed the five steps of the porch. And their mysterious books, wrapped in shopping-bag paper, remained on the table next to the door, closed firmly behind them.

An accident of geography sent me to a school where all my classmates were white, many the children of doctors and lawyers and business executives. All my classmates certainly must have been uneasy on that first day of school—as most children are uneasy—to find themselves apart from their families in the first institution of their lives. But I was astonished.

The nun said, in a friendly but oddly impersonal voice, 'Boys and girls, this is Richard Rodriguez.' (I heard her sound out: *Rich-heard Road-ree-guess.*) It was the first time I had heard anyone name me in English. 'Richard,' the nun repeated more slowly, writing my name down in her black leather book. Quickly I turned to see my mother's face dissolve in a watery blur behind the pebbled glass door.

* * *

5   Many years later there is something called bilingual education—a scheme proposed in the late 1960s by Hispanic-American social activists, later endorsed by a congressional vote. It is a program that seeks to permit non-English-speaking children, many from lower-class homes, to use their family language as the language of school. (Such is the goal its supporters announce.) I hear them and am forced to say no: It is not possible for a child—any child—ever to use his family's language in school. Not to understand this is to misunderstand the public uses of schooling and to trivialize the nature of intimate life—a family's 'language.'

Memory teaches me what I know of these matters; the boy reminds the adult. I was a bilingual child, a certain kind—socially disadvantaged—the son of working-class parents, both Mexican immigrants.

In the early years of my boyhood, my parents coped very well in America. My father had steady work. My mother managed at home. They were nobody's victims. Optimism and ambition led them to a house (our home) many blocks from the Mexican south side of town. We lived among *gringos* and only a block from the biggest, whitest houses. It never occurred to my parents that they couldn't live wherever they chose. Nor was the Sacramento of the fifties bent on teaching them a contrary lesson. My mother and father were more annoyed than intimidated by those two or three neighbors who tried initially to make us unwelcome. ('Keep your brats away from my sidewalk!') But despite all they achieved, perhaps because they had so much to achieve, any deep feeling of ease, the confidence of 'belonging' in public was withheld from them both. They regarded the people at work, the faces in crowds, as very distant from us. They were the others, *los gringos*. That term was interchangeable in their speech with another, even more telling, *los americanos*.

I grew up in a house where the only regular guests were my relations. For one day, enormous families of relatives would visit and there would be so many people that the noise and the bodies would spill out to the backyard and front porch. Then, for weeks, no one came by. (It was usually a salesman who rang the doorbell.) Our house stood apart. A gaudy yellow in a row of white bungalows. We were the people with the noisy dog. The people who raised pigeons and chickens. We were the foreigners on the block. A few neighbors smiled and waved. We waved back. But no one in the family knew the names of the old couple who lived next door; until I was seven years old, I did not know the names of the kids who lived across the street.

In public, my father and mother spoke a hesitant, accented, not always grammatical English. And they would have to strain—their bodies tense—to catch the sense of what was rapidly said by *los gringos*. At home they spoke Spanish. The language of their Mexican past sounded in counterpoint to the English of public society. The words would come quickly, with ease. Conveyed through those sounds was the pleasing, soothing, consoling reminder of being at home.

10 During those years when I was first conscious of hearing, my mother and father addressed me only in Spanish; in Spanish I learned to reply. By contrast, English (*inglés*), rarely heard in the house, was the language I came to associate with *gringos*. I learned my first words of English overhearing my parents speak to strangers. At five years of age, I knew just enough English for my mother to trust me on errands to stores one block away. No more.

I was a listening child, careful to hear the very different sounds of Spanish and English. Wide-eyed with hearing, I'd listen to sounds more than words. First, there were English (*gringo*) sounds. So many words were still unknown that when the butcher or the lady at the drugstore said something to me, exotic polysyllabic sounds would bloom in the midst of their sentences. Often, the speech of people in public seemed to me very loud, booming with confidence. The man behind the counter would literally ask, 'What can I do for you?' But by being so firm and so clear, the sound of his voice said that he was a *gringo*; he belonged in public society.

I would also hear then the high nasal notes of middle-class American speech. The air stirred with sound. Sometimes, even now, when I have been traveling abroad for several weeks, I will hear what I heard as a boy. In hotel lobbies or airports, in Turkey or Brazil, some Americans will pass, and suddenly I will hear it again—the high sound of American voices. For a few seconds I will hear it with pleasure, for it is now the sound of *my* society—a reminder of home. But inevitably—already on the flight headed for home—the sound fades with repetition. I will be unable to hear it anymore.

When I was a boy, things were different. The accent of *los gringos* was never pleasing nor was it hard to hear. Crowds at Safeway or at bus stops would be noisy with sound. And I would be forced to edge away from the chirping chatter above me.

I was unable to hear my own sounds, but I knew very well that I spoke English poorly. My words could not stretch far enough to form complete thoughts. And the words I did speak I didn't know well enough to make into distinct sounds. (Listeners would usually lower their heads, better to hear what I was trying to say.) But it was one thing for *me* to speak English with difficulty. It was more troubling for me to hear my parents speak in public: their high-whining vowels and guttural consonants; their sentences that got stuck with 'eh' and 'ah' sounds; the confused syntax; the hesitant rhythm of sounds so different from the way *gringos* spoke. I'd notice, moreover, that my parent's voices were softer than those of *gringos* we'd meet.

15   I am tempted now to say that none of this mattered. In adulthood I am embarrassed by childhood fears. And, in a way, it didn't matter very much that my parents could not speak English with case. Their linguistic difficulties had no serious consequences. My mother and father made themselves understood at the county hospital clinic and at government offices. And yet, in another way, it mattered very much—it was unsettling to hear my parents struggle with English. Hearing them, I'd grow nervous, my clutching trust in their protection and power weakened.

There were many times like the night at a brightly lit gasoline station (a blaring white memory) when I stood uneasily, hearing my father. He was talking to a teenaged attendant. I do not recall what they were saying, but I cannot forget the sounds my father made as he spoke. At one point his words slid together to form one word—sounds as confused as the threads of blue and green oil in the puddle next to my shoes. His voice rushed through what he had left to say. And, toward the end, reached falsetto notes, appealing to his listener's understanding. I looked away to the lights of passing automobiles. I tried not to hear anymore. But I heard only too well the calm, easy tones in the attendant's reply. Shortly afterward, walking toward home with my father, I shivered when he put his hand on my shoulder. The very first chance that I got, I evaded his grasp and ran on ahead into the dark, skipping with feigned boyish exuberance.

But then there was Spanish. *Español*: my family's language. *Español*: the language that seemed to me a private language. I'd hear strangers on the radio and in the Mexican Catholic church across town speaking in Spanish, but I couldn't really believe that Spanish was a public language, like English. Spanish speakers, rather, seemed related to me, for I sensed that we shared—through our language—the experience of feeling apart from *los gringos*. It was thus a ghetto Spanish that I heard and I spoke. Like those whose lives are bound by a barrio, I was reminded by Spanish of my separateness from *los otros, los gringos* in power. But more intensely than for most barrio children—because I did not live in a barrio—Spanish seemed to me the language of home. (Most days it was only at home that I'd hear it.) It became the language of joyful return.

A family member would say something to me and I would feel myself specially recognized. My parents would say something to me and I would feel embraced by the sounds of their words. Those sounds said: *I am speaking with ease in Spanish. I am addressing you in words I never use with* los gringos. *I recognize you as someone special, close, like no one outside. You belong with us. In the family.*

Ricardo.

20   At the age of five, six, well past the time when most other children no longer easily notice the difference between sounds uttered at home and words spoken in public, I had a different experience. I lived in a world magically compounded of sounds. I remained a child longer than most; I lingered too long, poised at the edge of language—often frightened by the sounds of *los gringos,* delighted by the sounds of Spanish at home. I shared with my family a language that was startlingly different from that used in the great city around us.

For me there were none of the gradations between public and private society so normal to a maturing child. Outside the house was public society; inside the house was private. Just opening or closing the screen door behind me was an important experience. I'd rarely leave home all alone or without reluctance. Walking down the sidewalk, under the canopy of tall trees, I'd warily notice the—suddenly—silent neighborhood kids who stood warily watching me. Nervously, I'd arrive at the grocery store to hear there the sounds of the *gringo*—foreign to me—reminding me that in this world so big, I was a foreigner. But then I'd return. Walking back toward our house, climbing the steps from the sidewalk, when the front door was open in summer, I'd hear voices beyond the screen door talking in Spanish. For a second or two, I'd stay, linger there, listening. Smiling, I'd hear my mother call out, saying in Spanish (words): 'Is that you, Richard?' All the while her sounds would assure me: *You are home now; come closer: inside. With us.*

'*Sí*', I'd reply.

Once more inside the house I would resume (assume) my place in the family. The sounds would dim, grow harder to hear. Once more at home, I would grow less aware of that fact. It required, however, no more than the blurt of the doorbell to alert me to listen to sounds all over again. The house would turn instantly still while my mother went to the door. I'd hear her hard English sounds. I'd wait to hear her voice return to soft-sounding Spanish, which assured me, as surely as did the clicking tongue of the lock on the door, that the stranger was gone.

Plainly, it is not healthy to hear such sounds so often. It is not healthy to distinguish public words from private sounds so easily. I remained cloistered by sounds, timid and shy in public, too dependent on voices at home. And yet it needs to be emphasized: I was an extremely happy child at home. I remember many nights when my father would come back from work, and I'd hear him call out to my mother in Spanish, sounding relieved. In Spanish, he'd sound light and free notes he never could manage in English. Some nights I'd jump up just at hearing his voice. With *mis hermanos* I would come running into the room where he was with my mother. Our laughing (so deep was the pleasure!) became screaming. Like others who know the pain of public alienation, we transformed the knowledge of our public separateness and made it consoling—the reminder of intimacy. Excited, we joined our voices in a celebration of sounds. *We are speaking now the way we never speak out in public. We are alone—together,* voices sounded, surrounded to tell me. Some nights, no one seemed willing to loosen the hold sounds had on us. At dinner, we invented new words. (Ours sounded Spanish, but made sense only to us.) We pieced together new words by taking, say, an English verb and giving it Spanish endings. My mother's instructions at bedtime would be lacquered with mock-urgent tones. Or a word like *si* would become, in several notes, able to convey added measures of feeling. Tongues explored the edges of words, especially the fat vowels. And we happily sounded that military drum roll, the twirling roar of the Spanish *r*. Family language: my family's sounds. The voices of my parents and sisters and brother. Their voices insisting: *You belong here. We are family members. Related. Special to one another. Listen!* Voices singing and sighing, rising, straining, then surging, teeming with pleasure that burst syllables into fragments of laughter. At times it seemed there was steady quiet only when, from another room, the rustling whispers of my parents faded and I moved closer to sleep.

2

25   Supporters of bilingual education today imply that students like me miss a great deal by not being taught in their family's language. What they seem not to recognize is that, as a socially disadvantaged child, I considered Spanish to be a private language. What I needed to learn in school was that I had the right—and the obligation—to speak the public language of *los gringos*. The odd truth is that my first-grade classmates could have become bilingual, in the conventional sense of that word, more easily than I. Had they been taught (as upper-middle-class children are often taught early) a second language like Spanish or French, they could have regarded it simply as that: another public language. In my case such bilingualism could not have been so quickly achieved. What I did not believe was that I could speak a single public language.

      Without question, it would have pleased me to hear my teachers address me in Spanish when I entered the classroom. I would have felt much less afraid. I would have trusted them and responded with ease. But I would have delayed—for how long postponed?—having to learn the language of public society. I would have evaded—and for how long could I have afforded to delay?—learning the great lesson of school, that I had a public identity.

      Fortunately, my teachers were unsentimental about their responsibility. What they understood was that I needed to speak a public language. So their voices would search me out, asking me questions. Each time I'd hear them, I'd look up in surprise to see a nun's face frowning at me. I'd mumble, not really meaning to answer. The nun would persist, 'Richard, stand up. Don't look at the floor. Speak up. Speak to the entire class, not just to me!' But I couldn't believe that the English language was mine to use. (In part, I did not want to believe it.) I continued to mumble. I resisted the teacher's demands. (Did I somehow suspect that once I learned public language my pleasing family life would be changed?) Silent, waiting for the bell to sound, I remained dazed, diffident, afraid.

Because I wrongly imagined that English was intrinsically a public language and Spanish an intrinsically private one, I easily noted the difference between classroom language and the language of home. At school, words were directed to a general audience of listeners. ('Boys and girls.') Words were meaningfully ordered. And the point was not self-expression alone but to make oneself understood by many others. The teacher quizzed: 'Boys and girls, why do we use that word in this sentence? Could we think of a better word to use there? Would the sentence change its meaning if the words were differently arranged? And wasn't there a better way of saying much the same thing?' (I couldn't say. I wouldn't try to say.)

Three months. Five. Half a year passed. Unsmiling, ever watchful, my teachers noted my silence. They began to connect my behavior with the difficult progress my older sister and brother were making. Until one Saturday morning three nuns arrived at the house to talk to our parents. Stiffly, they sat on the blue living room sofa. From the doorway of another room, spying the visitors, I noted the incongruity—the clash of two worlds, the faces and voices of school intruding upon the familiar setting of home. I overheard one voice gently wondering, 'Do your children speak only Spanish at home, Mrs. Rodriguez?' While another voice added, 'That Richard especially seems so timid and shy.'

30   *That Rich-heard!*

With great tact the visitors continued, 'Is it possible for you and your husband to encourage your children to practice their English when they are home?' Of course, my parents complied. What would they not do for their children's well-being? And how could they have questioned the Church's authority which those women represented? In an instant, they agreed to give up the language (the sounds) that had revealed and accentuated our family's closeness. The moment after the visitors left, the change was observed. '*Ahora,* speak to us *en inglés,*' my father and mother united to tell us.

At first, it seemed a kind of game. After dinner each night, the family gathered to practice 'our' English. (It was still then *inglés,* a language foreign to us, so we felt drawn as strangers to it.) Laughing, we would try to define words we could not pronounce. We played with strange English sounds, often over-anglicizing our pronunciations. And we filled the smiling gaps of our sentences with familiar Spanish sounds. But that was cheating, somebody shouted. Everyone laughed. In school, meanwhile, like my brother and sister, I was required to attend a daily tutoring session. I needed a full year of special attention. I also needed my teachers to keep my attention from straying in class by calling out, *Rich-heard*—their English voices slowly prying loose my ties to my other name, its three notes, *Ri-car-do.* Most of all I needed to hear my mother and father speak to me in a moment of seriousness in broken—suddenly heartbreaking—English. The scene was inevitable: One Saturday morning I entered the kitchen where my parents were talking in Spanish. I did not realize that they were talking in Spanish however until, at the moment they saw me, I heard their voices change to speak English. Those *gringo* sounds they uttered startled me. Pushed me away. In that moment of trivial misunderstanding and profound insight, I felt my throat twisted by unsounded grief. I turned quickly and left the room. But I had no place to escape to with Spanish. (The spell was broken.) My brother and sisters were speaking English in another part of the house.

Again and again in the days following, increasingly angry, I was obliged to hear my mother and father: 'Speak to us *en inglés*'. (*Speak.*) Only then did I determine to learn classroom English. Weeks after, it happened: One day in school I raised my hand to volunteer an answer. I spoke out in a loud voice. And I did not think it remarkable when the entire class understood. That day, I moved very far from the disadvantaged child I had been only days earlier. The belief, the calming assurance that I belonged in public, had at last taken hold.

Shortly after, I stopped hearing the high and loud sounds of *los gringos*. A more and more confident speaker of English, I didn't trouble to listen to *how* strangers sounded, speaking to me. And there simply were too many English-speaking people in my day for me to hear American accents anymore. Conversations quickened. Listening to persons who sounded eccentrically pitched voices, I usually noted their sounds for an initial few seconds before I concentrated on *what* they were saying. Conversations became content-full. Transparent. Hearing someone's *tone* of voice— angry or questioning or sarcastic or happy or sad—I didn't distinguish it from the words it expressed. Sound and word were thus tightly wedded. At the end of a day, I was often bemused, always relieved, to realize how 'silent', though crowded with words, my day in public had been. (This public silence measured and quickened the change in my life.)

35   At last, seven years old, I came to believe what had been technically true since my birth: I was an American citizen.

But the special feeling of closeness at home was diminished by then. Gone was the desperate, urgent, intense feeling of being at home; rare was the experience of feeling myself individualized by family intimates. We remained a loving family, but one greatly changed. No longer so close; no longer bound tight by the pleasing and troubling knowledge of our public separateness. Neither my older brother nor sister rushed home after school anymore. Nor did I. When I arrived home there would often be neighborhood kids in the house. Or the house would be empty of sounds.

Following the dramatic Americanization of their children, even my parents grew more publicly confident. Especially my mother. She learned the names of all the people on our block. And she decided we needed to have a telephone installed in the house. My father continued to use the word *gringo*. But it was no longer charged with the old bitterness or distrust. (Stripped of any emotional content, the word simply became a name for those Americans not of Hispanic descent.) Hearing him, sometimes, I wasn't sure if he was pronouncing the Spanish word *gringo* or saying gringo in English.

Matching the silence I started hearing in public was a new quiet at home. The family's quiet was partly due to the fact that, as we children learned more and more English, we shared fewer and fewer words with our parents. Sentences needed to be spoken slowly when a child addressed his mother or father. (Often the parent wouldn't understand.) The child would need to repeat himself. (Still the parent misunderstood.) The young voice, frustrated, would end up saying, 'Never mind'—the subject was closed. Dinners would be noisy with the clinking of knives and forks against dishes. My mother would smile softly between her remarks; my father at the other end of the table would chew and chew at his food, while he stared over the heads of his children.

My *mother!* My *father!* After English became my primary language, I no longer knew what words to use in addressing my parents. The old Spanish words (those tender accents of sound) I had used earlier—*mamá* and *papá*—I couldn't use anymore. They would have been too painful reminders of how much had changed in my life. On the other hand, the words I heard neighborhood kids call *their* parents seemed equally unsatisfactory. *Mother* and *Father; Ma, Papa, Pa, Dad, Pop* (how I hated the all-American sound of that last word especially)—all these terms I felt were unsuitable, not really terms of address for *my* parents. As a result, I never used them at home. Whenever I'd speak to my parents, I would try to get their attention with eye contact alone. In public conversations, I'd refer to 'my parents' or 'my mother and father'.

40   My mother and father, for their part, responded differently, as their children spoke to them less. She grew restless, seemed troubled and anxious at the scarcity of words exchanged in the house. It was she who would question me about my day when I came home from school. She smiled at small talk. She pried at the edges of my sentences to get me to say something more. (What?) She'd join conversations she overheard, but her intrusions often stopped her children's talking. By contrast, my father seemed reconciled to the new quiet. Though his English improved somewhat, he retired into silence. At dinner he spoke very little. One night his children and even his wife helplessly giggled at his garbled English pronunciation of the Catholic Grace before Meals. Thereafter he made his wife recite the prayer at the start of each meal, even on formal occasions, when there were guests in the house. Hers became the public voice of the family. On official business, it was she, not my father, one would usually hear on the phone or in stores, talking to strangers. His children grew so accustomed to his silence that, years later, they would speak routinely of his shyness. (My mother would often try to explain: Both his parents died when he was eight. He was raised by an uncle who treated him like little more than a menial servant. He was never encouraged to speak. He grew up alone. A man of few words.) But my father was not shy, I realized, when I'd watch him speaking Spanish with relatives. Using Spanish, he was quickly effusive. Especially when talking with other men, his voice would spark, flicker, flare alive with sounds. In Spanish, he expressed ideas and feelings he rarely revealed in English. With firm Spanish sounds, he conveyed confidence and authority English would never allow him.

The silence at home, however, was finally more than a literal silence. Fewer words passed between parent and child, but more profound was the silence that resulted from my inattention to sounds. At about the time I no longer bothered to listen with care to the sounds of English in public, I grew careless about listening to the sounds family members made when they spoke. Most of the time I heard someone speaking at home and didn't distinguish his sounds from the words people uttered in public. I didn't even pay much attention to my parents' accented and ungrammatical speech. At least not at home. Only when I was with them in public would I grow alert to their accents. Though, even then, their sounds caused me less and less concern. For I was increasingly confident of my own public identity.

I would have been happier about my public success had I not sometimes recalled what it had been like earlier, when my family had conveyed its intimacy through a set of conveniently private sounds. Sometimes in public, hearing a stranger, I'd hark back to my past. A Mexican farmworker approached me downtown to ask directions to somewhere. 'Hijito . . . ?' he said. And his voice summoned deep longing. Another time, standing beside my mother in the visiting room of a Carmelite convent, before the dense screen which rendered the nuns shadowy figures, I heard several Spanish-speaking nuns—their busy, singsong overlapping voices—assure us that yes, yes, we were remembered, all our family was remembered in their prayers. (Their voices echoed faraway family sounds.) Another day, a dark-faced old woman—her hand light on my shoulder—steadied herself against me as she boarded a bus. She murmured something I couldn't quite comprehend. Her Spanish voice came near, like the face of a never-before-seen relative in the instant before I was kissed. Her voice, like so many of the Spanish voices I'd hear in public, recalled the golden age of my youth. Hearing Spanish then, I continued to be a careful, if sad, listener to sounds. Hearing a Spanish-speaking family walking behind me, I turned to look. I smiled for an instant, before my glance found the Hispanic-looking faces of strangers in the crowd going by.

* * *

Today I hear bilingual educators say that children lose a degree of 'individuality' by becoming assimilated into public society. (Bilingual schooling was popularized in the seventies, that decade when middle-class ethnics began to resist the process of assimilation—the American melting pot.) But the bilingualists simplistically scorn the value and necessity of assimilation. They do not seem to realize that there are *two* ways a person is individualized. So they do not realize that while one suffers a diminished sense of *private* individuality by becoming assimilated into public society, such assimilation makes possible the achievement of *public* individuality.

The bilingualists insist that a student should be reminded of his difference from others in mass society, his heritage. But they equate mere separateness with individuality. The fact is that only in private—with intimates—is separateness from the crowd a prerequisite for individuality. (An intimate draws me apart, tells me that I am unique, unlike all others.) In public, by contrast, full individuality is achieved, paradoxically, by those who are able to consider themselves members of the crowd. Thus it happened for me: Only when I was able to think of myself as an American, no longer an alien in *gringo* society, could I seek the rights and opportunities necessary for full public individuality. The social and political advantages I enjoy as a man result from the day that I came to believe that my name, indeed, is *Rich-heard Road-ree-guess*. It is true that my public society today is often impersonal. (My public society is usually mass society.) Yet despite the anonymity of the crowd and despite the fact that the individuality I achieve in public is often tenuous—because it depends on my being one in a crowd—I celebrate the day I acquired my new name. Those middle-class ethnics who scorn assimilation seem to me filled with decadent self-pity, obsessed by the burden of public life. Dangerously, they romanticize public separateness and they trivialize the dilemma of the socially disadvantaged.

45   My awkward childhood does not prove the necessity of bilingual education. My story discloses instead an essential myth of childhood—inevitable pain. If I rehearse here the changes in my private life after my Americanization, it is finally to emphasize the public gain. The loss implies the gain: The house I returned to each afternoon was

quiet. Intimate sounds no longer rushed to the door to greet me. There were other noises inside. The telephone rang. Neighborhood kids ran past the door of the bedroom where I was reading my schoolbooks—covered with shopping-bag paper. Once I learned public language, it would never again be easy for me to hear intimate family voices. More and more of my day was spent hearing words. But that may only be a way of saying that the day I raised my hand in class and spoke loudly to an entire roomful of faces, my childhood started to end.

Once you've read "Aria" and shared your responses to it with other readers, you'll discover that no two responses from participatory readings are alike. Even the same reader, rereading the essay a second time, will be struck by different things and have different responses, engaging in a new conversation with the text (and thus its writer) each time. College readers have responded to this essay in many ways as it evoked their own experiences, reminded them of something else they'd read, or presented an unfamiliar world that engaged their curiosity. Some have responded to young Rodriguez' embarrassment in the presence of his family, finding in his responses a reminder of moments when they had similar reactions to their own parents. Others have been disturbed by his "speaking negatively about his parents" in a public way—a violation of the respect due to parents in their own families and cultures. Some have been reminded of their own school experience, of a moment where a teacher took some action on their behalf, of a time when there were misunderstandings between home and school, or for some students, of their experience with nuns and Catholic schools. Some speakers of English as a second language have been reminded of their own experience with or without bilingual education. Still others, who know of the current bilingual education debate only second hand from observing the experience of a classmate or from reading newspaper accounts, have found in the details of Rodriguez' account a new perspective for thinking about these issues. These different responses nevertheless reflect similar processes of engaging in the conversation and interacting with the text— processes that underlie all of our participatory conversations.

When people participate in conversations, they typically do so in several ways: they make connections between what someone has said and their own experiences/their own perspectives; they try to understand more about how the speaker has come to the things he or she is saying from the speaker's perspective; they place these two perspectives—these two representations of experience—in relation to each other, seeing how the perspectives compare, and they see how a larger understanding (that may include a richer perception of differences) might be drawn from them. In other words, participants may:

- *recall* their own prior experiences, understandings, and perspectives (including those that they've gained from hearing of others' experiences in prior conversations and prior reading);
- *represent* the perspective of the writer;

■ *relate* these perspectives to each other; and

■ *reframe* what they discover from both perspectives to come to a new understanding.

This happens even in the simplest conversations. When Melanie introduces the topic of combat boot shoes at the kitchen table, Karen thinks about her own prior experience of this type of footwear—about another friend who has them, about the style her friend bought ("24 holes"), about what she's heard them called ("Doc Martens"). She tries to learn more about Melanie's perspective—about what Melanie wants—and to represent and understand that perspective ("Oh, those?"). She relates and reframes both perspectives, matching up her understanding and what Melanie's saying to make "combat boots" and "Doc Martens" come together into a common understanding of a shoe style. And she moves back and forth between these acts of reflecting, trying on another perspective, relating and reframing at different moments in the conversation. The shared knowledge that the girls gradually create through their conversations emerges from their ongoing process of bringing together their different understandings and working with them.

Readers likewise reflect on their prior experiences and perspectives, try on the new ones they're gaining through their reading, relate these to each other, and reframe them into new understandings. And, like speakers, they move back and forth among these ways of participating at various moments, not only while they're reading, but sometimes for long afterwards. All of these acts of participation go on almost simultaneously during reading. If you look back at the ways in which you glossed "Aria," you'll probably find examples of each of these ways of participating in the conversation, ways that you'll build on in academic settings.

Recalling

For most readers, there will be many points of connection with the story Rodriguez is telling, many parts of his text that resonate in some way with their own experience. Rodriguez has framed his own story in a particular way, and he speaks to us here from one view that he holds of himself and his experience— that of a person who became bilingual without bilingual education. Many of his readers will not have had the same experience of moving between languages (and he is writing primarily for readers who won't have had that experience—to let them know what it was like from his perspective). But all of his readers will have been children who've had to move from the intimacy of home to the larger world of school, all will have had school experiences in which they felt less or more at home in the classroom, and all will remember moments where their participation was played out in language (or in silence)—moments like the ones Rodriguez reconstructs from his classroom or around the family dinner table. Their memories of such moments will be triggered by something Rodriguez has said.

Here is what one reader recalled of his own experiences, stimulated by a first, participatory reading of "Aria":

It wasn't too soon that my sister and I started communicating to each other in English. And that's where the relationship with our parents started to drift away. Because we were young, English came to us much easier than it did to our parents, as it still does. So the fact that we communicated with each other in English made it harder for my parents to understand us. I remember times when we would sit at the dinner table together and my parents would carry out a conversation (in Russian) and my sister and I would stare at each other from under our spoons. **(Leon)**

While the first recollection relates an experience much like the one Rodriguez describes, his memoir leads a second reader to recall a somewhat different set of events.

I usually end up in Europe once a year for about a month at a time. . . When I am in Paris I stay and live and skate with my friends every day and they usually are all French. So after awhile I get used to their sounds, their polite way to each other, and easily pick up on the rude loud Americans, which I am one because I am no good at the French language and probably sound like a fool speaking it. **(Matt O.)**

Representing

At other moments, readers may work to "try on" or represent Rodriguez's perspective, to see how the world looks through his eyes. As in a spoken conversation, a reader can come to understand (if not agree with) what Rodriguez has to say about his experience, seeing all of the ways his perspective makes sense in light of everything else he tells us. A participant might say something to the effect of "I see what you're saying. It fits with all of these other things you've told us." Here's one reader's representation of what he understands as Rodriguez's perspective.

I think that the writer, Rodriguez, says throughout the text that life for a bilingual child is sometimes harsh and unfair. The trials and tribulations that bilingual children face are amazing. They have to suffer through so much anguish. I feel so terrible for what is happening to them. . . . I was very naive in trying to understand what they are going through. They face things I have never dreamt about, being a privileged child. **(Tom)**

Relating

Readers may also put different perspectives and experiences into relationship with one another, seeing how they can be compared and what can be learned from their similarities and differences. One way of doing this is by placing two actual experiences against each other, seeing how they compare, and making that comparison explicit, as this reader has done.

Richard Rodriguez's childhood almost mirrors mine. My parents could speak better English than Rick's but I almost felt like I was reading my own childhood. The only difference of course is that I spoke Greek and he spoke Spanish. I didn't feel as alienated has he did though. I was shy for most of elementary school but gradually, like Rick, it went away the more comfortable I felt speaking English. **(John)**

Another way is by translating Rodriguez's experience into more familiar terms, as another reader does.

> Making the transition from Spanish could be compared to playing hockey. If the only way you have known how to play hockey is street hockey, then there really isn't a problem. This is like Rodriguez only knowing how to speak Spanish. Then one day you find out you are on a new hockey team, except it's an ice hockey team. You don't know how to skate so there is a barrier that stops you. This is like Rodriguez having to speak English. You have all the skills to do everything except for one major factor in both cases. So what you must do to play hockey is practice hard to become part of the team. Rodriguez did this. He studied hard and became part of society. **(Jim)**

Reframing

Reframing involves taking an example that a writer has framed in one way (as Rodriguez has framed his own experience as an argument against bilingual education in schools) and seeing it in a different way. Readers of "Aria," for example, could reframe Rodriguez's story as an example of larger tensions between home and school, between private language and public language, between maintaining the culture of one's family and becoming assimilated into American society—tensions that could be found across many different experiences. Reframing often involves connecting what the writer has written with a different theme, one that links it to other stories and other examples. Here a reader has reframed Rodriguez's experience with the theme of assimilation into American culture.

> What I thought was most interesting about the story is how Rodriguez realizes that to become assimilated into American culture and language does not make you (as a foreigner) cultureless but more able to realize what things make your culture different by experiencing the country you live in. **(Shayna)**

Another reader's response suggests that two experiences (Rodriguez's and her own) can be reframed by the theme of tensions between traditional and modern ways.

> I do not value family language as deeply as Rodriguez. I think we, as people, become more modern, the family's heritage dies. My brother and I will not carry on the Philippine traditions as well as the generation before us. **(Jayme)**

Moving back and forth through all of these ways of connecting allows readers to participate most fully in the conversation invited by the writer.

Rodriguez's essay can be particularly difficult for some readers to connect with at first, particularly readers who have had no experience of growing up with a different language or culture from neighbors and classmates. But in looking more closely, we can almost always discover ways of relating to any human experience. Here's the reflection of a writer who grew up in an Irish community in Boston in the 1990s on this very concern:

One might ask—how does the difficulty of a Spanish-speaking kid in the 50's in California growing up relate to me? That's it there—the fact that he is growing up and has similar experiences as a child as we all do. For example, we can relate to possibly his difficulty in school or how his relationship with his parents suffered as a result of him becoming a part of society. These are experiences we can share and "converse" about through writing in hope of acquiring a common knowledge about something. For me right now it is knowledge about myself.

As an 18 year old kid still unsure of where I am headed, it always interests me to find out other people's experience with growing up. It's a conversation I think we all have with each other—whether it be through reading another's writing or introducing yourself to a stranger or spending time with friends. The end result is hopefully a better understanding about yourself and others. **(Matt S.)**

Note how this reader has *represented* Rodriguez's experience ("the difficulty of a Spanish-speaking kid in the 50's in California growing up"), has explored possible ways to *relate* to this experience from his own experience ("difficulty in school" or "relationship with parents"), and has found a way of *reframing* the two experiences ("experience with growing up," gaining "a better understanding about yourself"), bringing together several participatory ways of responding to a text, which in turn helps him to reflect again on his own understandings about himself. These aren't separate steps or isolated parts of our thinking, but they flow together as we work towards new understandings.

Finally, there will be moments when the ways in which we've reframed the writer's experience offer us other ways of jumping into the conversation the writer has invited—not just connecting, but disagreeing, arguing, and presenting other points of view. These too are ways in which you might want to participate.

READING RESPONSE

Look back at your glossings of "Aria." See where the connections you made involved recalling some aspect of your own experience. See where you have attempted to represent Rodriguez's experience or his understanding of that experience in your own words—to capture or sum up what you think he's saying. See where you have not only reflected on a connection with your own experience but where you've identified (or could identify) what the relationship is between his experience and your own or where you can put his experience into terms that are more familiar to you. See if there are places where you named a theme or idea, or can now name a theme or idea that can be used to reframe Rodriguez's experience in relationship to experiences that you, and many other people, might have had.

Write a journal response in which you follow out one or more of the ways in which you've connected with Rodriguez's memoir as a participatory reader. Draw the points in Rodriguez's text that are significant to these connections into your own writing by quoting them, creating the sense of a two way conversation. See what new understandings you can come to about Rodriguez's experience and/or your own as you build on the connections you've made.

Reading Analytically and Evaluatively

While we've been focusing on the sort of participatory reading that extends a conversation with an author, other approaches to reading call for stepping back out of the conversation—to understand why it worked the way it did, and to evaluate how well it worked. Seeing why a piece of writing works as it does, and evaluating how well it works will be helpful to you, not only as a reader, but as a writer who will be writing a memoir of your own (Chapter 3) and making choices similar to the ones Rodriguez has made.

As you step back from a written conversation, you can begin to see more clearly how the writer has built his part of it—not only what he has included, but how much, in what order, and how the picture he portrays or the argument he sets forth moves from step to step. This type of reading can be termed *analytical*, and it's the sort of reading we're more likely to do when we return to the text a second or third time.

What the writer includes depends on what he or she thinks you (the imagined reader) already know. Rodriguez assumes an audience of contemporary American readers who will have heard some of the public debates on bilingual education: readers who will be familiar with some aspects of the immigrant experience, but who, for the most part, won't have had that experience themselves. At times he'll remind his readers of the shared knowledge they already have as background to his story, or fill in what he thinks they might not know. He defines bilingual education for his readers, for example, though he defines it in his own way: as a "scheme" proposed by Hispanic-American social activists, whose goal is "to permit non-English-speaking children . . . to use their family language as the language of school" (p. 28). In doing so, he's evoking some shared knowledge that makes a story which speaks to the issue of bilingual education worth reading (answering the implied question: "So what?" "Why are you telling me this?"). But he also wants to have this conversation on his own terms, to establish his own definition as the basis for interpreting the story that will follow. In this way, as he tells the story of his own experience, creating new shared knowledge, he'll also, he hopes, create a shared interpretation of the experience as part of that knowledge.

As a first step in an analytical reading, then, you might look at <u>what</u> is being shared.

- What's being talked about?
- What are some key points in the text that seem to state what it's about most strongly?
- What are the themes that keep reappearing, the words that are repeated?

Because this essay contrasts Rodriguez's experiences of the linguistic worlds (or discourse communities) of home and school, one way of beginning to analyze the essay is to create two lists of words and phrases from the text—those associated with home and those associated with school. But Rodriguez also interrupts his portrayal of home and school at points to make some larger points about public issues, and you might also want to note where he does that, asking what elements of his personal experience he draws on to make those points and what information he has included about the public debate.

What Rodriguez talks about connects to why he talks about it. Part of his purpose involves making an argument against a public policy of supporting bilingual education in schools, though in choosing to write this essay in the genre of a memoir about his own experience, he most likely has some more personal goals as well: the memoir gives him a chance to revisit, reinterpret, and make more sense of his own experience, for himself as well as for us.

At this point we can analyze how Rodriguez has constructed his argument—how he has developed both the story and the framework through which he wants us to interpret it. Rodriguez wants to make some larger points, but he knows that his readers won't accept those points unless he engages them in some way, lets them see the issues as he has seen them, through the lens of his own experience, so part of the how is telling the story of that experience. At the same time, if he just told the story, without saying something about why he's telling it, his readers might turn away with a shrug and a "So what?" He thinks others will want to hear his story because he has something to contribute to a larger, public conversation about language and schooling—and it's that public conversation that gives his private experience its significance to other readers.

How Rodriguez tells his story includes the way he begins (with his memory of his first day of school), the way he moves among those memories and what he thinks they say about bilingual education, the points at which he moves in close to give us detailed images or moves back to give a more general picture of what his life was like at that time, and the words he chooses (including Spanish terms—*los gringos, mis hermanos*). Many of the places in the text that caught your attention in your first, participatory reading may be points you come back to, to analyze. The point of an *analytical reading* is to see how the text works in itself (apart from connections it might make to experiences you've had or read about), and reading others' texts in this way will be particularly valuable to you as a writer.

At this point you might also engage in a third type of reading: an *evaluative reading* that looks at *how well* the essay works to accomplish the writer's purpose. Maybe the evidence isn't convincing or doesn't take into account likely objections. Maybe the writer has told a powerful story, but that story leads you to a different conclusion than the one the writer has presented, or at least to a qualification of that conclusion. Rodriguez may have offered evidence from his own life which convinces you that there's a separation between intimate, family language and school language for "any child," but not that it makes a sufficient case for opposing the use of two public languages such as Spanish and English in a school bilingual education program. An evaluative response can focus on what works in the essay, as well as what's not completely involving or convincing. You might ask, "What do I find to be the most effective moments in this essay?" and "Why are they effective?" While our primary focus will be on participatory and then analytical readings in the next few chapters, trying on an evaluative stance with the work of other writers can help you become a better evaluative reader as you work on drafts and revisions of your own writing.

This is a good moment to reread "Aria" from an analytical and/or evaluative perspective. For a second reading, particularly when you're reading as a writer who will also be writing a memoir, you'll want to step away from the conversation invited by a written text to reflect more consciously on what it includes, what it's purpose is, and how it works. For this sort of reading, you'll want to take a close look at your glosses from a first reading, and add to them as you reread analytically. A paragraph-by-paragraph glossing to note the main point or main focus of each paragraph in the margin will be particularly useful for an analytical reading.

Responding Analytically

Look closely at the <u>what</u> of Rodriguez's memoir—tracing his ideas, his main points, his examples—through your glossing. Then step back to look at the <u>how</u> and the <u>why</u> of this essay, considering these questions:

—How does Rodriguez structure this essay? What examples does he bring in? How does he pull you into his own experiences? Where does he move in close to give us details from his experience of language in his family? Where does he step back from his story and make larger comments about what he sees as its meaning?

— Why does he structure this essay in this way? Why does he move as he does from past to more recent moments? Why does he interrupt his narrative to comment on it from his present perspective?

Choose one section of the memoir that most interested you and write a journal response in which you analyze what Rodriguez has written about and how, and the ways in which this section contributes to the larger structure and purposes of his memoir, including and quoting specific examples from the text that illustrate the points you make.

Responding Evaluatively

After you've reread the essay analytically, you may also want to respond evaluatively, imagining yourself in a conversation with the writer where you talk about where you connected with the text, what you liked in it (or didn't), and why. Imagining such conversations will also give you practice for responding to the writing of other student writers in your class.

Write an evaluative response in which you talk directly to Rodriguez about how he has written this section, describing the interaction between what he has written and your own response as a reader and why you find what he's written to be effective or confusing in addressing his apparent purposes as a writer.

Evaluative readings are often linked to our expectations about *genres*—to expectations that have been built up from our other experiences with a particular sort of text. We expect sitcoms, for example, to have laugh tracks, and producers who have tried to make sitcoms without them have found that their audiences were confused and discomfited. We expect horror/thriller movies to have appropriate background music, and it can be disconcerting to viewers if there is no music to signal when a terrifying moment is about to happen. Genres like the sitcom, the horror movie, the mystery or science-fiction story take on certain conventions over time, and while writers and directors may have good reasons for experimenting with the forms they've inherited, even those experiments depend on the prior expectations that viewers and readers have about the form. Again, genres arise when particular styles and formats are developed in response to a recurring situation, where similar needs or expectations are met over and over again.

The genre Rodriguez uses, the memoir, has been used most often when someone who is a public figure (often a published writer) goes back to share some aspect of his or her experience. Readers aren't generally interested in the trivia of even the most famous person's daily life, and how effectively a memoir works generally depends on how well the writer identifies and brings out themes from a particular life that speak to more general concerns. Part I includes several examples of the memoir genre that focus on a variety of experiences: moments in families, in schools, in neighborhoods, by writers from many different backgrounds. You may want to turn to one of them at this point, applying the ways of reading that we've explored here to another reading.

OBSERVING CONVERSATIONS IN WRITING CLASSROOMS

Readers whose purposes are guided by a course assignment most often bring what they've discovered in the written conversation back to a spoken conversation in the classroom. There, the text that has been read and the ways in which readers have responded to it become part of the new shared knowledge that the classroom community is creating. The conversations in college writing classrooms typically have the larger purpose of building some of the shared knowledge about academic literacy—about what's involved in reading and writing and carrying on conversations in college settings—that students will need for all of their courses. But this purpose is carried out in somewhat different ways in different classrooms, and in different moments of classroom conversation.

We can see some of these ways and purposes if we look at a moment of classroom conversation about "Aria" that took place in a college writing class. As you read this conversation and the discussion of it that follows, you'll also want to begin to think about the conversations that are going on in your own writing class, and you may want to take detailed notes on or even record some of your own classroom conversation so that you can look at what's going on in it together.

Conversation 2: In the College Classroom

TEACHER: Or another place in the text, if you see it somewhere else too. Is . . . Is home . . . Is home homey? (Students laugh.) For the lack of a better word? Ummm.

STUDENT 1: Doesn't he have intense pressure? (Teacher doesn't respond.)

TEACHER: Is it a dysfunctional family?

STUDENT 2: No.

TEACHER: Okay. All right. Home life is what? (*Teacher turns to write "home life" on the board.*)

STUDENT 2: Cold. It may be dysfunctional in a way . . . without the other two children. . . . He has a regular childhood before he got his education. . . . Well, I kinda developed my own thoughts. (*Students laugh.*)

TEACHER: Hey, he's making meaning, okay? He's making meaning. Okay, um . . . home life is—I think he uses the word "intimate" (*teacher writes "intimate" on the board*)—and school life is what?

STUDENT 2: Uhh . . . lonely reason.

TEACHER: Okay. (*Teacher writes "school life" and then "lonely reason" on the board.*) So as a young child, all right, as a young child he, he goes to school and he's told this is the way to act and speak and think. And he goes home and he says, "No, no, no, you know, you're the son of Mexican immigrants. Don't ever forget that." So how, how is an eight year old supposed to deal with that? And what are the alternatives? What could his parents have done? What could his teachers have done?

STUDENT 3: They could have told him that when you are at school, you know, be like other people. When you are at home, be yourself.

TEACHER: They could have helped him . . . right?

STUDENT 4: Or they could have gotten together, you know, and just sat down and talked to him, his teachers and his parents . . . that way he would have had both values . . . you know . . . he could have looked up to his parents for one thing and his teachers for another instead of having to choose between one and another.

Pause here for a moment and make your own observations in response to the questions we asked about the girls' conversation in the introduction:

- ■ <u>What</u>? What is the conversation about? What shared understandings are necessary to allow the conversation to continue?

- ■ <u>Why</u>? Why is this conversation taking place? What is its primary purpose? What other intentions and purposes might it serve?

- ■ <u>How</u>? What do you notice about how the participants go about achieving these purposes and building these understandings?

- ■ Finally, is there more you'd like to know about the <u>situation</u> in which the conversation is taking place?

If you compare your responses to the questions about the girls' kitchen table conversation and this classroom conversation, you'll see of course that what's being talked about is different, but that why its being talked about is different too. That difference in purpose reflects the fact that this conversation is taking place within the more formal setting of a classroom.

There are two concerns with this conversation—to keep it going, keep people participating, and to create a shared understanding of the topic. The reason for having most classroom conversations is not primarily to build an interpersonal relationship among the people in the classroom (though that's likely to happen to some degree), but to allow certain kinds of learning to take place. Here the balance of the two conversational concerns is reversed. Instead of building shared knowledge for the purpose of maintaining the sort of personal interaction that will support a friendship, the participants in this sort of academic conversation are interacting with each other for the purpose of building the shared understandings that the course curriculum calls for. Because of the strong direction toward the building up of specific shared knowledge in academic settings, the focus usually remains firmly on the topic.

In the more formal discourse communities of classrooms—where people have defined roles (teacher and students) and a defined goal (to accomplish the work of the course), the shared knowledge, shared purposes, and shared ways are likely to have specific characteristics, ones that we'll want to look at more closely for this classroom conversation and that you'll want to consider for a conversation in your classroom.

Shared Knowledge

Let's first consider the specific nature of the shared knowledge that's being built up in this academic conversation. As in any conversation, the teacher and students need some shared knowledge of what they're discussing:

- They need to have read the selection from Rodriguez's memoir, to have the information it contains about Rodriguez's experience. This *shared information* and a *shared general understanding* of what the reading is about is necessary for the conversation to continue, though the participants don't have to agree on exactly what this text means.

- Through their discussions, they'll also build a shared understanding of some *shared key concepts* that are important for the areas of study that the course will focus on. In this classroom we can see that one of those concepts is "making meaning"—the idea that speakers, like writers, aren't just stating what's obvious, but trying out new understandings.

- Over the course of this classroom conversation, the teacher and students try out various terms to describe Rodriguez's home and family life on the one hand, and his school experience on the other, gradually building a shared picture of some of the ways that those experiences might be seen, some *shared meanings* about and *interpretations* of that experience.

- They also develop a set of *shared terms* or *common vocabulary*—both from Rodriguez's text and from their own discussion—for describing that picture.

Shared Purpose

For the teacher and the students in this writing course, the general purpose of many conversations is to have the sort of discussion that will be helpful to writers, so they'll have some ideas about the reading that they can draw on in their papers. This segment, with its naming of the characteristics of home and school life sets up a comparison of the two that may be a future essay topic. The course itself guides the ways that participants will read and the meanings they'll make from their reading. It *frames* the readings with the focus of the course, guiding students to read from that perspective.

It's usually the teacher's role to structure specific classes to realize specific purposes. The teacher of this writing course is concerned about more than just having the students know who Richard Rodriguez is and what information is included in the text they've read. She's guiding them to think and talk in some of the ways that are characteristic of academic discourse communities:

- She wants them *to participate in particular ways of thinking*—to compare the two worlds of home and school that Rodriguez writes about.

- She wants them *to use language in particular ways* —*to name,* or *characterize,* each world, and to include some ways of naming that are more representative of academic terminology (so she goes from asking "Is home 'homey'?" to asking whether the family is "disfunctional").

- She wants them *to work with texts in particular ways,* to look closely at the text to support their ideas, so she points them to a word Rodriguez himself uses to characterize his home life: "intimate."

All the while she is listing these terms on the board, making two lists—one for home and one for school—so that they can step back and see what key points might be made in comparing the two. She is inviting the students in this class to participate in the sort of conversation that will go on, in talk and in writing, in many of the discourse communities they'll find in their college courses.

Shared Sense of How the Conversation Should Proceed

The <u>how</u> of classroom conversations, even in the same type of course, will vary. The pattern we see in this conversation is typical of the sort of conversation (the *genre* of classroom talk) referred to as *discussion.* In this classroom, the teacher is the leader who introduces the topic and guides the conversation, in accordance with a generally shared understanding of her role. But, as we've seen, she also guides the conversation in specific directions that fit with the framework of the course, and the shared knowledge/shared meanings that are important to the purposes of conversations in freshman writing classrooms. As in most classroom discussions:

- The ways in which participants contribute are closely *linked to their roles.* Here the teacher asks questions and the students respond to the teacher's questions. The discussion goes back and forth between the teacher and individual students, never from one student directly to another. The teacher doesn't respond to Student 1's response ("Doesn't he have intense pressure?") and his turn ends. But the exchange with Student 2 goes on for several turns (probably because that student's responses fit more with what she expected for answers).

- There are specific ways in which an individual response becomes part of the *official shared knowledge of the classroom* (or doesn't). Here the teacher responds in several ways: not answering, and following up with a new question (implying that the student's statement doesn't make a relevant contribution); giving a positive response ("all right") followed by a new question; encouraging the student to continue thinking along that line; or even writing the student's words on the board. With this last response, the teacher shows that she accepts the student's contribution as significant and is making it part of the official public language of the classroom. But it also ends that student's turn, and it's followed by new questions that she directs toward other students.

- There are different *segments within the conversation* related to the knowledge that's being built—moments in which the shared knowledge that's being created is summed up, and something new begins. The teacher sums up Rodriguez's experience as a young child and goes on to ask a new question: "What could his teachers have done?" prompting responses from Students 3 and 4.

- What gets built on in a discussion is linked to *the shared knowledge* that the course is building. For the purposes of this classroom, participants' contributions need to add to a shared understanding of Rodriguez's memoir but also to an understanding of the ways in which different writers' accounts of their experiences speak to a larger theme: moving from the private and intimate settings of home to the more formal and public ones of educational settings—a theme that's assumed to be of shared interest to the students and writers in this classroom.

The Situation

Again, as in the girls' conversation, it's the situation—who's participating and when and where—that determines what's important and meaningful in this conversation. In this classroom, as in many classrooms, the teacher plays a large role in this determination. At this point, early in the semester, it's the teacher's sense of what makes a meaningful contribution in this classroom discussion, what she sees as adding to a growing understanding of Rodriguez's memoir and of the larger theme of the course, that most strongly shapes this particular classroom conversation. Yet because all of the students have had their own conversation with Rodriguez's text, they bring their own perspectives to the classroom discussion—perspectives that may help to stretch the boundaries of what's significant and relevant to this conversation and open the way to new understandings for classmates and teacher alike.

OBSERVATION ACCOUNT

Observe and take detailed notes on a segment of your own classroom conversation.

1. Identify the different types of shared knowledge being developed, including:
   —general understandings about what you're discussing;
   —working concepts, representing ideas that you'll draw on and apply in other discussions and to other examples;
   —ideas and meanings that are repeated and expanded on;
   —other shared terms and common vocabulary.

   Are there other types of shared knowledge being built here? What gets written on the board, if anything? What do you think will become part of the official shared knowledge of the classroom—concepts and ideas and understandings that everyone will be assumed to share and to work from?

   What sorts of prior knowledge and experience do you think the students are bringing to this conversation that helps them participate?

2. Identify the shared purposes of this conversation.

   What do you think the larger purposes of your classroom conversations are and how does the moment you're analyzing fit into those purposes? Do the purposes include:
   —engaging in particular ways of thinking;
   —using particular ways of talking and naming what you're thinking about or what you observe?
   —drawing on a text in particular ways, if this segment focuses on the discussion of a text?
   —preparing for a follow-up activity?

   What other purposes (including interpersonal ones) do you see being fostered within this segment of a conversation?

3. Identify the shared ways of this conversation.

   What do you notice about the process of carrying out this classroom conversation?

   (continued)

How would you name the genre of that conversation (lecture, teacher-led discussion, another discussion format)?

Does everyone participate? (Who does and who doesn't?) In what ways? Are particular sorts of contributions associated with specific roles in the classroom?

How are contributions taken up as part of the shared knowledge of the classroom, or not?

Do you see small segments or movements of classroom exchange that mark phases in the development of shared knowledge or in classroom activity?

Do you see ways in which links are made between the shared knowledge of this conversational segment and the larger shared knowledge and shared purposes of the course?

4. Consider the situation—who, where, and when—of this segment of a classroom conversation, to see what it adds to your understanding of the shared knowledge, shared purposes, and shared ways.

In your observation account, take these elements into account, to describe the shared knowledge that's being created, the shared purposes that are being addressed, and the shared ways in which the conversation is being carried out in this classroom moment in relationship to what you've come to understand about the knowledge, purposes, and ways of the course. You might also look at your own role in the conversation. Your response will be most useful to your class's reflection on its conversations if you draw on specific examples that illustrate what you've come to understand from this observation and analysis. Compare these responses in class and create some shared understandings about whole class and group work.

REFLECTING ON HOW CONTEXT SHAPES READING

Sometimes, as readers, we are less interested in the way the writer has framed the conversation and more interested in what a text contributes to a conversation of our own. Each new conversation provides its own new situation and whatever is brought to that situation is adapted to new purposes. *Resituating* what someone has said or written involves making it fit into a new conversation. The girls at the kitchen table bring in what they know from the other worlds they inhabit and resituate that knowledge and even the words of those prior conversations in their present conversations. They talk about current styles or music or TV shows, often drawing from other texts (like those of songs or advertisements) that are available to them in popular culture.

The conversations in writing that take place in the academic world depend on prior conversations set forth in other written texts. Much of the shared knowledge of a field or a discipline, or of a generally educated person, resides in the texts that everyone has read. One of the most striking characteristics of the discourse of academic communities is the extent to which it refers to and builds on prior texts—whether they are the plays of Shakespeare, the writings of Freud, or the research reports of current researchers in physics or biochemistry. Drawing accurately from those prior texts—summarizing them, quoting them, and using them as a jumping-off point for further discussion, and for extending the literate conversation they've begun—is an important part of the discourse of the academic world.

When people write about texts, each writer, each contributor, extends the conversation that has been started, perhaps adding to it, perhaps taking it in a new direction, while acknowledging and giving credit to those people who have already contributed and reminding others of those earlier contributions. Each text, once it's published (or once its writer agrees that it can be made public), becomes available for new discussion, to be used in new conversations, directed to new purposes. The conversations represented in these chapters and the texts in the accompanying readings provide one illustration of how literate conversations work—identifying a topic or theme, drawing on what others have said about that topic by summarizing, restating, and quoting what has been written, and directing those prior contributions to a new purpose in a new conversation aimed at a new group of readers. (*Intertextuality* is a term used to name this quality, in written conversations, of referring to, evoking, or building on other texts.)

For Rodriguez, the conversations of home were shut off from the work of school, and later in his autobiography, he describes some of the effect his rigid separation of home and school had on him as a reader. Reading was a "chore" to do for school, one that left him feeling lonely and isolated. But he was determined to do well in school, so he read a lot.

> I entered high school having read hundreds of books. My habit of reading made me a confident speaker and writer of English. Reading also enabled me to sense something of the shape, the major concerns of Western thought. (I was able to say something about Dante and Descartes and Engels and James Baldwin in my high school term papers.) In these various ways, books brought me academic success as I hoped they would. But I was not a good reader. Merely bookish, I lacked a point of view when I read. I vacuumed books for epigrams, scraps of information, ideas, themes—anything to fill the hollow within me and make me feel educated. **(Hunger of Memory, 63–64)**

For Rodriguez, reading was not part of a conversation to which he could contribute his own ideas and understandings, in the way that he had in the spoken conversations of his family. Because he separated the "real" conversations of his childhood from his academic literacy, he was unable, until much later in his academic career, to engage in a thoughtful interaction with the texts he read in the ways we've explored in this chapter. But his experience provided the theme he began to explore as a writer. "If, because of my schooling, I had grown culturally separated from my parents, my education finally had given me ways of speaking and caring about that fact" (72). And his academic literacy gave him ways of stepping back and reflecting on his experience, to see what he and others could learn from it.

> REFLECTIVE
> INQUIRY
>
> This chapter has explored some of the different ways in which readers participate in the conversations that written texts invite. This is a good moment to step back and reflect on your own experience as a reader, reading for different purposes, in different settings. Are there specific moments in your own reading experience that you remember? Are there purposes for and ways of reading that you recall in relationship to any particular setting? Are there moments when reading became, for you, a conversation with the writer? Or did you associate reading with being "merely bookish," getting what you needed for school purposes but not interacting with the text beyond that? Have books or any other sorts of texts (crafted and formalized language—such as stories, song lyrics, sermons, whether read or heard) helped you to understand and explain your own experience? Are they something that you've carried with you into new settings and new conversations to use the insights they gave you for new purposes?
>
> In a journal response, try to capture and recreate some aspect of your reading experience, moving in closely to examine that experience and stepping back to explore how that experience represents your larger understandings about yourself as a reader, learner, text-user, and participant in conversations that take place with or draw from texts. Considering the ways in which reading has been described in this chapter, how might these prior experiences help shape your approach to new conversations with and about texts in academic settings?

All of the memoirs included in Part I are by writers who are exploring ways in which their experiences with language—the talk they heard around them in one setting or another, the words they remember, the ways they defined themselves in relationship to that talk and those words—have influenced who they are, what they think and write about, and how they write. So any of these memoirs can be resituated in relationship to a larger conversation about these concerns.

The next two chapters will move you more explicitly toward creating a memoir of your own, about your own experience within any of the discourse communities of your past and (implicitly or explicitly) how that contributes to who you are now as a reader, writer, and learner as you enter the new discourse communities of your academic study. Your own memoir will most likely focus on experiences that are very different from those of Rodriguez. But, as you recreate your experience in a past discourse community for your readers, you are very likely to try to recreate as well some of its conversations. Your own memoir need not make explicit reference to that of Rodriguez, but as you study and draw on the ways in which he has recreated moments in his own experience, you'll implicitly be bringing the conversation you've had with his text into your new conversation with your own readers, whether through the themes you explore or the ways in which you explore them.

<table>
<tr>
<td>

REFLECTIVE INQUIRY

</td>
<td>

Look back at the ways in which Rodriguez creates for us the feeling (and sometimes the actual words) of the conversations that took place at several points at his family dinner table, as well as the opening conversation of his first school day. Then remember a typical sort of conversation that went on in one of your own familiar settings, any moment where words were being used, even if only one person was actually speaking, in a kind of performance. Try to recreate it as he has (and as Cisneros has recreated a fictional version of conversations about a name), capturing its essence and the likely sorts of words that were spoken, even if you don't remember anything that was actually said. Use this inquiry to capture what you now see about that community, by reflecting back on your past experience, to let your readers come to those understandings through what you show them in your description of this moment (rather than through what you tell them explicitly).

</td>
</tr>
</table>

WRITING IN ACADEMIC GENRES

Part I is intended to guide you as a writer who will work within the genre of the memoir, but there are other ways in which a reading is typically resituated in new writing in academic settings, and this is a good moment to explore those as well.

Although there are many genres of academic writing, including the research report that we'll work on in later chapters, one of the most common genres is the *academic essay* (a broad genre that includes many sub-types). *Essay* is a useful term for a genre of writing that involves explorations guided, at least in part, by the writer's interests and purposes as opposed to a more directly utilitarian genre such as a letter of complaint or even a genre with a more specifically defined purpose, such as a lab report.

We've come to associate the term *essay* with school genres, written for school purposes, and with particular types or sub-genres of school essays, such as the "persuasive essay" that shows up on many standardized English tests. But *essay* can also refer to a genre of nonfiction that is intended not just to report information but to engage readers as participants in some experience or discovery or area of reflection, and that may be published in magazines or newspaper supplements or in collections by a writer or about a theme. Rodriguez's memoir is an essay of this sort.

Essays are also shaped by some shared expectations within a community of readers. In academic settings, it's the shared expectations that have been built up among writers and readers of the academic essay that matter most to writers who are entering academic conversations. This may be a good moment to try out some of the expectations in an exploratory way, so that you can continue your own classroom discussion about the ways of both spoken and written conversations in academic settings.

Each chapter will include suggestions for *exploratory essays* that follow from the work of the chapter. These are intended to guide you in giving shape to the ideas and observations you've explored in writing and discussion in ways that are typical of the academic essay in one of its forms. Exploratory essays offer you a chance to try out a particular type of academic essay and then talk about what you've tried with other writers in your class, seeing what some common expectations might be for such an essay.

Any of your exploratory essays might be turned into a piece of *formal writing*—a fully-developed and complete essay or report in a final, edited version. In that case the final form of the writing will be important, and you'll draw on the understandings you've developed with classmates about particular structures and forms to present your own finished piece of writing. In addition to the formal memoir at the end of Chapter 3, you may want to prepare other formal pieces of writing in Part I. Suggestions for drafting, revising, and editing your essays can be found in the Writing Strategies section.

The Essay in Response to a Reading

A common type of academic essay is one that asks you to write about a theme as it's presented in a particular reading or a question as it can be explored through a particular reading. While the themes for such essays are often assigned, when you've worked with an essay as you have with Rodriguez's memoir, you are likely to have discovered a theme or question that genuinely interests you—an idea that has allowed you to reframe Rodriguez's experience and to see how it might address some of your own experiences or concerns. Working with such an idea will allow your essay to be guided by your own interests and purposes (as an essay ideally should be).

Try thinking about your essay from three perspectives:

IDENTIFY AND EXPLORE A THEME

1. <u>What you want to explore and why</u>. You might begin by looking back at the informal writing you've done to see what ideas you really want to explore further, and then look back at the text of "Aria" to find places you've glossed that connect with one of those ideas. Or you might begin by turning again to a quotation that seems significant to you and working from that quotation, moving from what it suggests about a theme you might want to pursue to other parts of the text that add to the understanding you've gained in this one section. You might also generate a list of possible themes with members of your working group, to stimulate your own thinking.

   If you prefer to work with a set question that focuses on the theme of discourse communities, here's one you might explore: In "Aria," Richard Rodriguez describes his experiences in each of two discourse communities, home and school, exploring the understanding he has come to from those experiences.

(continued)

(*continued*)

How does he describe his experience in each of those discourse communities, and how does he draw on those experiences to show how he has come to his beliefs about private and public language?

2. <u>What your readers might be interested in and why</u>. You'll want to consider who your readers will be, what they already know and what you'll need to tell them. You'll also need to think about what you want to show them from the text, what evidence you want to give them, that will help them follow out your exploration with you and see the understanding you've come to.

3. <u>How to do all of this in the ways that are typical of the discourse community you're writing for</u>. You'll want to consider your writing community's assumptions and expectations for this type of essay. They will probably include drawing quotations directly from Rodriguez's text that illustrate the points you want to make to your readers.

Here are some other steps that you might take after drafting this essay:

Reflecting

When you've completed a draft of your essay, reflect on your process, purposes, and assumptions (what you did, what you were trying to do, and why).

- How did you go about writing this essay? What did you do first, second, etc.?

- What guidelines did you have in your own mind about how an essay like this might be structured? About other aspects of essay writing? How did you follow out your prior understandings as you made choices in your writing?

- What were your purposes in writing this essay? How did those purposes influence what you did as a writer?

Sharing

Share your essays with other readers to develop a shared understanding of what elements seem important in creating an essay about another essay (Rodriguez's memoir) that can bring readers into your own discoveries. Use this opportunity to discuss some of your assumptions and approaches as a class to begin to create shared understandings about the range of strategies and options available to you, and the ones that will be most significant in your present setting.

CHAPTER
2

Writing as Conversation

Chapter 2 focuses on written conversations from the perspective of the writer. At its center is a memoir by Barbara Mellix, "From Outside, In." In this essay, the author reflects on what was involved for her as she negotiated different dialects and different ways of thinking about language on her way to becoming a confident college writer. Working with Mellix's memoir, we'll consider what's involved in our competence as readers, writers, and speakers—a competence that allows us to communicate effectively within familiar settings and to move into new settings and acquire new ways of using language.

Chapter 2 pursues three lines of inquiry:

- In what ways are writers, like readers, participating in conversations in writing, and how can we identify the elements of competence that allow them to do so successfully?

- What can we learn about such competence by seeing what we do as we shift from telling to writing stories in a specific setting?

- What can we discover by reflecting on our own longstanding experience as writers?

These inquiries contribute to the larger questions of Part I by adding new perspectives on the question of who you are and what you bring to the academic conversations in which you're now a participant. The chapter ends with suggestions for writing in some of the genres that are common in academic writing: applying a question to a reading, writing a comparison essay, and writing a short research report.

If a reader is taking part in a conversation in writing, the writer must be as well. A writer must imagine the conversation, consider what will capture the reader's attention, and keep the reader involved, just as if they were talking. Readers bring their own understandings and expectations to the conversation, and the writer must anticipate the sort of back and forth exchange with those readers that might occur if they were in the same room.

To write for readers (as opposed to writing in a private journal or working notebook), you have to take on the roles of both speaker and listener, imagining the listener's response to what you've said and how to shape or reshape what you'll say to evoke a particular response (or at least some response). What do you bring, as a writer, to such conversations? You bring an understanding of how to participate in conversations, developed through your experience in many conversations in many discourse communities—your *discourse competence*. You bring all of your experience in altering your language and style in ways that are appropriate to the changing contexts you're in. And you bring your own experience as a writer.

READING A WRITER'S REFLECTIONS ON COMMUNITY AND COMPETENCE

All college writers have to figure out how to take what they already know and adapt it to the new circumstances in which they are writing. As they move into and among different communities, they need to be sensitive to subtle differences not only in what people talk and write about, but in the ways they talk and write about it. Reading about the experiences of others who have made significant adaptations will help you think about the subtle shifts you make every day as a speaker and writer and the discourse competence these shifts represent.

In her memoir "From Outside, In," Barbara Mellix explores what she came to learn as a college writer by going back to reflect on her experience of language in different settings. Like many African Americans, Mellix uses a distinct variety of English, which she refers to as "black English," with close friends and family, even as she speaks and writes the mainstream version of the language (which she calls "standard English") in less intimate circumstances. In her memoir, she draws on her experience of language in different settings to explore what she's learned about shifting her language for different contexts, using what she has come to understand as a speaker to see her own development as a writer in different settings.

As you turn to Mellix's memoir, you are once again entering a new conversation—the one that she invites with her readers—but one now situated in the larger context of this book, the work of Cisneros and Rodriguez, the stories you've heard from classmates, and your own reflections and rememberings. So this time the written conversation isn't wholly new, and you're not wholly an outsider. One aspect of discourse competence involves paying attention to the prior knowledge that you bring and can build on when you start a new reading.

Look at the title, "From Outside, In" and think about what it suggests in relationship to the themes of this book so far. Glance quickly through the pages of Mellix's memoir to get some sense of <u>what</u> this reading is about, and then reflect on the background knowledge you bring to this topic. Think also about Mellix's possible purposes for writing as well as your purposes for reading in the context of this chapter. Those purposes affect <u>how</u> you read. If you're just reading to find examples of Mellix crossing discourse communities or displaying her discourse competence, you might skim quickly to get that information. But this is a memoir—a narrative of someone's experience—not a textbook chapter, so that may lead you to approach the reading in a different way, as might the fact that you too are a writer who will be writing a memoir.

READING RESPONSE

Gloss Mellix's text as you read. Afterward, look back through your glossings and find a few places that particularly capture your interest or curiosity. Copy the words (with a page number) to start your journal response. Working with each quotation, explore in your response what you think Mellix is saying and why you think it's interesting or important (drawing on the ways of responding through representing, recalling, relating and/or reframing that you explored in Chapter 1). How does it contribute to the meanings Mellix is trying to express in the immediate context of the surrounding paragraph(s)? In the larger memoir? Are there questions that it raises or answers for you about what's involved in moving between discourse communities as a speaker and writer? Are there connections it makes for you to the memoir by Rodriguez (or others) or to your own experience? (You may want to use a double-entry notebook format, described in Strategies, pp. 502–503, for working with readings in this way.)

As you discuss this essay, drawing on the quotations you've chosen, you might want to consider the following questions:

What are some of the distinct discourse communities Mellix describes and what makes them distinct? How does she name them, or how would you name them?

How does Mellix try to characterize and make sense of her experience in each community? What words and phrases does she use to try to explain her observations about these experiences?

What does Mellix's essay contribute to your understanding of discourse (language as used in social context) and discourse communities?

Does Mellix's essay lead you to recall anything more about your own experiences with discourse communities or add anything to your perspective on those experiences?

From Outside, In

Barbara Mellix

1   Two years ago, when I started writing this paper, trying to bring order out of chaos, my ten-year-old daughter was suffering from an acute attack of boredom. She drifted in and out of the room complaining that she had nothing to do, no one to "be with" because none of her friends were at home. Patiently I explained that I was working on something special and needed peace and quiet, and I suggested that she paint, read, or work with her computer. None of these interested her. Finally, she pulled up a chair to my desk and watched me, now and then heaving long, loud sighs. After two or three minutes (nine or ten sighs), I lost my patience. "Looka here, Allie," I said, "you too old for this kinda carryin' on. I done told you this is important. You wronger than dirt to be in here haggin' me like this and you know it. Now git on outta here and leave me off before I put my foot all the way down."

I was at home, alone with my family, and my daughter understood that this way of speaking was appropriate in that context. She knew, as a matter of fact, that it was almost inevitable; when I get angry at home, I speak some of my finest, most cherished black English. Had I been speaking to my daughter in this manner in certain other environments, she would have been shocked and probably worried that I had taken leave of my sense of propriety.

Like my children, I grew up speaking what I considered two distinctly different languages—black English and standard English (or as I thought of them then, the ordinary everyday speech of "country" coloreds and "proper" English)—and in the process of acquiring these languages, I developed an understanding of when, where, and how to use them. But unlike my children, I grew up in a world that was primarily black. My friends, neighbors, minister, teachers—almost everybody I associatetl with every day—were black. And we spoke to one another in our own special language: *That sho is a pretty dress you got on. If she don' soon leave me off I'm gon tell her head a mess. I was so mad I could'a pissed a blue nail. He all the time trying to low-rate somebody. Ain't that just about about the nastiest thing you ever set ears on?*

Then there were the "others," the "proper" blacks, transplanted relatives and one-time friends who came home from the city for weddings, funerals, and vacations. And the whites. To these we spoke standard English. "Ain't?" my mother would yell at me when I used the term in the presence of "others." "You *know* better than that." And I would hang my head in shame and say the "proper" word.

5   I remember one summer sitting in my grandmother's house in Greeleyville, South Carolina, when it was full of the chatter of city relatives who were home on vacation. My parents sat quietly, only now and then volunteering a comment or answering a question. My mother's face took on a strained expression when she spoke. I could see that she was being careful to say just the right words in just the right way. Her voice sounded thick, muffled. And when she finished speaking, she would lapse into silence, her proper smile on her face. My father was more articulate, more aggressive. He spoke quickly, his words sharp and clear. But he held his proud head higher, a signal that he, too, was uncomfortable. My sisters and brothers and I stared at our aunts, un-

cles, and cousins, speaking only when prompted. Even then, we hesitated, formed our sentences in our minds, then spoke softly, shyly.

My parents looked small and anxious during those occasions, and I waited impatiently for our leave-taking when we would mock our relatives the moment we were out of their hearing. "Reeely," we would say to one another, flexing our wrists and rolling our eyes, "how dooo you stan' this heat? Chile, it just too hyooo-mid for words." Our relatives had made us feel "country," and this was our way of regaining pride in ourselves while getting a little revenge in the bargain. The words bubbled in our throats and rolled across our tongues, a balming.

As a child I fell this same doubleness in uptown Greeleyville where the whites lived. "Ain't that a pretty dress you're wearing!" Toby, the town policeman, said to me one day when I was fifteen. "Thank you very much," I replied, my voice barely audible in my own ears. The words felt wrong in my mouth, rigid, foreign. It was not that I had never spoken that phrase before—it was common in black English, too—but I was extremely conscious that this was an occasion for proper English. I had taken out my English and put it on as I did my church clothes, and I felt as if I were wearing my Sunday best in the middle of the week. It did not matter that Toby had not spoken grammatically correct English. He was white and could speak as he wished. I had something to prove. Toby did not.

Speaking standard English to whites was our way of demonstrating that we knew their language and could use it. Speaking it to standard-English-speaking blacks was our way of showing them that we, as well as they, could "put on airs." But when we spoke standard English, we acknowledged (to ourselves and to others—but primarily to ourselves) that our customary way of speaking was inferior. We felt foolish, embarrassed; somehow diminished because we were ashamed to be our real selves. We were reserved, shy in the presence of those who owned and/or spoke *the* language.

My parents never set aside time to drill us in standard English. Their forms of instruction were less formal. When my father was feeling particularly expansive, he would regale us with tales of his exploits in the outside world. In almost flawless English, complete with dialogue and flavored with gestures and embellishment, he told us about his attempt to get a haircut at a white barbershop; his refusal to acknowledge one of the town merchants until the man addressed him as "Mister"; the time he refused to step off the sidewalk uptown to let some whites pass; his airplane trip to New York City (to visit a sick relative) during which the stewardesses and porters— recognizing that he was a "gentleman"—addressed him as "Sir" I did not realize then—nor, I think, did my father—that he was teaching us, among other things, standard English and the relationship between language and power.

10   My mother's approach was different. Often, when one of us said, "I'm gon wash off my feet," she would say, "And what will you walk on if you wash them off?" Everyone would laugh at the victim of my mother's "proper" mood. But it was different when one of us children was in a proper mood. "You think you are so superior," I said to my oldest sister one day when we were arguing and she was winning. "Superior!" my sister mocked. "You mean I'm acting 'biggidy'?" My sisters and brothers sniggered, then joined in teasing me. Finally, my mother said, "Leave your sister alone. There's nothing wrong with using proper English." There was a half-smile on her face. I had gotten "uppity," had

"put on airs" for no good reason. I was at home, alone with the family, and I hadn't been prompted by one of my mother's proper moods. But there was also a proud light in my mother's eyes; her children were learning English very well.

Not until years later, as a college student, did I begin to understand our ambivalence toward English, our scorn of it, our need to master it, to own and be owned by it—an ambivalence that extended to the public-school classroom. In our school, where there were no whites, my teachers taught standard English but used black English to do it. When my grammar-school teachers wanted us to write, for example, they usually said something like, "I want y'all to write five sentences that make a statement. Anybody git done before the rest can color." It was probably almost those exact words that led me to write these sentences in 1953 when I was in the second grade:

> The white clouds are pretty.
> There are only 15 people in our room.
> We will go to gym.
> We have a new poster. We may go out doors.

Second grade came after "Little First" and "Big First," so by then I knew the implied rules that accompanied all writing assignments. Writing was an occasion for proper English. I was not to write in the way we spoke to one another: The white clouds pretty; There ain't but 15 people in our room; We going to gym; We got a new poster; We can go out in the yard. Rather I was to use the language of "other": clouds *are*, there *are*, we *will*, we *have*, we *may*.

My sentences were short, rigid, perfunctory, like the letters my mother wrote to relatives:

> Dear Papa,
> How are you? How is Mattie? Fine I hope. We are fine. We will come to see you Sunday. Cousin Ned will give us a ride.
> > Love,
> > Daughter

The language was not ours. It was something from outside us, something we used for special occasions.

15   But my coloring on the other side of that second-grade paper is different. I drew three hearts and a sun. The sun has a smiling face that radiates and envelops everything it touches. And although the sun and its world are enclosed in a circle, the colors I used—red, blue, green, purple, orange, yellow, black—indicate that I was less restricted with drawing and coloring than I was with writing standard English. My valentines were not just red. My sun was not just a yellow ball in the sky.

By the time I reached the twelfth grade, speaking and writing standard English had taken on new importance. Each year, about half of the newly graduated seniors of our school moved to large cities—particularly in the North—to live with relatives and find work. Our English teacher constantly corrected our grammar: "Not 'ain't,' but 'isn't.' " We seldom wrote papers, and even those few were usually plot summaries of short stories. When our teacher returned the papers, she usually lectured on the importance of using standard English: "I *am*; you *are*; he, she, or it *is*," she would say, writing on the chalkboard as she spoke. "How you gon git a job talking about 'I is,' or 'I isn't' or 'I ain't?'"

In Pittsburgh, where I moved after graduation, I watched my aunt and uncle—who had always spoken standard English when in Greeleyville—switch from black English to standard English to a mixture of the two, according to where they were or who they were with. At home and with certain close relatives, friends, and neighbors, they spoke black English. With those less close, they spoke a mixture. In public and with strangers, they generally spoke standard English.

In time, I learned to speak standard English with ease and to switch smoothly from black to standard or a mixture, and back again. But no matter where I was, no matter what the situation or occasion. I continued to write as I had in school:

Dear Mommie,
How are you? How is everybody else? Fine I hope. I am fine. So are Aunt and Uncle. Tell everyone I said hello. I will write again soon.
                    Love,
                    Barbara

At work, at a health insurance company, I learned to write letters to customers. I studied form letters and letters written by co-workers, memorizing the phrases and the ways in which they were used. I dictated:

20   Thank you for your letter of January 5. We have made the changes in your coverage you requested. Your new premium will be $150 every three months. We are pleased to have been of service to you.

In a sense, I was proud of the letters I wrote for the company: they were proof of my ability to survive in the city, the outside world—an indication of my growing mastery of English. But they also indicate that writing was still mechanical for me, something that didn't require much thought.

Reading also became a more significant part of my life during those early years in Pittsburgh. I had always liked reading, but now I devoted more and more of my spare time to it. I read romances, mysteries, popular novels. Looking back, I realize that the books I liked best were simple, unambiguous: good versus bad and right versus wrong with right rewarded and wrong punished, mysteries unraveled and all set right in the end. It was how I remembered life in Greeleyville.

Of course I was romanticizing. Life in Greeleyville had not been so very uncomplicated. Back there I had been—first as a child, then as a young woman with limited experience in the outside world—living in a relatively closed-in society. But there were implicit and explicit principles that guided our way of life and shaped our relationships with one another and the people outside—principles that a newcomer would find elusive and baffling. In Pittsburgh, I had matured, become more experienced: I had worked at three different jobs, associated with a wider range of people, married, had children. This new environment with different prescripts for living required that I speak standard English much of the time, and slowly, imperceptibly, I had ceased seeing a sharp distinction between myself and "others." Reading romances and mysteries, characterized by dichotomy, was a way of shying away from change, from the person I was becoming.

But that other part of me—that part which took great pride in my ability to hold a job writing business letters—was increasingly drawn to the new developments in my life and the attending possibilities, opportunities for even greater change. If I could write letters for a nationally known business, could I not also do something better, more challenging, more important? Could I not, perhaps, go to college and become a school teacher? For years, afraid and a little embarrassed, I did no more than imagine this different me, this possible me. But sixteen years after coming north, when my youngest daughter entered kindergarten, I found myself unable—or unwilling—to resist the lure of possibility. I enrolled in my first college course: Basic Writing, at the University of Pittsburgh.

25   For the first time in my life, I was required to write extensively about myself. Using the most formal English at my command, I wrote these sentences near the beginning of the term:

> One of my duties as a homemaker is simply picking up after others. A day seldom passes that I don't search for a mislaid toy, book, or gym shoe, etc. I change the Ty-D-Bol, fight "ring around the collar," and keep our laundry smelling "April fresh." Occasionally, I settle arguments between my children and suggest things to do when they're bored. Taking telephone messages for my oldest daughter is my newest (and sometimes most aggravating) chore. Hanging the toilet paper roll is my most insignificant.

My concern was to use "appropriate" language, to sound as if I belonged in a college classroom. But I felt separate from the language—as if it did not and could not belong to me. I couldn't think and feel genuinely in that language, couldn't make it express what I thought and felt about being a housewife. A part of me resented, among other things, being judged by such things as the appearance of my family's laundry and toilet bowl, but in that language I could only imagine and write about a conventional housewife.

For the most part, the remainder of the term was a period of adjustment, a time of trying to find my bearings as a student in a college composition class, to learn to shut out my black English whenever I composed, and to prevent it from creeping into my formulations; a time for trying to grasp the language of the classroom and reproduce it in my prose; for trying to talk about myself in that language, reach others through it. Each experience of writing was like standing naked and revealing my imperfection, my "otherness." And each new assignment was another chance to make myself over in language, reshape myself, make myself "better" in my rapidly changing image of a student in a college composition class.

But writing became increasingly unmanageable as the term progressed, and by the end of the semester, my sentences sounded like this:

30   My excitement was soon dampened, however, by what seemed like a small voice in the back of my head saying that I should be careful with my long awaited opportunity, I felt frustrated and this seemed to make it difficult to concentrate.

There is a poverty of language in these sentences. By this point, I knew that the clichéd language of my Housewife essay was unacceptable, and I generally recognized trite expressions. At the same time, I hadn't yet mastered the language of the classroom, hadn't yet come to see it as belonging to me. Most notable is the lifelessness of the prose, the apparent absence of a person behind the words. I wanted those sentences—and the rest of the essay—to convey the anguish of yearning to, at once, become something more and yet remain the same. I had the sensation of being split in two, part of me going into a future the other part didn't believe possible. As that person, the student writer at that moment, I was essentially mute. I could not—in the process of composing—use the language of the old me, yet I couldn't imagine myself in the language of "others."

I found this particularly discouraging because at midsemester I had been writing in a much different way. Note the language of this introduction to an essay I had written then, near the middle of the term:

> Pain is a constant companion to the people in "Footwork." Their jobs are physically damaging. Employers are insensitive to their feelings and in many cases add to their problems. The general public wounds them further by treating them with disgrace because of what they do for a living. Although the workers are as diverse as they are similar, there is a definite link between them. They suffer a great deal of abuse.

The voice here is stronger, more confident, appropriating terms like "physically damaging," "wounds them further," "insensitive," "diverse"—terms I couldn't have imagined using when writing about my own experience—and shaping them into sentences like, "Although the workers are as diverse as they are similar, there is a definite link between them." And there is the sense of a personality behind the prose, someone who sympathizes with the workers: "The general public wounds them further by treating them with disgrace because of what they do for a living."

35   What caused these differences? I was, I believed, explaining other people's thoughts and feelings, and I was free to move about in the language of "others" so long as I was speaking *of* others. I was unaware that I was transforming into my best classroom language my own thoughts and feelings about people whose experiences and ways of speaking were in many ways similar to mine.

The following year, unable to turn back or to let go of what had become something of an obsession with language (and hoping to catch and hold the sense of control that had eluded me in Basic Writing), I enrolled in a research writing course. I spent most of the term learning how to prepare for and write a research paper. I chose sex education as my subject and spent hours in libraries, searching for information, reading, taking notes. Then (not without messiness and often-demoralizing frustration) I organized my information into categories, wrote a thesis statement, and composed my paper—a series of paraphrases and quotations spaced between carefully constructed transitions. The process and results felt artificial, but as I would later come to realize I was passing through a necessary stage. My sentences sounded like this:

> This reserve becomes understandable with examination of who the abusers are. In an overwhelming number of cases, they are people the victims know and trust.

Family members, relatives, neighbors and close family friends commit seventy-five percent of all reported sex crimes against children, and parents, parent substitutes and relatives are the offenders in thirty to eighty percent of all reported cases. While assault by strangers does occur, it is less common, and is usually a single episode. But abuse by family members, relatives and acquaintances may continue for an extended period of time. In cases of incest, for example, children are abused repeatedly for an average of eight years. In such cases, "the use of physical force is rarely necessary because of the child's trusting, dependent relationship with the offender. The child's cooperation is often facilitated by the adult's position of dominance, an offer of material goods, a threat of physical violence, or a misrepresentation of moral standards."

The completed paper gave me a sense of profound satisfaction, and I read it often after my professor returned it. I know now that what I was pleased with was the language I used and the professional voice it helped me maintain. "Use better words," my teacher had snapped at me one day after reading the notes I'd begun accumulating from my research, and slowly I began taking on the language of my sources. In my next set of notes, I used the word "vacillating"; my professor applauded. And by the time I composed the final draft, I felt at ease with terms like "overwhelming number of cases," "single episode," and "reserve," and I shaped them into sentences similar to those of my "expert" sources.

If I were writing the paper today, I would of course do some things differently. Rather than open with an anecdote—as my teacher suggested—I would begin simply with a quotation that caught my interest as I was researching my paper (and which I scribbled, without its source, in the margin of my notebook): "Truth does not do so much good in the world as the semblance of truth does evil." The quotation felt right because it captured what was for me the central idea of my essay—an idea that emerged gradually during the making of my paper—and expressed it in a way I would like to have said it. The anecdote, a hypothetical situation I invented to conform to the information in the paper, felt forced and insincere because it represented—to a great degree—my teacher's understanding of the essay, *her* idea of what in it was most significant. Improving upon my previous experiences with writing, I was beginning to think and feel in the language I used, to find my own voices in it, to sense that how one speaks influences how one means. But I was not yet secure enough, comfortable enough with the language to trust my intuition.

40   Now that I know that to seek knowledge, freedom, and autonomy means always to be in the concentrated process of becoming—always to be venturing into new territory, feeling one's way at first, then getting one's balance, negotiating, accommodating, discovering one's self in ways that previously defined "others"— I sometimes get tired. And I ask myself why I keep on participating in this highbrow form of violence, this slamming against perplexity. But there is no real futility in the question, no hint of that part of the old me who stood outside standard English, hugging to herself a disabling mistrust of a language she thought could not represent a person with her history and experience. Rather, the question represents a person who feels the consequence of her education, the weight of her possibilities as a teacher and writer and

human being, a voice in society. And I would not change that person, would not give back the good burden that accompanies my growing expertise, my increasing power to shape myself in language and share that self with "others."

"To speak," says Frantz Fanon, "means to be in a position to use a certain syntax, to grasp the morphology of this or that language, but it means above all to assume a culture, to support the weight of a civilization."* To write means to do the same, but in a more profound sense. However, Fanon also says that to achieve mastery means to "get" in a position of power, to "grasp," to "assume." This, I have learned—both as a student and subsequently as a teacher—can involve tremendous emotional and psychological conflict for those attempting to master academic discourse. Although as a beginning student writer I had a fairly good grasp of ordinary spoken English and was proficient at what Labov calls "code-switching" (and what John Baugh In *Black Street Speech* terms "style shifting"), when I came face to face with the demands of academic writing, I grew increasingly self-conscious, constantly aware of my status as a black and a speaker of one of the many black English vernaculars—a traditional outsider. For the first time, I experienced my sense of doubleness as something menacing, a built-in enemy. Whenever I turned inward for salvation, the balm so available during my childhood, I found instead this new fragmentation which spoke to me in many voices. It was the voice of my desire to prosper, but at the same time it spoke of what I had relinquished and could not regain: a safe way of being, a state of powerlessness which exempted me from responsibility for who I was and might be. And it accused me of betrayal, of turning away from blackness. To recover balance, I had to take on the language of the academy, the language of "others." And to do that, I had to learn to imagine myself a part of the culture of that language, and therefore someone free to manage that language, to take liberties with it. Writing and rewriting, practicing, experimenting, I came to comprehend more fully the generative power of language. I discovered—with the help of some especially sensitive teachers—that through writing one can continually bring new selves into being, each with new responsibilities and difficulties, but also with new possibilities. Remarkable power, indeed. I write and continually give birth to myself.

Mellix's memoir enriches our picture of what's involved in moving between discourse communities, but it also provides a way of looking at some specific elements of *discourse competence* that you'll look at in your own speaking and writing. These elements include:

■ sensitivity to context;

■ attention to shared knowledge, purposes, and ways within a discourse community;

■ a sense of the different expectations of different discourse communities;

Black Skin, White Masks (1952; rpt. New York: Grove Press, 1967), pp. 17–18.

- flexible understanding of appropriate language and style;
- willingness to take risks and try out different ways of saying something, in speaking or in writing.

As we consider each of these, you may want to look back again at your glossed text to think about the examples Mellix gives and see precisely how these elements of discourse competence work for her.

Sensitivity to context. Mellix tells us how aware she was, even as a child, that you have to pay attention to the context in which you're speaking. Her examples show that she understood implicitly (and was sometimes told explicitly) that her family's "own special language" was reserved for some contexts and that the common language of the larger society was to be used in others. She's able to draw on this awareness of context as she thinks about her work as a writer.

Attention to the shared knowledge, purposes, and ways of a discourse community. Within each discourse community that Mellix spends time in, she comes to understand what's known and expected by insiders to that community. Part of what's shared within each community is not only what you talk about at home or in a business letter, but also how you talk about it, and what the purposes are (like showing your daughter that you're really angry about being interrupted when you're trying to write, or maintaining a smooth business relationship with customers). In writing this memoir, she's also writing for an implied discourse community, one made up of other college writers and college writing teachers, and you can see how she has addressed her readers' likely purposes, created the shared knowledge they need, and done so in ways that will keep them moving with her through the conversation.

A sense of the different expectations of different discourse communities. Because she moves among such very different discourse communities, Mellix quickly comes to understand not only that a given community has particular ways of interacting, but also that there are different expectations for each one. We see her paying attention to those expectations as she moves from home to school, to her first job, and to college. Acquiring the ways of using language that are characteristic of each new setting is a slow process, but her awareness that she needs to pay attention to differences helps her adapt to each one as a speaker. And she gives us examples of her adaptation of her written language as well, from the letters she writes home, to the business letters she writes at work, to the writing she does for her courses.

In all of this Mellix demonstrates *a flexible understanding of appropriate language and style.* She tries on the discourse of each setting she's in, speaking and writing in ways that will let her get along within that setting. Most of the time she acquires new ways of using language naturally through participating in a setting, but other speakers sometimes call her attention to particular features: "'Ain't?' my mother would yell at me when I used the term in the presence of *others.*" Sometimes she and her siblings mock her relatives' fancy English, and sometimes they mock each other's: when she charges her sister with acting "superior" rather than "biggidy," she gets accused of getting "uppity" and is told that she has "put on airs." And in school, her English teacher constantly corrects her grammar: "Not 'ain't' but 'isn't'." Yet despite hearing these rules, her own experience in different communities lets her see that they can't be applied rigidly but have to be adapted to different contexts and her own purposes.

Finally, what really fuels Mellix's acquisition of new discourses is her *willingness to take risks*—to try out the ways she observes others using language in a setting, to work to say or write things in the new discourse, even though she might not get it quite right the first time.

We'll return to Mellix's reflections on what she had to learn as a college writer after you begin your own inquiry into your own discourse competence.

EXPLORING SPOKEN AND WRITTEN STORYTELLING

Here we'll explore the concept of discourse competence in more detail, seeing how it appears in one sort of classroom conversation—the telling of stories in the classroom, and how that carries over to a written version of the same conversation. In the following excerpt from a classroom conversation, students in a college writing class are telling each other stories. Their purposes are partly to get to know each other early in the semester, partly to begin their thinking about possible incidents that they can draw on for a memoir, and partly to see whether there are any differences in the ways they tell their stories to each other and the ways in which they write them (so they tape-record and transcribe the stories they tell). To see what kinds of competence students bring to this conversation, we'll look at a story told by one student, Dana, in two modes—speaking and writing. The context of this writing class is still somewhat new for Dana early in the semester, so we can see him trying out strategies that he's brought from other settings as he's talking. And because the context stays the same when he writes, we can see how those strategies are built on or altered as he tries to carry on the same conversation through writing.

OBSERVATION ACCOUNT

To look at your own discourse competence in the ways in which we'll look at Dana's you'll want first to tape-record a story of a moment in your experience as you tell it to classmates or to a friend or family member outside of the class. It's important to have a real audience for your story, because you'll want to be able to see the ways in which you respond to an actual listener. As you decide what to tell, think about what you might want to write about in your own memoir. Are there stories that you've told before? If so, how might one of those stories capture something typical about the ways of thinking and talking that characterize one of your discourse communities? Or you might want to use this moment to tell something that you haven't told before, to explore the possibilities

(*continued*)

(continued)

of recapturing a moment in your past language and literacy experiences that you want to think some more about. The story you choose at this point does not have to be included in your memoir; telling one story may give you ideas for others that you'll want to write about in the end. (You'll find suggestions for generating ideas in the *prewriting* section of Writing Strategies.)

Telling stories in the classroom can also serve a number of other purposes: it can give you a chance to get to know more about other members of your class or of your writing group; it can give you a sense of the audience you'll be writing for and of what you do to capture their interest; and it can allow you to explore and reflect on common themes in your different experiences.

When you've finished telling and recording your story, transcribe it, trying to capture your actual telling as accurately as possible, including pauses and hesitations. You may want to use a sequence of three dots (. . .) instead of conventional punctuation to show pauses, using the example of Dana's transcription.

Next, create a written version of your story. If you'd told your story to members of your class, for example, and were now contributing that story to a class collection, how would you write it? Decide how you'll begin, what you'll include, how you'll end, if your purpose is to recreate the same basic story in writing for the same audience.

See "Conducting Field Research" for additional information on taping and transcribing spoken conversations (Strategies, pp. 538–39).

The story Dana first tells the class isn't about a discourse community experience in any immediate and obvious way, but it does capture some of the ways of talking and thinking that are characteristic of Dana, his father, and his brother. Later, as Dana begins to think about the ways his father talks about this event and his own telling of it, he also notices some significant discourse differences across generations. At this moment though, Dana has just chosen a familiar story that he thinks will amuse his classmates—a story about the time his brother smashed up his father's truck.

The thing is you gotta know my father . . . he's the ultimate . . . ah . . . perfectionist . . . he . . . the person that like . . . ah . . . I heard you talking before that has a schedule of events of everything and wears like a tie to bed . . . he and . . . a . . . on the other hand my brother . . . if I may . . . ah . . . be so coarse . . . as to say . . . is the ultimate hard ass . . . and the thing is that I . . . I think is hilarious . . . no one else does . . . what my father did was he bought a brand new truck . . . one of those short Isuzu . . . ah . . . pick-ups and . . . ah . . . it was nice . . . it was shiny . . . and the thing is you got . . . you have to earn . . . you have to earn the respect from my father . . . I shouldn't say points or anything . . . but to be able to use it . . . and he was . . . and he used the truck . . . and he took it up a . . . ah . . . up a . . . one of those parking garages . . . yes . . . and how it went was . . . it goes up a ramp and curves around . . . like where it's gonna . . .

and you park it and . . . ah . . . a funny thing was he didn't put the emergency brake on and it was in neutral and . . . ironic . . . its funny because the truck rolled down the hill missing like . . . Jaguars . . . Mercedes . . . you know . . . its coming down and its missing everything . . . and it slams into like . . . a gate thing . . . ah . . . concrete fixture somewhat like . . . you know . . . that over there . . . to only come home . . . yah . . . to come home and I . . . and I did . . . I wasn't there so I wasn't able to see my father's face but to see . . . you know . . . the look in his eyes as my brother was . . . ah . . . you know . . . who was . . . it would've been hilarious . . . nnah . . . to this day my brother contends that its not that bad . . . I look at the truck and like there's no rear quarter and its . . . its totally . . . ah . . . disheveled and I . . . I think . . . I . . . its kinda weird of me to think that that's a good thing that happened to him . . . but . . . ah . . . I think its kinda funny.

As Dana talks, his classmates nod knowingly or laugh, and in many of his pauses he looks around the room, to see whether his listeners really are following what he says, and whether they are responding. When he's finished, they ask questions about whether his brother was punished, and they respond with driving mistakes of their own. As they go on sharing stories and responses, they begin to build a community, in the classroom, of people who can share common references "like Dana's brother and the truck," and a common vocabulary, repeating a term Dana uses: "the ultimate hard ass" to apply to other people who could fill that role. They also develop a sense of how long a turn they can take and keep their listeners' attention, of when it's OK to interrupt the speaker, of how to let the others know when they've just paused to think, or that their story has ended. They do the things people always do when they begin to form a new discourse community, a community that will be held together by the things its members talk about and the ways they talk.

As he talks in this classroom setting, Dana displays his *discourse competence*—a competence that involves being sensitive to a particular context, being aware of how that context might shape the <u>what</u>, <u>why</u>, and <u>how</u> of a conversation, and adapting what he knows from other contexts to participating in this one.

Analyzing a Spoken Story

Look back at the transcript of Dana's spoken story for a minute, and see what you can determine about how the classroom context might influence his thinking about:

- <u>what</u> he tells and what shared knowledge he needs to create;
- <u>why</u> he tells the story he does and what he has to share about his intentions; and
- <u>how</u> he tells the story, particularly its shape and style, the specific language he uses and the language he doesn't use.

In thinking about the <u>what</u>, <u>why</u>, and <u>how</u> of Dana's spoken story, you might have begun to notice the extent to which he's trying out ways to adapt his story to this particular conversation.

In deciding <u>what</u> to talk about, Dana has to decide what will interest his classmates (mostly first year college students). But he also has to decide what will be appropriate to this classroom setting (and there are probably some stories that he'd tell some of the same students if they were in the cafeteria or at a party that he wouldn't want to tell in the classroom with a teacher). Dana doesn't know this community all that well yet, so he pays a lot of attention to whether his listeners can follow what he's saying, using "you know" frequently, partly to fill in while he thinks of what he wants to say next, but partly to see whether his listeners do know—whether they've had experiences that make what he's telling them familiar. He explicitly ties his story to the others that have been told ("I heard you talking before") so that he can build on the shared knowledge that this community is developing. But there are other kinds of shared knowledge that he does assume in this community—"Isuzus," "Mercedes," "Jaguars": he effectively exploits the differences in these kinds of cars, in who is likely to own them and in how costly it's likely to be to smash them up, to build the drama of the pick-up's run down the ramp.

<u>Why</u> he's telling a story—the main purpose of this classroom conversation— is already established, but here too, Dana is trying out what he can do within that purpose. He wants to share a story that he thinks his classmates might also find funny, but he doesn't want to sound too critical of his father or brother, although in other settings he has probably told this story in much more critical ways. We can see his uncertainty, his testing out of what his own stance should be towards the events he's telling, when he says of himself, "it's kinda weird of me to think that that's a good thing that happened to him."

Although he's stepping into a new community, Dana also has a sense of some of the rules for <u>how</u> things can be said here, or he's checking them out, based on his past school experience. "If I may be so coarse as to say" shows his uncertainty about whether terms like "the ultimate hard ass" are really appropriate to this new context, and his description of the smashed-up truck as "disheveled" probably reflects his attempt to find a word that will feel right in the classroom. We can see from Dana's story that he is concerned with using language in ways that are "appropriate" for the context. We can also see that the concept of *appropriateness* can be complex, that it involves not only using a style of language that's not "too coarse" and not too refined for this setting, but also, for example, figuring out that a humorous story will be appropriate in this setting. And it also involves working out shared ways of proceeding—telling a story that's not too much longer or shorter than others' stories, and one that takes listeners into a past event, for example.

We can see then that Dana enters this composition class with many kinds of knowledge—about the world, about what a particular group of people are likely to know, about linguistic structures and styles, about strategies for communication, and about when and how to test out what will work and what won't in this new context. All of this is part of the discourse competence that he has developed in other settings. But Dana is also entering a community of writers. And in that context, he'll draw on the same discourse competence that he has drawn on naturally as a speaker, as we'll see when we turn to his written story.

OBSERVATION ACCOUNT

To analyze your spoken story, look to see (and gloss) <u>what</u> you talked about—the events you told, the words you used, the details you included, the shared knowledge you created for your listeners. Look also at <u>how</u> you talked about these things, at where you began and ended, at where you stepped into the events and where you stepped back and commented about them. Working from your gloss, try to determine <u>why</u> you talked about these things in these ways. What guided your moment-to-moment choices as the teller of this story? Are there ways in which the particular situation—telling this story in the classroom, following on the stories told by others—affected your choices?

In listening to your tape, were there parts you particularly liked? Things you might say differently if you were to tell the story again? What do you think was most effective about your telling of this story?

In your account of this inquiry, move through your story, describing what you've seen about what you were saying and why and how at each moment, and considering what that shows about your discourse competence—about the understandings you brought to bear on telling this story in this context.

Discourse Competence in Writing

As a writer, Dana draws on both his conversational discourse competence and his prior understandings about written discourse. Although he is writing for the same classroom audience that he has told his story to, he also brings prior understandings about writing in school contexts, and these shape the ways in which he applies familiar discourse strategies. Although it's not so obvious without the pauses that were present in the transcribed spoken version, Dana is still testing out what might work in this situation—as you will do in your own writing. Dana's written version of his story has the title "Perfectly Imperfect."

My father is a very meticulous person: always pointing out details, doing things by the book and, if it is possible, showing no imperfections. My brother, although nothing of the sort, likes to think he is just like him.

It all happened a year ago when my father bought a brand new small bed pick-up truck, and my brother finally got a chance to drive it. Apparently what had happened when my brother Don took the truck out was that he did not pull the emergency brake on all the way when he parked it. It would not have been so bad if the truck was not parked at the top of a curvy hill in a parking garage. Needless to say, the truck rolled down the hill only to smash into a cement wall structure at the bottom of the garage.

> I guess the only luck to come out of this adventure was the fact that the truck did not hit any parked cars on the way down the hill. It would have been a personal thrill for me to see the look on my father's face as my brother brought the truck in the driveway. My brother finally realized he did a stupid thing and that he was not that perfect anymore.

Up to this point, Dana's classmates have been participants in this conversation: as listeners who have nodded, agreed or disagreed, or made comments of their own. But at this point they step out of that participatory mode to look analytically at Dana's written text and how it differs from the spoken one. By asking the familiar questions, we too can see how Dana's understandings about writing in school contexts have shaped what he's done here, including:

- <u>what</u> Dana includes in this written version and how it differs from what was included in the spoken one;
- <u>why</u> Dana seems to be making the choices he does and what his intentions are in writing this version; and
- <u>how</u> Dana shapes his written version and the choices he makes about wording and style.

In Dana's written text, you have probably noticed differences, first in <u>what</u> is talked about. The basic story remains the same and some core words and phrases appear in both: father, brother, truck, pick-up, emergency brake, truck rolled down the hill, look on my father's face. Other core ideas are expressed differently: Dana's father was "the ultimate perfectionist" in the spoken version and a "meticulous person" in the written. And others appear in only one version: for example, the term "hard ass," and the names of cars.

As for <u>why</u> it is talked about, Dana's intentions in the spoken version were, at least in part, to connect to the prior conversation, to entertain his listeners, and to keep them interested in what he has to say, and the details he includes there work towards those purposes. And because it's Dana who was telling the story and building an interpersonal connection with other students, it's his own response to the events that was highlighted. His second version, though, while intended for his same classmates as readers, doesn't really seem to be written to entertain his audience and fellow-participants in a conversation in the same way, but has taken on the purposes of a school writing task (which it is).

What he assumes about these school purposes affects <u>how</u> Dana tells his story in this written version. <u>How</u> includes what gets added and what gets left out, and the shape the story takes, as well as its actual wording. Dana focuses on the theme of perfect father and would-be perfect brother, he adds a conclusion that fits explicitly with that theme, and he eliminates both the details that were intended to let readers imagine the events as they were happening and most of his own response to these events. Although he could have shaped his written story in many different ways, he chooses to write it as a school essay with several traditional elements:

— a clear introduction,

— a central narrative of events in the past, and

— a conclusion that shows the significance of the events and points back to the theme raised in the introduction.

The shape Dana gives this essay reflects his intention to take this opportunity to show that he knows how to do some of what's typically called for in school writing.

Sensitivity to Context   Because Dana is writing within an academic context, he has followed a common expectation of academic writing—that the point of any written text, its lesson or meaning, is made explicitly. This accounts for the emphasis in typical writing instruction on the *thesis statement*, that says up front what the point of the essay will be, as well as on a conclusion that expands and restates what the essay has shown about that point. While Dana states his thesis explicitly toward the end of his story, he makes the point about his brother being less perfect than he thinks he is in several places, from the title "Perfectly Imperfect" to "nothing of the sort" in the first paragraph, to the concluding sentence.

The forms of academic writing are actually more varied than the thesis-statement model suggests (and we'll look at many different ways in which writers have made their points). But the convention of *explicitness* holds true even for narratives (and we've seen that Rodriguez steps out of the stories he is telling to say what understandings he's drawn from these experiences). When you're writing fiction or telling a story to friends on a street-corner, you're more likely to let the reader or listener infer the point of the story from the events and descriptions it contains. But when you use narrative in an academic essay you're most likely to make your point explicitly, several times, beginning with your title and ending with the final statement, just as Dana has.

Attention to Shared Knowledge, Purposes, and Ways   When writing, you need to be able to imagine the background knowledge readers are likely to bring and add whatever new shared knowledge is needed. And you need a sense of what readers will expect in this sort of writing, for this purpose. Dana has eliminated some of the specific information that appeared in his oral story—like the kinds of cars parked in the garage (though such detail would have helped to create a shared world with his readers, as it did with his listeners). But he still assumes some common knowledge, at least of a parking garage, and perhaps of sibling relationships. In his written story, though, Dana also depends on a shared understanding of *formal conventions*—a title, paragraphs, definite statements of introduction and conclusion. While Dana, the speaker, can draw on the shared environment of the classroom, pointing to something in the room and saying "It slams into . . . a concrete fixture somewhat like, you know, that over there." Dana, the writer, can't just point over there, so he names "a cement wall structure," even if he doesn't have precise words to describe it.

Writing for school purposes also tends to be formal in diction, and Dana eliminates phrases like "you gotta" and "the ultimate hard ass." In speaking, Dana was clearly addressing an audience of peers. In writing, we usually assume that anyone, not just friends or peers, might read what we've written.

A Sense of a Discourse Community   When you write, as when you speak, you are addressing real audiences in real communities, even if your readers aren't people you know directly. You write for readers with whom you can assume some shared knowledge and interests, your readers will respond (at least in their heads) with questions and new ideas, and the focus is on the communication of meanings. Journalists write for newspaper readers (and for particular readers who choose to read specific newspapers). Physicists write for other physicists, and physics students write in the ways their professors have come to expect that physicists will write. Even writers of personal memoirs, like Cisneros and Rodriguez, can imagine a likely audience of readers—for Cisneros, readers who have already read her fiction and might now want to know more about the writer behind the stories she has written; for Rodriguez, readers who are interested in education and specifically the educational experience of someone who is bilingual, as well as readers who are focused on the political issue of bilingual education.

A Flexible Understanding of Appropriate Language and Style   Most often such flexibility or versatility is not what comes to mind about language when we step back as writers. From our school experience, we tend to think in terms of fixed rules for what is right and what is wrong. But from our discourse community experience, we know that those fixed rules don't really account for what we do in different settings. Indeed, as speakers, we don't have to think much about how we use language when we're insiders to a setting. It's only when we switch settings, or switch modes of communication from speaking to writing, that we begin to think that there might be a problem with the sentences we speak or write and the words we use.

As he talks, Dana hesitates and restarts to make his sentences fit his ideas, and if we try to apply punctuation to what he's transcribed, we might find in places that we have only fragments of complete sentences that don't quite fit with what comes before or after. Because he has more time to think as he writes, Dana has probably produced fewer of these glitches in writing, and he has certainly edited them all out of his final version (another sign of his awareness of what's important in producing written texts for school contexts). But if he hadn't, it wouldn't be because he lacked knowledge of how to form sentences, but because he was carrying some of what was natural in his speaking into his writing.

A Willingness to Take Risks and Try Out Different Ways of Saying Something
When you're speaking and writing, you're continually responding to different

contexts, and you can't possibly know all of the implicit rules that people share for what's appropriate or "correct" for each context. You can only learn what's appropriate by testing different ways of saying things and seeing how your listeners or readers respond.

We can see this testing process in the spoken version of Dana's story, in the way he tries out the word "disheveled" to see if it works to describe his father's smashed-up truck to this audience (and we can see that he has paused to think before choosing this word). Dana takes fewer risks in his written version of the story however, and in the final, edited version most traces of any earlier risk-taking process have disappeared. One choice Dana has made about writing for school contexts seems to be to play it safe.

When you're writing in exploratory ways for a writing class, however, it's important to take the risks that will allow you to test out what's effective in presenting your ideas and engaging your readers. You may find, for example, that some of the strategies you use in speaking will work in your writing as well. Dana could have tried giving details and creating strong images like "Jaguars, Mercedes," repeating syntactic patterns ("It's coming down," "It's missing everything") and sometimes even bringing in moments of actual dialogue. Trying out these strategies could have made his written story as lively as his spoken one.

OBSERVATION ACCOUNT

To look at differences in the two versions of your story, begin by glossing the written version, looking particularly for changes you made from your oral telling. You'll want to indicate what words, events, or ideas appear only in one version, what things appear in both, and what appears but is reshaped or altered in the second version.

After glossing what appears in these two versions of your stories, see what you can tell about the purposes and assumptions that were implicit in your decisions as a writer, and the ways in which these purposes and assumptions affected the choices you made about how you told your story in the written version.

What examples can you find of the ways in which you:

—adjusted to the contexts for which you were speaking and writing;

—paid attention to shared knowledge, purposes, and ways;

—drew on your sense of the classroom discourse community;

—made choices in language and style that were appropriate to what you were trying to accomplish, at a particular moment, in your telling or writing your stories;

—took risks and tried out different ways of saying something.

In your account of this work, write about the choices you've made in each version of your story and what they show about your discourse competence as speaker and writer.

REFLECTING ON THE ELEMENTS OF YOUR WRITER'S REPERTOIRE

You may find it reassuring, as a writer, to think about the many aspects of discourse competence you can draw on as you write for new settings. But there are still several areas of concern that many writers struggle with. Writers are typically concerned about the correctness of the language they use and about avoiding grammatical errors. They may also be concerned with developing a style that will engage their readers and still fit the purposes of the writing they may be assigned to do. Sometimes, like Cisneros, they're concerned with developing a voice. These concerns often affect their writing process—how they begin, how they work through a piece of writing, and how many sheets of paper they crumple up or screens of text they delete along the way. Because these four concerns are related, we'll consider them together to guide your reflective inquiry into your own experience of any or all of them. We'll also look back to see where Mellix has raised any of these concerns, and how her reflections on her own experience might speak to them for other writers.

Language

Our concerns about whether the language we write is grammatically correct typically come early in our schooling, when we get the first paper returned with red pencil markings. But we can usually trace an awareness of the fact that people use different grammatical forms to moments when we move outside of our most familiar settings and into new ones. The concept of *language variation* can help us in thinking about this concern. Any widely spoken common language, like English, has a great deal of variation in ways that it is spoken, and there are many *varieties of English* that are associated with different communities, different regions of the country, different countries, and/or different social status. Whether or not we're speakers of a distinct variety of English—of the different varieties spoken in Appalachia or Texas or Maine or New York City or in black communities throughout the U.S.—most of us have had moments when we've suddenly become self-conscious about our ordinary way of speaking. Perhaps we've found ourselves hesitating suddenly, worrying about the pronunciation of a word or whether we're using it correctly, or whether we should be saying "who" or "whom." And, unfortunately, most of us have also had moments of noticing some feature of another person's language in a negative way.

When student writers are asked to comment on moments when they worried about or changed something in their own language, or when they noticed something about someone else's, they voice a variety of observations and concerns. They note times when they shifted the way they talked to something they saw as more mainstream.

> I grew up in Revere where the letter "r" does not exist. I once had a heavy Revere accent, but in high school I moved to Northhampton. I still remember my sister

saying to me that people would think I was stupid if they heard me speak. (I also pluralized the word "you" to "yous"). Being an impressionable person, I listened to those around me and quickly changed my patterns of speech. **(Lorraine)**

They remember times when they judged others by their language.

When I heard the kids I went to school with leaving out "r's," I automatically assumed that these kids were not very smart. Apparently the kids at school picked up on the difference too, because I remember in approximately fifth grade being teased for putting such emphasis on "r's" and "ing's" and being accused of being nerdy. Although I don't believe anymore that people who speak without "r's" are any less intelligent or of a lower social class, I still find that when I am around people who speak this way I try not to put such emphasis on my "r's" or "ing's." Perhaps, unconsciously, I'm still worried that they may find me to be nerdy or snobby. **(Melissa)**

They describe conflicts about varieties of language use even within their own families.

While my boyfriend's family thought nothing of saying "mines," my mom would definitely cringe at the thought. I noticed though that when my mom and his mom talked together, they each gave in a bit and moved their levels . . . My mom has always bothered me about using correct grammar. While she says "For what class are you doing this," I say, "What class are you doing it for?" She feels and tells me that it's practically a sin to end a sentence with a preposition! I, on the other hand, could care little about this because when I'm with my friends I fit in! I place little emphasis on spoken syntax because I think that trying too hard to choose the right phrase order, etc. takes away from the meaning of the conversation. My mom and I have disagreed on this point for years. **(Joan)**

Most often they try to do whatever they see as necessary to fit in to the discourse communities they value most (as Joan does with her friends).

Some varieties of English are distinguished primarily by pronunciation or vocabulary. Others have distinct grammatical features (like "yous" to show a plural form of you). But those distinctions have regular patterns—patterns that are recognizable by both insiders and outsiders. And those patterns are required if you're going to sound like an insider to a community that uses that variety. Such varieties may reflect regional differences, but they also carry social meaning that is sometimes negative. At the same time, though, they also serve positive social purposes, and these varieties continue to exist because they express a particular connection among people of a community and contribute a sense of identity. When people move from one area of the country to another, for example, they often hold on to a regional accent or to some of the ways they would have said something back home instead of switching to an equivalent term like "tonic," or "soda," or "pop." The sense that your variety of language helps you stay connected with your community is especially true for speakers of what Mellix calls "Black English." While most of its speakers (like Mellix) also speak the more public and common English of the wider society, many (again like Mellix) choose to use their "finest, most-cherished black English" at home and in the Black community, as a style of discourse that affirms values and ways of seeing the world that are widely shared within that community.

In college, Mellix becomes particularly worried that features of the language she speaks with friends and family will carry into her writing and she tries to learn "to shut out my black English" whenever she composes, "to prevent it from creeping into my formulations" (p. 64). On the one hand, it's a "special language" that she doesn't want to leave behind in her life because she doesn't want to sacrifice the intimacy of her relationships with family and friends in the way that Rodriguez did. But her feelings about that language are complicated because she knows that many people in the larger world see it as inferior, although from a linguistic perspective it is not.

Like Mellix, we can value the insider language of our particular community, and still have some ambivalent feelings about it as we move into the larger world. Most of us have learned to think that some varieties of language are inherently better than others—that they are more correct or have more expressive power. But the truth is that what we think of as good and bad or correct and incorrect language is connected to political and social circumstances, as Mellix has come to recognize. The features of any particular variety, even the "standard" variety, aren't inherently better or worse than those of another variety. All are fully grammatical languages offering equal resources for communication, and each variety is appropriate in its own context.

Mellix's variety, "Black English," now more often referred to as African American Vernacular English (AAVE) or Ebonics by linguists and scholars, was shaped by the interaction of African-based languages and English (resulting in the creation of a new and wholly grammatical creole language) when enslaved Africans were first brought to the United States. Its history gives it some grammatical features that are significantly different from those of more common or mainstream or "standard" English. Mellix points to a few of these in her essay when she gives examples of the sentences she knew she couldn't write in school. It doesn't use the verb "to be" in some places where other varieties do use it, as in "The white clouds pretty"; "We going to gym;" and it sometimes uses a different verb, as in "We got a new poster," instead of "We have a new poster."

There are many other significant features of Black English, enough to make linguists argue about whether it should be classified as a separate language rather than just a dialect of English. But there are several things that are important for all of us to understand about this or any variety:

- different varieties aren't better or worse—just different;
- grammatical correctness isn't absolute but depends on the variety of language being used in a context (so that what's correct in standard En-

glish is incorrect if you want to function as an insider among speakers of Ebonics, or even in parts of a town like Revere where, as Lorraine noted, "yous" replaces the plural "you"); and

■ our natural facility with language allows us to try out and acquire new forms in a regular way, as we move from one variety of language to another.

Why do these understandings matter to you as a writer? For several reasons. One is that it is difficult to feel comfortable taking risks with new varieties, styles and uses of language if you feel that you'll be judged as inferior when what you'd say in one setting mixes in with the variety that's used in the new setting. It's hard to become a fluent speaker and writer in a new setting if you have to spend a lot of your time trying to keep something you'd say elsewhere from "creeping into [your] formulations." You do need to look for such mixed forms when you're editing something you've written, but that should be your last worry, not your first. When you're learning a new language or variety, the mixed forms or "errors" that appear in your own writing fall into patterns that keep changing as you read and write more. While you may have gotten a paper back that has twenty things marked wrong, if you analyze those markings closely you'll probably find that you've really made the same two or three errors a number of times. You may need to watch for only a few concerns to correct those patterns that don't match the written variety of a language you're aiming for.

You can find specific strategies for identifying patterns of mixed forms in your own writing in the Editing Strategies section of Part IV.

REFLECTIVE INQUIRY

What has shaped your own experience with language as a speaker and writer as you've moved through different contexts? What do you remember about the most common concerns with grammar, and punctuation that you've had as a writer, or those that have been pointed out to you most often?

Look back through papers you've written that have a teacher's markings. If "errors" have been marked, try to list these, put them into categories, and see if you can find patterns in these markings. (Or exchange pieces of unedited, first draft or very informal writing with a classmate and mark mixed and unconventional forms.) If you have more than one paper to look at, do you see any differences in the unconventional forms that appear when you're writing for different contexts, for different purposes? What sorts of "problems" have appeared in your writing in the past, and do they still seem to be present? Drawing on the discussion of this chapter, why do you think any repeated unconventional or mixed forms that have appeared repeatedly have done so? Do you understand the convention in standard written English for what has been marked? If not, give examples of these forms and markings.

Style

It doesn't make sense to talk about rules of language apart from context. Language, as it's actually used, is not inherently right or wrong. But it can make a good or bad fit with the setting it's being used in, showing the speaker to be an insider or outsider to that setting. Most of what we worry about as rules of grammar are really rules of *discourse style*, an explicit or implicit understanding of what's appropriate in a setting. A professor who regularly used *ain't* rather than *isn't* in class lectures would seem very strange indeed, like a bridegroom who showed up for a formal wedding ceremony wearing ratty jeans instead of a tux. But there are settings in which *isn't* would also be strange, and so the students in the classroom might well be discussing a short story where believable characters would only use the form *ain't*. And speakers who want to fit in will often find themselves "moving levels," as Joan observed, to make a conversation work better.

Using the metaphor of clothing style is one of the easiest ways to grasp the ways in which we move between the informal styles we use in some contexts (which may be associated with a particular variety of language), and the more formal styles we use in others. Mellix herself uses this metaphor when she says about her very polite and standard response to a police officer: "I had taken out my English and put it on as I did my church clothes, and I felt as if I were wearing my Sunday best in the middle of the week" (p. 61).

New styles are something to *add* to your repertoire, like adding to your current wardrobe the style of clothing you need for a particular event. The more styles you possess, the more you can clothe your body or your voice comfortably for a variety of settings, and the more easily you can shift styles of language in ways that are appropriate to each setting. You already possess the appropriate styles of language (and the right languages/varieties) for your conversations in the communities you've been part of, whether at home or at work, and you probably don't want to throw them out if you plan to keep spending time in those communities. As Rodriguez's experience tells us, the personal cost of doing so, of no longer being comfortable at home, is too high.

But our awareness of style also affects what we do in the conversations we try to create as we write: trying to choose the words and phrases that seem appropriate for writing in a particular setting, that seem close to what others write in that context. Mellix describes her freshman writing experience as "a time for trying to grasp the language of the classroom and reproduce it in my prose; for trying to talk about myself in that language, reach others through it" (p. 64). As she looks back at the essays she produced in her early college courses, Mellix finds evidence of her own attempts to try on new styles. She's pretty hard on herself as she looks at what she's written though, complaining about "a poverty of language in these sentences," and pointing to words and phrases she sees as "clichéd." The examples she gives us do show that she's drawing on phrases that are commonly used: "My excitement was soon dampened"; "a small voice in the back of my head"; "my long awaited opportunity." But we're always drawing on the words of others (particularly if we're trying to avoid having our most comfortable language creep into what we're saying), and trying out these phrases is a sign of Mellix's discourse competence. The problem though is that they aren't quite right for what she's trying to say.

Part of the problem for Mellix is that she's not really comfortable yet in this new discourse community. The styles of language she's aiming for don't quite fit her yet, because, as a new freshman, she's just beginning a process of becoming an insider. As she looks back at that moment in her experience, she sees that:

> As that person, the student writer at that moment, I was essentially mute. I could not—in the process of composing—use the language of the old me, yet I couldn't imagine myself in the language of "others" (p. 65).

Looking at an essay she wrote in mid-semester, she finds "the voice here is stronger, more confident" with terms like "physically damaging," "insensitive," and "diverse." And still later, in a paper for a research writing course, she sees that she has begun to take on the language of the books and articles she has been reading, and she finds terms like "overwhelming number of cases" and "single episode."

Mellix concludes her essay with an understanding about what was involved for her in moving, as a writer, into an academic discourse community: "I had to take on the language of the academy, the language of 'others.' And to do that I had to learn to imagine myself a part of the culture of that language, and therefore someone free to take liberties with it" (p. 67). In other words, she acquired the style of her new discourse community in two ways: by taking risks in trying out what she observed about how people talked and wrote there; and by participating actively in that context as a reader, a writer, and a member of a classroom community, as she gradually became an insider.

Reread some of the writing you have done in different contexts. Look at notes you have written to friends, letters you have written to distant relations, essays you have written for class, entries you have written in a journal, e-mails you have sent, more formal research papers or reports you have composed, and any poems or songs you have written. As you read two or three of these different texts, what do you notice about the style of writing you employ in each? In what ways do you structure this writing? What kinds of language do you use? Why did you use this language in particular? Is there a particular kind of rhythm to your writing? In what ways do you address or relate to your assumed audience? What changes do you find you make when writing for different contexts? Why do you make these changes? What do you see at this point about style in writing or about your style as a writer?

REFLECTIVE INQUIRY

Voice

What does Mellix mean when she describes her own voice as a writer as "stronger" in her later essays, or when she talks about the "professional voice" that the language she used in a research paper helped her to maintain? What do any writers mean when they use the term *voice*?

You may think of your voice as drawing on the graceful, comfortable, and mostly unconscious ways you speak, with subtle alterations as you move from one setting to another—from your parents' dinner table to work to an evening with your friends—in any setting in which you feel at home. You probably think of your voice as including what others hear—pitch, tone, accent, the speed at which someone talks. But you can also think of it as involving a characteristic style that includes typical words and expressions, patterns of sentences, and even elements like humor or insults or abruptness. These characteristic elements are influenced most strongly by our experience in our primary discourse communities—our homes and families—but reshaped by our experience in the many other discourse communities we become members of in the larger world. Even siblings won't end up sounding exactly alike as their voices are affected by their participation in conversations of males or females, of different peer groups, in different classes, perhaps at different schools.

Much of your sense of what sounds like you is likely to be influenced strongly by your primary discourse community and by the different voices you heard there. But you've also been part of other discourse communities and tried on other ways of talking as well. As a result, you have a number of different voices, or different ways of using the voice you first developed at home to draw on as a writer. As you write for new settings, you'll try on new styles that seem to fit them, perhaps awkwardly at first, but gradually developing a voice of your own to fit in that setting, just as Mellix developed a "professional voice" for writing a research paper.

When we apply the concept of voice to writing, we are using the term as a metaphor, to some extent, since there is no physical sound from the words on the page. Yet in a writer's choice of words, in the typical rhythms of sentences, in patterns of repetition, in the ways that stories or examples are brought in, we can find much that sounds like a particular person speaking in a particular context. This sense of the writer's voice is especially strong in personal essays like the memoirs that we are focusing on in this unit.

Many writers talk about finding their voice, about how they couldn't begin to write in an effective, powerful way until they did so. It isn't always a new voice that they are discovering, but more often an old one—one that they had and lost and are now trying to recapture, as Sandra Cisneros does. In the memoirs, included at the end of the next chapter, several other writers tell of their own discoveries that some of what they were looking for as writers was there all along, in the language of their homes, their families, and their communities. As writers they had to accept that language in order to bring its resources into their writing.

You may want to think not of voice but of voices—all of the different ways your own voice sounds, from your accent to your tone to the words you choose as you use your voice in different settings. Listening with appreciation to some of your voices and the voices of others in informal, private settings is an essential part of developing a confident voice for public purposes. Reflecting on such moments may help you to better understand how the voices you've used and heard contribute to your repertoire as a writer.

Look at one of your informal journal responses that you liked and felt comfortable about writing. Mark places where the language feels most right to you (perhaps looking at the words you chose, the ways you phrased your ideas, and/or the rhythm of your sentences). Do you associate that language with home? With other discourse communities you've participated in? With the language of classroom discussions you've been part of or texts you've been reading? With other reading that you do for your own nonschool purposes? To what degree can you see yourself bringing into your informal academic writing voice some of the other voices you've been developing in other conversations?

REFLECTIVE INQUIRY

Process

As someone who has done a lot of writing for school settings, you've probably developed specific strategies for getting that writing done (and maybe some global anxieties *about* getting the writing done). You may also have had some formal instruction about the writing process, requiring that you move from activities that help you generate ideas (brainstorming lists or maps), to organizing those ideas (outlines), to writing those ideas in several drafts and revisions of those drafts, to editing and proofreading your final versions. Most writers don't move as neatly through this process as these steps suggest—they're likely to have new ideas to fit in even as they're working on what they hope will be their final version of an essay, for example. (We'll learn more about one student writer's process in the next chapter.) But to try out your ideas in a comfortable and familiar voice while thinking your way into a new conversation in a new setting, you'll want to make some space in your own process of writing to use that voice to think in long before you worry about what you'll eventually say in a final form for a specific audience. If you want to begin to find the strengths of your own voices in new settings you'll need sometimes to follow out your ideas as they come, without always interrupting yourself to worry about "correctness" in terms of school style. If you're writing in a second language, you may even need to draw on words from your first language sometimes, so that you don't interrupt the flow of your ideas while you find the word or phrase you want in the new language.

Most of the time, even when you're generating ideas, you're doing so within the context of an ongoing conversation within a particular community.

In academic communities, most writing builds on and applies the thinking of others. It draws on the shared knowledge that thinking represents, the shared purposes for thinking about that topic, and the shared ways people have talked about it. The conversational dialogue with others is implied at every stage of the writing process.

One of the things that writing classes try to do is make this implied dialogue explicit—to bring the hidden conversation out into the open. They may do this by moving back and forth between texts that are read and those that students write, exploring ways of working with those prior texts and ways of writing about them and bringing them into current written conversations. They may do it by having students read and respond to each other's writing, so that the ways in which the individual writer's text contributes to and fits with a larger ongoing conversation become more visible. And in almost all writing classes, the teacher also makes the implied dialogue explicit, by writing responses to each student's writing, reading what the student writes in response, and so on.

Barbara Mellix doesn't tell us much about the sorts of conversations that went on in her own writing classes or how they contributed to her own writing process. But she does tell us about some of her teachers' responses to her writing, and how the dialogue with one teacher worked for her, when she looks at the strategy she used in starting off her research paper. Her teacher suggested that she begin with an anecdote, and she did that, inventing a hypothetical situation to fit with the information she was conveying in the paper. But, she tells us,

> [It] felt forced and insincere because it represented—to a great degree—my teacher's understanding of the essay, *her* idea of what in it was most significant. . . . I was beginning to think and feel in the language I used, to find my own voices in it, to sense that how one speaks influences how one means. But I was not yet secure enough, comfortable enough with the language to trust my intuition (p. 66).

It's hard for teachers, student writers, and even other peer writers in the classroom to have conversations that suggest ways of approaching a piece of writing that won't sometimes feel forced and insincere. Even this part of the conversation about writing needs to be dialogical, bringing together the words and strategies that others have tried or might try for this piece of writing and the writer's own efforts, trying out possibilities, and seeing what will work for both writer and readers. Both writer and readers have to be good listeners and good risk takers in this conversation, and that is hard work (as you'll see when you have such conversations about the memoirs that you write).

But the potential rewards are great. By drawing on her existing discourse competence and her awareness of what it meant to talk in ways that were appropriate to a context, by trying on new words and new styles as she participated in new settings, by developing voices that more comfortably represented her as she became an insider to those settings, and by "writing and rewriting, practicing, experimenting" Mellix discovered the "generative power of language."

> I discovered—with the help of some especially sensitive teachers, that through writing one can continually bring new selves into being, each with new responsibilities and difficulties, but also with new possibilities (p. 72).

Reading and writing lets us greatly extend the range of conversations in which we participate, and those conversations can offer us many new possibilities for learning about ourselves and the world.

Reflect on a piece of writing that you've done for this or another class.

REFLECTIVE INQUIRY

- What sort of assignment is it and what does it call for you to do? If you have written guidelines for the assignment, what do you do when you read those guidelines? Which words have you focused on in this instance and how do you use them to guide your process?

- What do you do when you write for an assignment like this? Do you have a specific place where you like to work? Do you begin with a pencil or at a computer? Do you scratch some notes about different things you want to say in different sections or begin with a section that seems central, or do you begin working on your opening sentence or paragraph and try to follow on through? Have you followed your typical pattern this time?

- What do you do when you get stuck? Do you get a snack or go for a walk? Do you try to work on a different section? Do you reread what you've written so far and try to regain the thread of your thinking?

- Do you reorganize or rewrite paragraphs or sentences as you go along? Or do you wait until you've written a complete draft to make changes?

- How do you structure your writing time? Do you write the paper all in one sitting or at different times? Do you write it the night before it's due, or do you start earlier? How long, in total writing time, did you end up spending on this particular assignment?

- How do you decide when you're finished? Do you reread what you've written? Do you read it to a listener or have someone else read it? Do you make changes after you feel you've gotten to the end, and if so, of what sort?

- When and how do you try to see what you've written from a reader's perspective? Do you step back and try on that perspective yourself at various points in your writing? At the end? Do you read your text aloud to yourself? To others? Do you have others read it? If so, do you always turn to the same readers, or do you have different readers for different sorts of writing? Did you call on another reader for this piece of writing? If so, what did you have that reader look (or listen) for?

(continued)

(continued)

What have you found noticeable or unusual about the way in which you've worked on this particular assignment? Is there anything about the situation that has served to reinforce your usual patterns or that has led you to work somewhat differently?

If you do much writing outside of academic contexts, how does your process in writing for academic tasks differ from your process for writing elsewhere?

WRITING IN ACADEMIC GENRES

The inquiries you've pursued in this chapter offer several possibilities for shaping your ideas in more formal ways in exploratory essays and reports. Again you'll want to generate shared assumptions in your writing community for working with any of these types of essay or report.

As you work with any of these essay suggestions, you may want to turn to the Writing Strategies section for ideas about drafting, writing, revising, and editing your essay. There are also two essays by student writers that were written in response to these suggestions in the additional readings for Part I that follow Chapter 3.

EXPLORATORY ESSAY 1   Drawing on a theme or question or understanding that has emerged from your informal writing and sharing responses, write a more extended response in which you draw from Mellix's memoir and show how it supports or leads to that theme or understanding or responds to that question. Your purpose here is to give more formal shape to the ideas that you were exploring earlier, to take a reader into consideration as you present them, guiding the reader through your ideas and the supporting evidence from Mellix's memoir in a way that shows the reader "this is what I've come to understand and why."

EXPLORATORY ESSAY 2   Relate what you've found in the memoirs you've been reading. In what ways were the experiences of Rodriguez and Mellix in moving between the discourse of home and the discourses of the wider society, and/or their perspectives on those experiences similar? Different? Can you apply Rodriguez's key working concepts "private identity" and "public identity"—to Mellix's experience? Can you apply Mellix's term "appropriateness" to the experience of Rodriguez? To your own experience? To your classmates?

Putting these different experiences and ways of thinking and talking about these experiences together, what might be several common elements involved in moving from (or between) the discourse community of home and family into those of a larger, less intimate, and more public world? What understandings can you draw about the relationship between the experiences people have had, the personal understandings they've drawn from their experiences, and the public meanings they are contributing to a larger conversation, in writing about those experiences?

Compare your spoken and written stories. The essay genre of *comparison and contrast* is a common one across academic disciplines because comparing and contrasting is a way of placing things in relationship to each other that helps us to develop larger, meta-level understandings of the things being compared. You can draw on the observations you've already made about these stories, to shape a more formally structured essay in which you identify some significant aspects of your discourse competence and compare the ways in which they can be seen in your spoken story and in your written story.

EXPLORATORY ESSAY 3

You might also write in the genre of the *research report*. The work you've just done represents a mini-research project—an inquiry that follows from a question like: "What are some of the ways in which I respond, as a speaker and writer, to the specific demands of the speaking or writing situation?" You've now found some of these ways, you have examples (evidence) to support what you say about these ways, and you have a basis for saying what you've come to understand and even what you might want to try to discover next that follows from what you've done. So you may want to try out the genre of the research report with some of its typical elements:

BRIEF RESEARCH REPORT

—introducing the issue and guiding question that you were exploring (perhaps a variation on the one above);

—telling what you did to explore it, how you went about your inquiry;

—naming the main things you learned, with supporting evidence;

—drawing a conclusion, perhaps considering the implications of what you've learned, why these understandings might be important within a given context. (You can find further guidelines for research reports at the end of Chapter 6.)

CHAPTER

3

Reading and Writing Memoirs

In Chapter 3, you'll continue exploring your experience with language and literacy in past discourse communities and the ways that experience situates you now, as you enter new academic communities. You'll read more memoirs by other writers, including one by a college writer, along with her discussion of the creative process that led from her first draft to her final memoir.

In this chapter, you'll pursue the following lines of inquiry:

■ What is the relationship between the discourses you've acquired in different communities and the social identities that have shaped your participation in the world?

■ How have the past experiences of other writers influenced their present ways of seeing, understanding, and naming the world and how does the discourse of new communities allow them to reframe and rename the past?

■ From reading other memoirs, what do you observe about the writer's craft? How might these ways of shaping and representing experience guide your own shaping of a memoir of your experience in a particular community?

Part I ends with further suggestions for writing in the genre of the memoir as you draft and revise your own and for sharing the memoirs you've created. The memoir is a form of personal essay that's particularly suited to exploring the issues of language and social identity that are a common concern of writers, focusing as it does, on how past moments of experience can be seen from the perspective of present understandings. We've seen that perspective—the past through the present—in the memoirs of Rodriguez and Mellix, and we'll see it again in the other memoirs that are included at the end of Part I.

Moving into new discourse communities often involves the difficult process of shaping new social identities and new ways of defining ourselves. We shape these identities partly by how we talk and write—by the new discourses we acquire, each representing a particular community with a particular way of seeing the world. But we shape them as well by how we name what we see in the world and our own positions in it. College is a particularly critical time for reflecting on issues of social identity, as students step out of the familiar worlds of family and friends and into new settings. College continues the movement that Rodriguez describes from a private identity to a public one, from an identity that's defined largely in relationship to people who know us well to one that may have many facets, each shaped to a significant degree by the ways in which we present ourselves to a larger world. Because these issues are so significant to the freshman year of college, the typical freshman writing course includes some consideration of them—drawing on readings like the ones that are included in these chapters and encouraging the writing of personal reflective essays such as the memoir that reframe private experience in a public text.

REFLECTING ON EXPERIENCES WITH LANGUAGE AND SOCIAL IDENTITY

Memoirs often focus on writers' experiences with language. This may be because language is so close to the self, so deeply connected to our strongest sense of who we are, but also to the many versions of that self. We may identify ourselves at different times by our racial and ethnic backgrounds, by the churches we go to, by the region of the country we grew up in, by our professional roles (whether English professor or college student), and when we're in settings where we share one of these aspects of our own identity with others, we're likely to slip unconsciously into the particular ways of talking and seeing the world that we have in common with them.

Identity and Discourse

The sociolinguist Jim Gee describes the discourse we acquire in each community as an *identity kit*: it involves not only a way of talking (or writing) but shared beliefs, values, and ways of seeing the world. When we're insiders to a particular community and we're fluent in the discourse of that community, we unconsciously act and think (at least some of the time) like other members of that community, and the discourse of the community becomes part of our identity. Some aspects of our identity—the ones we grow up with—are fundamental to our experience of the world, and Gee refers to these ways of talking, thinking, and being in the world as our *primary discourses*. Other discourses—those associated with schools, academic disciplines, or professional roles—are ones we take on later, generally as part of our movement into a larger, public world, and we may move in and out of those social identities and the ways of talking and thinking we associate with them, putting them on and off as it suits us. Gee calls these *secondary discourses*. (You can read how Gee discusses these concepts in "Literacy, Discourse, and Linguistics," a reading that's included at the end of Part III.)

As children, the language we acquire first—our primary discourse—is the intimate, private language of the family and the immediate community. We can see the distinction between primary and secondary discourses most clearly in the case of Rodriguez because for him they involve two different languages. Rodriguez describes his experience of language at home from the time before his parents were told they should speak to their children only in English, recalling the intense intimacy created by their family language.

> Excited, we joined our voices in a celebration of sounds. *We are speaking now the way we never speak out in public.* We are alone—together, voices surrounded to tell me. Some nights, no one seemed willing to loosen the hold sounds had on us . . . Family language: my family's sounds. The voices of my parents and sisters and brother. Their voices insisting: *You belong here. We are family members. Related. Special to one another. Listen!* (p. 32)

As Rodriguez remembers these private moments, he captures one aspect of his own identity—a child within a particular family. His memories are of the special intimacy he felt in that experience. It is only later, when he has added the identities of schoolboy, of someone who is acquiring English as second language, and retrospectively, in response to public debates, of someone who had a bilingual childhood, that he sees the language being used in those family moments as significant.

In his memoir, as he looks back on his experience of moving out beyond the language of the family, Rodriguez describes that movement as being one that took him away from a private identity to face the task, in school, of learning the language of public society and of finding his public identity. It's a task that confronts everyone, whether or not it involves moving between languages, and it is one that is central to the work of all writers. Though we don't all share Rodriguez's problem of having to move between languages as we negotiate our private and public worlds, we do in fact move between our primary discourses—the ways of speaking that we've developed with those we're closest to—and the secondary discourses that characterize more public worlds.

Negotiating New Social Identities

In the present moment you are developing a new social identity as college student, one that has both social/personal and academic aspects and, in that context, you're also developing an identity as an academic writer. To the identity of college writer, you bring your past identities as a student, as a writer in and out of school contexts, as a person who is placed in a more or less comfortable way in relationship to a current classroom community by your past experiences, and as a language-user who will bring the full repertoire of language from all of these identities into the college classroom.

We can see this process of negotiating a new college student identity reflected in the responses of one student writer—Melissa. She is a young freshman who has come to college directly from high school. Melissa reflects on her past student identity in high school—the identity of the good student—placing that experience in relationship to the uncertainty she feels in the present moment. Here's how she begins:

> High school was a piece of cake. There were so many familiar faces and hallways. Each class was another easy "A." I can remember sitting in my trigonometry class, feeling completely in control. I understood the material and was able to follow the teacher easily. Often times when the class was unable to answer a question asked of them by the teacher, Mrs. C would call on me. I can still remember this vividly: "Melissa, do you know it?" she would say in a voice that expressed confidence in me, and most of the time I would. The people around me would wonder how I was able to get such good grades in the class. Many of my friends would come over to my house the night before the exam so that I could explain the material to them. I felt so bad for them because they were so confused with things that seemed so simple to me.

Melissa places her high school identity, which she characterizes in terms of "confidence in myself" against the way she feels as she starts college:

> Here at the big university, I wander around each day, unsure of my self. I attend each class but feel as though I was not properly prepared for it. I pay attention in class but am unable to follow or understand what is being said to me. I get extremely overwhelmed when I look around and realize that the other students seem to know what they are doing. I know now that the roles have changed from what they were in high school. I have become the classmate that I felt so bad for in the past. I hear myself asking other students around me to explain what is going on.

In each setting we can see Melissa defining herself in relation to others—to those who were confused in high school, and to those who seem to know what they're doing in college. But even as she does so, she's trying to reframe her experience to encompass both her old and new student identities, and she does so by asserting other aspects of her identity: She says, for example, "I'm normally not a quitter and I like to be in control, which is why I'm not giving up easily." Then, from the nonquitter identity, she starts to name college as "a gigantic challenge for me to overcome." She notices aspects of a new college identity that is bringing with it "the new feeling of independence and maturity." And she begins to imagine what will happen as she participates in this new community:

> Without even noticing it, I will become like the others around me who have more confidence and understanding. I will belong and will obtain my confidence back again. . . . If I do not . . . then I will know that this is not where I belong.

Reflecting on her experience in these ways allows Melissa to imagine the process of becoming an insider to the world of successful college students. The students who are most academically successful in the long run are those who don't see learning as a simple matter of "you get it or you don't," but who understand that real learning (and real scholarly inquiry) means pushing against the boundaries of what you understand easily, and developing strategies for trying again with what seems impossibly difficult to make sense of. As she reframes her academic identity, Melissa is beginning to reposition herself as a learner in ways that will better support her long-term academic goals. Soon, as she finds ways to keep working to understand new and difficult material, she'll add "biology major" to her college identity.

REFLECTIVE INQUIRY	Think about your varied discourse community experiences in relationship to your current identity kit. What has significance for who you are now, for the social identities that are most important at this moment in your life? If you were packing up a kit of ways of talking, thinking, seeing the world, valuing, and believing that you think will influence your present and future social roles and identities, what would you put in it?
	Have you included the identities of student and writer? These may not seem significant, but they will particularly influence the ways in which you approach the student or writer aspects of your present academic identity. If you have not, in an earlier inquiry, described your past identity in one of those roles, you might want to do so now. What terms would you use to capture how you saw yourself? How might you have been described by others (by other students, by teachers)? Did you see any conflict or reinforcement between this aspect of your identity and other aspects (diligent student and party animal, for example)? Do you see ways in which that aspect of your past identity interacts with the academic aspect of your identity in the present?

READING MEMOIRS

Memoirs may focus on very different experiences in very different communities, but they are likely to represent the writers' social identities in some common ways—ways that suggest the extent to which our various social identities are constituted in language. As you think back about the memoirs we've already read and look to the additional memoirs at the end of Part I, you'll find that, together, they explore a number of elements of social identity.

Social Identities Involve Naming

One aspect of our social identities has to do with the ways in which they are named by ourselves, or by others, in the words that are available to us from the society around us. It includes how we hear, respond to, and use those words, and how they influence us in our own process of defining ourselves or being defined. We've already seen how Rodriguez names his family and his school identities as "private" and "public," and how, in Mellix's family, she is named as someone who is "getting uppity" and "putting on airs" when she steps out of the family's special language in family settings. Melissa too, when says she's "not a quitter," uses this way of naming herself to focus on an aspect of her identity that she'll draw on in her new college setting.

When you turn to the memoirs following this chapter, you will see how some writers have responded to the ways that others have named them or have named some aspect of their experience, as well as the ways the writers themselves have named themselves or that experience.

- In "I Just Wanna be Average," Mike Rose recalls some ways of naming kids in the vocational track of high school and tells of one student's determination to define himself in the ways he has been defined—as "average."

- bell hooks, in "talking back," explains how, having been reprimanded as a child for talking back, she has redefined "talking back," using the term to name the ways in which she tries to challenge injustice and oppression. (She has even renamed herself as a writer, taking the name of a great-grandmother who had had a reputation for talking back.)

- Dave Eggers, in a selection from *A Heartbreaking Work of Staggering Genius*, tells of taking his younger brother to a school open house (their parents have died), where he tries to figure out how the other parents are seeing them ("Sad and sickly? Or glamorous and new?") while he names them in turn ("interesting in only their prototypical Berkleyness") as he tries to figure out who he is in his new parental role.

- Amy Tan, in "Mother Tongue," recalls the many names that she and others have used for the English that her mother, a Chinese immigrant, speaks: "broken," "fractured," "limited," "simple," and why, as a daughter and writer, she won't dismiss but will use "all of the Englishes" she grew up with.

- Tommi Avicolli, in "He Defies You Still. Memoirs of a Sissy," recalls the labels he has confronted—faggot, sissy, queer—and counters with his own defiant use of the term sissy to represent an identity he'll embrace.

- Annie Dillard presents her parents as joke tellers, realizing that she and her siblings were cast in the role of "straight man."

You'll find that several memoirs by student writers reflect these themes as well. Sean's grandmother used terms like "floozy" and "sassmouth" to name styles and behaviors she disapproved of. James names himself (partly ironically) a Writer-King. Dina reflects on how others' perceptions of her as "Russian" or "Jewish" play against her own sense of her identity as she moves between countries.

Social Identities Are Shaped Through Dialogue and Difference

The "doubleness" Mellix felt to be part of her identity as a child—being part of an intimate black community where people draw on a particular discourse and its ways of seeing the world, and then stepping into a public "white" discourse with different ways—reflects that dialogue. Likewise, at Rose's high school, there weren't just "voc-ed" students. That term took on meaning in relationship to the existence of another group, another track, called "college prep," with different ways of talking, acting, dressing, and valuing things.

We Can Have Multiple Social Identities.   Some are associated with roles we play like parent, child, worker, student, others with our interests ("computer geek"), still others with our cultural, racial or religious heritage, and others with our talents ("rebounder" or "cellist"). Though we might emphasize one such identity in some moments, our sense of who we are draws in complex ways from each of them, and any one can be evoked in a particular moment, brought into the present, and explored or reframed. It's Mellix's multiple social identities—as parent, as an insider to a black community, as student and academic writer—that she tries to put into relationship with one another.

Our Past Social Identities Influence Who We Are in the Present While Our Present Social Identities Influence the Way We See the Past.   The writers of these memoirs, as they bring the past into the present, are also exploring the past through the present, seeing how each influences and shapes the other. Rodriguez's bilingual past and his present beliefs about education are each reframed by the other perspective. Avicolli explores how his current social identity as a gay man has been influenced by his childhood experiences, but also how that identity leads him to resee these experiences.

Do these characteristics seem relevant to your own experiences with social identities?

READING RESPONSE	Skim through the memoirs following this chapter and choose one that interests you. You'll be working with this memoir through several activities—exploring the ways in which it addresses the theme of social identity, and seeing how the writer has worked in creating this memoir.

Read the memoir, glossing it in the ways suggested in Reading Strategies (p. 499). Then write a journal response in which you consider what the writer has written about, and why she/he might be writing about this (what the writer is trying to come to an understanding about, and what she/he wants readers to understand).

In what ways do the characteristics of social identity listed above seem relevant to the memoir you've chosen:

- Does it involve naming and being named?
- Is the writer's identity defined from both insider and outsider perspectives?

(continued)

- Does the writer discuss multiple social identities?
- Does the writer bring any past social identities into the ways in which he or she views things in the present?

What does this writer show about a past moment or moments and what does the writer seem to think about that moment from the perspective of the present?

WRITING MEMOIRS

When readers and writers begin to place themselves within the conversations that go on within a particular community, they do so using not only the language and style of writing of that community, but also the genres of that community. Genres arise when people repeatedly speak or write about the same sorts of things, for similar purposes, within similar settings. Shopping lists, office memos, grant proposals, e-mail messages are all genres that have arisen because the activities they represent are so similar that they soon take on a familiar form, one that gets further refined as it's used. So the genres that are common within a discourse community can also tell you something of what's valued within that community (brevity, for example, in fast-paced e-mail and on-line chat exchanges, where part of the shared discourse is a set of understood abbreviations). Adding new discourses—new ways of talking and thinking about the world—and the genres that go with them, is a necessary part of the work of writers as they move into larger, more public worlds.

Working Within the Genre of Memoir as a Writer

The memoir is closely linked to the personal essay genre that's often taught in schools and required on college applications. However, it's not just a school genre, but one that appears in magazines and literary journals, or, as in Rodriguez's case, within a longer autobiography made up of a series of memoirs. A memoir, as a formal genre, offers a way for writers to reflect on their past experiences and explore their relevance to the present, but also to make those private past experiences public in a way that will speak to a larger audience. And because it is a formal genre, different from the sorts of informal reflections about the same events a writer might write in a private journal or in letters to family or friends, reading others' memoirs and writing your own can help you focus on questions of shape and form in a way that moves beyond fixed rules and structures (like the five paragraph essay that many writers have learned) to see multiple possibilities for addressing the key elements of a genre.

For college writers who are moving between the social worlds of home, family, old friends, and familiar classrooms and the new and still uncertain worlds that they're entering, the memoir can be a way of taking stock of where they are and considering where they might be going. As you write your own memoir, you'll want to reflect on the experiences that have influenced you as a writer and language user, and/or that have contributed to one or more of your social identities—perhaps as a member of a family or a cultural group, as a student, as a writer.

DRAFTING A MEMOIR

You've reflected on many aspects of your experience in communities through a variety of journal responses.

- Begin by reading back through these responses, highlighting thoughts and moments that you might want to explore through a memoir.

- Then, with the understandings you've gained from those reflections as background, select a particular experience within a discourse community that has contributed in a significant way to an aspect of your own social identity and that you feel comfortable sharing in a more public way.

- Write a memoir (of about 3 typed pages) about that experience. This an exploratory piece of writing, where your goal is to discover a new understanding about a past experience for yourself and to share both the experience and the understanding with your readers. You'll want to decide on a moment that captures your own experience of insiderness or outsiderness to a community's ways of thinking and talking—a moment that you might see in new terms from your present perspective. Include a specific moment or incident that was significant for you, or a characteristic scene, making it as real to your readers as possible by showing it in detail and by capturing some of the language that was associated with it. Pause to visualize that moment. Then show what that moment or scene felt like, and reflect on how you now see its significance, in retrospect, for you in the present.

This exploratory version of your memoir will serve as a first draft of a final version, one that you'll revisit after looking more closely at some of the ways in which other memoirs have been shaped, and after sharing your memoir with other readers.

Reading the Memoir of Another College Writer

To see how a college writer uses the genre of memoir to explore the social identities associated with different discourse communities, to reexamine and rename her past experiences from a present perspective, and to give a shape to what she writes that fits both her own purposes and the needs and expectations of the more public audience of her readers, we'll turn now to a memoir written by a student writer, Karen (whom we saw in the kitchen table conversation in the introduction), in her freshman year of college. Because she was asked to reflect on her writing process as she worked on this memoir, responding to questions like the ones included at the end of the last chapter, we can see not only the final version of what she wrote, but the way she went about writing it. (Remember, as you read, that this is Karen's <u>final</u> version, after she brainstormed, drafted, received feedback and suggestions from other readers, revised, and edited.)

READING RESPONSE

Read and gloss Karen's memoir, looking at <u>what</u> she writes about, <u>why</u> she writes about it, and <u>how</u> she writes about it. Write a response that captures what you might say to her if you were responding to her memoir in a peer writing response group. What might you say about <u>what</u> she's included here? Is there anything else you might want to know about <u>why</u> she has included the things she's written and why these events and details are significant to the understandings she seems to be trying to frame for herself and her readers. Then consider <u>how</u> she writes this memoir, from a peer writer's perspective. What do you notice in particular about the choices she's made in structuring the memoir? In the details she includes?

Continue to read on in the chapter through Karen's account of her process in writing this memoir. Does her account of her process and choices lead you to think in any different ways about what you might do as you work on the next draft of your memoir?

Karen's Memoir

I was born in the Congo
I walked to the fertile crescent and built
    the sphinx
I designed a pyramid so that a star
    that only glows every one hundred years falls
    into the center giving divine perfect light
I am bad

We are less then halfway through Nikki Giovanni's seven stanza poem "Ego-tripping" as the tightly packed crowd of the Shiloh Baptist Church erupts; a mix of laughter, applause, and echoes of our words. There are ten of us, ages four to thirteen, lined up across the stage: all but two statuesque, perhaps majestic, hands clasped, heads nodding respectfully at the audience's applause. The two, my best friend Melanie and I, ages five and four respectively, stand center stage, hands locked and swinging with wild abandon. The poem starts up again, each child reciting a verse. When my turn comes along, Melanie and I say the line together and get such an outpouring of laughter that we continue on, reciting the entirety of the poem, with little regard for whose turn it actually is to speak.

Alike in our coveting of attention, as in so many other ways, this was not the first time my best friend and I stole the show, only one of the most memorable. On dress-up days for our preschool group, I usually wore the bunny suit, Melanie the clown, but inspired by the other's performance we'd switch our costumes and roles. Neither of us wanted to be categorized.

Perhaps it was there, in the little brown church on the corner, that I learned my love for poetry. More certainly it was there, where I gained my sense of identity. I grew up in two different families, mine and that of my best friend; one White, one Black, in a Black community that accepted me as one of its own. "Blackness" was as much a part of my identity as anything else. I grew up singing Gospel, learning about Malcolm, listening to Billie Holiday, rapping with RUN DMC, and trying to get my hair to stay in the cornrows and beads Melanie always wore. At the same time though, I also grew up singing "On the good ship, Lollipop" and learning Latin hymns from my Catholic grandmother in a section of the city where Melanie's black skin made her an outsider. But these moments fell into separate categories only when I grew older, when I learned how others viewed the world. Race was never an issue to me or Melanie, and we always knew we were sisters. Skin color was not a defining element.

As I grew older, though, I began to struggle with society's definition of who I was. In my two families, my town, my church and within my group of friends I was always Karen, no further explanation required. But as my social universe began to expand, strangers began to label me. I struggled with these labels because they always left out a part of my essence, of my identity, and I never fit into the categories that were "created" for me. Initially, I was always judged as white or sometimes Puerto Rican, which always left out a major part of who I was. My friends would argue for my Blackness or, alternatively, for my uniqueness, while I'd reply to the frequently asked question "What are you really?" with "Oh, I'm real mixed up," though I did not always feel that way. I just did not fit the categories that others saw the world in.

5   In my high school years, I struggled—I was trying to define myself within the implied standards of individuals and the larger society, I needed to evade the racial divisions and often battles at my high school, and I wanted to find ways of fighting both the individual prejudice that assaulted me and my friends and the systemic racism that limited my friends' plans and possibilities. These years left me with deep wounds, as I learned how much a white privilege that I didn't want would deny the Black parts of my identity. At the same time, I began to perceive, through my friends' eyes, what Dubois referred to as "double-consciousness"—an awareness not only of their Black identity but also of the way that identity was defined by a racist society. But that perception left me even more confused about where I fit.

It wasn't until about halfway through my teenage years, that I realized I did not need to fit perfectly within society's "jar," as William Carlos Williams would say. I came to see that while most people believed in "black and white" categories of Black and White, we didn't need to. It was at that point where I began to understand what I've learned to name in college "the social construction of race."

So now I question categories, while I try to learn the psychology behind humans' impulses to classify, segregate, and often degrade people. My best friend and I are still sisters, studying together the "Psychology of the African-American Experience," reading DuBois and Appiah, West and Dyson, and trying on arguments instead of dress-ups.

Fifteen years later, I stand before a group of peers, reciting a poem of my own, still trying to make sense of the world by bringing together the diverse pieces of my own experience, still trying to move beyond simple categories.

You're a bowl of Alphabet Soup:
Four drops Pythagoras
and a handful of village elder
With a dash of Snoop savvy for ghetto navigation.

You're Brooklyn Tech at Harvard Yard and
Radical Exponents on the Metro.

You're five chapters Malcolm
Ten stanzas Giovanni
and one primed Vivaldi composition.

What are some of the things we can learn from Karen's memoir if we use our analytical tools of looking at <u>what</u> she writes about, <u>why</u> she writes about it, and <u>how</u> she writes about it in relationship to the discourse *context*?

The context is set partly by the assignment to write about an aspect of her past experience that she feels is significant to who she is now and to her current values and beliefs. It's set partly by her position as a college freshman whose thinking is being influenced by a number of her courses. And it's set partly by the fact that she has written this essay in a setting where she has been receiving feedback from a number of readers. Let's look first at what she's had to say about her writing of this memoir.

Here's what Karen says about deciding <u>what</u> to write about:

I had a hard time thinking about what to write about. I had some ideas, but I didn't really know what anyone else would find interesting. And I had already written a lot before about growing up in a racially-mixed neighborhood and what it was like being part of my best friend's family, who were Black, so I didn't think I really had anything new to say about that, even though it seemed like a good topic to write about for this memoir.

I started out trying to write some stuff about how I felt in high school and about the racial divisions there, and I got something written, but I didn't really like it. (I ended up throwing a lot of this out when I got going on my final memoir. A few of the ideas seemed important to keep, but all the details about things that happened in high school would have made it too long, and they just didn't fit in the end.)

The other thing was that I sort of knew how I wanted the memoir to go. I knew I needed to talk about a specific moment in my experience, and I wanted to describe that moment. So I started out making a list of moments I might want to write about. At first my list was mostly about high school, but then I got out an album of old pictures and I started remembering earlier times. I found a picture of me and Melanie in the clown and bunny costumes we used to wear in pre-school and some other pictures of us at Shiloh Baptist Church, and I remembered the way we used to give performances of poetry with the big kids.

I didn't really remember what poems we recited at Shiloh, but I knew from what my mom and Melanie's mom told us that they were mostly poems by Black women. And it just happened that I was reading the poems of Nikki Giovanni for my poetry course. So I asked my mother if this one poem, "Ego-tripping" was one we might have read, and she actually had saved the programs from our perform-ances and the copies of the poems we all got when we were learning them (though Melanie and I couldn't read yet). So I found the actual poem, an old pur-ple copy made on one of those old ditto machines. And once I found that, I knew I had the memoir and the rest was pretty easy.

From what she's said so far, we can see <u>why</u> Karen finally decides to include the events that she does and how much those decisions are shaped by the context for which she is writing. Her first ideas are strongly influenced by the fact that she is writing this for a college assignment and that she needs to make choices that will fit the terms of that assignment. She's also trying to interest her readers and herself and not just to write again about things she's written about earlier. But <u>why</u> she's made particular choices also has a certain element of luck—that she tried the strategy of looking in a photo album to get some ideas and found a picture of herself with her friend Melanie in their favorite costumes, and that she found a copy of one of the poems they would have read at the church performance. Of course, having decided to focus on the performance as a significant moment in the past, she could have guessed at a poem they might have performed. But finding the actual copy gave her confidence that she was on the right track.

We can see more about <u>what</u> and <u>why</u>, but also about <u>how</u> Karen finally writes this memoir as her reflections on her process continue.

> Melanie and I are also in a course on the Psychology of the African-American Ex-perience, and we've been reading DuBois, and we talked about what I was think-ing about as I was writing this memoir, and when I went back to try to write some more, his words about double-consciousness seemed to fit exactly with what I was trying to say. And being in that course together also made me think it would be good to show what we're doing together now, not just in the past.
>
> I still didn't have an ending though. One of my readers, who knows I'm in a creative writing class and that I've been writing poetry, asked if there was any-thing in my own poetry that would fit with what I was saying. I was sort of reluc-tant to use my own poetry, which seems sort of personal, in an essay like this. But I looked at a poem where I had referred to Nikki Giovanni, and it turned out to say exactly how I felt about how it's good to be a mixture of many things and move beyond simple categories. So I put that part in, and read through and spell-checked again, and that was it. My readers helped me with a little more editing and proofreading in the end, but I felt as if I had it the way I wanted it. (And hon-estly, I just didn't have any more time to work on it with everything I have to do for my other courses.)

So <u>how</u> for this writer involves not only the final choices she makes about ways to set up her essay that will interest her readers, but getting the responses of real readers to see whether what she's written is clear, and hearing their sug-gestions as well. It's not just the conversation with readers that she imagines as a writer, but the real conversations she has with real readers, that help her to shape her essay in a way that satisfies her.

If we look back now at the final version, we can see some more about those choices and how they've allowed Karen to address issues of social identity and the crossing of discourse communities that are central to this chapter.

<u>What</u>? Writing About Identity and Discourse

Karen definitely uses the occasion of writing this memoir to focus in on an aspect of her own social identity that is important to her now, as she's entering a new discourse community—her experience with friendship outside of racial categories and her conviction that such categories are limiting and should be questioned. She could have chosen to write about other significant aspects of her identity—her years as an athlete, her relationship with an older brother, what she's learned from her relationship with a disabled cousin—topics that made her first brainstormed list. Her choice may reflect the fact that issues of race and of multiculturalism are being addressed in several of her courses (courses that she has probably selected, in turn, because of her interest in these issues), and those courses give her a new lens through which to examine her familiar experience.

<u>How</u>? Using the Language and Style of a New Community

Just as Mellix takes on the language of the community she's writing for and writing within, using phrases like "appropriating terms," and quoting the words of Fanon (who writes about colonialism and relationships of power) to link speaking (or writing) with assuming a culture, Karen uses the terms of her new community to understand her past experience in new ways. She works with a concept defined by the writer of black intellectual history, W. E. B. Dubois—"double consciousness" (which represents the ways in which African Americans have had to see the world and themselves simultaneously from the perspective of their own culture and the dominant white culture). Then she goes on to use another new term, telling us that "I began to understand what I've learned to name in college 'the social construction of race.' "

Karen has also taken on some of the larger elements of the discourse style of her new college community. Using contrasting details—as she does to suggest differences between the community she grew up in and the one her grandmother lived in—is one element of that style. Other elements include taking what others have written as a source of authority, and interweaving the words from those written texts with her own evolving text. In this way, Karen places herself within a larger, ongoing conversation that takes place in writing, mentioning not only the work of DuBois, but the poet William Carlos Williams, as well as Nikki Giovanni. And she also makes good hypotheses about what constitutes shared knowledge in the academic community she is writing for—that her readers will know who these poets are, who DuBois is (and what Appiah, West, and Dyson are likely to write about if they're being read in a course on the African-American experience). But in crossing communities, she also assumes other shared knowledge with her readers—about RUN DMC, and about all of the elements of shared knowledge from different worlds she stirs into the mix of her own poem. Finally, the strategy of beginning and ending with quotations from poems is also one that's familiar in this new discourse community (not unlike Mellix's teacher's suggestion that she start a paper with an anecdote).

<u>Why</u>? Seeking New Understandings of Past Experiences

We can also see that Karen's social identities have involved the ways in which she has been named by others and the ways in which she tried to avoid others' ways of naming the world as black or white. So she has had to negotiate her own social identities in dialogue with the perspectives of others. While she speaks in this memoir from the identity of someone who has been trying to move across racial categories, we see that other identities come into play here—the grandchild of a Catholic grandmother, the college student who is studying psychology, even perhaps the beginning poet, who is trying out new forms for representing her understandings and experience. Some of these identities, at least, affect the ways in which she approaches the present moment.

Karen's ideas about her memoir have been drawn from her own experience, but her ways of shaping those ideas have been influenced by her conversations with other readers, who react to her drafts, telling her what they like and what interests them, asking her questions, and helping her see what else she might add. Writing from the perspective of one's readers, as well as oneself, is an important skill for writers to develop.

Writers who want to invite an extended conversation with their readers in a way that's particularly effective in memoirs may want to draw on some of the discourse strategies they've learned as speakers, using dialogue, recreating details, using repetition. (Notice how Karen uses repetition to build up the different elements of her experience: "I grew up in two different families . . . I grew up singing Gospel . . . I also grew up singing 'On the good ship Lollipop.'")

To write with readers in mind, you can keep shifting between writing and reading, stepping back to act as a reader of your own writing. But the most straightforward way to find out whether a piece of writing will evoke the response the writer intends is to share it with real readers, as Karen has done. Writers may ask readers to respond to their writing, or they may talk out their ideas with a willing listener (as Karen has done with Melanie).

PEER RESPONSE	Reading and responding to the memoirs of other college writers is a good way of helping them see how the written conversation they've created is working. At the same time, reading others' memoirs carefully helps you to see how to step back from your own and take a reader's perspective as you move through drafts. This is a good moment to read and respond to drafts written by a classmate. You might also want to read, respond, and discuss your responses to one of the memoirs of student writers included at the end of the chapter. Finally, you will want to apply the same style of reading and responding to your own draft.

(continued)

You can read and respond:

- from a participatory perspective—focusing on what interested you, what confused you, where you would like to know more;

- from an analytical perspective—focusing on what you've found about the <u>what</u>, <u>why</u>, and <u>how</u> of this memoir;

- from an evaluative perspective—focusing on how well the memoir works in terms of the <u>what</u>, <u>why</u>, and <u>how</u>; on whether enough information and details and examples are included to meet your needs for shared knowledge as a reader; how well the writing works to show or tell you the significance of these events and where you'd need to be shown or told more to see the writer's meaning; how well the overall structuring works to help you see and follow this meaning and whether the style works consistently throughout to let you hear the writer's voice.

Reading and Comparing Memoirs as a Writer

One reason for reading a number of memoirs is to get a sense of the strategies and approaches other writers have used, and you can read these memoirs as a source of inspiration—with a writer's eye—to see the different ways in which others have worked within this genre. Reading in this way, in any genre, adds another important strategy to your repertoire as a writer as you discover the quite different ways in which writers have worked with common elements

- Memoirs invite you into the experience of a writer in a number of ways. Unlike more traditional academic essays, where there's usually an introduction that states pretty clearly what the writer intends to explore in the essay and how, memoirs are likely to have a wider range of structures. Here are some of the ways memoir writers have begun.

  With a moment of past experience (Rodriguez, Rose)

  With a broader statement of a theme "Our parents would sooner have left us out of Christmas than leave us out of a joke." (Dillard)

  With a comment on some aspect of the theme ("'talking back' meant speaking as equal to an authority figure"—hooks), ("the power of language" and "I use all the Englishes I grew up with"—Tan)

  With a quotation (from a poem by Nikki Giovanni—Karen)

  With a larger historical context—(the Rose excerpt comes from a larger chapter that Rose begins by giving some information about Italian immigration to the United States, setting his own experience of schooling within a broad pattern in U.S. history)

Likewise these writers have structured their memoirs in different ways, bringing out their larger themes or understandings in different places in their narrative. But they do all link their immediate experiences to larger understandings in a way that their readers can recapture.

STUDENT VOICES

Look at this opening from a memoir by a student writer about her experience of moving to the United States from Jamaica. Laysian begins with specific words she recalls her mother saying. Are there words that you recall that capture a theme in the experience you're writing about?

> "Speak betta Inglish likle gal" my mother would always say to me. She always expects me to practice and speak English clearly. She believes that by practicing our English we would have it easier when we get to the outside community of socializing. In Jamaica, even though we all speak broken English, in a certain situation we are still expected to speak Standard English. Not because people won't understand us if we don't but because we believe it's a better way to communicate with each other in public, especially to people we don't know. **(Laysian)**

■ Memoirs involve the selection and ordering of personal experience. The writer has to select those moments that are meaningful when seeing his/her life from a particular perspective. Not all moments, not all details, are equally significant, and the writer must choose what will best represent that aspect of his life from the perspective being explored.

Eggers, for example, has written a book of over 500 pages to recount the first several years after his parents' deaths (which occurred when he was still in college), years in which he was trying to figure out how to be a parent, a brother, and a young adult simultaneously. But he has still had to select from the whole of his experience of those years. In the selection included here, he imagines his and his brother's performance at a school parents' meeting as a performance onstage, creating a script that captures the words of that performance and the roles they've played out at that moment.

Avicolli, in a memoir of a few pages, takes us into several significant scenes in his life that have led to his understanding about the aspect of his identity associated with sexual preference.

Karen gives one scene in detail and then points to other moments in her experience that add to what that opening scene offers from the perspective of her larger argument for rejecting racial categories.

■ Memoirs are written from a particular stance, from particular ways of seeing the world, and it's that stance that guides the selection and ordering of experience. A memoir may involve a negotiation of different ways, as we found in Mellix's attempt to bring together the ways and stance of the academic writer and of the speaker of "cherished" black

English, but even in this negotiation, the lens through which the experiences are being viewed is evident. By naming the writer's stance, you can see how the writer is "reading" the experiences being recounted. By virtue of the fact that the writer is located in a different time (and perhaps place) from that in which the events took place, the writer is no longer participating in those events as an insider, but is now a partial outsider, writing from a new perspective.

Here's what Eggers has to say about that perspective.

> There is, intrinsic to the process of a memoir, the resulting destruction of one's former self. Writing about those years, and being as cruel to who I was as I could be implicitly means that you are killing that person. Yes, you are sometimes celebrating that person's better thoughts, but overall you are saying: This was me then, and I can look at that person from the distance I now have and throw water balloons on his stupid fat head.

Although the events Eggers recounts are tragic, he's not approaching them from such a stance, but trying to hold off the sense of the tragic by undercutting it.

- In memoirs, the writer's stance is closely connected to the writer's voice. The voices of most of the writers of the memoirs in this unit might be described as serious, sincere, appreciative or maybe critical or challenging. But Eggers' stance towards his former self is rather unsympathetic, distant, ironic, sometimes comic, and these are terms one could apply to the qualities of his voice here as well. In his case, both that stance and that voice evolve in part from his expectations about his readers:

> While writing the original text, I had in my head, not the usual Writer's Ideal Reader, but instead my own potential reading person, the Mean/Jaded/Skimming Reader—the person I had been for many years.

If you're writing for a mean, jaded reader who might mock you if you take yourself too seriously, you'll want to mock yourself first. But assuming this voice and this stance (and writing this memoir at all) offers Eggers a way to make some emotional distance for himself from the painful loss of his parents and even from the immature self who didn't quite know how to handle the life he was left with.

Karen too tried out a comic voice, with exaggeration and mis-namings, as she fooled around earlier with some ideas for a story about her experience. However, it wasn't an appropriate voice for the serious exploration of racial categorization that she finally focuses on for her memoir (as you can see) and she didn't use it in what she wrote later.

> I was a toddler junkie. I nearly OD'd on drugs when I was less than two years old. I guess I was also a purse snatcher, since it was my mother's purse that I found the drugs in. I was caught in the act though, and thus was saved from either a premature death or a life of crime, when I walked into the

kitchen to proudly show off a handful of the pretty yellow antihistamines I had already stuffed into my mouth.

A writer who used an opening like this one might be setting up a memoir that explores being the black sheep of a family—the kid who gets into trouble. Or it could create a stance that might work in a memoir that went on to explore the complexities of a friend's experience with drugs. In Karen's case though, it remained just an amusing family story, not a moment that was significant to an aspect of her identity or from which she could discover something in the present, so she set it aside.

■ Writers often bring the words of other writers into their memoirs in ways that help them make larger connections and bring their personal understandings together with what others have come to understand and express. It's not surprising that writers, who are also readers, will find connections in what they're reading that help them make sense of their own experiences. We've seen, for example, that Mellix quotes the words of Fanon: "To speak . . . means . . . to assume a culture, to support the weight of a civilization." Other writers, while not quoting the words they've read, still point to defining concepts they've drawn from their readings: Karen points to DuBois; hooks points to the work of the psychologist Alice Miller on childhood trauma.

STUDENT VOICES

Many writers find that it's words from popular culture that most resonate with their own experience. Deni uses the words of the Dave Matthews Band, "So Much to Say," as the title for her memoir, and then explains that title with the following opening paragraph.

> I love music. Or more exactly: I need music. The worst punishment I ever had was when my parents instead of grounding me took away my stereo. I collect it: CDs, a few records I can't listen to but there . . . and tapes. Mix tapes that I make for myself and some that my friends make for me—although most times I mix some for them. It's one of the best forms of communication, I think. There's something about letting someone listen to what you truly love, and you don't need to say anything, explain anything, just listen.

Deni goes on to describe a tape made for her by her friend Jore, and to recapture a period of her life, the end of her senior year of high school, through the songs recorded there.

Does something that you've read or heard (a song lyric, a line from a movie, a poem you've read, a poem you've written, etc.) capture what you think to be true of the experience you're recounting? You may want to use the quotation as an epigraph—something that stands alone as an introduction to your memoir (with or without your commenting on the quotation directly), or you may want to work it into your text, as Mellix has done with her quotation from Fanon.

■ Memoirs also end in different ways, capturing the understandings they've represented in different forms for readers to take away. Avicolli ends with a poem he has written, as does Karen. Rodriguez ends with a moment of speaking confidently before others that contrasts with his opening classroom moment. Tan, who has explored the ways in which she has come to think about her mother's "Englishes" as a writer, ends with her mother's verdict on her own writing. "So easy to read." And Mellix ends with a final statement of the understanding she has gained as a writer in academic settings, that "through writing one can continually bring new selves into being."

Look quickly again at the memoirs at the end of Part I, this time noting how each is set up in terms of how it begins and ends, what it seems to include, and what stance the writer takes and voice the writer uses. Then choose one or two new memoirs from the set, read and gloss the memoir, then look at each memoir in more detail and write a response in which you consider these elements of <u>how</u>:

READING RESPONSE

- the way the writer has begun;

- the ways in which the writer has selected and ordered what is told;

- the stance the writer is taking towards what's told (the attitude the writer seems to have towards what's told);

- the voice the writer uses (perhaps a voice the writer would use in telling a story to friends, or an academic voice, or a poetic voice);

- the ways in which the writer brings in and connects to the writing of others (if he or she does so);

- the way in which the writer ends the memoir.

By analyzing the <u>how</u> in this way, do you come to any new understandings about <u>why</u>, about what the writer's meanings and purposes are in this memoir? What understandings do you come to about the choices and strategies available to writers of memoirs?

WRITING IN A PUBLIC GENRE: THE FORMAL MEMOIR

The process of going from an exploratory draft to a final, formal piece of writing rarely follows a set of neat steps. It's more likely to be messy in the ways that Karen described, as she moved back and forth in different parts of what she was writing until she saw how it could all be shaped together. As you work with the earlier draft of your memoir and begin to make decisions about its final form, you may want first to try out different ways of beginning, selecting and ordering, and ending, before you make decisions about your final version.

One way of finding new possibilities is to play with the text of your memoir. Try writing it in another voice, beginning and ending it in another way, changing the order of your telling. Set aside your draft version and, on separate sheets of paper, experiment with two or three elements. You might want to try out a particular approach that a writer of one of the memoirs has used, mimicking that approach to test its effectiveness for what you're doing, and writing in the style of hooks or Dillard or Eggers. Finally, however, you'll produce a draft version that feels as if it works in the ways you want it to, that seems close to a final and formal version that you'd be willing to share with a wider, public audience. At that point, you're ready to step back one more time do a final revision of your memoir.

The word "revision" means "reseeing." It often takes stepping away from what you've written, trying on the perspectives of other readers, and stepping into the role of reader yourself, to allow you to resee your first version of a piece of writing—to see it with new eyes and to find in it new possibilities. After you've had feedback from your writing group, looked closely at the ways in which other writers have crafted their memoirs, and experimented with some new forms, you have a new perspective from which to resee the exploratory draft versions of your memoir and to write a final version.

REVISE YOUR MEMOIR

As you step back to resee what you've written, think about both what you've come to understand about the significance of the moments you've portrayed and how you've brought out the significance of these moments to your readers. Here are some things you'll want to consider in your revision process:

- Getting the comments of other readers—classmates, friends, family members, teacher—as well as your own reader's perspective. (You might also try reading aloud to listeners.)

- Looking again at <u>how</u> you've said what you have to say. How have you gained your readers' interest and brought them into the experiences you've written about? How have you made those experiences come alive for them? How have you brought them to see the larger understandings that you've gained from these experiences?

- Rereading from the perspective of the general expectations associated with this genre. These might include:
  - ☐ a particular experience or event in the past
  - ☐ told with details that allow the reader to share/understand the experience
  - ☐ a focus on a particular theme, issue, or concern
  - ☐ a sense of what new understanding has been gained by reseeing that experience in the present (or what new questions have emerged)
  - ☐ frequently, one or more quotations connecting this understanding to another memoir or other reading

(continued)

When you're satisfied with, or at least finished with, the overall shape of the final text you've produced, reread again, perhaps out loud, to make sure your sentences are smooth and clear, and that you haven't created mixed or unconventional forms, editing wherever it's needed. And finally proofread carefully.

(The Writing Strategies section of Part IV offers further suggestions on revising, editing, and proofreading.)

Extending Your Inquiry

You may want to resee your memoir in another way, going beyond its boundaries and extending your inquiry. Most memoirs offer an opening up rather than a closing down of the possibilities for seeing and interpreting the meaning of the writer's experience. And it's often the case that writing one memoir is only the beginning of an inquiry that you'll want to take further. There are a number of ways of extending the inquiry that you've begun in writing your own memoir: broadening your perspective on the themes and concerns it raises, trying on new perspectives or points of view about the events or types of events that you've recounted, or placing your own experience in a broader socio-cultural, historical, or psychological context.

■ The memoir you've written may connect your own experience to those of others in terms of social identity and social roles, and you may want to follow out a theme in your memoir as it appears in other memoirs, using others' experiences as a way of further gaining perspective on your own. For example, if Karen were to expand on her own experience of moving between black and white communities, what might Mellix's perspective offer? If your memoir explores ways in which you, like bell hooks, were a child who talked back, placing her memoir against yours might give you a way to explore the meaning of that experience in deeper ways. (Or if you were the opposite, the silent child, the contrast with hooks could give you a way of exploring the meanings and the possibilities of such silence.) Or you may find several memoirs among those written by members of your class that evoke themes of sibling relationships, friendship, school challenges; placing your memoir within a set focusing on a common theme, and exploring the connections that make you see them as a set, can be another way to broaden your framework of understanding about your own experience.

■ The memoir you've written represents your own point of view about the events that you have described, and you may want to discover the perspectives of other participants in these events, placing them in dialogue with your own. For example, if Karen were to interview Melanie about her experience of growing up in the same community, within the same two families, to what degree would their perspectives and understandings match, and what different memories, interpretations, and understandings of these events might Melanie have? How might her perspective further extend the understandings Karen is working toward?

■ The memoir you've written may be about a local, seemingly personal event, but those events are always located within a larger social/cultural/historical/psychological context. For example, Karen points to the roles her readings play in her course the Psychology of the African-American Experience. They are playing roles in enlarging and reframing her understandings. Using one of those readings to explore the broader historical or psychological context in which racial categorization and separation has gone on in the United States might let her continue to construct a broader framework for understanding what she has experienced or observed. Your understanding of the context for any specific experience can be enlarged in this way—by finding out something about the history of immigration to your community or the psychological experience of being the youngest sibling or the theory of reading or writing or bilingual language instruction that seems to have shaped the context for your defining classroom experience.

We can explore the significance of our experiences in discourse communities by moving in close to examine the workings of that experience in detail, and by moving out, to understand the larger contexts in which those experiences take place. We'll continue to explore the relationship between specific moments, immediate situations and larger contexts in Part II, as we turn from memories of past experiences in discourse communities to study current settings and the conversations that take place in them.

EXPLORATORY ESSAY: AN EXTENDED INQUIRY

Suggestions:

1. Start your own thinking with a guiding question. What more do you want to learn about the theme or issue you're exploring that you think you can learn from the people and texts you have available to you?

2. Use one of the ways discussed above to extend your inquiry beyond what you've captured in your memoir:

   ■ Connect your own experience to those of others in terms of social identity and social roles, by following out a theme as it appears across your memoir and other memoirs.

   ■ Get the perspectives of other participants in the events you've described.

   ■ Locate the events you've written about within a larger socio-cultural, historical, or psychological context.

(continued)

Within any of these options, you should have more than one text—your memoir and another text, reading, or interview—that you are putting in dialogue with each other.

3. Using the texts you've chosen or collected, you'll want to reread them with your guiding question in mind, glossing and pulling out places that speak to that question. Make notes of all the ideas and connections that interest you. Then look for key points you're finding that connect to your question.

4. Set up a structured organizer to help you see the relationships between these key points. (See Planning, Drafting, and Shaping Strategies p. 511.) Try to generate and name several key points that these texts speak to in some way. Not every text has to address every point. Sometimes when one text addresses a key point that another doesn't, that can show a significant difference in perspective.

5. What do you think you've learned about your question by working in this way with these texts? Write an exploratory essay/report in which you introduce your question and some of your initial thinking about it, address key points that connect these texts and shed light on your question, and tell your readers what new understandings you've gained. Include quotations from the texts or interviews you draw on. Shape your essay in whatever way best allows you to explore and convey the understandings you've come to.

Additional Readings

Mike Rose, "I Just Wanna Be Average" (from *Lives on the Boundary*)

In *Lives on the Boundary* (1989), Mike Rose uses his own teaching experience in urban schools and as a professor at UCLA to reflect on the promise that students from diverse backgrounds bring to the classroom and on ways he has found of helping students succeed. But he begins his book by relating his own experience growing up in an Italian immigrant family in South Los Angeles. Rose describes what, in his own education, could have thwarted his parents' dreams for him, and what helped him to move forward. One critical moment came in high school, when his records got mixed up with those of another student and he was placed in a vocational track.

In this excerpt, Rose focuses not on home, but on one of the communities of high school—that of students who are tracked away from serious academic work. He describes the ways of talking and seeing the world that such students share as they protect themselves from the insult implied in their school placement, proclaiming through their words and their actions, "I just want to be average," and he shows how he, too, took on that social identity. His memoir suggests that it's not just differences between home and school languages or dialects that affect students' futures as writers and learners, but differeneces in "discourse"—in the social identity kit that speakers and writers develop from the worlds they've been part of. Rose, the writer, shows us how the social identity of "average" or "vocational student" gets shaped.

After two years in the vocational track, Rose was switched to the academic track. But by then he was an outsider to the ways of thinking and talking that were expected in that very different discourse community. His own experience led him to see students' academic achievement as shaped, not so much by their intelligence, but more by differences in their social situations and their familiarity with the shared knowledge and shared ways of talking and writing that are assumed in academic settings.

(Chapter 8 includes a later section from *Lives on the Boundary* that demonstrates what Rose has to say about what's assumed as shared knowledge in the discourse of college courses.)

I Just Wanna Be Average

Mike Rose

1 It took two buses to get to Our Lady of Mercy. The first started deep in South Los Angeles and caught me at midpoint. The second drifted through neighborhoods with trees, parks, big lawns, and lots of flowers. The rides were long but were livened up by a

group of South L.A. veterans whose parents also thought that Hope had set up shop in the west end of the county. There was Christy Biggars, who, at sixteen, was dealing and was, according to rumor, a pimp as well. There were Bill Cobb and Johnny Gonzales, grease-pencil artists extraordinaire, who left Nembutal-enhanced swirls of "Cobb" and "Johnny" on the corrugated walls of the bus. And then there was Tyrrell Wilson. Tyrrell was the coolest kid I knew. He ran the dozens like a metric halfback, laid down a rap that outrhymed and outpointed Cobb, whose rap was good but not great—the curse of a moderately soulful kid trapped in white skin. But it was Cobb who would sneak a radio onto the bus, and thus underwrote his patter with Little Richard, Fats Domino, Chuck Berry, the Coasters, and Ernie K. Doe's mother-in-law, an awful woman who was "sent from down below." And so it was that Christy and Cobb and Johnny G. and Tyrrell and I and assorted others picked up along the way passed our days in the back of the bus, a funny mix brought together by geography and parental desire.

Entrance to school brings with it forms and releases and assessments. Mercy relied on a series of tests, mostly the Stanford-Binet, for placement, and somehow the results of my tests got confused with those of another student named Rose. The other Rose apparently didn't do very well, for I was placed in the vocational track, a euphemism for the bottom level. Neither I nor my parents realized what this meant. We had no sense that Business Math, Typing, and English–Level D were dead ends. The current spate of reports on the schools criticizes parents for not involving themselves in the education of their children. But how would someone like Tommy Rose, with his two years of Italian schooling, know what to ask? And what sort of pressure could an exhausted waitress apply? The error went undetected, and I remained in the vocational track for two years. What a place.

My homeroom was supervised by Brother Dill, a troubled and unstable man who also taught freshman English. When his class drifted away from him, which was often, his voice would rise in paranoid accusations, and occasionally he would lose control and shake or smack us. I hadn't been there two months when one of his brisk, face-turning slaps had my glasses sliding down the aisle. Physical education was also pretty harsh. Our teacher was a stubby ex-lineman who had played old-time pro ball in the Midwest. He routinely had us grabbing our ankles to receive his stinging paddle across our butts. He did that, he said, to make men of us. "Rose," he bellowed on our first encounter; me standing geeky in line in my baggy shorts. "'Rose'? What the hell kind of name is that?"

"Italian, sir," I squeaked.

5   "Italian! Ho. Rose, do you know the sound a bag of shit makes when it hits the wall?"

"No, sir."

"Wop!"

Sophomore English was taught by Mr. Mitropetros. He was a large, bejeweled man who managed the parking lot at the Shrine Auditorium. He would crow and preen and list for us the stars he'd brushed against. We'd ask questions and glance knowingly and snicker, and all that fueled the poor guy to brag some more. Parking cars was his night job. He had little training in English, so his lesson plan for his day work had us reading the district's required text, *Julius Caesar,* aloud for the semester. We'd finish the play way before the twenty weeks was up, so he'd have us switch parts again and again and start again: Dave Snyder, the fastest guy at Mercy, muscling through Caesar to the breathless squeals of Calpurnia, as interpreted by Steve Fusco, a surfer who owned the school's most envied paneled wagon. Week ten and Dave and Steve would take on new roles, as would we all, and render a water-logged Cassius and a Brutus that are beyond my powers of description.

Spanish I—taken in the second year—fell into the hands of a new recruit. Mr. Montez was a tiny man, slight, five foot six at the most, soft-spoken and delicate. Spanish was a particularly rowdy class, and Mr. Montez was as prepared for it as a doily maker at a hammer throw. He would tap his pencil to a room in which Steve Fusco was propelling spitballs from his heavy lips, in which Mike Dweetz was taunting Billy Hawk, a half-Indian, half-Spanish, reed-thin, quietly explosive boy. The vocational track at Our Lady of Mercy mixed kids traveling in from South L.A. with South Bay surfers and a few Slavs and Chicanos from the harbors of San Pedro. This was a dangerous miscellany: surfers hodads and South-Central blacks all ablaze to the metronomic tapping of Hector Montez's pencil.

10   One day Billy lost it. Out of the corner of my eye I saw him strike out with his right arm and catch Dweetz across the neck. Quick as a spasm, Dweetz was out of his seat, scattering desks, cracking Billy on the side of the head, right behind the eye. Snyder and Fusco and others broke it up, but the room felt hot and close and naked. Mr. Montez's tenuous authority was finally ripped to shreds, and I think everyone felt a little strange about that. The charade was over, and when it came down to it, I don't think any of the kids really wanted it to end this way. They had pushed and pushed and bullied their way into a freedom that both scared and embarrassed them.

* * *

Students will float to the mark you set. I and the others in the vocational classes were bobbing in pretty shallow water. Vocational education has aimed at increasing the economic opportunities of students who do not do well in our schools. Some serious programs succeed in doing that, and through exceptional teachers—like Mr. Gross in *Horace's Compromise*—students learn to develop hypotheses and troubleshoot, reason through a problem, and communicate effectively—the true job skills. The vocational track, however, is most often a place for those who are just not making it, a dumping ground for the disaffected. There were a few teachers who worked hard at education; young Brother Slattery, for example, combined a stern voice with weekly quizzes to try to pass along to us a skeletal outline of world history. But mostly the teachers had no idea of how to engage the imaginations of us kids who were scuttling along at the bottom of the pond.

And the teachers would have needed some inventiveness, for none of us was groomed for the classroom. It wasn't just that I didn't know things—didn't know how to simplify algebraic fractions, couldn't identify different kinds of clauses, bungled Spanish translations—but that I had developed various faulty and inadequate ways of doing algebra and making sense of Spanish. Worse yet, the years of defensive tuning out in elementary school had given me a way to escape quickly while seeming at least half alert. During my time in Voc. Ed., I developed further into a mediocre student and a somnambulant problem solver, and that affected the subjects I did have the wherewithal to handle: I detested Shakespeare; I got bored with history. My attention flitted here and there. I fooled around in class and read my books indifferently—the intellectual equivalent of playing with your food. I did what I had to do to get by, and I did it with half a mind.

But I did learn things about people and eventually came into my own socially. I liked the guys in Voc. Ed. Growing up where I did, I understood and admired physical prowess, and there was an abundance of muscle here. There was Dave Snyder, a sprinter and halfback of true quality. Dave's ability and his quick wit gave him a natural appeal, and he was welcome in any clique, though he always kept a little independent. He enjoyed acting the fool and could care less about studies, but he possessed a certain maturity and never caused the faculty much trouble. It was a testament to his independence that he included me among his friends—I eventually went out for track, but I was no jock. Owing to the Latin alphabet and a dearth of *R*s and *S*s, Snyder sat behind Rose, and we started exchanging one-liners and became friends.

There was Ted Richard, a much-touted Little League pitcher. He was chunky and had a baby face and came to Our Lady of Mercy as a seasoned street fighter. Ted was quick to laugh and he had a loud, jolly laugh, but when he got angry he'd smile a little smile, the kind that simply raises the corner of the mouth a quarter of an inch. For those who knew, it was an eerie signal. Those who didn't found themselves in big trouble, for Ted was very quick. He loved to carry on what we would come to call philosophical discussions: What is courage? Does God exist? He also loved words, enjoyed picking up big ones like *salubrious* and *equivocal* and using them in our conversations—laughing at himself as the word hit a chuckhole rolling off his tongue. Ted didn't do all that well in school—baseball and parties and testing the courage he'd speculated about took up his time. His textbooks were *Argosy* and *Field and Stream*, whatever newspapers he'd find on the bus stop—from *the Daily Worker* to pornography—conversations with uncles or hobos or businessmen he'd meet in a coffee shop, *The Old Man and the Sea*. With hindsight, I can see that Ted was developing into one of those rough-hewn intellectuals whose sources are a mix of the learned and the apocryphal, whose discussions are both assured and sad.

15   And then there was Ken Harvey. Ken was good-looking in a puffy way and had a full and oily ducktail and was a car enthusiast . . . a hodad. One day in religion class, he said the sentence that turned out to be one of the most memorable of the hundreds of thousands I heard in those Voc. Ed. years. We were talking about the parable of the talents, about achievement, working hard, doing the best you can do, blah-blah-blah, when the teacher called on the restive Ken Harvey for an opinion. Ken thought about it, but just for a second, and said (with studied, minimal affect), "I just wanna be average." That woke me up. Average?! Who wants to be average? Then the athletes chimed in with the clichés that make you want to laryngectomize them, and the exchange became a platitudinous melee. At the time, I thought Ken's assertion was stupid, and I wrote him off. But his sentence has stayed with me all these years, and I think I am finally coming to understand it.

Ken Harvey was gasping for air. School can be a tremendously disorienting place. No matter how bad the school, you're going to encounter notions that don't fit with the assumptions and beliefs that you grew up with—maybe you'll hear these dissonant notions from teachers, maybe from the other students, and maybe you'll read them. You'll also be thrown in with all kinds of kids from all kinds of backgrounds, and that can be unsettling—this is especially true in places of rich ethnic and linguistic mix, like the L.A. basin. You'll see a handful of students far excel you in courses that sound exotic and that are only in the curriculum of the elite: French, physics, trigonometry. And all this is happening while you're trying to shape an identity, your body is changing, and your emotions are running wild. If you're a working-class kid in the vocational track, the options you'll have to deal with this will be constrained in certain ways: You're defined by your school as "slow"; you're placed in a curriculum that isn't designed to liberate you but to occupy you, or, if you're lucky, train you, though the training is for work the society does not esteem; other students are picking up the cues from your school and your curriculum and interacting with you in particular ways. If you're a kid like Ted Richard, you turn your back on all this and let your mind roam where it may. But youngsters like Ted are rare. What Ken and so many others do is protect themselves from such suffocating madness by taking on with a vengeance the identity implied in the vocational track. Reject the confusion and frustration by openly defining yourself as the Common Joe. Champion the average. Rely on your own good sense. Fuck this bullshit. Bullshit, of course, is everything you—and the others—fear is beyond you: books, essays, tests, academic scrambling, complexity, scientific reasoning, philosophical inquiry.

The tragedy is that you have to twist the knife in your own gray matter to make this defense work. You'll have to shut down, have to reject intellectual stimuli or diffuse them with sarcasm, have to cultivate stupidity, have to convert boredom from a malady into a way of confronting the world. Keep your vocabulary simple, act stoned when you're not or act more stoned than you are, flaunt ignorance, materialize your dreams. It is a powerful and effective defense—it neutralizes the insult and the frustration of being a vocational kid and, when perfected, it drives teachers up the wall, a delightful secondary effect. But like all strong magic, it exacts a price.

* * *

My own deliverance from the Voc. Ed. world began with sophomore biology. Every student, college prep to vocational, had to take biology, and unlike the other courses, the same person taught all sections. When teaching the vocational group, Brother Clint probably slowed down a bit or omitted a little of the fundamental biochemistry, but he used the same book and more or less the same syllabus across the board. If one class got tough, he could get tougher. He was young and powerful and very handsome, and looks and physical strength were high currency. No one gave him any trouble.

I was pretty bad at the dissecting table, but the lectures and the textbook were interesting: plastic overlays that, with each turned page, peeled away skin, then veins and muscle, then organs, down to the very bones that Brother Clint, pointer in hand, would tap out on our hanging skeleton. Dave Snyder was in big trouble, for the study of life—versus the living of it—was sticking in his craw. We worked out a code for our multiple-choice exams. He'd poke me in the back: once for the answer under A, twice for B, and so on; and when he'd hit the right one, I'd look up to the ceiling as though I were lost in thought. Poke: cytoplasm. Poke, poke: methane. Poke, poke, poke: William Harvey. Poke, poke, poke, poke: islets of Langerhans. This didn't work out perfectly, but Dave passed the course, and I mastered the dreamy look of a guy on a record jacket. And something else happened. Brother Clint puzzled over this Voc. Ed. kid who was racking up 98s and 99s on his tests. He checked the school's records and discovered the error. He recommended that I begin my junior year in the College Prep program. According to all I've read since, such a shift, as one report put it, is virtually impossible. Kids at that level rarely cross tracks. The telling thing is how chancy both my placement into and exit from Voc. Ed. was; neither I nor my parents had anything to do with it. I lived in one world during spring semester, and when I came back to school in the fall, I was living in another.

20   Switching to College Prep was a mixed blessing. I was an erratic student. I was undisciplined. And I hadn't caught onto the rules of the game: Why work hard in a class that didn't grab my fancy? I was also hopelessly behind in math. Chemistry was hard; toying with my chemistry set years before hadn't prepared me for the chemist's equations. Fortunately, the priest who taught both chemistry and second-year algebra was also the school's athletic director. Membership on the track team covered me; I knew I wouldn't get lower than a C. U.S. history was taught pretty well, and I did okay. But civics was taken over by a football coach who had trouble reading the textbook aloud—and reading aloud was the centerpiece of his pedagogy. College Prep at Mercy was certainly an improvement over the vocational program—at least it carried some status—but the social science curriculum was weak, and the mathematics and physical sciences were simply beyond me. I had a miserable quantitative background and ended up copying some assignments and finessing the rest as best I could. Let me try to explain how it feels to see again and again material you should once have learned but didn't.

You are given a problem. It requires you to simplify algebraic fractions or to multiply expressions containing square roots. You know this is pretty basic material because you've seen it for years. Once a teacher took some time with you, and you learned how to carry out these operations. Simple versions, anyway. But that was a year or two or more in the past, and these are more complex versions, and now you're not sure. And this, you keep telling yourself, is ninth- or even eighth-grade stuff.

Next it's a word problem. This is also old hat. The basic elements are as familiar as story characters: trains speeding so many miles per hour or shadows of buildings angling so many degrees. Maybe you know enough, have sat through enough explanations, to be able to begin setting up the problem: "If one train is going this fast . . ." or "This shadow is really one line of a triangle. . . ." Then: "Let's see . . ." "How did Jones do this?" "Hmmmm." "No." "No, that won't work." Your attention wavers. You wonder about other things: a football game, a dance, that cute new checker at the market. You try to focus on the problem again. You scribble on paper for a while, but the tension wins out and your attention flits elsewhere. You crumple the paper and begin daydreaming to ease the frustration.

The particulars will vary, but in essence this is what a number of students go through, especially those in so-called remedial classes. They open their textbooks and see once again the familiar and impenetrable formulas and diagrams and terms that have stumped them for years. There is no excitement here. *No* excitement. Regardless of what the teacher says, this is not a new challenge. There is, rather, embarrassment and frustration and, not surprisingly, some anger in being reminded once again of long-standing inadequacies. No wonder so many students finally attribute their difficulties to

something inborn, organic: "That part of my brain just doesn't work." Given the troubling histories many of these students have, it's miraculous that any of them can lift the
shroud of hopelessness sufficiently to make deliverance from these classes possible.

**READING
RESPONSE**

1. Reflecting on discourse, identity, and context
   Mike Rose shows us how the identity of vocational education students (like students in other high school tracks) is reinforced by their interactions with each
   other and with their teachers. He offers small, generally appreciative, portraits
   of several of his high school classmates and generally less-appreciative portraits
   of several teachers.

   ■ What details of behavior and language does Rose capture for each person?
     What does each example contribute to the larger picture he is creating?
     What is he trying to recreate about his high school experience as it felt to
     him as a student? How is his perspective different as he revisits the experi-
     ence from his present identity as a teacher? How do both perspectives con-
     tribute to the larger concerns Rose explores?

   ■ How did the teachers view students in the vocational track? How was their
     view of students in the college track different? Have you or someone you
     know ever been identified as part of a vocational track? How might such
     identities look different from an insider's perspective? From the perspective
     of a vocational education advocate?

2. Reading from a writer's perspective
   Rose crafts his memoir in several ways that you may want to think about in creating a final version of your own memoir.

   ■ Consider how Rose invites you into his experience as he takes you on his
     long bus ride from his home to his high school and describes the classmates
     who accompanied him from his end of town into an unfamiliar school
     world. How does this bus ride serve to suggest some of the themes of the es-
     say? How might the idea of distance or journey work on a metaphorical
     level?

   ■ Observe how, like Rodriguez, Rose moves in closely at some moments of
     experience, and steps back at others to comment on these moments from a
     present perspective, in relationship to the issues that most concern him.
     Where does he make these shifts in perspective, and how does he signal
     them?

   ■ Rose uses as one point of reference, a book, *Horace's Compromise*, by a
     contemporary advocate of school reform, Ted Sizer, assuming familiarity
     with this book as part of the shared knowledge his readers will bring. How
     does that reference help suggest his larger concerns?

   ■ What do you take as Rose's purpose in writing this memoir? How has (or
     hasn't) this structure allowed him to achieve it from your perspective as a
     reader?

bell hooks, "Talking Back"

bell hooks (who spells her name with lower-case letters) writes of growing up in a southern black community, where young women were not supposed to "talk back," and certainly weren't supposed to talk in public. Yet she too found herself in a world of rich and poetic women's language at home. Like Rodriguez, she had to struggle with the problem of reconciling a private, family voice and a public, academic one. But for hooks this was made more difficult because, as a girl, she wasn't supposed to question authority at home or claim authority outside of it.

As she began to "talk back" as a writer and teacher, and to gain a public voice, hooks did not give up the language of home and family, but chose to maintain two voices, side by side. Later in her book *Talking Back* (1989), from which this excerpt is taken, she explains how she learned, when she left Kentucky and became a college student at Stanford, "to speak differently while maintaining the speech of my region, the sound of my family and community" (79). She wants to present an alternative to Richard Rodriguez's insistence that the language of "community and kin" impedes one's educational progress (particularly at institutions like Stanford, which he also attended), and she asserts her own position:

> Language reflects the culture from which we emerge. To deny ourselves daily use of speech patterns that are common and familiar, that embody the unique and distinctive aspects of our self, is one of the ways that we become estranged and alienated from our past. It is important for us to have as many languages on hand as we can know or learn. (79–80)

Talking Back

bell hooks

1   In the world of the southern black community I grew up in, "back talk" and "talking back" meant speaking as an equal to an authority figure. It meant daring to disagree and sometimes it just meant having an opinion. In the "old school," children were meant to be seen and not heard. My great-grandparents, grandparents, and parents were all from the old school. To make yourself heard if you were a child was to invite punishment, the back-hand lick, the slap across the face that would catch you unaware, or the feel of switches stinging your arms and legs.

To speak then when one was not spoken to was a courageous act—an act of risk and daring. And yet it was hard not to speak in warm rooms where heated discussions began at the crack of dawn, women's voices filling the air, giving orders, making threats, fussing. Black men may have excelled in the art of poetic preaching in the male-dominated church, but in the church of the home, where the everyday rules of how to live and how to act were established, it was black women who preached. There, black women spoke in a language so rich, so poetic, that it felt to me like being shut off from life, smothered to death if one were not allowed to participate.

It was in that world of woman talk (the men were often silent, often absent) that was born in me the craving to speak, to have a voice, and not just any voice but one that could be identified as belonging to me. To make my voice, I had to speak, to hear myself talk—and talk I did—darting in and out of grown folks' conversations and dialogues, answering questions that were not directed at me, endlessly asking questions, making speeches. Needless to say, the punishments for these acts of speech seemed endless. They were intended to silence me—the child—and more particularly the girl child. Had I been a boy, they might have encouraged me to speak believing that I might someday be called to preach. There was no "calling" for talking girls, no legitimized rewarded speech. The punishments I received for "talking back" were intended to suppress all possibility that I would create my own speech. That speech was to be suppressed so that the "right speech of womanhood" would emerge.

Within feminist circles, silence is often seen as the sexist "right speech of womanhood"—the sign of woman's submission to patriarchal authority. This emphasis on woman's silence may be an accurate remembering of what has taken place in the households of women from WASP backgrounds in the United States, but in black communities (and diverse ethnic communities), women have not been silent. Their voices can be heard. Certainly for black women, our struggle has not been to emerge from silence into speech but to change the nature and direction of our speech, to make a speech that compels listeners, one that is heard.

5   Our speech, "the right speech of womanhood," was often the soliloquy, the talking into thin air, the talking to ears that do not hear you—the talk that is simply not listened to. Unlike the black male preacher whose speech was to be heard, who was to be listened to, whose words were to be remembered, the voices of black women—giving orders, making threats, fussing—could be tuned out, could become a kind of background music, audible but not acknowledged as significant speech. Dialogue—the sharing of speech and recognition—took place not between mother and child or mother and male authority figure but among black women. I can remember watching fascinated as our mother talked with her mother, sisters, and women friends. The intimacy and intensity of their speech—the satisfaction they received from talking to one another, the pleasure, the joy. It was in this world of woman speech, loud talk, angry words, women with tongues quick and sharp, tender sweet tongues, touching our world with their words, that I made speech my birthright—and the right to voice, to authorship, a privilege I would not be denied. It was in that world and because of it that I came to dream of writing, to write.

Writing was a way to capture speech, to hold onto it, keep it close. And so I wrote down bits and pieces of conversations, confessing in cheap diaries that soon fell apart from too much handling, expressing the intensity of my sorrow, the anguish of speech—for I was always saying the wrong thing, asking the wrong questions. I could not confine my speech to the necessary corners and concerns of life. I hid these writings under my bed, in pillow stuffings, among faded underwear. When my sisters found and read them, they ridiculed and mocked me—poking fun. I felt violated, ashamed, as if the secret parts of my self had been exposed, brought into the open, and hung like newly clean laundry, out in the air for everyone to see. The fear of exposure, the fear that one's deepest emotions and innermost thoughts will be dismissed as mere nonsense, felt by so many young girls keeping diaries, holding and hiding speech, seems to me now one of the barriers that women have always needed and still need to destroy so that we are no longer pushed into secrecy or silence.

Despite my feelings of violation, of exposure, I continued to speak and write, choosing my hiding places well, learning to destroy work when no safe place could be found. I was never taught absolute silence, I was taught that it was important to speak but to talk a talk that was in itself a silence. Taught to speak and yet beware of the betrayal of too much heard speech, I experienced intense confusion and deep anxiety in my efforts to speak and write. Reciting poems at Sunday afternoon church service might be rewarded. Writing a poem (when one's time could be "better" spent sweeping, ironing, learning to cook) was luxurious activity, indulged in at the expense of others. Questioning authority, raising issues that were not deemed appropriate subjects brought pain, punishments—like telling mama I wanted to die before her because I could not live without her—that was crazy talk, crazy speech, the kind that would lead you to end up in a mental institution. "Little girl," I would be told, "if you don't stop all this crazy talk and crazy acting you are going to end up right out there at Western State."

Madness, not just physical abuse, was the punishment for too much talk if you were female. Yet even as this fear of madness haunted me, hanging over my writing like a monstrous shadow, I could not stop the words, making thought, writing speech. For this terrible madness which I feared, which I was sure was the destiny of daring women born to intense speech (after all, the authorities emphasized this point daily), was not as threatening as imposed silence, as suppressed speech.

Safety and sanity were to be sacrificed if I was to experience defiant speech. Though I risked them both, deep-seated fears and anxieties characterized my childhood days. I would speak but I would not ride a bike, play hardball, or hold the gray kitten. Writing about the ways we are traumatized in our growing-up years, psychoanalyst Alice Miller makes the point In *For Your Own Good* that it is not clear why childhood wounds become for some folk an opportunity to grow, to move forward rather than backward in the process of self-realization. Certainly, when I reflect on the trials of my growing-up years, the many punishments, I can see now that in resistance I learned to be vigilant in the nourishment of my spirit, to be tough, to courageously protect that spirit from forces that would break it.

10   While punishing me, my parents often spoke about the necessity of breaking my spirit. Now when I ponder the silences, the voices that are not heard, the voices of those wounded and/or oppressed individuals who do not speak or write, I contemplate the acts of persecution, torture—the terrorism that breaks spirits, that makes creativity impossible. I write these words to bear witness to the primacy of resistance struggle in any situation of domination (even within family life); to the strength and power that emerges from sustained resistance and the profound conviction that these forces can be healing, can protect us from dehumanization and despair.

These early trials, wherein I learned to stand my ground, to keep my spirit intact, came vividly to mind after I published *Ain't I A Woman* and the book was sharply and harshly criticized. While I had expected a climate of critical dialogue, I was not expecting a critical avalanche that had the power in its intensity to crush the spirit, to push one into silence. Since that time, I have heard stories about black women, about women of color, who write and publish (even when the work is quite successful) having nervous breakdowns, being made mad because they cannot bear the harsh responses of family, friends, and unknown critics, or becoming silent, unproductive. Surely, the absence of a humane critical response has tremendous impact on the writer from any oppressed, colonized group who endeavors to speak. For us, true speaking is not solely an expression of creative power; it is an act of resistance, a political gesture that challenges politics of domination that would render us nameless and voiceless. As such, it is a courageous act—as such, it represents a threat. To those who wield oppressive power, that which is threatening must necessarily be wiped out, annihilated, silenced.

Recently, efforts by black women writers to call attention to our work serve to highlight both our presence and absence. Whenever I peruse women's bookstores, I am struck not by the rapidly growing body of feminist writing by black women, but by the paucity of available published material. Those of us who write and are published remain few in number. The context of silence is varied and multi-dimensional. Most obvious are the ways racism, sexism, and class exploitation act to suppress and silence. Less obvious are the inner struggles, the efforts made to gain the necessary confidence to write, to re-write, to fully develop craft and skill—and the extent to which such efforts fail.

Although I have wanted writing to be my life-work since childhood, it has been difficult for me to claim "writer" as part of that which identifies and shapes my everyday reality. Even after publishing books, I would often speak of wanting to be a writer as though these works did not exist. And though I would be told, "you are a writer," I was not yet ready to fully affirm this truth. Part of myself was still held captive by domineering forces of history, of familial life that had charted a map of silence, of right speech. I had not completely let go of the fear of saying the wrong thing, of being punished. Somewhere in the deep recesses of my mind, I believed I could avoid both responsibility and punishment if I did not declare myself a writer.

One of the many reasons I chose to write using the pseudonym bell hooks, a family name (mother to Sarah Oldham, grandmother to Rosa Bell Oldham, great-grandmother to me), was to construct a writer-identity that would challenge and subdue all impulses leading me away from speech into silence. I was a young girl buying bubble gum at the corner store when I first really heard the full name bell hooks, I had just "talked back" to a grown person. Even now I can recall the surprised look, the mocking tones that informed me I must be kin to bell hooks—a sharp-tongued woman, a woman who spoke her mind, a woman who was not afraid to talk back. I claimed this legacy of defiance, of will, of courage, affirming my link to female ancestors who were bold and daring in their speech. Unlike my bold and daring mother and grandmother, who were not supportive of talking back, even though they were assertive and powerful in their speech, bell hooks as I discovered, claimed, and invented her was my ally, my support.

15   That initial act of talking back outside the home was empowering. It was the first of many acts of defiant speech that would make it possible for me to emerge as an independent thinker and writer. In retrospect, "talking back" became for me a rite of initiation, testing my courage, strengthening my commitment, preparing me for the days ahead—the days when writing, rejection notices, periods of silence, publication, ongoing development seem impossible but necessary.

Moving from silence into speech is for the oppressed, the colonized, the exploited, and those who stand and struggle side by side a gesture of defiance that heals, that makes new life and new growth possible. It is that act of speech, of "talking back," that is no mere gesture of empty words, that is the expression of our movement from object to subject—the liberated voice.

READING RESPONSE

1. <u>Reflecting on discourse, identity, and context</u>
   - bell hooks shows us how the rules of discourse in the southern black community of her childhood were also shaped by age and gender. What does she show of the distinguishing features of men's talk versus women's talk, of what was allowed for adult women, "grown folks," that was not allowed for children?
   - hooks describes some of the ways in which she sought to develop and maintain an identity that was different from the one expected for her and the responses she received from others when she violated the norms of her community. How do those earlier experiences connect with her present efforts to maintain an identity as an independent black woman writer? Are there any parallels between her experience and your own?
   - hooks places her own experience in a larger political context, connecting it to a larger understanding of what it means for any people to be colonized, oppressed, and exploited. How and where does she move from the personal to the political? Do the understandings she presents here connect to those in other memoirs you've read?

2. <u>Reading from a writer's perspective</u>
   As you think about creating a final version of your own memoir, look back at the ways in which hooks has shaped hers.
   - Consider how hooks introduces her memoir by defining the key terms, "back talk" and "talking back" in the ways in which the community of her childhood would define them. How does she trace out varying notions of "talk" and "back talk" and work with a set of talk-related terms to provide movement through this memoir, from this early definition to her final appropriation of these terms for her own uses?
   - hooks makes reference to the work of the psychoanalyst Alice Miller on the ways in which children are traumatized in their growing up years. What does she draw from this connection to Miller and how does she use Miller's ideas to further (and to give authority to) the points she is making about her own experience?
   - Rather than moving back and forth between early moments of experience and present interpretations, hooks presents a more linear account that moves from her childhood experience to her recent experience as a writer, drawing

   (continued)

> parallels between the two. How do those parallels work to support the understandings and directions she draws from her more recent experience?
>
> ■ What do you take as hooks's purpose in writing this memoir? How has (or hasn't) this structure allowed her to achieve it from your perspective as a reader?

Dave Eggers, "A Heartbreaking Work of Staggering Genius"

In the book *A Heartbreaking Work of Staggering Genius* (2000), Dave Eggers chronicles five years of his life, beginning with a period in which both his parents were dying of cancer. With their deaths, he had to assume, as a twenty-one-year old who hadn't completed college, responsibilty for raising his seven-year-old brother.

Although the experience was tragic, Eggers tries to get another perspective on that tragic experience by writing about it in a mocking, ironic, and sometimes comic voice. He mocks his uncertain efforts at being a parent at the same time he's a brother, even as he makes it clear that he assumes the role quite seriously.

In this excerpt, Eggers recreates for us a moment in which he and his brother go to a parents' open house at his brother's school. He shows how he and his brother are attempting to define themselves and their roles by presenting the moment as a performance, in which they say the right words and play the right parts to go along with their new social identities.

A Heartbreaking Work of Staggering Genius

Dave Eggers

7:52 P.M.

1   The open house is still full—it goes until nine, not eight, as I had thought—and we are both overdressed. We walk in. Toph immediately untucks his shirt.

The walls are covered with corrected papers about slavery, and the first-graders' unsettling self-portraits.

Heads turn. This is our first open house, and people are not sure what to make of us. I am surprised, having expected that everyone would have been briefed about our arrival. Kids look at Toph and say hi.

"Hi, Chris."

5   And then they look at me and squint.

They are scared. They are jealous.

We are pathetic. We are stars.

We are either sad and sickly or we are glamorous and new. We walk in and the choices race through my head. Sad and sickly? Or glamorous and new? Sad/sickly or glamorous/new? Sad/sickly? Glamorous/new?

We are unusual and tragic and alive.

10   We walk into the throng of parents and children.

We are disadvantaged but young and virile. We walk the halls and the playground, and we are taller, we radiate. We are orphans. As orphans, we are celebrities. We are foreign exchange people, from a place where there are still orphans. Russia? Romania? Somewhere raw and exotic. We are the bright new stars born of a screaming black hole, the nascent suns burst from the darkness, from the grasping void of space that folds and swallows—a darkness that would devour anyone not as strong as we. We are oddities, sideshows, talk show subjects. We capture everyone's imagination. That's why Matthew wants Beth and me dead in a plane crash. His parents are old, bald, square, wear glasses, are wooden and gray, are cardboard boxes, folded, closeted, dead to the world—We ate at their house actually, not long ago, accepting a neighborly invitation sometime before Matthew's plane crash comment. And we were bored to tears in their stillborn house, its wooden floors and bare walls—the daughter even played the piano for us, the father so haughtily proud of her, the poor bald guy. They owned no TV, there were no toys anywhere, the place was airless, a coffin—

But we!—we are great-looking! We have a style, which is messy, rakish, yet intriguingly so, singular. We are new and everyone else is old. We are the chosen ones, obviously, the queens to their drones—the rest of those gathered at this open house are aging, past their prime, sad, hopeless. They are crinkly and no longer have random sex, as only I among them am still capable of. They are done with such things; even thinking about them having sex is unappealing. They cannot run without looking silly. They cannot coach the soccer team without making a mockery of themselves and the sport. Oh, they are over. They are walking corpses, especially that imbecile smoking out in the courtyard. Toph and I are the future, a terrifyingly bright future, a future that has come from Chicago, two terrible boys from far away, cast away and left for dead, shipwrecked, forgotten, but yet, but yet, here, resurfaced, bolder and more fearless, bruised and unshaven, sure, their pant legs frayed, their stomachs full of salt water, but now unstoppable, insurmountable, ready to kick the saggy asses of the gray-haired, thickly bespectacled, slump-shouldered of Berkeley's glowering parentiscenti!

Can you see this?

We walk around the classrooms. In his homeroom, on the walls, there are papers about Africa. His paper is not on the wall.

15   "Where's your paper?"

"I don't know. Ms. Richardson didn't like it, I guess."

"Hmmph."

Who is this Ms. Richardson? She must be a moron. I want this "Ms. Richardson" brought out and driven before me!

The school is full of nice children but eccentric children, delicate and oddly shaped. They are what my friends and I, growing up in public schools, always envisioned private school kids were like—a little too precious, their innate peculiarities amplified, not muted, for better and worse. Kids who think that they are pirates, and are encouraged to dress the part, in school. Kids who program computers and collect military magazines. Chubby boys with big heads and very long hair. Skinny girls who wear sandals and carry flowers.

20   After about ten minutes, we're bored. My main reason for coming has gone bust. I was looking to score.

I expected flirting. I expected attractive single mothers and flirting. My goal, a goal I honestly thought was fairly realistic, was to meet an attractive single mother and have Toph befriend the mother's son so we can arrange playdates, during which the mother and I will go upstairs and screw around while the kids play outside. I expected meaningful glances and carefully worded propositions. I imagine that the world of schools and parents is oozing with intrigue and debauchery, that under its concerned and well-meaning facade, its two-parent families, conferences with teachers and thoughtful questions directed to the history teacher about Harriet Tubman, everyone is swinging.

But by and large they're ugly. I scan the crowd milling in the courtyard. The parents are interesting only in their prototypical Berkeley-ness. They wear baggy tie-dyed, truly tie-dyed, pants, and do not comb their hair. Most are over forty. All of the men have beards, and are short. Many of the women are old enough to have mothered me, and look it. I am disheartened by the lack of possibility. I am closer in age to most of the children. Oh but there is one mother, a small-headed woman with long, long, straight black hair, thick and wild like a horse's tail. She looks exactly like her daughter, same oval face, same sad dark eyes. I've seen her before, when I've driven Toph to school, and have guessed that she's single; the father is never present.

"I'm gonna ask her out," I say.

25   "Please, don't. Please," Toph says. He really thinks I might.

"Do you like the daughter at all? This could be fun—we could double date!"

"Please, please don't."

Of course I won't. I have no nerve. But he does not know that yet. We walk the halls decorated with construction paper and student work. I meet Ms. Richardson, the homeroom teacher, who is tall and black and severe—with distended, angry eyes. I meet the science teacher who looks precisely like Bill Clinton and stutters. There is a girl in Toph's class who, at nine, is taller than her parents, and heavier than me. I want Toph to be her friend and make her happy.

A woman nearby is looking at us. People look at us. They look and wonder. They wonder if I am a teacher, not knowing how to place me, thinking maybe that because I have scraggly facial hair and am wearing old shoes that I will take and molest their children. I surely look threatening. The woman, this one looking at us, has long gray hair and large glasses. She is wearing a floor-length patterned skirt and sandals. She leans toward us, points her finger to me and to Toph and back, smiles. Then we find our places and read the script:

30   MOTHER: Hi. This is your . . . son?

BROTHER: Uh . . . no.

MOTHER: BROTHER?

BROTHER: Yeah.

MOTHER: *(squinting to make sure)* Oh, you can tell right away.

35 BROTHER: *(though knowing that it is not really true, that he is old and severe-looking, and his brother glows)* Yeah, people say that.

MOTHER: Having fun?

BROTHER: Sure. Sure.

MOTHER: You go to school at Cal?

BROTHER: No, no, I finished school a few years ago.

40 MOTHER: And you live around here?

BROTHER: Yeah, we live a few miles north. Close to Albany.

MOTHER: So you live with your folks?

BROTHER: No, just us.

MOTHER: But . . . where are your parents?

45 BROTHER: *(thinking, thinking: "They're not here." "They couldn't make it." "I have no idea, actually; if only you knew just how little idea I have. Oh it's a doozy, that story. Do you know what it's like, to have no idea, no idea at all of their exact whereabouts, I mean, the actual place that they are right now, as we speak? That is a weird feeling, oh man. You want to talk about it? You have a few hours?")* Oh, they died a few years ago.

MOTHER: *(grabbing Brother's forearm)* Oh, I'm sorry.

BROTHER: No, no, don't worry. *(wanting to add, as he sometimes does, "It wasn't your fault." He loves that line, especially when he tacks on: "Or was it?")*

MOTHER: So he lives with you?

BROTHER: Yeah.

50 MOTHER: Oh, gosh. That's interesting.

BROTHER: *(thinking of the state of the house. It is interesting.)* Well, we have fun. What grade is your . . .

MOTHER: Daughter. Fourth. Amanda. If I may, can I ask how they died?

BROTHER: *(again scanning possibilities for the entertainment of him and his brother. Plane crash. Train crash. Terrorists. Wolves. He has made up things before, and he was amused, though younger brother's amusement level was unclear.)* Cancer.

MOTHER: But . . . at the same time?

55 BROTHER: About five weeks apart.

MOTHER: Oh my god.

BROTHER: *(with inexplicable little chuckle)* Yeah, it was weird.

MOTHER: How long ago was this?

BROTHER: A few winters ago. (Brother *thinks about how much he likes the "a few winters ago" line. It's new. It sounds dramatic, vaguely poetic. For a while it was "last year." Then it was "a year and a half ago." Now, much to* Brother's *relief, it's "a few years ago." "A few years ago" has a comfortable distance. The blood is dry, the scabs hardened, peeled. Early on was different. Shortly before leaving Chicago,* Brothers *went to the barber to have* Toph's *hair cut, and* Brother *doesn't remember how it came up, and* BROTHER *was really hoping it wouldn't come up, but when it did come up,* BROTHER *answered, "A few weeks ago." At that the haircutting woman stopped, went through the antique saloon-style doors to the back room, and stayed there for a while. She came back red-eyed.* BROTHER *felt terrible. He is always feeling terrible, when the innocent, benign questions of unsuspecting strangers yield the bizarre answer he must provide. Like someone asking about the weather and being told of nuclear winter. But it does have its advantages. In this case,* BROTHERS *got a free haircut.)*

60   MOTHER: *(holding Brother's forearm again)* Well. Good for you! What a good brother you are!

BROTHER: *(Smiling. Wonders: What does that mean? He is often told this. At soccer games, at school fund-raisers, at the beach, at the baseball card shows, at the pet store. Sometimes the person telling him this knows their full biography and sometimes she or he does not. Brother doesn't understand the line, both what it means and when it became a standard sort of expression that many different people use. What a good brother you are! *BROTHER *had never heard the saying before, but now it comes out of all kinds of people's mouths, always phrased the same way, the same words, the same inflections—a rising sort of cadence:*

        What   a   good   bro-ther   you   are!

    What *does that mean? He smiles, and if Toph is close, he'll punch him in the arm, or try to trip him—look at us horsing around! Light as air!—then Brother will say the same thing he always says after they say their words, the thing that seems to deflate the mounting tension, the uncomfortable drama swelling in the conversation, while also throwing it back at the questioner, because he often wants the questioner to think about what he or she is saying. What he says, with a cute little shrug, or a sigh, is:)*
Well, what are you gonna do?

    *(*MOTHER *smiles and squeezes* BROTHER's *forearm one more time, then pats it.* BROTHERS *look to* AUDIENCE, *wink, and then break into a fabulous Fossean dance number, lots of kicks and high-stepping, a few throws and catches, a big sliding-across-the-stage-on-their-knees thing, then some more jumping, some strutting, and finally, a crossing-in-midair front flip via hidden trampoline, with both of them landing perfectly, just before the orchestra, on one knee, hands extended toward audience, grinning while breathing heavily. The crowd stands and thunders. The curtain falls. They thunder still.)*

FIN

As the crowd stomps the floor for a curtain call, we sneak through the back door and make off like superheroes.

1. <u>Reflecting on discourse, identity, and context</u>

READING RESPONSE

- In this scene, Eggers moves back and forth between the ways in which he sees the parents and children around him at the school open house and his projection of the ways in which those parents and children must be seeing him and his brother. What are some of the terms he uses to name the others, and what are the terms he imagines others using to name him? What is the effect of these contrasting terms (all arising from his own imagination) on the identity he assumes or creates? How does his attempt to assume contrasting perspectives on his situation, his own as an insider and that of outsiders, shape what he perceives? To what degree might both views represent his own conflicting understandings of his situation?

- Eggers resists assuming an adult, parental identity, even as he must carry out that role. How does he represent that resistance through the ways he portrays this scene?

- How do the seemingly innocuous words exchanged by "mother" and "brother" and his own parenthetical commentary on his responses to the mother's questions contribute to the picture he offers of the underlying concerns he is grappling with?

2. <u>Reading from a writer's perspective</u>

As you think about creating a final version of your own memoir, look back at the ways in which Eggers has shaped his.

- Consider how Eggers moves in the early parts of this scene at the school's open house from a few observed details to his interpretations and projections of the ways in which he and his brothers are being seen. Underline the sentences that offer the core narrative and the actual observed details. What does Eggers add to this core, and how does each addition contribute to the larger picture he's presenting?

- Eggers moves from recreating and commenting on a scene to offering a dramatization of a particular moment of interaction, one in which he and his brother "find our places and read the script." What roles does he see as scripted for them in this encounter? What does recreating that script add to his portrayal of this scene?

- Eggers works within a particular stance here. You can find his own commentary on that stance on p. 107. What elements contribute to the ironic, self-mocking style he is trying to create? What effect does that style have on your response as a reader?

- What do you take as Eggers's purpose in writing this memoir? How has (or hasn't) this structure and style allowed him to achieve that purpose from your perspective as a reader?

Amy Tan, "Mother Tongue"

Becoming alienated from our past selves can have a profound effect on our writing, no matter what our background. Amy Tan, author of *The Joy Luck Club,* writes about the fact that it took a long time to accept the English of her home—the English she learned from her mother—as a resource rather than a problem:

> To me, my mother's English is perfectly clear, perfectly natural. It's my mother tongue. Her language, as I hear it, is vivid, direct, full of observation and imagery. That was the language that helped shape the way I saw things, expressed things, made sense of the world.

But others see her mother's English as "broken" or "fractured," and for a long time, Tan did too. Tan describes how the ways she had learned to see the world, from her mother's perspective, made the sorts of questions on standardized tests hard for her to answer, which made her think of herself as not being good in English. Unlike hooks, she spent her college years rejecting the language of home before she learned, as a writer, to draw on "all of the Englishes I grew up with."

Mother Tongue

Amy Tan

1   I am not a scholar of English or literature. I cannot give you much more than personal opinions on the English language and its variations in this country or others.

I am a writer. And by that definition, I am someone who has always loved language. I am fascinated by language in daily life. I spend a great deal of my time thinking about the power of language—the way it can evoke an emotion, a visual image, a complex idea, or a simple truth. Language is the tool of my trade. And I use them all—all the Englishes I grew up with.

Recently, I was made keenly aware of the different Englishes I do use. I was giving a talk to a large group of people, the same talk I had already given to half a dozen other groups. The nature of the talk was about my writing, my life, and my book, *The Joy Luck Club.* The talk was going along well enough, until I remembered one major difference that made the whole talk sound wrong. My mother was in the room. And it was perhaps the first time she had heard me give a lengthy speech, using the kind of English I have never used with her. I was saying things like, "The intersection of memory upon imagination" and "There is an aspect of my fiction that relates to thus-and-thus"—a speech filled with carefully wrought grammatical phrases, burdened, it suddenly seemed to me, with nominalized forms, past perfect tenses, conditional phrases, all the forms of standard English that I had learned in school and through books, the forms of English I did not use at home with my mother.

Just last week, I was walking down the street with my mother, and I again found myself conscious of the English I was using, the English I do use with her. We were talking about the price of new and used furniture and I heard myself saying this: "Not waste money that way." My husband was with us as well, and he didn't notice any switch in my English. And then I realized why. It's because over the twenty years we've been together I've often used that same kind of English with him, and sometimes he even uses it with me. It has become our language of intimacy, a different sort of English that relates to family talk, the language I grew up with.

5   So you'll have some idea of what this family talk I heard sounds like, I'll quote what my mother said during a recent conversation which I videotaped and then transcribed. During this conversation, my mother was talking about a political gangster in Shanghai who had the same last name as her family's, Du, and how the gangster in this early years wanted to be adopted by her family, which was rich by comparison. Later, the gangster became more powerful, far richer than my mother's family, and one day showed up at my mother's wedding to pay his respects. Here's what she said in part:

"Du Yusong having business like fruit stand. Like off the sheet kind. He is Du like Du Zong—but not Tsung-ming Island people. The local people call putong, the river east side, he belong to that side local people. That man want to ask Du Zong father take him in like become own family. Du Zong father wasn't look down on him, but didn't take seriously, until that man big like become a mafia. Now important person, very hard to inviting him. Chinese way, came only to show respect, don't stay for dinner. Respect for making big celebration, he shows up. Mean gives lots of respect. Chinese custom. Chinese social life that way. If too important won't have to stay too long. He come to my wedding. I didn't see, I heard it. I gone to boy's side, they have YMCA dinner. Chinese age I was nineteen."

You should know that my mother's expressive command of English belies how much she actually understands. She reads the *Forbes* report, listens to *Wall Street Week,* converses daily with her stockbroker, reads all of Shirley MacLaine's books with ease—all kinds of things I can't begin to understand. Yet some of my friends tell me they understand 50 percent of what my mother says. Some say they understand 80 to 90 percent. Some say they understand none of it, as if she were speaking pure Chinese. But to me, my mother's English is perfectly clear, perfectly natural. It's my mother tongue. Her language, as I hear it, is vivid, direct, full of observation and imagery. That was the language that helped shape the way I saw things, expressed things, made sense of the world.

* * *

Lately, I've been giving more thought to the kind of English my mother speaks. Like others, I have described it to people as "broken" or "fractured" English. But I wince when I say that. It has always bothered me that I can think of no way to describe it other than "broken," as if it were damaged and needed to be fixed, as if it lacked a certain wholeness and soundness. I've heard other terms used, "limited English," for example. But they seem just as bad, as if everything is limited, including people's perceptions of the limited English speaker.

I know this for a fact, because when I was growing up, my mother's "limited" English limited *my* perception of her. I was ashamed of her English. I believed that her

English reflected the quality of what she had to say. That is, because she expressed them imperfectly her thoughts were imperfect. And I had plenty of empirical evidence to support me: the fact that people in department stores, at banks, and at restaurants did not take her seriously, did not give her good service, pretended not to understand her, or even acted as if they did not hear her.

10   My mother has long realized the limitations of her English as well. When I was fifteen, she used to have me call people on the phone to pretend I was she. In this guise, I was forced to ask for information or even to complain and yell at people who had been rude to her. One time it was a call to her stockbroker in New York. She had cashed out her small portfolio and it just so happened we were going to go to New York the next week, our very first trip outside California. I had to get on the phone and say in an adolescent voice that was not very convincing, "This is Mrs. Tan."

And my mother was standing in the back whispering loudly, "Why he don't send me check, already two weeks late. So mad he lie to me, losing me money."

And then I said in perfect English, "Yes, I'm getting rather concerned. You had agreed to send the check two weeks ago, but it hasn't arrived."

Then she began to talk more loudly. "What he want, I come to New York tell him front of his boss, you cheating me?" And I was trying to calm her down, make her be quiet, while telling the stockbroker, "I can't tolerate any more excuses. If I don't receive the check immediately, I am going to have to speak to your manager when I'm in New York next week." And sure enough, the following week there we were in front of this astonished stockbroker, and I was sitting there red-faced and quiet, and my mother, the real Mrs. Tan, was shouting at his boss in her impeccable broken English.

We used a similar routine just five days ago, for a situation that was far less humorous. My mother had gone to the hospital for an appointment, to find out about a benign brain tumor a CAT scan had revealed a month ago. She said she had spoken very good English, her best English, no mistakes. Still, she said, the hospital did not apologize when they said they had lost the CAT scan and she had come for nothing. She said they did not seem to have any sympathy when she told them she was anxious to know the exact diagnosis, since her husband and son had both died of brain tumors. She said they would not give her any more information until the next time and she would have to make another appointment for that. So she said she would not leave until the doctor called her daughter. She wouldn't budge. And when the doctor finally called her daughter, me, who spoke in perfect English—lo and behold—we had assurance the CAT scan would be found, promise that a conference call on Monday would be held, and apologies for any suffering my mother had gone through for a most regrettable mistake.

15   I think my mother's English almost had an effect on limiting my possibilities in life as well. Sociologists and linguists probably will tell you that a person's developing language skills are more influenced by peers. But I do think that the language spoken in the family, especially in immigrant families which are more insular, plays a large role in shaping the language of the child. And I believe that it affected my results on achievement tests, IQ tests, and the SAT. While my English skills were never judged as poor, compared to math, English could not be considered my strong suit. In grade school I did modertely well, getting perhaps B's, sometimes B-pluses in English and scoring

perhaps in the sixtieth or seventieth percentile on achievement tests. But those scores were not good enough to override the opinion that my true abilities lay in math and science, because in those areas I achieved A's and scored in the ninetieth percentile or higher.

This was understandable. Math is precise; there is only one correct answer. Whereas, for me at least, the answers on English tests were always a judgment call, a matter of opinion and personal experience. Those tests were constructed around items like fill-in-the-blank sentence completion, such as, "Even though Tom was_____, Mary thought he was_____." And the correct answer always seemed to be the most bland combinations of thoughts, for example, "Even though Tom was shy, Mary thought he was charming," with the grammatical structure "even though" limiting the correct answer to some sort of semantic opposites, so you wouldn't get answers like, "Even though Tom was foolish, Mary thought he was ridiculous." Well, according to my mother, there were very few limitations as to what Tom could have been and what Mary might have thought of him. So I never did well on tests like that.

The same was true with word analogies, pairs of words in which you were supposed to find some sort of logical, semantic relationship—for example, "*Sunset* is to *nightfall* as_____ is to_____." And here you would be presented with a list of four possible pairs, one of which showed the same kind of relationship: *red* is to *stoplight, bus* is to *arrival, chills* is to *fever, yawn* is to *boring.* Well, I could never think that way. I knew what the tests were asking, but I could not block out of my mind the images already created by the first pair, "*sunset* is to *nightfall*"—and I would see a burst of color against a darkening sky, the moon rising, the lowering of a curtain of stars. And all the other pairs of word—red, bus, stoplight, boring—just threw up a mass of confusing images, making it impossible for me to sort out something as logical as saying: "A sunset precedes nightfall" is the same as "a chill precedes a fever." The only way I would have gotten that answer right would have been to imagine an associative situation, for example, by being disobedient and staying out past sunset, catching a chill at night which turns into feverish pneumonia as punishment, which indeed did happen to me.

* * *

I have been thinking about all this lately, about my mother's English, about achievement tests. Because lately I've been asked, as a writer, why there are not more Asian Americans represented in American literature. Why are there few Asian Americans enrolled in creative writing programs? Why do so many Chinese students go into engineering? Well, these are broad sociological questions I can't begin to answer. But I have noticed in surveys—in fact, just last week—that Asian students, as a whole, always do significantly better on math achievement tests than in English. And this makes me think that there are other Asian-American students whose English spoken in the home might also be described as "broken" or "limited." And perhaps they also have teachers who are steering them away from writing and into math and science, which is what happened to me.

Fortunately, I happen to be rebellious in nature and enjoy the challenge of disproving assumptions made about me. I became an English major my first year in college, after being enrolled as pre-med. I started writing nonfiction as a freelancer the week after I was told by my former boss that writing was my worst skill and I should hone my talents toward account management.

20   But it wasn't until 1985 that I finally began to write fiction. And at first I wrote using what I thought to be wittily crafted sentences, sentences that would finally prove I had mastery over the English language. Here's an example from the first draft of a story that later made its way into *The Joy Luck Club,* but without this line: "That was my mental quandary in its nascent state." A terrible line, which I can hardly pronounce.

Fortunately, for reasons I won't get into today, I later decided I should envision a reader for the stories I would write. And the reader I decided upon was my mother, because these were stories about mothers. So with this reader in mind—and in fact she did read my early drafts—I began to write stories using all the Englishes I grew up with: the English I spoke to my mother, which for lack of a better term might be described as "simple"; the English she used with me, which for lack of a better term might be described as "broken"; my translation of her Chinese, which could certainly be described as "watered down"; and what I imagine to be her translation of her Chinese if she could speak in perfect English, her internal language, and for that I sought to preserve the essence, but neither an English nor a Chinese structure. I wanted to capture what language ability tests can never reveal: her intent, her passion, her imagery, the rhythms of her speech and the nature of her thoughts.

Apart from what any critic had to say about my writing, I knew I had succeeded where it counted when my mother finished reading my book and gave me her verdict: "So easy to read."

READING RESPONSE

1. Reflecting on discourse, identity, and context

- Amy Tan begins her memoir by recalling a recent moment of her experience, a moment when she was giving a talk about her writing to a roomful of people that included her mother. What does that moment illustrate about her own intersecting identities and the language that represents them?

- Tan tells us that, in her writing, she uses "all the Englishes I grew up with." What are some of the examples she gives of her different Englishes, and what do they suggest about her different identities as she speaks and writes in different contexts, for different purposes? If you have had experience in speaking significantly different Englishes, does her account of her experience resonate with your own?

- Tan describes her own struggle with naming: the names she has given to her mother's English in the past, the names others have given to it, and some of the understandings that she has found to accompany these namings. How does her exploration of such naming help her (and her readers) to gain new understandings?

- Tan moves from her recent experiences with and reflection on language to some of her earlier experiences—to the limitations her mother's "limited" English almost placed on her own possibilities. What does her analysis of her earlier school experience with language add to the larger picture she is presenting here?

2. <u>Reading from a writer's perspective</u>

As you think about creating a final version of your own memoir, look back at the ways in which Tan has shaped hers.

- Tan includes in her memoir a number of examples of her mother's English and of the different Englishes she herself uses in different contexts. How do her examples, as well as her descriptions, of these Englishes contribute to your understanding, as a reader, of why all of them would be important to her?

- Tan begins her memoir by recalling moments in her recent past and then moves back to earlier moments. How does this movement work to help her represent her understandings? Are there ways in which you might imagine altering this structure?

- What do you take as Tan's purpose in writing this memoir? How has (or hasn't) its structure and style allowed her to achieve that purpose from your perspective as a reader? Why does she start and end with moments of seeing her own work through her mother's eyes?

Tommi Avicolli, "He Defies You Still: The Memoirs of a Sissy"

In "He Defies You Still" (1985), Tommi Avicolli presents five moments in "the memoirs of a sissy"—moments which were powerful ones for defining how he would be seen and named by the rest of society and that were consequently powerful for how he came to name and define himself. In presenting five discrete moments of his experience, he allows his readers to see the continuity in that experience, even across separate events, when seen, in retrospect, from the perspective of his identity as a gay man.

He Defies You Still
The Memoirs of a Sissy

Tommi Avicolli

> You're just a faggot
> No history faces you this morning
> A faggot's dreams are scarlet
> Bad blood bled from words that scarred[1]

---

[1] Tommi Avicolli, "Faggot", published in *GPU News*, Sept. 1979.

SCENE ONE

1   A homeroom in a Catholic high school in South Philadelphia. The boy sits quietly in the first aisle, third desk, reading a book. He does not look up, not even for a moment. He is hoping no one will remember he is sitting there. He wishes he were invisible. The teacher is not yet in the classroom so the other boys are talking and laughing loudly.

Suddenly, a voice from beside him:

"Hey, you're a faggot, ain't you?"

The boy does not answer. He goes on reading his book, or rather pretending he is reading his book. It is impossible to actually read the book now.

5   "Hey, I'm talking to you!"

The boy still does not look up. He is so scared his heart is thumping madly; it feels like it is leaping out of his chest and into his throat. But he can't look up.

"Faggot, I'm talking to you!"

To look up is to meet the eyes of the tormentor.

Suddenly, a sharpened pencil point is thrust into the boy's arm. He jolts, shaking off the pencil, aware that there is blood seeping from the wound.

10   "What did you do that for?" he asks timidly.

"Cause I hate faggots," the other boy says, laughing. Some other boys begin to laugh, too. A symphony of laughter. The boy feels as if he's going to cry. But he must not cry. Must not cry. So he holds back the tears and tries to read the book again. He must read the book. Read the book.

When the teacher arrives a few minutes later, the class quiets down. The boy does not tell the teacher what has happened. He spits on the wound to clean it, dabbing it with a tissue until the bleeding stops. For weeks he fears some dreadful infection from the lead in the pencil point.

SCENE TWO

The boy is walking home from school. A group of boys (two, maybe three, he is not certain) grab him from behind, drag him into an alley and beat him up. When he gets home, he races up to his room, refusing dinner ("I don't feel well," he tells his mother through the locked door) and spends the night alone in the dark wishing he would die. . . .

These are not fictitious accounts—I *was* that boy. Having been branded a sissy by neighborhood children because I preferred jump rope to baseball and dolls to playing soldiers, I was often taunted with "hey sissy" or "hey faggot" or "yoo hoo honey" (in a mocking voice) when I left the house.

15   To avoid harassment, I spent many summers alone in my room. I went out on rainy days when the street was empty.

I came to like being alone. I didn't need anyone, I told myself over and over again. I was an island. Contact with others meant pain. Alone, I was protected. I began writing poems, then short stories. There was no reason to go outside anymore. I had a world of my own.

In the schoolyard today
they'll single you out

Their laughter will leave your ears ringing
like the church bells
which once awed you. . . . [2]

School was one of the more painful experiences of my youth. The neighborhood bullies could be avoided. The taunts of the children living in those endless repetitive row houses could be evaded by staying in my room. But school was something I had to face day after day for some two hundred mornings a year.

I had few friends in school. I was a pariah. Some kids would talk to me, but few wanted to be known as my close friend. Afraid of labels. If I was a sissy, then he had to be a sissy, too. I was condemned to loneliness.

Fortunately, a new boy moved into our neighborhood and befriended me; he wasn't afraid of the labels. He protected me when the other guys threatened to beat me up. He walked me home from school; he broke through the terrible loneliness. We were in third or fourth grade at the time.

20   We spent a summer or two together. Then his parents sent him to camp and I was once again confined to my room.

SCENE THREE

High school lunchroom. The boy sits at a table near the back of the room. Without warning, his lunch bag is grabbed and tossed to another table. Someone opens it and confiscates a package of Tastykakes; another boy takes the sandwich. The empty bag is tossed back to the boy who stares at it, dumbfounded. He should be used to this; it has happened before.

Someone screams, "faggot," laughing. There is always laughter. It does not annoy him anymore.

There is no teacher nearby. There is never a teacher around. And what would he say if there were? Could he report the crime? He would be jumped after school if he did. Besides, it would be his word against theirs. Teachers never noticed anything. They never heard the taunts. Never heard the word, "faggot." They were the great deaf mutes, pillars of indifference; a sissy's pain was not relevant to history and geography and god made me to love honor and obey him, amen.

SCENE FOUR

High school Religion class. Someone has a copy of *Playboy*. Father N. is not in the room yet; he's late, as usual. Someone taps the boy roughly on the shoulder. He turns. A finger points to the centerfold model, pink fleshy body, thin and sleek. Almost painted. Not real. The other asks, mocking voice, "Hey, does she turn you on? Look at those tits!"

25   The boy smiles, nodding meekly; turns away.

The other jabs him harder on the shoulder, "Hey, whatsamatter, don't you like girls?"

Laughter. Thousands of mouths; unbearable din of laughter. In the Arena: thumbs down. Don't spare the queer.

---

[2] Tommi Avicolli, "Faggot."

"Wanna suck my dick? Huh? That turn you on, faggot!"
The laughter seems to go on forever. . .

Behind you, the sound of their laughter
echoes a million times
in a soundless place
They watch you walk/sit/stand/breathe. . . .[3]

30   What did being a sissy really mean? It was a way of walking (from the hips rather than the shoulders); it was a way of talking (often with a lisp or in a high-pitched voice); it was a way of relating to others (gently, not wanting to fight, or hurt anyone's feelings). It was being intelligent ("an egghead" they called it sometimes); getting good grades. It means not being interested in sports, not playing football in the street after school; not discussing teams and scores and playoffs. And it involved not showing fervent interest in girls, not talking about scoring with tits or *Playboy* centerfolds. Not concealing naked women in your history book; or porno books in your locker.

On the other hand, anyone could be a "faggot." It was a catch-all. If you did something that didn't conform to what was the acceptable behavior of the group, then you risked being called a faggot. If you didn't get along with the "in" crowd, you were a faggot. It was the most commonly used put-down. It kept guys in line. They became angry when somebody called them a faggot. More fights started over someone calling someone else a faggot than anything else. The word had power. It toppled the male ego, shattered his delicate facade, violated the image he projected. He was tough. Without feeling. Faggot cut through all this. It made him vulnerable. Feminine. And feminine was the worst thing he could possibly be. Girls were fine for fucking, but no boy in his right mind wanted to be like them. A boy was the opposite of a girl. He was not feminine. He was not feeling. He was not weak.

Just look at the gym teacher who growled like a dog; or the priest with the black belt who threw kids against the wall in rage when they didn't know their Latin. They were men, they got respect.

But not the physics teacher who preached pacifism during lectures on the nature of atoms. Everybody knew what he was—and why he believed in the anti-war movement.

My parents only knew that the neighborhood kids called me names. They begged me to act more like the other boys. My brothers were ashamed of me. They never said it, but I knew. Just as I knew that my parents were embarrassed by my behavior.

35   At times, they tried to get me to act differently. Once my father lectured me on how to walk right. I'm still not clear on what that means. Not from the hips, I guess, don't "swish" like faggots do.

A nun in elementary school told my mother at Open House that there was "something wrong with me." I had draped my sweater over my shoulders like a girl, she said. I was a smart kid, but I should know better than to wear my sweater like a girl!

---

[3]*Ibid.*

My mother stood there, mute. I wanted her to say something, to chastise the nun; to defend me. But how could she? This was a nun talking—representative of Jesus, protector of all that was good and decent.

An uncle once told me I should start "acting like a boy" instead of like a girl. Everybody seemed ashamed of me. And I guess I was ashamed of myself, too. It was hard not to be.

SCENE FIVE

PRIEST: Do you like girls, Mark?

40   MARK: Uh-huh.

PRIEST: I mean *really* like them?

MARK: Yeah—they're okay.

PRIEST: There's a role they play in your salvation. Do you understand it, Mark?

MARK: Yeah.

45   PRIEST: You've got to like girls. Even if you should decide to enter the seminary, it's important to keep in mind God's plan for a man and a woman.[4]

Catholicism of course condemned homosexuality. Effeminacy was tolerated as long as the effeminate person did not admit to being gay. Thus priests could be effeminate because they weren't gay.

As a sissy, I could count on no support from the church. A male's sole purpose in life was to father children—souls for the church to save. The only hope a homosexual had of attaining salvation was by remaining totally celibate. Don't even think of touching another boy. To think of a sin was a sin. And to sin was to put a mark upon the soul. Sin—if it was a serious offense against god—led to hell. There was no way around it. If you sinned, you were doomed.

Realizing I was gay was not an easy task. Although I knew I was attracted to boys by the time I was about eleven, I didn't connect this attraction to homosexuality. I was not queer. Not I. I was merely appreciating a boy's good looks, his fine features, his proportions. It didn't seem to matter that I didn't appreciate a girl's looks in the same way. There was no twitching in my thighs when I gazed upon a beautiful girl. But I wasn't queer.

I resisted that label—queer—for the longest time. Even when everything pointed to it, I refused to see it. I was certainly not queer. Not I.

---

[4]Tommi Avicolli, *Judgment of the Roaches,* produced in Philadelphia at the Gay Community Center, the Painted Bride Arts Center and the University of Pennsylvania; aired over WXPN-FM, in four parts; and presented at the Lesbian/Gay Conference in Norfolk, VA, July, 1980.

50   We sat through endless English classes, and History courses about the wars between men who were not allowed to love each other. No gay history was ever
taught. No history faces you this morning. You're just a faggot. Homosexuals had never
contributed to the human race. God destroyed the queers in Sodom and Gomorrah.

          We learned about Michelangelo, Oscar Wilde, Gertrude Stein—but never that
they were queer. They were not queer. Walt Whitman, the "father of American poetry," was not queer. No one was queer. I was alone, totally unique. One of a kind.
Were there others like me somewhere? Another planet, perhaps?

          In school, they never talked of the queers. They did not exist. The only hint we
got of this other species was in religion class. And even then it was clouded in
mystery—never spelled out. It was sin. Like masturbation. Like looking at *Playboy* and
getting a hard-on. A sin.

          Once a progressive priest in senior year religion class actually mentioned
homosexuals—he said the word—but was into Erich Fromm, into homosexuals as
pathetic and sick. Fixated at some early stage; penis, anal, whatever. Only hetero-
sexuals passed on to the nirvana of sexual development.

          No other images from the halls of the Catholic high school except those the
other boys knew: swishy faggot sucking cock in an alley somewhere grabbing asses in
the bathroom. Never mentioning how much straight boys craved blow jobs, it was
part of the secret.

55   It was all a secret. You were not supposed to talk about the queers. Whisper
maybe. Laugh about them, yes. But don't be open, honest; don't try to understand.
Don't cite their accomplishments. No history faces you this morning. You're just a
faggot—no history just a faggot.

EPILOGUE

          The boy marching down the Parkway. Hundreds of queers. Signs proclaiming gay
pride. Speakers. Tables with literature from gay groups. A miracle, he is thinking. Tears
are coming loose now. Someone hugs him.

> You could not control
> the sissy in me
> nor could you exorcise him
> nor electrocute him
> You declared him illegal illegitimate
> insane and immature
> But he defies you still.[5]

------

[5]"Sissy Poem," published in *Magic Doesn't Live Here Anymore* (Philadelphia: Spruce Street Press, 1976).

1. Reflecting on discourse, identity, and context

   ■ Tommi Avicolli focuses in particular on the ways in which he has been named by others. How does such naming affect the ways in which he sees his own identity? What does he gain by doing his own naming?

   ■ Many high school students, whether or not they are homosexual, have been called "faggot" or the equivalent, seriously or in jest. What does Avicolli suggest about the effect of these terms on everyone? What were some of the derogatory terms commonly used in your own high school and how did those terms affect the identities that were available to students?

2. Reading from a writer's perspective
   As you think about creating a final version of your own memoir, look back at the ways in which Avicolli has shaped his.

   ■ Consider how Avicolli (like Karen) begins and ends his memoir with excerpts from his poems. How do these poems work to frame the memoir? What do they add to the understandings that he represents in his prose?

   ■ Avicolli presents his memoir in five scenes. How does this structure affect the picture he presents, and what does each scene that he has chosen add to that picture? How is the effect different from what it might have been if he had created one continuous narrative?

   ■ Avicolli tells each scene in the third person, writing about "the boy." In scenes two, four, and five, he then moves into the first person, telling us "I *was* that boy," and reexamining these events and their meanings from his personal perspective. What effect does the third person narration and the shifting of perspective have on the reader's perception of the events he is portraying and the understandings he is representing?

   ■ What do you take as Avicolli's purpose in writing this memoir? How has (or hasn't) its structure and style allowed him to achieve that purpose from your perspective as a reader?

Annie Dillard, "An American Childhood"

Annie Dillard writes essays and books in a number of genres: fiction, poetry, autobiography, and nonfiction. Her best-known book, one that received the Pulitzer Prize, is *The Pilgrim at Tinker Creek,* in which she describes her close observations of nature during a year when she was living alone in a rural cabin. The following selection comes from *An American Childhood (1987),* in which she recounts experiences that influenced the ways in which she sees and writes about the world. In "The Art of the Joke," Dillard recalls the ways in which a common genre became central to the ways in which her family interacted.

An American Childhood

Annie Dillard

1   Our parents would sooner have left us out of Christmas than leave us out of a joke. They explained a joke to us while they were still laughing at it; they tore a still-kicking joke apart, so we could see how it worked. When we got the first Tom Lehrer album in 1954, Mother went through the album with me, cut by cut, explaining. B.V.D.s are men's underwear. Radiation makes you sterile, and lead protects from radiation, so the joke is. . . .

Our father kept in his breast pocket a little black notebook. There he noted jokes he wanted to remember. Remembering jokes was a moral obligation. People who said, "I can never remember jokes," were like people who said, obliviously, "I can never re-member names," or "I don't bathe."

"No one tells jokes like your father," Mother said. Telling a good joke well—successfully, perfectly—was the highest art. It was an art because it was up to you: if you did not get the laugh, you had told it wrong. Work on it, and do better next time. It would have been reprehensible to blame the joke, or, worse, the audience.

As we children got older, our parents discussed with us every technical, theoretical, and moral aspect of the art. We tinkered with a joke's narrative structure: "Maybe you should begin with the Indians." We polished the wording. There is a Julia Randall story set in Baltimore which we smoothed together for years. How does the lady word the question? Does she say, "How are you called?" No, that is needlessly awkward. She just says, "What's your name?" And he says, "Folks generally call me Bominitious." No, he can just say, "They call me Bominitious."

5   We analyzed many kinds of pacing. We admired with Father the leisurely meanders of the shaggy-dog story. "A young couple moved to the Swiss Alps," one story of his began, "with their grand piano"; and ended, to a blizzard of thrown napkins, ". . . Oppernockity tunes but once." "Frog goes into a bank," another story began, to my enduring pleasure. The joke was not great, but with what a sweet light splash you could launch it! "Frog goes into a bank," you said, and your canoe had slipped delicately and surely into the water, into Lake Champlain with painted Indians behind every tree, and there was no turning back.

Father was also very fond of stories set in bars that starred zoo animals or insects. These creatures apparently came into bars all over America, either accompanied or alone, and sat down to face incredulous, sarcastic bartenders. (It was a wonder the bartenders were always so surprised to see talking dogs or drinking monkeys or performing ants, so surprised year after year, when clearly this sort of thing was the very essence of bar life.) In the years he had been loose, swinging aloft in the airy interval between college and marriage, Father had frequented bars in New York, listening to jazz. Bars had no place whatever in the small Pittsburgh world he had grown up in, and lived in now. Bars were so far from our experience that I had assumed, in my detective work, that their customers were ipso facto crooks. Father's bar jokes—"and there were the regulars, all sitting around"—gave him the raffish air of a man who was at home anywhere. (How poignant were his "you knows" directed at me: you know how bartenders are; you know how the regulars would all be sitting around. For either I, a nine-year-old girl, knew what he was talking about, then or ever, or nobody did. Only because I read a lot, I often knew.)

Our mother favored a staccato, stand-up style; if our father could perorate, she could condense. Fellow goes to a psychiatrist. "You're crazy." "I want a second opinion!" "You're ugly." "How do you get an elephant out of the theater? You can't; it's in his blood."

What else in life so required, and so rewarded, such care?

"Tell the girls the one about the four-by-twos, Frank."

10   "Let's see. Let's see."

"Fellow goes into a lumberyard. . . ."

"Yes, but it's tricky. It's a matter of point of view." And Father would leave the dining room, rubbing his face in concentration, or as if he were smearing on greasepaint, and return when he was ready.

"Ready with the four-by-twos?" Mother said.

Our father hung his hands in his pockets and regarded the far ceiling with fond reminiscence.

15   "Fellow comes into a lumberyard," he began.

"Says to the guy, 'I need some four-by-twos.' 'You mean two-by-fours?' 'Just a minute. I'll find out.' He walks out to the parking lot, where his buddies are waiting in the car. They roll down the car window. He confers with them awhile and comes back across the parking lot and says to the lumberyard guy, 'Yes. I mean two-by-fours.'

"Lumberyard guy says, 'How long do you want them?' 'Just a minute,' fellow says, 'I'll find out.' He goes out across the parking lot and confers with the people in the car and comes back across the parking lot to the lumberyard and says to the guy, 'A long time. We're building a house.'"

After any performance Father rubbed the top of his face with both hands, as if it had all been a dream. He sat back down at the dining-room table, laughing and shaking his head. "And when you tell a joke," Mother said to Amy and me, "laugh. It's mean not to."

* * *

We were brought up on the classics. Our parents told us all the great old American jokes, practically by number. They collaborated on, and for our benefit specialized in, the painstaking paleontological reconstruction of vanished jokes from extant tag lines. They could vivify old *New Yorker* cartoons, source of many tag lines. The lines themselves—"Back to the old drawing board," and "I say it's spinach and I say the hell with it," and "A simple yes or no will suffice"—were no longer funny; they were instead something better, they were fixtures in the language. The tag lines of old jokes were the most powerful expressions we learned at our parents' knees. A few words suggested a complete story and a wealth of feelings. Learning our culture backward, Amy and Molly and I heard only later about *The Divine Comedy* and the Sistine Chapel ceiling, and still later about the Greek and Roman myths, which held no residue of feeling for us at all—certainly not the vibrant suggestiveness of old American jokes and cartoons.

* * *

20   Our parents were both sympathetic to what professional comedians call flop sweat. Boldness was all at our house, and of course you would lose some. Anyone could be misled by poor judgment into telling a "woulda hadda been there." Telling a funny story was harder than telling a joke; it was trying out, as a tidy unit, some raveling shred of the day's fabric. You learned to gauge what sorts of thing would "tell." You learned that some people, notably your parents, could rescue some things by careful narration from the category "woulda hadda been there" to the category "it tells."

At the heart of originating a funny story was recognizing it as it floated by. You scooped the potentially solid tale from the flux of history. Once I overheard my parents arguing over a thirty-year-old story's credit line. "It was my mother who said that," Mother said. "Yes, but"—Father was downright smug—"I was the one who noticed she said that."

* * *

The sight gag was a noble form, and the running gag was a noble form. In combination they produced the top of the line, the running sight gag, like the sincere and deadpan Nairobi Trio interludes on Ernie Kovacs. How splendid it was when my parents could get a running sight gag going. We heard about these legendary occasions with a thrill of family pride, as other children hear about their progenitors' war exploits.

The sight gag could blur with the practical joke—not a noble form but a friendly one, which helps the years pass. My parents favored practical jokes of the sort you set up and then retire from, much as one writes books, possibly because imagining people's reactions beats witnessing them. They procured a living hen and "hypnotized" it by setting it on the sink before the bathroom mirror in a friend's cottage by the New Jersey shore. They spent weeks constructing a ten-foot sea monster—from truck inner tubes, cement blocks, broomsticks, lumber, pillows—and set it afloat in a friend's pond. On Sanibel Island, Florida, they baffled the shell collectors each Saint Patrick's Day by boiling a bucketful of fine shells in green dye and strewing the green shells up and down the beach before dawn. I woke one Christmas morning to find in my stocking, hung from the mantel with care, a leg. Mother had charmed a department store display manager into lending her one.

When I visited my friends, I was well advised to rise when their parents entered the room. When my friends visited me, they were well advised to duck.

* * *

25   Central in the orders of merit, and the very bread and butter of everyday life, was the crack. Our mother excelled at the crack. We learned early to feed her lines just to watch her speed to the draw. If someone else fired a crack simultaneously, we compared their concision and pointedness and declared a winner.

Feeding our mother lines, we were training as straight men. The straight man's was an honorable calling, a bit like that of the rodeo clown: despised by the ignorant masses, perhaps, but revered among experts who understood the skills required and the risks run. We children mastered the deliberate misunderstanding, the planted pun, the Gracie Allen know-nothing remark, which can make of any interlocutor an instant hero.

How very gracious is the straight man—or, in this case, the straight girl. She spreads before her friend a gift-wrapped, beribboned gag line he can claim for his own, if only he will pick it up instead of pausing to contemplate what a nitwit he's talking to.

---

1. Reflecting on discourse, identity, and context

   Dillard focuses not so much on specific moments in the life of her family, but on typical patterns that occurred over time and that helped to create a family identity.

   - What does Dillard's account tell you about the shared identity of these family members—about what's important to them and the values they have in common? What do you learn about the characteristics of individual family members within the world they share?

   - Dillard doesn't explicitly discuss how the family history of joke-telling might have influenced her as a writer (particularly as a writer who typically writes in a serious vein), but many of the details she includes suggest that influence. What do those details suggest about the significance of this past experience for the present life of the writer?

   - Most of the jokes that Dillard's family told were ones they'd heard or read, ones that had already been told by others. How did these commonly-told jokes nevertheless help to define what it meant to be an insider in this family?

2. Reading from a writer's perspective

   As you think about creating a final version of your own memoir, look back at the ways in which Dillard has shaped hers.

   - In her opening paragraphs, Dillard focuses more on her family's concern with the art of joke-telling than on the actual jokes they told, and it's not until the seventh or eight paragraph that she includes full examples of specific jokes. How does that framing work for you as a reader? Do you see alternative ways in which she might have framed this narrative?

   - In the opening paragraph, Dillard writes as if her readers will bring shared knowledge of the songs of Tom Lehrer, a satirical song-writer who wrote in a comic way about political issues like the threat of nuclear war. In a parenthetical statement at the end of the sixth paragraph, she comments on how her father told stories about barrooms, acting as if she, as a nine-year old, would share that knowledge. What does her own account suggest about the advantages and disadvantages of assuming such shared knowledge in a joke or a memoir?

   - What do you take as Dillard's purpose in writing this memoir? How has (or hasn't) this structure and style allowed her to achieve that purpose from your perspective as a reader?

READING RESPONSE

Sean Smith, "Language Memoir"

Sean wrote this memoir as a college freshman. At first, after reading about others' experiences with moving between languages and cultures, he was uncertain that there was anything significant in his own experience growing up in one mainstream English-speaking community to write about. But as he found his own connections to the memoirs he was reading, he decided to write about his own memories of his grandparents. In his memoir, Sean recalls not only the things they did together but the things his grandfather and grandmother would say. His memoir may trigger memories of your own.

Language Memoir

Sean Smith

1   As I read the memoirs assigned in the course book about how the author's language was affected as a child, I remembered my grandparents on my mother's side. Both of who lived with my parents before I was born.

Since my grandfather was born in 1919 in upstate New York and my grandmother to a poor section of Boston in 1918, they both had their way of speaking that would sound strange to anyone who didn't know them. My parents both worked the same hours in the same office, so they were gone during the day. This left me with my grandparents most of the day, so I picked up on most of their odd words and phrases before I was even in school. Most of which I still use on occasion.

My mother and grandmother always had a close relationship. Almost every night, while everyone had gone their separate ways for the night, those two would be in the kitchen talking about their days over mugs of tea. Since my mother grew up in a house with a father and two brothers, she had only her mother to relate to and bond with over the years. This is why she wanted to take my grandmother in when her health began to fail instead of putting her in a home. Wanting to be together, my grandfather moved in also. One of the ailments that affected my grandmother was her poor circulation, which didn't allow her to climb long flights of stairs or walk long distances. She took the bedroom on the first floor. Since it wasn't big enough for two, my grandfather lived upstairs. This arrangement worked well, that is until my mother was expectant with me.

Since they both had separate rooms, there would not have been enough room for me when I arrived. My grandfather, the half of the couple in better health, volunteered to move out. He only moved one town over, but this probably didn't come easy to him since it would be the first time he lived alone in 40 years. Well, almost alone since he visited my grandmother and I daily.

5   One thing I remember my grandfather doing when he would visit was to take me on walks. It didn't matter what time of year it was, he hated to sit inside. Even in the winter when it was "so cold your words freeze and you have to read 'em," we'd be out walking.

When we walked in the fall he and I would sometimes collect acorns from an oak tree down the street from my house. Once I had filled all my pockets with acorns we would walk back home (usually this took longer than the walk down, since when you're little a pocketful of acorns really weighs you down) and pile all of them into a knothole in a tree in the front yard. We'd then sit on the "piazza" (or porch to most) and watch the family of squirrels that lived up in the tree come down and take some to the nest and bury others. He'd say they buried them so far down that they were in "Casey Jones' locker". Who is Casey Jones? I still don't know. I'm not sure my grandfather did either.

On the summer days, the days that it was "hotter than the hobs of Hell" we'd walk about a mile to the center of town where there was a convenience store. He'd buy us both a Coke. He always told me he had no idea why he drank it. "The worst thing in the world for ya. Will eat the rust right off metal!" It didn't *feel* like it was doing me any harm. I always figured it was because mine was a soda and his was a "pop."

Whenever we weren't outside, the thing he liked most was card games. Most of the time we bet M&Ms. Each color being its own denomination. He taught me how to shuffle and deal. When I dealt him a bad hand, he'd claim that I gave him "a hand like a foot." Most of the time this wasn't true. He usually let me win. Which meant I got most of the candy. And that usually meant I'd hear my grandmother yell "You're all wound up! Stop running, you'd make a cup of coffee nervous." My grandmother hardly ever yelled though. She was a patient woman and I was usually pretty well behaved, not "hell on two legs" as she described some other kids. She spent most of her time with me while I was inside. We usually watched game shows. *Scrabble* was always her favorite. After that was over, the *Price is Right* came on and then ended at noon. As soon as Bob Barker said his good-byes. I knew it was time for lunch. This meant my grandfather would soon be there and my grandmother would make me my peanut butter and jelly sandwich (she'd use the butter knife to draw a heart in the peanut butter once she spread it) with my glass of milk.

As my grandfather's territory was outside, my grandmother's was inside. Every Thursday, despite her circulatory problem, she cleaned house. The scrubbing floors and dusting sometimes had to be carried over to Friday morning, depending on how well she felt. I suppose she figured that she owed her daughter something for taking her in and taking care of her. It was appreciated, but it wasn't necessary. She didn't have to earn her keep. My mother later told me that my grandmother was the best friend she ever had. I think that was payment enough.

10   With my grandmother, some words were too harsh or embarrassing for her liking. Any woman who appeared to be of loose morals was a "floozy, chippy, harlot or a trollop." I, having no idea what she really meant, thought that a "trollop" was anyone who dressed colorfully. Anyone who smelled nice ("more perfume than a French whore" as my grandmother would say) I thought was classified as a "floozy." I had no idea what she really meant, and since they seemed like compliments to me (colorful and smelling good) I figured I'd use them myself. Who doesn't like to be complimented? Apparently my mother who told me never to repeat any word I heard from my grandmother and made a bee line upstairs to change.

Some words she used seemed to be made up all together. I wasn't toilet trained, I was trained to use the "hopper." My family didn't own a couch, we owned a "davenport." "Sean, keep your feet off the davenport, please." If I gave her any trouble with this request, she'd tell me not to give her any "sassmouth." If this wasn't enough to scare me straight, she'd tell me I was "cruisin for a bruisin." I never pushed my luck far enough to find out what she meant by that.

Every meal to her was dinner. I woke up and had some "dinner," after the *Price is Right* I ate "dinner" again and once my parents got home, my mother made a third "dinner" for me. She soon got out of this habit when I told her my mother let me have dessert if I ate all my "dinner." Since this was such a vague term, I tried to eat pudding shortly after breakfast. She wasn't too keen on this idea. She always managed to keep up with me and whatever trouble I was about to get into. A year ago this month she passed away. She never really left though in essence. I always think of her whenever someone asks me if I want "a cup of coffee" or how the *Price is Right* leads me right into noon (minus the sandwiches with the hearts drawn in them). This helps somewhat, whenever I remember that I'll never hear her voice. At least I can hear her words.

My grandfather isn't in the best shape either. He recently had colon cancer which spread and couldn't be removed completely. Even though he may not be here for too much longer and our "squirrel tree" is a stump cut down just above the knothole, the words he planted in my mind, like the forgotten acorns that grow into trees, will be around long after their source is gone.

READING RESPONSE

1. Reflecting on discourse, identity, and context

   ■ Sean provides some background information that sets the stage for the important roles his grandparents would play in his parents' life and in his own. What does that background contribute to your understanding of the significance of these relationships to him?

   ■ What Sean tells us about his grandparents, and what he shows us about each of them as he recalls the things he did with them and recreates the things they said, work together to characterize each of them. What was each grandparent like, and what did he appreciate most in each of them?

2. Reading from a writer's perspective

   ■ To create portraits of his grandparents, Sean captures the words and phrases he most associates with each of them. How do those words and phrases contribute to those portraits? As you recall moments with people who were significant in your own life, do any of their words and phrases come to mind that help to capture what they were like for you?

   ■ Sean ends his memoir with a reference to the "squirrel tree" he and his grandfather planted, using it as a metaphor to capture the ideas he's been trying to convey. What does that metaphor add to your understanding of his meaning? Is there a metaphor that might capture the understandings you're presenting in your own memoir?

   ■ What do you take as Sean's purpose in writing this memoir? How has (or hasn't) this structure and style allowed him to achieve that purpose from your perspective as a reader?

James R. Jean, "Memoirs of an Indivisible Man"

In much of his work for his writing class, James Jean played with style, using a written story-telling style, for example, that his classmates described as "mock-heroic." In this memoir, James recounts much of his own experience with language and literacy up to this point in his experience. James feels that his own interest in style may have come partly from his own experience in different settings: "I lived in the ghetto . . . I picked up on the slang, the tone of voice. I had to speak one way in school, but I couldn't speak the same way in the hood . . . It wasn't working." As he began writing poetry, he found himself paying more attention to the style of what he read and wrote. He noticed that "you could have the same topic, but different styles affect you differently," and he began to be interested in trying on different styles as a writer. He loves the mood achieved by Edgar Allen Poe, and the seemingly simple style of Robert Frost, but he has also enjoyed participating in poetry slams and trying on the stand-up style of hip-hop-inspired poetry performances. See how he works with style in this memoir of his literary life.

Memoirs of an Indivisible Man

James R. Jean

1   Yesterday is history, tomorrow is a mystery, and today is the gift. This is my memoir, a composition of history, mystery, and a gift. It is a story of sewing feelings to form thoughts, thoughts to form words, words to form language, and language to return to its infant state and become feelings once again. Beyond the purple moons of Gaea, there is a world consisting of a crystal ocean, living glass menageries that talk, and magicians casting ancient spells from dark and ancient legends along the shores of eternity. I am not yet born. Welcome to one of my many disposable worlds. I am the Writer-King and you are the reader. We are both powerful. You give life to my words and my words may teach or entertain you. I am indebted to you. You have a choice to make. You can be immersed into my thoughts and be fully united with me in this spectacle or you can remain an outsider and not get the full understanding of what I am trying to convey. I am the Writer-King and I present to you this memoir of my literary life.

> I am not yet born; O hear me.
> Let not the bloodsucking bat or the rat or the stoat or
> The club-footed ghoul come near me.—Louise MacNeice

I am not a great or an accomplished writer yet, or hold any semblance to one, but darn it I will f*&^%$# write with the liberty and freedom I am allotted by 'free speech' and the prerogatives and privileges held by he who so ever wields the ever-mighty pen. Conformity, are you not the bloodsucking bat, the rat, the stoat? I bite my thumb at thee, for thou art a saucy knave—a fool bearing no discrepancy from Puck himself. "Who is this impersonator of William Shakespeare my greatest foe." Conformity replies, "That should come and defy me, cursing for no reason, and mocking me as though he were a gifted writer? Are you to create your own words too?" Here is my reply to you Conformity. I am, as the early hunters and gatherers were, experimenting, victim to progress therefore victim to trial and error. Listen to this Conformity and tell me what you think:

> I am not yet born, rehearse me.
> In the parts I must play and the cues I must take when
>   Old men lecture me, bureaucrats hector me . . .
> Let them not make me a stone and let them not spill me
> Otherwise kill me.

Aha! You are speechless!

Does Louise MacNeice's poem not seem as though it were especially written to allude to how I am continually being modeled and shaped as a writer? Though 'I am not yet born', I have a voice. I have many voices. I create voices. My voice is the voice of many, but still it is one voice. If I were to label it, it would be called *priblic;* a combination of the private and public languages I have come to experience on this little potpourri dish called earth.

I am often times unconsciously cued by various communities to speak in *those voices,* in the *priblic* way. So often am I cued by certain conditions to *play roles* that I can lose track of the unspoken rules of language—what I like to call the 'who, what, when, wheres of discourse' (WWWWD). Does this suggest that I am stippled with duplicity and being double minded? No! Duplicity and being double minded suggest that there is a sort of conflict between opposing parts. Though I have many voices, therefore many parts, there is no real conflict between the different voices—merely disagreements among them. That is what the process is about, smoothing down those rough jagged-edges.

5   As I look at what I am now as a writer, I can say that I am a scavenger, seeking to gather the richness and to harness the power associated with the spoken and written language. Even as I write this memoir, I experiment. I toy with word selection, structure, style, tone, context, adding and removing myself from the writing (as will be seen later), etc., etc. As I try to walk along paths I've yet taken, I will and may have already erred; but that is the price I must pay if the possibility of being a great writer is a hope that can one day be grasped. But enough of this! 'Who is this Writer-King?' you must be asking. Let us both sit back and listen to *History's story:*

* * *

"*Uh uhm.* All right, listen carefully as I tell you the story of the Writer-King. I am Old Man History. I am one but I will speak for Mystery and Gift. For within this trilogy is one story and I have been chosen to narrate it. I was chosen because of my ability to navigate back and forth through time. I am in essence a part of time. But without further adieu, here is the story of the Writer-King through the voice and eyes of all seeing History:

First of all James is not a king at all. Let us face it, he is not even that great of a writer. Surely he is no Shakespeare, Dante, Chaucer, or even a Hemingway (yes, not even Hemingway), though he grew up reading their works. He is of a different stock, a different breed, and a weird one. He is the product of all the different communities he has been a part of since childhood. James grew up in the inner city. A product of urban idealism and culture coupled with the suburban experience clichéd by the white picket fences and such words as 'wicked' used as an adjective and an adverb; i.e. That car was *wicked*.—adjective; That test was *wicked* hard.—adverb. He is the fabrication of the U.S. *melting pot*. In all sense, he is the son of Truth yet the product of many lies. Among his many fathers in language were the books that he read and the shows that he watched. He's all mixed up and all of that shows in the style of his writing and the 'special languages' he sometimes chooses to use to express himself. That is not necessarily a bad thing—it is rather, a tad different.

It is amazing how much James is more a formulation of childhood experiences (more or less before high school) then of more current experiences. Those pre high school years were really what shaped his rudimentary views on language and its uses. These views only now, are being looked back for a clearer understanding into how this writer has come to write the way he does (or thinks he should).

His first and very important confrontation with the power of language (or lack there of) came in his elementary school years. Being the son of Haitian parents, he spoke English with a mild yet noticeable accent. I bet you he still remembers those days in the first grade when he used to be teased by his peers because he really did not know the language. I'm sure he still remembers being teased for being different, teased for the way he pronounced the word 'beach' which sounded like that wonderful cuss word we have become ever so familiar with. I'm sure that those experiences forced him to become a mild recluse because he could not participate in the communities set up by his 'peers' who spoke the same way. I'm almost certain that when they would circle around and talk about the wrestling matches the night before, James would have plenty to say, but couldn't—because words would get in the way. These interactions with the kids that were not in his bilingual class were difficult yet crucial. To understand the relationship between language and power in that fashion was painful—but Life got its point across.

10   It did not take too long for James to learn the intricacies of the English language and to speak it with a fluency that became admired by others in the bilingual class that he was in. The progress was one of trial and error. There was a lot of listening to different conversations and practicing what was heard with different groups. "Hey dawg, you saw the Monday Night Raw last night, yo that was mad fatt. Nigga I'm telling you Hogan can't be seen and ain't no one got nothin on him."

Along this journey many words and expressions were learned. James realized though that they were unique to kids and learned quickly what not to say in front of adults.

Oh I remember the excitement James felt when the word the 'beach' meant what it was suppose to mean because it was pronounced correctly. I remember the way his mouth became a fountain of words and he was like a mad scientist from then on, experimenting wildly. Words became formulas and different combinations of words and phrases produced different responses and made him and other people feel different ways. He spoke *it* well and was proud; proud, not only because he could *fit in* now, but also because he was now able to make a choice—"To be or not to be." He chose not to be; not be completely assimilated into any one group, not to be labeled as being of one kind, not be conformed by a single community. He could now speak his mind and his heart in a way that had only been envied of in the past. And thus a new journey began—to understand the gift.

Those early elementary years' experiences created a key understanding of relationships. He had learned that there is a relationship between language and power. As his language improved and the accent faded, so did his fears and insecurities in communicating with others. He was now *allowed* to set up his own little groups because he understood a small yet important concept in the whole scheme of Language; to speak or write was to establish a relationship between him and his audience. As greater ease and mobility was established with the English language, James was moved from the bilingual program in the fourth grade, to the Advance Class Program with all English speaking students—and there was no problem. So James quickly learned two major personal lessons: to speak was to define yourself to others; and in communication, the speaker or writer holds a certain power, whether to captivate the heart or to persuade it to take action.

James is not there yet as a complete writer, but he is at least moving forward in searching. But as I am History and I am the future-yet-to-be, I see James getting an 'A+' in his English 101 class (That's just my personal opinion). But in any event, James is trying to define who he is as a writer and all that he has experienced in the past has been part of the difficult building process. Some treasures are worth keeping and others can be discarded said the scavenger. James has tasted the fruit of power and its affiliation with language and he has found it to be ever so sweet. I am old man History—and the train stops here.

15   Actually, let me not stop here. This is another vignette into the life of the Writer-King. To be young and full of dreams, to thirst and to seek to drink deep from the spring of knowledge, to walk along trails that lead to nowhere, to yearn for the mysticism that Language holds, and to search to understand the magic kettle that produces words; these were the thoughts that captivated the mind of the Writer-Prince. He swims in a dry lakebed and some how ends up soaking wet. He is able to feed off the air and find it very much fulfilling. This sounds like nonsense, but it is not. James sees words as threads to be knitted into whatever his mind dares to conceive. As the saying goes, if you keep pulling on the thread, the whole sweater will unravel. So James tugs and tugs to understand the mystery and relationship between language and power and to unravel the secret within them lies.

James was taught by life and its sometimes-cruel lessons that writing with emotion rather then the strict, factual, and stringent style that he was accustomed to had a different effect than the emotional approach. He learned this one during a summer program in the sixth grade. He had to write an essay on our experiences during the summer and how the program had enriched him. James wrote his essay error-free. He stood up and read it wonderfully with changes in tone and hand motion. But this certain girl got up and read hers also. It was beautiful! It was littered with emotions and imagery. It was written with a certain freedom that was remarkable. He fell in love with that approach and so he grew to include it in his entourage. He learned that to really be able to move back and forth between different communities he had to be versatile with words and not fear adjusting tone and context or overall style to better communicate or relate a point across.

"I have been more sinned against than sin" is one way of saying that one has been dearly wronged. But when little ol' James used this Shakespearean line in conversation with friends, the reply was "Shut up you idiot". What was wrong? Well duh it's obvious. It was out of place. This seemingly small *incident* in middle school (the seventh grade) was another required episode in the 'process' of James improving into a better writer and relatable speaker.

The sum product of these experiences was an understanding that language was not something that was singular but rather it was plural. There were relationships between language and various concepts such as power, being able to relate, and defining oneself. By self-definition I mean setting up who you are and your role in a particular group or community. By these small and tiny episodes, James gained a greater realization that there was a bigger picture to speaking and writing, but all these thoughts and concepts were just notions, misplaced and undefined.

Though there was probably no definition or working concept behind these ideas during the pre-collegiate years, there was an unconscious mechanism telling him "Okay no swearing in your term paper James." I now skip to the college years (the college 2 months) of James' life. To see and understand the concepts that in the past were but unconsciously cued mechanisms is a great thing for this Writer-King. It allows him to breakdown ideas and analyze word choice, structure, etc. and understand how they create ideas and feelings. But in any effect, I tire so I end here with this thought from the Writer-King himself:

> To understand or to seek to understand the knitting of feelings to form thoughts, thoughts to form words, words to form language, and language to return to its infant state and become feelings once again is something that is very much incredible. History and the experiences that it has put me through was my initial teacher about Language and its promiscuity with other concepts. History has knitted me into an unfinished glove. One day I'll be complete.
>
> The mystery is in the gift. The gift is words and the ability to combine them to create images and ideas is amazing. The mystery that lies within words lies in the way it can be made to increase in its richness depending on how it is used and combined, and part of the mystery is that I do not know the extent of its powers. I am still the Writer-King by self-definition. And by self-definition I am a lifetime student to the art of language. Contend me in these thoughts but still, in the words of Ancient Wisdom "I think therefore I am." I am the writer you are the reader and as this is the conclusion, I am more powerful. Beyond earth's new moon, there is no crystal lake. There are no glass menageries that are talking. There are no magicians casting ancient spells along the pebbled shores of eternity. But still, I am the Writer-King. And still, I am not yet born.

READING RESPONSE

1. <u>Reflecting on discourse, identity, and context</u>

   ■ James explores his own identity as a writer by taking on the persona of the "Writer-King" engaging in a debate with Old Man History. What points does Old Man History make that balance and temper the Writer-King's ambitions as a writer? Might the persona of Old Man History represent another side of the writer himself? What understanding of James's identity and concerns as a writer do you get from reading what's said through each of these personas?

   ■ James, like Rodriguez, was the child of immigrant parents and (unlike Rodriguez) he was in bilingual classrooms until the fourth grade. Do you think he would agree with Rodriguez's position that, to gain a public identity, a child must leave his family's language and private identity behind? Do you find evidence in the details James offers of his experience to support the position you think he'd take? Does his coining of the word "priblic" contribute to your sense of how he'd see this issue?

   ■ What are the most significant understandings that James comes to, in his memoir, about language, identity, and the different contexts of his life?

2. <u>Reading from a writer's perspective</u>

   ■ The Writer-King describes himself as a scavenger, "seeking to gather the richness and to harness the power associated with the spoken and written language." Where do you find examples of scavenged language in this memoir? Where has he scavenged language from, and what effect does each instance of such scavenging contribute to the whole?

   ■ James draws on the words of the poet Louise MacNeice at the beginning of his memoir, and echoes those words again at the end. What do MacNeice's words contribute to your understanding of what comes in the middle? Has the writer come back to his starting point, or has something changed through the narrative itself? As you write your memoir, are there words from another source—a poem, a song—that capture something essential about the experience you want to convey? Can you imagine using them in a circular frame, as James has?

   ■ Adopting two personas and casting his memoir as a debate between them allows James to present two opposing views of his own history with language and writing. How effective is this device for you as a reader? Does it suggest alternative ways in which you might represent aspects of your own identity or structure multiple views of your own experience?

   ■ What do you take as James's purpose in writing this memoir? How has (or hasn't) this structure and style allowed him to achieve that purpose from your perspective as a reader?

Dina Tsirelson, "Memoir"

Dina Tsirelson was born in Russia and moved with her family to Israel when she was five years old. Then, just three years before she entered college, her family moved again, to the United States. She says, "I always thought that in the area of language I was quite lucky since I had the opportunity to live in three countries with fundamentally different languages and to learn these languages while confronting them face to face, in their natural discourse communities. I consider myself fortunate not to be limited to the rules of just one language, but being able to think and express myself in several ways." Now she finds herself to be most comfortable, most an insider, with those few people who share all three of her languages—Russian, Hebrew, and English. Yet she recalls that, immediately after September 11th, when reading of the moment when Rodriguez speaks out in class and understands that he has become part of American society, "I remembered that earlier that same day, in a class discussion about the tragedy that befell this country, I had used a word in a way I've never done before. I said the word 'we' to mean America and its people, including myself among them for the first time."

In writing her memoir, Dina chose to focus on two significant and related transitions in her life, her family's emigration from Russia to Israel and more recently from Israel to the United States. Then, after reading Tommi Avicolli's memoir, she experimented with using a different structure for her own, recasting it into scenes, using Avicolli's model. Both versions are included here.

Memoir

Dina Tsirelson

1   After seven hours of flight, a plane lands in Tel-Aviv, Israel. We step out on a long flight of stairs into the typical Israeli October heat dressed for the Russian autumn cold. The first thing I see is a tall, slightly crooked, almost naked palm tree. The only place where I have seen palms before is a hothouse in Leningrad, where they were well taken care of, lively and green. I imagined that in Israel they would be even more lavish. And my first words in this new land are uttered in disbelief: "why are the palms here so tattered?"

That was at the time when I spoke only one language—Russian. Since then, there have been quite a few more. The moment marks my first transition into a different world, a move that we awaited eagerly for many years when leaving Russia was not permitted. But it turned out to be not the only one. Almost exactly ten years later our plane landed in Logan airport and into a new life once again, under quite different circumstances. I tend to think of these two transitions as separating the events of my life into three "eras": Russia, Israel, and America. These transitions from one country to another brought with them the transitions between languages that have become such an integral part of my life.

The physical transition to Israel might have taken a moment or a few hours at most, but the passage through languages that followed took somewhat longer. Unlike the palm tree, Israel was not a disappointment, although I did not feel at home right from the start. Of course, it took time for me to learn the language and get accustomed to the new society. In the few years after we arrived, my mother was in seventh heaven just from thinking that she now lived where she belonged, among Jews, after escaping the blatant antisemitism of soviet Russia. Since I did not experience antisemitism myself, I had no such distinct euphoric feelings. One thing I remember distinctly from that time is kids calling "Hey Russian, go back to Russia!" Sometimes they would ask, "Are you Russian?" I could never be sure what they meant. I always wished they were more specific, so that I would know if I should take offense or not. 'If by "Russian" you mean someone who was born in Russia and spoke Russian, then yes, I am; but if you are implying that I am not Jewish and do not belong here, you are sadly mistaken.' I wished I could explain that to them, but what do kids know anyway.

I could not bring myself to say anything because other than being shy I was afraid to speak in the foreign tongue. But that soon changed since at that age I quickly picked up the language and all the aspects of culture that come with it, a kid's culture that includes slang, games, ideas, misconceptions. I was soon speaking Hebrew fluently even with Russian-speaking friends and acquired Hebrew-speaking friends as well. Once I had mastered the language, I became part of the whole, an insider to the Israeli elementary school community.

5   Since living in the third "era," I have come to think of these three languages as equally my own, although each one has a different connotation and its own appropriate uses, placing me in different discourse communities. Before I moved to America, Hebrew was my main everyday language outside of home. It was the language of school and friends. At home, however, I always kept speaking Russian although I left Russia when I was only five and never learned to read and write in it very well. I've recently realized the irony in this—that my actual 'native language,' the language I learned first and the only one in which I have no accent is not the language I know best.

But what distinguished my discourse with Russian-speakers in Israel was that I could use all three languages freely, without ever worrying that a word from a different language would not be understood in this context. This was, and still is, particularly visible in the way I speak at home. My Russian is not exactly 'pure,' but rather a mix of the expressions I learned from relatives and friends and what I could muster without ever officially learning it, including outdated slang and childish formulations. Often due to my own limitations in Russian, when I could not find just the word I was looking for the moment I needed it, I turned to a nonsense verb whose meaning could still be very much understood from its suffixes and prefixes. When I speak to someone my age who had just moved from Russia, it sometimes seems like we don't speak exactly the same language and can't understand each other perfectly. With my family, I played with the languages freely, inventing new words and switching from one to another to a mix of all three. I consider myself fortunate not to be limited to the rules of just one language, but to be able to think and express myself in several ways.

However, having three languages so intertwined in one head causes inevitable slip-ups. It happened more than once that while talking to my Israeli friends a Russian word would slip from my mouth. Certain everyday terms are so much engraved in my mind in their Hebrew form that I do not always notice that they *are* in fact Hebrew and that they will not be understood in some situations. Even my grandmother who does not speak Hebrew practically at all says such words as 'microwave' 'traffic-light' and 'air-conditioner' to her Russian-speaking friends in Hebrew and often has to face their annoyance with not understanding her.

I did not remember much of Russia and Israel is where my life was. I did most of my growing-up there and all my friends were there. I was used to that life and did not know any other. Hebrew became like a native language to me and I did not know how I would be able to switch completely to a new one, start all over again. When it was time to move again, I was ten years older and had many reasons to dislike the move. It was much more difficult this time. The feeling was different. My excitement was not so much from happy anticipation as from anxiety. There were no first words and no special and unique memories of the moment.

America was in many ways a cultural shock for me. All the expected difficulties were there: another language, different units of measure, school subjects, people, customs. But there was also something else, something that I did not anticipate. Suddenly I could not take the fact that I was Jewish for granted. My holidays and traditions were not commonly understood by everyone. I had to explain things that were always obvious before. I had to explain that Yom Kippur is not the equivalent of New-Year's; I had to explain that matzah was not made from matzo-flour, but the other way around. Although I appreciated learning so much about different cultures, I became isolated from my own. At a certain point I had realized that we do not even have a Jewish calendar, and had almost missed a holiday. It had slipped my mind because the whole country was not celebrating with me. I had to constantly remind myself who I was and force myself to keep some traditions that were part of everyday life back in Israel.

10   Nevertheless, this was not my biggest problem with the move to America. Both because I grew up in Israel, where my Jewishness was nothing to pay particular attention to, and because I was never strictly religious, I never defined myself by my religion. Language always played a much greater role in my life, and even more so since I made my second transition. Now a third language, one that I had only studied a little as a foreign language before, was to become my primary school language. I found myself sitting in my first high-school class, a history class, in front of a teacher speaking quickly in English and a whole class that followed, responding, answering, sometimes laughing. At times, whole sentences blended into long, indistinguishable strings of syllables. The first days, I dragged along from class to class, often getting lost in the school's maze-like hallways. I could not follow the reading in class and did not speak up because English was impossible to pronounce. I had to think over and plan in my mind the whole sentence before I could say it, and then it was too late to say it—the conversation had moved elsewhere. Speaking English felt sometimes like my tongue stepped into a piece of gum, and while trying to get unstuck from it, managed to stick to another gum. Speaking was hard, but writing was a pure nightmare. I shudder to think how impossible it seemed to formulate complex thoughts for an analytical paper with such a limited vocabulary and no idea of the right phrase to express established concepts. My escape was writing letters in Hebrew, talking to a few

Russian-speakers at school, and most of all, coming home to speak my way and make fun of the English language all together.

Now, three years later, I have gotten so used to writing and speaking in English that it seems to be taking over its predecessors in my head. Lately I have gotten too neglectful of the way I speak Russian, so much that sometimes my sentences are just not grammatically correct. I was having trouble writing a simple letter in Hebrew because only English sentences came to mind. It was about a year into my life here when my mother asked me what language I was thinking in, and at that moment I realized that it was now English.

Nonetheless, English is still not the language I am most comfortable with. I still use them all equally, but my ability to use them depends on the moment. Sometimes one comes more easily, sometimes another. My three languages are precious to me and I don't want to forget any one of them. I am truly most comfortable when I can use the three of them together. But apparently, three was not enough—I am taking a Spanish course this year. Already, Spanish words sometimes come to mind for no reason. Things are bound to get even more complicated soon enough.

Memoir—Restructured

Dina Tsirelson

SCENE 1

A girl is walking home from school. Some kids from her school are nearby. When she gets closer, a boy approaches her and asks, "Are you Russian?" It is not intended as a real question. He knows the answer. She, however, is never sure what he means. She wants to explain to him that although she was born in Russia and happens to speak Russian, she is just as Jewish as he is and belongs in the same country, but she can't. Therefore she just keeps walking. She has learned to ignore this. The boy yells after her, "Go back to your Russia!"

SCENE 2

Early evening in a dormitory on a field trip. Two people making casual conversation. One asks the other where she's from. The girl says that she's from Israel. That is who she considers herself to be. After further conversation, she has to explain how come she can speak Russian, so she says that she moved from Russia to Israel first. In response to a question, she says that both her parents are from Russia. The asker then asks why they moved to Israel. The girl stammers, then snickers. She starts going "Ah . . . well . . . ," then thinks for a while. The other interprets this to mean that the girl does not exactly know the reason. The girl quickly says "no, no . . . I know" but still can't answer the question. She has often been asked why they decided to move from Israel to America, but never why they moved to Israel. This question comes as a complete surprise for her. It was something she took for granted and therefore never thought about it. What reason could there possibly be other than the one most obvious, that they were returning to their homeland after two thousand years of diaspora?

SCENE 3

A college English class discussing in small groups papers they wrote about some experience of theirs. The girl again is asked how did it happen that she speaks both Russian and Hebrew. She explains, like she is long used to, that she lived in Israel for ten years after moving there from Russia. Someone in her group comes to the conclusion that the girl must not be Jewish. She is a little surprised. The girl asks her why does she think so. The answer: "I just didn't know that there were Russians who practiced Judaism." The girl is completely bewildered. She does not know what to make of that response. How can someone say that? What needs to be explained here? She thought that that was common knowledge, something obvious, like the fact that there are Jews in America. It is not Russians practicing Judaism, but Jews living in Russia because they had no place else to be. That is, until they moved to Israel.

SCENE 4

Same field trip. Two people are cleaning up in the kitchen, talking.

5 "Can I ask you a question?" He is a little uncomfortable; he is not sure if the question is appropriate.

"Sure, ask." Now she is curious.

"Do women in Israel wear . . ." he makes a motion with his hand over his face ". . . ?"

"Oh, no, no," she laughs.

Just a little cultural misunderstanding, really, no big deal. So what if he doesn't know the difference between Jewish and Muslim. Maybe somewhere along the way he got the impression that everyone in the Middle East must look the same. But what *did* he know? What *is* common knowledge about these things in this country?

* * *

10 The first scene takes place in Israel. The other three, in America. Before that, there was Russia. But there are no scenes from Russia, just stories I heard much later. They were stories of secret Jewish life in soviet Russia, and stories of persecution. I heard about the secret library of Jewish books hidden in my grandfather's house, of political prisoners, of an underground Jewish Theater. We were nothing but "Jews." When you were labeled as such, you did not have much perspective. Hebrew, back then, was not permitted. Officially, it did not even exist. I heard one story from a friend of ours: he applied for a license to be a Hebrew teacher. He received a polite response: "we could grant you this license if there was such a language, but since this language does not exist, you cannot be a Hebrew teacher." This was in the seventies, when the Israeli song "Halleluia" was playing even on Russian radios after winning first place in the Eurovision.

After many years of being "refuseniks," those whose request to immigrate out of Russia the government refused, we were finally let go and came to Israel—a dream come true. For a while, my mother was in seventh heaven just from thinking that she now lived where she belonged, among Jews, after escaping the blatant antisemitism of soviet Russia. Since I did not experience antisemitism myself, I had no such distinct euphoric feelings. I was only five and had to get used to living in a new place and learning a new language. Fortunately, at that age it did not take that long. I quickly picked up the language and all the aspects of culture that come with it, a kid's culture that includes slang, games, ideas, misconceptions. I was soon speaking Hebrew fluently even with Russian speaking friends and have acquired Hebrew-speaking friends as well. Once I had mastered the language, I became part of the whole, an insider to the Israeli elementary school community.

But for a while at least, I was still "Russian." The irony is unbelievable. In Russia, I was a Jew. In Israel, I was Russian. And here, here I am both—or neither. Depends on what idea people get from what I tell them. I always had trouble defining myself this way. If someone asks, I tend to answer "Israeli." But I never know how people understand this, especially when I say that I was born in Russia.

There were two transitions, two moves from one country to another that in the most part established the way I see myself. The two transitions are separated by ten years of time and span three continents. I tend to think of them as separating the events of my life into three distinct periods: Russia, Israel, and America. The most dividing thing between them is the language. But as I moved from one to the other, I did not just switch to the new language. Rather, I added the language to my cache of ways of thinking and speaking, learning to be a part in new communities and using the discourses of them all.

My favorite identity—the multilingual.

READING RESPONSE

1. Reflecting on discourse, identity, and context

- Dina sees her life as divided into three 'eras,' each marked by a different country, culture, and language. Yet the identities she experiences and that others give her as she moves from one era into the next are not so clearly separated. What are some of the complex threads of language, culture, and religion that cross these different eras of her life, and, how do they affect her sense of what it means to belong in each place?

- In Dina's restructured memoir, she presents several scenes of key moments in her experience. How do these scenes recast the themes of identity that are raised in the first version of the memoir?

- In her portfolio overview/reflection, Dina commented that she ended up addressing somewhat different aspects of her social identity in the second version, in a way that "seemed to me a little darker, less pleasant." Do you find that difference in mood in the second version? If so, what elements do you feel contribute to it?

2. Reading from a writer's perspective

- Drawing on your experience, as a reader, of Dina's restructuring of her memoir, what do you find to be the advantages, disadvantages, of each way that she has presented her experience? Might you work with either of these structures in your own memoir?

(continued)

- In her portfolio overview, Dina said she has come to think that "a memoir is not a definitive account but a representation of how I saw some aspect of my life or identity at the particular moment when I was writing it." How would you characterize how she sees her life or identity at the moment of writing these two versions of her memoir? Do you see yourself, in your own memoir, as representing a particular view of your life that you hold at this moment, one that might change at a different time?

- Dina hasn't given her memoir a title. What might you suggest?

- What do you take as Dina's purpose in writing this memoir? How have (or haven't) these variations in structure and style allowed her to achieve that purpose from your perspective as a reader?

ESSAYS IN ACADEMIC GENRES

The two essays that follow were written in response to the prompts at the end of Chapter 2. Each writer has found his own way to follow out an idea that has come up for him in the work of these early chapters, doing so in a more formal academic essay structure. Each essay includes an introduction stating a theme, thesis or question, a body or middle section that develops that idea, exploring what evidence there is from one or more readings that supports that idea or helps to answer that question, and concluding with a final point of discovery or a restatement of what was discovered.

Bryan Gangemi, "The Birth of a New Writer"

Bryan chose to return to Mellix's essay to pursue a question that had arisen for him in his informal journal responses. As a freshman who was thinking about how he could further his own development as a writer, Bryan was particularly interested in how other writers had learned to write in effective and powerful ways. In his essay he analyzes Mellix's text closely for evidence that will answer his question, "What factors led to a gifted writer's ability to blend words and ideas together to create beautifully crafted works?" This sort of detailed look at how a text works and what it offers in relationship to a particular theme or question is sometimes referred to as *textual analysis*.

The Birth of a New Writer

Bryan Gangemi

1   As an admirer of fine writing, I became quite interested in learning the steps Mellix took in developing her art form. What factors lead to a gifted writer's ability to blend words and ideas together to create beautifully crafted works? Writers speak in numerous voices to a variety of audiences. There are numerous styles that writers can attach to and use as their weapon of choice in attacking projects. Some writers like Mellix, fit the Darwinian theory of evolution. They begin their writing paths with innate qualities and through gradual change become more adaptive to their environment. In essence Mellix became adaptive to her readers and adapted to each environment as an equal member who could communicate effectively with her audience. Gaining a clear understanding of the Mellix evolutionary path is my focus in this paper. Through an analysis of her piece "From Outside, In," I will examine the elements that contributed to her discourse competence and the many unique voices of writing she speaks in.

Mellix in a sense grew up as a bilingual child. She used both "Black" English and "standard" English, each of which she used as means of communication for the appropriate setting she was in. Although each style is a form of the same language, there are so many differences present in each version that essentially, they exist as separate languages. Mellix spoke "Black" English quite well and felt a deep connection and comfort with it. When Mellix needed to speak "standard" English, the comfort level she had with "Black" English vanished. "We felt foolish, embarrassed, and somehow diminished because we were afraid to be our real selves" (p. 61).

Despite her discomfort, the very use of "standard" English proved to be her earliest and most important exposure to discourse competence. This movement towards "standard" English allowed her to develop a new voice that traveled far beyond the perimeter of "Black" English. Mellix's experience of both forms of English gave birth to her ability to move readily between different discourse communities.

Upon graduating high school Mellix moved to Pittsburgh. This move provided her with many rich experiences that further developed her speaking and writing. "In time, I learned to speak "standard" English with ease and to switch smoothly from Black to standard or a mixture, and back again" (p. 63). This quote exemplifies the smooth transitions that were beginning to occur between her styles of speech. Not only was switching back and forth going more fluidly but a new job helped her realize what her limitations were as a writer and what direction she wanted to set her writing.

5   Mellix's new job was a position at a health care company. This position required her to write to customers about issues pertaining to medical coverage. "In a sense, I was proud of the letters I wrote for the company: they were proof of my ability to survive in the city, the outside world—an indication of my growing mastery of English. But they also indicate that writing was still mechanical for me, something that didn't require much thought" (p. 63). Although she began to use the "standard" English language like it was her own, she wanted to go beyond a mechanized way of writing. She was typing away like a programmed robot with very little thinking involved and no emotional expression, just a specific task to complete in the most standardized of

ways. She came to realize how restricted she was in writing at this position and the desire to break free from this system started to foment from within.

With three jobs behind her, a new family, new friends, and a renewed pleasure in reading, Mellix was ready to take the next step towards furthering her writing skills. Her next step—in what would become her birth as a great writer—was enrolling in a writing course at the University of Pittsburgh. It was here that she realized the lifelessness that was tied in with her prose and she became fully aware of her need to make a significant change in her approach. Most importantly, she learned that to best communicate with an audience, she needed to become one with the people she was writing about. "I was, I believed, explaining other people's thoughts and feelings, and I was free to move about in the language of "others" as long as I was speaking of others" (p. 65).

Realizing that to be an effective writer one must speak the "other's" language, she started to work on the fine-tuning of her writing skill. As a writer, she was beginning to comprehend the intricacies of the "other's" language. However the discomfort she felt during childhood still was with her as an adult. Her new ventures into writing resulted in "the psychological conflict for those attempting to master academic discourse" (p. 67). As she was growing closer to her new found methods of writing, she felt she was growing distant from her "blackness"—*the one source of absolute comfort she had with language*. Her intimate connection to "Black" English had been with her since early childhood and her transition into the "other's" language presented her with conflicting feelings.

To be a successful writer still grounded to her roots, she figured out she had to mentally project herself as an important and equal part to the language she was speaking with. "I had to imagine myself a part of the culture of that language." Once Mellix was able to work with this delicate balance, immersion into the language—in an imagined sense—became her key to maintaining her true identity and venturing into new writing. Comparatively, actors must go through a similar process to that of Mellix. When preparing for a role in theater or film, many great actors immerse themselves in the character's surroundings and state of mind to become one with the role. Actors only imagine themselves as these characters and still have with them a strong background and identity, which can be preserved in this process.

"I write and continually give birth to myself" (p. 67). With her final words in the piece capturing her ability to adapt to various environments, Mellix affirms her continuous growth as a writer fit to become a member of many discourse communities. Most importantly she is able to maintain a strong link to her heritage, which influenced and inspired her so greatly.

In his essay, Bryan has stuck very closely to Mellix's memoir, discussing it from beginning to end. What makes his essay different from a summary of the memoir that would be intended to provide a more condensed representation of its contents? How has Bryan's question guided him in selecting and emphasizing particular aspects of the memoir? What understandings of Bryan's perspective do you get as he points to and comments on aspects of Mellix's experience?

READING RESPONSE

Jake Wark, "Alone Among the Others"

Jake 's interest at this point was different from Bryan's. Having sometimes felt, himself, like a social outsider, he became interested in that theme as it was developed in the memoirs he had been reading (including the full text of Cisneros's "Ghosts and Voices"). He decided that the memoirs give evidence of self-doubt and alienation but also that language plays a role as the writers establish a more confident identity, and those are the two points—alienation/aloneness and finding an identity through language—that he would look for in each one. Jake chose not to offer a detailed comparison of these memoirs, but rather to capture the main points each one makes with reference to his controlling idea in what might be described as a *critical summary*, working towards a *synthesis*—a bringing together—of the related ideas in all three.

Alone Among the Others
Cisneros, Rodriguez, and Mellix

Jake Wark

I   The role of social outsider, though painful to live through, can provide an author with a valuable experience with which to engage the reader. Such is the case with Sandra Cisneros, Richard Rodriguez, and Barbara Mellix, whose memoirs all draw on recollections of self-doubt, alienation, and aloneness. Each found strength and courage in their struggle, however, and each succeeded in their efforts to discover their true and whole identity through the use of a language that once made them different.

Sandra Cisneros begins and ends her memoir "Ghosts and Voices" with the suggestion that her outsider role led to her success as a writer. As a child, gender was the main issue: "I was born an only daughter in a family of sons," she writes, " . . . leaving me odd-woman-out forever" (p. 2). With no sisters to act as comrades or confidantes, Cisneros lived a "solitary childhood" (p. 3) among her six brothers in an impoverished urban neighborhood "where the best friend I was always waiting for never materialized" (p. 3). When she left her home for Iowa College, she felt a different sort of aloneness: with a heritage as different as her own was from those of her classmates', Cisneros felt isolated on a socioeconomic level. "I only knew that for the first time in my life I felt 'other'" (p. 4). Only by dropping her pretensions and imitations, by embracing the things that made her different from her colleagues, did she find her voice—"the voice I'd been suppressing all along" (p. 4).

In "Aria," Richard Rodriguez also had the outsider role thrust upon him as a child. The lone Latino in his classroom and the son of blue-collar Mexican immigrants, Rodriguez was alone among peers who "were White, many the children of doctors and lawyers and business executives" (p. 28). Even out of school, "our house stood apart. . . . We were the foreigners on the block". Ethnicity was an issue on both sides of the equation: the phrases "*los gringos*" and "*los americanos*" (p. 29) were synonymous in his home, implying that his family was separate and different from the Americans outside their door. Rodriguez' native Spanish, which he identified so closely with his family identity, was a reminder "of my separateness from *los otros*" (p. 30), a warning that "in this world so big, I was a foreigner" (p. 31). Rodriguez ultimately eschews his familial insider role to become an insider of the larger world, the public world, quite a different tack from that taken by Cisneros, but one that still maintains identity and individuality.

Barbara Mellix' identity was shaped by language, as well, but the issue described in "From Outside, In" was knowing when, not how, to speak the public language of "the others" (p. 60). Mellix and her kin were taught implicitly that the "ordinary, everyday speech" (p. 60) used informally by her peers and family was invalid and inferior to that of the dominant social group. Pressured to use "proper" English among Whites—and even unfamiliar Blacks—Mellix and her siblings "felt foolish, embarrassed . . . diminished because we were ashamed to be our true selves" (p. 61). Use of the "proper" language with intimates "for no good reason" (p. 62)—that is, among the family rather than the Whites for whom it was reserved—drew snide remarks. It was considered "'uppity'" (p. 61)—a word that implies a normative outsider role for African-Americans by describing a departure from it. "The language," she writes, "was not ours" (p. 62). Indeed, she viewed standard English and her local variation as "two distinctly different languages" (p. 60), and approached the former as a novice student might study a foreign tongue: "stud[ying] form letters . . . memorizing the phrases" (p. 63), looking at formula rather than style, even admitting that her writing was "still mechanical" (p. 63). This was not due to a lack of free thought: Mellix recounts her rich and emotive drawing as a child, indicating that it was the language, not the creative ability, by which she felt "restricted" (p. 62).

5   Through her own initiative and hard work, and with the help of her professors, Mellix began to make the language her own. Like Cisneros, Mellix had to forsake the shame she felt for her background; like Rodriguez, she had to take a risk in exposing herself and her "otherness" (p. 64) in order to feel comfortable with the language she began to slip into. She had to "imagine myself a part of the culture of that language" (p. 67) in order to fully become a part of it, to carry that "good burden" (p. 67).

Once content in their familial intimacy, later outsiders in an often unfriendly environment, all of these authors found their identities and voices by stepping beyond the limits defined by themselves or others. Each took a risk, walking treacherous ground in unfamiliar territory, to marry themselves to a greater culture. Each stepped away from the world they knew best, but in so doing they further solidified their individuality. Whether through language, culture, or life experience, we are all unique, all different in some way from the person next to us, all with a story to tell.

| How do Jake's ideas about overcoming alienation and finding identity through language affect what he chooses to draw from each of these memoirs? By placing these memoirs alongside each other, does he seem to have gained for himself, or has he offered you as a reader, any new understandings, new ways of thinking about what each memoir offers? | **READING RESPONSE** |

PART II

Studying Everyday Conversations

The next three chapters invite you to participate in the type of *primary* or *field research* that is currently going on in a number of academic disciplines. You'll begin by identifying a community that you want to study, one where you're an insider and where you currently spend time. Then you'll consider some of the ways other writers and researchers have tried to capture the ways of particular communities. The larger questions in Part II focus on how a community carries out its conversations and how the shared knowledge, purposes, and ways of those conversations connect to the shared beliefs and values of this community, large or small. As an insider to the community, as well as a researcher, you'll be viewing the community from both perspectives, and your study may also help you see more about what you seek and value at a moment when you're also identifying a new path for yourself through the academic communities that you'll study in Part III.

The particular form of field research you'll be undertaking is ethnographic research, a method of inquiry developed in the field of anthropology to look at how communities and societies created their own cultures. The readings include several ethnographic studies of particular cultural settings (such as a college dorm, a college bar, an on-line game). The reading selections also include short stories and other types of writing in which the writer tries to capture and recreate the talk, values, and ways of a particular community.

Each chapter will include inquiries that focus on reading, observation, and reflection. Because the observations you'll be doing in these chapters will provide much of the material for the longer research report that you'll write at the end of Chapter 6, they'll be labeled as *research memos*. The research memo, as a genre of informal writing, is similar to the observational account that you worked with in earlier chapters. But it is intended to contribute to one larger, focused inquiry and to your report on that larger inquiry—to serve as a sort of progress report on what each new angle contributes to your ongoing research. These research memos are intended to be cumulative, and you'll want to keep adding to your earlier observations (rather than repeating something you've already noted). Suggestions for writing exploratory essays in other academic genres will appear at the end of each chapter.

LEARNING GOALS

- To extend the process of becoming an insider to academic communities by undertaking some of the typical research and writing done in those communities.

- To extend your repertoire as a reader, writer, and researcher by focusing on analytical reading and writing.

- To discover more about the shared ways and values of a particular discourse community, so that you can come to a deeper understanding of your own competence as an insider to an informal community, and how that connects to the competence you're developing in a more formal, academic one.

CHAPTER

4

Identifying Communities

Chapter 4 focuses on a short story by Flannery O'Connor, whose writing was deeply rooted in the talk of small southern towns like the one she lived in for most of her life. The story dramatizes a conflict between two very different discourse communities. Reading a literary text will allow us to enter these fictional discourse communities together and to develop some shared understandings about how to look at what goes on there. A close reading of this story will help to frame several key inquiry strands:

- What's involved in entering the world of a short story as a reader?

- What can literature teach us about discourse communities and what distinguishes them from one another—including not only differences in what people talk about and how, but the differences in perspective, values, and social identity that lie behind the words?

- How might our prior experiences in reading literature in other settings contribute to our understandings of this story?

Through our analysis of the O'Connor story, we'll see what it means to be an insider or an outsider to a community. We'll discover the extent to which insiderness is shaped, not only by what's said and how it's said, but by the unstated, implicit understandings that underlie the actual words. And we'll find how the ways people talk are connected to the values they share. Chapter 4 introduces some concepts and ideas we can use when we turn to the different communities that we actually participate in and to some studies that contemporary researchers have done of such communities. It offers ways of analyzing what goes on in discourse communities that you can then apply to your own study of a familiar community (and before you begin the work of this chapter, you may want to turn to the beginning of Chapter 5—to think about the community you'll choose to study). It also suggests some ways of reading, analyzing, and writing about literary texts that are common in academic settings.

ENTERING THE WORLD OF A SHORT STORY AS A READER

Before you embark on your own research into a familiar community we'll consider how a piece of literature can provide insights into how and why discourse communities work the way they do. Literature typically reflects the experiences of people in the immediate contexts of their lives, drawing on their ways of talking, their ways of thinking, their ways of seeing the world. At the same time, literature invites a reader into the world it portrays, to visit that setting and to experience some of what insiders know or don't know.

Flannery O'Connor's short story, "The River," presents us with characters who represent two quite different communities, including a child who must move between the two, creating his own understanding of their meanings. Because her short story makes specific demands on readers who would try to enter the conversation O'Connor has initiated, it offers an opportunity for extending your repertoire as a reader to include a genre of modern fiction. And because we'll be looking analytically at the ways in which O'Connor's story works, it offers, as well, an opportunity for extending your repertoire as a writer to include the genre of critical analysis. As you think about the fictional communities O'Connor portrays, you'll also be trying out some of the analytical tools that you'll use in studying a real-world community.

Entering "The River" as a Participatory Reader

Unlike the memoir, the literary genre of fiction focuses not on actual events but on possible events within human experience and in human communities. Modern short fiction also typically moves away from both the explicit creation of shared background knowledge for the reader and from explicit statements about the meaning of events that characterize the memoir. Both of these moves affect our participation as readers.

The simplest way for a fiction writer to create shared knowledge with a reader would be to start off by giving all of the necessary background information in the beginning of a story or a novel—describing the situation, the setting and the characters: the who, where, and when (in much the way news reporters are expected to write). But most modern fiction doesn't do that. Instead, writers are more likely to drop readers right into the middle of whatever's going on, without any introduction or explanation, forcing us to be more active in developing an understanding of the story's possible meanings.

Like most contemporary fiction writers, Flannery O'Connor begins her story without offering any background information to tell the reader when and where the story is taking place or what has happened to lead up to the moments she'll describe (nor does she back up later to fill us in). Since we know by now that all conversations, whether actual or implied, whether spoken or written, are shaped not only by what's talked about, but also by, why—by the participants' intentions and purposes—we must assume that O'Connor does have particular intentions in starting this way, intentions that we may come to understand as we read. To understand the sort of conversation this story invites, as well as what it might tell us about discourse communities, you'll have to read it at least twice—once as a participant, and then a second time to look analytically at how the story works. Let's consider first how you might approach the text from a participatory perspective.

In your first reading, you'll enter "The River" as a participant in the conversation that the writer invites, trying to go along with its flow and to fill in any gaps in your understanding by making your best guesses about what's going on. O'Connor intentionally forces us to respond as if we've stepped into a conversation that's already in progress—a conversation about people and events we know nothing about, and one for which we lack necessary shared knowledge.

The opening section of "The River" introduces two of the main characters of the story—the father and the babysitter—and begins to characterize them through what they say and the objects they value. It also introduces the child who is shoved out of the door of one world and into another. Although it doesn't provide a lot of background information, it does create some beginning shared knowledge that you can build on as you go along.

You'll find that your understanding of what's happening gradually builds, even though much remains implied rather than stated in the story. For the reader in a participatory reading, you have to let the story do the talking, keeping up with it as best you can and trying to fill in the gaps in your understanding as you read. As you continue your participatory reading, let yourself be pulled into the story, doing your best to make sense of it, and don't worry too much about any moments of confusion—just go along with the story and let yourself be part of the experience.

READING RESPONSE

Read through "The River" in one sitting, trying to get an overall sense of the conversation you've stepped into, of the story you're being told. Mark places where you have questions or experience gaps in your understanding and make a few quick notes about what you're thinking, but keep going with the flow of the story without really stopping to try to work out answers at this point.

When you reach the end, write an informal journal response in which you try to capture the first impressions you've had of "The River" as a participant reader. Look at the places you marked, the quick notes you made, and try to recount what happened for you as you proceeded through the text. How did your reading lead to certain impressions or insights? What parts of the text were most intriguing? Which were confusing or unclear? What questions do you have? Try to capture as much as possible the experience of reading the story for the first time.

The River

Flannery O'Connor

1   The child stood glum and limp in the middle of the dark living room while his father pulled him into a plaid coat. His right arm was hung in the sleeve but the father buttoned the coat anyway and pushed him forward toward a pale spotted hand that stuck through the half-open door.

"He ain't fixed right," a loud voice said from the hall.

"Well then for Christ's sake fix him," the father muttered.

"It's six o'clock in the morning." He was in his bathrobe and barefooted. When he got the child to the door and tried to shut it, he found her looming in it, a speckled skeleton in a long pea-green coat and felt helmet.

5   "And his and my carfare," she said. "It'll be twict we have to ride the car."

He went in the bedroom again to get the money and when he came back, she and the boy were both standing in the middle of the room. She was taking stock. "I couldn't smell those dead cigarette butts long if I was ever to come sit with you," she said, shaking him down in his coat.

"Here's the change," the father said. He went to the door and opened it wide and waited.

After she had counted the money she slipped it somewhere inside her coat and walked over to a watercolor hanging near the phonograph. "I know what time it is," she said, peering closely at the black lines crossing into broken planes of violent color. "I ought to. My shift goes on at 10 p.m. and don't get off till 5 and it takes me one hour to ride the Vine Street car."

"Oh, I see," he said; "well, we'll expect him back tonight, about eight or nine?"

10   "Maybe later," she said. "We're going to the river to a healing. This particular preacher don't get around this way often. I wouldn't have paid for that," she said, nodding at the painting, "I would have drew it myself."

"All right, Mrs. Connin, we'll see you then," he said, drumming on the door.

A toneless voice called from the bedroom, "Bring me an icepack."

"Too bad his mamma's sick," Mrs. Connin said. "What's her trouble?"

"We don't know," he muttered.

15   "We'll ask the preacher to pray for her. He's healed a lot of folks. The Reverend Bevel Summers. Maybe she ought to see him sometime."

"Maybe so," he said. "We'll see you tonight," and he disappeared into the bedroom and left them to go.

The little boy stared at her silently, his nose and eyes running. He was four or five. He had a long face and bulging chin and half-shut eyes set far apart. He seemed mute and patient, like an old sheep waiting to be let out.

"You'll like this preacher," she said. "The Reverend Bevel Summers. You ought to hear him sing."

The bedroom door opened suddenly and the father stuck his head out and said, "Good-by, old man. Have a good time."

20   "Good-by," the little boy said and jumped as if he had been shot.

Mrs. Connin gave the watercolor another look. Then they went out into the hall and rang for the elevator. "I wouldn't have drew it," she said.

Outside the gray morning was blocked off on either side by the unlit empty buildings. "It's going to fair up later," she said, "but this is the last time we'll be able to have any preaching at the river this year. Wipe your nose, Sugar Boy."

He began rubbing his sleeve across it but she stopped him. "That ain't nice," she said. "Where's your handkerchief?"

He put his hands in his pockets and pretended to look for it while she waited. "Some people don't care how they send one off," she murmured to her reflection in the coffee shop window. "You pervide." She took a red and blue flowered handkerchief out of her pocket and stooped down and began to work on his nose. "Now blow," she said and he blew. "You can borry it. Put it in your pocket."

25 He folded it up and put it in his pocket carefully and they walked on to the corner and leaned against the side of a closed drugstore to wait for the car. Mrs. Connin turned up her coat collar so that it met her hat in the back. Her eyelids began to droop and she looked as if she might go to sleep against the wall. The little boy put a slight pressure on her hand.

"What's your name?" she asked in a drowsy voice. "I don't know but only your last name. I should have found out your first name."

His name was Harry Ashfield and he had never thought at any time before of changing it. "Bevel," he said.

Mrs. Connin raised herself from the wall. "Why ain't that a coincident!" she said. "I told you that's the name of this preacher!"

"Bevel," he repeated.

30 She stood looking down at him as if he had become a marvel to her. "I'll have to see you meet him today," she said. "He's no ordinary preacher. He's a healer. He couldn't do nothing for Mr. Connin though. Mr. Connin didn't have the faith but he said he would try anything once. He had this griping in his gut."

The trolley appeared as a yellow spot at the end of the deserted street.

"He's gone to the government hospital now," she said, "and they taken one-third of his stomach. I tell him he better thank Jesus for what he's got left but he says he ain't thanking nobody. Well I declare," she murmured, "Bevel!"

They walked out to the tracks to wait. "Will he heal me?" Bevel asked.

"What you got?"

35 "I'm hungry," he decided finally.

"Didn't you have your breakfast?"

"I didn't have time to be hungry yet then," he said.

"Well when we get home we'll both have us something," she said. "I'm ready myself."

They got on the car and sat down a few seats behind the driver and Mrs. Connin took Bevel on her knees. "Now you be a good boy," she said, "and let me get some sleep. Just don't get off my lap." She lay her head back and as he watched, gradually her eyes closed and her mouth fell open to show a few long scattered teeth, some gold and some darker than her face; she began to whistle and blow like a musical skeleton. There was no one in the car but themselves and the driver and when he saw she was asleep, he took out the flowered handkerchief and unfolded it and examined it carefully. Then he folded it up again and unzipped a place in the innerlining of his coat and hid it in there and shortly he went to sleep himself.

40   Her house was a half-mile from the end of the car line, set back a little from the road. It was tan paper brick with a porch across the front of it and a tin top. On the porch there were three little boys of different sizes with identical speckled faces and one tall girl who had her hair up in so many aluminum curlers that it glared like the roof. The three boys followed them inside and closed in on Bevel. They looked at him silently, not smiling.

"That's Bevel," Mrs. Connin said, taking off her coat. "It's a coincident he's named the same as the preacher. These boys are J. C., Spivey, and Sinclair, and that's Sarah Mildred on the porch. Take off that coat and hang it on the bed post, Bevel."

The three boys watched him while he unbuttoned the coat and took it off. Then they watched him hang it on the bed post and then they stood, watching the coat. They turned abruptly and went out the door and had a conference on the porch.

Bevel stood looking around him at the room. It was part kitchen and part bedroom. The entire house was two rooms and two porches. Close to his foot the tail of a light-colored dog moved up and down between two floor boards as he scratched his back on the underside of the house. Bevel jumped on it but the hound was experienced and had already withdrawn when his feet hit the spot.

The walls were filled with pictures and calendars. There were two round photographs of an old man and woman with collapsed mouths and another picture of a man whose eyebrows dashed out of two bushes of hair and clashed in a heap on the bridge of his nose; the rest of his face stuck out like a bare cliff to fall from. "That's Mr. Connin," Mrs. Connin said, standing back from the stove for a second to admire the face with him, "but it don't favor him any more." Bevel turned from Mr. Connin to a colored picture over the bed of a man wearing a white sheet. He had long hair and a gold circle around his head and he was sawing on a board while some children stood watching him. He was going to ask who that was when the three boys came in again and motioned for him to follow them. He thought of crawling under the bed and hanging onto one of the legs but the three boys only stood there, speckled and silent, waiting, and after a second he followed them at a little distance out on the porch and around the corner of the house. They started off through a field of rough yellow weeds to the hog pen, a five-foot boarded square full of shoats, which they intended to ease him over into. When they reached it, they turned and waited silently, leaning against the side.

45   He was coming very slowly, deliberately bumping his feet together as if he had trouble walking. Once he had been beaten up in the park by some strange boys when his sitter forgot him, but he hadn't known anything was going to happen that time until it was over. He began to smell a strong odor of garbage and to hear the noises of a wild animal. He stopped a few feet from the pen and waited, pale but dogged.

The three boys didn't move. Something seemed to have happened to them. They stared over his head as if they saw something coming behind him but he was afraid to turn his own head and look. Their speckles were pale and their eyes were still and gray as glass. Only their ears twitched slightly. Nothing happened. Finally, the one in the middle said, "She'd kill us," and turned, dejected and hacked, and climbed up on the pen and hung over, staring in.

Bevel sat down on the ground, dazed with relief, and grinned up at them.

The one sitting on the pen glanced at him severely. "Hey you," he said after a second, "if you can't climb up and see these pigs you can lift that bottom board off and look in thataway." He appeared to offer this as a kindness.

Bevel had never seen a real pig but he had seen a pig in a book and knew they were small fat pink animals with curly tails and round grinning faces and bow ties. He leaned forward and pulled eagerly at the board.

50   "Pull harder," the littlest boy said. "It's nice and rotten. Just lift out thet nail."

He eased a long reddish nail out of the soft wood.

"Now you can lift up the board and put your face to the . . . " a quiet voice began.

He had already done it and another face, gray, wet and sour, was pushing into his, knocking him down and back as it scraped out under the plank. Something snorted over him and charged back again, rolling him over and pushing him up from behind and then sending him forward, screaming through the yellow field, while it bounded behind.

The three Connins watched from where they were. The one sitting on the pen held the loose board back with his dangling foot. Their stern faces didn't brighten any but they seemed to become less taut, as if some great need had been partly satisfied. "Maw ain't going to like him lettin out thet hawg," the smallest one said.

55   Mrs. Connin was on the back porch and caught Bevel up as he reached the steps. The hog ran under the house and subsided, panting, but the child screamed for five minutes. When she had finally calmed him down, she gave him his breakfast and let him sit on her lap while he ate it. The shoat climbed the two steps onto the back porch and stood outside the screen door, looking in with his head lowered sullenly. He was long-legged and hump-backed and part of one of his ears had been bitten off.

"Git away!" Mrs. Connin shouted. "That one yonder favors Mr. Paradise that has the gas station," she said. "You'll see him today at the healing. He's got the cancer over his ear. He always comes to show he ain't been healed."

The shoat stood squinting a few seconds longer and then moved off slowly. "I don't want to see him," Bevel said.

* * *

They walked to the river, Mrs. Connin in front with him and the three boys strung out behind and Sarah Mildred, the tall girl, at the end to holler if one of them ran out on the road. They looked like the skeleton of an old boat with two pointed ends, sailing slowly on the edge of the highway. The white Sunday sun followed at a little distance, climbing fast through a scum of gray cloud as if it meant to overtake them. Bevel walked on the outside edge, holding Mrs. Connin's hand and looking down into the orange and purple gulley that dropped off from the concrete.

It occurred to him that he was lucky this time that they had found Mrs. Connin who would take you away for the day instead of an ordinary sitter who only sat where you lived or went to the park. You found out more when you left where you lived. He had found out already this morning that he had been made by a carpenter named Jesus Christ. Before he had thought it had been a doctor named Sladewall, a fat man with a yellow mustache who gave him shots and thought his name was Herbert, but this must have been a joke. They joked a lot where he lived. If he had thought about it before, he would have thought Jesus Christ was a word like "oh" or "damm" or "God," or maybe somebody who had cheated them out of something sometime. When he had asked Mrs. Connin who the man in the sheet in the picture over her bed was, she had looked at him a while with her mouth open. Then she had said, "That's Jesus," and she had kept on looking at him.

60   In a few minutes she had got up and got a book out of the other room. "See here," she said, turning over the cover, "this belonged to my great grandmamma. I wouldn't part with it for nothing on earth." She ran her finger under some brown writing on a spotted page. "Emma Stevens Oakley, 1832," she said. "Ain't that something to have? And every word of it the gospel truth." She turned the next page and read him the name: "The Life of Jesus Christ for Readers Under Twelve." Then she read him the book.

It was a small book, pale brown on the outside with gold edges and a smell like old putty. It was full of pictures, one of the carpenter driving a crowd of pigs out of a man. They were real pigs, gray and sour-looking, and Mrs. Connin said Jesus had driven them all out of this one man. When she finished reading, she let him sit on the floor and look at the pictures again.

Just before they left for the healing, he had managed to get the book inside his innerlining without her seeing him. Now it made his coat hang down a little farther on one side than the other. His mind was dreamy and serene as they walked along and when they turned off the highway onto a long red clay road winding between banks of honeysuckle, he began to make wild leaps and pull forward on her hand as if he wanted to dash off and snatch the sun which was rolling away ahead of them now.

They walked on the dirt road for a while and then they crossed a field stippled with purple weeds and entered the shadows of a wood where the ground was covered with thick pine needles. He had never been in woods before and he walked carefully, looking from side to side as if he were entering a strange country. They moved along a bridle path that twisted downhill through crackling red leaves, and once, catching at a branch to keep himself from slipping, he looked into two frozen green-gold eyes enclosed in the darkness of a tree hole. At the bottom of the hill, the woods opened suddenly onto a pasture dotted here and there with black and white cows and sloping down, tier after tier, to a broad orange stream where the reflection of the sun was set like a diamond.

There were people standing on the near bank in a group, singing. Long tables were set up behind them and a few cars and trucks were parked in a road that came up by the river. They crossed the pasture, hurrying, because Mrs. Connin, using her hand for a shed over her eyes, saw the preacher already standing out in the water. She dropped her basket on one of the tables and pushed the three boys in front of her into the knot of people so that they wouldn't linger by the food. She kept Bevel by the hand and eased her way up to the front.

65   The preacher was standing about ten feet out in the stream where the water came up to his knees. He was a tall youth in khaki trousers that he had rolled up higher than the water. He had on a blue shirt and a red scarf around his neck but no

hat and his light-colored hair was cut in sideburns that curved into the hollows of his cheeks. His face was all bone and red light reflected from the river. He looked as if he might have been nineteen years old. He was singing in a high twangy voice, above the singing on the bank, and he kept his hands behind him and his head tilted back.

He ended the hymn on a high note and stood silent, looking down at the water and shifting his feet in it. Then he looked up at the people on the bank. They stood close together, waiting; their faces were solemn but expectant and every eye was on him. He shifted his feet again.

"Maybe I know why you come," he said in the twangy voice, "maybe I don't."

"If you ain't come for Jesus, you ain't come for me. If you just come to see can you leave your pain in the river, you ain't come for Jesus. You can't leave your pain in the river," he said. "I never told nobody that." He stopped and looked down at his knees.

"I seen you cure a woman oncet!" a sudden high voice shouted from the hump of people. "Seen that woman git up and walk out straight where she had limped in!"

70 The preacher lifted one foot and then the other. He seemed almost but not quite to smile. "You might as well go home if that's what you come for," he said.

Then he lifted his head and arms and shouted, "Listen to what I got to say, you people! There ain't but one river and that's the River of Life, made out of Jesus' Blood. That's the river you have to lay your pain in, in the River of Faith, in the River of Life, in the River of Love, in the rich red river of Jesus' Blood, you people!"

His voice grew soft and musical. "All the rivers come from that one River and go back to it like it was the ocean sea and if you believe, you can lay your pain in that River and get rid of it because that's the River that was made to carry sin. It's a River full of pain itself, pain itself, moving toward the Kingdom of Christ, to be washed away, slow, you people, slow as this here old red water river round my feet."

"Listen," he sang, "I read in Mark about an unclean man, I read in Luke about a blind man, I read in John about a dead man! Oh you people hear! The same blood that makes this River red, made that leper clean, made that blind man stare, made that dead man leap! You people with trouble," he cried, "lay it in that River of Blood, lay it in that River of Pain, and watch it move away toward the Kingdom of Christ."

While he preached, Bevel's eyes followed drowsily the slow circles of two silent birds revolving high in the air. Across the river there was a low red and gold grove of sassafras with hills of dark blue trees behind it and an occasional pine jutting over the skyline. Behind, in the distance, the city rose like a cluster of warts on the side of the mountain. The birds revolved downward and dropped lightly in the top of the highest pine and sat hunch-shouldered as if they were supporting the sky.

75 "If it's this River of Life you want to lay your pain in, then come up," the preacher said, "and lay your sorrow here. But don't be thinking this is the last of it because this old red river don't end here. This old red suffering stream goes on, you people, slow to the Kingdom of Christ. This old red river is good to Baptize in, good to lay your faith in, good to lay your pain in, but it ain't this muddy water here that saves you. I been all up and down this river this week," he said. "Tuesday I was in Fortune Lake, next day in Ideal, Friday me and my wife drove to Lulawillow to see a sick man there. Them people didn't see no healing," he said and his face burned redder for a second. "I never said they would."

While he was talking a fluttering figure had begun to move forward with a kind of butterfly movement—an old woman with flapping arms whose head wobbled as if it might fall off any second. She managed to lower herself at the edge of the bank and let her arms churn in the water. Then she bent farther and pushed her face down in it and raised herself up finally, streaming wet; and still flapping, she turned a time or two in a blind circle until someone reached out and pulled her back into the group.

"She's been that way for thirteen years," a rough voice shouted. "Pass the hat and give this kid his money. That's what he's here for." The shout, directed out to the boy in the river, came from a huge old man who sat like a humped stone on the bumper of a long ancient gray automobile. He had on a gray hat that was turned down over one ear and up over the other to expose a purple bulge on his left temple. He sat bent forward with his hands hanging between his knees and his small eyes half closed.

Bevel stared at him once and then moved into the folds of Mrs. Connin's coat and hid himself.

The boy in the river glanced at the old man quickly and raised his fist. "Believe Jesus or the devil!" he cried. "Testify to one or the other!"

80   "I know from my own self-experience," a woman's mysterious voice called from the knot of people, "I know from it that this preacher can heal. My eyes have been opened! I testify to Jesus!"

The preacher lifted his arms quickly and began to repeat all that he had said before about the River and the Kingdom of Christ and the old man sat on the bumper, fixing him with a narrow squint. From time to time Bevel stared at him again from around Mrs. Connin.

A man in overalls and a brown coat leaned forward and dipped his hand in the water quickly and shook it and leaned back, and a woman held a baby over the edge of the bank and splashed its feet with water. One man moved a little distance away and sat down on the bank and took off his shoes and waded out into the stream; he stood there for a few minutes with his face tilted as far back as it would go, then he waded back and put on his shoes. All this time, the preacher sang and did not appear to watch what went on.

As soon as he stopped singing, Mrs. Connin lifted Bevel up and said, "Listen here, preacher, I got a boy from town today that I'm keeping. His mamma's sick and he wants you to pray for her. And this is a coincident—his name is Bevel! Bevel," she said, turning to look at the people behind her, "same as his. Ain't that a coincident, though?"

There were some murmurs and Bevel turned and grinned over her shoulder at the faces looking at him. "Bevel," he said in a loud jaunty voice.

85   "Listen," Mrs. Connin said, "have you ever been Baptized, Bevel?"

He only grinned.

"I suspect he ain't ever been Baptized," Mrs. Connin said, raising her eyebrows at the preacher.

"Swang him over here," the preacher said and took a stride forward and caught him.

He held him in the crook of his arm and looked at the grinning face. Bevel rolled his eyes in a comical way and thrust his face forward, close to the preacher's. "My name is Bevvvuuuuul," he said in a loud deep voice and let the tip of his tongue slide across his mouth.

90   The preacher didn't smile. His bony face was rigid and his narrow gray eyes reflected the almost colorless sky. There was a loud laugh from the old man sitting on the car bumper and Bevel grasped the back of the preacher's collar and held it tightly. The grin had already disappeared from his face. He had the sudden feeling that this was not a joke. Where he lived everything was a joke. From the preacher's face, he knew immediately that nothing the preacher said or did was a joke. "My mother named me that," he said quickly.

"Have you ever been Baptized?" the preacher asked.

"What's that?" he murmured.

"If I Baptize you," the preacher said, "you'll be able to go to the Kingdom of Christ. You'll be washed in the river of suffering, son, and you'll go by the deep river of life. Do you want that?"

"Yes," the child said, and thought, I won't go back to the apartment then, I'll go under the river.

95   "You won't be the same again," the preacher said. "You'll count." Then he turned his face to the people and began to preach and Bevel looked over his shoulder at the pieces of the white sun scattered in the river. Suddenly the preacher said, "All right, I'm going to Baptize you now," and without more warning, he tightened his hold and swung him upside down and plunged his head into the water. He held him under while he said the words of Baptism and then he jerked him up again and looked sternly at the gasping child. Bevel's eyes were dark and dilated. "You count now," the preacher said. "You didn't even count before."

The little boy was too shocked to cry. He spit out the muddy water and rubbed his wet sleeve into his eyes and over his face.

"Don't forget his mamma," Mrs. Connin called. "He wants you to pray for his mamma. She's sick."

"Lord," the preacher said, "we pray for somebody in affliction who isn't here to testify. Is your mother sick in the hospital?" he asked. "Is she in pain?"

The child stared at him. "She hasn't got up yet," he said in a high dazed voice. "She has a hangover." The air was so quiet he could hear the broken pieces of the sun knocking in the water.

100   The preacher looked angry and startled. The red drained out of his face and the sky appeared to darken in his eyes. There was a loud guffaw from the bank and Mr. Paradise shouted, "Haw! Cure the afflicted woman with the hangover!" and began to beat his knee with his fist.

* * *

"He's had a long day," Mrs. Connin said, standing with him in the door of the apartment and looking sharply into the room where the party was going on. "I reckon it's past his regular bedtime." One of Bevel's eyes was closed and the other half closed; his nose was running and he kept his mouth open and breathed through it. The damp plaid coat dragged down on one side.

That would be her, Mrs. Connin decided, in the black britches—long black satin britches and barefoot sandals and red toenails. She was lying on half the sofa, with her knees crossed in the air and her head propped on the arm. She didn't get up.

"Hello Harry," she said. "Did you have a big day?" She had a long pale face, smooth and blank, and straight sweet-potato-colored hair, pulled back.

The father went off to get the money. There were two other couples. One of the men, blond with little violet-blue eyes, leaned out of his chair and said, "Well Harry, old man, have a big day?"

105   "His name ain't Harry. It's Bevel," Mrs. Connin said.

"His name is Harry," *she* said from the sofa. "Whoever heard of anybody named Bevel?"

The little boy had seemed to be going to sleep on his feet, his head drooping farther and farther forward; he pulled it back suddenly and opened one eye; the other was stuck.

"He told me this morning his name was Bevel," Mrs. Connin said in a shocked voice. "The same as our preacher. We been all day at a preaching and healing at the river. He said his name was Bevel, the same as the preacher's. That's what he told me."

"Bevel!" his mother said. "My God! what a name."

110   "This preacher is name Bevel and there's no better preacher around," Mrs. Connin said. "And furthermore," she added in a defiant tone, "he Baptized this child this morning!"

His mother sat straight up. "Well the nerve!" she muttered. "Furthermore," Mrs. Connin said, "he's a healer and he prayed for you to be healed."

"Healed!" she almost shouted. "Healed of what for Christ's sake?"

"Of your affliction," Mrs. Connin said icily.

The father had returned with the money and was standing near Mrs. Connin waiting to give it to her. His eyes were lined with red threads. "Go on, go on," he said, "I want to hear more about her affliction. The exact nature of it has escaped . . ." He waved the bill and his voice trailed off. "Healing by prayer is mighty inexpensive," he murmured.

115   Mrs. Connin stood a second, staring into the room, with a skeleton's appearance of seeing everything. Then, without taking the money, she turned and shut the door behind her. The father swung around, smiling vaguely, and shrugged. The rest of them were looking at Harry. The little boy began to shamble toward the bedroom.

"Come here, Harry," his mother said. He automatically shifted his direction toward her without opening his eye any farther. "Tell me what happened today," she said when he reached her. She began to pull off his coat.

"I don't know," he muttered.

"Yes you do know," she said, feeling the coat heavier on one side. She unzipped the innerlining and caught the book and a dirty handkerchief as they fell out. "Where did you get these?"

"I don't know," he said and grabbed for them. "They're mine. She gave them to me."

120   She threw the handkerchief down and held the book too high for him to reach and began to read it, her face after a second assuming an exaggerated comical expression. The others moved around and looked at it over her shoulder. "My God," somebody said.

One of the men peered at it sharply from behind a thick pair of glasses. "That's valuable," he said. "That's a collector's item," and he took it away from the rest of them and retired to another chair.

"Don't let George go off with that," his girl said.

"I tell you it's valuable," George said. "1832."

Bevel shifted his direction again toward the room where he slept. He shut the door behind him and moved slowly in the darkness to the bed and sat down and took off his shoes and got under the cover. After a minute a shaft of light let in the tall silhouette of his mother. She tiptoed lightly across the room and sat down on the edge of his bed. "What did that dolt of a preacher say about me?" she whispered. "What lies have you been telling today, honey?"

125   He shut his eye and heard her voice from a long way away, as if he were under the river and she on top of it. She shook his shoulder. "Harry," she said, leaning down and putting her mouth to his ear, "tell me what he said." She pulled him into a sitting position and he felt as if he had been drawn up from under the river. "Tell me," she whispered and her bitter breath covered his face.

He saw the pale oval close to him in the dark. "He said I'm not the same now," he muttered. "I count."

After a second, she lowered him by his shirt front onto the pillow. She hung over him an instant and brushed her lips against his forehead. Then she got up and moved away, swaying her hips lightly through the shaft of light.

* * *

He didn't wake up early but the apartment was still dark and close when he did. For a while he lay there, picking his nose and eyes. Then he sat up in bed and looked out the window. The sun came in palely, stained gray by the glass. Across the street at the Empire Hotel, a colored cleaning woman was looking down from an upper window, resting her face on her folded arms. He got up and put on his shoes and went to the bathroom and then into the front room. He ate two crackers spread with anchovy paste, that he found on the coffee table, and drank some ginger ale left in a bottle and looked around for his book but it was not there.

The apartment was silent except for the faint humming of the refrigerator. He went into the kitchen and found some raisin bread heels and spread a half jar of peanut butter between them and climbed up on the tall kitchen stool and sat chewing the sandwich slowly, wiping his nose every now and then on his shoulder. When he finished he found some chocolate milk and drank that. He would rather have had the ginger ale he saw but they left the bottle openers where he couldn't reach them. He studied what was left in the refrigerator for a while—some shriveled vegetables that she had forgot were there and a lot of brown oranges that she bought and didn't squeeze; there were three or four kinds of cheese and something fishy in a paper bag; the rest was a pork bone. He left the refrigerator door open and wandered back into the dark living room and sat down on the sofa.

130   He decided they would be out cold until one o'clock and that they would all have to go to a restaurant for lunch. He wasn't high enough for the table yet and the waiter would bring a highchair and he was too big for a highchair. He sat in the middle of the sofa, kicking it with his heels. Then he got up and wandered around the room, looking into the ashtrays at the butts as if this might be a habit. In his own room he had picture books and blocks but they were for the most part torn up; he found the

way to get new ones was to tear up the ones he had. There was very little to do at any time but eat; however, he was not a fat boy.

He decided he would empty a few of the ashtrays on the floor. If he only emptied a few, she would think they had fallen. He emptied two, rubbing the ashes carefully into the rug with his finger. Then he lay on the floor for a while, studying his feet which he held up in the air. His shoes were still damp and he began to think about the river.

Very slowly, his expression changed as if he were gradually seeing appear what he didn't know he'd been looking for. Then all of a sudden he knew what he wanted to do.

He got up and tiptoed into their bedroom and stood in the dim light there, looking for her pocketbook. His glance passed her long pale arm hanging off the edge of the bed down to the floor, and across the white mound his father made, and past the crowded bureau, until it rested on the pocketbook hung on the back of a chair. He took a car-token out of it and half a package of Life Savers. Then he left the apartment and caught the car at the corner. He hadn't taken a suitcase because there was nothing from there he wanted to keep.

He got off the car at the end of the line and started down the road he and Mrs. Connin had taken the day before. He knew there wouldn't be anybody at her house because the three boys and the girl went to school and Mrs. Connin had told him she went out to clean. He passed her yard and walked on the way they had gone to the river. The paper brick houses were far apart and after a while the dirt place to walk on ended and he had to walk on the edge of the highway. The sun was pale yellow and high and hot.

135   He passed a shack with an orange gas pump in front of it but he didn't see the old man looking out at nothing in particular from the doorway. Mr. Paradise was having an orange drink. He finished it slowly, squinting over the bottle at the small plaid-coated figure disappearing down the road. Then he set the empty bottle on a bench and, still squinting, wiped his sleeve over his mouth. He went in the shack and picked out a peppermint stick, a foot long and two inches thick, from the candy shelf, and stuck it in his hip pocket. Then he got in his car and drove slowly down the highway after the boy.

By the time Bevel came to the field speckled with purple weeds, he was dusty and sweating and he crossed it at a trot to get into the woods as fast as he could. Once inside, he wandered from tree to tree, trying to find the path they had taken yesterday. Finally he found a line worn in the pine needles and followed it until he saw the steep trail twisting down through the trees.

Mr. Paradise had left his automobile back some way on the road and had walked to the place where he was accustomed to sit almost every day, holding an unbaited fishline in the water while he stared at the river passing in front of him. Anyone looking at him from a distance would have seen an old boulder half hidden in the bushes.

Bevel didn't see him at all. He only saw the river, shimmering reddish yellow, and bounded into it with his shoes and his coat on and took a gulp. He swallowed some and spit the rest out and then he stood there in water up to his chest and looked around him. The sky was a clear pale blue, all in one piece—except for the hole the sun made—and fringed around the bottom with treetops. His coat floated to the surface and surrounded him like a strange gay lily pad and he stood grinning in the sun. He intended not to fool with preachers any more but to Baptize himself and to keep on going this time until he found the Kingdom of Christ in the river. He didn't mean to waste any more time. He put his head under the water at once and pushed forward.

In a second he began to gasp and sputter and his head reappeared on the surface; he started under again and the same thing happened. The river wouldn't have him. He tried again and came up, choking. This was the way it had been when the preacher held him under—he had had to fight with something that pushed him back in the face. He stopped and thought suddenly: it's another joke, it's just another joke! He thought how far he had come for nothing and he began to hit and splash and kick the filthy river. His feet were already treading on nothing. He gave one low cry of pain and indignation. Then he heard a shout and turned his head and saw something like a giant pig bounding after him, shaking a red and white club and shouting. He plunged under once and this time, the waiting current caught him like a long gentle hand and pulled him swiftly forward and down. For an instant he was overcome with surprise; then since he was moving quickly and knew that he was getting somewhere, all his fury and his fear left him.

140   Mr. Paradise's head appeared from time to time on the surface of the water. Finally, far downstream, the old man rose like some ancient water monster and stood empty-handed, staring with his dull eyes as far down the river line as he could see.

Reading "The River" Analytically

While a participatory reading is like stepping into a conversation, an analytical reading requires stepping in and out of it. Imagine that, after participating in a conversation, you and a friend stepped outside of the room to have a conversation of your own, where you talked about what you'd gotten from what you had been listening to—about what seemed to be going on, what you still couldn't figure out, and what the words were that led you to see the conversation in this way. At this point, you'd be moving toward a different sort of response—one where you pulled out elements of the conversation and began to analyze them. We move back and forth between participatory and analytical responses all of the time in our daily lives. Sometimes we "go with the flow" of a conversation, without thinking about it too much. Other times we step back and speculate: "I wonder why Jim said that," or "He told me about that earlier. I wonder why he's repeating it." Our first analytical responses are generally an attempt to answer the questions that we have found during our first participatory responses by looking back at what's been said to see what else we can learn.

The way you approach an analytical reading depends in part on what it is that you want to know, and on your purpose for reading. Generally your first purpose as a reader is to figure out what is going on, and what it all means, so that the story begins to make sense. In your writing course, your reading also has a second purpose: to add to your framework of understanding about the topic of discourse communities by entering a fictional world where two contrasting communities are portrayed. A second layer of analysis of "The River" will be aimed at discovering more about those communities and the ways O'Connor represents their words, their ways of seeing the world, and their contrasting beliefs and values. You're also reading as someone who is considering how people read and write in literate discourse communities. So a third layer of analysis will focus on the genre of modern short fiction and some of the ways in which people write and read in that genre.

Reading Analytically for Content and Meaning

The meaning of a text doesn't come exclusively from the words on the page, but rather from the interaction between those words and what we bring to them as readers. Readers who want first to make more sense of what they've read are likely to extend the ways they interact with it, using several strategies:

- *Identifying gaps.* O'Connor's story is difficult to fully understand and appreciate in a first reading because so much is implied rather than stated. In a second, more analytical reading, you can pay particular attention to the places that left gaps in your understanding as you read the first time, seeing whether you can fill in those gaps or, if not, noting those spots to return to again later.

- *Evoking prior knowledge.* O'Connor's story depends on some prior knowledge about the ways of particular communities. While you may not have prior knowledge of what it's like to live in an expensive apartment, give up-scale parties, and collect modern art, or of what it's like to live in a poor rural area, raise your own hogs, and go to healings by a river, you do have some general cultural knowledge about what these experiences might be like from what you've read or heard or seen on TV or in the movies. You can use that prior knowledge to help you make sense of the specific settings and events that O'Connor creates.

- *Looking closely at passages of the text.* Looking more closely at a particular passage can help you begin to answer some of the questions you had as a reader, questions like "what's going on here?" and "why does this young boy do the things he does?" If you focus on a few passages that seem particularly significant or even particularly confusing, you may begin to see how those passages work to shape the meanings of the whole story, and you can test some of those new understandings and insights against the clues of other portions of the text. Because your shared knowledge is being built continuously through your reading of a text, the meanings you gain from looking at earlier passages will also help you to understand later ones.

**READING
RESPONSE**

Return to "The River" for a second, analytical reading. This time, instead of going with the flow of the story, pause frequently to step out of it, annotating it as you go, with the purpose of:

—*Identifying and filling in gaps.* Note where you've found tentative answers to questions and gaps that you identified earlier, identify new questions and uncertainties, and note possible answers;

—*Evoking prior knowledge.* Note places where your hypotheses about these characters and their actions are informed by prior knowledge or assumptions you bring about the worlds represented here;

—*Looking closely at key passages of the text.* Mark a few passages that seem particularly significant to you in helping you shape an understanding of the story or especially puzzling to you as you grapple with an understanding.

When you've finished this reading, write an informal journal response in which you reflect on the understandings you've gained through this second reading. Choose one key passage that you've marked, and (noting its page number) write about the passage in particular: What does it contribute to the story? Why does it seem significant? What puzzles you about it or its place in the story?

ANALYZING DISCOURSE COMMUNITIES IN LITERATURE

"The River" could be read in relationship to a number of different themes and placed in different thematic groupings with other stories—the theme of religious belief or concepts of salvation, for example. Here, each reading has been chosen because it focuses in some way on the theme of discourse communities. How can "The River" contribute to our understanding of discourse communities? And how might the concept of a discourse community enhance our understanding of "The River"?

Members of discourse communities, as we've seen, are likely to share common interests, values, and ways of seeing the world, as well as particular ways of using language. Each of the two communities O'Connor portrays in "The River" can be described in terms of those shared elements. So too, the differences between the two communities can be described in terms not only of their different ways of talking and naming things, but also in terms of opposing values. As we saw in Chapter 3, our social identities are often shaped by a sense of difference from others who may occupy the same physical space—in the way that Mike Rose and his fellow Voc Ed students defined themselves through their difference from students in the college prep track. "The River," in showing us two sharply differentiated discourse communities, also lets us see how much the identities of participants in each community are shaped through contrast with the other. As we consider some aspects of how O'Connor creates her portraits of these two communities, you can begin to see how each of these elements comes into play in the community you've chosen to study. You'll build on these preliminary observations as you carry out your own discourse community research.

The Shared <u>What</u>

In analyzing fictional discourse communities, as in studying an actual one, you can begin to understand more about the community by looking at what people talk about and think about. In fiction, where a writer is selecting what to tell us about the world she has imagined, we can assume that everything in the story has been included because it is significant in some way to the story's possible meanings.

READING RESPONSE	Drawing on the text of the story, make two lists, one for the world associated with the parents and one for the world associated with the babysitter. List all of the important words and phrases that you recall, associated with each community. Then look back at the text of the story to see what other significant words you might want to add. Look at your two lists, and note your first impressions and observations about them.

Let's look first at the words that are associated with each community, representing what people talk about, think about, and value in each of these worlds. If you look at the words and phrases linked to each world, you'll find several aspects of what is named and talked about that are characteristic of the shared knowledge of any discourse community.

■ *Some words appear frequently in association with a community, suggesting some of the community's interests and concerns.* In the opening exchanges in the parents' apartment, you'll notice that Mrs. Connin uses the word "preacher" three times. The watercolor on the parents' wall is mentioned twice, as Mrs. Connin looks at it with disapproval. Throughout "The River" you'll find a number of words that are repeated within key sections of the story or across different moments in the story.

■ *Clusters of words are repeated within or in relationship to a discourse community, suggesting a network of related concerns.* You may have noticed, for example, that the world Harry/Bevel leaves is represented by *ashtrays* and *cigarette butts* and a mother who is *sick* with a *hangover*, while the world he enters is a world where *sin* and *pain* and *affliction* are *healed* with prayer.

■ *Words and objects may have different meanings across discourse communities.* In "The River," the word *Christ* is used differently in the parents' and

Mrs. Connin's worlds. Objects such as Mrs. Connin's book, <u>The Life of Jesus Christ for Readers Under Twelve</u>, can also represent different meanings in these two communities.

- *The same person or idea or object may have different names in different communities.* "Hog" and "shoat," for example, are alternative terms for a pig that are likely to be used by people who raise the animals, and less likely to be used by city folks like the child's parents.

- *Important aspects of shared insider knowledge are understood rather than stated explicitly.* Beyond the words themselves lies a whole world of knowledge that's shared, implicitly, by members of one community and that doesn't have to be named each time (though O'Connor has to let us see what it is). What constitutes insider knowledge in these two communities—the knowledge that can be assumed and doesn't always have to be stated? Insider knowledge in the world of Harry's parents includes knowledge of abstract art, of the value of collector's items. In Mrs. Connin's world, the insider knowledge (that Harry doesn't bring, even though he has changed his name) includes the whole system of meanings associated with a particular form of religion.

  One world "knows" and doesn't have to explain the shared knowledge gained in art museums and antique stores. The other world "knows" and doesn't have to explain the shared knowledge gained in these repeated preachings, healings, and baptisms. It is only when someone comes from outside that what's familiar to insiders is suddenly seen as strange.

- *Both the stated and implied insider knowledge of a community is linked to underlying shared values and beliefs.* Abstract art and collector's items are connected to a set of values associated with a world that values "high culture." Preachers and healings are associated with the practice of a particular style of Christianity, and a belief that Christ can be called on in direct ways to intervene in human experience. These values are seen in opposition at a number of points in the story.

Describe as much as you can about the insider knowledge that is shared by members of the parents' discourse community. Then shift focus and describe the corresponding language and knowledge in the babysitter's community. What values are associated with each community? How does the shared knowledge of each community point to deeper beliefs and understandings?

READING RESPONSE

The Shared <u>How</u>

O'Connor includes actual dialogue only at particular moments in the story, suggesting that wherever the characters speak, there is something significant that we should come to understand from their speaking. As in any community, the ways in which her characters talk and the styles of language they use, give us further clues to who they are and what they value.

READING RESPONSE   Turn to the places where there is dialogue in the story to see what you can observe about the ways the characters talk: about the styles of language they use and the connections between ways they talk and the roles they play. What do these observations add to the picture you've been developing of the differences between these two communities?

The ways of talking in "The River" suggest some important elements of talk in all discourse communities:

- *Participants in a discourse community use particular varieties or styles of English.* In the opening paragraph of "The River," we find words representing the different varieties of English associated with the different social classes that coexist in the white southern town where the story is set. For example, "He ain't fixed right," introduces the world of the white, freckled ("speckled") baby-sitter, who is immediately placed in a lower social class through her use of the nonstandard *ain't*, while the few words spoken by the boy's father at the beginning seem to represent a variety of standard English that would be spoken by educated, urban Southerners. Such distinctions continue throughout the story.

- *They talk in ways that are associated with specific roles.* Participants always have particular roles that they play in the exchanges of any discourse community. In "The River," Mrs. Connin plays the role of a parent/caretaker/concerned adult to Harry's innocent child, but she plays a somewhat different role in the larger, public gathering by the river, one that affects how she presents herself and the child. The preacher is playing the role of a preacher, speaking not as an individual, but in the metaphorical terms and the associated gestures and rituals that are common to many Christian religious practices. Indeed, there's enough of a common text for baptisms that this preacher's words to Bevel are an echo of those that might be spoken by any number of preachers in any number of settings.

- *They draw on a discourse community's genres.* We can see that within each of the two discourse communities, there are some larger patterns of talking and communicating, with particular names for those ways—for those genres. *Baptisms* and *healings* represent formal genres of talk with their own form and shape and style that are repeated in very similar ways from one of these events to another. The preacher knows how to carry out a good healing with his words as well as his actions. In the parent's world, it seems that nothing is taken seriously, and everything is a *joke*.

- *They know how and when to speak literally or metaphorically and know how to interpret the words of others.* The boy enters a world where "he knew immediately that nothing the preacher said or did was a joke"—the world of "gospel truth." But that does not mean that every statement is to be taken literally. All communities, even those that think of themselves as always speaking "the gospel truth," have ways of moving away from literal statements to other implied meanings. Harry/Bevel, because he is not an insider, has a hard time interpreting the ways that others talk in this new community.

■ *Their shared ways of talking are connected to shared values with a community.* Within the story, familiar ways of talking and interacting help to create and affirm the identity and values of the participants in each discourse community. The believers who gather by the river value ways of talking that point beyond the daily experience of people like Mrs. Connin— working the 9 P.M. to 5 A.M. shift and riding the streetcar for an hour to get home—to another level of meaning where pain will be carried away through faith. For the parents, the idea that everything is a joke, may suggest a distanced, ironic stance towards life, where there's value in not being too strongly committed to any particular position or set of values.

In a journal response, follow out, in detail, the ways in which one of these aspects of the ways in which people talk is important to your understanding of the story. Or read the following commentary by a student on the importance of the difference between literal and metaphorical meaning in "The River" and see what it contributes to your own understanding:

> Children always take things literally even though we may not mean something in the way we say it. When Bevel went to the river and heard the preacher talking about the river as being a way to the kingdom of Christ and that if he got baptized he would be able to go to the kingdom of Christ, he didn't take it metaphorically. Instead he believed that it was literally a way to get to a new place and to a new community where he would feel more comfortable and that he wouldn't have to go back to the apartment but instead he would go under the river to the Kingdom of Christ. Even though the preacher wasn't giving the listeners that kind of impression and the adults understood what the preacher was trying to say, Bevel took everything differently and took matters into his own hands. Bevel didn't want to fool with preachers anymore and decided to baptize himself until he found the kingdom of Christ, which he believed was in the river.
> **(Laysian)**

What other examples can you find to support this idea? Does this commentary help you to better understand the story? How would this line of reasoning help to interpret the ending of the story? Write a response to this comment, offering your own perspectives on how literal and metaphorical meanings are contrasted in "The River."

STUDENT VOICES

Understanding Why

Much of what makes "The River" confusing in a first reading is our uncertainty about the intentions that lie behind the words the characters speak and the actions they carry out. Is Mrs. Connin a "misguided fanatic" who wants to bring another soul to salvation, even if it's a child with no real understanding of what's happening to him? Or is she "a woman of faith" who believed that if she took this little boy to the preacher down at the river, that the preacher would be able to help him? Are the parents disinterested in their child, and mostly concerned with getting him out of the way? Why does Harry/Bevel lie and steal for no apparent reason? Think about your own questions and assumptions about the characters' intentions.

Some possible answers to such questions can be found by considering the ways in which intentions and purposes are represented in discourse communities.

- Intentions and purposes may sometimes be directly stated or they may be implied through peoples' actions.

  When Mrs. Connin pulls out her handkerchief to give to the boy, her actions speak as loudly as the words she says to herself, "You per-vide" [provide]. Later, when her sons stare at the boy and beckon to him that he should follow them into the yard, he knows from the way they look and the way they stand that they intend to cause him trouble, even though they say nothing.

- People are often trying to achieve multiple intentions and purposes with any one statement or action.

  One of the preacher's purposes with his preaching, for example, is likely to be to convince his listeners of the importance of faith and to confirm the value of the faith they have. Another may be to draw in his listeners with the power of his preaching (building his reputation as a preacher who has brought these listeners to the river). But he's not likely to intend that anyone should actually jump in and flow with the river through death and into paradise. Other characters, in any moment of their actions, are likely to have multiple purposes as well.

- Intentions and purposes, whether shown through words or actions, are typically framed in relationship to the shared values and ways of being of a discourse community.

  The father's immediate purposes as he pushes the boy towards the babysitter and then, in an afterthought, sticks his head out of the bed-room door saying, "Goodbye, old man," may be clear enough, but his larger intentions towards the child need to be seen in the context of everything that's shown about the parents. Likewise Mrs. Connin's purposes when she lifts the boy up towards the preacher are easier to imagine in the context of what's shown throughout the story about her beliefs and values.

As they wonder about <u>why</u> the characters act as they do in this story, readers tend to be concerned above all with the child's purposes at the end. Here are some questions that three other readers have had about the story's ending: (1) "I didn't understand why Harry wanted to die. The story confused me and I only understood that we were looking at a sad world through Harry's eyes." (2) "Is it possible he attempted to escape (at such a young age) who he really was—his mother, father, home life? The river brought him to Christ, to free-dom, to another place." (3) "Bevel 'knew that he was getting somewhere, all his fury and fear left him' (p. 185). Did he mean to die? Or is he up to the last mo-ment convinced he is going to some kingdom? Is the solution that only by dy-ing he will supposedly get there?"

The boy is shown as not fitting so simply within either discourse commu-nity, and his purposes aren't so simply defined by the values and beliefs of ei-ther, though his actions are shaped to some degree by what he understands of both. In his final actions, we're told directly what his intentions are: "He in-tended not to fool with preachers any more but to Baptize himself. . . . He didn't mean to waste any more time." But since those intentions exist against a background of his inability to interpret the preacher's words, they offer us little certainty about what he's really trying to achieve.

These questions about the characters' purposes lead to larger questions about the writer's purpose as well. O'Connor has created this story in which the characters have these interests and concerns, these ways of talking, these often ambiguous intentions and purposes. But why? What are her intentions with what she has and hasn't told us? What is the background of shared values and understandings and shared ways that can help us to interpret the mean-ings of her work? How can we move beyond the response of the reader who wrote: "Honestly, I don't think I understood the point of the story."

REFLECTING ON YOUR PRIOR KNOWLEDGE ABOUT LITERATURE

Flannery O'Connor, in choosing to write within the genre of the modern short story, is drawing on the familiar elements of that genre. Our primary purpose as readers has been to add to an understanding of discourse communities and the shared values represented within them, not to study the short story as you might in a literature class with the purpose of using the story to contribute to your un-derstanding of literature and how literary genres work. But you can understand more about the story by reading against the background of your knowledge about literature, drawing on your prior experience and some shared concepts. If you were asked to analyze a piece of literary fiction as literature, you might, for example, look at the story in terms of *setting*, seeing all of the details of time and place that are presented and how those details contribute to an understanding of the worlds in which the action of the story takes place. Or you might focus in on the details that help to create your sense of each *character*, from the moment when the father first appears in his bathrobe and greets the babysitter—"a loom-ing skeleton in a long pea green coat," and including much of what we've seen about the ways in which each character talks and acts throughout the story.

The writing of a literary work is also located in a particular context—a particular time and place with particular questions and concerns. Much mod-ern fiction implicitly asks the question: How do we really know what's true? How much can we rely on the perceptions and the "truth" of anyone else and, by implication, how do we know that our own understanding of the world is the "right" one? Writers of modern fiction often explore this question by showing us the world from the perspective of a particular character, letting us see the degree to which that perspective is limited—the ways in which the character doesn't understand or take into account everything that we as readers might think he or she should, but also the ways in which we feel our own understanding to be limited by the limitations in the character's perceptions. The field of literary studies has developed a useful concept for getting at this problem: *point of view*. The concept of "point of view" helps readers to answer two questions: "Whose meaning is it?" and "Can I trust that character's understanding?"

The memoirs we read in Part I consistently present events in the writer's voice (present or past), from the writer's first person perspective ("Quickly I turned to see my mother's face dissolve in a watery blur behind the pebbled glass door") and from the writer's point of view. When we read those memoirs, we always know who is speaking and whose version of events we're getting. In fiction, however, the author can choose to tell the story from a number of different perspectives. If the story is told in the first person, we are getting the perspective of the fictional narrator (not the author), but when the story is told in the third person, we have to look harder to see whose perspective we're getting.

In reading "The River," much of the trouble we have in understanding the purposes of characters has to do with this problem of the perspective or point of view from which we, as readers, are seeing places and events. To a great extent, in this story, we seem to be limited to how the world appears from the child's perspective. Sometimes we see what's happening from within his consciousness, with phrases that directly indicate his own uncertainty. For example, when Mrs. Connin's son suggests pulling the board off the pigpen, "he *appeared* to offer this as a kindness." Then the boys' faces "*seemed* to become less taut, as if some great need had been partly satisfied."

At other times, though we don't get any indication of what the child is thinking, we still seem to be standing in his shoes, seeing only what he can see: "The preacher was standing about ten feet out in the stream where the water came up to his knees." We also observe the boy himself: "Bevel rolled his eyes in a comical way and thrust his face close to the preacher's." But the focus is always on him—on what he does, on what he sees, and what he thinks—and through most of the story we understand the world only from Bevel's perspective.

Nevertheless, the subtle shifts in the point of view that O'Connor offers, from seeing what Harry/Bevel sees or does to knowing what he thinks, are significant in the story. By looking at where in the story our position as readers shifts from being outside of his head—observing him or what he observes—to inside his head and reading his thoughts, we can understand still more about the meaning he's making from the events going on around him, about what his own intentions might be in the actions he initiates, and about what the significance of his limited understanding might be in the context of the larger story and the worlds it portrays.

Return to "The River" to explore the way in which one aspect of the story as a literary genre contributes to its meaning, looking closely at the text of the story.

Setting. What's the larger setting in which the story takes place and what in the text tells you that? Where in the story does O'Connor give details about setting, what are those details, and why are they significant in relationship to the larger possible meanings of the story?

Character. Choose a character and look in detail at the ways in which O'Connor has portrayed that character through the way the character looks, talks, acts, etc. How do these details help to "characterize" the person you've chosen? What function does this character seem to have in the larger story, and how do the characterizing details contribute to the ways he/she functions and to his/her place in shaping the story's possible meanings?

Point of View. Look closely at a section of the story that you feel is important to your understanding of the whole story. What do you observe about the ways in which the story is narrated in that section? Where are you as a reader positioned from moment to moment in that section? How does that positioning affect the understandings you gain about what is going on in that section? How does it affect your sense of the larger possible meanings of the story?

Below is a student's first draft of an analytical essay that focuses on the question of a character's intentions (often referred to in literature courses as "character motivation"). Read this draft as a peer reviewer and make notes as you read. You may want to refer to the section on Peer Response Strategies in Part IV for more ideas on responding to drafts.

The question that interested me was "Why did Harry seem to want attention from everyone?" I think there were several reasons why he wanted attention.

First, his parents were very cold towards him. I don't think he felt as though they were giving him the attention he wanted. It seems to me he was rather neglected and he felt that. When he thought he was getting attention from them he "jumped as if he had been shot" (p. 174). This suggests how happy, surprised, and puzzled he was to have even a word from his parents directed to him. At this particular point I think he feels happy because he thought he was finally getting attention from them. At the same time he felt puzzled and surprised because he wasn't expecting them to say anything to him.

Since the attention wasn't given at home, he tried attaining it from others like Mrs. Connin. He did so by changing his name to Bevel since the preacher's name was also Bevel. This caused Mrs. Connin to not only be surprised but in excitement to introduce him to the Reverend also as Bevel. Now he would not only get attention from Mrs. Connin and the Reverend but the people also.

"He saw the oval close to him in the dark. 'He said I'm not the same now,' he muttered. 'I count.'" This passage helped me understand not only the story but in particular Bevel. You see, Bevel wanted to belong and again it leads to the first question. After

(continued)

(continued)

having gotten the attention he so much wanted (from the preacher) he felt as though he counted. As if he was someone now. It's like his whole self-esteem went up because of the preacher. In the end though he feels that the only place he was truly going to be counted was in the river. So he goes and is washed away by the current.

Bevel reminds us how people can be so cruel. People can hurt you, desert you, and well they take your soul if you let them. I think this story proves it. **(Abby)**

Look at Abby's exploration of the child's motivations. Do you agree that he was motivated by the need for attention? Are there points in the story that you would use to add to or alter the understanding that Abby is developing here?

Abby's exploration was a first draft of the ideas she wanted to pursue in a more extended exploratory essay. What do you observe about how she has structured this draft and what she has included in it. If you were responding to this draft, what responses would you make to Abby? Are there changes that would make what she's written clearer or more convincing to you as a reader? Are there additions or changes to the ideas she has presented here that you would suggest? Are there places where you would like to have more examples or evidence (perhaps another quotation), or more explanation (perhaps more discussion of a quotation she has included)? How do you think such additions or changes would contribute to a fuller, more finished essay?

Even after we've looked at the story together in these way, we're likely to come away with different understandings of its meaning—and perhaps different interpretations of the boy's drowning as tragic death or salvation. These are shaped in part by our perception of the writer's intentions and purposes, in part by our prior experiences—of other texts, of different religions and their discourse. But we know much more, not only about the discourse communities represented in the text, but also about how the discourse of the text and the writer's use of some of the conventions of the genre of modern fiction have contributed to our understandings. We can also enter into a new conversation about the author's intentions as she contributed this short story to a world of readers.

The Author's Purposes

Unlike actual discourse communities, fictional ones exist within a world created by a writer. It is possible to see Flannery O'Connor making a contribution to a larger conversation being carried out by writers and readers of modern fiction in English—a literate community that people can belong to by the literature they choose to read, write, talk about, and value. O'Connor contributes to that conversation through her writing, in private conversations, and also in public talks that she gave for many audiences (particularly for college students) around the country.

We can look for evidence of O'Connor's purposes as a writer and the meanings she was trying to represent in the many conversations she carried on about writing. But we also need to read her purposes and meanings against the background of her own beliefs and values (both as participant in a discourse community of writers of modern fiction and as a Southern and Catholic writer) just as we did for the characters in her story. In her talks and letters, O'Connor makes it clear that much of <u>how</u> she writes is connected to her identification with the work of modern fiction. (Note that in the following comments, written in the 1950's, O'Connor uses "he" to refer to all writers, both male and female.)

> Modern fiction often looks simpler than the fiction which preceded it, but in reality, it is more complex. A natural evolution has taken place. The author has for the most part absented himself from direct participation in the work and has left the reader to make his own way amid experience dramatically rendered and symbolically ordered. The modern novelist merges the reader in the experience: he tends to raise the passions he touches upon. If he is a good novelist, he raises them to effect by their order and clarity a new experience. ("Fiction is a Subject with a History," 851)

We can see that O'Connor, as a writer, intended to invite our participation as readers by bringing us into the experience she imagined and leaving us to make our own way (and to make our own meanings).

At the same time, O'Connor's understanding of how she wanted to write was shaped by her sense of her identity as a Southern writer. Although O'Connor had left the South to study at Iowa State and to be a writer in New York City, serious illness forced her to return to Georgia when she was 25, and she spent the rest of her life (another 25 years), living in the house she grew up in and writing about the particular world she knew best. She saw her writing as shaped profoundly by her experience of her community in much the way that Cisneros saw hers shaped by the cold-water flats of Chicago, and she saw all writers, from whatever regions, as having to write out of the particular understandings they would have from their own experience of particular communities.

> The knowledge [that] makes the Georgia writer different from the writer from Hollywood or New York . . . is the knowledge that the novelist finds in his community. When he ceases to find it there, he will cease to write, or at least he will cease to write anything enduring. The writer operates at a particular crossroads where time, place and eternity somehow meet. His problem is to find that location. ("The Regional Writer," 847–48)

While O'Connor saw herself as part of a larger world of writers of modern fiction, she also located her work firmly within a particular, local discourse community, the Southern town she spent most of her life in, and part of the <u>how</u> of her work involved capturing on the page the voices she heard there. But she also saw herself as a Catholic writer, one who believed in God, grace, and

redemption and who wanted to explore the meanings associated with such beliefs and to share that exploration with others. She described her combined
Southern and Catholic identity as bringing

> a distrust of the abstract, a sense of human dependence on the grace of God, and
> a knowledge that evil is not simply a problem to be solved but a mystery to be
> endured. ("The Catholic Novelist in the Protestant South," 862)

REFLECTIVE INQUIRY	Drawing on O'Connor's own comments about her work and her identity as a writer, write an informal response about the ways some aspect of what she said contributes to your understanding of the questions she might have wanted to explore with "The River." Reflect on how some aspect of "The River" helps you to understand better one of her comments as a writer.

When we read "The River" in relationship to the values and beliefs of its characters and their version of Christianity, we can draw on O'Connor's larger framing of her own beliefs to help us shape our understanding of the text. Her sense
that we don't always have clear answers and that much of what we don't understand about human experience will necessarily remain a mystery creates a level of
uncertainty and ambiguity in her writing, inviting us to continue to ask <u>why</u>.

In many stories, the shared values and ways of a discourse community
provide an important backdrop to the characters and their conflicts and motivations. Toni Cade Bambara's "The Lesson" is such a story. It appears in the
readings at the end of Part II, and you may want to turn to it at this point and
explore it in some of the ways we've drawn on in this chapter.

WRITING IN ACADEMIC GENRES: CRITICAL ANALYSIS

In writing analytically on any topic you'll want to allow time for three related activities:

- *Exploring.* The first draft of an essay is exploratory when it doesn't set a
  defined topic or format but suggests some possibilities within which
  you can begin to explore what ideas interest you about the story. In it,
  you want to develop your ideas and the supporting evidence for whatever question or idea you want to explore. But you also want to begin
  to think about how you'll present what you discover to other readers—
  how you'll introduce what you're aiming to do or learn through your
  analysis, how you'll present that analysis, and how you'll bring that
  analysis to some sort of closure that adds, finally, to your own and your
  reader's understandings of whatever you are exploring.

- *Focusing*. Having worked through your understanding of an idea or question, you'll want, in your second draft, to be sure that the idea or question is really the focus of your essay from beginning to end, and that everything included in the essay contributes to that focus. (This can be difficult when you're dealing with a complex work like "The River" where there are so many interrelated issues and ideas that can provide a possible focus.) Focusing typically involves stating the question/idea clearly for yourself (and your reader) at the beginning—then using whatever there is in your first draft that addresses your focus—shaping it to fit the that focus.

- *Elaborating*. As you work on a second draft you will also want to elaborate on what you've written—including whatever will help you explore your focus question more fully, explaining whatever information, details, quotations you've included, filling in gaps and being explicit (in the way that a fiction writer does not have to be) about what you see as the significance of the evidence you've included.

You can work on exploring, focusing, and elaborating as you write a critical analysis essay. More suggestions for drafting, revising, and editing your essay can be found in Writing Strategies in Part IV.

The purpose of this essay is for you to write a critical analysis of some aspect of the story, drawing on its details to guide you (and your readers) to a larger understanding of a question that interests you. Here are some possibilities:

THE CRITICAL ANALYSIS OF LITERATURE

- Return to a question that interested you and/or puzzled you that was not explored much in your class discussions and explore it more fully. Do you have some possible explanations or tentative answers? What clues in the text have helped you to find them?

- Choose another passage in the text, beyond the ones discussed in your class, and explore, in detail, what that passage contributes to your understanding of the story.

- Look in more detail at one or the other of the discourse communities that are presented in the story. Pull together the most significant things that you've come to understand about the ways in which the shared beliefs and values of the community are represented in its members' words, actions, valued possessions, or other ways of being in the world.

5

Analyzing Everyday Conversations

In Chapter 5 and Chapter 6, we'll be studying the talk that goes on in actual discourse communities. We'll look at everyday conversations through lenses provided by other researchers, and we'll also look directly at the community you have chosen to study and write about. Chapters 5 features a study of two rural discourse communities that have some similarities to the fictional communities O'Connor wrote about in her fiction. This study, by Shirley Brice Heath, draws on *ethnographic* research methods frequently used in field research. For your own study, this chapter suggests that you begin by looking closely at one small piece of data (a conversation that you record in your community) and analyze that conversation in relation to the situation in which it takes place and the insider knowledge represented in it. The selections from Heath's ethnographic study demonstrate how she draws on conversations to discover their relationship to larger patterns of beliefs and values in the communities she studied. You'll move back and forth between her study and your own as you draw on her ways of looking to further your own understandings.

The inquiries of this chapter focus on three questions:

- How do researchers study, systematically, the ways people talk in actual discourse communities?

- What can you learn about such research by reading another researcher's study and applying its ways to your own study?

- In what ways can you extend your preliminary research into the talk in your community to look at its literacy practices and its relationship to the wider culture?

Much of the knowledge shared in academic settings and passed on in courses is created through research into defined areas of inquiry. Researchers who are interested in how people live, act, and communicate in various cultural settings (including American subcultures like skateboarders or the communities formed in chat rooms), most often work within the genre of *ethnography*. Ethnographers attempt to capture the way that life goes on in a particular setting and to pull out the meanings that are represented in its typical moments of daily life and daily interaction. They assume that to understand the meaning of a particular behavior or expression, you need a rich and complex understanding of the *culture* it's imbedded in—of what we've been calling the shared knowledge, purposes and ways, and the shared values and beliefs—of people in that setting. So they typically observe all aspects of the life of a community: what people do, eat, wear, or use, as well as what they say. At the same time, they try to highlight the community's significant characteristics—the things that make it recognizable and distinctive. You'll do the same as you learn more about the community you choose to study—figuring out both what your community has in common with, for example, other communities of college-age male friends who listen to a particular type of music—and how it's different.

DOING ETHNOGRAPHIC RESEARCH

Ethnographic research depends on gathering real data about a community—gathering the evidence that can show others how the researcher has come to particular understandings about the community. In studying a discourse community, you want to observe and analyze the ways in which people use language and the beliefs, values, and ways of seeing the world that are imbedded in those ways.

Observing Discourse Communities

We are all insiders to some communities and outsiders to others. Most often in contemporary society, people move in and out of a number of smaller and overlapping speech communities in their daily lives, shifting their styles and altering their ways of using language as they step from one to another. If you survey your classmates to discover what communities they've been in, you'll find that they've grown up in different regions of the United States, in different countries, or maybe just in different neighborhoods of the same city. Together, you'll bring a variety of ethnic backgrounds to the classroom. Your parents will have different workplace and community affiliations, and you'll find that you yourselves will have worked in or may be working in pizza places, doctor's offices, retail stores, or summer camps. You'll socialize in different groups—sometimes single sex groups of young men drinking beer on a Friday night or young women hanging out after soccer practice, or mixed-age working bud-dies, or extended families. The worlds you and your classmates bring into the classroom in this way are very different—but similar in important ways. Each small community might have a different way of expressing meaning and get-ting things done with words. But each community has *some* ways of doing these things. And any of these communities will prove interesting to observe and to write about.

As you decide on the community you want to study, you'll want to choose a group and a setting that you spend time in regularly—where you're an insider. You may decide to focus on interactions at home, among a particular group of friends, at work, on a team, in a school activity, with a roommate, or with a classmate in the cafeteria. Studying a setting where people are just coming together, getting to know each other, and trying to build shared knowledge and discover shared values can also tell you a lot about how communication in a setting works, so for the purposes of this study, you might consider a newly-forming discourse community—such as new college dormmates—as well as long-established ones like a family or group of co-workers.

RESEARCH STRATEGY	*Choosing a community to study*: Begin by brainstorming communities you might find in-teresting to study, or reviewing a list you may have generated earlier. (Other student re-searchers have studied groups of friends with a particular interest like skateboarding or surfing; groups that have come together in a particular setting like a gym, a table in the cafeteria, a workplace, a dorm, or over the internet; as well as long-term communities of families, old friends, or church members, including communities where the conversa-tions are in another language.) You might try to think of all of the people you have com-municated with in the last week. Are these people that you interact with regularly? Do you use language in similar ways? Do you value some of the same things? Also consider which communities you have a lot of access to, and which will consent to this study and will give you permission to record a conversation (or conversations) that goes on there.
	For a community that interests you, reflect in writing about what you want to know and would like to learn about it. Who are its members, what experiences have you shared with them, and what do you value about being or becoming an insider?
	Observing a community: Once you decide on a community to study, you'll want to observe and record your observations in a systematic way, using a double-entry note-book format. (See Conducting Field Research in Part IV.) At first you'll want to capture as much as possible of what goes on there, because almost anything you observe might prove significant to what you finally want to show about this community. Who's present for its conversations? Where do they take place? What objects do people hold, carry, use, wear, or hang on their walls? What music do they listen to? What do they watch on TV? What sorts of movies do they like? The suggestions for research memos in this and the following chapter will guide you in making other observations.

Whatever setting or group you choose, you'll be taking a close look at the conversations that go on there, studying the style of communication that prevails and the ways in which that style connects to larger patterns of communication that exist across discourse communities. You may look as well at the ways in which literacy and written communication are used in the setting—at the sorts of reading and writing that are done or the ways in which written texts are referred to and brought into the shared arena of spoken conversations. Overall you'll be working toward creating the richest possible picture of communication in this community.

Studying Everyday Conversations

From looking closely at typical conversations, you can discover a lot about what's shared by insiders to a community. As you look at the ways they create and maintain shared knowledge, shared purposes, and shared ways of carrying out the conversation you can also come to learn what they worry about, what they believe, and what they value. One good way to begin to look at the typical conversations of a community is to record one—an ordinary, representative exchange that the members of this discourse community take part in.

RESEARCH STRATEGY

Begin by collecting one example of an ordinary conversation that occurs in your discourse community. Although it's possible to collect conversational data by taking careful notes on a conversation—recording who spoke and what they said as accurately as possible, it is difficult to do this effectively when you're also a participant in the conversation. It's better then, for the purposes of this study, to tape record a conversation.

You'll want to ask the participants for permission to record the conversation. (It's unethical to record someone's words and to play them or transcribe them for others to hear or read without permission.) Most people don't mind participating if they know you're looking at the way that conversations are structured as part of a school research project and that they don't have to be identified by name if they don't want to be. While verbal permission is sufficient for an informal project, your class may decide to use a common written permission form. (You'll find an example in Part IV on page 539.)

Choose a time when everyone will be gathered around, and record the actual conversation. Most participants generally forget that the tape recorder is on after they get five or ten minutes into the conversation. Only rarely has a student researcher had to turn to a different group or found that group members talked in ways that were too strained and uncomfortable to be representative of their ordinary conversations.

Tape record at least 30 minutes of the conversation. Then transcribe a short segment (about 3 to 5 minutes) that contains lively exchanges between two or more participants and that seems typical of the sort of interaction that takes place in this setting. In transcribing, try to get down the actual words as they were spoken, including repetitions and pauses and interruptions.

Here's an example of a conversation recorded by two students from a first-year writing class. Laura and Blanca had just met in the class and had gotten to know each other a little in their writing group. Both of them had been out of school for a few years. Both were newcomers to the city and didn't really know a lot of people there. Both happened to be married. They decided to get together one evening with their husbands and they recorded their first "getting-to-know-one-another" conversation, as they tried to find things in common to talk about. Here's the start of a portion they transcribed, where they talk about some cookies Laura made:

ANIKET: These are really good . . .

BLANCA: Uh-huhm

LAURA: Thank you, thank you . . .

(everybody laughing)

ANIKET: I mean, they're not really sweet, but they just have a little bit of sweet in em.

LAURA: I know . . . yeah . . . more like . . .

KELLY: Laura is a really good cook.

LAURA: No, I'm not . . .

KELLY: Yes, she is . . .

ANIKET: Really?

LAURA: No.

KELLY: Thai food, Italian food . . .

ANIKET: Oh, really?

LAURA: I am **not** a very good cook . . . no, really, I'm not trying to be **humble** or something.

ANIKET: We are both pretty bad.

BLANCA: Ahh. Well compared to us you're great! Ahhh.

LAURA: You're just lazy . . .

ANIKET: Well that too.

As we look closely at this conversation, we'll be focusing on the elements we considered in analyzing "The River," and that you'll want to look for in analyzing the conversation you've recorded.

First, consider <u>what</u> the participants in this conversation talk about:

■ The words and clusters of related words that appear (you can mark up your text and circle these words to make their patterns more evident, seeing what words each person introduces, which ones are picked up and repeated by others, which ones seem to build a theme);

■ Any words that seem to have particular or distinctive meanings in this discourse community;

■ The ways in which any participant is named or described by herself/himself or by others.

You've probably identified one topic of the conversation as Laura's cooking, since Kelly states that "Laura is a really good cook." You might have noticed that references to Laura (her name and the pronouns "she," "I," and "you," used to refer to Laura) in relationship to food or cooking occur six times, and that some different kinds of food she can cook are also named. If you have circled all of the words that concern Laura, her cooking, or food, you'll have circled many key words of the conversation. The participants are all involved in naming themselves as good, bad, or lazy in relationship to their idea of a good cook.

Next look at <u>how</u> the participants talk. Consider:

■ Their conversational style;

■ Any relationship you find between the way they talk, the turns they take, or what they say and their roles in this group;

■ Any genres of talk that they might be using;

■ Anything they say that might not be intended to be taken literally.

As you've looked at <u>how</u> the conversation is being carried out, you've probably noticed that the style is informal and that all four people take turns. The turns and what they say in them seem related to their roles and relationships. And there seems to be some disagreement among the participants about whether to take all that is said literally, in ways that we'll consider.

Now speculate about <u>why</u> they might be talking as they do:

■ What are their possible intentions and purposes with each contribution?

■ Do you think they might be trying to achieve more than one purpose at once?

■ Do their purposes match up, or might they be at cross-purposes at some moments?

■ Do their immediate purposes with any statement or question fit with what seem to be the larger purposes of the conversation?

When you've focused on <u>why</u>, on the speakers' purposes and intentions, you've probably found that the picture becomes more confusing. Aniket's first statement, that the cookies are really good, seems intended to compliment Laura, and Kelly's comment that she's a really good cook reinforces that compliment. But Laura keeps denying this, saying finally, "I am **not** a very good cook." And when Aniket and Blanca suggest she's better than they are, Laura adds what might be seen as an insult, "You're just lazy."

As outsiders it's hard for us to say much more than that. We don't really know why there's so much talk about Laura's cooking, or why Laura is so reluctant to accept the praise she's receiving, and why Kelly keeps insisting on the point. We know that the larger purpose of this conversation is for these couples to get to know each other as couples. But we don't really know what purposes the specific contributions to this exchange serve for each person at the moment. To understand more, we need more knowledge about the context—about the participants and their relationships and what the circumstances are in which this conversation takes place—knowledge that insiders have and that we don't.

In writing about this conversation, Blanca tells us more about the participants: "It is very important to know the nexus that there is between the four of us. Laura and I are both Europeans. We also have a lot of cultural connections because she grew up in Italy and I, in Catalunya [Catalan]." It's against that background knowledge that Blanca interprets the exchange about Laura's cooking. Here's what she says about this excerpt:

> When Kelly says, "Laura is really a good cook," we all look at her and acknowledge this by nodding our heads after having had some of her cookies. When she says, "I am not a very good cook . . . I'm not trying to be humble . . ." it is not that she is lying or actually being humble. To understand this, you probably need the insider knowledge that Laura and myself have from our backgrounds. We both come from countries where cooking tradition is deeply assimilated by everybody. Eating big and delicious meals is our tradition and every time we sit down for dinner we look forward to several hours of eating and talking. Traditionally, there are no fast meals on the run or small portions. It is commonly known that "good wives" know how to do all that; they know how to cook all the traditional dishes and they spend hours in front of the stove. That's why Laura says, "I'm not a very good cook." It all depends on the concept of a good cook.

Laura (who is actually German though she grew up in Italy) also mentions their European nationalities as being important to some of the understanding she and Blanca share. But she focuses also on the combinations of couples. She sees two subgroups here, one made up of two Europeans and two Americans, the other of one couple and another couple. Here's an excerpt from her analysis of the same conversation:

> In the beginning we have an example of insider information given from one couple to the other, when Kelly says, "Laura is really a good cook," to which Laura reacts right away with: "No, I'm not." Kelly does not only fill the others in on what he feels is noteworthy, but he also states that he is somewhat proud of Laura. Her first reaction shows that she disagrees, which in a setting like this one can have several reasons: she doesn't want to appear to be bragging, even if just by not modifying Kelly's statement; there isn't a common definition of what a "good cook" is and she can't be sure that the standards of a loving husband are the same as Blanca's and Aniket's. One might even point out what seems typical of a couple: one adds to the other's speech what they think was not correct or has been left out.
>
> Aniket takes a turn and relates the subject to themselves as a couple. "We are both pretty bad [with cooking]," to which Blanca adds: "Well, compared to us you're great!" This is a way of giving some information about themselves, and it relativizes the definition of a "good cook," implying that not much is needed to be regarded as that within this circle.

In discussing the larger conversation that this excerpt was taken from, Laura points to the larger implicit purpose behind this conversation: "to get to know one another better, solidify and continue the friendship." Blanca continues to focus on the cultural perspectives that different members of the group bring, finding that in getting to know each other better, they are pulling in their backgrounds to create new shared knowledge they can all draw on—what she describes as "a multinational tradition," a "multicultural insider knowledge."

This is a good moment to look back at the specific details you noted as you considered the <u>what</u>, <u>why</u>, and <u>how</u> of this conversation. Are there details that you can better understand now that you have more knowledge about the couples and their backgrounds and about the shared insider knowledge about their cultural backgrounds that Laura and Blanca think is important here?

It's also a good moment to consider the insider knowledge that's necessary to understanding the conversation you've recorded, perhaps by sharing your recording or transcript with outsiders (with others in your class) and seeing what else they need to know in order to make sense of what's going on here. Here is what Blanca learned about the insider knowledge of this conversation in that way.

> One of the things that helped me in analyzing the data was the discussion of our group in class about the conversation. I was surprised to find that without 'insider knowledge' another group member couldn't figure a lot of what was going on in the conversation, and that something that seemed pretty obvious to me needed an explanation for an outsider to comprehend it. I realized that as an outsider, you might wonder who is in the conversation: male or female? Their relationships to each other?
>
> Once you get all the information on someone's conversation, your perspective on the conversation changes. Then you are more of an 'insider.' You have more connections to make. But when analyzing my conversation I also tried to place myself as an outsider, to see the way outsiders would see it, although I found it extremely difficult to do.
>
> In attempting to take an outsider's perspective and to understand 'insider knowledge,' I've come to understand more about our discourse community.

Begin by glossing your transcript of the conversation, looking at what is said, why, and how, marking key words and phrases, and making notes in the margins.

Start with <u>what</u> the participants in this conversation talk about, marking and making notes in the right-hand margin about the elements of <u>what</u>, <u>why</u>, and <u>how</u> that we looked at for Laura and Blanca's conversation.

Add notes for anything else you observed that you think might be significant in understanding this conversation in this discourse community. Are there places where what

(continued)

RESEARCH MEMO 5.1

(*continued*)

is said and how it's said seems especially typical or characteristic of the participants in this community, of the things they care about, and of the ways they interact? What does your gloss show you that fits with the initial observations you've made of the typical words, objects, and activities of this community and of the typical ways in which they talk? How does this add to the picture you have been developing of this discourse community—of what's shared and what's valued there, of why the participants typically come together and have conversations like this, and of the roles they play there?

As you write up your analysis of this conversation in a journal response or exploratory essay, you'll want to give your readers a sense of what your discourse community is like by showing them what can be seen in one conversation. In other words, the conversation serves as an example that points to important aspects of life in this discourse community.

Begin by giving a general introduction to this segment of a conversation—to this "episode" in the life of the community, including the important background information that outsiders would have to know to make sense of this situation.

Then write up your analysis. You will want to talk your readers through the conversation represented in your transcript, telling them:

- what this exchange contributes to the larger, ongoing concerns and purposes of this discourse community; and

- exactly how the details of <u>what</u>, <u>why</u>, and <u>how</u> work in making that contribution.

You want to help your readers see what you've seen in the transcript as characteristic of conversations in your community.

Your goal here is to produce as rich and detailed an analysis as possible and then to say what you have learned from it, what it leads you to see about this conversation and about your discourse community. (Look back at Blanca's and Laura's analyses of their conversation. They both quote from the conversation, explaining not only what's being talked about, but *why* these people are talking about these things in the way they are.)

This analysis will eventually be incorporated into your larger study of your discourse community.

Attach the glossed copy of your transcript.

DRAWING ON A STUDY OF CONVERSATIONS AND COMMUNITIES

Getting to know each other and beginning to form a new friendship, as in the case of these two student couples, requires building new shared knowledge and creating shared ways of interacting. In established discourse communities where people have spent a lot of time together, much shared knowledge and a lot of the ways in which people interact can be assumed. Those assumed, shared ways were the focus of *Ways With Words* (1983), a classic study of discourse communities that was carried out by the anthropologist Shirley Brice Heath.

Heath went to live in the Piedmont area of the Carolinas—an area that's not unlike the Georgia towns that O'Connor's fiction captured—and she stayed there for ten years. She hung around in kitchens and stirred pots and held babies while people talked. She went to church meetings and bible study groups. She spent time in schools and classrooms. She found that there were two distinct rural communities around the town she studied, as distinct as the two worlds that O'Connor portrayed in "The River"; that each of those communities had its own insider knowledge and values and beliefs; and that these were reflected in the ways that people talked and what they talked about.

In the conversational data she gathered, Heath discovered particular speech genres that were repeated in each community, and she came to see one genre, the story, as playing a particularly important role in both of the rural communities (which she named Roadville and Trackton). Stories, narrative accounts of events, occurred in many conversations in both communities. But they took different forms and were used for different purposes, reflecting deeper cultural differences.

Stories in Roadville have a shared purpose: to make people laugh by making fun of either the storyteller or a close friend or family member who is present. A community member in Roadville described a story as "something you tell on yourself, or on your buddy, you, you know, it's all in good fun, and a li'l something to laugh about" (p. 210). People don't tell stories behind other

READING RESPONSE

Before you turn to read Heath's discussion of oral traditions, you can turn to p. 212 to see an example of a conversation in which a story is embedded (Roadville Text IV), and to prepare yourself for Heath's discussion by developing your own hypotheses about this text, and how it works, and why. As you read this transcript of part of a conversation, ask yourself the familiar questions: what, how, and why. What insider knowledge do you need to make more sense of this conversation?

Then turn to Part I of "Oral Traditions" to see what Heath reports about the discourse community of Roadville. Why does Heath see Roadville Text IV, with its representation of shared knowledge, shared purposes, and shared ways, as characteristic of the shared beliefs and values of that community?

Heath keeps moving back and forth between making generalizations about what goes on in this community and giving specific examples. As you gloss, note her movement between specifics and generalizations and mark the larger understandings that you think she wants her readers to take away from this discussion. Mark as well any places where what she's observed connects with something you've observed about your own discourse community.

What picture do you get of this community from Heath's discussion and the examples she gives? Write a brief journal entry about what you find from your reading and glossing.

people's backs. Roadville stories also have a shared form: they are always about something that actually happened, they stick close to the actual events, and they end with a moral or a lesson that reinforces what the expected behavior in the community should be.

Stories in Trackton are likewise intended to make people laugh. But people do sometimes tell stories about others who aren't present. And the shared form of Trackton stories is quite different from the form of Roadville stories: they begin with something that really happened, but they are often developed through creative exaggeration and invention. They don't typically end with a moral or lesson, but they do tend to show how someone cleverly overcame a difficult situation (even if that outcome is made-up). We'll see how stories work in Roadville as we turn to Part I of "Oral Traditions."

Oral Traditions: Ways with Words
Part I: In Roadville
Shirley Brice Heath

A PIECE OF TRUTH

1   Roadville residents worry about many things. Yet no Roadville home is a somber place where folks spend all their time worrying about money, their children's futures, and their fate at the hands of the mill. They create numerous occasions for celebration, most often with family members and church friends. On these occasions, they regale each other with "stories." To an outsider, these stories seem as though they should be embarrassing, even insulting to people present. It is difficult for the outsider to learn when to laugh, for Roadville people seem to laugh at the story's central character, usually the story-teller or someone else who is present.

A "story" in Roadville is "something you tell on yourself, or on your buddy, you know, it's all in good fun, and a li'l something to laugh about." Though this definition was given by a male, women define their stories in similar ways, stressing they are "good fun," and "don't mean no harm." Stories recount an actual event either witnessed by others or previously told in the presence of others and declared by them "a good story." Roadville residents recognize the purpose of the stories is to make people laugh by making fun of either the story-teller or a close friend in sharing an event and the particular actions of individuals within that event. However, stories "told on" someone other than the story-teller are never told unless the central character or someone who is clearly designated his representative is present. The Dee children sometimes tell stories on their father who died shortly after the family moved to Roadville, but they do so only in Mrs. Dee's presence with numerous positive adjectives describing their father's gruff nature. Rob Macken, on occasion, is the dominant character in stories which make fun of his ever-present willingness to point out where other folks are wrong. But Rob is always present on these occasions, and he is clearly included in the telling ("Ain't that right, Rob?" "Now you know that's the truth, hain't it?"), as story-tellers cautiously move through their tale about him, gauging how far to go by his response to the story.

Outside close family groups, stories are told only in sex-segregated groups. Women invite stories of other women, men regale each other with tales of their escapades on hunting and fishing trips, or their run-ins (quarrels) with their wives and children. Topics for women's stories are exploits in cooking, shopping, adventures at the beauty shop, bingo games, the local amusement park, their gardens, and sometimes events in their children's lives. Topics for men are big-fishing expeditions, escapades of their hunting dogs, times they have made fools of themselves, and exploits in particular areas of their expertise (gardening and raising a 90-lb pumpkin, a 30-lb cabbage, etc.). If a story is told to an initial audience and declared a good story on that occasion, this audience (or others who hear about the story) can then invite the story-teller to retell the story to yet other audiences. Thus, an invitation to tell a story is usually necessary. Stories are often requested with a question: "Has Betty burned any biscuits lately?" "Brought any possums home lately?" Marked behaviour— transgressions from the behavioral norm generally expected of a "good hunter," "good cook," "good handyman," or a "good Christian"—is the usual focus of the story. The foolishness in the tale is a piece of truth about everyone present, and all join in a mutual laugh at not only the story's central character, but at themselves as well. One story triggers another, as person after person reaffirms a familiarity with the kind of experience just recounted. Such stories test publicly the strength of relationships and openly declare bonds of kinship and friendship. When the social bond is currently strong, such stories can be told with no "hard feelings." Only rarely, and then generally under the influence of alcohol or the strain of a test in the relationship from another source (job competition, an unpaid loan), does a story-telling become the occasion for an open expression of hostility.

Common experience in events similar to those of the story becomes an expression of social unity, a commitment to maintenance of the norms of the church and of the roles within the mill community's life. In telling a story, an individual shows that he belongs to the group: he knows about either himself or the subject of the story, and he understands the norms which were broken by the story's central character. Old-timers, especially those who came to Roadville in the 1930s, frequently assert their long familiarity with certain norms as they tell stories on the young folks and on those members of their own family who moved away. There is always an unspoken understanding that some experiences common to the oldtimers can never be known by the young folks, yet they have benefited from the lessons and values these experiences enabled their parents to pass on to them.

5   In any social gathering, either the story-teller who himself announces he has a story or the individual who invites another to tell a story is, for the moment, in control of the entire group. He manages the flow of talk, the staging of the story, and dictates the topic to which all will adhere in at least those portions of their discourse which immediately follow the story-telling. At a church circle meeting, many of the neighborhood women had gathered, and Mrs. Macken was responsible for refreshments on this occasion. The business and lesson of the circle had ended, and she was

preparing the refreshments, while the women milled about waiting for her to signal she was ready for them. Mrs. Macken looked up from arranging cookies on a plate and announced Sue had a story to tell. This was something she could not normally have done, since as a relative newcomer, a schoolteacher, and a known malcontent in Roadville, her status was not high enough to allow her to announce a story for someone who was as much of an oldtimer as Sue. However, as the hostess of the circle, she had some temporary rank.

Roadville Text IV

MRS. MACKEN: Sue, you oughta tell about those rolls you made the other day, make folks glad you didn't try to serve fancy rolls today.

MRS. DEE: Sue, what'd you do, do you have a new recipe?

MRS. MACKEN: You might call it that

SUE: I, hh wanna

10   MARTHA: Now Millie [Mrs. Macken], you hush and let Sue give us *her* story.

SUE: Well, as a matter of fact, I did have this new recipe, one I got out of *Better Homes and Gardens*, and I though I'd try it, uh, you see, it called for scalded milk, and I had just started the milk when the telephone rang, and I went to get it. It was Leona /*casting her eyes at Mrs. Macken*/. I thought I turned the stove off, and when I came back, the burner was off, uh, so I didn't think anything about it, poured the milk in on the yeast, and went to kneading. Felt a little hot. Well, anyway, put the stuff out to rise, and came back, and it looked almost like Stone Mountain, thought that's a strange recipe, so I kneaded it again, and set it out in rolls. This time I had rocks, uh, sorta like 'em, the kind that roll up all smooth at the beach. Well, I wasn't gonna throw that stuff all out, so I cooked it. Turned out even harder than those rocks, if that's possible, and nobody would eat 'em, couldn't even soften 'em in buttermilk. I was trying to explain how the recipe was so funny, you know, see, how I didn't know what I did wrong, and Sally piped up and said 'Like yeah, when you was on the phone, I came in, saw this white stuff a-boiling, and I turned it off.' (pause). Then I knew, you know, that milk was too hot, killed the yeast /*looking around at the women*/. Guess I'll learn to keep my mind on my own business and off other folks?

The story was punctuated by gestures of kneading, turns of the head in puzzlement, and looks at the audience to see if they acknowledged understanding of the metaphors and similes. Stone Mountain is a campground in the region which everyone at the circle meeting had visited; it rises out of the ground like a giant smooth-backed whale. The beach is a favorite summer vacation spot for Roadville families, and the women often collect the smooth rocks from the beach to put on top of the dirt in their flower pots.

Several conventions of stories and story-telling in Roadville stand out in this incident. The highest status members present, Mrs. Dee and her granddaughter Martha, reannounce Sue's story and subtly convey that Mrs. Macken stepped out of line by asking Sue to tell a story on this occasion. Within her narrative, Sue follows a major requirement of a "good story"; it must be factual, and any exaggeration or hyperbole must be so qualified as to let the audience know the story-teller does not accept such descriptions as literally true. Sue qualifies her Stone Mountain description with "almost," her equation of the rolls with rocks by "sorta like 'em," and her final comparison of the rolls to rocks with "if that's possible." She attempts to stick strictly to the truth and exaggerates only with hedges and qualifications.

Perhaps the most obligatory convention Sue follows is that which requires a Roadville story to have a moral or summary message which highlights the weakness admitted in the tale. "Stories" in these settings are similar to testimonials given at revival meetings and prayer sessions. On these occasions, individuals are invited to give a testimonial or to "tell your story." These narratives are characterized by a factual detailing of temporal and spatial descriptions and recounting of conversations by direct quotation ("Then the Lord said to me:"). Such testimonials frequently have to do with "bringing a young man to his senses" and having received answers to specific prayers. The detailing of the actual event is often finished off with Scriptural quotation, making it clear that the story bears out the promise of "the Word." Sue's story is confession-like, and its summing up carries a double meaning, both a literal one ("on my own business" = cooking) and a figurative one ("on my own business" = general affairs). Any woman in the group can quote Scripture describing the sins of which the tongue is capable (for example, James 3:6 which likens the tongue to a fire which spreads evil).

Unspoken here is the sin of Sue and Leona—gossip—the recounting and evaluating of the activities and personalities of others. Gossip is a frequent sermon topic and a behavior looked upon as a characteristic female weakness. Leona, who is not present at the circle meeting, is a known gossip, who occasionally telephones several of the women to fill them in on news in the neighborhood. All of the women know, but none says explicitly, that any phone call with Leona is likely to bring trouble, both to those who are the topics of her phone conversation and to those who are weak enough to listen to her. The story, told at the end of a church circle meeting, appears to be an innocent piece of female chatter, but it carries a message to all present which reminds them of their own weakness in listening to Leona. All the women have gossiped, and all have given in to listening to Leona at one time or another. Yet on this public occasion, all avoid direct negative talk about either Leona or anyone else, since engaging in this censured activity in such a public setting where more than two individuals are present would be foolish. Instead Sue's story is an occasion in which all recognize their common, but unspoken, Christian ideal of disciplined tongue. The major understandings and background knowledge on which a full interpretation of the story depends are unarticulated.

Sue's story carries subtle messages about the values and practices of the culture out of which the story comes. She reaffirms that the most frequent gossip in Roadville takes place between only two people, with an unstated and often unfulfilled agreement that neither will reveal her participation to others; broaches of such trust are frequent causes of female disagreement. Moreover, Sue asserts her maintenance of certain community norms for homemakers: she makes her bread "from scratch" instead of buying store goods; she is unwilling to throw out food; she has obviously trained Sally, her daughter, to be attentive to kitchen matters. Picking up, or recognizing all of this information depends on the familiarity with Roadville's norms and daily customs which the women of the church circle share.

15   In several ways, stories such as Sue's are similar to Biblical parables, a frequent source for sermons and Bible lessons, and a literary source familiar to all. Parables told by Jesus recount daily experiences common to the people of his day. Often parables end with a summary statement which is both a condemnation of one or more of the story's characters and a warning to those who would hear and understand the parable for its relevance to their own lives. In a parable, two items or events are placed side by side for comparison. The details of the story bring out its principal point or primary meaning, but there is little or no emotional expressiveness within the story evaluating the actions of the characters. The action is named and detailed, but its meaning to the characters is not set forth in exposition or through a report of the emotions of those involved. Biblical parables often open with formulas such as "The Kingdom of heaven is like unto this . . . " (Matthew 13:24, 13:31, 13:33, 13:44, 13:45, 20:1, 25:1), or admonitions to listen: "Listen then if you have ears" (Matthew 13:9) and "Listen and understand" (Matthew 15:10). Roadville's parable-like stories often open with announcement of the comparison of the events of the story to another situation: "That's like what happened to me . . . " Both men and women often open their stories with the simple comment "They say . . . " or a metaphor such as "We've got another bulldog on our hands" (referring to a fighting personality who is the central character in an upcoming story). In ways similar to Biblical parables, Roadville folks share with their listeners experiences which provide a lesson with a meaning for the life of all. The story is told using direct discourse whenever possible: "And he goes 'Now, you look out.'" or "Like yeah when you was on the phone . . . "

For the best of the parable-like stories, that is, those which are told repeatedly or are handed down in families over generations, the retelling of the entire story is often not necessary. Only its summary point need be repeated to remind listeners of the lesson behind the story. Proverbs or well-known sayings also carry lessons stating the general will of the community and ideals of Roadville families. Understanding of these depends, as do parable-like stories, on comparing one thing to another, for example, seeing similarities across nature.

> A whistlin' girl and a crowin' hen will come to no good end.
> A rollin' stone gathers no moss.
> A stitch in time saves nine.
> Rain before seven, clear by eleven.

For those activities which are traditionally part of the daily routine of mill families' lives—agriculture, weather, male-female relations, pregnancy and childbirth—proverbial guides to behavior abound. Proverbs help determine when certain crops are planted and harvested, predict rain, sunshine, good fishing or bad, link personality traits to physical features, and dictate behaviors of mothers-to-be. The anonymous and collective voices of those who have abided by these lessons in their experiences remind Roadville residents of behavioral norms and reinforce expectations of predictable actions and attitudes among community members.

The Bible's parables and proverbs are sometimes quite consciously used as a written model for Roadville's oral stories and proverbs. However, few written sources, other than the Bible, seem to influence either the content or the structure of oral stories in Roadville. Access to written stories, other than those in the Bible, is relatively rare. Women buy home and garden magazines and read their stories of successful remodeling or sewing projects—testimonials on the merits of budget shopping, thriftiness, and tenacity in do-it-yourself projects. Some women buy "True Story" magazines and publications which feature the personal stories of movie and television personalities, but they do not usually read these publicly. Some women occasionally buy paperback novels, and when asked about their hobbies, they often include reading, but then add comments such as "There's no time for it, for reading, you know, for pleasure or anything like that."

In church-related activities, they not only use stories from the Bible, but they occasionally hear certain other types of content-related stories. The circle meeting at which Sue was asked to tell her story is an example of one such activity. In such meetings, women share study of a designated Bible passage or a book of the Bible. The leader often reads from other short story-like materials to illustrate the need to follow the precepts covered in the Biblical passage. Throughout the discussion, however, there are numerous references to "our own stories [the experiences of those present]" which better relate to the Bible message than do the printed materials supplied for Bible study. Men's and women's Bible study groups prefer that a pastor or an elder lead them. The pastor sometimes suggests to lay leaders that they use a book of exposition of the Scriptures (especially when the Bible study focuses on a particular book of the Bible, such as Revelation). Some members of the Bible study group may be assigned portions of supplementary materials to read and discuss at the next Bible study. However, such efforts usually fail miserably. Roadville men and women do not like to read in public and do not wish to admit their lack of understanding of expository materials. They state strong preferences that, if any written materials are used to expand on Biblical passages, the pastor, and not they, should do it. As Mrs. Turner's mother explained. "I believe what the preacher speaks to be the truth, because I feel he is our leader, and I don't feel, well, I feel like *he* is tellin' us the right thing."

Thus, in interpreting the Bible, church members prefer either their own stories or Biblical accounts to written stories—whether factual expositions or tales of the lives of other modern-day Christians. Their own stories are often modeled on Biblical parables, but they are also personal accounts of what God's Word has meant to them. They reject depersonalized written accounts which come from unfamiliar sources. They use their own stories told on themselves and their friends to entertain and instruct, as they highlight personal and communal weaknesses and their struggles either to overcome them or to live with them.

Heath's discussion of Roadville reinforces some of the understandings about discourse communities that we've been developing throughout this book. For example, Heath contributes to an understanding of the ways particular genres take shape in relationship to community expectations. She tells us that the story in Roadville Text IV is typical of what's considered a "good story" in Roadville. What characterizes a good example of that genre in Road-ville? Heath tells us it's based on:

- <u>What</u> is talked about. In Roadville, it's expected to be an actual incident, focusing on facts without too much exaggeration.

- <u>How</u> it's talked about. In Roadville, the *how* involves strict rules of turn-taking, according to people's roles. In this case, the hostess has the most status and gets to elicit the story, and though other women make comments, she quickly quiets them down and turns the floor over to Sue. All of the women know and accept these status rules for turn-taking.

    <u>How</u> also involves the form of the story, the expected pattern of structure and organization and the elements that will be included. The story ends, as most Roadville stories do, with a moral, "Guess I'll learn to keep my mind on my own business and off other folks." Sue knows how to tell her story to fit this pattern.

- <u>Why</u> it's talked about. Sue also understands why her story has been requested. It's really a lesson about not gossiping, and the telling of the story reinforces shared knowledge—that almost everyone does gossip in this community, and shared values—and that they really shouldn't do it. But there are other elements that contribute to a good example of the speech genre of the story in Roadville.

- It connects to other genres in the community. Those genres include sermons with messages and morals, parables from the Bible, and the les-

---

RESEARCH MEMO 5.2

Many discourse communities have stories as one of their important genres. If yours does, think about the stories that are told and how they're told, and what makes a good story, using some of the elements that Heath has named for Roadville stories. Think about:

- What a good story is about.
- How it's told, both in terms of who gets to tell it, and what patterns it follows.
- Why it's told.
- How it connects to other genres within the community.
- How it connects to values that are represented across genres.

If your discourse community has a genre that it relies on more than stories—the joke, for example—name that genre and describe what makes a good example of it in relationship to the sorts of elements Heath names. You may find examples of these genres in your observation notebook. If not, begin now to see if you can observe any forms that are used, repeatedly by members of your community, so that people share a sense of what a good _____ is.

Describe your discourse community's good story or other genre, giving an example and discussing what seems important to the community's shared understanding of the elements of this genre.

sons of Bible study meetings. These genres may be spoken or written. What matters is that they represent similar values, providing opportunities for reinforcing lessons about how people should live and act. Even the nonchurch-related materials that women (or rarely men) might read, like "True Story" magazines, bear a relationship to what's valued in the "good story."

■ It represents shared values in similar ways as do other aspects of communication within the community. Roadville residents value what they understand to be factually true, and so they don't create stories, they don't read fiction, they don't invent metaphorical language and only draw on what's written in the Bible, and they tend to emphasize memorization and recitation of prayers and lessons, so that they stay strictly to the original text.

Here's a student writer's response about the genre of the joke in her family discourse community.

STUDENT VOICES

There are jokes in our discourse community that only insiders would understand and think are funny. These jokes are told not only to lighten up the subject, but they are also told to make a statement. For example, when my mother makes the joke 'we're the last minute Shafers,' she is not only lightening up the subject but making a point. We were making our plans [for a high holiday] on a Thursday night; we planned to leave for New York at four or five on Friday morning. We were definitely making our plans at the last minute. Instead of feeling upset or embarrassed by this, my mother is making this familiar joke to validate our slack in making the plans earlier. She is in turn, teaching me a lesson, not to get caught up in the nonsignificant details, but to make light of them and relax. Most of all, she is teaching me to accept ourselves for who we are. My parents are the last minute Schafers, and that is ok.

Another example of this in the same conversation is when I asked jokingly 'should I bring a sleeping bag to lie on?' Here I was making a joke but also a statement. When my siblings and I were young, my parents would bring us to the Synagogue that their Rabbi ran in New York. In this special Synagogue, the prayers would take extra long, since they were said in a very special way. When my siblings and I would get tired and need to sleep, my parents would set up sleeping bags in the back of the Synagogue and we would sleep there until the services were over. My family became known as the 'sleeping bag family.' This has brought us closer to the people in New York and it is a sweet insider joke. I have been away from my house for two years, and therefore have not gone on these types of road trips to New York with my parents for a long time. I was making this joke but making a statement as well that I feel as though I have not been to the Synagogue since I was young and I felt out of touch with that discourse community. Through this joke, I felt instantly like an insider again. **(Reena)**

Drawing on the sorts of elements that we've been naming in looking at what makes a good story in a community, what would you say are the elements that make a good joke in Reena's discourse community?

The next selection of "Oral Traditions" focuses on Trackton, and the ways in which Trackton stories differ from Roadville stories. While in Roadville, stories are straight-forward factual accounts of real events, in Trackton stories are playful and imaginative—often partly fictional, though they may begin with some true incident, and they most often end with the teller gaining some sort of victory over difficult situations. This is true of the stories told by both children and adults, and even prayers in Trackton church services involve creative elaboration on an original text, rather than strict memorization and recitation.

This selection from Heath's larger discussion of storytelling in Trackton looks at children and adolescents, showing how Trackton children learn to play around with language, how they become good at "talking junk, " and how they begin to develop some of the creative language play that's valued in the larger community. Again, it's useful to start by looking at a particular text produced in the Trackton community, to develop your own picture of what's going on, before turning to Heath's larger discussion.

READING RESPONSE

Turn to Trackton Text VIII (p. 223), which involves one extended story told by a 12-year-old boy to a group of friends. As you read this transcript of a story, ask yourself:

- What Terry is talking about—why, and how.
- What do you notice about his language, his style, as well as about the ways he structures his story?
- What insider knowledge do you think you need to make more sense of this story, in this community?

Then turn to Part II of "Oral Traditions" to see what Heath reports about the discourse community of Trackton, why this story text is characteristic of some of the shared knowledge and shared beliefs and values of young people in that community, values that reflect to some degree those of the larger community. As you read and gloss, note points of comparison—similarities and differences—to what you've learned about the things that are valued in Roadville, as well as to what you're observing about your own community.

What picture do you get of this discourse community from Heath's discussion and the examples she gives? What do you find about this community in comparison to Roadville? Write a journal response about what you find from your reading and glossing.

Oral Traditions: Learning How to Talk Junk
Part II: In Trackton

Shirley Brice Heath

1   The stories of young children and the insults and playsongs of older children are similar in several ways. The structuring of repetitions with variations in both of these resembles patterns in adults' narratives (see Trackton Text II, for example). To under-

stand any of these, one must have some prior knowledge of the situation being re-counted and must accept the ritualized routine of the performance as having meaning in the context of community life. Descriptions of ritualized insults, such as playing the dozens, sounding and riddling, among black children have emphasized that listeners make sense of these only by knowing both background meanings and intentions. These elaborate word games, played by older children, parallel the type of verbal play, social interactional style, and treatment of themes which children who become suc-cessful story-tellers in Trackton learn to use.

On the plaza, school-age boys and girls model a wide range of methods of verbal play, imaginative exaggeration, and ways to vary treatment of themes in their ex-changes of insults and playsongs. When a ballgame or other play breaks into an alter-cation, the children either fuss or shout playsong-like insults at each other. Most of these include "mamma" or other members of the family and focus on personal char-acteristics or behaviors. Some are chanted in a sing-song pattern; others are simply shouted. Those which are chanted have a four-beat rhythm.

TRACKTON TEXT VI (BOYS AND GIRLS 9–12)

> Yó; má;, yó má
> Yo' gréasy gréasy grán' má
> Gót skínny légs 'n fát bohín'
> Enúf to scáre ol' Fránkenstéin
> Yóu gót a úgly héad
> Yóu néed sóme cornbréad
>
> 5
> Yóu kin róll yú' éyes
> But you cáin't contról yó' síze
>
> Shé so méan,
> Shé like Méan Jóe Gréen [a football player for a national team]

Both two-liners and four-line verses often have either internal or end rhyme, and spontaneous creations which have such rhyme are most likely to be picked up and used again and again by other children. When preschoolers first begin to mock ver-bally the behavior of their aggressors, there is great audience mirth, and enthusiastic response. They soon begin mocking their challengers by repeating the insults they hear older children use to each other. Young children, because of the extraordinary latitude they have in taking on varying roles and related language uses, can toss these insults out to community members, old and young. Thus they have numerous occa-sions for testing the degrees of approval insults of different form and content receive. Clever language play (rhyme, alliteration, etc.) plus skillful manipulation of content score the highest response from the audience.

Children experiment with these insults, usually by the age of three years. Some-times they are successful, sometimes not. Benjy was especially persistent in trying his own versions of insults; but he was late in grasping the fact that some characteristics of individuals were appropriate for mocking, and others were not.

> Yo' daddy have false teef. (3 years, 6 months)
> Yo' daddy name Brer. (3 years, 8 months)

Yo' daddy mamma eat po'k 'n beans. (4 years)
Yo' mamma wear combat boots. (4 years, 2 months)
Yo' mamma wear army drawers. (4 years, 8 months)
Yo' mamma wear a batman cape. (5 years)
Yo' mamma name Frankenstein. (5 years, 2 months)

10   Only gradually did Benjy come to recognize which characteristics would be incongruous or appropriate for a ritualized, not a personal, insult to a mamma or daddy. False teeth and adult nicknames such as Brer were neither uncommon nor incongruous; mammas wearing combat boots and named Frankenstein were both. Benjy, by the age of four, was consistently able to choose the correct content for the ridicule in his one-liners.

Before they go to school, children rarely create two-liners. The following from Benjy (5 years, 6 months) is a rare example, but it shows his level of control of both content and end-rhyme.

Yóu, snággle-toof mónster, yóu,
Becáuse you éat a rótten shóe. (said in a sing-song chant)

Benjy seemingly forces an effect on the verse, however, because he simply says the first line, almost as a one-liner, and then chants the second line. Though shoes are not often described as rotten in the community, Benjy has captured the insult power of accusing someone of eating rotten food (suggesting he is so poor he has nothing else), and he has made a causal connection between eating shoes and being snaggle-toothed.

At school, children hear many two-line insults, and boys especially acquire very quickly a much more extensive repertoire of these than they have in Trackton. Soon after they are settled in school, they begin bringing home their own two-liners. These always contain some rhyme, but they do not always successfully create a sense of the ridiculous or nonsensical. The rhyming requirements of two-liners seem to be learned earlier in the primary school years than are appropriate patterns of content for insults. By the second grade, Benjy brought home the following couplets. No doubt, he had heard them at school, and he had mixed several to make some of his own creations. The following were, however, all newly introduced to Trackton by Benjy.

Nóbody fíddle
Wid de óreo míddle. [a well-known school adaptation of a television commercial]

15   Héy fiddle díddle, de mán in de míddle
Wid de twó chéeks ón de síde. [portions of several insult verses combined]

Shít, Gód damn
Git off yó' áss 'n jám. [a "classic" among older primary-school children]

You ríde my áss [probably a line out of an older student's conversation Benjy
                          adopted]
I stéal yo' páss.

These last verses illustrate Benjy's efforts to incorporate "dirty words," taboo terms, into his verbal play. The one-liners below were among his earliest efforts; these were all brought home within the first school term.

20   My mámma ain't fúck Móther Góose.
         Yó' mamma gót a bíg áss.

Within the community, these do not receive particular reinforcement from adults. By the time they begin school, children are challenged for verbal dueling much less frequently by community adults than they are in their preschool years. Preschool occasions for verbal play and witty lighthearted exchanges between child and adult become more and more rare as children get older. Once a child begins school, adults lose interest in him as a partner for verbal challenge, and preschoolers coming along behind him in the community take his place on the plaza's stage.

School-age peers become the reinforcers for the use of these insults, and they acclaim and denounce certain types of insults in a developmental sequence of acceptability. In the earliest school years, children laugh, giggle, and act appropriately mock-shocked at any one-liner with taboo words. One-liners receive little reinforcement without these taboo words. Two-liners or four-line verses with rhyme, but with little punch in terms of insult, usually bring approval; those with both rhyme and insult are sure to win a direct announcement or gesture of praise if directed to a child higher in peer ranking, and an abdication by silent retreat if directed to a peer of equal or lesser rank. Boys engage in these verbal challenges at the bus stop, on the bus, and in the playground at school when they are certain they cannot be heard by school authorities. The use of these insults becomes most intense in the upper primary grades and junior high school (12–15 years). By the time the boys reach high school (15–18 years), they rarely use verbal challenges to establish and maintain status relations. Instead they use sports, direct challenges to a particular display of skill (for example, in a pool game), or direct physical confrontation. Verbal play appears to be viewed as the game of young boys, those who have neither the freedom of access to places suitable for direct challenges of skill or physical prowess nor the courage for them.

Among girls, many features found in boys' insults appear in their assertions of challenge and mockery in both insults and playsongs. During the early primary grades, girls rarely engage in insults through one-liners, couplets, or verses. Instead, they become apprentices of a sort to girls in the older grades who teach them playsongs which contain many linguistic and social features of insults. At school, certain groups of black girls, aged nine to twelve years, become known as performers, and at every possible opportunity, they segregate themselves to use their playsongs in jump-rope or hand-clap games. These playsongs carry generalized messages of mockery and assertion and tell of experiences the girls seem to see as their own. White girls or mixed groups never sing playsongs of the following type; these are performed only in all-black groups. They are chanted with a clear, four-beat rhythm.

TRACKTON TEXT VII

Sar dínes, wóo, 'n po'k 'n béans, wóo
Sar dínes, wóo, 'n po'k 'n béans, wóo
I kin téll by yo' héad
Dat ya éat cornbréad
Sar dínes, wóo, 'n po'k 'n béans, wóo
Sar dínes, wóo, 'n po'k 'n béans, wóo
I kin téll by yo' híp

> Dat you eat potáto chíp
> Sar dínes, wóo, 'n po'k 'n béans, wóo
> Sar dínes, wóo, 'n po'k 'n béans, wóo
> I got stéak in my pláte
> 'n I júst cain't wáit
> I got bóogers in my éyes
> 'n I don't táke no jíve
> Sar dínes, wóo, 'n po'k 'n béans, wóo
> Sar dínes, wóo, 'n po'k 'n béans, wóo

25   Several chunks of the language often included in insults (cf. Benjy's one-liner "Yo' mamma eat po'k 'n beans," and the couplet rhyming "head" and "cornbread") also appear in the playsongs. Throughout this playsong, foods associated with poverty—sardines, pork and beans, and cornbread—carry a message of what may be taken as mockery and ridicule from the speaker: you eat cornbread; sardines and pork and beans are pervasive in your life; I eat steak, and "I don't take no jive." The message is twofold: insult to listener and assertion of speaker's strength. Telling experiences—the eating of certain foods, participation in getting the spirit at church, having babies, playing the fool, and overcoming obstacles—appear again and again in these playsongs.

Girls usually come to use pieces of the language of playsongs in their one-liners, couplets, or verses by the time they are in the upper primary grades. However, in any serious challenge of peer relations, especially between girls from different communities, a physical confrontation is preferred over verbal challenges. The latter are usually reserved for challenges between friends or between girls for whom there is no serious confrontation in status relations. By the junior high school years, the girls stop performing the playsongs entirely. They seem to be regarded as child's play, and the older girls will participate in them only occasionally when they correct or comment on the performance of younger girls in their own community. However, at the junior and senior high levels, the girls transfer the skills they used in the playsongs and insults to cheers they make up for their school teams. The desegregation of schools and the closing of all-black schools cut off the major opportunity for the creation and performance of these cheers, though occasionally they can still be heard in all-black neighborhood functions. A few have been transferred into use by mixed cheerleading squads in the desegregated junior and senior high schools. Occasionally, a group of black cheerleaders from the mixed squad will perform one of the cheers formerly used in the all-black schools. These cheers are accompanied by more and different kinds of steps and hand-clapping routines than are the cheers performed by the entire squad. Often only black students in the crowd respond to these cheers.

> Óne, twó, three, four, fíve
> Hárlem Héights don't táke no jíve
> Síx séven, eight, nine tén
> Táke it úp 'n dó it agáin
>
> Say héy, hey, héy, héy, hey, héy
> Whát y gót-ta-say, whát ya gót-ta-say
> Whát ya gót-ta-say, whát ya gót-ta-say

Sáy [name of school] (drawn out over three beats)
Dey are súper (drawn out over three beats)

Immediately following *super*, a complicated clap and kick routine begins which continues for almost a minute. The entire cheer is repeated twice. The clapped ending the second time is the same as the first, with the exception of the final two measures, which provide a coda-type ending and final flourish. The following cheer has a similar pattern.

Thúnder, thúnder, thúnderátion
30   Wé de dévil's délegátion
Wé de right cómbinátion
Wé creáte a sénsátion
Thúnder, thúnder, thúnderátion

In this cheer, the five-line stanza given is punctuated by a syncopation of hand-clap and stomp which reinforces the four-beat measure of each line. The stanza given above is repeated three times; the final repetition ends with a giant jump and a shout to *THUNDER*.

Within these cheers, the strategies of insult, mockery, and assertion children use in insults and playsongs appear. The central message is one of victory, overcoming the adversary. Though these insults, playsongs, and cheers are not stories, they do provide opportunities for both boys and girls to practice the strategies and performance skills which good story-tellers must have in Trackton. These include:

word play (including rhyming, alliteration);

gestures and sound effects;

extensive use of metaphors and similes;

suggestion of behavioral and social attributes through repeated use of a single lexical item (po'k 'n beans = poverty);

involvement of public media figures (such as Spider Man).

"Sayin' it short" or wrapping description in lively but pithy statements characterizes good insults, playsongs, and "talkin' junk" in Trackton. Just as insults, playsongs, and cheers report strength in conflict, facility in struggle, and an ability to vary ways of defeating one's adversaries, so do good stories. In many ways, stories in both their form and content reflect the linguistic and role-playing lessons learned from an early age on the stage of Trackton's plaza.

35   Once they are in school, both boys and girls bring together the play with language and the experiences of knowing and feeling their preschool language learning has taught them. They continue to practice these skills and strategies in their peer language play. Twelve-year-old Terry, the son of one of Trackton's transients, told the following story to a group of boys after his first week in a new school.

TRACKTON TEXT VIII

You don't know me, but you will. I'm Terry Moore. You might think I look sissy, sittin' in dat class ackin' like I'm working, you know. But I'm de tough one around here, and I done been down to Mr.___ office more'n you can count. You know, I'm de onliest one what can stand up to dat paddle of his. He burn me up. I'ma tell you 'bout dat (pause). One day I was walkin' down de hall, now you ain't 'posed to do dat, 'less'n you got a pass, and I ain't had no pass on my ass. And all of a sudden I hear somebody comin', and dere was a feelin' like my ass was caught for sure. And it was Mr.___, and he come roun' de corner like he knowed I was dere. I took out runnin' (pause) now don't ever run 'less'n you know you don't hafta stop. Dat was my mistake. It was good while it lasted. I run all the way down Main, but my feet 'n legs start hurtin' and then I got me a strain, but den a power like Spider Man, and I look back, and dis web fall all over Mr.___, and he struggle (pause), and he struggle (pause), and he struggle. 'n den dis big old roach [cockroach] come outta de walls of dem ol' buildings on Main, and that roach start eatin' his head (pause), his fingers (pause), 'n his toes (pause) 'n he holler, 'n he holler, 'n I come to de end of Main, and I stop to watch.

"Hey Terry lis'n, hep me."

"Yea, I hep you, you gonna do what I say?"

"I do it, I do it. Just get me óutta here."

I just hold my sides laughing, and him getting madder and madder. So after I had me a good laugh, I go,

"You gonna burn dat paddle úp?"

He go, "You can háve it, you can háve it."

So I let 'im up, and call off dat roach and dat spider web, and we went back to school. But he didn't do what he say. He git me, 'n he took dat paddle to me, and to' [tore] me up (long pause). But somewhere out dere, old Spider Man, he know I'm takin' it for him, and he hep me out next time.

*　*　*

In this story, Terry has shown that he learned to "talk junk" well.

His story contains some internal rhyme (*pass, ass, Main, strain*), taboo words, similes, items associated with poverty (roach), and involvement of an outside agent of assistance—Spider Man. Terry suggests that the principal, once out of his own territory and onto Main (one of the most run-down sections of town), has no strength to overcome the forces there. The roach attacks, and the principal becomes Terry's victim, begging for help. Terry extols his own virtues—strength, wit, and wisdom. He offers some direct advice from a newcomer, showing he knows the school rules:

> You have to have a pass in the school hall; don't run away unless you are sure you can outrun your pursuer.

He also offers more subtle messages, showing he knows some rules which are not often explicitly stated: kids almost always get caught, and when a kid gets caught, he takes it like a man. Terry makes clear his undaunted spirit in spite of what may sound like defeat at the hands of the principal and abandonment by Spider Man.

Terry's story includes two double entendres. The first is in the principal's response "You can have it," and Terry does "get it" in the end. The second is his own in the question "You gonna burn dat paddle up?" The principal does "let him have it" and does "burn dat paddle up," but at Terry's expense. As children, especially boys, get older, their insults, playsongs, and stories carry numerous examples of double entendre: harmless references on the surface, but heavily suggestive—often of sexual refer-

ences. Boys delight in watching listeners to see if they catch both the literal and suggested meanings of certain expressions. Teachers and other authority figures are usually helpless either to respond to or to punish for these.

Terry's tale illustrates a type of story in which boys especially excel—the performance of a "true story" in which they "talk junk." In these, the story-teller is usually the star, and he gives highly detailed exaggerated accounts of his adventure. He
gestures wildly, contorts his face, grunts, groans, and offers other dramatizations of
the story's actions. The story may highlight the ridiculous, but it often also provides
illustration of the hard lessons of life the story-teller and the audience share.

As you've seen from your reading, "talking junk" is one way of talking
that's valued among young people of Trackton. Talking junk is not exactly a
genre, but more of a style of talking that extends across several genres—
playsongs, stories, ritual insults, and even high school cheers. Heath gives examples of a number of elements of that style, telling us that it typically involves:

- Repetition with variations
- Ritualization (requiring the same forms and elements for an appropri-
  ate performance, as in "Yo mama" ritual insults)
- Exaggeration
- Performance (with a public show or showing off)
- Verbal mocking
- Creative language play (rhyme, rhythm, alliteration)
- Taboo words

The style may be familiar to you, even if it's not used in one of your own
discourse communities. Although Heath finds it within a Black rural community, it has much in common with a style that's shared among many Black and
other urban adolescents, one that has provided the foundations for rap music,
performance poetry, and other contemporary genres.

In her larger study, Heath also looks at a number of different settings in
which the life of each community is carried out: kitchens and living rooms,
front porches, churches, schools, workplaces, and those settings have much in
common with similar settings in other communities. Where a conversation
takes place is very important in shaping what is talked about, why, and how,
and the participants who tell exaggerated or even risqué stories in one setting
will function quite differently in another. Nevertheless, some of the characteristic ways of a community are likely to be found across settings and genres. In
Trackton church settings, for example, participants draw on many of the elements of creative style that characterize other genres in the community, but
they use them in sermons and prayers.

STUDENT VOICES

Here are observations by two student researchers about style in the communities they are studying. What do they contribute to your understanding of how style might appear in a discourse community's conversations?

On the style of "modern day conversations" in an on-line discourse community of friends, communicating through instant messaging:

> "I never realized that on AIM [AOL Instant Messenger] in almost every sentence I used abbreviations. Also in the discourse community of my family or my friends, spelling and grammar don't matter as much. But I would pay more attention if I was talking to my coworkers.
>
> We not only use a lot of abbreviations, we have to go into details. On AIM when using feeling or action words a person would use*. For instance, "Doing hw . . . *sigh . . . *, but on the phone a person would know the expression of the word "sigh" by the tone of voice. Also on the phone or in person we would not say "brb," we would say "be right back." We're being polite, like when someone steps out and comes back, and the other person says "wb" (welcome back). **(Salina)**

On the style of high school friends in Mexico City:

> Teenagers in Mexico use swear words to find acceptance. Partnered with slang, it's a way in which we all communicate. Of course, the degrees of swearing change depending on how well one knows another and there are certain rules that seem to automatically be followed. First of all, one does not swear in the presence of parents or children. To a Mexican, politeness is incredibly important, and one cannot just go around swearing to everyone. Even though teenagers in Mexico City might seem very rude, it is very rare to have them swear in the presence of grownups. We acknowledge their higher standing and give them the respect they deserve. Children are respected because of their innocence. How much one swears and which specific curse words depend on your relationship to the other people. Whether you're older? Does the person you're talking to find swearing offensive or weak? How well do you know them? What is the setting? Is the group sex-segregated? Also be careful what and how much you say. The kids inexperienced in swearing stand out by using words they don't understand, by saying too many of them, and by being particularly vulgar. **(Deni)**

RESEARCH MEMO 5.3

Draw on these responses to think about some features of style that appear in the discourse community you are studying.

- Is there a characteristic style of talk?
- Does it involve the use of a particular variety of language?
- Does it draw on particular words or types of words?
- Does it tend to be carried across genres? Across settings?

(continued)

- How would you characterize that style?
- What are some of its features?
- Do you see examples of these features of style in the conversation you recorded? (If you haven't captured any examples of style in your observation notebook, begin now to watch for them.)
- Does style seem significant in other aspects of the life of the community?
- Do people dress in a particular style, or listen to music of a particular style, and does that seem to go along with the style of talk you've observed?

Write a brief research memo to capture your thinking so far about style in your community.

Heath's discussion of Roadville and Trackton continues with a comparison of storytelling in the two communities and of the ways in which each community's storytelling fits into its shared traditions and culture. She begins her comparison by looking at *how* stories are told in each community—at how they're structured, at how they're invited or introduced, at how one has to act in order to tell a story and have it be heard. She next discusses the <u>what</u> or the content of these stories. Then she goes on to discuss the purposes for storytelling in the two communities: both the purpose that's common in both settings—to entertain; and other purposes that differ. Throughout this comparison, she shows how each of these aspects of storytelling connects to the shared values of the community. She also places storytelling in the broader context of community life, showing how children learn the different ways of the two communities and describing the other models (spoken or written) they might encounter in books or sermons or Bible stories. As you read the final section on oral traditions, see how much of it fits with what you've already come to understand from your earlier reading about each of the communities and what new understandings you gain as she places the ways of the two communities against each other for direct comparison.

READING RESPONSE

From your reading and discussion of Part I and Part II of "Oral Traditions" you've developed a significant amount of shared knowledge about the ways with words of the two communities of Roadville and Trackton. From that prior knowledge, what do you predict that Heath will emphasize as she compares the storytelling traditions of the two communities?

As you read, gloss places where you find new information or where something you read earlier becomes clearer to you.

When you've read this section, write a response in which you consider what this portion of the reading adds to your earlier understanding. How does this direct comparison of the two communities help to highlight elements that might not have emerged so sharply from the discussion of each community in isolation?

Oral Traditions
Part III: The Traditions of Story-telling

Shirley Brice Heath

1   People in both Trackton and Roadville spend a lot of time telling stories. Yet the form, occasions, content, and functions of their stories differ greatly. They structure their stories differently; they hold different scales of features on which stories are recognized as *stories* and judged as good or bad. The patterns of interaction surrounding the actual telling of a story vary considerably from Roadville to Trackton. One community allows only stories which are factual and have little exaggeration; the other uses reality only as the germ of a highly creative fictionalized account. One uses stories to reaffirm group membership and behavioral norms, the other to assert individual strengths and powers. Children in the two communities hear different kinds of stories, they develop competence in telling stories in highly contrasting ways.

Roadville story-tellers use formulaic openings: a statement of a comparison or a question asked either by the story-teller or by the individual who has invited the telling of the story. Their stories maintain a strict chronicity, with direct discourse reported, and no explicit exposition of meaning or direct expression of evaluation of the behavior of the main character allowed. Stories end with a summary statement of a moral or a proverb, or a Biblical quotation. Trackton story-tellers use few formulaic openings, except the story-teller's own introduction of himself. Frequently, an abstract begins the story, asserting that the point of the story is to parade the strengths and victories of the story-teller. Stories maintain little chronicity; they move from event to event with numerous interspersions of evaluation of the behaviors of story characters and reiterations of the point of the story. Stories have no formulaic closing, but may have a reassertion of the strengths of the main character, which may be only the opening to yet another tale of adventure.

In Roadville, a story must be invited or announced by someone other than the story-teller. Only certain community members are designated good story-tellers. A story is recognized by the group as an assertion of community membership and agreement on behavioral norms. The marked behavior of the story-teller and audience alike is seen as exemplifying the weaknesses of all and the need for persistence in overcoming such weaknesses. Trackton story-tellers, from a young age, must be aggressive in inserting their stories into an on-going stream of discourse. Story-telling is highly competitive. Everyone in a conversation may want to tell a story, so only the most aggressive wins out. The stress is on the strengths of the individual who is the story's main character, and the story is not likely to unify listeners in any sort of agreement, but to provoke challenges and counterchallenges to the character's ways of overcoming an adversary. The "best stories" often call forth highly diverse additional stories, all designed not to unify the group, but to set out the individual merits of each member of the group.

Roadville members reaffirm their commitment to community and church values by giving factual accounts of their own weaknesses and the lessons learned in overcoming these. Trackton members announce boldly their individual strength in having been creative, persistent, and undaunted in the face of conflict. In Roadville, the sources of stories are personal experience and a familiarity with Biblical parables, church-related stories of Christian life, and testimonials given in church and home lesson-circles. Their stories are tales of transgressions which make the point of reiterating the expected norms of behavior of man, woman, hunter, fisherman, worker, and Christian. The stories of Roadville are true to the facts of an event; they qualify exaggeration and hedge if they might seem to be veering from an accurate reporting of events.

5   The content of Trackton's stories, on the other hand, ranges widely, and there is "truth" only in the universals of human strength and persistence praised and illustrated in the tale. Fact is often hard to find, though it is usually the seed of the story. Playsongs, ritual insults, cheers, and stories are assertions of the strong over the weak, of the power of the person featured in the story. Anyone other than the story-teller/main character may be subjected to mockery, ridicule, and challenges to show he is not weak, poor, or ugly.

In both communities, stories entertain; they provide fun, laughter, and frames for other speech events which provide a lesson or a witty display of verbal skill. In Road-ville, a proverb, witty saying, or Scriptural quotation inserted into a story adds to both the entertainment value of the story and to its unifying role. Group knowledge of a proverb or saying, or approval of Scriptural quotation reinforces the communal experi-ence which forms the basis of Roadville's stories. In Trackton, various types of language play, imitations of other community members or TV personalities, dramatic gestures and shifts of voice quality, and rhetorical questions and expressions of emotional evaluations add humor and draw out the interaction of story-teller and audience. Though both communities use their stories to entertain, Roadville adults see their stories as didactic: the purpose of a story is to make a point—a point about the conventions of behavior. Audience and story-teller are drawn together in a common bond through acceptance of the merits of the story's point for all. In Trackton, stories often have no point; they may go on as long as the audience enjoys the story-teller's entertainment. Thus a story-teller may intend on his first entry into a stream of discourse to tell only one story, but he may find the audience reception such that he can move from the first story into an-other, and yet another. Trackton audiences are unified by the story only in that they rec-ognize the entertainment value of the story, and they approve stories which extol the virtues of an individual. Stories do not teach lessons about proper behavior; they tell of individuals who excel by outwitting the rules of conventional behavior.

Children's stories and their story-telling opportunities are radically different in the two communities. Roadville parents provide their children with books; they read to them and ask questions about the books' contents. They choose books which em-phasize nursery rhymes, alphabet learning, animals, and simplified Bible stories, and they require their children to repeat from these books, and to answer formulaic ques-tions about their contents. Roadville adults similarly ask questions about oral stories which have a point relevant to some marked behavior of a child. They use proverbs and summary statements to remind their children of stories and to call on them for comparisons of the stories' contents to their own situations. Roadville parents coach children in their telling of stories, forcing them to tell a story of an incident as it has been precomposed in the head of the adult.

Trackton children tell story-poems from the age of two, and they embellish these with gestures, *inclusios*, questions asked of the audience, and repetitions with variations. They only gradually learn to work their way into any on-going discourse with their stories, and when they do, they are not asked questions about their stories, nor are they asked to repeat them. They must, however, be highly creative and entertaining to win a way into an on-going conversation. They practice the skills which they must learn in order to do so through ritualized insults, playsongs, and of course, continued attempts at telling stories to their peers.

In Roadville, children come to know a story as either a retold account from a book, or a factual account of a real event in which some type of marked behavior occurred, and there is a lesson to be learned. There are Bible stories, testimonials, sermons, and accounts of hunting, fishing, cooking, working, or other daily events. Any fictionalized account of a real event is viewed as a lie; reality is better than fiction. Roadville's church and community life admit no story other than that which meets the definition internal to the group.

10   The one kind of story Trackton prides itself on is the "true story," one in which the basis of the plot is a real event, but the details and even the outcome are exaggerated to such an extent that the story is ultimately anything but true to the facts. Boys excel in telling these stories and use them to establish and maintain status relations once they reach school age, and particularly during the preadolescent years. To Trackton people, the "true story" is the only narrative they term a "story," and the purpose of such stories is to entertain and to establish the story-teller's intimate knowledge of truths about life larger than the factual details of real events.

Three other types of stories are not termed such in Trackton: these are the retold story, the formulaic story, and the straightforward report or factual story. Girls, by the second or third grade (7–8 years), excel in telling stories they have themselves read or had read to them. They retell these stories, bringing every detail to life with exaggerated gestures, a sing-song intonation, and often an additional embellishment to the ending. They usually announce themselves before they begin the story: "I'm Zinnia, 'n I'm 'onna tell y'all sump'n." Girls particularly enjoy retelling tales in which there is a great deal of dialogue, for they play out the talking parts of characters with great relish. "Goldilocks and the Three Bears," "Billy Goat Gruff," and other stories in which animals engage in highly personalized styles of talking are favorites of the youngest school-age girls.

In formulaic stories large chunks of an oral story are retold in a frame which varies slightly from telling to telling. Both boys and girls tell these stories, as do adults in Trackton on occasion. The most common of these are stories based on Bible stories (cf. the mayor's tale of King Solomon to the quarreling boys) and ghost tales. Portions of these formulaic stories remain the same across generations, but the framework into which the chunks of dialogue, description of the ghost, or detailing of where the murder victim's wounds are placed is adapted in accordance with the situation which provoked the story. Often such stories are used as a form of social control by adults. If they do not want their children in a certain section of town, they tell ghost stories about things which happened there. Often the central character is not a ghost, but simply a scary figure who has taken on supernatural qualities and does not want his territory invaded. Respectables, when asked about these stories, link them to superstitions and to old-timey ways. They feel they are "not real stories, just ol' folks trying' to scare the young'uns."

The fourth type of story is simply a straightforward reporting of events. This is sometimes actually referred to as a "story" by Trackton children after they have begun attending school. Both boys and girls in school respond with this type of real-life report when asked to tell or write a story. They hear the primary school social studies lesson on Abraham Lincoln introduced as a story about his life, and they see that the lesson is a recounting of factual events in his life. They hear the term "story" used repeatedly in school to mean a factual reporting of what has happened or is happening, and they seem to adopt this definition for most of their in-school performances.

The classification of true, retold, formulaic, and factual stories is based only on the source of the stories, and is not one which would be regarded as making sense to the Trackton residents. For them, a "true story" calls for "talkin' junk," and only after one has learned to talk junk can one be a good story-teller. Trackton people admit, however, that children hear and read stories from books at school, and they themselves listen to "stories" [soap operas] on television. They also understand that people outside Trackton often mean a factual summary of an event when they ask Trackton folks to tell their "story" or "side of the story." But in Trackton, there is only the "true story," which would be to a Roadville resident anything but true. In contrast, neither Roadville's factual accounts nor tales from the Bible would be termed stories in Trackton. Since Trackton parents do not read books with their children and do not include these in their gifts to preschoolers, they have no occasion to talk of the stories in books. In short, for Roadville, Trackton's stories would be lies; for Trackton, Roadville's stories would not even count as stories.

Heath's work shows us that you can learn a lot about a discourse community not only by seeing it by itself, but also by comparing it to others. You may want to consider what you can learn, not only from her comparison, but by comparing what she's found for Roadville and Trackton to what you're finding for your own community, following the guidelines at the end of the chapter for a comparison essay.

EXTENDING YOUR RESEARCH

Heath's larger study of the ways with words in these communities extends beyond these oral traditions to encompass literate traditions as well. She observes all of the reading and writing that is done in the two communities. She looks at the sorts of texts that are read (not only the Bible and/or popular magazines, but job-related texts from the mill that many members of both communities work at, and letters containing information about schools or social services) or written (cards and letters to friends and family, notes to school). She looks at how they're read or written (including whether they're read by one reader or writer alone, or collaboratively within the community). She also looks at the purposes for reading and writing in the two communities. The sorts of purposes she names may be useful to you if you gather information about the uses of literacy in your own discourse community for your ethnographic study.

Exploring Uses of Literacy

Heath found that literacy was used for the following purposes in both Roadville and Trackton:

Reading

Instrumental: to gain information for practical needs of daily life (e.g. labels on products)

News-related: to gain information about things that were happening locally or beyond (e.g. newspapers and church bulletins)

Confirmational: to check and confirm facts or beliefs (e.g. the Bible, appliance directions)

Social-interactional: to get information related to social connections (e.g. greeting cards and letters, church newsletters, articles about children on sports pages)

Members of the Roadville community used reading for one additional purpose:

Recreational/Educational: to be entertained or to plan entertainment (e.g. comics, ads for movies)

Writing

Memory aids: to serve as a reminder (telephone numbers, notes, grocery lists)

Substitutes for oral messages: to communicate when direct oral communication wasn't possible (notes for school, greeting cards, letters)

Financial: to sign checks, write out amounts and purposes of expenditures

And in Roadville:

> *Social-interactional:* to maintain social connections (letters, thank you notes)

And in Trackton:

> *Public Records:* to announce the order of church services and forthcoming events and to record policy decisions (church bulletins, reports of committees)

In general, Heath found that people used literacy mostly to accomplish practical functions in their daily lives. Roadville members praised reading and kept reading materials around, but they didn't typically do any reading that wasn't immediately necessary. And with the exception of the social-interactional uses of writing in Roadville, members of both communities also wrote only when they needed to accomplish the specific functions Heath lists.

In the end, Heath found that the ways people read and wrote—the <u>what,</u> and <u>how</u>, and <u>why</u> of their literate traditions—in these communities wasn't very different from the ways of their oral traditions. Trackton residents who gathered on their front porches to tell stories in collaborative ways, building on each others' turns, tended also to gather on their front porch to read letters that came from schools or state agencies, engaging in a collaborative reading and interpretation that everyone would contribute to. Roadville residents who looked to the Bible and to sermons for strict models of how a story should be told also looked to the instructions in "how-to" magazines for models for carrying out other activities. The values and ways of the communities weren't different when it came to their practices of literacy, but were represented in them, and by studying the communities' literate practices as well as oral conversations, and stepping back to reflect on the connections between them, Heath reinforced her understandings of the values and beliefs each community shared.

	RESEARCH MEMO 5.4

While you're spending an hour or two in the discourse community you are studying, note every time a member of the community uses literacy directly (reading, writing, or using other forms of representation—symbols, numbers) or indirectly (referring in conversation to a written text, something someone read in the newspaper for example). Using your observation notebook, you may find it helpful to create the observation chart below, rather than the usual double entry format.

Then name the function for which this literacy activity is used, working from those Heath found in Roadville and Trackton, and adding your own terms where Heath's don't apply. Star any functions/purposes that aren't on Heath's list.

Time   Place   Literacy Activity   <u>What</u>   <u>How</u>   <u>Why</u>   (Function/purpose)

(continued)

(continued)

In a journal response, reflect on the most significant functions of literacy that you have observed in your discourse community. Does your discourse community typically use literacy for other functions that didn't appear on your observation chart? Comment particularly on the functions of literacy in your own discourse community that don't appear in Heath's communities. What characterizes them, what's their purpose, how do you decide when you've completed them and accomplished their functions? Has doing this observation led you to any new insights about the role of literacy in your discourse community? Do you find it to be distinct from or continuous with what you're discovering about conversations in your discourse community (about the <u>what</u>, <u>why</u>, and <u>how</u> of communication there)?

Are there other uses of literacy in other parts of your own life that aren't included here? Do they suggest other purposes and other values that aren't reflected in this discourse community? How do the values underlying some use of literacy in your discourse community compare to the values associated with the same use in Roadville or Trackton?

STUDENT VOICES

Here are selections from Blanca's reflection on literacy in her community:

My community uses literacy for the purpose of learning. In my community, we can find all sorts of different knowledge in general. Learning something new is always interesting and welcomed by us. By reading books we enrich ourselves and afterwards we can share what we learned, such as new vocabulary. For example, I remember how a few days ago Laura was asking the group the meaning of a word that she read somewhere and didn't understand. Aniket, Kelly, and myself were giving her different responses in search for the correct one. That shows the interest of learning that we have in our community. . . .

Our discourse community has totally different habits [from Roadville]. All of us like reading, just for the pleasure of it, and we always have at least one book we are in the process of reading. We comment on it and give ideas for new readings. . . .

In Roadville, people quote from the Bible for any need they have in every day life. We could never do that, not only because most of us don't know any passage by heart, but also because there's not one particular religion which we all have in common. Instead, we are familiar with different religions from our backgrounds such as Catholicism and Hinduism.

The biggest difference is created by the fact that people in Roadville have a small perspective of the world. I believe this is mainly because they have never been away from their town. All they know is what they've seen since they were children. That's the way they have been raised and those are the traditions that they follow. Different communities do things in different ways, but we really can't criticize them unless we have a good idea of why they do things that way. Even then, who is to say what is the right way or the wrong way of living.

(continued)

Earlier in this chapter you saw some excerpts from the conversation Blanca recorded and some of her discussion of that conversation and how it reflects insider knowledge and values. Do you find connections between what she said earlier and what she finds here about her community's literacy practices and the ways in which they differ from those of Roadville? Do you find evidence of continuity between the oral and written traditions of Blanca's community, in the way that Heath has found for Roadville?

Connecting the Local and the Wider Culture

One way in which communities may connect to a wider culture is through their literacy—through what they read and write and the written texts that others bring into their conversations. They also connect through television, movies, music—some of the other shared interests that you've explored. Although her primary focus was on the communities of Roadville and Trackton, Heath also compared their ways to those of the Maintown community—the townspeople who typically had more education and were more likely to hold professional positions than the people of Roadville or Trackton. What she found was that the values of the townspeople were less likely to be defined locally through only the interaction within the community, and more likely to be defined in relationship to other groups beyond the community—the professional associations that people belong to, for example. This connection was typically maintained through the things that people read and wrote. Here's what she had to say about the townspeople and their shared values values that carry into both their oral and literate traditions.

> The townspeople, black and white, are *mainstreamers*, people who see themselves as being in the mainstream of things. They look beyond the Piedmont for rules and guidance in ways of dressing, entertaining themselves, decorating their homes, and decision-making in their jobs. . . . Secondary sources, not the face-to-face network, are usually authoritative for mainstreamers. They choose their movies on the advice of critics; they select their automobile tires on the recommendations of consumers' guides; they seek out professional advice for marital problems, and for interior decorating and landscaping ideas. An individual's assertion of formal credentials—either university degrees or public awards and distinction—makes him an authority (1983, 236).

Maintowners, even when gathered in familiar local groups, carry into those groups their sense of connection to a wider culture.

While the informal and familiar discourse community that you are studying may have its own locally defined ways, it may also orient itself to a larger, more public culture—through music, for example, or internet technology—or a somewhat private subculture like skateboarding that extends through many communities around the world although outsiders are only minimally aware of it.

STUDENT VOICES

Both in the conversation you've been analyzing and in other exchanges and interactions, consider the ways in which your discourse community makes connections to a wider culture. Begin by reading the following reflections by a student writer on the connections she found in the dinner-time conversations of her Puerto Rican family:

> In this community Puerto Rican political movements, as well as important figures like Carlos Albizu Campos and Bernardo Vega, among others, are often discussed. Perhaps discussing these important matters during dinner time assures the participants' knowledge of their history. As we go into depth we realize there is a bigger picture presented here not only about Puerto Ricans but Hispanic families in the United States.
>
> In these dinner-time conversations we speak Spanglish. Today just about every Hispanic family residing in the United States uses Spanglish. However this language came about, one theory is for certain; after living in the United States for so long, many have forgotten words in their native tongue. But being able to use the two languages we grew up with, Spanish and English, is also a strong value in my community.
>
> The conversation begins when my sister Ingrid states the fact that to her Bernardo Vega was the best Puerto Rican writer. Her tone of voice sounded, to my mother, doubtful as if she was uncertain and so the statement is understood as a question, "Mami, verdad que the best writer Boricua era Bernardo Vega." The conversation gets interrupted by my older sister Diana who is distracted by other things. But my mother, on the other hand, extends the conversation about Puerto Rican writers to contribute to everyone's understanding. She extends the conversation so that knowing something about this becomes of importance and use to those present. **(Abby)**

RESEARCH MEMO 5.5

Thinking about what Abby discovered, look back at your transcribed conversation for examples of connections to the wider culture. Look also at some of the other exchanges and interactions in your discourse community that you've captured in your observation notebook. Are there times that members of that community take as their point of reference something in the larger culture—a movie, a book, a television program, a football team, a music group—or something in a larger cultural tradition associated with their religion or their racial or ethnic origins? Reflect on the significance of that connection and on what it contributes to the shared understandings, shared ways, and shared values of your community?

In the wider culture of those who are interested in studying communities and language, many researchers have drawn on Heath's study, bringing it into their own conversations and letting it guide their own work. Her work is significant because it was the first major study that looked so extensively at the communicative life of particular communities. It showed what we've been seeing in the examples in this book—that knowing how to talk or speak or read or write in the right ways for a particular community depends on becoming an insider to that community, and that insiders have rich communicative competence in their own communities.

WRITING IN ACADEMIC GENRES: THE COMPARISON ESSAY

Writers need to do the sort of thinking, talking, reading, writing, and research that typically goes on in an academic community. They need not only to have guidelines for writing in academic genres, but to participate in the work that specific genres of academic writing grow out of, as you are doing with your own research. Making comparisons, as Heath has done with Roadville and Trackton, is a common way of developing new understandings in academic work. An example of a student writer's comparison essay follows in *Student Voices*.

EXPLORATORY ESSAY

To compare your community to those Heath studied (or to those being studied by other classmates), begin by making a chart for the key elements or points of comparison you want to look at for each of the communities. (Two organizing strategies for comparison essays, the chart, and the Venn diagram, are discussed in Writing Strategies, pp. 511–512.) Consider <u>what</u> people talk about (their typical topics), <u>why</u> (their typical purposes and intentions), <u>how</u> (their typical genres, styles, and roles), what's important about the situation, and what shared beliefs and values are reflected. Add other points of comparison that you think might be important.

Then choose some elements of similarity or difference from your chart that seem significant, and write an essay in which you explore connections (similarities and/or differences) between what Heath observed in either (or both) community and what you've been discovering in your own, drawing supporting evidence from Heath's text and from your own data and journal entries thus far.

As you structure your essay, you can choose to discuss each point for one community and then for the other (with supporting evidence for each point). Or you can discuss the first point for both communities, the second for both communities, as Denise has done in the essay below. (These are the typical genre expectations for the structure of comparison and contrast essays.)

You'll also need an introduction to the comparison you're undertaking that says something about what you hope to learn from it (a question or thesis). And you'll need a conclusion that says something about what you did learn and how it has contributed to you developing understandings about discourse communities in general or about your own discourse community.

You'll draw on these ideas for your longer report on a discourse community—to place your study in the context of other work that has been done on a topic. (You'll see examples of this in the research reports by student writers that are included in the Part II readings.)

STUDENT VOICES
Denise has used the structure of comparison and contrast to bring out the similarities and differences she found between conversations and storytelling within her community of friends, in Roadville and in Trackton. Gloss her essay, to look for the points she makes about each community and to see how she has used this structure. Then look at the chart she has made. Has the chart served as an effective guide for the final structure she creates?

There are various uses for conversations within discourse communities. While exploring Heath's Roadville and Trackton communities, I found the theme of "social unity" as the main purposes for conversation within each of these two communities. After reviewing my transcription, I noticed that social unity was also the purpose or theme displayed through the conversation that took place within my own discourse community. While exploring the various "ways with words" in Roadville and Trackton, Heath found the following to be true of Roadville, "stories recount an actual event either witnessed by others or previously told in the presence of others and declared by them a "good story." This seems to be the basis for "stories" told within my discourse community as well.

The settings for each community are quite different. Roadville is a rural white community and Trackton is a rural black community. My discourse community is even a bit more different than these two. My community is set in an *urban* white area. "Stories" or conversations take on different meaning within each of the communities, although they all share a common purpose (social unity). Residents of Roadville use stories to recount true life experiences which are told in "good fun" and are never intended to bring harm to anybody. In Trackton, though, stories are recounted in an embellished and exaggerated fashion. My community's usage of "story telling" was similar to Roadville's as Buzzy's night of drinking (an actual event) was shared with the group.

I also noticed that the representation of members varied in each community. Heath indicates that in Roadville, "stories are told only in sex segregated groups." Trackton's storytelling sessions include both sexes and all ages. My community, as does Trackton's, includes members from both sexes, but unlike Trackton and Roadville, the age of each member in my community is similar.

My community and Roadville's community were exact when it came to the actual "telling of the story". In both communities, a story is requested with a question being asked. In Roadville, Mrs. Dee asks Sue, "Do you have a new recipe?" In my community, Jasmine asks Buzzy, "How did you feel the next morning?" The stories then proceed from there. The storyteller in Roadville sets the pace of the conversation and is in control of the group, but Buzzy, who is the storyteller in my community, is not the leader of the group. In fact, he is the follower as the other group members lead the conversation through the asking of various questions directed towards Buzzy, the storyteller.

An interesting characteristic of a Roadville story is that the story being told usually leads to the telling of another story that is similar to the present topic being discussed. Heath describes it as thus, "one story triggers another, as person after person reaffirms a familiarity with the kind of experience just recounted." Similarly, I found this pattern within my community's conversation. The story being told at one point is concerning Buzzy's broken finger. Jasmine can relate to a similar personal experience and offered the following, "I broke my shoulder and they sent me to the orthopedic surgeon the

(continued)

next day." Buzzy chimed in with an experience concerning somebody that he knew and added this, "A guy I know had three slipped discs." These separate stories were in relationship to the overall theme of the conversation. Buzzy could identify with the shared, familiar personal experiences that were similar to his own.

After reading Heath's study on the "Ways with Words" in Roadville and Trackton, I have gained new insight in the use of conversation within my own discourse community. It does not really matter what the topic of conversation is or who the storyteller is within my group. We participate in group conversation to "glue" us together socially. As in Roadville, our stories are frequently based upon actual events, but are very seldom told in a serious manner. The participants like to have fun with one another and do not like to venture into discussing topics that are "heavy" in nature. Conversation within my discourse community is used as a means of social interaction to increase the relationship ties between each of the participants. **(Denise)**

Are the points of comparison that Denise makes clear to you? Do you think the characteristics she identifies for Roadville and Trackton are a good representation of what Heath has had to say? Do you see ways in which her comparison to Roadville and Trackton sheds light on her own community? Does Denise provide enough shared knowledge so that you, as an outsider to her study (though not to Heath's) can make sense of what she's saying here?

DENISE'S COMPARISON CHART

Roadville	Trackton	My Community
Setting is a rural white community.	Setting is a rural black community.	Setting is an urban, white/Generation X.
Stories recount an actual event. They are used for good fun and do not mean any harm.	Stories are embellished and exaggerated.	Buzzy's story was based on an actual event laced with jokes.
Stories begin with a question (inquiry from a participant).	Story is told by one person voluntarily beginning with personal experience.	Story is told upon request. Question is asked of Buzzy by Jasmine.
Stories are told in sex-segregated groups.	All sexes and ages are present when stories are told.	Story is told where the gender is mixed but the ages are similar.
One story triggers another story.	Stories invite participation from all listeners. There isn't just one storyteller.	Story being told triggered stories from all participants.
Storyteller is in control of the conversation within the group.	All participants of the group are active in storytelling.	Participants/questioners were in charge of storytelling.
Story becomes an expression of social unity.	Stories are intended to intensify social interactions.	Story was used to "glue" the participants of the group together in a social setting.

CHAPTER

6

Writing in Ethnographic Genres

In Chapter 6, we'll focus on ways in which you can extend your research into the setting you've chosen, looking more closely at the nature of the setting, the roles participants play in it, and the patterns that emerge in ongoing interactions there. We'll consider the underlying shared values and beliefs that bring participants to that setting, or that participants develop in response to the setting itself. We'll read part of an ethnographic study of a college bar near a mid-western campus, done by anthropologist James Spradley and his student, Brenda Mann, to see how this study can guide your own inquiry. We'll also look at the ways researchers report on their studies, comparing the style and structure of Spradley and Mann's ethnography to Heath's. We'll consider the style and purpose of other examples of ethnographic writing included at the end of Part II, and explore ways for you to report on what you've learned, using the academic genre of a research report. The inquiries of this chapter will focus on three questions:

- What can you learn, as a researcher, by moving from a focused study of a conversation to a broader observation of patterns of interaction in your community?

- How can you use an ethnographic study by other researchers to guide your own research and to help you interpret what you find?

- As a writer, what can you discover about the ways others have reported on their studies to help you decide how to report on what you learn?

The communities that Heath studied in *Ways with Words* are ones that people have lived in their whole lives, where people have grown up with the understandings they share and where those shared understandings underlie their interactions in a number of specific settings—on front porches, in churches, at other gathering spots, and even to a significant degree at the mill where most members of these two communities worked. The communities Heath studied are *primary discourse communities*, reflecting the language and the ways of using language that their members grew up with. Residents of these communities don't spend much time in *secondary discourse communities* where they have to learn significantly different ways with words.

You may be studying a newly forming discourse community or a life-long discourse community of family or friends you grew up with. Or you may have chosen a setting that falls someplace in between—perhaps a specific location like a sport team's locker room or a workplace, where participants enter an ongoing culture and gradually become insiders to it, coming to participate in (and to contribute to and perhaps alter) its values and its ways. The participants in such secondary discourse settings have typically grown up in many different primary discourse communities, with many different ways of talking, and often different languages or dialects, but they've generally learned to adapt those ways fairly quickly to new settings as they need to. In semi-public settings that many different people enter over time, there's typically an established ongoing pattern of interaction that newcomers learn as they participate—a pattern that can be seen day after day, no matter which insiders happen to be present and that will continue in a similar form after current insiders go on to other places.

OBSERVING A SETTING AND THE WAYS PEOPLE INTERACT THERE

Workplace settings are typical examples of secondary discourse communities that people step into for a time, adopting new ways while sometimes bringing in old ones. Here's one such setting, a telemarketing office staffed mostly by college students, studied by Charles, an insider. The following description was taken from his final report. In it, he provides important background knowledge about the setting that his readers need to share:

> The discourse community that I decided to record and transcribe was at my job, which is in a telemarketing office. Here I am a fundraiser who calls people for contributions and the other people who were on the phone while I was recording are called verifiers. Their jobs are to confirm any contributions that I receive or anyone else at the job because our pay is based on how many pledges we can receive.

And here's a typical exchange:

TANYA: (*on the phone*) Hello.

MARITSA: He did not say whether he was there or not.

TANYA: May I please speak to Albert?

MARITSA: No.

TANYA: No message, I'll give him a call back.

SHARINE: God bless you.

MARITSA: I don't think I ever answered the phone in my mother's house saying
            [when asked] "Hello is such and such here?" "NO"

SHARINE: Me either.

MARITSA: and pause for like . . . five seconds, "NO"

TANYA: Hello, may I speak to Peter . . . alright, thank you.

TANYA: (*recreating phone call*) "No I'm sorry he is not in." (*slams the phone*)

EVERYONE: (*laughing*)

MARITSA: Tanya!

TANYA: (*recreating phone call*). "Can I please speak to Mr. Johnson?" "NO."
            (*Slams the phone and starts to laugh.*)

MICHAEL: I told you a classic one. When I call up sometimes they say "Well what
            do you want?" and I say "NOTHING!" klump, and I hang up on them.

MARITSA: (*laughs*)

MICHAEL: "What do you want?" "Nothing!"

Here the participants are doing what telemarketers do every evening in settings like this: making phone calls, asking if someone is home, making requests for donations (or trying to sign on customers for new goods and services) and getting occasional affirmative responses along with numerous rejections. Participants who come to work in this setting quickly learn to adopt the more formal style required for this sort of work—the polite phrases and tone of voice, the carefully enunciated requests, the open-ended responses when someone can't be reached. "I'll give him a call back." But they adopt other ways of this workplace community as well, and a second line of interaction runs parallel to the first—the recreating of the phone exchanges and the refusals that are heard, with much laughter, often followed by comments in a very different tone and style. Charles describes this pattern, as it appeared in this particular conversation:

Everyone had a story or experience that they wanted to share with everyone else. The main topic that everyone spoke about was how rude other people can be over the phone. One at a time, each of the participants took turns describing the rudeness of the people they have spoken to. As they each were recalling their own experiences, they would describe it as if the event just took place. Tanya describes how she was calling for this woman's husband and the woman just said "No, he's not here," and the woman slams the phone. She then imitates the woman and repeats the response and then slams the phone a couple of times. We also try to figure out the reasons why people are so rude.

The studies carried out by many student researchers in their workplace settings have shown similar dual patterns of interaction, one for interacting with the public, and another for interacting with fellow employees, and these patterns are often directly linked, as Charles has found, so that what goes on in the public side of the work is echoed and processed somehow in the moments when employees step back from their public roles.

Here's a description of another workplace:

> Dependable Cleaners . . . is a business . . . in which the employees consist mainly of young workers ranging from the ages of seventeen to twenty. The majority of customers that enter this store are older people who live in this area. The conversations and topics that are discussed vary dependent on the participants in the action. Certain behaviors that are characteristic of behind the counter would not be carried out to those that are over the counter. Actions such as bitching, swearing, gossiping, joking, and ridiculing take place only in the presence of other well-known employees. Greeting, talking, and "kissing ass" are actions portrayed to the customer. These types of speech acts are also characteristic of other communities that serve the initial purpose of serving customers in order to gain profit for a business. Certain behaviors are taught and required to be used in the presence of paying customers. The saying that "the customer is always right" is a needed piece of information in this particular type of community.
>
> As you are on the other side of the counter, you are automatically labeled as an outsider, which is someone who does not belong to the group of behind the counter insiders, unless of course you are a friend or family member, in which case the same rules of restraint do not apply as they do to other customers. **(Melissa)**

As Melissa sets the context for her study, her description of the setting shows how important the physical setting is to what goes on in it—the fact that there is a counter makes visible a division in the roles of participants into customers and employees—a division represented in 'other side of the counter' outsiders, and "behind the counter insiders." In the telemarketing office also, although Charles identifies distinct employee roles, the setting itself reinforces the major distinction in roles, between telemarketers who are sitting close together on the inside making phone calls to solicit money for a number of causes, and potential donors at the other end of the phone lines who accept or reject those phone calls.

Although it doesn't emerge strongly from either of these studies, another element that can often distinguish insiders in workplaces and other secondary discourse communities from outsiders is a specialized vocabulary. There are typically short-hand terms for food orders in restaurants, technical terms for technology workers, medical terms in hospital labs. The telemarketing office does have specialized names for the roles that people play—fundraisers and verifiers—and the meaning of the latter term might not be immediately clear to outsiders. Families too can have insider vocabulary, and friends often do. As you consider the setting, you'll want to identify any specialized insider terms that are used.

Melissa further differentiates the insiders and outsiders in this setting by identifying the sorts of actions that typically take place behind-the-counter and distinguishing these from those that would go on in the presence of customers—actions like "bitching," "gossiping," and "ridiculing," as opposed to "kissing ass." She has identified these actions through repeated and systematic observations, and her categorization of these as "types of speech acts" points to another concept that has become important to ethnographers of communication and another tool that such researchers use in understanding the settings they study.

RESEARCH MEMO 6.1

Begin by recording, in your observation notebook, moments in which the physical setting specifically influences what's going on in your discourse community, whether it's a car, a kitchen table, a gym, or an office. What physical objects contribute to what takes place among people in the setting? How are people arranged there? In the other column reflect on any connections you find between any aspect of the setting and the roles of participants, their interests, preoccupations, and concerns, and the ways in which they interact.

Next, record examples of insider terms—specialized vocabulary, common words that have taken on special meanings, made-up words or expressions, even nicknames, that are unique to this community or to communities like this one. In your double entry notebook, list the terms that you hear being used in this community and any others that you recall. Use the other column to reflect on the significance of these terms—why they are used in this community and what they contribute to insiders' shared identity and ways of seeing the world. Look back also at your transcribed conversation. Do you find any of these terms there? If so, how are they used in a conversational context? Include these examples in your notebook. How would you define any of these terms for outsiders?

Finally, record any sorts of interactions that differentiate outsiders and insiders if both are present. Again, in the other column, reflect on any patterns you begin to see and connections you can find to others' observations and interpretations (those of your classmates, or those represented in these chapters).

Write a research memo in which you report on anything you discovered from these observations of the physical setting, insider terms, and patterns of interaction that adds to the picture you've been developing of this discourse community. Create a glossary of insider terms if there are any that outsiders won't readily understand.

STUDENT VOICES

Here are a student researcher's comments on insider terms from his final report on his study of a discourse community of skateboarders.

Our discourse community as skateboarders is definitely an insider's world. Just knowing what a skateboard is would not really be able to help you much on being an insider on our speech and our actions . . . To understand a conversation you would need knowledge of many aspects of the sport. You would need to know the names and how certain tricks are done, also a knowledge of who is who in the skateboarding world. You would need to know the names that we have given to certain skateboard spots, a sort of skateboarding geography. Also knowing a history of skateboarding including what tricks have been done and in what videos would help.

Examples of this would be in my transcript. I am talking to Roger about what they had done at Donny. Roger replies, "Ummm Jerry backside nose blunt slid down and popped out."

To understand this conversation you would need to know what Donny is; Donny is the name skaters have given to a certain long ledge on Beacon Street in Boston. The reason we call it Donny is because the first person to do something down it was a kid named Donny Barley. Hence Donny Ledge. By giving it this name, we have made it much easier to talk about it instead of saying, "The ledge on Beacon Street that goes along the twelve stairs about three feet high." This is too time-consuming so we say "Donny."

Most skate spots in Boston and all over the world have nicknames. A skater from Boston could be talking to a skater from San Francisco and they could name off names like Black Rock, Hubba, Pier 7, Love Park, Brown Marble, Pullaskey, Bercy, and they would fully understand what the other person was talking about.

Now to understand more of the conversation, you would need insider knowledge on the names of tricks and how to perform them. For example, you would have to know what a back-side nose-blunt slide is. A back-side nose-blunt slide is a very difficult trick; it's when the rider turns ninety degrees and places the nose of the board and wheels on top of the ledge or object and travels a distance on top of the ledge and rolls away. Now for Jerry to do this down Donny is basically impossible, so now the person listening to the conversation knows that Roger is being sarcastic. **(Matt O)**

Are any of these specialized skateboarding terms familiar to you? Do you get enough of an explanation, or enough sense from the context in which they are used, to understand what they refer to as an outsider? Do these specialized terms remind you of any others in your own discourse community that you haven't yet thought of?

Looking specifically at the characteristic *speech acts* of a setting is a good way to look more broadly at many sorts of exchanges, to complement the picture you've been getting by looking closely at one conversation. It provides another way of beginning to see more about the culture of a discourse community—to understand its values, meanings, what insiderness involves, and what the elements are in the identity kit that will allow someone to function as an insider in that setting.

A *speech act* has been defined by philosophers of language as a way of doing things with words. In our ordinary lives, we are constantly using our words to make things happen and to have an effect on those around us: greeting, apologizing, promising, reprimanding, gossiping, even lying. Thinking of our words as acts, intended to accomplish something, helps us to focus on the <u>why</u>—on the intentions and purposes behind what we say. Knowing how to interpret a speech act, being able to read the intentions behind the words that are spoken, is a fundamental aspect of shared knowledge within a discourse community. Such knowledge often separates insiders from outsiders.

The term *speech act* is usually used to refer to specific utterances but not usually to a larger string of them. A conversation generally has a number of different speech acts—moments when speakers are informing, teasing, apologizing. Longer stretches of these acts make up larger *speech events*, and when a particular speech event, like cheering for a team (which may include specific speech acts like praising, urging, insulting the other team) goes on often and takes on a set form with identifiable elements, those elements make it recognizable as a *speech genre*—in this case, cheering.

Being an insider always depends on both your *performance* and your *interpretation* of all the speech acts and speech genres of the community you're in. To be an insider, you must be able to perform correctly the speech acts that are most common—to know how to joke, or to pray or to "testify," for example (as we saw in "The River"). You must know how to turn an experience with burnt rolls into a moral lesson in Roadville, or to give an appropriately worded insult in Trackton. The student couples whose conversation Laura and Blanca recorded know how to give compliments appropriately, in ways that are understood by the others. The student telemarketers know how to perform the speech acts involved in soliciting money in ways that will be seen as appropriate, even if the larger speech event of solicitation itself isn't appreciated. And workers at Dependable Cleaners know how to "kiss ass" at some times, as well as to bitch and ridicule at others. At the same time, the particpants in all of these settings need to know when others are offering an insult, giving a compliment, or "kissing ass."

The challenge for the insider researcher, however, is *naming* what you know. As an insider you already know how to participate in these speech acts—to perform them and to interpret them when they're performed by others. But it's hard to step back from the setting and name the implicit knowledge that allows you to participate successfully, to put your interpretations of what goes on there into words. Being systematic in your observation and applying methods that other researchers have used will help you to make the implicit explicit.

You can begin to observe speech acts in your discourse community by listing, in your observation notebook, the actions you see people trying to accomplish with words. Every time you think you see someone trying to do something through words (something we do with all of the words that we speak), make note of the words that are said. Then reflect on

> <u>What</u>—what the words themselves refer to,
>
> <u>How</u>—what you notice about the form/style of those words,
>
> <u>Why</u>—the apparent intentions and purposes of the speaker: what the speaker seems to be trying to accomplish with those words.

At this point, turn back to your transcript of a conversation and gloss it for speech acts. Where do you find speakers actively trying to accomplish something with their words, what do you think they're trying to accomplish, and why?

RESEARCH MEMO 6.2

LEARNING FROM AN ETHNOGRAPHIC STUDY

"How to Ask for a Drink" by James Spradley and Brenda Mann explores the meanings and values of a cultural setting by looking at the speech acts that go on there. It comes from a book, *The Cocktail Waitress,* in which Spradley and Mann report on what they learned about a particular work setting—a "college bar" in a Midwestern city where many of the customers and most of the waitresses were also college students. At the time of the study, Brenda Mann was an insider participant in this setting, working as a waitress while she was going to school. James Spradley was her professor and an outside observer/researcher. Together they collected different sorts of data that would help them understand what went on in the bar and the values represented in the interactions that were taking place there, including data on the ways people talked to each other and what they were trying to do with their words—their speech acts. They then interpreted those data together from both insider and outsider perspectives.

As they report on this setting, Spradley and Mann are involved in both naming and renaming. On the one hand, they wanted to understand the setting from an insider perspective so, as they observed interactions and cataloged the common speech acts, they asked waitresses about what they observed, and they recorded the words the waitresses use to name what was going on. At the same time, however, as they report on what they found, they are renaming it in the terms used by other researchers who carry out ethnographic studies of communication—translating the insider knowledge of the bar into the insider knowledge of an academic field, using the specialized vocabulary that represents key concepts in the field. Many of the terms they use highlight ways of interacting that have been found across cultural settings. As a reader, you'll want to note them and consider how they might apply to your own setting.

While Heath reported on Roadville and Trackton in a narrative form, telling the story of life in the two communities and imbedding her analysis in that narrative, Spradley and Mann report on their research in a form that's more characteristic of the traditional research report. They aren't trying to tell a story that recreates the bar experience for you or that lets you participate in it as a reader. So you won't have the same participatory reading experience that you have had with earlier readings. Nevertheless, in your first reading of this selection, you are still going to be participating in a way of seeing this setting that Spradley and Mann have framed—taking in what they have to tell you, seeing the setting through their eyes, finding your own connections with what they have to say and bringing in your own examples of the phenomena they describe. Because they're speaking to an audience of other researchers who are interested in studying cultural settings—both faculty researchers like Spradley and student researchers like Mann—they present their study in ways that will be familiar to many researchers who might want to carry out studies like this one.

You'll want to approach this reading from the stance of a researcher who is carrying out a similar study, to see what you can learn from their approach. You may be interested in learning about Brady's Bar, but for this moment it's most important to see how researchers study settings like this, what elements they look at that may be useful to look at in your setting, and how these researchers name what they find—the key concepts that will help you to name what you observe in your setting.

Read through the Spradley and Mann selection now to get an idea of how they went about their study of speech acts so that you can borrow from their approach and their key concepts as you continue to identify and analyze speech acts in your discourse community. Later, you will want to go back to read more analytically from the perspective of the writer of a research report— looking at what went into the report they've written, how they've structured it, and for what purposes.

READING RESPONSE

1. Before you begin to read "How to Ask for a Drink," look through the whole article.

   - Think about the title. What do you think this study will be about?

   - Look at the section headings, and note what you bring from your prior knowledge. What do you expect each section ("The Ethnography of Speaking," "Speech Acts") to tell you? Are there headings that you do not have enough prior knowledge (from your study this semester or from your out-of-school experience) to speculate about?

   - What do you predict that you might learn from this study of speech acts in a bar room setting, based on what you see in these headings?

   (continued)

Taking a minute to write a page or so in response to these questions will give you the opportunity to reflect on the expectations you form and the understandings that you bring as a reader, and will allow you to situate yourself in relation to this text. It's a useful technique to use when approaching any new reading, especially an academic study.

2. As you read, gloss this text from the perspective of a reader and a researcher. Try to get a sense of how Spradley and Mann are using the concept of a speech act along with a general sense of this discourse community and the shared knowledge and values insiders there have. As a researcher, consider the following:

- The questions Spradley and Mann are asking

- The ways they go about trying to answer those questions

- The examples they give of speech acts and speech events at Brady's Bar, and their understanding and interpretation of these acts and events

- The key concepts they use in studying this setting and these acts

- How the examples they've included and their discussion of those examples offer you an understanding of some key concepts

- The extent to which the key concepts offer you ways of thinking about and talking about what you're observing in your own discourse community setting

3. Many of the terms Spradley and Mann use to talk about the language used at Brady's Bar are specific to the study of cultural settings as such studies are carried out by anthropologists and anthropological linguists. These specific terms from the field can provide you with new ways of thinking about and framing your own study. To add these terms to your repertoire of ways of speaking about language and about discourse communities, you should create a glossary as you read, writing down each new term you come to and making a few notes about your working definition of each one and/or an example (from Spradley and Mann's study or from your own) that you think will fit it.

How to Ask for a Drink

James Spradley and Brenda Mann

1   Brady's Bar is obviously a place to drink. Every night a crowd of college-age men and women visit the bar for this purpose. But even a casual observer could not miss the fact that Brady's is also a place to *talk*. Drinking and talking are inseparable. The lonely drinker who sits in silence is either drawn into conversation or leaves the bar. Everyone feels the anxious insecurity of such a person, seemingly alone in the crowd at Brady's. It is also believed that drinking affects the way people talk, lubricating the social interchange. If liquor flows each night in Brady's like a stream from behind the bar, talking, laughing, joking, and dozens of simultaneous conversations cascade like a

torrent from every corner of the bar. Early in our research we became aware that our ethnography would have to include an investigation of this speech behavior.

The importance of drinking and talking has also been observed by anthropologists in other societies. Take, for example, the Subanun of the Philippine Islands, studied by Charles Frake.[1] Deep in the tropical rain forests of Zamboanga Peninsula on the island of Mindanao, these people live in small family groups, practicing swidden agriculture. Social ties outside the family are maintained by networks to kin and neighbors rather than through some larger formal organization. Social encounters beyond the family occur on frequent festive occasions that always include "beer" drinking. Unlike Brady's Bar with separate glasses for each person, the Subanun place fermented mash in a single, large Chinese jar and drink from this common container by using a long bamboo straw. A drinking group gathers around the jar, water is poured over the mash, and each person in turn sucks beer from the bottom of the jar. As the water passes through the mash it is transformed into a potent alcoholic beverage. There are elaborate rules for these drinking sessions that govern such activities as competitive drinking, opposite-sexed partners drinking together under the cover of a blanket, and games where drinking is done in chugalug fashion. But the drinking is secondary to the talking on these occasions and what Frake has said about the Subanun might easily apply to Brady's Bar:

> The Subanun expression for drinking talk, . . . "talk from the straw," suggests an image of the drinking straw as a channel not only of the drink but also of drinking talk. The two activities, drinking and talking, are closely interrelated in that how one talks bears on how much one drinks and the converse is, quite obviously, also true . . . Especially for an adult male, one's role in the society at large, insofar as it is subject to manipulation, depends to a considerable extent on one's verbal performance during drinking encounters.[2]

In this chapter we will examine the verbal performances of those who participate in the social life at Brady's. We focus on a single speech event, *asking for a drink*, and the social function of this event. This chapter is intended as a partial ethnography of speaking, a description of the cultural rules at Brady's Bar for using speech.

THE ETHNOGRAPHY OF SPEAKING[3]

5   Throughout each of the preceding chapters our description has aimed at answering the fundamental ethnographic question: "What would a stranger have to know to act appropriately as a cocktail waitress and to interpret behavior from her perspec-

---

[1] This discussion is based on Charles O. Frake, "How to Ask for a Drink in Subanun" (1964b). This classic article provided many insights as well as the framework for the material presented in this chapter.

[2] Ibid. (1964b:128–129).

[3] One of the earliest formulations of the approach to a cultural description of speaking behavior used in this chapter is Dell H. Hymes, "The Ethnography of Speaking" (1962). Many earlier works in language and culture implicitly deal with the same issues. See Dell H. Hymes, ed., Language, Culture and Society: A Reader in Linguistics and Anthropology (1964) for the best of this earlier literature. Since 1962 Dell H. Hymes has published a series of articles that elaborate on his early formulation of the ethnography of speaking. This chapter and the next one draw heavily from these works. See especially his "Introduction: Toward Ethnographies of Communication" (1964);

tive?" An ethnography of speaking asks this question in reference to the way people talk. It goes beyond the usual linguistic study that analyzes speech in abstraction from its usage. Instead of describing linguistic rules that generate *meaningful* utterances, we sought to discover the sociolinguistic rules that generate *appropriate* utterances. This approach is extremely important because people at Brady's are not interested in merely saying things that make sense; they seek instead to say things that reveal to others their skill in verbal performances. Indeed, this often requires that a person utter nonsense, at least so it seems to the outsider.

In order to discover the rules for using speech, we began by recording what people said to one another, noting whenever possible the gestures, tone of voice, setting, and other features of the verbal interaction. Then we examined these samples of speech usage for recurrent patterns and went back to listen for more instances. At first we sought to identify the major speech events that were typical of the bar. A speech event refers to activities that are directly governed by rules for speaking.[4] On any evening the waitress participates in many different speech events. For example, Denise enters the bar shortly after 6:30 in the evening and almost her first act is to exchange some form of *greeting* with the bartender, the day employees who are present, and any regulars she recognizes. At the bar she *asks for a drink*, saying to John, "I'd like a gin gimlet." This particular speech event takes many forms and is one that Denise will hear repeatedly from customers throughout the evening. She will also label this speech event *taking an order*. John refuses her request, fixes a Coke instead, and replies, "You know you can't have a drink now, you start work in thirty minutes."

The evening begins slowly so Denise stands at her station talking to a regular customer. They are participating in a speech event called a *conversation*. As more customers arrive, Denise will say, "Hi, Bill," "Good to see you, George. Where have you been lately?" "Hi, how are things at the 'U' these days?" and other things to *greet* people as they walk in. She will *give orders* to the bartender, *answer the phone*, make an *announcement* about last call, and possibly get into an *argument* with one table when she tries to get them to leave on time. Like the other girls, Denise has learned the cultural rules in this bar for identifying particular speech events and participating in the verbal exchanges they involve. She has acquired the rules for greeting people, for arguing, and for giving orders, rules that define the appropriate ways to speak in such events.

It wouldn't take long for a stranger to see that *asking for a drink* is probably the most frequent speech event that occurs in the bar. But, although it is an important activity, it appears to be a rather simple act. A stranger would only have to know the

"Directions in (Ethno-) Linguistic Theory" (1964); "Models of The Interaction of Language and Social Setting" (1965); "Sociolinguistics and the Ethnography of Speaking" (1971); and "Models of the Interaction of Language and Social Life" (1972). One of the earliest empirical studies based directly on Hymes' formulation of the ethnography of speaking was Charles O. Frake, "How to Ask for a Drink in Subanun" (1964b). This was published in a special issue of the American Anthropologist, "The Ethnography of Communication," edited by John J. Gumperz and Dell Hymes (1964), and contains other important articles in this area. For a recent collection of studies, see John J. Gumperz and Dell Hymes, eds., The Ethnography of Communication: Directions in Sociolinguistics (1972).*
[4]*This definition of a speech event is based on Dell Hymes (1972:56).*

name of one drink, say Pabst Beer, and any simple English utterance that expresses a desire in order to appropriately ask for a drink. The waitress approaches the table, asks, "What would you like?" and a customer can simply say, "I'll have a Pabst." And once a person knows all the names for the other beverages it is possible to use this sentence to ask for any drink the bartenders can provide. A stranger might even go out of the bar thinking that asking for a drink is a rather trivial kind of speech behavior. That was certainly our impression during the first few weeks of fieldwork.

But as time went on we discovered that this speech event is performed in dozens of different ways. The people who come to Brady's have elaborated on a routine event, creating alternative ways for its execution. The well socialized individual knows the rules for selecting among these alternatives and for manipulating them to his own advantage. Asking for a drink thus becomes a kind of stage on which the customer can perform for the waitress and also the audience of other customers. A newcomer to the bar is frequently inept at these verbal performances, and one can observe regulars and employees smiling at one another or even laughing at some ill-timed and poorly performed effort at asking for a drink. Our goal was not to predict what people would say when they asked for a drink but to specify the alternative ways they could ask for a drink, the rules for selecting one or another alternative, and the social function of these ways of talking.[5] We especially wanted to know how the waitress would interpret the alternatives she encountered in the course of her work. At the heart of the diverse ways to ask for a drink was a large set of speech acts, and it was largely through observing the way people manipulated these different acts that we discovered how to ask for a drink in Brady's Bar.

SPEECH ACTS

10   In order to describe the way people *use* speech we begin with the speech act as the minimal unit for analysis. In every society people use language to accomplish purposes: to insult, to gather information, to persuade, to greet others, to curse, to communicate, etc. An act of speaking to accomplish such purposes can be a single word, a sentence, a paragraph, or even an entire book. A speech act refers to the way any utterance, whether short or long, is used and the rules for this use.[6]

---

[5]We agree with Frake who maintains that the goal of ethnography is not prediction but identification of culturally-appropriate alternatives. In his "Notes on Queries in Ethnography," he writes:

> The aims of ethnography, then, differ from those of stimulus-response psychology in at least two respects. First, it is not, I think, the ethnographer's task to predict behavior per se, but rather to state the rules of culturally appropriate behavior. In this respect the ethnographer is again akin to the linguist who does not attempt to predict what people will say but to state rules for constructing utterances which native speakers will judge as grammatically appropriate. The model of an ethnographic statement is not: "if a person is confronted with stimulus X, he will do Y," but: "if a person is in situation X, performance Y will be judged appropriate by native actors." The second difference is that the ethnographer seeks to discover, not prescribe, the significant stimuli in the subject's world. He attempts to describe each act in terms of the cultural situations which appropriately evoke it and each situation in terms of the acts it appropriately evokes (1964a:133).

[6]Our definition of a speech act is based on Dell Hymes (1972:56–57).

Our informants at Brady's Bar recognized many different categories of speech acts. They not only identified them for us but would frequently refer to one or another speech act during conversations in the bar. For example, at the end of a typically long evening the employees and a few real regulars are sitting around the bar talking about the events of the night. "Those guys in the upper section tonight were really obnoxious," recalls Sue. "They started off *giving me shit* about the way I took their orders and then all night long they kept *calling* my name. After last call they kept *hustling* me and when I finally came right out and said no, they really *slammed* me." The other waitress, Sandy, talks of the seven Annies who were sitting at one of her tables: "They kept *asking* me to tell them what went into drinks and they were drinking Brandy Alexanders, Singapore Slings, Brandy Manhattans, and Peapickers. Then they kept *muttering* their orders all evening so I could hardly hear and *bickering* over the prices and *bitching* about the noise—it was really awful."

Giving shit, calling, hustling, slamming, asking, muttering, bickering, and *bitching* are all ways to talk; they are speech acts used at Brady's Bar. There are at least 35 such named speech acts that our informants recognized and these form a folk taxonomy shown in Figure 6.1.

Components of Speech Acts[7]

The terms shown in this taxonomy refer to the *form* that messages take. But, in order to understand any speech act and the rules for its use, one must examine the various *components* of such acts. For instance, a waitress who hears a customer say, "Hey, sexy, what are you doing after work tonight?" also pays attention to the time and place of this utterance, who said it, the intention of the speaker, the tone of voice, and many other components. If said by a female customer, the waitresses would probably be shocked and offended. On the other hand, such an utterance by a *regular* male customer, especially early in the evening, might be interpreted as *teasing.* If said in a serious tone of voice by a male a few minutes before closing, the waitress would see this as *hustling.* Each of these components enters into the rules for using speech acts. Let's take a typical event to look briefly at the components that are the most important in asking for a drink.

It is Friday evening shortly before 10 P.M. In a few minutes the bouncer will assume his duties at the door. Some tables are empty in both sections but the waitresses expect a rush of customers before 10:30. Two males enter and go directly to vacant stools at the bar; Sandy stands idly at her station watching them. The bartender has his back turned when they sit down, but when he turns around one of the newcomers asks quickly and firmly: "Could I please have a Schlitz?" The other one immediately adds, "Make mine Miller's." Without a word the bartender, who has never seen these two customers before, gets the beers, opens the bottles, and sets them down on the bar with two glasses. He collects their money and returns some change before turning to check other customers' needs. Sandy, her tables taken care of, has watched the brief interaction and thinks to herself, "If those *boys* had sat in my section I would

---

[7]*See Dell Hymes (1972) for an extended discussion of the components of speech acts. We have also found Joe Sherzer and Regna Darnell, "Outline Guide for the Ethnographic Study of Speech Use" (1972) especially helpful.*

WAYS TO TALK AT BRADY'S BAR	Slamming
	Talking
	Telling
	Giving shit
	Asking
	Begging
	Begging off
	Gossiping
	Joking
	Teasing
	Muttering
	Ordering
	Swearing
	Sweet talking
	Pressuring
	Arguing
	Bantering
	Lying
	Bitching
	P.R.ing
	Babbling
	Harping
	Crying over a beer
	Hustling
	Introducing
	Flirting
	Daring
	Bickering
	Apologizing
	Calling
	Greeting
	Bullshitting
	Hassling
	Admitting
	Giving orders

FIGURE 6.1   Some Speech Acts Used in Brady's Bar

have carded them both and asked them to leave—they can't be a day over 17." About
five minutes later when the bartender has his attention on other matters, the two
customers quietly move to one of the tables in Sandy's section and finish their beers.
Later, when Sandy checks their table, one of them orders again, "Could we please
have another round?" Without a word she clears their empty bottles and brings another Schlitz and Miller's. Let us look more closely at the components of these
speech acts the two young customers have used to ask for drinks.

15　　1. *Purpose.* Because asking for a drink can be done with any number of different
speech acts, customers tend to select ones that will achieve certain ends. In addition
to a drink they may want to tell others something about themselves, demonstrate
their prowess with females generally, set the stage for later interaction with the waitress, etc. In this case, the two customers want to gain admittance to the adult world
of male drinking. Even more, they want to pass as *men*, circumventing entirely the
stigma of merely being *boys*. They could probably borrow I.D. cards from college
friends that would legitimize their presence. But such a tactic would also announce to
everyone, through the public experience of being carded, that they had not yet gained
unquestioned right to participation in this male world. They have learned that the skillful use of language can be an effective substitute for age and manliness.

2. *Message Content.* Schlitz and Miller's are both common drinks for young
males. Had either of these customers asked for a daiquiri, a Marguerita on the rocks,
or a Smith and Currants, it would have created suspicion. Not that male customers
never drink these beverages—they do on rare occasions. But because these are female drinks it would have called attention to other characteristics of the customers.
Instead of creating the impression that they were "ordinary men," such a request
would have made others wonder whether they were *ordinary*, and even more important, whether they were really *men*. An order of scotch and soda, bourbon and seven,
whiskey and water, or gin and tonic would not have cast doubt on their maleness but
might have been a reason for others to question their age. Men often order such
drinks but, in this case, asking for any one of these would obviously contrast with
their youthful appearance. By ordering two usual drinks of young men—common
beers like Schlitz and Miller's—they effectively created a protective screen around
their true identities.

3. *Message Form.* "Could I please have a . . ." is the polite form of *asking* in
Brady's Bar. The second customer also *asked* when he added, "Make mine . . ." But
they could have *ordered* in a more direct statement. They might have *asked for information* with a question about the kinds of beers available. They could have *muttered* an
order in an effort to avoid attention. Other forms were also available but asking politely helped insure an impression of knowledgeable confidence. Other speech acts
could easily bring suspicion in the same way that ordering an unusual drink might
have done.

4. *Channel.* People at Brady's ask for drinks by using one of several different channels. A person who regularly drinks the same beverage and does so repeatedly on a
single night may receive a drink on the house. By his drinking *behavior* he can thus be

asking for a free drink. When a regular enters the bar, his very presence asks for a drink, and he can merely take a place at the bar or a table and the drink appears. Various gestures are another frequently used channel as when a regular walks in and holds up his index finger or nods his head. The waitress takes his order from memory and delivers it to the waiting customer. Asking for a drink by gesture instead of the verbal channel was not possible for the two young customers because of their status as persons off the street. When someone does use one of these other channels it serves as a public announcement of status in the bar.

5. *Setting.* The setting of a speech act refers to the time and place it is spoken. Even though Brady's is a small bar, the place where a person speaks can change the social significance of what is said. Individuals at the bar tend to take on some of the "sacred maleness" associated with that location. Drinking at the tables tends to convey less experience and, combined with an appearance of youth, can be sufficient reason for carding a customer. A person who enters, and walks confidently to the bar, communicates the unstated message that he is a man, a mature drinker, one whose presence at the bar is not to be questioned. By timing their entry prior to 10:00 PM they also circumvent the possibility of being carded by the bouncer. Once a drink is served at the bar, the same customers who would have been carded at a table, and probably excluded, can move with immunity to a table in either section. In order for a waitress to ask them for I.D.'s at that point would require that she violate the implicit rule that bartenders know better than waitresses, something few girls are eager to do in such a public manner. By timing the round ordered from a waitress to follow the drinks ordered from a bartender, the customer can ask for a drink and also accomplish other desired ends.

20   6. *Tone.* A customer who enters the bar is probably not always aware of the manner or tone he uses to ask for a drink. It may have been days since he asked for a drink in any bar and his tone of voice and general manner of speech may be conditioned by experiences earlier in the day. But, to the waitress who hears hundreds of people asking for drinks, the tone communicates a great deal. The person who asks questions about drinks or who hesitates, communicates more than the kind of drink desired. The customer who uses this occasion to hustle the waitress or tease her must carefully manipulate the tone of any utterance to avoid being seen as inept or crude. The two customers who asked for a Schlitz and Miller's exuded confidence in their manner of speaking. By eliminating any hesitancy from the speech act they effectively communicated to the bartender as well as to other customers that they were men who knew their way around in bars.

7. *Participants.* Speech acts are used between two people or between groups of people. In Brady's Bar, the participants in any communicative event can change the meaning and consequences in the same way that other components do. Asking the *bartender* instead of the *waitress* allows underage males to escape the emasculation of being carded by females. When a couple enters the bar and the girl is underage, a quick firm order for both by the male will mask the girl's discomfort and keep her from being carded. An underage *regular*, on the other hand, can order from either the bartender or waitress without worrying about being carded. As we shall see, *who* is

talking to *whom* is one of the most significant variables in understanding the way people talk.[8]

But asking for a drink is not merely a communication between a customer and employee. Nearby customers and employees participate in the exchanges as an attentive audience. Many speech acts cannot be understood at Brady's unless we consider the audience before whom a speaker performs. The two young men who ordered at the bar were not only seeking to get around the barrier of carding but also to communicate their claim to adult male status, especially to those at the center of this male-oriented social world.

8. *Outcome.* The regular participants in the social life at Brady's learn to use language successfully and thereby achieve a variety of ends. Not everyone who manipulates the various features of a speech act accomplish their intentions. Some customers *hustle* a waitress when asking for a drink but to no avail. Some seek to avoid being carded, only to find themselves required to show their I.D. or leave. Others make a claim to privileged intimacy or special status, only to find their performance inept and open to derision. But there are other outcomes that often lie outside the awareness of the actors. In this case the two customers successfully escaped the degradation of carding, demonstrated their manliness and adulthood to their audience, and paved the way for an evening of uninterrupted drinking at a table served by a cocktail waitress. But equally important, their skillful performance in asking for a drink set in motion the social processes that could eventually change their status in Brady's Bar from underage persons-off-the-street to regular customers. For having escaped the carding process once, they have established their right to drink at Brady's, and subsequent visits will reinforce this right.

RITUALS OF MASCULINITY

Probably the most important outcome of the various ways to ask for a drink at Brady's Bar is related to the way they symbolize the values of *masculinity* that lie at the heart of bar culture. During our observations of the way male customers asked for drinks it became clear that these performances had a ritual quality about them. Goffman has identified the nature of this ceremonial or ritual quality in social interaction:

> To the degree that a performance highlights the common official values of the society in which it occurs, we may look upon it, in the manner of Durkheim and Radcliffe-Brown, as a ceremony—as an expressive rejuvenation and reaffirmation of the moral values of the community.[9]

25   In a sense, the routine performances of asking for a drink at Brady's Bar have been transformed into rituals that express important male values. Customers and

---

[8]*The participants in any speech event at Brady's Bar depends on their particular identity at the time of speaking. The range of social identities in the bar have been examined in our discussion of the social structure of Brady's Bar in Chapter 4.*

[9]*Erving Goffman, The Presentation of Self in Everyday Life (1959:35). Our discussion of masculinity rituals in this section has drawn many insights from this book as well as Interaction Ritual (1967) and Encounters (1961) by Goffman.*

other members of this community seldom view these speech events as rituals, but nevertheless they function in this manner. These ritual performances reinforce masculine virtues and symbolize full membership in the male world of Brady's Bar.

Furthermore, these rituals take on an added meaning when we consider that the ongoing social life at Brady's often obscures the presence of a deep structural conflict. It stems from the fact that the bar functions both as a *business* and as a *men's ceremonial center* where masculine values are reaffirmed. The conflict between these two features of the bar is partially mediated by a set of speech acts that customers employ to ask for drinks. We need to examine this structural conflict briefly.

On the one hand, the bar is a business establishment that is organized to sell drinks for a profit. It has no membership dues, no initiation rituals, no rules except legal age that restrict certain classes of people from buying drinks. Any adult can open the doors, walk into the bar, and order any drink in the house. The only requirement for drinking is payment of the usual fees. As a business establishment Brady's Bar has an air of efficiency, casualness, and impersonality. There is no readily apparent organization except the division between employees and customers. Even the spatial arrangement can be seen purely in economic terms with the bar and tables arranged for the efficient distribution of drinks. It is possible for an individual to stop in for a drink without ever suspecting that the bar is much different from a restaurant, a bank, or department store except for the menu, small services rendered, or items sold. At one level, then, Brady's is primarily a place of business.

On the other hand, Brady's Bar is a *men's ceremonial center*. As we have seen in earlier chapters, there is a formal social structure that ascribes to men the places of high status. The spatial patterns in the bar reflect the values of a male-oriented culture with certain places having an almost sacred atmosphere. The language patterns also serve to reaffirm male values, providing an important symbol of membership in the informal men's association. Even the division of labor that appears to be a strict business function reflects the subordinate position of women in the bar as well as the wider society. At another level, then, Brady's Bar is primarily a place where men can come to play out exaggerated masculine roles, acting out their fantasies of sexual prowess, and reaffirming their own male identities.

The essence of the *ceremonial function is to reaffirm the official values of manhood in our culture*. But this is difficult to do when women enter almost every night to drink and talk. Some even select the same drinks as men and all have the right to sit at the bar itself. Strangers visit Brady's frequently for a quick drink, never entering into the social and ceremonial life of the bar. Students tend to be a transient group that results in a constant turnover of customers. Relationships among people in the bar are frequently impersonal and businesslike. All of this works counter to the ceremonial function that requires some common public expression of the moral values on which masculine identities are constructed. It requires some way to highlight the virtues of strength, toughness, aggressiveness, and dominance over females. Most important, it requires some corporate group of males staging the ritual performances together. It is possible that these ceremonial functions could be carried out by restricting membership to men in a formal way as done by athletic clubs or men's associations in certain New Guinea societies. Some "male only" bars still employ this device. The moral values of masculinity could be reaffirmed by aggressive physical activity from which women were excluded as is done in competitive football from Little League teams for boys to the National Football League. But Brady's managers do not even allow the escalation of the rare fights that do occur but halt them before they hardly begin. Drinks at Brady's could be restricted to men alone or special uniforms and ceremonial regalia could be created to symbolize their corporate unity and importance. But Brady's has none of these. Instead, *male values are reaffirmed by the use of elaborate patterns of language*. It is not so much *what* people say but *how* they speak that serves to mediate between the business and ceremonial functions of the bar.

30   Language is used to symbolize status and masculinity in public displays. Equally important, customers use speech performances to create a sense of corporate belonging, a feeling of full membership in the men's association that constitutes the hub of this society. Asking for a drink becomes not only a display of an individual's masculinity but a membership ritual announcing to those present that the speaker *belongs*, he is a man who has ties with other men, a male who is at home in a truly male world. Such rituals occur during *dominance displays*, *ritual reversals*, *reciprocal exchanges*, *drinking contests*, and *asking for the wrong drink*. We shall consider each of these in turn.

DOMINANCE DISPLAYS

One frequent way that men ask for a drink is not to ask for a drink at all. In the situation where it is appropriate to ask for a drink, they ask instead for the waitress. This may be done in the form of *teasing*, *hustling*, *hassling* or some other speech act. But, whatever the form, it serves as a ritual in which masculine values are symbolized for the people at Brady's. Consider the following example of hassling.

Sandy is working the upper section. She walks up to the corner table where there is a group of five she has never seen before: four guys and a girl who are loud and boisterous. She steps up to the table and asks, "Are you ready to order now?" One of the males grabs her by the waist and jerks her towards him. "I already know what I want, I'll take you," he says as he smiles innocently up at her. Sandy removes his hand and steps back from the table. She takes the orders from the others at the table and then turns back to the first man. He reaches over and pulls her towards him, prolonging the ritual of asking for a drink with a question, "What's good here, do you know?" Sandy patiently removes his hand for the second time, "If you haven't decided yet what you want to drink, I can come back in a few minutes." "Oh, please, don't leave me!" He grabs her by the leg this time, the only part of her he can reach and inquires, "What's your name, honey? Are you new here? I don't think I've seen you before? What nights do you work?" The others at the table begin to smile and chuckle, making the situation worse; Sandy knows that several nearby customers are also watching the encounter. Finally, in desperation she heads for the bar and he calls out, "I'll have a Screwdriver."

Back at her station, she gives the bartender the order and tells Mike, a regular sitting by her station, about the *obnoxo* in the upper section. Mike listens and puts his arm protectively around her, "Look, just make them come down to the bar if they want to order. If they give you any more shit tell me and I'll take care of them." The order is ready and Sandy balances her tray as she heads back to the waiting customers, planning to stand on the opposite side of the table in hopes of avoiding a repeat performance.

This kind of performance is not exceptional. For the waitresses it is a recurrent feature of each night's work. The details vary from customer to customer but the basic features remain constant. She approaches a table where, instead of asking for a drink, a customer seizes upon the brief encounter to display his manly skills. "Where have you been all my life?" asks one. "Sit down and talk to us," says another. "Have I ever told you that I love you?" "Haven't I seen you someplace before?" "Wouldn't you like to sit on my lap?" And often the verbal requests are punctuated with attempts to invade the personal space of the waitress. One customer asks for his drink in a low, muffled voice, requiring the waitress to move closer or bend down so she can hear. Another grabs her as she starts to leave. Some pinch, grab a wrist, pat, or securely retain the waitress with an arm around her waist. Except for the regular customer whom she knows well, these direct attempts at physical contact are obvious violations of the usual rules governing interaction between men and women. Indeed, their value seems to lie in this fact, as if to say that here is a real man, one who can act out his aggressive fantasies.

35   Thus Brady's Bar provides male customers with a stage where they can perform; it offers an audience to appreciate their displays of manliness. Furthermore, this ritual setting gives a special legitimacy to expressing one's masculinity. Asking for a drink becomes an occasion to act out fantasies that would be unthinkable in the classroom, on the street, and even perhaps when alone with a female. But here, in the protective safety of the bar, a customer can demonstrate to others that he has acquired the masculine attributes so important in our culture.

But the masculinity rituals would not be effective without the cooperation of the waitress. She has learned to respond demurely to taunts, invitations, and physical invasions of her personal space. She smiles, laughs, patiently removes hands, ignores the questions, and moves coyly out of reach. It is precisely these qualities of her response that complement the performance of male customers. When she meets a particularly aggressive and obnoxious customer she may complain to bartenders or regulars, providing these men with their opportunity to demonstrate another aspect of manliness—the protector role. But the cultural expectations are clear: *she should remain dependent and passive.* As waitresses move back and forth between the bar and their tables, they also move between these two kinds of encounters—warding off the tough, aggressive males, and leaning on the strong, protective males.

Although the girls know it is important to keep their place during these encounters, it is also clear they *could* act otherwise in dealing with aggressive customers. Like the bartenders, they might refuse to allow customers to act in offensive ways. They could become aggressive themselves, "tough broads" who brusquely reprimand customers and have them removed from the bar. On occasion the girls all have acted in this way towards a customer, something it would be *possible* to do with relative frequency. For example, one night Joyce was making her way to the table in the corner of the upper section and she had a tray load of expensive cocktails. Doug, a regular, stepped out in front of her, blocking the path. "C'mon, Doug. Don't make me spill these drinks." He was drunk. "I'll move if you give me a kiss," he replied. "Not now, Doug. I have to get these drinks to that table. Now *please* move!" Doug stood his ground, refusing to budge an inch. "If you don't move, Doug, I'm gonna kick you in the shins, and I mean it!" Doug didn't move, but instead, beer in one hand, he reached out to put the other arm around Joyce. That was all it took. Joyce gave him a good hard kick in the shins, and then, to her surprise, Doug kicked her back! Joyce glared at him and he finally let her through to the table. She felt both angry and proud as she carried the tray of ten heavy drinks to the table. Most of the frozen daiquiris were melting and the Bacardis had spilled over the tops of glasses. But for one brief moment an encounter with an aggressive male had been changed into a relationship in which she felt on equal footing. But in the process she had destroyed the ritual quality of Doug's attempt to demonstrate his manliness.

RITUAL REVERSALS

The ritual quality of asking for a drink does not always have a serious tone. Waitresses and customers often work together to create humorous scenes for the audiences around them, using speech acts like *bantering*, *joking*, and *teasing*, in ways that appear to be serious. These performances are particularly effective in symbolizing masculine values when they call attention to subtle possibilities that some individual is *not* acting like a woman or man. Two examples may serve to illuminate this complex use of language in asking for a drink. The first one humorously suggests that the waitress is sexually aggressive in the way reserved for men. The second implies that the male customer is less than a man because of homosexual tendencies.

Recall an earlier example when Sue waited on a Cougar regular who came to Brady's with three friends. When she approached their table they were engrossed in conversation and to get their attention she placed her hand on one customer's shoulder. He turned to see who it was and then said loudly in mock anger, "Don't you touch me!" Sue jumped back, pretending to be affected by his response. "I'm sorry. Do you want another beer?" He smiled. "No, thanks, a little later." She continued on her circular path around the section. A few minutes later she was back in the area and as she passed the same table the customer reached out and grabbed her by the waist. "Watch the hands," she said. "I'll have another Pabst now," the regular said. She brought him the beer. "That was fast!" he commented as she set the bottle down. "I'm a fast girl," was her response.

40 "Oh, you mean with the beer?" To which she answered, as she collected the money and turned to leave, "What did you think I meant?" In this encounter, first the customer and then the waitress *jokingly* suggest that she may be a sexually aggressive female, thereby underscoring the important cultural value of actually being a passive female.

During the course of our research, a popular song included in the juke box selections at the bar had to do with a football player called Bruiser LaRue, an implied homosexual. Playing this song or making loud requests for someone to play it, provided abundant opportunities for treating homosexuality in a humorous manner. One such opportunity involved asking for a drink. Holly notices two regulars come in the door and because it is crowded they end up along the wall at the back of the lower section where she has just taken an order for another round. Because of the crowd and noise, neither bartender sees these well-known regulars or has a chance to greet them. Holly already knows their drinks so does not need to wait for their orders, but one of them says with a smile, "I'll have a Pink Lady, tell him it's for Bruiser LaRue." At

the bar when Holly passes the message on, the bartender immediately scans her section to see who this "Bruiser LaRue" might be. Smiles and laughter are quickly exchanged across the noisy bar, and the ritual is complete. If either bartender or customer were to admit even the possibility of being homosexual or accuse another
male of such behavior, it would be a serious violation of cultural norms. By joking
about it in the presence of a waitress, they uphold the dominant masculine values, saying, in effect, "We are so manly we can even joke about being effeminate." In a similar
fashion, it is not uncommon for a waitress to approach a table of male customers
who have just sat down and one will say, "My friend here wants a Pink Lady," or "Bill
wants a Gold Cadillac." The waitress smiles, the customers poke one another, smile,
laugh, and add other comments. The incongruity of "a man like one of us" having a "female drink" has provided a brief ritual reversal of the sacred values. Because it occurs
in a humorous context, no one is threatened and all settle down to a night of drinking, comfortable in their sense of manhood.

RECIPROCAL EXCHANGES

There are several contexts in which customers order drinks for other people
with an expectation of reciprocity. Buying in rounds is the most frequent kind of exchange and occurs with almost every group of men who stay for any length of time in
the bar. A typical sequence goes something like this. Six men take their places at a
table and begin with separate orders: a scotch and soda, two Buds, a Lowenbrau, a
Brandy Manhattan, and a whiskey tonic. The waitress brings the drinks, arranged in order on her tray, and places each one down for the respective customer. Fred, who is
sitting on the corner where the waitress stands announces, "I'll get this one," and
hands her a ten dollar bill. He has assumed the temporary responsibility to ask for
drinks desired by anyone at the table. Half an hour later the waitress checks the table:
"How're you doin' here?" Fred shakes his head that they aren't quite ready, and the
others keep right on talking. But the question has signaled the group to prepare to
order soon. The next time the waitress approaches their table, Bill, sitting next to
Fred, looks up and says, "Another round." The responsibility for asking has now shifted
to him and he orders for everyone. In this case he might check individually or act on a
knowledge of his friends' drinking habits. When the drinks arrive he pays for the second round. Soon another member of the group will take over, and before the evening
ends each of the six customers will have taken one or more turns. It is not uncommon for the composition of a table to change, adding new drinkers, losing some to
other tables, expanding and contracting with the ebb and flow of people, creating ever
widening circles of reciprocal exchange.

These exchanges did not seem unusual to us until we discovered that female customers almost never order or pay in rounds. Those who do are usually waitresses
from other bars; they know that this practice eases the work-load for the cocktail
waitress, both in taking orders and making change. Why then do men almost always
order in rounds, asking for drinks in this reciprocal fashion? When we observed the
other ways that men typically make work difficult for waitresses it seems improbable
that ordering in rounds was intended to assist the cocktail waitresses. Whatever the
reason for this practice, it is a continual reminder that *males belong to groups of men in*

the bar. The individual nature of asking for a drink is transformed into a shared, social experience. When men request drinks and pay for them in rounds they reaffirm their ties to one another and their common membership in a kind of men's association.

Numerous occasions occur when a single individual will buy for another person or a whole group at another table. The reciprocity in these exchanges may never occur or it can take place at a later date, but the expectation of a return drink underlies the action. In the course of an evening the waitress may have frequent orders of this nature. Two guys and a girl are drinking at a table near the lower waitress station. One of the guys signals the waitress and says, "Would you take a drink to Mark, over there? It's his birthday. Tell him it's from us." Drawing on her recollection of Mark's original order she asks the bartender for a whiskey sour and delivers it to Mark who hasn't even finished his first drink. Another friend of Mark's sitting nearby sees the extra drink arrive and when he learns it is Mark's birthday, he orders a round for everyone at the table, again in honor of the occasion.

45   As the bar becomes more crowded, waitresses are often kept running to take drinks to an acquaintance here who was recently engaged, a friend there who got a new job, or someone else a customer hasn't seen for a while. "Take a drink to that guy over there in the red shirt who just came in, a gin and tonic, and tell him Bob sent it," a customer tells the waitress, pointing across the bar. Fighting her way back through the crowd to the bar and then over to the man in the red shirt, the waitress says, "This is from Bob." The surprised and pleased customer looks over the crowd, locates Bob at his table and calls loudly, "Thanks, Bob, I'll talk to you later." Other people notice, look briefly in his direction, and the noisy hum of activity continues at a steady pace.

A regular at the bar motions for Stephanie: "I owe Randy one from last week. Do you know what he's drinking? Whatever it is, send him one from me." Randy is in the other waitresses section so Stephanie passes the word on to Joyce and soon Randy has an unrequested drink arrive at his table. He remembers the debt when the waitress identifies the regular; a wave and shouted words of thanks that cannot be heard above the noise complete the transaction. Later the same night customers will ask for other drinks to be delivered at other places. "I want another round for Alan—tell him congratulations on his new job." "I hear Ron got engaged, take him a drink from me."

In these and similar cases, the drink is purchased, not because someone wants a drink, but rather as a symbol of a friendship tie. On many occasions these exchanges are followed by shouting and gestures that serve not only to communicate between friends but to announce to others that the participants are inside members of the bar crowd. Even when the transaction is known only to the buyer, recipient, and waitress, the ritual performance has fulfilled its function. The customers have both demonstrated they are not alone in an impersonal, business establishment. They know people here and are known by others. The very act of establishing social ties in this manner gives these customers an additional reason for being in the bar. Their claim to membership has been announced, acknowledged, and confirmed.

Sometimes reciprocal exchanges are done in a humorous manner, emphasizing certain masculine values as well as reaffirming membership in the men's association. Recall an earlier example when one night a man at the bar called Holly over and said, "I want you to take a drink to the guy over there in the sport coat and tell him Dan said to get fucked." When the message and drink were delivered they brought a return order—a Harvey Wallbanger for Dan and a 75¢ tip for Holly. The message with its overtones of a tough man who could even use obscenity in the presence of a woman was clear. The return order of a Harvey Wallbanger, a drink with sexual connotations, brought smiles to the faces of bartenders, waitress, and customers alike. In addition, the exchange highlighted publicly the social ties between two customers.

Later on that same evening, Holly was asked to take a double vodka tonic to Gene, a regular, who was already quite intoxicated. A friend across the bar had observed Gene's steady drinking all night and increasingly boisterous behavior. Gene was finishing the last drink he would order when the "gift" arrived. "This is from Bill," said Holly with a smile, loud enough for others at the table to hear. Faced with the choice of increasing physical discomfort and a reputation that he wasn't man enough to down another drink, Gene raised the drink in a smilingly reluctant toast and finished off the double vodka tonic.

50   On a typical evening drinks criss-cross the bar in these ways with considerable frequency. The senders and receivers come to be recognized as full members of the bar society. Even those who do not participate in these rituals themselves gain a secure sense that there is a lot of action at Brady's. They are reassured that this is a place where male customers, in general, and themselves, in particular, truly belong.

DRINKING CONTESTS

Sometimes customers ask for drinks that involve a challenge to another man's ability to drink. In an earlier chapter we mentioned how waitresses become customer's "lucky charms" in these contests. The night is slow and two guys sitting at Joyce's station pass the time by "chugging", a kind of drinking contest. A coin was flipped and first one customer called and then the other. If a call identified the correct side of the coin, the customer who called was not required to down his drink in a single gulp. Each failure to call the coin correctly meant asking for another drink and chugging it down until one or the other contestants called a halt, thereby losing the game.

At times, such contests involve the entire bar, as customers become spectators cheering on the early demise of the participants. One evening, several of the Cougars were seated at the bar. It was late and they had been there most of the evening. The bar was noisy, but suddenly became quiet as John ceremoniously placed six empty shot glasses in front of one of the football players. "Okay, Larry, ol' boy, let's see you handle this!" Holly and Sue crowded together into the lower waitress station to get a better look as John slowly filled each shot glass with tequila. People seated at tables stood to get a better view. Someone had dared Larry to drink six straight shots of tequila and he was going to do it. John finished pouring and stepped back, bowing in deference to Larry, "It's all yours," he added. Larry picked up the first glass, toasted his audience, and downed it. Everyone applauded and cheered. He picked up the second, toasted again, and downed it too. Again, the group applauded and so it went until all six glasses were empty. Larry had met the challenge and the game was over. Someone slapped Larry on the back, he reddened and headed for the men's room. Activity returned to normal. The contest was over.

While this was one of the more dramatic contests, similar ones take place frequently at Brady's. Such drinking contests bring males together in a competitive sport, one they are allowed to play inside the bar, but in a way which symbolizes desirable masculine traits—a willingness to compete, strength, endurance, and the ability to imbibe great quantities of strong liquor. It is a contest that places emphasis on *how* one plays the game rather than who wins. Larry may have made a fast retreat to the bathroom, but he *had* played the game, and that is what counted. In addition, those who participated as spectators demonstrated their ties with Larry and others in the bar.

ASKING FOR THE WRONG DRINK

One of the most curious ways that males ask for drinks involves intentional errors in ordering. This kind of asking for a drink appears to involve a combination of two speech acts: *ordering* and *telling*, or giving information. Consider the following example. Two young men enter the bar and take a table next to the wall in the lower section. The waitress approaches their table and places a napkin in front of each one. She waits in silence for their order. One of them looks up at her and says calmly:

55   "Two double Sloe Screws on the rocks, uhhhh, for Joe and Bill."

The waitress turns quickly, goes to the bar, and in a moment returns with two, tall, dark bottles of Hamm's beer. A stranger might think this interaction strange, and at first this kind of "asking for a drink" seemed out of place, but in time we noted other similarly strange games being played. For example, someone comes in and says, "I'll have a banana Daiquiri with Drambuie," or another person says, "Make mine a double Harvey Wallbanger." As you watch the waitress in these and other situations, you observe that frequently the drinks people ask for are not served. A scotch and soda is given instead of the banana daiquiri, a bourbon and water is served instead of the double Harvey Wallbanger, two Hamm's are delivered instead of two double Sloe Screws on the rocks.

In no case where a person asks for one drink and is given another, at least in situations like the examples noted, does the customer complain that he received the wrong drink. Two factors complicate the situation. First, sometimes people do order "Sloe Screws" or "Harvey Wallbangers" and the waitress brings these drinks. Second, occasionally the bartender mixes the wrong drink or the waitress serves the wrong drink and the customer *does* complain. If we return to our original ethnographic goal, we can now ask, "What does a stranger to Brady's Bar have to know in order to ask for a drink in this manner, or to interpret correctly when someone else asks for a drink in this manner? Furthermore, why does this kind of "asking" go on?

If the stranger were to assume the role of cocktail waitress, she would have to know at least the following:

1. That the drink requested was not actually desired.
2. That another drink was actually being requested.
3. What that other drink was.

Waitresses do acquire the rules for correctly interpreting these kinds of requests. But what are these rules and how do they operate?

Let's go back to the customer who said, "Two double sloe screws on the rocks, uhhhh, for Joe and Bill." In addition to the utterance itself, he also communicates a *metamessage*, a message about the message, that serves to identify the kind of speech act he intends it to be. The metamessage says something like, "Don't take us seriously, we really don't want two double Sloe Screws on the rocks. We aren't *ordering* but only *teasing.* " But how is such a metamessage sent and how does the waitress interpret it correctly? Sometimes this information is sent by the *tone* of a speech act or by accompanying gestures or facial expressions. But when a customer uses these metamessage forms he also signals to others that he is teasing or joking. He may then be seen as a "ham," someone unsophisticated in bar culture. The ideal is to ask for a double Sloe Screw on the rocks or a banana Daquiri with Drambuie in a perfectly serious tone of voice and manner, *sending metamessages in ways that are not obvious* to the surrounding audience. At least three alternatives are open to the sophisticated, well-enculturated customer.

60   First, he may choose to make a referential mistake that the waitress will recognize but other, less sophisticated customers will not. Let's take the order for two double Sloe Screws on the rocks. "On the rocks" is a feature of several drinks at Brady's. It means that liquor will be served only with ice and not the usual additional liquid. Whiskey on the rocks, for example, is whiskey without soda, water, or anything except ice. Vodka on the rocks is vodka and ice, nothing more. If a customer wants to order something "on the rocks," it usually means naming a type of liquor, not a fancy drink containing liquor and other mixtures. For example, if you order a Screwdriver on the rocks (vodka and orange juice), it would mean a screwdriver without orange juice, the same thing as vodka on the rocks. This order would be quickly recognized by waitresses as a *referential mistake*. It is a name that sounds like a drink, but no one knowledgeable in the ways of the bar would ask for this drink, unless perhaps as a joke. A Sloe Screw is a mixture of sloe gin and orange juice. When the customer said, "Two double sloe screws on the rocks," he was talking nonsense. He asked for a drink that doesn't exist at Brady's Bar, but when he made this obvious and intentional error of reference, he also signaled to the waitress that he was *teasing*, not *ordering*. He might have asked for sloe gin on the rocks, in which case the waitress could have brought the two customers each a glass of sloe gin and ice.

A second way to unobtrusively let the waitress know that a named drink is not desired involves the connotations of certain drinks. If they are clearly female drinks such as a Pink Lady or Gold Cadillac, this can signal that the customer doesn't really want them. Both a "Sloe Screw" and a "Harvey Wallbanger" have implicit sexual connotations that are widely recognized by the people at Brady's. "A glass full of tequila" carries the connotation of an impending contest and other features of the setting can make it clear that no contest is planned. If a regular wants to tease the waitress, he will not name a scotch and soda or gin and tonic for these ordinary drinks do not have the special connotations that could signal the use of a different speech act.

Finally, customers can signal the intended speech act by combining two or more speech acts. When the customer asked for two double sloe screws on the rocks, he added, "for Joe and Bill." He was *telling* the waitress something else, in addition to the apparent order. The waitress can quickly guess that the customers are teasing, but how will she know to bring them bottles of Hamm's beer? If she doesn't recognize the two customers as regulars or know their customary drinks, she can use this additional information to check with the bartenders: "What do Joe and Bill over there in the corner usually drink?"

These complicated ways of asking for drinks have many functions for both the customer and waitress. Most important, they clearly demonstrate that the customer has mastered the use of bar language. As an individual learns to use the language of this culture with skill, he also becomes recognized as a regular, one who has gained entrance to the inner circle of this little society.

CONCLUSION

When we began to discover the enormous range of ways that men ask for drinks and how all these patterns of talking reaffirmed masculine values as well as symbolizing full membership in the bar community, we went back to examine the way women ask for drinks. Certainly our interpretation of the significance of male speech acts would be questionable if female customers ordered drinks in the same way as males. One would expect that to women customers the bar would be seen much more as a business establishment, a place to get drinks and perhaps meet men but not a place to participate in ceremonial performances that emphasized male values. The contrast between the way men and women ordered drinks was striking. Furthermore, it shed light on why female customers seemed to unwittingly create problems for the cocktail waitresses, a topic we discussed in Chapter 4. If we exclude the few women who came to the bar as experienced cocktail waitresses, the following significant differences are present.

65

1. *Female customers order separately, never in rounds.* The bar is more like a restaurant to them; they have come to purchase drinks, to get out of the dormitories for a time, perhaps to meet men, but not to become part of a ceremonial women's association.

2. *Female customers ask numerous questions about drinks.* To them, a drink is not something to use in establishing an identity as a regular customer. It is much more like an item on a restaurant menu and so it seems appropriate to inquire about the range of drinks available and their contents. After all, Brady's Bar is a place of business that sells drinks. Men hardly ever ask about drinks because such questions would reveal their ignorance and weaken the value of drinks as ceremonial markers of adulthood, masculinity, and full membership in the bar. Women, on the other hand, see drinks more as something to taste, to drink, to purchase for yourself.

3. *Female customers pay separately for their drinks.* The shared experience of ordering and paying hold little significance to women. Like a group of men who go out to lunch in a restaurant and pay separately, the women who visit Brady's are merely following the rules for purchasing things in a business establishment.

4. *Female customers are never ready to order at the same time.* Unlike the men who form small drinking *groups*, women treat the entire process of asking for a drink as an individual economic exchange between themselves and the waitress. The girls at a table who require the waitress to make six or seven trips to the bar for individual orders are not trying to create difficulties for her. They see these trips as simple acts of service for which they have paid.

5. *Female customers change their drinks frequently.* Men find it useful to stay with the same drink. They can then order in rounds. Because employees tend to recognize

people by drinks, asking for the same thing on every occasion establishes one's identity as a regular, a continuing member of the bar society. Sending drinks to other people becomes easier when the waitress knows what a customer "always" drinks. But these ceremonial qualities are hardly significant to a female and so she tries new drinks, changing often for the sake of variety or in search of a drink which has little or no taste of alcohol to it.

70   6. *Female customers almost never tip.* We suspect that the entire cultural atmosphere of the bar communicates to women that men are receiving a special service in the form of opportunities to express their manhood. Undoubtedly competition between the female customer and the cocktail waitress also influences their reluctance to tip.

7. *Female customers never engage in reciprocal exchanges.* As we noted, they do not order in rounds. They do not send drinks across the bar to a friend who has not been seen for a time. They do not send drinks as jokes nor to a friend who gets engaged or locates a new job. The only occasion when female customers sent drinks to others, and these were rare, was on birthdays.

8. *Female customers never intentionally ask for the wrong drink.* Because the inner circle at Brady's is not open to these women, the skilled use of bar language is unimportant. Their status is relatively fixed and manipulating speech acts cannot change it.

9. *Female customers never engage in drinking contests.* Again, the symbolic meaning of such activities is only meaningful to males in the context of the bar.

It is clear that asking for a drink in Brady's Bar means one thing to men, another to women. For the female customer it is a simple economic transaction, one that takes only a few alternative speech acts. For the male customer it is an opportunity to manipulate language for a variety of ends. What Charles Frake has concluded about asking for a drink in Subanum could also apply to the men who come to Brady's Bar for drinking and talking.

75   The Subanun drinking encounter thus provides a structured setting within which one's social relationships beyond his everyday associates can be extended, defined, and manipulated through the use of speech. The cultural patterning of drinking talk lays out an ordered scheme of role play through the use of terms of address, through discussion and argument, and through display of verbal art. The most skilled in "talking from the straw" are the *de facto* leaders of the society. In instructing our stranger to Subanun society how to ask for a drink, we have at the same time instructed him how to get ahead socially.[10]

---

[10]*Charles O. Frake, "How to Ask for a Drink in Subanun" (1964b).*

You can see that Spradley and Mann have carefully observed some of the elements that you've been observing in your own discourse community. They give a clear picture of the *setting*, for example, creating a rich picture of the scene where drinking and talking are going on. Even if you've never been in a bar, or in any setting where people are drinking, you can probably picture the scene from what they say and from your general knowledge of popular culture (perhaps from television reruns of a bar-setting sitcom like *Cheers*).

Spradley and Mann also show us the *participants*. In the setting of Brady's Bar, the participants are defined by their roles: the waitresses, the bartender, and the customers. Although individual participants may come and go, the bar will always be a place where people drink and talk, and it will always have waitresses or waiters, a bartender, and customers. It's the setting and the roles connected to that setting, more than specific individuals, that shape the interactions that go on here.

Even though specific individuals don't matter so much in terms of the ongoing culture of Brady's Bar, types of participants do matter. A regular male customer can say something like, "Hi, sexy, what are you doing after work tonight?" and the waitress is likely to interpret that as teasing, while if an unfamiliar male customer says roughly the same thing, and does so late in the evening, the waitress will see it as hustling. Outsiders—two young (probably underage) males—try to pass as insiders as they carry out the speech act of ordering a drink. (That the young men are able to get by suggests that knowing how to play a role at least adequately, without overplaying it, is a step on the way to temporary or eventual insiderness.)

These details of setting and participants help to create a rich portrait of the community for readers.

READING RESPONSE

To see how the details that Spradley and Mann provide to help visualize the discourse community at Brady's Bar, try creating your own portrait of the world they've shown us, drawing on the examples and details they've provided. Recreate the picture you get of this discourse community, of what it means to be an insider there, and of the beliefs and values that are shared among groups within the discourse community and the ways in which these beliefs and values are demonstrated. (You'll want to bring in Spradley and Mann's words and examples to enrich your portrait.) Share your portrait with other writers to see whether their perspectives add to or complement your own.

Consider your own earlier responses about the setting you're studying and the participants in that setting. From reading Spradley and Mann's study, do you have any further ideas about the details you'll want to emphasize in creating a portrait of your own community for your readers?

In addition to portraying the setting and the participants, Spradley and Mann do a number of other things in their study that you can draw on as you continue your own. They look closely at the participants' interactions and they look for repeated routines and rituals in those interactions. They also interpret those interactions, seeing what shared values they suggest, and how these values might be represented in the genres that are common in the setting.

Observing and Analyzing Interactions

Spradley and Mann focus on speech acts as a way of observing and analyzing the interactions at Brady's Bar, observing both larger speech events and the smaller speech acts that make up those events. They find that the most typical speech event in the college bar is *asking for a drink*. But as they observe the ways in which drinks are ordered, they find that this is not one simple act. Rather there are many possible speech acts that go on in the process—joking, teasing, sweet-talking, flirting. The insider-regulars to this bar know how to maintain a friendly interaction with the waitresses without talking in a way the waitresses find obnoxious. But when outsiders come in, they might "bicker" or "bitch" or ask for unnecessary details about how the drinks are made, violating the general expectations that make this local community work. Spradley and Mann not only observe these acts, but they find out the insider terms for the acts they observe.

Spradley and Mann also look at what goes into a speech act, using a schema with eight elements. That schema was developed by the sociolinguist Dell Hymes to try to take into account everything that insiders had to be able to manage successfully in order to display their communicative competence, and it's a schema that has been used widely by others doing the ethnography of communication.

The first three elements of this schema correspond roughly to the ones we have been using throughout this book: the *purpose* (<u>why</u>), the *message content* (<u>what</u>), and the *message form* (<u>how</u>). We've been looking at two other elements—the *setting* (<u>where</u> and <u>when</u>), and the *participants* (<u>who</u>), as part of the context. This schema adds several new elements, however: the *channel*, a way of capturing the fact that people can communicate through actions and gestures as well as through words (as when Tanya keeps slamming the phone down in the telemarketing office); the *tone* of voice (again an important feature of the telemarketing conversation); and the *outcome*—the important consideration of whether people perform their speech acts in the ways that will actually accomplish what they intend them to accomplish.

Analyzing speech acts, like analyzing a conversation, offers a way to see how the details of interaction are linked to larger patterns and meanings. Analyzing a common speech act in your own setting using this eight element schema may highlight aspects of communication in that setting that weren't so clear to you before.

**RESEARCH
MEMO 6.3**   List the speech acts you've observed in your community. Then look again at the eight components of a speech act (purpose, content, form, channel, setting, tone, participants, and outcome) that Spradley and Mann use to analyze the ways in which two young (and probably underage) men have asked for drinks (pp. 255–257). Choose one specific example of a typical speech in your setting and analyze it with the terms/components that Spradley and Mann have set forth, based on the example below.

Here's how a student researcher analyzed the eight components of a speech act common in his discourse community of male friends. He began by cataloging "the speech acts available in the community": talking, asking, joking, ballbustin, swearing, arguing, telling, whining, calling, ordering, crying, bitching, kidding, lying, screaming, bullshitting (B.S.ing), scheming, hassling, sweating, teasing, mumbling, taunting, ass kissing. He then chose to analyze "ballbustin" according to Spradley and Mann's eight components.

1. **Purpose**—The main purpose of "ballbustin" is to get a laugh out of some people while, at the same time, giving somebody a hard time. This can be done in a friendly way, or sometimes it may be done in a not so friendly way. Even though you are giving someone a hard time, it is often done in good spirit.

2. **Message Content**—the content of the message will focus on something that someone did or might do, in a certain situation. It can be silly or serious, and often times it is just simply hassling someone about something that they have done. A member of the discourse community that I am studying named Mike is always saying the same catch phrase when he talks, like "can I get a drink *or . . .*" and "are we going *or. . . .*" It is such a regular occurrence that we have given him the nickname "Bobby Orr," [the name of a professional hockey player] because he is always saying "*or. . . .*"

3. **Message Form**—Sticking with the same example, the way people would "bust Mike's balls" would be to add "*or . . .*" to everything they say around him. You could simply say something innocent like, "Are you guys ready to leave *or . . . ,*" and everyone would know that you were "bustin Mike's balls." Another way to emphasize the effect is to stress the word "*or . . .*" so it stands out from everything else you just said.

4. **Channel**—You would usually find yourself "ballbustin" with someone who you know, but it could be possible to indirectly "bust someone's balls." If you were just meeting someone for the first time, and they were wearing a shirt that had a weird design on it, you might say something like "I once had a shirt like that before," and some people would understand that you were "busting that person's balls," while others might not.

5. **Setting**—"Ballbustin" seems to take place in all types of settings, rather than just certain situations. It can be used as a way to break tension and get a laugh, or it might be used to harass someone you don't particularly like. I've "busted balls" in all types of settings, as well as having my own "balls busted" in different situations as well. One thing that I do notice is that you are less likely to "bust someone's balls," if you do not know that person well enough. "Ballbustin" tends to take place amongst people who are familiar with one another.

6. **Tone**—Tone is an important part of "ballbustin" because you need to emphasize certain areas of your speech to get the right effect. In the discourse community that I am studying, you can usually tell when a person is serious or joking, and the way you tell this is by recognizing the tone of their voice and their body language. If you were an "outsider" in a certain discourse community, you might not pick up on unique little things that take place, because they are disguised by tone and body language that only the "insiders" are familiar with.

(continued)

(*continued*)

7. **Participants**—The people involved in "ballbustin" are usually people who are familiar with each other. It is rare, as well as difficult, to "bust someone's balls" if you are not familiar with that person. To "ballbust," you need to have a certain topic to attack that person on. It is much easier if you know that person well, and you are able to draw from a larger list of things to talk about.

8. **Outcome**—The usual outcome to "ballbustin" is a good laugh between the people involved. Sometimes someone might not be in a good mood, and they might take it seriously. This can lead to arguing and possibly even fighting. Although fighting is a rare occurrence, it is sometimes an outcome that can be the result of "ballbustin." Overall, I have done my share of "ballbustin," as well as receiving it, and the results are usually a good laugh between friends. **(Robert C.)**

Robert has used the components Spradley and Mann name quite effectively to discover more about a familiar way of interacting among his friends. The one place where his analysis differs from theirs is with his use of the term *channel*. They use it to distinguish an activity that's carried out verbally from one that is signalled through nonverbal behavior—using a gesture to order a drink, for example. Robert, instead, focuses on whether the speech act is carried out directly or indirectly—another significant feature. Nevertheless, his use of Spradley and Mann's schema helps him discover quite a bit about this speech act in his community. What picture of his community do you get from this analysis of one speech act?

Seeing Repeated Routines and Rituals

In most settings, a sense of insiderness is maintained through the repetition of certain routines. Maybe a parent always begins a dinner table conversation by asking the kids how school was that day. Maybe a boss always reminds workers at the beginning of a shift that "the customer is always right." With repetition these actions become *rituals*—formalized routines that everyone knows and can anticipate.

Rituals typically involve some level of performance—with an awareness of carrying out a routine in the view of others to gain their attention and approval, not just carrying out an action for oneself—and performers often participate in an extended routine. Spradley and Mann find several characteristic, attention-getting routines at Brady's Bar, such as the "reciprocal exchange" where customers order drinks for other customers in the bar (not just for the group they're sitting with). Only insiders would know how to carry out all of the turns in these exchanges and how to interpret what's serious and what's a joke. As you look at your own data, you'll want to consider the extent to which the exchanges there have a ritualized quality from the repetition of key elements across exchanges and whether there's an element of performance for others.

Spradley and Mann also suggest that the repeated rituals of regulars contribute to shared cultural expectations—in this case a particular model of manliness—in a bar where the real insiders are young adult males who go there frequently. They interpret the larger exchanges that go on there as "rituals of masculinity"—rituals that "symbolize the values of *masculinity* that lie at the heart of bar culture" (p. 257).

The cultural expectations that are reinforced within any setting are likely to be aligned in some way with those of the larger society—either reinforcing or challenging dominant values. As Spradley and Mann observe more about the shared values that are expressed in Brady's Bar, they uncover some values that many of us would find uncomfortable or seriously objectionable— attitudes towards women and the expectation that they "should remain de- pendent and passive," and narrow norms of "manliness," with anti-homosexual innuendo used as one of the ways of reinforcing those norms. In the 1970's, when this study was carried out, such norms were only beginning to be chal- lenged in the larger society. Since then the socially acceptable ways of con- structing a gendered identity as a man or woman, an identity that doesn't restrict sexual preference, have gradually expanded in many, but not all, settings.

One of the issues that arises as soon as you start to study real-world com- munities is that people in those communities (even communities you're part of) sometimes talk in ways that reflect values that you wouldn't want people to hold and that may even prove deeply offensive to you or other members of your classroom community. As a researcher, you may nevertheless want to ex- amine such data, as Spradley and Mann do, if they seem central to the talk that goes on in your setting, using your research group to help you interpret what you find and reflect on the issues that are raised.

RESEARCH MEMO 6.4

Look again at the rituals that Spradley and Mann describe at Brady's Bar: dominance displays, ritual reversals, reciprocal exchanges, drinking contests, and asking for the wrong drink. Do you find any comparable rituals in your own community? Do some speech acts, whatever their immediate function, serve a broader social one as well? Are key elements repeated and ritualized? Are they "performed" for others' apprecia- tion? Are there underlying values that they help to maintain? To what degree do these shared values reflect some aspects of the norms and values of a larger culture or sub- culture within society? To what degree do they go with constructing a certain type of identity?

Robert might find that "ballbustin," for example, serves primarily a social function, giving this group of friends an easy way of being playful with each other. It does involve repeated elements, as in the example he gives of repeating "Or." Members of the group do seem to perform their variations on this ritual for the whole group's appreciation. "Ballbustin" is similar to what other groups of male friends do, but perhaps with a differ- ent name. And there are certainly shared values that the group maintains in this way that Robert could name, values that help to place this group within the larger society.

STUDENT VOICES	Here are a student researcher's observations about the values she's found in the typical interactions of the community of friends she is studying. Her response might help you generate more ideas about values in your own community.

> My discourse community is formed by a group of Korean friends who are living in the United States. Some of them came to the U.S. a few months ago and one has been raised in the US between American and Korean cultures. . . . Our main purpose of the communication is to share the difficulties that we face as immigrants. We talk about how American culture differs from Korean culture, the easiest way to learn English, and our school. We also share funny stories to each other, and so forth. My discourse community is different from groups of friends of any Americans because we speak more than one language and we are between two worlds where we are educated and influenced by two different cultures. . . .
>
>   Most of the time we talk about Korean songs, singers, actors, and TV shows. Constantly, my friends visit Korean web sites and download Korean songs which most of the time they are our favorite songs. We try to update with new songs, new actors, and new TV shows. The most updated person is the leader of the conversation in our community. . . . Surprisingly immigrants tend to value their nationality and seek their country's stuff. For instance, my friends, who came to the US a few months ago, were "America" lovers; they liked American clothes, they listened to American music, they liked "pizza" (referring to American food) and so forth. But once they came to the US, their attitude toward Korean manufactures and food has changed. Now living in the new country, they seek for Korean stuff: Korean food, Korean songs, Korean clothes. I think the reason is that living in a foreign country people think more about their identity and love things that can represent his/her nationality. **(Sophie)**

READING ETHNOGRAPHY FROM A WRITER'S PERSPECTIVE

Now that you've gathered data about a discourse community, analyzed it, and interpreted its meanings, you'll want to begin to think about how you'll present what you've learned—to think as a writer about the *what*, but especially about the *why*, and the *how* of ethnographic writing. There are a variety of approaches to writing within the larger genre of ethnography as it is used by academic researchers. And there are other genres of ethnographic writing—writing that focuses on cultural settings and on the values insiders share—that are directed to a more general audience of readers outside of the academic setting. The reading you've done and the additional readings included at the end of this chapter offer a range of models to examine closely as you begin to plan your own report.

Looking at Spradley and Mann's Report

Spradley and Mann are working within a written genre that has taken shape over time, that has routine elements, and that reflects the shared values of a discourse community—a community of researchers who are interested in the study of cultural settings. That genre—the *ethnography* or the shorter *ethnographic report*—like the speech events at Brady's Bar, has been shaped by ongoing social interaction among people who read and write anthropological studies. It evokes shared knowledge about culture and identity and about how to study these issues, shared understandings about the purposes of such study, and a shared sense of how to report on what's been studied. These shared ways help to make up the social identity associated with the academic discourse community of anthropologists and their students—a community whose speech acts (or writing acts) can also be studied.

If you turn back to Spradley and Mann's study and reread it analytically, as a writer, you'll see how these writers handle elements common to the genre of the ethnographic report.

- *They frame their report in a way that will set a context for readers—offering some background knowledge that they want their readers to bring to what follows, and suggesting the lens through which the rest of the study should be interpreted and understood*. Spradley and Mann place their study in the context of other anthropological studies of drinking and talking behavior in other societies and they use common anthropological concepts—describing the bar, for example, as a "male ceremonial center," like the Native American kiva or the men's associations of New Guinea.

- *They state the question they're trying to answer and how it relates to the way they approached the portion of their study that's described in this chapter*. Spradley and Mann tell us that their study "has aimed at answering the fundamental ethnographic question: 'What would a stranger have to know to act appropriately as a cocktail waitress and to interpret behavior from her perspective?'" (p. 250). They then go on to explain what this means when applied to this portion of their study, where they look at how people talk.

- *They discuss the methods they used for their study—how they collected data, what data they collected, and how they analyzed it*. Spradley and Mann explain that for this portion of their study they use methods related to the ethnography of speaking—and they explain how those methods relate to their purposes in carrying out the study (p. 251).

- *They consider the cultural meaning and shared values represented in what they've observed*. For all of the speech acts and speech events that Spradley and Mann study, they look at: "the way they symbolize the values of *masculinity* that lie at the heart of bar culture" (p. 257) and at how they become part of routines and rituals that function as ceremonies in affirming those values.

- *They conclude in a way that reiterates, adds to or highlights the significant understandings that have come out of this study*. Spradley and Mann do this in two ways. First they describe the ways female customers order drinks, in contrast to what males do, presenting further evidence that what they've been describing is a distinctive male style, since women don't participate in it. Then, in their final paragraph, they again point to the parallels between what they've seen in Brady's Bar and what has been learned about the Subanum drinking encounter: that it provides an opportunity for men to display a particular social skill that's valued in that culture; and that such a setting is an appropriate one to study if you want to look at shared cultural understandings about masculinity in a society,

The themes that emerge in this part of the study are echoed in other parts of *The Cocktail Waitress*. Spradley and Mann intended their study to cast light on an important aspect of culture—how culture defines male and female roles—by seeing how these roles are defined in one common setting in American culture. They conclude, from their larger study, that "manhood and womanhood are defined in the process of social interaction"—that gender identities are shaped by the sorts of exchanges (in many different settings) that go on between men and women.

READING RESPONSE

By now you know Spradley and Mann's study very well, and as you return to the conversation they've invited, you'll be reading it as an insider to that conversation. As the writer of an ethnographic report, you'll want to look more analytically at how they've written their report, seeing how they've presented the understandings they've gained from their study and their purposes as writers. As a reader, at this point, you may also begin to read evaluatively, considering how effectively what they've done works for you.

<u>What</u> have they included? Do they give the right amount of detail for you to understand their examples, or too much, or too little? Do they provide enough background shared knowledge about the context of Brady's Bar or about other studies they refer to?

<u>Why</u> have they included it? Do they give you a clear sense of their purposes with the study, and of the relationship between what they've included and those purposes?

<u>How</u> have they constructed this report on their study and can you see why they've constructed it this way? What purposes do the various elements of their report serve for readers who are interested in studies of cultural settings?

Note places that you'll want to return to as you write your own report—either to see how Spradley and Mann have accomplished a part of their discussion that you have found particularly effective or to remind yourself of something ineffective, that you'll want to alter as you write your own report.

Comparing Ethnographic Studies

Although Spradley and Mann and Heath have written ethnographies, they differ in their styles of reporting—in how they write about what they've learned. Spradley and Mann, as we've seen, write in the genre of a formal report. Heath, on the other hand, tells the story of the two communities she studied. In fact she uses the term "story" in the prologue to her book, telling readers how they should approach what she's written.

The reader should see *Ways with Words* as an unfinished story, in which the characters are real people whose lives go on beyond the decade covered in this book and for whom we cannot, within these pages, either resolve the plot or complete the story. Through these pages, however, the reader should move very close to a living understanding of the ways of behaving, feeling, believing, and valuing of the children, their community members, and their townspeople teachers (1983, 13).

Both styles of reporting are common to the field of anthropology, although "telling the story" of a cultural group is a particularly frequent approach. Recently, some anthropologists have been experimenting with this form, having different members of the community speak directly about their own experiences and their interpretation of those experience, in their own voices, for example. Genres are always taking new shapes to fit the needs and interests of the people who use them.

At this point you may want to turn to other ethnographic studies to see how other researchers have reported on their research. At the end of Part II you'll find several such studies, including some by student researchers, focusing on the worlds of working class high school students in Great Britain, students in a college dormitory in the United States, a group of college classmates in a cafeteria, a group of long-term friends in an apartment several of them share, and the participants in an on-line video game. These researchers have asked somewhat different questions about their communities, highlighted different themes, framed their studies in different ways, and drawn on different pieces of the data they collected. And not all ethnographic writing takes the form of an ethnographic report. Any writer who wants to offer a rich understanding of the culture of a setting may draw on ethnographic methods of observation, analysis, and interpretation but write about what is learned in nonreport genres, as you can see if you look at the essay "Good Craic," Edie Shillue's account of her visit to a bar when she was traveling in Northern Ireland.

As you plan your own report or ethnographic essay, you'll want to use your own response as a reader to help you decide how you prefer to present your study to other readers—whether you prefer to write a more straightforward report of the sort that Spradley and Mann have produced or to represent your understandings about the community in a narrative style more like Heath's.

READING RESPONSE

To compare the different ways ethnographic studies might be set up and organized, look back at Spradley and Mann's study, rereading the first few pages to remind yourself of how they've framed their report, and then looking quickly through the whole to see the headings they've used to organize and pull out larger points from their study, and finally rereading their conclusion.

Then look in the same way at the chapter from Heath's study, again thinking about framing, structure and headings, and conclusion.   *(continued)*

(continued)

What elements do you find in one or more of these studies that you would now consider to be part of the genre of the ethnographic report?

After comparing the ways these ethnographic reports are organized, use what you've seen and learned to sketch out a plan for your report on your own study, bringing together as much as possible what you've learned from the work you've been doing in Part II:

—How will you introduce your study and frame it in the beginning of the paper? What key points/ideas/themes or ways of seeing what follows will you want your reader to understand at the beginning?

—How will you organize and present all that you've learned about this discourse community? What do you think you'll use for headings and (briefly) what do you think you'll include under each one?

—Where will you bring in the connections you see between your study and other research on discourse communities (from the other studies in this book)?

READING RESPONSE   Preview the additional selections of ethnographic writing at the end of the chapter and then choose one to read and gloss carefully and to respond to.

USING THE GENRES OF ETHNOGRAPHIC WRITING

The focus of Chapters 5 and 6 has been on carrying out field research within the academic genre of the ethnographic report, and the inquiries of this chapter have been leading you toward writing within that genre. But you may also want to think about other ways to present what you have learned, in addition to or in place of the ethnographic report.

You might provide a journalistic account of that setting, as a reporter would do, in a way that says less about your personal responses, but more about what a wider audience of readers might want to know about this little segment of the world. You could even recreate the life of the community imaginatively, in the script for a sitcom, a play, or a dialogue-filled short story. If you return to the example of "The River" or turn to "The Lesson" in the readings for Part II and consider the ways in which O'Connor and Bambara have represented in their short stories some of the characteristic ways of the communities around them, you may be inspired to work within that genre. There are many possible audiences for your insider perspective on the discourse community you have been studying, and many genres of writing that you can draw on to share your understandings with those audiences. Whatever genre you choose, as you move from observing speech acts and analyzing individual conversations that you've gathered in the community you're studying to writing a ethnographic account of that community, you'll want to use your observations to give as rich a picture as possible of community life.

You'll want to bring out the larger patterns of meaning you've found and how these can be seen in, and are supported by, the specific details of the data you've collected. Discovering patterns and generalizations and knowing how to back these up in ways convincing to readers by using detailed supporting evidence are important aspects of the ways with words of academic research communities. Using the same details to involve readers or viewers in an experience that will lead them to experience and understand these the larger characterizations is one of the ways of creative writers.

WRITING IN A NON-REPORT GENRE

If your class allows a choice of genres for writing about the discourse community you've been studying, or if you have the opportunity to write about this community in both an ethnographic report and in another genre, experiment with reporting as a travel writer, as a journalist, as a fiction writer. You'll want to ask yourself:

—How do writers typically present characteristic moments of experience in this genre?

—How do they work with those moments to bring out some of the underlying shared concerns, interests, and values of the community?

—How do they create shared background knowledge for their readers/listeners?

—How do they meet other expectations of the genre—in fiction, for example, that there will be a "plot" with some sort of action that leads to a resolution or outcome?

Plan how you will address these elements in a way that both captures your discourse community and meets readers' expectations for the genre you have chosen and then draft your writing in the genre you've chosen.

WRITING IN AN ACADEMIC RESEARCH GENRE: THE ETHNOGRAPHIC REPORT

As a researcher, you've undertaken a process of discovery, not necessarily knowing what you would find. Now that you've been through that process, you want to report on what you did find, in a way that will be convincing to readers. What are some of the significant things that you've learned about the community you've been studying? What, in the data you gathered and analyzed, helped you to see these things? What do you want to show your readers? You can begin to think about these questions by reviewing the writing that you've been doing throughout this study.

DRAWING ON YOUR NOTES, RESEARCH MEMOS, AND JOURNAL RESPONSES	Look back through all of your writing for Chapters 5 and 6. Highlight and gloss places that seem to give strong evidence of something you want to show about your community, places where you've come to some new insight, places where you've found points of contact with the work of other researchers—anything that you think you might want to draw into your final report. Then see where you can draw these pieces into your plan or how you can adapt your plan to encompass these pieces. Making an outline, with points that you can finally use as headings, can help you organize this.

Once you've reminded yourself of all that you've discovered, there are several further steps that you'll find helpful in preparing to write:

1. *Decide how to characterize your discourse community.* What do you now want to show about it? What does this sense of your community lead you to emphasize as you introduce the study, give background information about it, discuss the conversation that you recorded there, and give other examples of speech acts and speech events that go on in that setting? What points of contact does it lead you to see with other studies you've read?

CHARACTER-IZING YOUR COMMUNITY	Here are some questions you'll want to consider as you think about the general, ongoing life of the community. ■ What seem to be the significant characteristics of the community and its members? You might consider its location; the age, education, occupation, sex, or social position of participants; their racial/ethnic identity; their relationship to each other; or anything else that seems important. ■ Does it exist within a larger definable community (like a youth group within a church)? ■ How would you name this community? And how is it both typical and atypical of other communities that might be named in the same way? (If you're studying a group of college-age male friends, for example, in what ways is your group of friends likely to be typical of that category, and in what ways do you think it's different?) ■ What larger understandings about this community have you come to through your study that you want your readers to take away from reading your report? What are you trying to show?

STUDENT VOICES	Notice how Jonathon introduces his study, "Guy Talk," by characterizing his group of male friends in terms of their style of guy talk and their interest in guy stuff. (A female classmate helped him to focus on these characteristics when she observed, "That's just the way guys talk. My friends would never talk that way.") (continued)

> Guys, we truly are a different breed. From the way we talk to what we talk about, we really do have our own style. If you are a guy, you probably don't even notice it, but it's true, when we are with our friends we talk about stuff that we wouldn't talk to others about, we talk about "guy stuff." I recorded a typical conversation between myself and a few of my friends, and I found that the stuff we talk about tends to be more male-oriented. For example, we go into cars and parties at great length. Now women may talk about these things too; however, they probably don't talk about them in the same way.

2. *Frame your study.* At this point in your work, you'll want to begin to think about how to place your study itself into a context—creating a frame for readers. For Spradley and Mann, the research context of other studies of drinking and talking behavior provides the frame they want to use to guide readers into their own study, because they're foregrounding the placement of their study within the field of anthropology. Other researchers/writers might want to frame their studies in other ways. If she were writing a report on the barroom discourse community she entered in Northern Ireland, Edie Shillue, might frame it with some of what she says in her interview—with something about her own travels in Vietnam and the contrast in her own position in Ireland, or with some historical background about the Troubles in Northern Ireland. How you choose to introduce and frame your study provides a lens through which the reader will see what follows. You can see some examples of the ways student researchers framed their studies below.

Matt S. frames his report, "A Slice of City Living," by characterizing his neighborhood and then placing his small community of male friends into that wider context.   **STUDENT VOICES**

> Our neighborhood does not have a genuine sense of community. It is predominately a white, Irish-Catholic. We are unified only technically by the church, and by the fact that the majority of people are from working, middle class families. The local church plays no unifying role in any of my friend's lives and those of many parents. No social gatherings occur to meet others from the parish. Everyone tends to their own business. It's a nice neighborhood to raise a family. It is well kept up. It's not dangerous yet it still has its perils. It has the perils that can ruin lives—drugs and alcohol. Drugs are not the major problem, though. Drugs can be found anywhere. It is the personal weakness to frequently use them and lose control. The choice is the source of the problem. I am not saying that my friends have been severe drug addicts through their teenage years, but drugs have taken their toll in some way or another on many of the kids that I am familiar with. . . .

Agnes introduces her study of friends, "My Chosen Family," with a definition of culture that she's read for another course and her understanding of American culture (she's a Polish-American who spent her high school years in Poland).   *(continued)*

(continued)

According to the British anthropologist Sir Edward Burnett Tylor, culture is "that complex whole which includes knowledge, belief, art, law, morals, custom and other capabilities and habits acquired by man as a member of society." Culture is a set of abstract values, ideals and perceptions shared by people belonging to the same society, that allow people to interpret events. Behavior is the manifestation of culture.

United States is a pluralistic society, made up of people of different cultures. This is the reason all inhabitants must be open and tolerant towards others, as they are all members of the American society. Most tend to be tolerant of diversity. My small discourse community seems to fulfill these "requirements." Therefore its openness makes every person, stranger or acquaintance, feel welcome.

3. *Find points of contact and connect your research to other studies.* If you don't follow Spradley and Mann's example of using a connection with other studies to frame your own, you'll want to include those connections at another appropriate place—to position yourself as an insider to an academic discourse community of researchers by showing how the shared knowledge of the field has led you to see some aspect of the data you've gathered, and showing how your examples reinforce and contribute to understandings that others have developed. What do you find in other studies that connects with what you've found in your own?

STUDENT VOICES

Look at the ways in which Shayna, in her study of the moving company where she works, makes a larger connection between what she's recorded and what has been found in other studies. This section begins with a statement from a co-worker:

Nino started to laugh and said, "She didn't say to bullshit." Nino figured out from the confusing talk between Sharon and I, that he was faking it, and we all found it really amusing. As I studied this aspect of our conversation, I realized that it was quite similar to a study Shirley Brice Heath did in a small town called Trackton. She studied the way in which they talked to each other, and she determined that the most appreciated style of talking was "talkin junk." The people there would base their stories around an actual event but lay on wild exaggerations and fictional details to the factual truth. The more junk you could effectively relate, the better story teller you were. Heath discovered an interesting idea through analyzing the way they converse with each other. She states that, "Trackton's stories are intended to intensify the social interactions and to give all parties an opportunity to share not only in the unity of the common experience on which the story may be based, but also in the humor of the wide-ranging language play and imagination which embellish the narrative" (1983, p. 166). This idea directly relates to the way Nino and I relate to Sharon. **(Shayna)**

4. *Working from your organizational plan, write a draft of your final report.* After you've characterized your community, decided how to introduce and frame your report, and discovered the connections to other research that you want to make, you're ready to write your draft. Your draft report will require that you move out in several ways from the detailed work of analysis that you've been doing in these last chapters

---

DRAFTING YOUR REPORT

a. You'll want to share with your readers the necessary information about the immediate situation of the conversations and speech acts you studied: who's involved in these interactions, when and where they take place, what sorts of knowledge about the world is drawn on if that's relevant.

b. You'll want to highlight the bigger themes that have emerged, the bigger <u>why</u> imbedded in the conversations and other speech acts, events, and genres that take place in your community. Then you'll want to draw from your analysis and from examples in your transcript or in your observation of speech acts to give supporting evidence for what you've found, highlighting key points, and using actual examples from your transcript and notes. You'll want to choose specific examples from all of the data you've gathered— from your analysis of a conversation, from your observations of speech acts— that illustrate what you've learned about the community and support the larger understandings you want readers to get from your report.

c. As you discuss examples, you'll want to highlight what insiders know and can do, in terms of both shared background knowledge and shared ways of interacting. How would you characterize the discourse of a speaker who gets attention and respect in this community's conversations and how can we see this in an example you've chosen? What does such a speaker have to be able to do to demonstrate the expected communicative competence of an insider to the community?

d. You'll want to bring in the connections you've found to a research context— commenting on what has been learned from other studies that have some points of contact with or some relevance to your own, quoting from those studies, and providing citations.

e. You'll want to leave your readers with some significant new understandings that have been gained from this work.

---

5. *Preparing a final version of your essay or report.* Once you've drafted your report, you'll want to get feedback from readers to use in revising, and then prepare your final version.

FINAL STEPS

- Add a title that captures something about the way you'd characterize your discourse community;

- Add headings (if you're working in a typical report format) that highlight key sections and ideas and that guide your readers through the major elements of your report;

- Add a Works Cited page (or References, if you use APA style) with complete information for the works you cite. (See Part IV, Documenting Sources (pp. 552–559) for details on MLA and APA styles for cited sources.)

- You will also need to edit and proofread very carefully.

Additional Readings

Each of the readings that follows offers a portrait of a particular setting or experience in a way that captures the perspectives of the insiders to a community. The writers/researchers may be insiders themselves, who have stepped back from their daily experience in the community to observe and to analyze what they've observed there. Or they may have stepped into these communities as outsiders, trying to see what life in the community is like from the inside. Whether working in the genres of fiction, the ethnographic report, or the personal essay, each of these writers has captured not only the ways in which insiders to the community talk but what they share as concerns, beliefs, and values. You'll want to consider what you can discover about the shared knowledge, purposes, and ways of insiders and the context that has helped to shape them as you look at these portraits.

Toni Cade Bambara, "The Lesson"

Toni Cade Bambara brought a variety of experiences to her writing of short stories. She grew up in poor neighborhoods in New York and New Jersey, and after graduating from college as an English and theater major, she worked for the welfare department and ran a local community center as well as continuing to study theater and literature. As a writer, she once said in an interview (in *Black Women Writers at Work*), "One's got to see what the factory worker sees, what the prisoner sees, what the welfare children see, what the scholar sees, got to see what the ruling-class mythmakers see as well, in order to tell the truth and not get trapped." That close observation, discovering what's seen by the insider participants in any setting, feeds fiction as well as ethnography, as the writer recreates people's worlds and their ways of seeing those worlds. The short story, "The Lesson," from her collection *Gorilla, My Love* (1972), presents a moment of experience from the perspective of a child living in an impoverished section of a city.

The Lesson

Toni Cade Bambara

1   Back in the days when everyone was old and stupid or young and foolish and me and Sugar were the only ones just right, this lady moved on our block with nappy hair and proper speech and no makeup. And quite naturally we laughed at her, laughed the way we did at the junk man who went about his business like he was some big-time president and his sorry-ass horse his secretary. And we kinda hated her too, hated the way we did the winos who cluttered up our parks and pissed on our handball walls and stank up our hallways and stairs so you couldn't halfway play hide-and-seek without a goddamn gas mask. Miss Moore was her name. The only woman on the block

285

with no first name. And she was black as hell, cept for her feet, which were fish-white and spooky. And she was always planning these boring-ass things for us to do, us being my cousin, mostly, who lived on the block cause we all moved North the same time and to the same apartment then spread out gradual to breathe. And our parents would yank our heads into some kinda shape and crisp up our clothes so we'd be presentable for travel with Miss Moore, who always looked like she was going to church, though she never did. Which is just one of the things the grownups talked about when they talked behind her back like a dog. But when she came calling with some sachet she'd sewed up or some gingerbread she'd made or some book, why then they'd all be too embarrassed to turn her down and we'd get handed over all spruced up. She'd been to college and said it was only right that she should take responsibility for the young ones' education, and she not even related by marriage or blood. So they'd go for it. Specially Aunt Gretchen. She was the main gofer in the family. You got some ole dumb shit foolishness you want somebody to go for, you send for Aunt Gretchen. She been screwed into the go-along for so long, it's a blood-deep natural thing with her. Which is how she got saddled with me and Sugar and Junior in the first place while our mothers were in a la-de-da apartment up the block having a good ole time.

So this one day Miss Moore rounds us all up at the mailbox and it's puredee hot and she's knockin herself out about arithmetic. And school suppose to let up in summer I heard, but she don't never let up. And the starch in my pinafore scratching the shit outta me and I'm really hating this nappy-head bitch and her goddamn college degree. I'd much rather go to the pool or to the show where it's cool. So me and Sugar leaning on the mailbox being surly, which is a Miss Moore word. And Flyboy checking out what everybody brought for lunch. And Fat Butt already wasting his peanut-butter-and-jelly sandwich like the pig he is. And Junebug punchin on Q.T.'s arm for potato chips. And Rosie Giraffe shifting from one hip to the other waiting for somebody to step on her foot or ask her if she from Georgia so she can kick ass, preferably Mercedes'. And Miss Moore asking us do we know what money is, like we a bunch of retards. I mean real money, she say, like it's only poker chips or monopoly papers we lay on the grocer. So right away I'm tired of this and say so. And would much rather snatch Sugar and go to the Sunset and terrorize the West Indian kids and take their hair ribbons and their money too. And Miss Moore files that remark away for next week's lesson on brotherhood, I can tell. And finally I say we oughta get to the subway cause it's cooler and besides we might meet some cute boys. Sugar done swiped her mama's lipstick, so we ready.

So we heading down the street and she's boring us silly about what things cost and what our parents make and how much goes for rent and how money ain't divided up right in this country. And then she gets to the part about we all poor and live in the slums, which I don't feature. And I'm ready to speak on that, but she steps out in the street and hails two cabs just like that. Then she hustles half the crew in with her and hands me a five-dollar bill and tells me to calculate 10 percent tip for the driver. And we're off. Me and Sugar and Junebug and Flyboy hangin out the window and hollering to everybody, putting lipstick on each other cause Flyboy a faggot anyway, and making farts with our sweaty armpits. But I'm mostly trying to figure how to spend this money. But they all fascinated with the meter ticking and Junebug starts laying bets as to how much it'll read when Flyboy can't hold his breath no more. Then Sugar lays bets as to how much it'll be when we get there. So I'm stuck. Don't nobody want to go for my plan, which is to jump out at the next light and run off to the first bar-b-que we can find. Then the driver tells us to get the hell out cause we there already. And the meter reads eighty-five cents. And I'm stalling to figure out the tip and Sugar say give him a dime. And I decide he don't need it bad as I do, so later for him. But then he tries to take off with Junebug foot still in the door so we talk about his mama something ferocious. Then we check out that we on Fifth Avenue and everybody dressed up in stockings. One lady in a fur coat, hot as it is. White folks crazy.

"This is the place," Miss Moore say, presenting it to us in the voice she uses at the museum. "Let's look in the windows before we go in."

5   "Can we steal?" Sugar asks very serious like she's getting the ground rules squared away before she plays. "I beg your pardon," say Miss Moore, and we fall out. So she leads us around the windows of the toy store and me and Sugar screamin, "This is mine, that's mine, I gotta have that, that was made for me, I was born for that," till Big Butt drowns us out.

"Hey, I'm goin to buy that there."

"That there? You don't even know what it is, stupid."

"I do so," he say punchin on Rosie Giraffe. "It's a microscope."

"Whatcha gonna do with a microscope, fool?"

10   "Look at things."

"Like what, Ronald?" ask Miss Moore. And Big Butt ain't got the first notion. So here go Miss Moore gabbing about the thousands of bacteria in a drop of water and the somethinorother in a speck of blood and the million and one living things in the air around us is invisible to the naked eye. And what she say that for? Junebug go to town on that "naked" and we rolling. Then Miss Moore ask what it cost. So we all jam into the window smudgin it up and the price tag say $300. So then she ask how long'd take for Big Butt and Junebug to save up their allowances. "Too long," I say. "Yeh," adds Sugar, "outgrown it by that time." And Miss Moore say no, you never outgrow learning instruments. "Why, even medical students and interns and," blah, blah, blah. And we ready to choke Big Butt for bringing it up in the first damn place.

"This here costs four hundred eighty dollars," says Rosie Giraffe. So we pile up all over her to see what she pointin out. My eyes tell me it's a chunk of glass cracked with something heavy, and different-color inks dripped into the splits, then the whole thing put into a oven or something. But for $480 it don't make sense.

"That's a paperweight made of semi-precious stones fused together under tremendous pressure," she explains slowly, with her hands doing the mining and all the factory work.

"So what's a paperweight?" asks Rosie Giraffe.

15   "To weigh paper with, dumbbell," say Flyboy, the wise man from the East.

"Not exactly," say Miss Moore, which is what she say when you warm or way off too. "It's to weigh paper down so it won't scatter and make your desk untidy." So right away me and Sugar curtsy to each other and then to Mercedes who is more the tidy type.

"We don't keep paper on top of the desk in my class," say Junebug, figuring Miss Moore crazy or lyin one.

"At home, then," she say. "Don't you have a calendar and pencil case and a blotter and a letter-opener on your desk at home where you do your homework?" And she know damn well what our homes look like cause she nosys around in them every chance she gets.

"I don't even have a desk," say Junebug. "Do we?"

20   "No. And I don't get no homework neither," says Big Butt.

"And I don't even have a home," say Flyboy like he do at school to keep the white folks off his back and sorry for him. Send this poor kid to camp posters, is his specialty.

"I do," says Mercedes. "I have a box of stationery on my desk and a picture of my cat. My godmother bought the stationery and the desk. There's a big rose on each sheet and the envelopes smell like roses."

"Who wants to know about your smelly-ass stationery," say Rosie Giraffe fore I can get my two cents in.

"It's important to have a work area all your own so that . . ."

25   "Will you look at this sailboat, please," say Flyboy, cuttin her off and pointin to the thing like it was his. So once again we tumble all over each other to gaze at this magnificent thing in the toy store which is just big enough to maybe sail two kittens across the pond if you strap them to the posts tight. We all start reciting the price tag like we in assembly. "Handcrafted sailboat of fiberglass at one thousand one hundred ninety-five dollars."

"Unbelievable," I hear myself say and am really stunned. I read it again for myself just in case the group recitation put me in a trance. Same thing. For some reason this pisses me off. We look at Miss Moore and she lookin at us, waiting for I dunno what.

"Who'd pay all that when you can buy a sailboat set for a quarter at Pop's, a tube of glue for a dime, and a ball of string for eight cents? It must have a motor and a whole lot else besides," I say. "My sailboat cost me about fifty cents."

"But will it take water?" say Mercedes with her smart ass.

"Took mine to Alley Pond Park once," say Flyboy. "String broke. Lost it. Pity."

30   "Sailed mine in Central Park and it keeled over and sank. Had to ask my father for another dollar."

"And you got the strap," laugh Big Butt. "The jerk didn't even have a string on it. My old man wailed on his behind."

Little Q.T. was staring hard at the sailboat and you could see he wanted it bad. But he too little and somebody'd just take it from him. So what the hell. "This boat for kids, Miss Moore?"

"Parents silly to buy something like that just to get all broke up," say Rosie Giraffe.

"That much money it should last forever," I figure.

35   "My father'd buy it for me if I wanted it."

"Your father, my ass," say Rosie Giraffe getting a chance to finally push Mercedes.

"Must be rich people shop here," say Q.T.

"You are a very bright boy," say Flyboy. "What was your first clue?" And he rap him on the head with the back of his knuckles, since Q.T. the only one he could get away with. Though Q.T. liable to come up behind you years later and get his licks in when you half expect it.

"What I want to know is," I says to Miss Moore though I never talk to her, I wouldn't give the bitch that satisfaction, "is how much a real boat costs? I figure a thousand'd get you a yacht any day."

"Why don't you check that out," she says, "and report back to the group?" Which really pains my ass. If you gonna mess up a perfectly good swim day least you could do is have some answers. "Let's go in," she say like she got something up her sleeve. Only she don't lead the way. So me and Sugar turn the corner to where the entrance is, but when we get there I kinda hang back. Not that I'm scared, what's there to be afraid of, just a toy store. But I feel funny, shame. But what I got to be shamed about? Got as much right to go in as anybody. But somehow I can't seem to get hold of the door, so I step away for Sugar to lead. But she hangs back too. And I look at her and she looks at me and this is ridiculous. I mean, damn, I have never ever been shy about doing nothing or going nowhere. But then Mercedes steps up and then Rosie Giraffe and Big Butt crowd in behind and shove, and next thing we all stuffed into the doorway with only Mercedes squeezing past us, smoothing out her jumper and walking right down the aisle. Then the rest of us tumble in like a glued-together jigsaw done all wrong. And people lookin at us. And it's like the time me and Sugar crashed into the Catholic church on a dare. But once we got in there and everything so hushed and holy and the candles and the bowin and the handkerchiefs on all the drooping heads, I just couldn't go through with the plan. Which was for me to run up to the altar and do a tap dance while Sugar played the nose flute and messed around in the holy water. And Sugar kept givin me the elbow. Then later teased me so bad I tied her up in the shower and turned it on and locked her in. And she'd be there till this day if Aunt Gretchen hadn't finally figured I was lyin about the boarder takin a shower.

Same thing in the store. We all walkin on tiptoe and hardly touchin the games and puzzles and things. And I watched Miss Moore who is steady watchin us like she waitin for a sign. Like Mama Drewery watches the sky and sniffs the air and takes note of just how much slant is in the bird formation. Then me and Sugar bump smack into each other, so busy gazing at the toys, specially the sailboat. But we don't laugh and go into our fat-lady bump-stomach routine. We just stare at that price tag. Then Sugar run a finger over the whole boat. And I'm jealous and want to hit her. Maybe not her, but I sure want to punch somebody in the mouth.

"Watcha bring us here for, Miss Moore?"

"You sound angry, Sylvia. Are you mad about something?" Givin me one of them grins like she tellin a grown-up joke that never turns out to be funny. And she's lookin very closely at me like maybe she planning to do my portrait from memory. I'm mad, but I won't give her that satisfaction. So I slouch around the store bein very bored and say, "Let's go."

Me and Sugar at the back of the train watchin the tracks whizzin by large then small then getting gobbled up in the dark. I'm thinkin about this tricky toy I saw in the store. A clown that somersaults on a bar then does chin-ups just cause you yank lightly at his leg. Cost $35. I could see me askin my mother for a $35 birthday clown. "You wanna who that costs what?" she'd say, cocking her head to the side to get a better view of the hole in my head. Thirty-five dollars could buy new bunk beds for

Junior and Gretchen's boy. Thirty-five dollars and the whole household could go visit Granddaddy Nelson in the country. Thirty-five dollars would pay for the rent and the piano bill too. Who are these people that spend that much for performing clowns and $1000 for toy sailboats? What kinda work they do and how they live and how come we ain't in on it? Where we are is who we are, Miss Moore always pointin out. But it don't necessarily have to be that way, she always adds then waits for somebody to say that poor people have to wake up and demand their share of the pie and don't none of us know what kind of pie she talking about in the first damn place. But she ain't so smart cause I still got her four dollars from the taxi and she sure ain't gettin it. Messin up my day with this shit. Sugar nudges me in my pocket and winks.

45   Miss Moore lines us up in front of the mailbox where we started from, seem like years ago, and I got a headache for thinkin so hard. And we lean all over each other so we can hold up under the draggy-ass lecture she always finishes us off with at the end before we thank her for borin us to tears. But she just looks at us like she readin tea leaves. Finally she say, "Well, what did you think of F.A.O. Schwarz?"

Rosie Giraffe mumbles, "White folks crazy." "I'd like to go there again when I get my birthday money," says Mercedes, and we shove her out the pack so she has to lean on the mailbox by herself.

"I'd like a shower. Tiring day," say Flyboy. Then Sugar surprises me by sayin, "You know, Miss Moore, I don't think all of us here put together eat in a year what that sailboat costs." And Miss Moore lights up like somebody goosed her. "And?" she say, urging Sugar on. Only I'm standin on her foot so she don't continue.

"Imagine for a minute what kind of society it is in which some people can spend on a toy what it would cost to feed a family of six or seven. What do you think?"

"I think," say Sugar pushing me off her feet like she never done before, cause I whip her ass in a minute, "that this is not much of a democracy if you ask me. Equal chance to pursue happiness means an equal crack at the dough, don't it?" Miss Moore is beside herself and I am disgusted with Sugar's treachery. So I stand on her foot one more time to see if she'll shove me. She shuts up, and Miss Moore looks at me, sorrowfully I'm thinkin. And somethin weird is goin on, I can feel it in my chest.

50   "Anybody else learn anything today?" lookin dead at me. I walk away and Sugar has to run to catch up and don't even seem to notice when I shrug her arm off my shoulder.

"Well, we got four dollars anyway," she says.

"Uh hunh."

"We could go to Hascombs and get half a chocolate layer and then go to the Sunset and still have plenty money for potato chips and ice cream sodas."

"Un hunh."

55   "Race you to Hascombs," she say.

We start down the block and she gets ahead which is O.K. by me cause I'm going to the West End and then over to the Drive to think this day through. She can run if she want to and even run faster. But ain't nobody gonna beat me at nuthin.

1. <u>Reflecting on discourse, identity, and community</u>

   ■ The narrator sets out to tell about Miss Moore, the lady with proper speech whom everyone hated. How do the details the narrator presents about Miss Moore contribute to your picture not only of Miss Moore's concerns and values but of the narrator and her friends as well?

   ■ Bambara has chosen to tell this story from a child's point of view. How might the story be different if told from the perspective of Miss Moore?

   ■ Miss Moore takes the children out of their familiar setting and into a new one (much like the baby sitter in "The River" does with young Harry). How much sense can these children make of the ways of the unfamiliar world they enter? How appropriate are the insider understandings they bring from their prior experience to the world that Miss Moore takes them to? How do the objects and experiences they're unfamiliar with reflect back on their own worlds?

   ■ What, finally, is the lesson Miss Moore wants them to learn? What do you think the narrator takes away from this experience? What does the final paragraph suggest about how the narrator is positioned as the story ends?

2. <u>Reading from a writer's/researcher's perspective</u>

   ■ Bambara presents, through her narrator, a general picture of the period of time when Miss Moore entered the community, and then focuses in on a particular, representative moment of experience that captures "the problem" Miss Moore presented to them. What does the framing of the story's opening contribute to what follows? What meanings are you left to discover, and how do you discover them? What gaps does Bambara leave that you have to fill in as a reader?

   ■ In this first-person narration, what does the narrator's discourse style contribute to the picture you get of her world? What does the direct representation of dialogue add to that picture?

   ■ If you've read one or more ethnographic research reports at the time that you turn to this story, what do you see as significantly different about the way this piece of fiction works and the way a report works. If you were portraying the community you are studying through the genre of the short story, how might you craft that story?

Paul Willis, "The Informal Group"

Paul Willis, a sociologist, focused his research on the social institution of the school. He wanted to know more about how schools work in maintaining the existing balance of "cultural capital" in a society—how they contribute to a social structure where there is often relatively little movement between classes (where children of middle class parents stay in the middle class, and where working class kids go on to working class jobs). That interest led him to look at what goes on in the informal school culture of groups of students in contrast to the formal and approved school ways. In *Learning to Labor* (1981), from which the following excerpt is taken, he looked at the ways in which working class boys in a British school carried out an ongoing rebellion against school authority. The meanings the boys find in school each day are located in the informal community of their peers, and are defined in opposition to the formal school expectations. The boys call themselves "the lads" in contrast to the more serious students, whom they call "ear'oles." They spend their days "wagging off" (ducking out of school) or trying to "have a laff" at the expense of school authorities. Their working class British dialect may be unfamiliar to you, but their oppositional stance towards school has its counterpart among groups of students in most American high schools. Even though Willis's original study— now a classic in the field of sociology—was carried out in the late 1960's, the insights it offers into the complex relationship between social class and schooling inform many contemporary studies. You may find Willis's identification of informal group values and how they are shaped in opposition to a formal culture to be particularly useful if you are studying an informal group.

The Informal Group

Paul Willis

On a night we go out on
the street
Troubling other people,
I suppose we're anti-social,
But we enjoy it.

The older generation
They don't like our hair,
Or the clothes we wear
They seem to love running
us down,

I don't know what I would
do if I didn't have the gang.

(Extract from a poem by Derek written in an English class.)

1   In many respects the opposition we have been looking at can be understood as a classic example of the opposition between the formal and the informal. The school is the zone of the formal. It has a clear structure: the school building, school rules, pedagogic practice, a staff hierarchy with powers ultimately sanctioned—as we have seen in a small way—by the state, the pomp and majesty of the law, and the repressive arm of state apparatus, the police. The 'ear'oles' invest in this formal structure, and in exchange for some loss in autonomy expect the official guardians to keep the holy rules—often above and beyond their actual call to duty. What is freely sacrificed by the faithful must be taken from the unfaithful.

Counter-school culture is the zone of the informal. It is where the incursive demands of the formal are denied—even if the price is the expression of opposition in style, micro-interactions and non-public discourses. In working class culture generally opposition is frequently marked by a withdrawal into the informal and expressed in its characteristic modes just beyond the reach of 'the rule'.

Even though there are no public rules, physical structures, recognised hierarchies or institutionalised sanctions in the counter-school culture, it cannot run on air. It must have its own material base, its own infrastructure. This is, of course, the social group. The informal group is the basic unit of this culture, the fundamental and elemental source of its resistance. It locates and makes possible all other elements of the culture, and its presence decisively distinguishes 'the lads' from the 'ear'oles'.

The importance of the group is very clear to members of the counter-school culture.

[In a group discussion]

5   WILL: (. . .) we see each other every day, don't we, at school (. . .)

JOEY: That's it, we've developed certain ways of talking, certain ways of acting, and we developed disregards for Pakis, Jamaicans and all different . . . for all the scrubs and the fucking ear'oles and all that (. . .) We're getting to know it now, like we're getting to know all the cracks, like, how to get out of lessons and things, and we know where to have a crafty smoke. You can come over here to the youth wing and do summat, and er'm . . . all your friends are here, you know, it's sort of what's there, what's always going to be there for the next year, like, and you know you have to come to school today, if you're feeling bad, your mate'll soon cheer yer up like, 'cos you couldn't go without ten minutes in this school, without having a laff at something or other.

PW: Are your mates a really big important thing at school now?

—   Yeah.

—   Yeah.

— Yeah.

10 JOEY: They're about the best thing actually.

The essence of being 'one of the lads' lies within the group. It is impossible to form a distinctive culture by yourself. You cannot generate fun, atmosphere and a social identity by yourself. Joining the counter-school culture means joining a group, and enjoying it means being with the group:

[In a group discussion on being 'one of the lads']

JOEY: (. . .) when you'm dossing on your own, it's no good, but when you'm dossing with your mates, then you're all together, you're having a laff and it's a doss.

BILL: If you don't do what the others do, you feel out.

15 FRED: You feel out, yeah, yeah. They sort of, you feel, like, thinking the others are . . .

WILL: In the second years . . .

SPANKSY: I can imagine . . . you know, when I have a day off school, when you come back the next day, and something happened like in the day you've been off, you feel, 'Why did I have that day off', you know, 'I could have been enjoying myself'. You know what I mean? You come back and they're saying, 'Ooth, you should have been here yesterday', you know.

WILL: (. . .) like in the first and second years, you can say er'm . . . you're a bit of an ear'ole right. Then you want to try what it's like to be er'm . . . say, one of the boys like, you want to have a taste of that, not an ear'ole, and so you like the taste of that.

Though informal, such groups nevertheless have rules of a kind which can be described—though they are characteristically framed in contrast to what 'rules' are normally taken to mean.

20 PW: (. . .) Are there any rules between you lot?

PETE: We just break the other rules.

FUZZ: We ain't got no rules between us though, have we? (. . .)

PETE: Changed 'em round.

WILL: We ain't got rules but we do things between us, but we do things that y'know, like er . . . say, I wouldn't knock off anybody's missus or Joey's missus, and they wouldn't do it to me, y'know what I mean? Things like that or, er . . . yer give 'im a fag, you expect one back, like, or summat like that.

25 FRED: T'ain't rules, it's just an understanding really.

WILL: That's it, yes.

PW: (. . .) What would these understandings be?

WILL: Er . . . I think, not to . . . meself, I think there ain't many of us that play up the first or second years, it really is that, but y'know, say if Fred had cum to me and sez, 'er . . . I just got two bob off that second year over there', I'd think, 'What a cunt', you know. (. . .)

30 FRED: We're as thick as thieves, that's what they say, stick together.

There is a universal taboo amongst informal groups on the yielding of incriminating information about others to those with formal power. Informing contravenes the essence of the informal group's nature: the maintenance of oppositional meanings against the penetration of 'the rule'. The Hammertown lads call it 'grassing'. Staff call it telling the truth. 'Truth' is the formal complement of 'grassing'. It is only by getting someone to 'grass'—forcing them to break the solemnest taboo—that the primacy of the formal organisation can be maintained. No wonder then, that a whole school can be shaken with paroxysms over a major incident and the purge which follows it. It is an atavistic struggle about authority and the legitimacy of authority. The school has to win, and someone, finally, has to 'grass': this is one of the ways in which the school itself is reproduced and the faith of the 'ear'oles' restored. But whoever has done the 'grassing' becomes special, weak and marked. There is a massive retrospective and on-going re-appraisal amongst 'the lads' of the fatal flaw in his personality which had always been immanent but not fully disclosed till now:

[In a group discussion of the infamous 'fire extinguisher incident' in which 'the lads' took a hydrant out of school and let it off in the local park]

PW: It's been the biggest incident of the year as it's turned out, hasn't it?

JOEY: It's been blown up into something fucking terrific. It was just like that [snapping his fingers], a gob in the ocean as far as I'm concerned when we did it, just like smoking round the corner, or going down the shop for some crisps.

35 PW: What happened (. . .)?

— Webby [on the fringes of the counter-school culture] grassed.

JOEY: Simmondsy had me on me own and he said, 'One of the group owned up and tried to put all the blame on Fuzz'. But he'd only had Webby in there.

SPANKSY: We was smoking out here.

SPIKE: He's like that, you'd got a fag, hadn't you [to Fuzz].

40 SPANKSY: And Webby asks for a drag, so he give Webby the fag. Rogers [a teacher] walked through the door, and he went like that [demonstrating] and he says, 'It ain't mine sir, I'm just holding it for Fuzz'.

WILL: Down the park before, (. . .) this loose thing, me and Eddie pulled it off, didn't we, me and Eddie, and the parky was coming round like, he was running round, wor'he, so me and Eddie we went round the other side, and just sat there, like you know, two monkeys. And Webby was standing there, and the parky come up to him and says, 'Come on, get out. Get out of this park. You'm banned'. And he says, he walks past us, me and Eddie, and he says, 'I know you warn't there, you was sitting here'. And Webby went, 'It warn't me, it was . . .', and he was just about to say summat, warn't he?

EDDIE: That's it, and I said, 'Shhh', and he just about remembered not to grass us.

Membership of the informal group sensitises the individual to the unseen informal dimension of life in general. Whole hinterlands open up of what lies behind the official definition of things. A kind of double capacity develops to register public descriptions and objectives on the one hand, and to look behind them, consider their implications, and work out what will actually happen, on the other. This interpretative ability is felt very often as a kind of maturation, a feeling of becoming 'worldliwise', of knowing 'how things really work when it comes to it'. It supplies the real 'insider' knowledge which actually helps you get through the day.

> PW: Do you think you've learnt anything at school, has it changed or moulded your values?

45   JOEY: I don't think school does fucking anything to you (. . .) It never has had much effect on anybody I don't think [after] you've learnt the basics. I mean school, it's fucking four hours a day. But it ain't the teachers who mould you, it's the fucking kids you meet. You'm only with the teachers 30 per cent of the time in school, the other fucking two-thirds are just talking, fucking pickin' an argument, messing about.

The group also supplies those contacts which allow the individual to build up alternative maps of social reality, it gives the bits and pieces of information for the individual to work out himself what makes things tick. It is basically only through the group that other groups are met, and through them successions of other groups. School groups coalesce and further link up with neighbourhood groups, forming a network for the passing on of distinctive kinds of knowledge and perspectives that progressively place school at a tangent to the overall experience of being a working class teenager in an industrial city. It is the infrastructure of the informal group which makes at all possible a distinctive kind of *class* contact, or class culture, as distinct from the dominant one.

Counter-school culture already has a developed form of unofficial bartering and exchange based on 'nicking', 'fiddles', and 'the foreigner'—a pattern which, of course, emerges much more fully in the adult working class world:

> FUZZ: If, say, somebody was to say something like, 'I'm looking, I want a cassette on the cheap like'. Right, talk about it, one of us hears about a cassette on the cheap, y'know, kind of do the deal for 'em and then say, 'Ah, I'll get you the cassette'.

Cultural values and interpretations circulate 'illicitly' and informally just as do commodities.

DOSSING, BLAGGING AND WAGGING

50   Opposition to the school is principally manifested in the struggle to win symbolic and physical space from the institution and its rules and to defeat its main perceived purpose: to make you 'work'. Both the winning and the prize—a form of self-direction—profoundly develop informal cultural meanings and practices. The dynamic aspects of the staff/pupil relationship will be examined later on. By the time a counter-school culture is fully developed its members have become adept at managing the formal system, and limiting its demands to the absolute minimum. Exploiting the com-

plexity of modern regimes of mixed ability groupings, blocked timetabling and multiple RSLA options, in many cases this minimum is simply the act of registration.

[In a group discussion on the school curriculum]

JOEY: (. . .) of a Monday afternoon, we'd have nothing right? Nothing hardly relating to school work, Tuesday afternoon we have swimming and they stick you in a classroom for the rest of the afternoon, Wednesday afternoon you have games and there's only Thursday and Friday afternoon that you work, if you call that work. The last lesson Friday afternoon we used to go and doss, half of us wagged out o' lessons and the other half go into the classroom, sit down and just go to sleep (. . .)

SPANKSY: (. . .) Skive this lesson, go up on the bank, have a smoke, and the next lesson go to a teacher who, you know, 'll call the register (. . .)

BILL: It's easy to go home as well, like him [Eddie] . . . last Wednesday afternoon, he got his mark and went home (. . .)

55   EDDIE: I ain't supposed to be in school this afternoon, I'm supposed to be at college. [on a link course where students spend one day a week at college for vocational instruction]

PW: What's the last time you've done some writing?

WILL: When we done some writing?

FUZZ: Oh are, last time was in careers, 'cos I writ 'yes' on a piece of paper, that broke me heart.

PW: Why did it break your heart?

60   FUZZ: I mean to write, 'cos I was going to try and go through the term without writing anything. 'Cos since we've cum back, I ain't dun nothing [it was half way through term].

Truancy is only a very imprecise—even meaningless—measure of rejection of school. This is not only because of the practice of stopping in school for registration before 'wagging off' (developed to a fine art amongst 'the lads'), but also because it only measures one aspect of what we might more accurately describe as informal student mobility. Some of 'the lads' develop the ability of moving about the school at their own will to a remarkable degree. They construct virtually their own day from what is offered by the school. Truancy is only one relatively unimportant and crude variant of this principle of self-direction which ranges across vast chunks of the syllabus and covers many diverse activities: being free out of class, being in class and doing no work, being in the wrong class, roaming the corridors looking for excitement, being asleep in private. The core skill which articulates these possibilities is being able to get out of any given class: the preservation of personal mobility.

[In a group discussion]

PW: But doesn't anybody worry about your not being in their class?

FUZZ: I get a note off the cooks saying I'm helping them (. . .)

65   JOHN: You just go up to him [a teacher] and say, 'Can I go and do a job'. He'll say, 'Certainly, by all means', 'cos they want to get rid of you like.

FUZZ: Specially when I ask 'em.

PETE: You know the holes in the corridor, I didn't want to go to games, he told me to fetch his keys, so I dropped them down the hole in the corridor, and had to go and get a torch and find them.

For the successful, there can be an embarrassment of riches. It can become difficult to choose between self-organised routes through the day.

WILL: (. . .) what we been doing, playing cards in this room 'cos we can lock the door.

70   PW: Which room's this now?

WILL: Resources centre, where we're making the frames [a new stage for the deputy head], s'posed to be.

PW: Oh! You're still making the frames!

WILL: We should have had it finished, we just lie there on top of the frame, playing cards, or trying to get to sleep (. . .) Well, it gets a bit boring, I'd rather go and sit in the classroom, you know.

PW: What sort of lessons would you think of going into?

75   WILL: Uh, science, I think, 'cos you can have a laff in there sometimes.

This self-direction and thwarting of formal organisational aims is also an assault on official notions of time. The most arduous task of the deputy head is the construction of the timetables. In large schools, with several options open to the fifth year, everything has to be fitted in with the greatest of care. The first weeks of term are spent in continuous revision, as junior members of staff complain, and particular combinations are shown to be unworkable. Time, like money, is valuable and not to be squandered. Everything has to be ordered into a kind of massive critical path of the school's purpose. Subjects become measured blocks of time in careful relation to each other. Quite as much as the school buildings the institution over time *is* the syllabus. The complex charts on the deputy's wall shows how it works. In theory it is possible to check where every individual is at every moment of the day. But for 'the lads' this never seems to work. If one wishes to contact them, it is much more important to know and understand their own rhythms and patterns of movement. These rhythms reject the obvious purposes of the timetable and their implicit notions of time. The common complaint about 'the lads' from staff and the 'earoles' is that they 'waste valuable time'. Time for 'the lads' is not something you carefully husband and thoughtfully spend on the achievement of desired objectives in the future. For 'the lads' time is something they want to claim for themselves now as an aspect of their immediate identity and self-direction. Time is used for the preservation of a state—being with 'the lads'—not for the achievement of a goal—qualifications.

Of course there is a sense of urgency sometimes, and individuals can see the end of term approaching and the need to get a job. But as far as their culture is concerned time is importantly simply the state of being free from institutional time. Its own time all passes as essentially the same thing, in the same units. It is not planned, and is not counted in loss, or expected exchange.

'HAVING A LAFF'
'Even communists laff' **(Joey)**

The space won from the school and its rules by the informal group is used for the shaping and development of particular cultural skills principally devoted to 'having a laff'. The 'laff' is a multi-faceted implement of extraordinary importance in the counter-school culture. As we saw before, the ability to produce it is one of the defining characteristics of being one of 'the lads'—'We can make them laff, they can't make us laff'. But it is also used in many other contexts: to defeat boredom and fear, to overcome hardship and problems—as a way out of almost anything. In many respects the 'laff' is the privileged instrument of the informal, as the command is of the formal. Certainly 'the lads' understand the special importance of the 'laff':

[In an individual discussion]

80   JOEY: I think fuckin' laffing is the most important thing in fuckin' everything. Nothing ever stops me laffing (. . .) I remember once, there was me, John, and this other kid, right, and these two kids cum up and bashed me for some fuckin' reason or another. John and this other kid were away, off (. . .) I tried to give 'em one, but I kept fuckin' coppin' it . . . so I ran off, and as I ran off, I scooped a handful of fuckin' snow up, and put it right over me face, and I was laffing me bollocks off. They kept saying, 'You can't fuckin' laff'. I should have been scared but I was fuckin' laffing (. . .)

PW: What is it about having a laugh, (. . .) why is it so important?

JOEY: (. . .) I don't know why I want to laff, I dunno why it's so fuckin' important. It just is (. . .) I think it's just a good gift, that's all, because you can get out of any situation. If you can laff, if you can make yourself laff, I mean really convincingly, it can get you out of millions of things (. . .) You'd go fuckin' berserk if you didn't have a laff occasionally.

The school is generally a fertile ground for the 'laff'. The school importantly develops and shapes the particular ambience of 'the lads' distinctive humour. We will look at particular pedagogic styles as material for comic and cultural development in a later chapter. For the moment, however, we can note the ways in which specific themes of authority are explored, played with and used in their humour. Many of their pranks and jokes would not mean the same thing or even be funny anywhere else. When a teacher comes into a classroom he is told, 'It's alright, sir, the deputy's taking us, you can go. He said you could have the period off'. 'The lads' stop second and third years around the school and say, 'Mr Argyle wants to see you, you'm in trouble I think'. Mr Argyle's room is soon choked with worried kids. A new teacher is stopped and told, 'I'm new in the school, the head says could you show me around please'. The new teacher starts to do just that before the turned away laughs give the game away. As a rumour circulates that the head is checking everyone's handwriting to discover who has defaced plaster in the new block, Fuzz boasts, 'The fucker can't check mine, I ain't done none'. In a humorous exploration of the crucial point where authority connects with the informal code through the sacred taboo on informing, there is a stream of telltale stories half goading the teacher into playing his formal role more effectively: 'Please sir, please sir, Joey's talking/pinching some compasses/picking his nose/killing Percival/having a wank/let your car tyres down'.

85　　　In a more general sense, the 'laff' is part of an irreverent marauding misbehaviour. Like an army of occupation of the unseen, informal dimension 'the lads' pour over the countryside in a search for incidents to amuse, subvert and incite. Even strict and well-patrolled formal areas like assembly yield many possibilities in this other mode. During assembly Spanksy empties the side jacket pocket of someone sitting in front of him, and asks ostentatiously 'Whose these belong to', as Joey is clipping jackets to seats, and the others ruin the collective singing:

> JOEY:　The chief occupation when we'm all in the hall is playing with all the little clips what holds the chairs together. You take them off and you clip someone's coat to his chair and just wait until he gets up . . . and you never really listen . . . you have to be really discreet like, so as the Clark [the deputy head] won't see yer, call you out, the other teachers don't matter. (. . .)
>
> JOEY:　Even on the hymn . . . when they mek you sing—
>
> PW:　But do they make you sing? I didn't notice many of you singing—
>
> —　I was just standing there, moving my mouth.
>
> —　We've only got one of them books between all our class. We've got one between twenty-five—
>
> —　When we do sing we make a joke of it.
>
> 90　FUZZ:　Sing the wrong verses . . . So if you're supposed to be singing verse one, you're singing verse three.
>
> [LAUGHTER]

READING RESPONSE

1. Reflecting on discourse, identity, and community

- What are the shared interests and concerns of "the lads" and what do they show you about what the boys value? What do their concerns suggest about the interests and values of the other group at the school, "the ear'oles"?

- In addition, to the physical acts of getting out of the classroom and/or its work and hanging out together (that the lads refer to as dossing, blagging, and wagging), Willis points to two specific speech acts that are important to

(continued)

the group: "grassing" and "having a laff." Spradley and Mann, in their analysis of the components of a speech act on pages 255–257, look at an act's purpose, content, form, etc., but also at its outcome. What makes a successful outcome for "grassing" and "having a laff?" How do the lads know that the purpose of each of these acts has been achieved?

- While Willis focuses his attention on what goes on in the school setting, both the lads' comments and his own discussion point to the ways in which the "rules" and values for group behavior in the school carry into the outside world. What do the lads say that connects to that larger world, and what does Willis say about how these small groups are positioned in a larger social world? Do you find evidence that their school identity contributes to their social class identity?

- Willis wants to know why and how children of working class parents in Great Britain typically rebel against middle class school values and choose to leave school for the same sorts of jobs their parents have held. What do you learn from this small portion of his study that might suggest an answer?

2. Reading from a writer's/researcher's perspective

- Willis moves back and forth between presenting the actual words of students in their conversations with him and his own analysis of the significance of what's said. Can you find an example of that connection between actual words and analysis where the two worked together to increase your understanding in a way that one or the other alone would not have?

- Other than "grassing," Willis doesn't really define the terms the lads use but lets the examples they give help to represent their meaning. As a reader, do you find this to be effective in bringing you into the world of insiders and giving a sense of the meanings they're conveying? Are there places where you might include more translations of terms for outsiders if you were writing this report?

- Look at the ways in which Willis has constructed this part of his report. What are the elements that make up its structure? How has he shaped his ways of reporting to his questions and purposes? Does each contribute to your own ability to navigate through the report as a reader and to understand the meanings Willis is presenting?

- How does the larger opposition Willis suggests between the values of the formal school culture and the values of the informal group help you to make sense of what he has found in this study? Does an opposition between the informal and the formal come into play in your own discourse community study? If so, what contrasting values are represented in each? (It's a typical characteristic of smaller and more personal discourse communities to define themselves in contrast to some larger and more formal setting.)

Michael Moffatt, "Coming of Age in New Jersey"

Michael Moffat is an anthropologist who, as a young faculty member at Rutgers, decided to discover more about the life of undergraduates by taking on the role of a slightly over-age, out-of-state freshman and moving into the dorms, showing up "dressed in jeans, a T-shirt, and sneakers, and carrying a battered old suitcase." He met his roommates (with whom he shared his true identity), attended orientation sessions with his new classmates, and joined the crowd in the dining hall, and generally blended into the ongoing student life. Over several years he undertook such participant-observation several times, living in the dorms at intervals over extended periods of time. He took observation notes on how students dressed and how they behaved, on their roles and relationships, and on what they talked about and how. He recorded typical conversations (with permission), and interviewed individual students about their experiences, interests, and concerns. He asked them to create personal maps of the campus (as in the examples following this reading). And he shared his data with successive classes of students, asking them to help him in interpreting what he'd found. The resulting study, *Coming of Age in New Jersey* (1989), explores the dorm community as he and his "dormmates" experienced it. In the selections that follow, Moffat considers the nature of the community that's established in the dorm and shows what he discovered about the discourse of the dorm and the concerns and values that discourse reflected.

Coming of Age in New Jersey

Michael Moffatt

1   A dormitory is a place to store possessions and sleep at night—but a residence hall is much more. It is an interdependent community where students care about and respect one another and a place where people can share and learn from one another—Shaping a Community: A Guide to Residence Life at Rutgers College.

COMMUNITY?

Rutgers students enjoyed much of the fun of college life, especially in their freshman and sophomore years, on their coed dorm floors among the sixty other young women and men with whom they happened to share the same level of a college residence hall in any given year. They did not need to form personal groups with these particular youths. The students could have lived anonymously in the dorms, side by side like strangers in a New York apartment house. But their own peer culture, and the deans, encouraged them to link up with everyone else on their floor. And on nearly one hundred dorm floors at Rutgers every year, they almost invariably did so.

The deans characterized these student groups in an officialese that was uniquely their own. It emphasized student choice and it obfuscated deanly authority. Dorm floors should be "interdependent communities of caring individuals" who "enhanced their college experiences" together, the deans recommended. The deans "fostered" student "community-building" through the "residence life" infrastructure, through "role-models," "mediation," "programming," "non-credit courses," and "hall government." Power did not really exist in this voluntaristic world of deanly fantasy. Collective standards somehow emerged without agents; the deans were simply the custodians of an impersonal democratic process:

> To protect the rights of all students, community standards have been developed. The Residence Life staff strives to uphold these standards. They provide constraints for those students who demonstrate an unwillingness to monitor their own behavior without unduly inhibiting the freedoms of those students who do. With the support of all community members, behavior problems can be kept to a minimum.

5   The students thought about these same groups in somewhat different ways. They recognized deanly authority and power, to begin with. As my student preceptor on Gate Third in 1977 put it, "There are some mean things I have to do." But if the deans believed that *they* "developed" the undergraduates through residence life—that the shaping of the students' extracurricular values was their expert task—the undergraduates, conversely, saw the dorms at their best as places for real student autonomy. The less a given dorm activity was obviously influenced by the deans, the better the undergraduates in the residence halls tended to enjoy it.

Like the deans, the students also wanted the dorm floors to be amiable places without lots of personal conflict on them. But the term "community," like "residence hall," rarely passed from their lips. Somehow "community" made the dorm floor groups sound much more earnest and intentional than they really were in student experience. A good dorm floor, most students believed, should be a relaxed place full of girls and guys who "got along," who were able to enjoy the informal pleasures of college life in an easy, personal atmosphere of their own making. Rather than being communities, dorm floors, according to student conceptions, should simply be "friendly places."

"Community" was a suspect term for another reason: its established position in the official rhetoric of late-twentieth-century American individualism. For, in addition to being open, friendly individuals, well-socialized American adults in the 1980s are supposed to desire community. Real communities in Western or Third World societies consist of people who have to get along with one another on a daily basis. They usually do not have much choice about the matter. Real communities thus constrain or even define the individual. A village in south India is one example; a department of tenured faculty members in an American university is another. "Community," in its contemporary American ideological sense, on the other hand, is often an individualistic concept masquerading as a sociological one. It usually means something like "people who choose to live together or work together due to common interests." Moreover, it is a word used by leaders, spokespersons, and publicists much more often than it is by ordinary folk. The late-twentieth-century political meaning of "community" tends to be "people who *ought* to choose to live or work together due to some common interest, as defined by me."

These meanings aside, "community," like "diversity" and the other key phrases of modern American individualism, is almost empty of specific content. It no longer even necessarily has to refer to a face-to-face group with a small, well-defined territorial base. Thus, cartoonist Gary Trudeau can make one of his characters belong to "the homeless community." Thus, Rutgers undergraduates can live in the "greater New York community," the "Rutgers community," the "undergraduate community" and their own "dorm communities."

Communities or not, the friendly groups of students who formed on every dorm floor every year at Rutgers did have certain recurrent sociological characteristics in common, however. Their human ingredients: undergraduates from similar provincial suburban hometowns of central and northern New Jersey. Their cultural contexts: contemporary American popular culture in its late-adolescent version, "college life" and American individualism as sources of shared interests and values among many of the residents. Their ecologies: similar spatial layouts for student sociability. Their micropolitical structures: standard bureaucratized systems of local control under the supervision of the deans (residence counselors, preceptors, and so on). And an ideal: a loosely formulated but very pervasive one concerning collective harmony or friendliness.

10   No two dorm floors ever worked out alike, however, and neither floor community nor floor friendliness was easily achieved. Most actual dorm floor groups amounted to varying mixes of collective success and failure. The members of every dorm floor acted out, over the course of a year of common residence and personal acquaintanceship, their own collective dramas, which they themselves reviewed and summed up now and again. This chapter is the story of one such annual student collectivity as I was able to know it, on the fourth floor of Hasbrouck Hall, where I did research a day and night a week in the academic year starting in 1984. Who were the main actors? What was the stage on which they performed? And what collective script did they write, half-deliberately and half-accidentally, in collaboration with one another all year long?

THE DISCOURSE OF THE DORM

In the lounges, the sophomores also soon taught the freshmen to talk the dominant mode of discourse in the undergraduate peer group. It might be labeled "Undergraduate Cynical." In different forms, it is probably a very old speech genre in American college culture. It can be seen as the polar opposite of Deanly Officialese, or of Faculty Lofty. Its attitudinal stance is "wise to the ways of the world." In it, moral, ethical, and intellectual positions are rapidly reduced to the earthiest possible motives of those who articulate them; in it, everyone who participates or is referred to is treated in the same way—leveled—made equal by the joke-and-insult-impregnated discourse of contemporary American friendly busting.

As the students spoke Undergraduate Cynical in the dorms, friends and acquaintances and one's own self were mocked at firsthand, and other people and other kinds of pretension were made fun of at a distance. The students might complain to one another about the rigors of higher education:

I really hate the teaching in my poly sci classes. They give you a lot of reading and lectures and then tell you to figure things out for yourself. There's a thousand questions the professor can ask. "Relate this to that." . . . I wish they'd have textbooks that just told you everything you need to know. Enough of this enlightened bullshit!—Freshman male, Erewhon Third, 1978

Or they might discuss among themselves various ways of beating the system, as did two upperclassmen on Hasbrouck Fourth in the spring of 1985.

15   AL: Hey, John, how was that exam? Was it a cake exam?

JOHN: Yeah. The prof said up to five answers were correct for every question.

AL: Good, good. That means you can definitely argue points with him.

At first I mistook Undergraduate Cynical for a privileged form of truth, for what the undergraduates really thought among themselves when all their defenses were down. Eventually I realized that, as a code of spoken discourse, Undergraduate Cynical could be just as mandatory and just as coercive as other forms of discourse. You could say some very important things in it, things that you really were not allowed to say elsewhere. It was definitely fun to talk it once you learned its rules, and I certainly enjoyed my regular bouts of it throughout my research. But you could not necessarily say everything that you really thought in it, any more than a dean speaking in public could easily stop emphasizing consensus and community among all those who "worked together" at Rutgers and suddenly start ventilating her or his personal animosities toward a particular administrative rival.

Imagine, for instance, that you were an undergraduate who had been reading a sonnet by the poet Shelley for a classroom assignment, and that it had really swept you away. Unless you enjoyed being a figure of fun, you would not have dared to articulate your feelings for the poem with any honesty in the average peer-group talk in the average dorm lounge. You might, on the other hand, have discussed such sentiments more privately with trusted friends. Ordinarily, the dorm lounge and its near-mandatory code did not allow you to say what the "real you" believed, either intellectually or in other ways. The dorm lounge was more often an arena for peer-group posing in which, acting *friendly,* you presented the "as if" you.

20   There were many nuances, subtleties, and variations in the modes of lounge talk, however. In unpredictable ways, peer-group talk could shift from purely cynical into more sincere, earnest expressions of meanings and feelings, even when it was not between close friends. In mid-September, while I was still getting to know the residents of Hasbrouck Fourth and while they were still sorting each other out, I touched off one of these talk sessions. In it, the student voices moved back and forth through a number of stances. Sometimes they were bullshitting. Sometimes they were simply being playful. Sometimes they were talking from the heart, evidently trying to present the "real me." Often they were trying to seize conversational control. And almost always, they were performing.

Louie had been hustling as usual, in an ironic mode he often used, simultaneously making fun of himself for hustling as he hustled: "Here I am, Mike, an unknown college sophomore, lost in the dorms at Rutgers. You're my big chance. You can make me famous. When are you gonna interview me? You *gotta* interview me!" So I decided to give him an interview I had been developing privately to elicit some simple cultural meanings. Except, as an experiment, I decided to give it to Louie around his peers rather than in private. We sat down with a tape recorder in a corner of the high-side lounge at about seven o'clock one evening early in the semester. Fifteen feet away, Carrie was quietly reading a book and apparently minding her own business; two freshmen girls sat near her.

I led off with my standard opening question in this interview. I was a man from Mars, I told Louie. I understood about colleges educationally. Earthlings did not have preprogrammed knowledge like we did on Mars. But I did not understand about college "dorms" on Earth. Why did young Earthlings leave big comfortable homes a few miles away, where all their needs were provided for by their parents, and come to live in these crowded, noisy confines, packed together like sardines?

> LOUIE: Well, part of college is to grow, and not only to grow intellectually but to grow independentlywise. . . . When you come to college, it's not exactly the real world but it's one step towards it, it's kinda like a plateau. You become more independent. You have to do your own laundry. . . . And you feel a togetherness because there's sixty of you on the floor and all stuck in the same boat . . .

Louie went on in this vein for five minutes, answering a few of my Martian's follow-up questions. Then, possibly aware that Carrie and the freshmen women were
25   listening in, he paused and soliloquized: "How I bullshit! You want some real answers now? I don't know why anyone's here. They're all just getting ripped off!"

This gave Carrie her opening. "Do you really believe all that stuff you just said, Louie?" she asked. Louie moved over closer to Carrie, and I followed him, carrying my tape recorder in a visible position. Louie said that he really did not know what he believed, so Carrie offered her answer to the Martian's question:

> College is a place where suburban brats come, to hang out for four years. . . .
> I think it's a step *away* from the real world. . . . I don't think a lot of people here
> *want* an education, whether from college itself or from interacting with other
> people. . . . And when they get out of here, they're just going into Mom and
> Dad's business, or Mom and Dad is going to pay for their apartment for three
> years until they get a real job. . . . Which is really fucked up.

Louie recognized the critique, but he did not consider himself a spoiled college kid. He answered Carrie by telling her that his father was divorced from his mother and was not putting him through Rutgers; he had to work hard at several jobs to stay in school. He talked about how hard he worked and how much money he made. A lot of other Rutgers undergraduates were serious, hardworking youths like him, he concluded. Carrie agreed that she was, but she was not sure about many others; and whatever the state of Louie's finances, she still thought his opinions were screwy: "I don't know, I see a lot of bullshit and a lot of bullshit people here. . . . And a lot of that stuff you were saying, I thought that was pretty *zorbo*. I said to myself, Louie man, if that's the way you think, I don't know. . . . "

Louie challenged her to tell him what in the world was *not* bullshit? She made a case for the caring self, for "how you feel about yourself and how you feel about those closest to you. That's all that really matters." "*I'm* proud of myself," Louie replied, "so that's not bullshit, right? According to your definition?" Carrie agreed that it was good that Louie was proud of himself, but she thought Louie's pride was misplaced, since it was really just rooted in his ability to make money. And that, she said, still struck her as "zorbo bullshit."

At this point, one of the freshman listeners cut in. "What exactly is 'zorbo'?" she asked deferentially. "I've never heard the phrase." "Bullshit," Louie explained in a dismissive tone. "Nothing," Carrie added. Later I discovered that Louie had never heard the word either and was bluffing. Carrie had coined it the year before in an old clique on a different dorm floor. It was her synonym for "nerd." A real loser, she had decided for some private reason, a hopeless case, should have the name "Zorbo McBladeoff." Anything that such a character did was a "zorbo" thing to do. She was not able to sell the word to Hasbrouck Fourth in 1984, however; despite Louie's implication that it was a perfectly ordinary term in the talk of knowledgeable upperclassmen at Rutgers, I never heard it again.

Carrie and Louie went back to their argument. Carrie thought that the most important things in life had nothing to do with money. Finding something you really wanted to do was more important. So was helping and influencing others. "If you can do that for a friend, and one friend starts to think the way you do, that's two of you now, and if two of you can go out. . . . I want to be able to change the way America is. I'm serious! This place is so fucked up."

Louie replied that helping others often did you no good at all: "Like, if you believe in something, and every time you try to do it, nine times out of ten it gets pushed back in your face . . . Where does that get you? That and fifty cents and you can buy a cup of coffee." Right now, Louie decided, what *he* believed in was "*nothin'*." And he got bored easily, he said, so he liked to try lots of different jobs and he liked to date lots of different girls. In deference to Carrie, Louie did not refer to his erotic prey with his normal label for them, "chicks."

While Carrie and Louie were in the middle of this colloquy, Jay walked in and sat down. He had been working on a paper for an English course; "Does anyone here understand Isaac Babel?" he asked the group at large. "No," Carrie answered abruptly, and went back to her argument. Jay did not like being ignored; he listened for a minute and then tried to change the mood of the session: "Oh, *I* get it, we're being *cosmic!*" Carrie told him to shut up, so he began busting on her directly. She had been talking about personal satisfaction through an artistic vocation. "Carrie wants to be a really incredible actress," Jay declared to the group, now augmented by three more passing residents, "perhaps on the order of Bo Derek or Ursula Andress." Carrie did not look much like either of these two ridiculous Nordic icons. That ploy did not succeed either, however, and a few minutes later Jay walked away.

Carrie and Louie went on arguing, and after another ten minutes, an upperclassman strode confidently into the lounge from the elevators. He was a skinny, self-assured young man wearing a worn black sports jacket; I had never seen him before on the floor,

and I never saw him again. Carrie stopped talking and gave him a big hello, without intro-
35 ducing him to anyone else, and they alluded briefly to unexplained old intimacies:

> CARRIE: Heeey! It's you! It's the crazy man! What's up?
>
> STRANGER: So good to see you alive, kid.
>
> CARRIE: I know. I got through it.

Then Carrie went back to the meaning of life with Louie. The stranger listened for a
few minutes, apparently felt he had caught the drift, and then stood up and actually
danced around the lounge intoning the following paean to the self. He had a certain
hypnotic charm, reinforced by the reiterative phrases he used, and a man-of-the-world
authority reinforced by the density of his easy vulgarisms:

> If you want to go out and be a success, you're gonna have to go to school and do
> well, you're gonna go to college, and you're gonna find out you can live on your
> own [Louie: "You're 150 per cent right!"] And you're gonna find out it's you! You
> know that song croons: "It is yooooou, Oh yeah, Oh yeah"? [Back to normal
> voice] I can tell a person what's gone right for me, how I've gotten where I've
> gotten, how I've fucked up.
>   And that's all I can do. It's them, you know, it's got to come from them. . . If
> they want to benefit, that's great. If they want to say, "You're an asshole," that's
> fine too. It hurts me to see them fuck up, but that's the way it's gonna be. And I
> don't get upset and say [tone of fake emotion], "You're fuckin' up, you're fuckin'
> up." I walk up calmly and say [calm tone], "You're fuckin' up." You know, "You
40 could do it that way or you could do it that way." And it's gonna come from you.
> Nobody's gonna hand you anything.
>   That's the way I feel. You know, it's different for everyone, but that's the way I
> feel.

I was not sure what this tone poem had to do with the substance of Carrie and
Louie's debate. But the stranger had captured everybody's attention, including my own.
Everyone sat in rapt silence as he ended his spiel. Then, apparently deliberately, he
punctured the mildly reverent mood he himself had created: "Yeah, and there's another
thing. I don't like to *dog* anyone. I present myself, not *degrade* somebody else. And you
know, it's rush week, everybody. And this is a lot of what my fraternity's all about. . . ."
The audience guffawed. The stranger laughed happily and made a quick exit. He had
achieved what Jay had failed to do. He had popped the "cosmic" bubble. This little talk
session was over, and the participants wandered off to other interests of the evening.

1. Reflecting on discourse, identity and context

   ■ In the opening section of this selection, Moffat raises questions about the nature of the "community" created in the college dormitories, presenting the
   official institutional perspective presented by administrators and the contrasting views of students, and exploring some of the difficulties of applying the
   term "community" to a dorm floor. From reading the later selection from this
   chapter on the discourse of the dormitory, would you define the particular
   dorm floor Moffat is reporting on as a discourse community? What in his example of a typical conversation leads you to see it in the way you do?

   ■ Moffat shows how, within the semi-public world of the dormitory lounge,
   students assume an identity that may be different from the one that they take
   on in private with their closest friends or in public in the classroom. What
   contributes to that identity and how is it represented in what people talk
   about and how?

   ■ Moffat names the most common style of talk in the dorm "Undergraduate
   Cynical." What are the features of this style of talk, what role does it play in
   campus life and relationships, and why do you think Moffat suggests that it
   "could be just as mandatory and just as coercive as other forms of discourse?"

2. Reading from a writer's/researcher's perspective

   ■ Moffat structures this chapter by introducing the official residence guide definition of a residence hall as an independent community, and then, looking
   closely at what goes on in this community. In what ways does his framing
   guide your reading of the details he presents?

   ■ At the end of his introductory section, Moffat says that he will look at the
   actors, their stage, and the script they wrote. How does the metaphor of the
   theater affect the ways in which he presents what he sees? While this excerpt
   skips over his discussion of the actors and the stage, it does focus on the
   script in the form of a characteristic moment of dorm discourse. Do you find
   the term script appropriate for what you read there? How does that notion
   affect the way in which you, as a reader, understand what follows?

   ■ Why do you think, out of all of the conversations Moffat taped, he chose this
   one to represent the discourse of the dorm? He provides a largely narrative
   account of this conversation, with interspersed dialogue, but without the sort
   of definitive analysis of each segment that Willis presents. Does his interpretation of the significance of these conversational moments emerge clearly for
   you as a reader? If you were writing this, might you intersperse a more explicit analysis with the presentation of the conversation, follow that presentation with a more explicit analysis, or leave it as it is, offering some introductory analysis and then leaving more space for the reader to do the
   interpretation?

EDIE SHILLUE, "GOOD CRAIC" AND AUTHOR INTERVIEW

Edie Shillue is both a teacher of writing and a professional writer. She is especially interested in the ways in which ordinary people interact in places that have been devastated by conflict; an earlier book *Earth and Water: Encounters in Vietnam* (1997) focuses on her experiences traveling and teaching in Vietnam. "Good Craic" is from a new book, *Peace Comes Dropping Slow: Conversations in Northern Ireland* (2003). In this chapter, she captures a conversation that took place when she entered a hotel bar in Belfast and she was included in the talk that went on among insiders there.

Although her graduate study was in applied linguistics, and her long-term interest in exploring how language is used in different communities began with her own studies as a student of conversations in familiar discourse communities, Shillue is not trying to study the communities she encounters using the formal tools of linguists or sociologists or anthropologists. Rather, she uses her writer's ear to listen and to try to hear what people say, and to understand how they think, and what they value. In "Good Craic," she recreates the bar conversation in a way that shows how it helped her gain a clearer sense of the meaning of an Irish discourse term, "craic" and some of the shared values of Irish culture. Nor is she writing about this conversation within the genre of the ethnographic report, and "Good Craic" might be closest to the genre of personal travel narrative, even with its specific focus on a country in conflict.

Included with this selection is an interview with the writer, in which she responded to the questions of student researchers who were themselves, at that moment, writing about their studies of discourse communities. You may find it interesting to discover what she herself has to say about writing this piece.

Good Craic

Edie Shillue

1   For most of the evening Frank "chatted me up" moving deftly from Heaney, his classmate, to Orwell, back to me, to Carson, his friend, to The Art of War as practiced by the great Chinese philosophers and/or the Celts. I'd look over to him, then turn to invite Prince Charming of the Blonde Hair to join in the conversation, but he'd refrain. Finally, I gave him my classic woman's look, hands forward, head shaking softly; the well-are-you-going-to-say-something? look.

"When," I have something to say, I'll say it," he replied, lighting a cigarette with his silver butane lighter, then snapping it shut.

"Well," I said, cheerily, "I'll have to remember to be there."

His stone face broke into a laugh. Nice Eyes was all bluster, with his smart remarks and unpleasant quips; many Irish men challenged you that way, tested your nerve, tried to make you win their respect before you even knew them. It is an ancient form of sabre rattling I am familiar with, since I was raised in an Irish-American household. Of course, that doesn't mean I like it. I'd sooner come back with my mother's well practiced reply; it is an icy, if polite, tolerance followed by a swiftly delivered, "knock it off." She was like her own mother with comebacks. In fact, as I thought about it, all the snappiest one liners I had in my arsenal were from the women of my tribe.

5   Still, the battle of wits is one that's perpetual in Ireland and I admire the Irish for it. Later, after Nice Eyes and I had broken the ice a little further he told me that writing about Ireland was quite a formidable task: "I mean, I've seen places here so pretty they'd make a stone cry." I smiled, understanding already what he meant. A drive through the countryside, up the Antrim coast towards Giant's Causeway, where I had been during my summer trip, left me intimidated and nervous. Ireland is small, but feels huge for a writer. Like other oral cultures it's full of stories and myths, (some dangerous, some charming) and everywhere you turn there's someone playing with words like they're clay. Verbal arts are bone deep here, making up the heart of celebration and daily life both. After I first arrived it seemed every conversation I had was a challenge to come up with something enjoyable to hear, be it the sound of the English or the content of the remark. Either or both these things had to sparkle. The charm of it verged on stereotype and I was always suspicious of being put on. But conversation in Ireland tugged at something inside me and as each sentence began I could feel myself planning my reply to work in a kind of musical harmony with it. That didn't mean agreement—in Northern Ireland there's little of that—it meant an exchange of sounds to create a short piece of music. It was, surely, the heart of "good craic".

"Craic" (or "Crack") is an untouchable, unseeable element that fuels interactions in Ireland and keeps them moving forward. If a party was particularly fun—no fights, no excessive drunkenness, good food, good music, lots of interesting stories told with immensely exaggerated detail—the craic was referred to as "grand" as in, "sure last night at Annie's the craic was grand." In fact, often a visitor to Ireland will come across the following dialogue:

"How was your weekend in Donegal/at Rob's/Joe's/Kate's?"

"Ach, Great Craic."

The end. No further explanation necessary. Anything else would be a sort of cruel tease. Something like, "so and so played music for hours, what's-his-name was there, your man told the funniest stories, he just kept going on all night, the beer was flowing, we showed up at the restaurant just as it was closing and stayed 'till three! The next day we sat around the kitchen eatin' Ulster Fry and nursin' hangovers. Aw, you shoulda been there."

10   Still, even that's not enough, so most people leave it at—"Good Craic" or "Great Craic" and that's that. All the rest is understood.

Irish "Crack" is defined by a wide range of scholars, journalists and ordinary people as: "social exchange." I think this is most inadequate and one day some time into my exploration of the place I dramatically spit on that definition during conversation with an academic. It took four and one half columns for the writers of the Oxford English Dictionary to explain it, and still that's not good enough.

"Crack" is also defined as "news or gossip, talk". This is the case only when the word is contained in the greeting: "Hey, what's the craic?" In the United States it finds its equivalent in, "What's up?" and, as in the United States, an answer is not always expected. It is also possible to describe someone as "good craic"—as in, "yeah, he's good craic, so he is."

Craic is the "atmosphere" the Irish Tourist Board tries so hard to describe in its brochures and media ads. A British friend relocated to Cork touched on it as he tried to explain his move: "I love the passion here, I don't know about you but I think . . . I think the Irish have great passion . . ." He stuttered on, trying to describe, in his Midlands restraint, the openness on the island that was such a relief to his system. I understood both the words and the pauses in his description and said, "yeah, it's nice . . . there's no pretentiousness here . . . it's . . . yeah, I like it too." However, for all the prevalance of the word, true "good craic" is rare and once you've experienced it "a good time" pales. In the end I shrug over the mystery of it, because I'm too busy enjoying what it awakens in me.

If 'craic' weren't so mysterious and elusive the Irish wouldn't be searching for it all the time, either. Sometimes I walked out in the early evenings and I would see men standing frozen in doorways, like dogs sniffing the air, and then they'd wander city and village streets like boats unmoored, trying to hook up with this thing no one can see or touch.

15   Craic is unique to Ireland and, for my money, it's all about talk and story. It is impossible to record, without painstaking adaptation to the limits of print and even when recorded successfully it succumbs to the rather frustrating feeling that 'you had to be there.' It is kept in the turn-of-phrase, the chat and the rhythm. It's accompaniment is live music, often, but not always, traditional Irish. It is based on complete and utter sincerity and it results in a sense of coming together spontaneously and creating a shared moment. It is a laugh, mostly, but it's verbal music too.

On top of the challenge to capture craic, Ireland has a landscape that renders both camera and pen useless. I could see the place unfold before me on each of my brief trips. It crinkled like a map being unrolled. The Mourne Mountains rumbled, the sun set late at night over Carlingford Lough and they looked like they floated above the water. Village and city streets unwound, twisting and turning and merging dangerously, water ran in streams through sentences and winked at me from hillsides as I drove the M1 and M2 highways around each of the six counties. Just prior to my winter arrival I had spent an evening with American friends showing slides from my first, summer trip. They "oohed" and "awed" while I sat in the back of the room puzzled.

"Oh, these things aren't even close to capturing what it looked like," I explained. But why? That I couldn't say. The pictures were flat and boring and Ireland—well, sure it's something else, not flat.

Frank gestured to my wine glass with his hand. It was nearing the dangerously low, buy-you-a-drink level.

"Let me buy you a drink," he said earnestly, like he was asking me a favor. "No," I answered, "I'm set."

20   He replied with a dramatic sullen face, as if to tell me I had saddened him, invited tragedy to the table, brought up an unpleasant subject. He put on a pout and looked dramatically *hurt*. I laughed out loud at him. For me it was a point won, bait not taken.

"It's dangerous talking to the Irish," I said to a friend in the US one evening during dinner, "I mean you better be ready to hold up your end of the conversation or they'll just hypnotize you."

She broke into loud laughter and speculated that it must be the accent. I said I wasn't convinced it was the accent so much as a deep, volcanic love for words, something that was literally unquenchable. Liam O' Muirthile, a poet from Cork, stated it this way: "*deep down inside us there is a language inseparable from us.*" His reference was to the Irish language, but for me it was the Irish English I ran into all over the island. Belfast was notorious for its indecipherable sound, the north in general was scorned for its heavy roll and turn, but I liked all of the island's accents. Irish itself sounded like volcanic rock to me. It sounded as if it was covered ember, undampable, never snuffed out. I could hear it and see it all over the nationalist sections of the north—it was flung in my face by people on the Falls Road, recited proudly by young schoolchildren, painted onto murals and store signs all over west Belfast, Derry and other areas. During my first trip to the Student's Union at Queen's University, I was embroiled in a scandal involving bilingual signs at student organization offices, with people complaining that signs with Irish and English posted around campus was an empty political gesture meant to insult the majority population. Those in favor of the bilingual signs found the opposite to be true. I'm not particularly interested in Irish—it doesn't appeal to me—but I've always been interested in language debates and the politics of language. In the United States I endured, with little patience, comments and complaints about Spanish or Chinese or Vietnamese being spoken in public. In Belfast, the university debate ended with an unannounced, sudden removal of the Irish language signs during summer break. Language in Ireland was a battlefield as surely as it was a weapon. I had already learned that mere introduction could get you into trouble. Even "Craic" itself was a debatable term, both in meaning and origin. For years it had been spelled as an English word—Crack—but was picked up at some point and turned into the Gaelic looking "Craic". Purists sneered their disdain, but I'm from the United States and we've been bastardizing languages for a couple hundred years now. I found "Craic" preferable.

* * *

"Irish is filled with murmuring", O'Muirthile said. The same could be said of Irish English, with its many varieties. It is impossible for the traveler not to lean as she first encounters the Irish, in-country or out. As I traveled I constantly found myself pulling forward and back with the people I met; my long, thin neck craning out from skinny shoulders, "Sorry? what did you say?" I asked politely. But clarity always seemed to elude me in Ireland. People and things changed in front of me, shifting and shaping like quicksilver; rude monsters turned into sentimental giants, the seemingly untrustworthy made me laugh. Sure I was in trouble trying to keep up with the verbal competition of the place.

O' Muirthile found inspiration for work everywhere in Ireland, saying the earth gave him all that he needed to write. Its hard not to be moved by Ireland's landscape, but the slipperiness of creative inspiration may have been fooling him. One of his poems began at the edge of the words of a well-digger: "I dig down deep for the place where the two streams meet. I dig for the dry September." He was digging into the ground for poems. In Belfast, Frank was out in city streets reaching for the words of Heaney and Carson, but most of us who write of and about Ireland find the muse shifting and slipping around the mouths of her citizens.

25   As the winter evening waned, I sat perched comfortably on my stool. I was thinking about poets, interesting conversation and "good craic". I was happy to have held

my own in the challenge of conversations and made a mental note of thanking my female ancestors for my inheritance. The bar was getting crowded with Eurokids at this
point and Frank wanted to say goodnight. He threw back the dregs of his Guinness
and said I was welcome in Ireland.

"You've got a very charmin' accent, so you do, very charmin' Edie from Boston."

And there it was . . . the compliment to make me blush, the laugh that disarmed
me, the flattery stolen from my own scheming mind. Game, Set, Match.

An Interview with the Writer
of "Good Craic," Edie Shillue

By Students Doing Discourse Community Studies

1   QUESTION: Why did you choose Northern Ireland?'

RESPONSE: "I chose it for a couple of reasons. One, I am interested in societies
in conflict and this is now referred to as a post-war society, so I am interested in
what happens when war is over so that's one of the things that brought me
there. The other thing, of course, I am Irish American, so I am very interested in it
from that perspective. I began to look at the society and to look at books about
the place and I was very distressed to see that there was so much about the war
but very little about the culture and how people talk to each other and it was
that sense of dissatisfaction that drove me to take a look. I determined that I was
going to write putting language, people, daily culture, daily life in the foreground
and moving the troubles to the background and it happens to be that they are at
that historic moment now.

QUESTION: "Was there a point when you were having the conversations with
people or listening to what they were saying and you would go back and begin
to feel like you were an insider in some of these conversations or were you always an outsider?"

RESPONSE: "I always feel that I am an outsider but I think that a lot of that has to
do with the fact that I got my training in Asia so that I was by virtue of skin color,
language, all of these things, I was the perpetual outsider. It didn't matter that I
would begin to learn the local language and stuff. In Ireland it was different because of my Irish American status and people would begin to say 'you understand
us, you understand this place' so I think the thing that might have got me in were
things like my accent because people wanted to know where I was from. But
then I would stay for a while and it wasn't necessarily just that I could pick up the
local slang, like using "we" or "sure" at the beginning of sentences or something,
but it was that I could understand what they were saying to me without having
them elaborate or explain and sort of just how I responded to any given situation. It was important to them to know that I was connected to Ireland but still I
learned never to assume insider status at any point ever."

5   QUESTION: "When you were there, did you tape all these conversations?"

RESPONSE: "No I didn't tape them at all. I have actually tried to tape conversations in the past and at one point I was having really good craic with one of the guys and I thought if only I could get my tape recorder right now and I just knew, we were talking about music and funny stories, they were full of funny stories about soldiers and the troubles and things, and I knew that if I ran to get my tape recorder out of my bag they would shut down immediately and I just kept saying to myself 'I have to get this down.' One of the great frustrations of the book overall is that you can't really capture everything. In spite of the fact that I record almost, like if I have a conversation with somebody I'll go home at the end of it and record as much of it as I can but once you start putting something on the page you move from the oral to print and it's a very frustrating experience trying to capture it on the page."

QUESTION: "Can you say more about how you worked on this as a writer?"

RESPONSE: "I know in your case you are studying discourse communities so it's a sort of an intellectual undertaking of studying how people communicate but for me it was how can I present this creatively and how can I present it intellectually so people understand that it was about slagging and it was about making me feel welcome in two different ways. I had to explain slag at some point, I thought it was a great conversation and if you are an insider you know what slag is but if you are an outsider, I knew that I would have to explain what slagging is so its just a matter of working at it as your own writing is the text. I do a lot of reading out loud and that really helps me to feel comfortable with what I've got on the page and to know that it doesn't just have to look good but for me it has to sound good. And you gather more information, I may have not understood the conversation when I first experienced it but over days, weeks, and other conversations with people about Ireland, I understood what had happened."

QUESTION: "When you read this to us, I felt like I had been there, you took us there very well. How do you do that? Is it just rewriting and practice?"

10   RESPONSE: "A lot of it is just rewriting and a lot of it is just relaxing. One of the things that writers find, whether it's for an academic paper or it's creative, the biggest obstacle is getting rid of this self-censorship, that says you have to present yourself as something that's more valuable than the self that you are, you have to use a voice that isn't your own. If somebody said, 'What's your voice like? What is the tone of your writing like?' I couldn't answer that question. I only know that the more I revise and the more I talk about my subject matter with people, or the more I read about my subject matter and take notes, the more I can identify when I am putting on airs or presenting a fake voice or trying to be somebody that I am not, which doesn't mean that you can't change your writing but it's really through something that others can't teach you which is learning to accept that what you do is valuable and can be further developed—and detail, details, details."

<table>
<tr><td>

**READING
RESPONSE**

</td><td>

1. <u>Reflecting on discourse, identity, and community</u>

   ■ In her travels, Shillue has depended on informal conversations with people she encounters (rather than formal interviews) to understand more about their country and its people. How does she negotiate this conversation? What understandings about conversations in Northern Ireland has she needed in order to make this one work?

   ■ What understandings do you get of some of the underlying concerns and values that are shared within this community and what leads you to those understandings?

   ■ How do the exchanges Shillue recounts in this bar compare with the ones studied by Spradley and Mann? How would you compare the concerns, interests, and values of participants in the two settings?

   ■ The genre of the personal essay allows room for the writer's own reflections on what she is learning and how she is thinking in the moments she describes. What does Shillue's self-reflection add to this account of a conversation at a bar that makes it different from a less personal research report? (Imagine Brenda Mann writing "How to Ask for a Drink" from her own perspective as a college student/waitress and including what she was thinking as the interactions that report describes were going on.)

2. <u>Reading from a writer's/researcher's perspective</u>

   ■ What has Shillue included in her account of her evening of good conversation—of "good craic" in the bar in Northern Ireland? What doesn't she include that might appear in more traditional ethnographic reports? How has she chosen to structure this account and what does she do to recreate her experience? Why do you think she makes these choices, and how do they work for you as a reader?

   ■ If you've read other people's accounts of their travels, in the genre of personal travel writing, or their accounts of their participation in particular settings in other personal essays, how does this piece compare to those other examples? If you're writing about a discourse community in the genre of the personal essay, are there any aspects of what Shillue has done here that might influence how you shape your own essay?

   ■ From reading the interview with the writer, what do you discover about her interests and purposes as a writer and how they've influenced both what she's written about and how she has written about it? Is there anything she says that particularly interests you as a researcher or writer? Are there other questions that you'd have liked to ask if you'd been a participant in this interview?

</td></tr>
</table>

Pebely Vargas, "DSP Continues"

Pebely chose to study the community of a group of new college friends who had gotten to know each other in a summer program, Directions for Student Potential (DSP), that provides extra academic support, before the freshman year, for students entering college. For Pebely, a strong student, it was life circumstances, returning to school as the single mother of a very young child, that brought her to this support program. Pebely found that the program allowed her to enter her freshman year with an already-established community of college friends. Pebely describes herself as bicultural, with a white mother who speaks only English and a Puerto Rican father who is bilingual. Raised speaking only English, she felt herself to be an outsider to her father's Spanish-speaking family; she regrets that she grew up speaking only one language, and she appreciates the fact that her father is now teaching her young son Spanish. Her new college friends represent diverse backgrounds and include students whose families immigrated from Haiti, Jamaica, and quite recently, Albania. Writing about her choice to study her friends from DSP, she says, "We are all very supportive of each other. We are all beginning to face the difficulties of college together, so we know how overwhelming it can be." As you read her study, and her transcript, you might think about the sorts of interactions that have gone on among your closest college friends, and the sorts of support they have provided for you in your own transition to college.

DSP Continues

Pebely Vargas

1   College is a place where friendships are made. These relationships are easily formed in Freshmen year because these students are all entering a new situation. Over the summer in the Direction for Student Potential program (which is a program to give students extra support and skills needed to perform well in college) a new discourse community was formed. These members are Laysian, Benny, Dorian, Abby and myself. In the past six months, we have become really good friends. We are comfortable enough with each other to talk about what's bothering us and just about anything that is on our mind. We came together because we all were unsure of what to expect in college. We became close because we relied on each other for a small period of time and became attached.

This specific conversation that I am analyzing took place in the McCormick Café. Laysian, Benny and I were eating lunch. This is an activity that takes place every Monday, Wednesday and Friday. It is one of the few places that we can actually sit down and have a reasonable amount of time to spend time together and relieve some stress. The conversations between our groups of friends change topics every couple of minutes in an attempt to keep the conversation fresh and continuous.

THEMES

In this conversation, along with many others, our stories "may highlight the ridiculous, but [they] often also provides illustration of hard lessons of life the story-teller and the audience share" (Heath, 225). We are all city kids who attended public school and we are not from the most privileged families, so life hasn't always been easy on us. However, we have the ability to joke and tease about this. We begin our conversation by talking about Benny's eating habits and then it turns into a conversation about not wasting food. Our next topic is whether or not it is better to have a phone with a paperclip on it or not to have a phone at all. We then discuss what is "ghetto", like watering down the ketchup and using the ketchup packets that come from places like Burger King. All of these exchanges are examples of how our lives haven't been easy, but we don't let them bring us down. We use them for the opposite of what they actually are. These exchanges are used to bring our moods up. We joke about them in a way so that it seems amusing to live life the way we have.

Another major theme in our discourse community is supporting each other. There are many times when we are stressed out because of school, home and other life issues. When we get together we just spill what's on our minds and everybody will try to make you feel better about the situation. For example, Dorian was a little behind with his homework. We all told him that if he needed any help that he can call us and we would try to help him as best as we could. We all have the understanding that we will be there for each other as much as possible.

SPEECH ACTS

5   In my discourse community there are many speech acts. Some of the most commonly used speech acts include greeting, talking, joking, teasing, grade exchanges, helping, supporting, gossiping and naming things "ghetto". These speech acts contribute to every conversation. There are also many words that can be found in every conversation such as yo (a way to call attention), dude (man, guy), phat (cool, good), dogg (friend) and chill (to relax). These are all words that we use in our speech acts that are brought from the wider community that we all belong to, which is the City of Boston.

TEASING

One of the most commonly used and amusing speech acts is teasing. Benny is almost always on the receiving end. When we first started DSP classes in the summer, he told us about a situation he was once in where he had to run from a girl. Ever since he told us, it became a ritual for us to tease him about it because it is not common for a guy to run from a girl in our neighborhoods. In the recorded conversation, Laysian and I tease Benny. Laysian initiates the teasing by saying, "you would run like them girls." She states it simply because she knows that I will say something in return to back her up. It is no different when Dorian and Abby are present. Someone makes a remark about Benny and someone else joins in.

There are also other ways we tease Benny. The main reason that we are always trying to put Benny on the spot is because he takes it in the way it was intended; for humorous purposes. He knows that we are only joking around with him and he'll defend himself in a joking way. Anyone other than Benny would get offended very quickly and an argument would result.

DEFINING "GHETTO"

Another characteristic of my discourse community is naming things ghetto. Anything that is foreign, funny or just plain weird to us is named ghetto. Ghetto is something that not everyone would do, such as "watering down ketchup." When something one of us have done or said is named ghetto, it is to give us something to joke about. It is acknowledging that we do crazy things. In the dialogue, our discussion about what is ghetto is very involving. This is because it is fun to distinguish what is ghetto between each other. It allows us to feel that we do belong to the group because we all have something that is considered ghetto in our lives.

Benny brings to our attention that a "dude" has a paperclip as the antenna on his cellular phone. We all agree that this is ghetto. Laysian tries to put Benny on the spot by saying, "Do you have a phone Benny." Benny answers, "I rather not have a phone than have a paperclip as an antenna on it." That would be announcing to everybody who sees him with the phone that he is ghetto. Being ghetto is something that you try to hide because it is admitting that you are different than others. The only reason that being ghetto is accepted in our group is because it is used for humorous purposes, and we don't look down on each other. We all have aspects in our lives that might be considered "ghetto."

CONNECTIONS

10   I think my discourse community resembles the Trackton community in "Oral Traditions" by Shirley Brice Heath. The members of the Trackton community know what it's like to live a hard life. The members of this community tell stories about incidents that have happened to them and they play around with these stories and interactions, in the same manner that we would in my discourse community. They make their stories interesting so that people will want to take the time to listen to them. We also make, or try to make, our stories more amusing because we want to entertain everyone. A good storyteller in both Trackton and my discourse community is the person who makes their stories the most entertaining. We both have to be "aggressive in inserting [our] stories into an on-going stream of discourse" (Heath, 228).

CONCLUSIONS

What I learned through studying my discourse community was that we all bring a piece of our other discourse communities with us to college. This is one reason why we actually came together, because we were already from one of the same discourse communities (the city of Boston) and entering a new one (UMass Boston). We weren't sure of what to expect in this new place so we clung on to each other for support. This new community reminded us of how things were before college, giving us a sense of security.

We are able to bring both these worlds together. We are able to bring our neighborhoods into the group by using words that are characteristic of our neighborhoods. We also tell stories relating to issues that have to do with where we are from. An example of this would be when Benny told us about how he ran from a girl. He brought a story from outside of college and we tease him about it in a way that we would tease members of our larger community for doing this. In our communities teasing is a way of having fun. We use our little community to represent who we truly are.

Conversation Transcription of My Discourse Community

Pebely Vargas

1   Setting: McCormack Café
Participants: Laysian, Benny, and Pebely
When: October 23, 2000 11:00 a.m.

PEBELY: Damn Benny (*Laysian and me laughing*).

BENNY: Yo, yo.

PEBELY: You see that? It was only like three minutes and you ate that whole thing.

5   BENNY: Yo . . . I'm a pig man . . . Alright I'm not a pig, I just know how to eat.

PEBELY: No, no, no wasting food.

BENNY: I don't, I don't. All those hungry kids out there.

LAYSIAN: You will get along with my mother cause she eat everything like you were eating.

PEBELY: Fa real.

10   LAYSIAN: She always do that like I don't.

BENNY: She does what?

PEBELY: My aunt used to make us eat every grain of rice. Every grain. Like I'm talking about you know like rice and beans in a plate, how sometimes you can't get that last grain you have to use your finger and like (*shows gestures*). Its nasty.

BENNY: My parents were like that. They were like if you don't eat all of it, I'm gonna shove it all in your nose. I was like thanks ma.

PEBELY: Right. It makes you not want to eat it.

15   LAYSIAN: You should just hide and just throw it outside.

PEBELY: My aunt sits right there and watches. If you put like that much juice (*gestures*) you got to drink all of it. I remember one time I had to go to the bathroom and she would not let me get up even to go to the bathroom until I finished that cup. I was like six years old and it was a big cup of juice.

LAYSIAN: You poured it right?

PEBELY: Yeah, cause you know when you are little, you pour whatever you want . . . you think you're grown.

BENNY: Yeah, I had my uh eight year old little cousin, she just got here from Haiti, and she's the same way. Like she'll put like a bowl of cereal, like a big bowl of cereal, a big bowl that I'll eat.

20   LAYSIAN: Was you born here?

BENNY: Nah, she was born in Haiti. And then.

LAYSIAN: Nah, I'm talking about you.

BENNY: Yeah, I was born here. I come in the middle of the day and what do I see a bowl of cereal all soggyed up and my mom was like do you want it? I was like nah.

PEBELY: I eat but I'm not that greedy . . . You ever see that show Popular on the WB?

25   BENNY: Nah

PEBELY: No, cause that dude over there looks like the fat dude.

BENNY: Where, oh.

PEBELY: I don't know why it is but he reminds me of him.

LAYSIAN: Look at Benny staring at him. I hate when I tell someone something and . . .

30   PEBELY: Yeah

BENNY: He got a paper clip for the antenna on his phone.

PEBELY: He got a what? (*all laughing*) . . . a paperclip.

BENNY: It is and then . . . . no isn't it? It is. Ghetto. It isn't my fault

LAYSIAN: Do you have a phone Benny?

35   BENNY: What happened?

LAYSIAN: Do you have a phone?

BENNY: I don't.

LAYSIAN: No you don't so don't (*laughing*) .

BENNY: Yo, I rather not have a phone than have a paperclip as an antenna on it.

40   LAYSIAN: I rather have a phone and a paperclip on it.

BENNY: Not me man. I only use paperclips for television.

PEBELY: And that makes it better?

BENNY: That does. No one else can see it.

PEBELY: Ok. Lets say that you're ghetto. Lets say that you're ghetto if there's that much ketchup in the bottle (*gestures*) would you add water?

45   BENNY: Nah dog.

PEBELY: Would you?

LAYSIAN: Yep.

PEBELY: We do it all the time. You just be shaking it up.

LAYSIAN: Shake it up. But I don't put a lot cause then its just like watery. I only use enough.

50   PEBELY: Yeah.

LAYSIAN: I leaned that in Jamaica cause stuff are mad expensive there.

PEBELY: They say that's when you're ghetto.

LAYSIAN: We be like in Burger King and we get the ketchup. We don't throw it away. We just throw it in the bottle. It tastes funny.

BENNY: I need to chill. He's kinda a big guy.

55   PEBELY: Right

BENNY: Come over here like you'll be talking about me.

LAYSIAN: You would run like them girls. (*Laysian and me laughing*)

PEBELY: Right

BENNY: You'll got jokes right.

60   LAYSIAN: No, no that's funny seeing Benny run.

PEBELY: He won't run from him, but if a girl came up behind him.

BENNY: Yo it was just an incident.

PEBELY: Really? You were scared.

BENNY: She didn't scare me man, I just had to get home.

READING RESPONSE

1. Reflecting on discourse, identity, and community

   ■ In the transcript of the cafeteria conversation, we see this group of friends exchanging little stories of their families. What do we learn from the transcript of the identities that these friends are bringing to this college setting from their prior experiences?

   ■ Pebely focuses on the speech acts that are common in her community. What is the purpose and the desired outcome of these speech acts, and do they appear to achieve that outcome?

   ■ In this community, the ways in which things are named is very important, and much of the conversation is spent defining the word "ghetto." Why is this particular term significant in the context of this college cafeteria conversation? In relationship to the friends' college student identities?

2. Reading from a writer's/researcher's perspective

   ■ Pebely frames her study with her understanding that college is a place where new friendships are made. How does this frame fit with the information that follows? Do the points that follow show something about how new friendships are formed among college newcomers?

   ■ Pebely structures her paper as a report, using headings to guide the reader through her presentation of key ideas and supporting data from her observations and transcribed conversation. How effectively do her headings guide you as a reader? Would you suggest any alternatives?

   ■ Pebely makes a connection between what she has observed and what Heath found about storytelling in Trackton? To what extent does that connection help to reinforce the central understandings she has been presenting?

   ■ Look again at Pebely's conclusion. What does she finally see as significant about this particular, shared friendship? Have the points she's made led you, as a reader, to anticipate this conclusion?

Jake M. Wark, "Means and Motives"

Jake Wark decided to study the discourse community of long-term friends who had worked together at the same army-navy store and who typically hung out together in an apartment that some of them rent. Jake was returning to school as a somewhat older freshman after a number of years of working at service jobs. When asked about his favorite piece of his own writing, Jake recalled the small magazine CRANK that he wrote and published from his apartment in the mid 1990's: "Twenty pages of speed-damaged and strip-club-inspired verbosity filtered through half a decade of convenience-store clerking and attendant class resentment." But he also acknowledged feeling "a little unsure of myself as a writer, 10+ years out of academia," and he noticed a tendency to write in an overly formal way at first, though he began to loosen up and write in a more natural voice as he became more comfortable in the classroom. In this report, Jake keeps his distance, reporting effectively as a researcher/observer on a group where he's really an insider, and using such terms from the discourse of research as "the subjects."

Means and Motives

Jake M. Wark

INTRODUCTION

1   Cambridge, Massachusetts, is widely regarded as a city that values diversity, intellectual achievement, and individuality. Hosting a variety of ethnic groups and a number of universities, Cambridge is a center of activity for artists, musicians, wordsmiths, and performers from across the country and around the world. Due south of the city's most prominent landmark, Harvard University, and just east of the river that separates Cambridge from Boston, is a quiet residential neighborhood known as Cambridgeport.

Under examination is a Cambridgeport apartment that houses three individuals from distinctly different backgrounds: Sonny, a guitar player and pharmacist from Long Island, NY; Dave, an artist/musician and medical student from Lima, Ohio; and Tezeta, a writer and newsletter editor born in Addis Ababa, Ethiopia. Visitors and hangers-on include Cathy, a massage therapist and bakery worker from Hawaii; and the author, a criminal justice student and shop clerk, native to the area, acting with consent as a participant observer. Almost all of the subjects draw a distinction between their primary interests and the work that they do to subsidize it: all of them have done their time in the low-wage workplace and understand the broad gulf that often separates dreams and demands.

The subjects met between 1994 and 1998 while working at a now-defunct clothing and accessory store in central Cambridge. Over the course of those years, they found that they shared a great deal in terms of musical taste, preference in television and film, and personal philosophy. This is due in part to their age; in their late twenties and early thirties, they are part of the age group known as Generation X, and were exposed in youth to the same trends in popular culture. More relevant, however, is that they are all uncomfortable in mainstream society. None of them appear overtly deviant from the norm, but each has played the role of outsider for a long or significant enough time that they have internalized it.

STORIES

5   In *Ways with Words* (1983), Shirley Brice Heath compares and contrasts the telling of stories by the white, self-identified Christian adults and the black schoolchildren in towns she calls Roadville and Trackton. Both milieus are rural, working-class, and situated in the American South. In the former, where community values are interpretations of Biblical scripture, a woman named Sue tells a self-deprecatory kitchen parable to acknowledge her indulgence of gossip and the trouble to which it led (pp. 212–214). In the latter, where Heath found that children are more apt to tell stories and sing songs that aggrandize themselves and "mock . . . the behavior of their aggressors" (p. 219), a young boy named Terry weaves a fantastical story of evading an authority figure and luring him into a trap sprung by a "big old roach" and Terry's friend, "old Spider Man" (p. 224).

In Cambridgeport, where rock music and its loser-makes-good ethos are among the community's underpinnings, Sonny recounts the tale of a drunken teenager named Dustin who gets over on a prospective salesman by feigning expertise:

> He was playing with 4-Play, his band, at some kid's Bar Mitzvah . . . and he was outside like drunk afterwards, standing in the driveway of some guy's house and looking at this like, old Cadillac or something from the seventies . . . and the guy comes out and he's like "You like the car? You want to buy it?" . . . and the guy starts like talking him up on buying the car and he popped the hood for him and Dustin was just like "Well, you're going to have to replace the sytometer and the timing belt is off," you know, and he doesn't know anything, but he . . . made up all sorts of problems that the car had, and the guy finally was like "Just take the car." He drove it for like eight months before it died. It was the "Yom Kippur Clipper." (Wark, 2001, p. 3)

In each community, the story depends on the shared knowledge of its listeners. The scriptural passages concerning "sins of the tongue" (Heath, 1983, p. 213), for instance, are common knowledge in Roadville. Among Trackton's children, reference points include television personalities like Spider Man and the parts of town run-down enough to host cockroaches. In Cambridgeport, a moniker like "4-Play" is recognizable as both a sexual double-entendre and as a reference to the classic four-part rock-band line-up of singer, guitarist, bass player, and drummer. Sonny also knows that his listeners are familiar with Bar Mitzvahs and Yom Kippur, and knows that they will forgive his mispronunciation of the latter for the sake of a humorous rhyme.

Each story topic is emblematic of a belief system: that gossip will detract from one's "own business" (Heath, 1983, p. 212), that outwitting adults requires supernatural powers and even then may fail, or that one may bluff one's way into anything, even a free car, if one is skillful and lucky enough. Sue, Terry, and Sonny are implicitly affirming a shared social or philosophical value in the telling of their stories.

QUOTING

10   In their essay "How to ask for a Drink" (1975), James Spradley and Brenda Mann define a "speech act" as the use of "a single word, a sentence, a paragraph, or even an entire book" to accomplish a specific goal, whether "to insult, to gather information, to persuade others, to greet others, to curse," or any of innumerable other ends (p. 252). They list eight components that comprise this unit of communication, and several stand out as particularly relevant here.

A common speech act in Cambridgeport is that of quoting: the application of a song lyric, film dialog, television catchphrase, notorious headline, or other previously linked words to the situation or conversation at hand. It occurs frequently and in many contexts, but this example is part of a casual exchange between two residents and a visitor at the apartment:

DAVE: . . . I'm going to a party tonight.

JAKE: What kind of party?

SONNY: Is it a drug party in 222?

15   DAVE & JAKE [*turn to Sonny in confusion*].   *What?* What is *that?*

SONNY: It's a GBH song. "Drug Party in Room 222."

(Wark, recorded 27 October 2001)

The *Purpose* of quoting is to demonstrate the depth of one's cultural literacy while carrying on the conversation. In the absence of a serious comment or observation, someone else's words may be the next best thing: in this case, Sonny has chosen a musical reference from a band with which his listeners are only marginally familiar.

Message Content refers to the meta-level meaning of the speech act. Sonny has not just asked a question here: by working the title of an obscure 1979 punk single into a conversation about a party, he has demonstrated just how encyclopedic his musical knowledge is. This acknowledges the interests of his audience while issuing a subtle challenge. *Message Form* is the vehicle in which the speech act is carried out: Sonny could have answered for Dave, or he could have simply sung the line without placing it into context. In this case, he has asked a gag question—Dave is in medical school, and isn't going to any drug parties anywhere.

Tone is an interpretational aid offered by the speaker. The quote, in this case, can be issued with accompanying gestures, facial expression, accent, or other interpretational aid, or it may be delivered deadpan, as Sonny's was here. In so doing, he withheld from his listeners a vital clue in deciphering the reference, perhaps to savor the satisfaction of explaining its origin.

20   Any speaker desires a given *Outcome* to their speech act. If the goal of quoting is to display cultural literacy, Sonny has won this round. In other circumstances, though, one quote may inspire another, more relevant or more esoteric, quotation, and its speaker would earn the bragging rights. Ideally, a listener would be able to complete

the lyric or cite an even more obscure phrase. A particularly dramatic choice might even be a point of reference later: "That was a good line you had the other night."

SERIOUS QUESTIONS AND SNAPPY ANSWERS

Spradley and Mann (1975) have noted that certain speech acts, when repeated and formalized, become rituals that express the values of the community: "routine performances reinforce . . . virtues and symbolize full membership" in the group (p. 257). Speech acts in Cambridgeport are not always so artful or measured as Sonny's story. Sometimes they are spontaneous and scatological:

SONNY: "What smells so good?"

JAKE: "Donuts."

DAVE: "My ass."

25   TEZETA: "What are struts?"

DAVE: "That's how you walk."

JAKE: "When Dave goes from point A to point B . . ."

DAVE: "I struts."

(Wark, 2001. pp. 1, 3)

Sonny was referring to Tezeta's vanilla-scented lotion and Tezeta was asking about his car, but both of them got a pair of wisecracks before anyone answered their questions. Similar gags and one-liners pepper all of the Cambridgeport conversations: an innocuous question or observation will often be followed by an ironic or sarcastic rejoinder, almost exclusively by one or more of the males in the group. These may be self-deprecatory or simply cheap and obvious, but not insulting or derogatory.

30   While they carry little in the way of virtue, these performances do affirm the speaker's membership in the group in that the respondents are speaking not only to the initial questioner, but also to the group at large. The reflect an emphasis on wit and speaking ability that is understood among the participants: while these examples might not be called poetic or even lyrical, they display a fondness for double meanings and the ability to play with words.

DEFYING STEREOTYPES

The sociologist Charles Horton Cooley (1956/1902) coined the phrase "looking glass self" to describe "the reflection of our self that we think we see in the behaviors of others toward us" (Kornblum, 1998, p. 100). The vulgar wisecrack in Cambridgeport is an ironic response to the participants' standing in the socio-professional circles they inhabit: as real or imagined underachievers, they may not receive the same degree of respect or deference that their bosses, high-level co-workers, successful acquaintances, or privileged fellow students mandate. By momentarily embracing the role of foul-mouthed lowbrow, they acknowledge and mock what they imagine is an outsider's perception of them as unskilled, untalented, or average.

In relation to many of his fellow medical students, Dave's convenience store employment history, delayed entry into graduate school, and informal attire mark him as an outsider. At home, however, he is aware of his position as the group's frontrunner in terms of accomplishment, with a clear view of his career path and financial aid that relieves him of the need to work. Dave compensates for this awkward singularity by directing the conversation away from serious discussion of academics and long-term goals. Tezeta, on the other hand, is drawn to academia but bound by financial restraints, and takes the opposite tack of waxing eloquent at the slightest provocation. As an African-American woman, she is well aware of the stereotypes and limitations assigned to her by institutional racism and sexism, and responds by alternating between ethnic vernacular and articulate exposition.

"HAVIN' A LAFF"

Inciting laughter is a recurring motive for speech in Cambridgeport and most other communities. The British "lads" of Paul Willis' *Learning to Labor* (1981) see "havin' a laff" as "the most important thing in . . . everything" (p. 299). Heath's Roadville residents find "a li'l something to laugh about" (p. 210) in good stories; the children she describes in Trackton inspire "great audience mirth and enthusiastic response" (p. 219) when they make fun of teachers and other children. Sonny's intent is no doubt the same when he inserts the "Yom Kippur Clipper" rhyme at the end of his story after a dramatic pause, and all of the snappy answers are offered in hopes of a similar outcome. Without the common element of humor or wit, none of the stories named here would be as interesting or entertaining: they would simply be platitudes of varying moral standards.

CULTURAL LITERACY

Cambridgeport speakers also demonstrate cultural literacy with their speech. Names from television police dramas, heavy metal music groups, and local politics are dropped into conversation with frequency. Rarely are they the subject of discussion; more often they are used as analogies, as in this case, where a defective car is compared to a rock band renowned for their elaborate pyrotechnic stage shows:

35   SONNY: "[My car] is blowing like blue smoke . . . I feel really trashy blowing blue smoke."

JAKE: "You feel like you're at a Kiss concert." (Wark, 2001, p. 3)

Naming specific icons, whether Kiss or Spider Man, reinforces the bond between the speaker, who recognizes them as common to all present, and the listeners, who can personalize their significance individually. The choice of icon, of course, must be both appropriate to the context and suitable to the speaker's motive: in "chatting [her] up" (p. 332), Edie Shillue's pub denizen Frank shows off a knowledge of literary figures that includes the Poet-Laureate of Ireland and a prominent English author/essayist that the ethnographer is bound to recognize and appreciate. Heath's subject, Terry, may have less sophisticated cultural references, but he, too, submits names that his audience recognizes as powerful and familiar. Fringe culture in general and its music in particular are among the factors unifying the Cambridgeport subjects, and serve as pools of shared knowledge from which they often draw references.

CONCLUSION

Whether because of race, economic background, delayed educational attainment, or personal experience, what makes the Cambridgeport subjects different from the larger culture is what makes them similar to each other. This much is understood among the group members: they respect each other regardless of, and in contradiction to, the perceived cultural emphasis on financial success and academic degrees. As inhabitants of a counterculture, their methods of discourse may be unique in their specifics, but they also have broader features that have been studied in numerous and diverse communities and community subsets. Sonny, Tezeta, Dave, and the others may not be aware of it, but the means and motives of their speech reflect patterns that connect them as social beings to the very culture from which they distance themselves.

REFERENCES

Heath, S. B. (1983). Ways with Words. Cambridge: Cambridge University Press.

Kornblum, W. (1998). Sociology: The Central Questions. Fort Worth: Harcourt Brace College Publishers.

Shillue, E. (1999). Good Craic. In E. Kutz (Ed.). English 101 Course Packet. Boston: University of Massachusetts Boston, Wheatley Copy Center.

Spradley, J. & Mann, B. (1975). The Cocktail Waitress: Women's Work in a Man's World. New York: Wiley.

Wark, J. M. (Ed.). (2001, October 27). Cambridgeport Conversation (Transcription). Boston: University of Massachusetts Boston.

Willis, P. (1981). Learning to Labor: How Working Class Kids Get Working Class Jobs. New York: Columbia University Press.

Cambridgeport Apartment

Jake Wark

1   SONNY: What smells good?

JAKE: Donuts.

CATHY: What's that

SONNY: Wow . . . look at that.

5   CATHY: Who smells so good?

DAVE: My ass.

CATHY: Smells like lotion or something.

DAVE: Yeah, it is, it's lotion.

(Conversation moves to kitchen; portion inaudible)

10   JAKE: No, the tape didn't come out last night so . . .

CATHY: Aww . . .

SONNY: Is it on now?

JAKE: It's, yes, it's taping now.

SONNY: Did you do a test first?

15   JAKE: Yes, I did a test . . .

CATHY: Ah, very good.

JAKE: It's working properly . . .

DAVE: Why do a test?

JAKE: We have proper modulation.

20   SONNY: We're finna go to the Idiot.

JAKE: No you're not.

TEZETA: It's like 9:30 in the morning.

JAKE: Have some donuts.

DAVE: It's 9:00 in the morning.

25   SONNY: I wish it was 9:00 in the morning.

JAKE: Mangia, baby.

SONNY: Chocolate donuts . . .

CATHY: Mmmm.

SONNY: So my car that I might buy is outside.

30   JAKE: Oh, alright. Congratulations.

SONNY: I gotta think about it, I gotta figure this out. (*Produces emissions chart or something*) Here's what he was working on.

DAVE: Dude, flow sytrometry. (?) Kid!

SONNY: What does that tell you about it?

DAVE: Whose is this?

35   SONNY: The owner's. Fabiano, the owner of the car.

TEZETA: What is that?

DAVE: Oh, this is what he does?

TEZETA: Is that—is that—oh.

DAVE: Oh, I see this, activated NKT cells.

40   TEZETA: Is he a physicist?

CATHY: Have a seat.

SONNY: Something.

DAVE: He's very sloppy on CT three.

SONNY: (*Unintelligible*)

45   TEZETA: Sonny, um . . .

DAVE: You know what?

TEZETA: Did you buy it? Are you gonna buy it?

SONNY: I don't know, I'm thinking about it.

TEZETA: What did the mechanic say? Was it mixed reviews?

50   SONNY: Yeah, it was a mixed review.

TEZETA: . . . Better than that, I mean, you didn't expect raves. It's an 11-year-old car.

SONNY: It will, perhaps, at some point in the future, need new struts.

TEZETA: What's that?

SONNY: Six hundred bucks.

55   DAVE: That's how you walk.

CATHY: That's a lot of money.

TEZETA: What's struts?

SONNY: The suspension.

JAKE: Well, when Dave goes from point A to point B . . .

60   DAVE: I struts. I think it's the thing that holds the wheels where they be at.

SONNY: Shocks and struts.

TEZETA: Oh, I see.

SONNY: So it's bumpy. And it's burning oil. It's blowing like blue smoke. At least at first. Which he said goes away, but then I still saw it. I don't know. That's embarrassing. I like a real—I feel really trashy blowing blue smoke.

JAKE: You feel like you're at a Kiss concert.

65   DAVE: The ah . . . (*Hands back emissions chart*)

SONNY: I don't want to mess it up.

DAVE: Is this for real?

SONNY: So he just like yeah, you know, nine hundred bucks . . .

DAVE: Tell him that you will give him one thousand dollars, minus the six hundred dollars for the struts, and whatever else, and you will take the car, and he owes you seventy-five dollars.

70   SONNY: Dustin got a car that way once when he was in high school. He was playing with Four-Play, his band, at some kid's bar-mitzvah or something like that, and he was outside like drunk afterwards, standing in the driveway, of some guy's house and looking at this like, old Cadillac or something from the Seventies, and he's staring at it drunkenly, and the guy comes out and he's like "You like the car? You want to buy it?" He's like "Well . . ." and so the guy starts like talking him up on buying the car, and he popped the hood for him and Dustin was just like "Well, you're going to have to replace the sytometer, and the timing belt is off," you know, and he doesn't know anything, but he just like picked through the engine while he was drunk and like picked it apart and made up all sorts of problems that the car had, and the guy finally was like "Just take the car." He drove it for like eight months before it died. It was the "Yom Kippur Clipper."

1. Reflecting on discourse, identity, and community

   ■ Jake provides a number of details about the backgrounds of the apartment insiders, their jobs and interests. How might you characterize this group of friends? And what do you think brings and holds them together?

   ■ Jake tells us that the members of this group "draw a distinction between their primary interests and the work that they do to subsidize it." What does this information contribute to the ways in which they perceive their own identities? How does it fit with what they talk about in the examples of exchanges that Jake offers?

   ■ Drawing on Spradley and Mann's model for studying speech acts, Jake analyzes the way quoting and snappy answers are used in his community. How do these analyses contribute to the understandings you're developing about this community? Are there any other exchanges that appear in the transcript of a conversation that you wish he'd analyzed?

   ■ What, finally, do you think Jake has come to understand about his community that he might not have seen so clearly before this study?

2. Reading from a writer's/researcher's perspective

   ■ Jake frames his study with a description of Cambridge. Why do you think it's significant that this apartment is located in the sort of city he describes? How does that larger context contribute to the portrait of the apartment insiders that emerges?

   ■ Jake makes several connections to other studies he has read. How does what he draws from each of these studies help to elucidate what he has observed in his own community?

   ■ Look back at the ways in which Jake has structured his report and the headings he uses. How effectively do his structure and his headings work to guide you, as a reader, through this report? Is there anything you would alter in the way that this report is structured or in the headings that signal that structure?

   ■ Jake includes a heading and a section on "Cultural Literacy." What does he see as cultural literacy in his community and how does he name it? How does it connect to the speech acts of quoting and giving snappy answers? As you consider your own community's relationship to the wider culture, do you find that the participants likewise share a cultural literacy that is featured in many of their interactions? How would you name that culture?

Richard Corrente, "The Dragon Court World"

Richard Corrente decided to focus his study of a familiar discourse community, on an on-line community that he had been participating in for some time: the world of an on-line game called Dragon Court. Rich's own interest in the game grew out of a general interest in and comfort with computers and the ease he felt in on-line communication. Through his involvement with this game, he has been able to communicate with and develop shared interests with players from around the world. If you haven't entered the world of an on-line game (or MUD/multi-user dimension, as it's formally named), you may be surprised to learn how complex a world such a game creates. If you are involved in a different on-line game, you may be interested in seeing how the world it creates compares to that of Dragon Court.

The Dragon Court World

Richard Corrente

INTRODUCTION

1   The discourse community I have chosen to study is a multi-user dimension, often referred to as a MUD, called Dragon Court (Dragon Court™ v1.2 ©1997–2001, Fred's Friends, Inc. [www.FFriends.com]), in which people from all over the world can meet each other. A discourse community is a group in which all the members share one or more things in common. Discourse communities can be anything from classrooms and groups of friends to church groups and workplaces. Ranging in membership from a few people to thousands, discourse communities come in all sizes. These communities can get together everyday or just once a month, and its members may meet in person, over the phone, or through the Internet.

Dragon Court is a Java-based role playing game, also known as an rgp, that is played online. In the game, players assume the role of an adventurer traveling through a medieval world in search of fame and treasure. In the game, players can trade items they have found and send letters to each other using the game's post office. Outside of the game, players have several other methods of communicating with each other. The ways of communicating include the forums, the chat rooms, instant messenger, and E-mail. Before looking at the ways of communicating, it is important to find out who is communicating and what is the game that brought us all together.

Dragon Court is set in a medieval world that is divided into several areas. The areas that a player can first access when they begin the game are Salamander Township and the Fields. Salamander Township is where players can save their game, buy items and equipment, and store items. The set up of the chat rooms is also based on the combination of Salamander Township and the Castle. The Fields is the first area where players can quest for treasure. As the game goes on, new areas become available to players. From the Fields, you can get to the Mounds and the Forest. The Mounds is an underground area which has several small places to quest in. The Mounds also include a place where you can fight the evil twin of the game's creator, Fred Haslam, most noted for being one of the original creators of Sim City (Sim City 2000™ ©1994–2001, Maxis, Inc. [www.maxis.com]). The Forest is another place for players to quest, and also includes a store, a place for players to practice their skills, and access to the Mountains. The Mountains offer two places to quest, as well as two shops. From Salamander Township, you can eventually access an area called the Castle. The Castle is where the post office, called DC Mail, is. The Castle also contains a place where players can join clans, special communities created by other players, and can raise their social status. Like the other areas in Dragon Court, the Castle also has places where players can quest.

PLAYERS' BACKGROUND

Knowing what the game is like is important for understanding the community of Dragon Court, but it is also important to know who the people are. As was previously stated, the players of Dragon Court come from all over the world. I polled many of the participants in the game, asking where they came from, what age they are, and if they are male or female. While the information reflects only sixty members of the community, including myself, it does provide a fairly accurate reading of what the entire community is like. Unfortunately, because not everyone participated in my polling, not all the countries of represented in Dragon Court were included in my findings. Despite that though, I was able to find out several key facts.

5   The most highly represented country in Dragon Court was the United States. Thirty-five of the sixty people were American, accounting for 58.3% of the total participants. The next highest country was Canada, which had eleven people making up 18.3% of the participants. 6.6% of the participants were from Great Britain, which was represented by 4 people. Australia and Norway both had two people, giving each country 3.3% of the total. The other five that were represented each had one participant, giving each of the countries 1.6% of the total. These five countries included Singapore, Belgium, Denmark, France, and Sweden. The remaining one person and 1.6% of the total went into the category "undisclosed", because that person did not give their country.

Of these sixty people, fifty-three were male. This makes up 88.3% of the people. The seven females who participated made up 11.6% of the group. Fifty-eight of the sixty people were willing to give their age. One of the undisclosed said he was "under 25, and that's all you need to know", and the other replied that she was "old enough to know better, but too young to care". For the participants who did give their age, the average ended up at about twenty to twenty-one years old. The oldest participant was forty-seven years old, and the youngest was only twelve. Two of the people who participated are cousins, showing that some members know each other in real life. One person had a wife who plays, one had a son who plays, and one had a brother and friend who play, but none of them participated in the poll along with the people they knew.

These different backgrounds provide the Dragon Court community with several important qualities. First, it allows for more diverse opinions in debates, and for other points of view to be explored. Second, the different languages brought in make some people more comfortable with the community, which mostly uses standard English. Third, it gives members of Dragon Court the chance to learn about other cultures.

Fourth, it gives everyone something to tease each other about, like asking one of the Scottish members if he can make everyone some haggis or battling between the Americans and Canadians about who has the better country. All these different backgrounds make communication between the players more interesting.

COMMUNICATION BETWEEN PLAYERS

Players communicate using several different methods. The most common methods are the forums and the chat rooms. For more private conversations, players will use E-mail, DC Mail, and instant messenger. Each of the different ways of communicating have their own purposes, and have important functions within the community.

The forums and chat rooms have several sections to them, and require a large amount of exploring to show them. I will be designating the next section to that, but I will provide you with an overview now. The forums are divided into nine sections, each with their own specific purpose. The nine sections are the Tavern, Clan Hall, Tome of History, Trade Forum, War Stories, Peasant Forum, Congress of Nobles, House of Lords, and Bugs Forum. The chat room is made up of several small chat rooms. The central chat room is the Commons. Off of the Commons are Market Place, Tavern, Clan Hall, Adventurers' Guild, and Queen's Court. The Market Place then splits off into the Armor Shoppe, Weapon Smith, Dry Goods, and the Temple. The Tavern contains many other temporary chat rooms created by players in Dragon Court. The Adventurers' Guild has the Mage's Wing, Trader's Wing, and Warrior's Wing. Off of the Queen's Court are the Grand Ballroom, Dining Hall, House of Lords, and Council of Regents.

10   The other three methods players have to communicate with are E-mail, DC Mail, and instant messenger. E-mail is probably the most used of these three methods. E-mail messages do not require the person receiving the message to be online when you send it. E-mail also allows you to send any form of graphic or music along with your messages, not just writing. DC Mail is probably the least used way of communication, as it takes one day for the mail to arrive at its mailbox. DC Mail also allows only small messages to be sent, about two-hundred fifty-five characters long. Sometimes, it will take two or three different messages just to send one complete paragraph. The good side of using DC Mail though is that you can send mail to someone simply by knowing their name, which saves you from scouting around to find the person's E-mail or instant messenger address. Instant messenger is the easiest to use, and allows direct conversations between people. The most common instant messenger programs used are America Online Instant Messenger (America Online Instant Messanger™ v4.7 ©1996–2001, America Online, Inc. [www.aol.com]) and Microsoft Network Instant Messenger (MSN Messenger™ v4.5 ©1997–2001, Microsoft Corporation [www.microsoft.com]), both of which have almost identical functions. The down side to instant messenger is that the person must be logged into their account in order for you to send them a message. All three ways give members ways to communicate to each other in the privacy of their own, smaller communities.

IN DEPTH COMMUNICATION

Of all the ways of communicating found in Dragon Court, the forums are the most popular. These nine areas are used by most of the people in the game, and serve as the main way of communicating with the rest of the community. The Tavern is the place where anyone can go to talk, and is usually the main place to find polls and questions from other players. Clan Hall is based on one area in the game, where you can go to join a clan. The Clan Hall forum is where clans post advertisements about their clan and what it has to offer to potential members. The Tome of History is the main forum for poetry, and also includes many romance, adventure, and comedy stories. The continual posters in the Tome of History usually vary their style of writing. The Trade Forum is for players in the game to trade items and weapons they have found with each other. This forum is mostly controlled by the people with lots of money, such as the older players and hackers. The presence of hackers in the game is a large problem, but the administration does not do much to keep them in line. The War Stories forum is mostly made up of a small group of people who post their stories and have everyone else tell them how great it is. The posters here seem less like they are trying to critic each other, and more as though they only want to be nice so the others will also post kind words to them. The Peasant Forum used to be a place for members of the lower social class in Dragon Court to meet. Now, due to lack of caring on the part of the moderators, the forum is a combination of the Trading Post and Clan Hall, where clans fight to buy new members who have recently joined the community. The Congress of Nobles is for the members of the middle class in Dragon Court. This forum was used mostly for talking between the middle class and for telling stories, myself being one of the storytellers there. Due to some problems the Dragon Court administration has been having with the forum, it has begun resetting itself once or twice a day, causing all the writing on the forum to erase. Once this problem has been fixed, there will hopefully be more people joining the forum again. The House of Lords is the meeting place of the upper class in Dragon Court. Because of the problem with the Congress of Nobles, I raised my social status and have begun posting in the more stable forum. I still have a middle class character who can post in the Congress once it is working right again. The Bugs Forum is where problems with the game, the forums, the chat rooms, and the hackers in the Trade Forum can be reported. Sadly enough, this seems to be one of the more popular forums among the players, but pretty much ignored by the administration.

The chat rooms work differently than the forums. The forums usually have the same groups of people in the same forums. The chat rooms usually have several groups of people who will all go in one chat room together, but will not always meet in the same one when the group gets together again. The most popular meeting place for groups is the Commons, which is the default room you go to when signing on to the chat rooms. The Market Place is not usually used, except for going to its Temple when players have a wedding, which is taken seriously despite the fact that it is a game. Several members who have met in Dragon Court have also gone on to get married in real life. The Clan Hall and Adventurers' Guild get almost no one in them, and it is rare to ever find one of them in use two days in a row. The Tavern and Queen's Court are the two of the more frequented chat rooms. In the Tavern, players can create their own chat rooms, so this area is constantly changing. The chat rooms players can create can be open to all other people or password protected so only certain people are allowed in. It is usually in these player made chat rooms or in the

Queen's Court that online parties are held. The Queen's Court is also used by members of the middle and upper class for meeting, though its use has declined somewhat in recent months. It seems that the groups who post in the Tavern forum are the most likely to use the chat rooms. This can be seen by the large number of "You'd have to hang out in the chat rooms to get it." remarks made by people in the Tavern who have their own insider knowledge into the chat room communities.

HOW WE TALK

Not only are there many methods for communicating within Dragon Court, but also many ways in which to talk. These ways include telling comedy and adventure stories, as well as poetry. Other ways include joking around, polling other players, bringing up questions, responding and commenting to other posts, fighting, getting angry, being polite, bringing peace, judging, introducing, and recruiting.

Of all these different ways of talking, the most common two are introducing and recruiting. Whenever someone new comes to the forums, they introduce themselves to everyone. Also, when a person moves up from the Peasant Forum to the Congress of Nobles and from the Congress of Nobles to the House of Lords they will introduce themselves so everyone else knows they are around now. Recruiting also goes on a lot, and in several different ways. Clans will recruit in Clan Hall to get new members into their groups. Storytellers, including me, will recruit people to be in new stories, which I believe makes the story more meaningful to the readers who joined. Another way of recruiting is to get people to join behind you on an idea. Sometimes people have something they want others to help with, such as cracking down on hacking, and will recruit people to raise support for the issue.

15   Other speech acts are used to have fun, such as fighting and polling. Though it may seem like fighting would be hurtful to the community, it really isn't. As was stated earlier, sometimes groups from the same country will fight with groups from other countries, such as Americans verse Canadians and Irish verse English. Sometimes there will be role playing fights between everyone in a community, such as when everyone in the entire House of Lords got into a giant pie fight with everyone else. Although hitting someone with a pie isn't as funny over the Internet as it is in real life, it was still a hilarious battle. Speech acts like this bring the community closer together.

VALUES FOUND IN SPEECH

The different speech acts and methods also are used to communicate shared values through the community. These values include a player's position on matters such as hacking, having fun, personal attacks, and cheating. Other than hackers and cheaters, the community shares the values of being against hacking and cheating. Some cheaters claim they do not like hacking, yet they have no reluctance in using the weapons and items hackers have created using cheating programs. Although hackers, cheaters, and one corrupt moderator do their best to keep the players of Dragon Court from having fun, the rest of us still hold it as an important value. The hackers, cheaters, and the corrupt moderator usually use personal attacks against members of the community to disrupt the fun, and most of the players are against this.

By looking at posts found in the forums, you see these values displayed. Having fun can be seen in the stories and poems written, in the friendly fights between players, and in jokes told around the forums. Hacking and cheating can be seen most commonly in the Trade Forum, but you can also see the fight to stop these online terrorists there. Personal attacks go on most commonly in the Trade Forum and in the Tavern, and this is also where you can see the people trying to stop them.

CONCLUSION

Despite the trouble-making made by some members of the community, there is a culture behind the game. This culture was started by people from all over the world finding a game called Dragon Court, which appealed to them. The people who came to Dragon Court met other people who shared the same interest in gaming, and they formed a community. This community has now grown to over sixty-six thousand registered characters.

This online culture has became what it is due to several factors. The first factor is the background everyone shares. People in Dragon Court have the chance to talk with people from all over the world, and have the chance to learn about the culture others have grown up in. Another factor is the many ways people have to communicate with, which helps to spread ideas and talk no matter what the conditions are. The forums and chat rooms also allow members of the community to talk to large numbers of people at one time. A third factor is the large number of ways the players have of talking. You can find a way that fits your idea, as well as one that fits the method you are communicating with.

20   When you look at the whole community, there is much that can be learned. One thing is how people get along with each other. Though there are the problem causing people, like can be found in any community, most of the players get along with each other. Even the people you would think would be fighting, like the members of the community from Israel and the Arab states, get along very well in each other's company. You also can learn that there is always someone with power who enjoys assaulting the people without it, such as the corrupt moderator. A third thing you can learn is how people separate their larger communities into smaller ones that are based on more common interests the smaller one shares than the larger one does. Overall, you learn how a community works.

Conversation

Richard Corrente

1   Here are a few things that should be pointed out to understand the conversation:

- All spelling mistakes were made during the conversation, not during my typing. I left the mistakes in to illustrate the fact that Dragon Court is a diverse group, and not everyone speaks English a first language. It also illustrates that some people are just bad typers, but that is beside the point.

- The conversation started before I arrived, and continued after I left.
- The conversation takes place in a chat room called "The Commons", which is a grassy area just outside the tavern.

5
- I don't know anyone in this conversation. I don't usually hang around in the chat rooms.

Key:
> public talk
>> action
<< private talk
( ) note made by me

>JACK OF KNIVES: "i'm no mage"

>RYU-OJI: "So? Ever heard of kerosine?"

>>*Jack of knives turns to SM*

10
>>*Guardian.K smiles bck her, hetting his hands rest where they are now, with hers on his*

>JACK OF KNIVES: "journey where?

>>*Kyliene skips through the commons toward the tavern.*

>STARLIGHT MOON: "they had to journey to town to watch a performance . . they should return in apprximately 2 hours"

>>*Martin Eastwind blinks like an owl, still slightly affected with AFK (I don't remember what AFK means.)*

15
>>*Jack of knives looks crestfallen*

>>RYU-OJI: *waves his hand in front of Martin*

>RYU-OJI: "Eastwind, any relation to Eastwood? Oooooh, are you a gunslinger?"

>>MARTIN EASTWOOD: *glares slightly at Ryu* "please don't do that"

>RYU-OJI: "Oh, I apologize."

20
>MARTIN EASTWIND: "no i an not"

<<STARLIGHT MOON: *whispers to you* "ahh. so we are at this game . . . well . . . you could call me star . . . that would be appropriate"

>>*Devilish breaths softly, then kisses Gk's cheek (Gk refers to Guardian.K.)*

>>*Martin Eastwind taps the hilt of the broadsword strapped across his back*

>>*Eshia tackles martin*

25
>RYU-OJI: "Ready for battle, I see?"

>>*Guardian.K smiles, kissing hers in return.*

>>*Martin Eastwind yelps*

<<STARLIGHT MOON: *whispers to you* "Sorry . . . miswisper"

>MARTIN EASTWIND: "heya!!!"

READING RESPONSE

1. Reflecting on discourse, identity, and community

   ■ Rich introduces his study by defining Dragon Court as a discourse community. From reading his study, do you agree with that definition? How does or doesn't the picture he presents reflect your conception of what a discourse community might be?

   ■ Participants in the world of Dragon Court join in creating an alternate, virtual word that reflects in many ways the actual world. What do you learn from Rich's study about the ways of Dragon Court that suggests this mirroring?

   ■ Rich names some of the most common speech acts and discusses the values that are reflected in them. What picture do those acts and those values give you of the concerns of this community?

   ■ In his conclusion, Rich suggests some of what can be learned by studying and participating in such a community. If you've participated in the community created through an on-line game, have you found that your own experience supports those conclusions?

2. Reading from a writer's/researcher's perspective

   ■ In his introduction, and continuing into later sections, Rich provides a great deal of background knowledge about the workings of the community he is studying. Depending on how familiar you are with the world of on-line games, you may find the amount of background he gives to be too little (assuming that you already share some knowledge of internet terms that you don't) or too much (reiterating information that you think most readers would already know). How appropriate do you feel the level of background information Rich has given is to the typical college-age reader?

   ■ Rich also provides a lot of information about the people who play the game, having polled a number of players as part of his study. Why is this knowledge about the players important in relationship to Rich's specific focus on communication among the players? If you've decided to study a large and spread-out group, do you think a poll might provide useful information for your own study?

   ■ Rich has attached a print-out of a portion of an actual conversation that took place in one of the chat rooms. As you read through these exchanges, do they add to your understanding of what might go on in a typical Dragon Court chat room conversation? Are there parts of this transcript that you would have wanted the researcher to analyze and interpret for you? Do you see any examples here that might have supported the points that Rich is making in the body of his report?

Participating in Academic Conversations

In the following chapters, you'll turn your attention to the more formal discourse communities that are formed in classes and disciplines (and ultimately in various academic and professional fields), looking at them from the perspectives of a student participant and a researcher, and seeing what you find as you try out each perspective. For your larger inquiry, you'll choose an academic discourse community represented by one of your introductory courses, and carry out a research study much like that in Part II. Here, your study will be framed and guided by particular questions that you want to explore, and it will draw on library research as well as field research.

The chapters include readings that explore three interrelated strands of your larger inquiry—focusing on your self, the discourse community of the course you've chosen, and the field or discipline the course represents:

1. Who am I as I approach this area of study? What have I become interested in and come to value as I've moved through other discourse communities? What do I bring as background knowledge and experience that seems relevant to this discipline? Why do I think I'm interested in it?

2. What are the ways in which this course presents this discipline—the <u>what</u>, <u>why</u>, and <u>how</u> of the work that goes on there? In what ways does it build on and expand the frameworks of knowledge that learners bring to it?

3. What are some of the larger goals and purposes of study in this discipline? What do insiders look at and try to learn about in their research? How do people talk, write, and think about what they're discovering? What values might underlie these ways?

LEARNING GOALS

■ To approach the academic discourse community you choose to study with your own stance, your own perspective, seeing what you bring to the work of that community, what you make of what goes on there, how you can see that work from the perspective of what interests or concerns you in the world.

■ To approach the academic discourse community as a community, studying it in the ways that we've been using, and seeing what you can learn about its values and its ways.

■ To see how knowledge is made and research is carried out in that academic community and how you can begin to work as a writer/ researcher in that context.

As you work toward your final research report for Part III, you may choose to proceed in one of two ways:

A. By completing a field (or primary) research study of the discourse community of the course you've selected (like the research report in Part II), adding a component in which you use the library to discover more about the sorts of research that are carried out in the discipline the course represents;

B. By completing a library (or secondary) research study, following up on a topic that you've found to be of interest to you as you reflect on the knowledge and interests you bring to the course and the ways in which the course has introduced the possible areas of study within the discipline.

In either case, your report will draw on your understandings about your own interests and identity as a learner, as well as on the picture you've developed of what this discipline focuses on and how.

It's also possible to extend the research you did in Part II, to see, through library research, what others have learned about a topic that you've identified through your field research—for example, the role of some aspect of popular culture, such as music, in defining a generational identity; the ways gender differences affect the ways people talk in different situations; or the ways in which the roles of congregants are defined in various church communities.

7

Researching Academic
Discourse Communities

Chapter 7 focuses on the intersection between your social identity as a student and the academic identities you're trying on as you study within particular disciplines. It features the report of a study that follows one student, Eric, through an introductory course in physics, drawing on a journal he keeps about his experience in the course. As you read "The Eric 'Experiment'" you'll plan your own study of an academic discourse community, drawing on that reading as you begin to look at your own position in the course you choose to study and/or consider what sorts of underpinnings it offers for a topic you'd like to research.

The inquiries in Chapter 7 address three questions:

- What understandings and perspectives do you bring to the introductory academic discourse communities of your courses?

- What can reading a study of another student's experience in such a course contribute to your thinking about the course you've chosen to focus on? What sort of model does it provide for studying the kind of academic community a course offers and introduces?

- What engages you in the course? What interests and questions does it lead you to? What implications are there for your work as a learner and a writer across academic settings?

The communities formed in classrooms and academic disciplines are similar in many ways to the informal discourse communities you studied in Part II. Their members share knowledge about particular aspects of the world. They have shared purposes in studying those aspects. And they have common ways of carrying out their research and communicating with others about what they've learned and what they still want to learn, along with some common beliefs and values.

In your studies of informal discourse communities, you've probably found that much of the purpose of conversations was social—that people were trying to form and maintain social relationships even when they had another shared purpose like practicing their religion or getting a job done. Academic discourse communities fulfill social purposes too. People come to identify with others in their classes, in their majors, in a discipline, and to form social connections and friendships with others in that community. But academic communities have larger nonsocial purposes as well, to study:

the physical and biological world (the sciences),

the cultural and social worlds that humans create (the social sciences),

the ways humans have sought to know and understand these worlds and their ways of representing them (the humanities), and

the ways people act on and effect changes in their worlds (the professions).

So one way in which academic discourse communities are likely to differ from the other communities you've studied is that study and learning, creating and sharing knowledge, are central to their shared purposes and to their "ways with words," and indeed such knowledge is highly valued.

Another is that a large portion of the conversation goes on in writing. The participants may not know each other personally—they can be working in different countries, speaking different languages—and they carry on their conversations through the writing they do in scholarly journals, even if they can't carry them on in person.

Finally, in academic discourse communities, both talk and writing will be informed by the *assumed shared knowledge* of other written conversations—knowledge of the important texts of the field. Part of what's assumed to be shared, and what's evoked in conversations, is what's been said by others who have written before, whether Freud, Kant, Newton, or more recent scholars. So becoming a member of an academic discourse community also involves reading and understanding some of the significant texts that have formed the history of the discipline as well as more recent texts that propose current directions and arguments.

These features—a focus on creating and sharing knowledge, on carrying out conversations in writing, and on building on the assumed shared knowledge represented in texts—significantly affect how people participate in academic communities, including introductory ones.

PREPARING TO STUDY AN ACADEMIC SETTING

As you choose one of your courses to study as an academic discourse community, you'll be approaching it as both a participant and a researcher. You'll want to analyze the workings of the discourse community as a researcher, but you'll also want to be able to draw on what you learn, as a college student, to help you to see your own questions, values, and concerns as a participant. So you'll want to choose to study a course that poses some significant questions or issues for you. You may want to consider what it is that you like or dislike or find easy or difficult, whether the course represents a field in which you might continue your study, or how you can use your experience in the course to help you decide what other sorts of courses you might want to explore. If you're following Strand B and preparing a library research report, you may want to begin by considering some topics and questions that a course has introduced and that you'd like to explore further—questions that you've begun to develop some background knowledge about. Or you might begin by looking at some studies by other student researchers at the end of Part III, to see whether their questions and interests might guide your own.

Vanessa decides to undertake a field research study in which she will look at the introduction to the field of music provided by her current courses. She planned to major in physics but she is now considering whether she wants to prepare to perform music professionally, and she begins by asking questions that help her move toward that decision.

> What is valuable to the insiders of the music discourse community? . . . What makes the music classes in college different from other classes? Who participates in them? What is the shared knowledge required to be an insider? What is the purpose of it? What are the types of work that professional musicians and students have to do? What are the questions that students are asked to write about in academic studies?

These questions frame the inquiry that Vanessa undertakes and her final research report on that inquiry. They may also help her to make a decision about whether this is a field she wants to enter. She'll try to answer these questions by collecting and analyzing data from her music class—the sorts of readings that are used, assignments that are given, the classroom conversations that go on, and the written conversations that get published in the music journals.

Juliette, on the other hand, already knows that she wants to major in science and that she'll use her biology class as a jumping off point for a library research report. She asks a different sort of question:

> Are women under-represented in the broad field of science, and if so, is it the result of negative societal and peer conditioning? This is the question I realized I was asking as I began to study my experience and the classroom discourse in my

Introductory Biology (Bio 111) class. It came to me as I was reflecting on my reasons for returning to college to seek out a science degree at 28 years old. I never thought too much before about gender differences in different fields of study, other than in a theoretical kind of way.

Juliette will draw on the same sources of data that Vanessa uses, but her question will take her beyond the biology classroom, into the library, where she'll try to discover more about the history and present status of women's representation in the sciences. (Both Vanessa's and Juliette's final research reports are included in the readings at the end of Part III).

Whether you focus your study on the academic discourse community created within a course or pursue questions that course raises through library research, you'll want to explore:

- The ways in which the course represents the shared knowledge and purposes of the discipline it provides an entry to, and what that course tells you about the sort of discourse community represented by the discipline;
- The possibilities that the course and your interests suggest for further topics to explore in discipline, moving beyond the classroom.

You may also want to examine the ways in which the course functions from the perspective of a student participant—how insiders in the classroom discourse community participate successfully, and how you might better understand your own experience, whether as insider or outsider, in that classroom academic community.

For this study, you'll proceed much in the way in which you did in studying nonacademic communities, focusing on the layered conversation—the talk, reading, and writing—that goes on in a discipline's introductory courses. But there will be three significant differences in this study:

1. Your research will be guided by some specific questions that you formulate—that represent what you want to know and discover.
2. You'll follow out a question through library research or supplement your field research with some library research, where you'll discover more about the shared knowledge being created and written about in academic journals by insiders to the field.
3. As a researcher, you may try shifting from an analytical to an *evaluative stance*, not only analyzing the ways of the discourse community you study, but evaluating what you find there, from a perspective that you name.

In studying an academic discourse community, you may want to work with other student researchers who are enrolled in the same course or in other courses in the discipline, working together to create a picture of this disciplinary community. Much of the research in many disciplines goes on collaboratively, and forming research groups is another way of participating in academic communities in the ways that insiders do.

Reflect on which of your current courses, or which questions or topics arising from one of those courses, you'll choose for your research. As you make your decision about an academic discourse community to study, consider:

RESEARCH MEMO 7.1

   —the significant questions and issues the course raises for you as a participant;

   —your interest in thinking about the shared knowledge, purposes and ways of the course and the discipline and perhaps in continuing your work in that discipline;

   —the sorts of data you're likely to collect and analyze and whether such data will be available and/or interesting for you to look at;

   —the actual work that you have left to do in the course and whether your study can help you thinking about that work (for example, examining and analyzing the course text might help with your preparation for a final exam; analyzing an assignment and how you work with it might help you work on a major writing assignment; finding journal articles in the field might help you if you have library research to do);

   —the other researchers in your classroom community who may be interested in studying the same or a related academic discourse community, and whether you want to form research teams or groups.

What academic discourse community do you finally decide on and why? Will you follow Strand A and carry out field research on an academic discourse community, using your library research to gather evidence of the shared knowledge, purposes, and ways of insiders to the discipline? Or will you follow Strand B and carry out a library research study, drawing on what you're learning from your course about the shared knowledge, purposes, and ways of this community to guide you in pursuing a particular topic and question that insiders have studied?

Once you've decided on the academic discipline or discourse community you'll study, you'll want to begin right away to collect data of several sorts:

RESEARCH STRATEGY

   • *Observational data.* As in your earlier study, you'll probably find a double-entry notebook most useful for making observation notes. (For more on using this notebook format for observation notes, look at Strategies for Field Research in Part IV.) This format is particularly useful for classroom observations because you can keep your class notes on one side of the page, recording the shared <u>what</u> of the classroom conversation, while adding reflections, questions, and connections on the other. If you begin to use this format right away for all of your notes, you'll find it easy to build a set of observation notes for your study while continuing your ordinary work in the course you are studying. If

(continued)

(*continued*)

you plan a library research report, you can also use this format to record and reflect on any relevant ideas and topics that are introduced in class.

• *Written artifacts.* You'll want to create a folder with the written materials that you might examine as part of your study—the syllabus, some interesting or problematic assignments or tests, and examples of your own work that you might want to explore. If you plan a library research report, you'll want to begin to gather relevant readings and any other possible sources of information from your course materials.

• *Conversational data.* For a field study, you'll want to look closely at how shared knowledge, shared purposes, and shared ways are built within the classroom, and for that purpose you'll want to gather actual speech data from your academic discourse community, either by recording and transcribing part of a class session (with permission from faculty and students), or by taking careful notes and trying to capture the same sort of details you would get in a recording—who speaks and what they say (approximately) for each speaker.

• *Interviews.* As your own question for this study becomes clearer, you may also want to arrange interviews with your professor, with classmates, or with more advanced students in the discipline who have taken this course at an earlier time.

• *Library resources.* You'll draw on journal articles, books, and reference materials in the academic discipline most closely associated with the course and/or most relevant to a research topic you've decided to pursue.

The research memos in Chapters 7 and 8 will guide you in analyzing field research data and/or drawing from them to do some preliminary thinking about your library research questions. The research memos in Chapter 9 will guide you in library research and in thinking about what that research can show you about the insider ways of a particular academic discourse community.

Matt, a freshman, has been studying his history class as an academic discourse community. In summing up what he has observed around him, he speculates about the interest and motivation of the students in the class. Earlier in the semester, he studied the discourse community of his long-term, neighborhood friends, looking closely at what they know as insiders. Now he uses the notion of insiderness that he has developed to think about how students participate and the different extent to which they're involved in this history classroom.

Some students in this class are much into history. This class may be included in their major or they may have taken the class as an elective they know they would enjoy. These people could be considered insiders to this classroom community. They give their attention and thoughts to the teacher's words. How much interest and time given to the course determines how much of an insider you are. It can be assumed that these students will add more to the classroom study. Others in the class may have taken it in order to fill distribution requirements or to fill their schedule as an incoming freshman. They might even hate the class. The class is not enjoyable and does not mean much to these students. Then there are those in the middle who are there to work no matter what course they are in. They get their work done, but history is not their favorite subject and they are not there to vigorously discover historical knowledge.

A range of insiderness, therefore, exists. Picture it as a scale from 1–10, ten designating the most involved insider. Each student could be assigned a number on this scale. If the class average were high, it would make for a more productive community of learners, each working diligently to provide new knowledge to the field of history.

Matt doesn't identify his own position on this scale of insiderness at this moment, but he's interested enough in this community to choose to study it.

For your study of a familiar and informal discourse community, you probably chose a setting in which you were a full insider—somewhere you wanted to be, and where you didn't have to think about what you had to do to participate fully and easily in any conversation. (In fact, your implicit insider knowledge probably made it hard sometimes to step back and name those things explicitly.) But you're in a different position in the academic discourse communities that make up your courses, and you may experience yourself as being anywhere from 1 to 10 on the scale of insiderness that Matt proposes.

Courses are, by design, introductions to the shared knowledge, shared purposes, and shared ways of thinking, talking, and writing that make up particular academic disciplines (or, for interdisciplinary courses, introductions to a theme or topic that bring together the ways in which several disciplines have pursued it). So not only are there different levels of insiderness within a classroom, there are also different levels within the discipline as a whole. The highest level is to be a full participant in the work of that discipline, in the ways graduate students are typically learning to be as they work alongside their professors in conducting physics experiments, carrying out therapeutic interviews in clinical psychology, preparing and critiquing their own exhibitions of photography or painting, or studying composition and the ways in which writing works in academic discourse communities. Graduate students are participating in the community of an academic discipline as apprentices— doing the same work as long-term members and having the same conversations about that work that long-term faculty insiders have. Because teaching is part of the work of academic insiders, graduate students typically do that work as well, and some of the teachers for your own courses may also be graduate students.

Undergraduate courses are structured to introduce students gradually not only to the knowledge that academic insiders to a discipline share, but also to ways of creating and thinking about that knowledge, to pave the way for those who will eventually enter that discipline as research physicists or clinical psychologists. Some students, like the "10's" in Matt's class, find themselves more and more at home in particular courses, and gradually come to identify with the discipline, to major in it, perhaps to continue their study and/or work in a related field when they graduate, as the most involved history insiders may do. But these courses are also intended to provide, for all students, the underpinnings of a general education: to give you enough understanding so that you can read and think about a new scientific discovery, or newly-discovered historical documents, or a new therapeutic direction being used with troubled kids, and perhaps enough of an introduction to the published scholarship in a field that you know how to draw on those resources to pursue answers to your own questions. In a complex society, we all need to have a great deal of shared knowledge about how the physical world, human societies, and people within them work, about how they've been studied, about how we might propose to learn more, in order to be informed and responsible participants in the society. It's that sort of general knowledge that introductory courses are designed to offer.

In addition, though, there's another way in which to think about the space you'll occupy among students of a discipline, and the space the discipline will occupy in your head. As you move through various discourse communities, nonacademic as well as academic, you are expanding both your own *personal framework of understanding*—your own layers of background knowledge—and the ways in which you use this framework to make sense of the world and what you'll do in it. Everything is a potential resource in this process, even courses you don't particularly like or that you're taking just to fill a requirement. You, as a learner and knower, are really at the center of your own journey through academic discourse communities, and it's worth your while to reflect on what you can use from each stage of the journey.

REFLECTIVE INQUIRY

This is a good moment to pause and map the terrain of your own personal knowledge and the knowledge you'd like to acquire.

Brainstorm a list or create a map for all of the areas of learning that you've begun to explore, that you feel you have some preliminary knowledge in, or that have captured your interest, whether through formal study or your own informal explorations. Then add a new list or overlay of areas and fields in which you think or know you'd like to learn more, and of subfields within those fields. How might you use your research to extend your knowledge in or beyond one of these areas? How might you use your general education to fill in more of what you want to learn?

Are any of your classmates focusing their studies on fields you might be interested in but haven't studied yet? If so, you might want to join with them in a research group, to see what you can learn from their research.

READING AN ACADEMIC STUDY

The following study of a learner's experience in one course, "Introductory Physics: The Eric 'Experiment'," was done as part of an effort to find out why students who did well in other subjects and who had the necessary math background often chose not to take science courses. Eric was a humanities major who was asked to take an introductory physics course as a "participant observer"—as someone who would both participate in the activities of this classroom discourse community and observe the nature of those activities and his own response to them. The researcher conducting the study, Sheila Tobias, was trying to discover how more students might be attracted to the sciences and to counter the assumption of too many science professors that those students who opted out of science just weren't smart enough to do well. She gave her larger study, in which she followed a number of very successful non-science students through their experience of science courses, the title *They're Not Dumb, They're Different.*

Our reading selection includes Eric's descriptions of what went on in his physics class and homework assignments along with his reflections on those activities. It's not surprising that many of his reflections focus on differences between what happens in the physics course and what happens in a literature course, and on what the underlying values might be that these differences reflect. Eric is trying to characterize an unfamiliar academic discourse community in terms of a familiar one in which he feels like an insider. As you read this selection, think about questions of <u>what</u>, <u>why</u>, and <u>how</u>—looking at them through Eric's eyes as a classroom participant. What does Eric see as the <u>what</u> of physics study? <u>How</u> does he find such study to be carried out in this course? And <u>why</u> does he think the work focuses on these things in these ways?

READING RESPONSE

As a student, your first reading of this study may be strongly participatory, as you step into this account of Eric's experiences and reflect on your own.

When you have finished reading and glossing, write a response in which you capture what you have learned about Eric as a student and as a member of this classroom community from this reading. What is his position, both literally and figuratively, in this classroom? Where do you see him sitting and how much interaction do you see him engaging in with the other students? Where do you think he fits according to Matt's scale of insiderness and why? What do you think contributes to the position you see him placed in?

Then, to better understand and position yourself as a student, write a description of yourself in the class you are focusing on. Where do you sit in this class? What do you have out on your desk? What do you typically do when the professor is speaking? Do you speak in this class? What kinds of things do you say? Write a description of yourself as a student in this class that would help an outsider (someone not in your class) see you as other students in the class or your professor might see you.

What strikes you as you look at what you've said about Eric's position and about your own? Why do you think you're positioned in this classroom, both physically and metaphorically, in the way that you are? How does that positioning affect the questions you want to address and the topics you're interested in pursuing?

As you read, you'll notice from Eric's journal entries that he has already acquired some amount of insider knowledge about physics. If you haven't taken a college physics class, you may not understand some specific details in Eric's notes, but his overall sense of what's going on in the class and why it works as it does will be clear enough.

Introductory Physics
The Eric "Experiment"
Sheila Tobias

The notion of a 'calling' is deeply ingrained in the mythology and history of science. If we assume that all students are 'called' in the same way and by the same age, we fix what is inherently variable— the size and composition of the talent pool.

—Daryl Chubin[1]

Eric found it "strange" to be in class again, especially in a lecture class where "everyone looks tired" and no one seemed particularly excited by the prospect of the five-week introductory physics course that lay ahead. His fellow classmates, as he perceived them, were either "bored" or "scared," he noted on the first page of the daily journal he was keeping of his reactions as a literature student to introductory physics. In even the most obscure literature class, he wrote, "there are always people who are intensely interested, at least at the outset. Is it simply the nature of the subject that makes elementary science classes appear unexciting, or is it the teaching style?"[2] Part of his assignment, as a participant-observer for a project supported by Research Corporation, was to find out.

Because it was a summer session, Eric would not experience the anonymity of the larger classes that characterize introductory physics. He shared his course with only 30 others, 20 men and 10 women (not the gender balance he was used to, as he recorded in his journal). But the habit of teaching large classes and the demands of the fast-paced summer-school schedule prevented his instructor from modifying the lecture format. One look at the assignment sheets and at the weight of the text[3] gave Eric some sense of the amount of material to be covered, and some anxiety. To add to his travail, he discovered his calculator wouldn't handle exponents when he began to work the problems that first evening (he borrowed an HP 15-C the next day). More serious was his worry that, although he had taken college calculus (a condition of his assignment as participant observer in this course), his brain wouldn't handle the computations. And it was clear there would be no respite either from the pace or the ex-

[1]Daryl Chubin of the Office of Technology Assessment, U.S. Congress, made these remarks during a talk at the AAAS National Meeting, New Orleans, Feb. 17, 1990. Quoted with his permission.
[2]Eric, of course, was not around after class when the few students who were intensely interested in the subject went up to speak to the instructor.
[3]*Halliday and Resnick, Fundamentals of Physics,* Third Edition, New York: John Wiley, 1988.

pectations. "The instructor gave the class the impression," Eric noted on the first day, "that since *he* had had to make it through the 'elementary grind,' so must we."[4] Literary studies offer a different kind of challenge, Eric noted right away. "In literature," he wrote, "the cutting edge is accessible, even if it is unlikely to be mastered by a beginner. In physics, a correct solution may be harder to figure out, but once done it will be indistinguishable from the professor's own." This insight soon became palpable for Eric when he discovered the "one nice thing" about physics: "as I try and endure, the understanding comes. And this does not necessarily happen in the humanities."

On the second day Eric began to notice more profound differences between the "values," as he put it, of a person in the humanities and those of a scientist.

> In a discussion of one of the homework problems, we were to judge the best clock for timekeeping, given a record of five clocks' readings at exactly noon. The professor chose the clock that gained exactly 51 seconds every day. I picked the clock that was within seven seconds of noon, day after day. A scientist wants predictability. I would rather have convenience.[5]

5 But the first "real day" of lecture disappointed him.

> The class consisted basically of problem solving and not of any interesting or inspiring exchange of ideas. The professor spent the first 15 minutes defining terms and apparently that was all the new information we were going to get on kinematics. Then he spent 50 minutes doing problems from chapter 1. He was not particularly good at explaining why he did what he did to solve the problems, nor did he have any real patience for people who wanted explanations.

Eric was learning that, for the most part, "why" questions are neither asked nor answered. The preference is for "how" questions. Perhaps because of this, his initial assessment of the teaching mode (compared to what he was used to) was negative.

> I do not feel that what this professor is doing can be considered teaching in any complex or complete sense. My understanding is that we are to learn primarily by reading the text, secondarily by doing problems on our own and comparing our solutions to those on sale in the physics office, and thirdly by mimicking the professor's problem-solving examples. Simply by intuition, I know physics, and more generally science, to involve creativity and finesse; but this man makes it into a craft, like cooking, where if someone follows the recipe, he or she will do well.

There was, indeed, a discrepancy between Eric's expectations and those of his professor (note 4).

---

[4] The instructor, reading these comments, did not recall ever using the term "elementary grind," but agreed that he brought to his teaching certain prejudices about who takes summer school physics and why: he assumed his students were "preprofessionals who, have already decided on a career in science and are in class to learn problem solving." After reading these comments, he conceded he needed to be "more guarded about what I say . . ." and that "extreme care must be taken to set a good mood for the course, and to offset the prejudices students bring with them."

[5] Page 11 in the text, question 30P.

10   By the end of the first week, classes seemed a little better or maybe, as Eric wondered, he was just getting "used to the way [the course] is being 'taught.'" Still, he felt patronized by the teaching style.

> I still get the feeling that unlike a humanities course, here the professor is the keeper of the information, the one who knows all the answers. This does little to propagate discussion or dissent. The professor does examples the "right way" and we are to mimic this as accurately as possible. Our opinions are not valued, especially since there is only one right answer, and at this level, usually only one [right] way to get it.

It was not the physics that bothered him. In later segments of his journal he would praise the text, a book borrowed from the physics undergraduate office that he begged to be able to keep when the course was over. He found his old love of math coming back. In the quiet of the university library where he spent afternoons trying to work the problems, he was "really quite content," he wrote. It was the class that bothered him most at the beginning, but he was honest enough to realize that as he "got more into the physics," he liked it better.

> As I am able to ask more knowledgeable questions, class becomes more interesting. I am finding that while the professor is happy to do example problems for the entire period, he will discuss the real world ramifications of a theory if asked.

His classmates didn't appreciate his interruptions, however. They seemed to "lose patience" with his "silly 'why' questions." These got in the way of the mechanics of finding the right solution to their assigned problems. And this was what, as Eric perceived it, physics was all about—for them.

15   He was finding more differences between doing physics and doing literary analysis. The professor's suggestion that setting up the problem and understanding concepts is more important than doing the arithmetic reduced Eric's homework time from six hours per night to three. He was happy to be relieved of some of the computation, but bothered, too. "Imagine being asked to show only that you *could* write a paper on the use of gender in *Tom Sawyer* without having actually to do so," he wrote in his journal that night.

Two weeks into the course, Eric was becoming skeptical about some of the models. His attention to language and his continuing need for answers to "why" questions was decidedly getting in his way. His July 9 entry reads:

> OK, I might as well admit it now. I don't really believe Newtonian mechanics. It works, yet somehow I think there are various forces which are made up—not really understood—just to make the calculations work out. Is there really a normal force?[6] The force which pushes a book down on a table is gravity. Yet the "normal" force which comprises the table pushing back on the book, seems a little strange. Why should a table push on a book? Maybe it should be called the

---

[6]Eric knew full well by then that the normal force in physics is the force perpendicular to the contact surface. He was playing with language.

"abnormal" force? And action-reaction seems to me to be a misnomer . . .
"Action-reaction" presupposes a cause and effect relationship which implies
duration, but in physics the "action-reaction" happens simultaneously.[7]

By then he was starting to look around a bit more at the students in the class.
Everyone looked clean cut and serious, he noted. Yet, there were a few people who
caught his eye.

There is one man with a crew cut who always sits in the front row and always
wears a hat that says, "Life is too short to dance with ugly women." Another
extremely muscular "frat boy type" catches my attention only because he always
mutters the right answer several seconds before anyone else. I have decided he is
either a genius or he has taken the course a few times before. There is a Hispanic
woman who sits next to me who is already having trouble with the material. She
tells me she spends seven hours a night on homework and needs to get an "A"
to receive an ROTC scholarship for next year. A pretty blonde premed sits
behind me. She acts like she wants to be friends, but her conversations always
eventually turn to, ". . . By the way, what did you get on problem 57?"

20   Yet, even though the class was small, there was "no sense of community within
the class," Eric noted, a fact he would later comment on at length. He attributed this
to the lecture format and to the subject, devoid, as he put it, of "personal expression."

Nobody seems particularly interested in making friends or seeing each other
outside of class. This may be one reason people dislike math and science classes,
their lack of community.

The first exam gave Eric some important insights both into how physics is taught
and why the sense of community was so lacking. He personally found the exam "easy,"
easier than the homework which, as he expressed it, "involved the use of multiple
concepts and numerical manipulations." In contrast, he wrote in his journal, "the exam
problems asked only for a simple exhibition of skills acquired." He was "frustrated" to
have spent so much time on problems which he would not encounter on tests. Later
he concluded that the homework problems were really too hard, "discouraging rather
than encouraging. Sometimes you are asked to display a knowledge of so many concepts at once, it is hard to get a hold of things."

But the real impact of the exam was felt when the exams were returned to the
class.

When we got our exams back this week, everyone was concerned about how
other people scored. I understand that natural curiosity and in my literature

---

[7]According to Arnold Arons, professor emeritus of physics, University of Washington, Eric's question
concerning time intervals elapsing in connection with force adjustments having to do with Newton's third
law, "is one of the deepest questions arising in classical physics. The question must be planted deliberately,
and students must be led to think about and discuss it. There are very very few Erics who raise it
spontaneously." (Personal communication to the author.)

classes there was always some comparing done between friends. However, I've never experienced the intense questioning that has happened this week. Almost everyone I talk to at some point or another asks me about my grade. When I respond I scored an "A,"[8] I get hostile and sometimes panicked looks. It is not until I explain that I'm only auditing and that my score certainly will not be figured into the curve, that these timid interrogators relax.

25   There was, in fact, no "grading on a curve" in Eric's course. The course handout had specifically stated this. Primed by other courses in science, students assumed they would be graded on a curve. The fact that the professor posted a histogram after each exam with the break points for the letter grades may have confused them. The professor said later, "maybe the students think a histogram implies a curve." His classmates' behavior, however, suggested to Eric that they fully believed grading was on a curve.

> It wasn't until this afternoon that a classmate explained to me that students in a science class try to identify people who score well and then constantly compare their scores (or time studying or answers on homework) to their own. I have never been in a class before where my grade had any effect, real or perceived, on anyone else.

Even more basic, for Eric, was the class' fixation on grades.

> Why is it so difficult to get a good grade? For one thing, there are less of them. Due to [perceived] curving in physics, the grades are based on the class average which kills any spirit of enjoyment. The message (though surely not intended) seems to be that no matter how hard you work—so long as everyone else works as hard or has more talent or experience—you *cannot* improve your grade.

Eric found the "sense of competition" in no way beneficial. "It automatically precludes any desire to work with or to help other people," he wrote. "Suddenly your classmates are your enemies." No wonder the class was not "fun," and there was so much hostility between students.

30   My class is full of intellectual warriors who will some day hold jobs in technologically-based companies where they will be assigned to teams or groups in order to collectively work on projects. [But] these people will have had no training in working collectively. In fact, their experience will have taught them to fear cooperation, and that another person's intellectual achievement will be detrimental to their own.[9]

Still, he was impressed with his fellow students. Although the class continued to look "tired and bored" to him, he noticed that they "stick with it." He found there to be a "much more practical attitude about this class" than he had experienced in hu-

---

[8]Eric did very well in the class. He never got the grade on his final exam but he averaged 92 during most of the course. See below for more of his comments about the examinations and the grading system used in his course.

[9]The issue of teamwork is a centerpiece of modern science. See Daryl Chubin et al, *Interdisciplinary Analysis and Research*, Lomond, 1986.

manities. People think "yes, this is dull, but I have to complete this course to get my degree or to get a good job."

> In my literature classes it was much harder to rationalize this way. People took courses mainly because of interest in the topic or because they thought the professor would be good. It is not that a science course cannot be or isn't interesting, only that it's not required or expected by the students that it be so.

While some of the concepts were difficult for him and he continued to be bothered by the "constant qualifiers" such as "assume a frictionless surface," it was the pace of the course that he found "excessive, almost insane."[10]

> I usually give myself three hours for homework and never finish . . . I feel, though, that I have sufficient control of the subject matter [studying this way] to do well on the exams. Most of the other students I have talked to take six or seven hours a day to do the work. . . . Aside from the pure misery of devoting that much of your life to physics, I wonder how much they, or rather we, will retain. I think that a slower pace and more in-depth discussions of the contents would, in the end, prove [more] beneficial.

35   He found the time demanded to be considerably more than he ever spent in literature—three hours per course hour in physics versus two hours per course hour in literature. Moreover, as he wrote during the third week, "physics homework demands a more intense, highly active type of thought."

> Reading, however critically done, is a more reflective activity. There isn't the demand for almost instantaneous application of the information. The result of this difference is that two hours of physics is much more demanding and tiring than two hours even of [academic] reading.

The drawbacks of this amount of time spent may not be immediately apparent, he wrote. However,

> with my extra time [as an undergraduate majoring in literature], I was able to pursue many different and independent types of educational experiences. Some of this included designing and running my own course, and [when an upperclassman] writing a grant-supported research paper. The science student is more often than not limited to the struggle of just completing required work.

When Eric asked himself, midway in the course, "what makes science hard?" he came to a preliminary conclusion that students will perceive a course to be "hard" when it is: 1) difficult to get a good grade; 2) time consuming; or 3) boring, dull, or simply not fun. Physics he found to be all of the above. But why introductory physics should be thought of as "dull" intrigued him. He kept coming back to the lack of community and the lecture format.

---

[10]The professor himself admitted that the pace was "preposterous." Mindful that a summer school course is not typical, we continued the experiment with semester-long courses in the following fall. See *infra*.

40   The lack of community, together with the lack of interchange between the professor and the students combines to produce a totally passive classroom experience. . . . The best classes I had were classes in which I was constantly engaged, constantly questioning and pushing the limits of the subject and myself. The way this course is organized accounts for the lack of student involvement. . . . The students are given premasticated information simply to mimic and apply to problems. Let them, rather, be exposed to conceptual problems, try to find solutions to them on their own, and then help them to understand the mistakes they make along the way.

But the concepts weren't easy and sometimes they didn't get cleared up at all.

For some reason I am unable or secretly unwilling to complete these statics problems. Nothing seems to make sense and for the first time since my initial anxiety attack, I feel a cloud of bewilderment around my head. . . . Tomorrow will give me a good opportunity, however, to see what venues are open to a student who is "lost." I will try buying a solution sheet and see if the problems make sense. If they still don't, I will go to office hours, an activity I've always hated. Someone who is clever will always get by; but what of someone who isn't? Is the measure of a course how much a bright student learns or how much someone who is "lost" can be made to comprehend?

Getting help was not easy for Eric or, he thought, for the others, despite the small size of the summer school class.

If you find you do not understand something from the last chapter, you must wait until after class to see either the professor or the teaching assistant. The professor's office hour is busy and there is not much time for in-depth help. The teaching assistant, while well-meaning, has problems communicating in English, and is only around on certain days of the week. Even if you start to feel that you understand, you are faced with the task of the next chapter's homework, so you really can't afford the luxury of spending yet another evening tackling the same problems.

45   As he lost some of his footing, Eric noted that it was much harder to "cram" for physics than for literature; hence it was not possible, as undergraduates are wont to do, to let the class "go" for a few days while he concentrated on something else.
The "best class" in Eric's view was one where the professor brought in five or six demonstrations, the results of which were counterintuitive, and then asked the class to speculate as to why specific results occurred. In this class, there was substantial interchange. It led Eric to wonder whether a class could be designed that was "half lab, half lecture." But even more, he longed for study groups, arranged by the instructor for the class.

The homework problems are hard and take an enormous amount of energy and patience. I think working together might engender an attitude that problems are enjoyable exercises . . . rather than aggravating stumbling blocks.

Worse yet, on any given day, the class worked on three separate chapters at once.

Take June 13 for example. On this day, the professor answered questions on the homework problems from chapter 6, did some sample problems from chapter 7, gave us a quiz on the material from chapter 6, did some demonstrations pertaining to chapter 7, and began to lecture on chapter 8.

50   A consequence of the fact that students did their work "in private," Eric thought, was the absence of any opportunity for them to *talk* about the physics they were studying. They seemed inhibited, he observed, even about asking questions. Eric continued to do well on the exams and quizzes and was always surprised, even "shocked" at how low the class average tended to be.

What this means is that there are a good many confused people sitting quietly and not asking questions. This is always the case to some extent in college, but physics seems harder on these people than the humanities. So much is based on what you should have learned the day before, that the course is a bit like a race where if you falter and don't immediately recover, you are sure to go down and be trampled.

The lack of "discussion" continued to fascinate and to bother Eric. He found that when he asked his classmates about what they were studying, they weren't able to "articulate an answer."

I wonder if this is because they lack communication skills or because they haven't yet had the time to reflect on what they have learned, or perhaps because they don't really *know* much about their subject—if knowledge is defined to mean a deep, thoughtful understanding, rather than a superficial ability to regurgitate formulas.

One possible explanation might have been that in a course where answers are so critical, there is an inordinate fear of "making mistakes."

55   One of the most frustrating things about the class is that the material comes so quickly. Once you stop "making mistakes" and master one chapter, you must move on right away to the next. Almost by definition, you wind up with more wrong answers than right ones. Learning physics becomes a process of making fewer and fewer mistakes, and moving on. There is no time to enjoy the success, no time to use those skills in order to discover more or dig deeper.

Still Eric was able to go deeper. He began to ponder the differences between mathematics and physics.

Today I asked the professor why you figure *work* with a dot product. I got a different answer than I expected. Instead of talking about vectors and scalars, he talked about "what works." I realized that in physics, unlike math, you are much more concerned with getting real and usable figures than in the mathematical integrity of the operation. This is interesting because until this point, I did not really understand the difference between pure math and math as applied to science.

By the last week of class even the professor was "tired," or so he appeared to Eric. The class was but a shadow of what it had been. One-third of the students enrolled had either dropped out or were just not attending anymore. Eric noticed that the ratio of men to women, however, had remained about the same. The professor made numerous mistakes in explanation, and like everyone else, Eric thought, "just wants this class to be over." The "sudden shifts from particles to waves and then from waves to heat and temperature, without a pause, had everyone scrambling."

> There are no sad faces on this, the last day of class. No one will miss this chore. No one will say to himself or herself, "I really enjoyed that," or "that was an interesting learning experience." Instead, people will congratulate themselves on having made it, will be happy with their "B" or their "C," and will very soon forget anything pertaining to physics.[11]

60   For Eric, the final exam was a compressed version of everything that the course had and had not been, absent the "big picture." Eric had found all four exams in the class "biased toward computation and away from conceptual understanding." He understood that to be able to complete the computations required "some level of conceptual understanding." But that level was "not particularly high," he wrote.

> The problems [on exams] seldom required the use of more than one concept or physical principle. Only once were we asked to explain or comment on something rather than complete a calculation.

Eric thought the final, which was cumulative, would be the ". . . ideal place to tie things up and ask comparative and conceptual questions." Instead, he found that the questions entailed some fill-in-the-blanks definitions with terms found in a list. This caused him to reflect on the course more generally.

> We had marched through the chapters, doing the required work, but never digging deeper. . . . I was able to keep myself on track by concentrating on one chapter at a time. But I never really got the idea that the professor had any understanding of how the concepts were related, as he rarely tied together information from more than one chapter. His lectures did not seem to build upon each other, and he gave no indication of a linear movement through a group of concepts. . . . The final then asked the most primary basic questions about only the most important laws of physics. We were not required, at any time, to interrelate concepts or to try and understand the "bigger picture."

It was not that the connective tissue was unavailable to the instructor; it was simply not featured. From the beginning of the course, Eric had liked the textbook and felt he had learned best from it. His ability to read through it on his own contributed to his early success in mastering the course. He noticed right away that the daily homework included an approximately equal number of two very different kinds of questions. One

---

[11]Research by Hestenes et al confirms the failure of conventional physics instruction to overcome students' naive misconceptions about motion. Ibrahim Abou Halloun and David Hestenes, "The initial knowledge state of college physics students," and "Common sense concepts about motion," *Am. J. Phys.* 53 (11) Nov. 1985, p. 1043, ff.

kind, for Eric, were only "exercises" and were assigned as homework problems. At one point in his journal he described these as "mathematical in nature and varying in difficulty from easy to nearly impossible." The second kind of questions were of a more "complex, conceptual nature." This latter kind interested Eric very much, but

65   . . . [since] these questions were never even mentioned by the instructor after the first day, nobody ever bothered to look at them. I feel that the professor misjudged the value of these questions and missed an opportunity to use them as launching points for discussions of the concepts.

After the final exam, Eric wrote that for him "the greatest stumbling block to understanding" was the lack of identifiable goals and the absence of linkage between concepts. He noted these deficiencies in answering a question we had posed: what makes science hard in general and for students like Eric coming to these disciplines as outsiders? He wrote:

To some extent science is hard because it simply *is* hard. That is to say, the material to be learned involves a great many concepts, some of which are very counterintuitive. The process of mastering these concepts and being able to demonstrate a computational understanding of actual or theoretical situations requires a great deal of time and devotion. In my experience, this fact is well understood by the students, the professor and the general public. What is not as well understood are the various ways in which this already hard subject matter is made even harder and more frustrating by the pedagogy itself.

He feels that some "skeletal plan" would have helped him enormously to see how each individual property and theory is related to the "big picture." Comparing his introductory physics experience with that of the humanities, he wrote, "A professor who lectures on American literature of the 19th century might oversimplify the various social factors involved in each novel by referring to long-term historical events and trends, but at least his or her students would have some foundation on which to build impressions and judgments of the works."

The other "most difficult aspect" of the course for Eric was the "lack of student involvement" in lectures, and in discussion outside of class. Simply being "talked *at*" suited this particular literature student not at all. He attributed his classmates' inability to articulate their subject matter directly to the fact that they got no practice "talking physics" in class.

70   Finally, he concluded, the "pressure involved in grade wars" goes much too far. He leaves us with the following advice:

If one is truly interested in reforming physics education in particular and science education more generally, de-emphasizing numeric scales of achievement and rethinking the grading curve is certainly one place to start.

You are observing an academic discourse community in ways quite similar to what Eric was doing. But, unlike Eric, your position is also that of the researcher whose questions are guiding the study. After your first responses to Tobias's study of Eric's experience, you'll want to go back and reread it, approaching it both analytically and evaluatively from the perspective of a researcher.

READING RESPONSE

In reading analytically as a researcher, you'll want to ask the following questions:

- What is Tobias's purpose in conducting and reporting on this study?

- What has she chosen to include in this report from all of the data she has gathered? (From Eric's complete semester-long observation and reflection journal, for example).

- How has she organized and structured it? What are the main points she makes?

- In what ways does Tobias use Eric's observations to address what she wants to show about the *what*, the *why* and the *how* of his physics class?

- What sorts of comments does she make about his observations and reflections (which provide the data she's analyzing)? How is she using them as evidence, and what is she showing with them?

For an evaluative reading, you'll want to ask how well the study does these things:

- How well is its purpose and guiding question defined?

- Is it set up and structured in such a way that it can adequately address that purpose and question?

- Is the representation of Eric's observations sufficient to make the points that Tobias wants to make, and do you find her interpretation of those observations convincing?

- Do you find that her report provides a convincing representation of a discourse community as seen through a participant's eyes?

- Does it provide a convincing representation of some of the problems of introductory physics education to its potential readers (and who might those readers be)?

Do your analytical and evaluative readings of Tobias's study suggest any things you'll want to pay attention to in thinking about your own study?

SEEING FROM THE PERSPECTIVE OF A RESEARCHER

Eric's role in this study is to participate in the work of the course and to keep a detailed journal in which he records both his observations of what goes on in the class and his own experience and reflections. Eric is contributing to a study as a participant-observer, he's not the researcher who has designed the study, who has asked its guiding questions, or who has planned ways to carry it out. His position or stance is therefore different from your own. But imagine that Eric, rather than Tobias, was the researcher as well as the participant in this study.

Generating Questions

The working concepts of shared knowledge, ways, and purposes that we've been using can help us to make sense of what we see, through Eric's eyes, as he observes the context and the texts of his own classroom. He describes physics study in terms of the <u>what</u> of concepts like force and gravity and Newtonian mechanics but also in terms of textbook problems to be solved for homework. He describes <u>how</u> in this classroom as consisting of lectures in which the teacher defines terms and demonstrates how to do problems, of homework where students read chapters and solve the problems at the end, and of exams where more problems are solved. The answer to <u>why</u> the class is taught in this way eludes Eric, however. It seems to him that there might be other ways to introduce the study of physics, and he starts noticing *underlying values* that seem to stress doing problems the right way rather than exploring the thinking behind them or showing how they relate to larger questions about the physical world.

Many of Eric's own questions are related to the <u>why</u> of the work students are being asked to do in the course: why is there such an emphasis on doing the computation for problems and so little on working with the larger concepts these problems point to, for example. Others have to do with the apparent shared values that underlie the work in the course, with the implicit question of whether these are also the shared values of professionals in the discipline. Eric speculates a lot about the experiences and motivations of the other students, also suggesting possible questions. Finally, Eric keeps wondering about the big picture, wanting to know more about the sorts of understandings physicists are developing when they build on the foundations being introduced in this course, and those wonderings might lead him to topics he would want to research on his own, whether to follow upon areas the course introduced or to gain understandings his course hasn't offered him. Thinking about the questions that would help Eric shape a study of his own might help you to think about the questions that emerge from your academic setting.

RESEARCH MEMO 7.2

Take some time to generate a list of possible research questions. Think about what you are interested in relationship to this academic course and the field it introduces. Don't worry about answers to these questions or to how you could possibly find answers to these questions: think only about coming up with at least ten questions. These questions can come directly from your own experiences as a student in this class. (That is, if you have trouble on the exams given in this class, you may want to ask, "Why am I having trouble passing exams in this class?") Or your questions may be broader questions

(continued)

(*continued*)

about the discipline, like Vanessa's. Or they may lead beyond the classroom itself, like Juliette's, and they can guide your research in the library if you are following research strand B.

Then reflect on what prior knowledge you bring to this study. What do you have as background knowledge or experience in relationship to any of the questions you might decide to pursue? What do you know from your prior experience as a researcher—from carrying out a primary research study of a familiar discourse community, and/or from doing other secondary, library research that might be relevant to deciding what questions to pursue and how? What do you know from reading other studies of academic settings (such as Tobias's) about how researchers pursue their questions about these settings through field research? What do you know from reading other studies in the field you've focused on about the sorts of questions researchers ask and the ways in which they go about answering them?

What does this self-inventory suggest about the questions that interest you most and how you might go about trying to answer them?

Examining Course Materials

If you're doing a field study, the methods that were used for Tobias's study can also help you consider possible methods for your own. Tobias's primary method of gathering data was to have Eric keep a journal of his observations and experiences. In those observations he also considered the written materials of the course—the textbook, the assignments, the exams.

Much of the work of an academic discourse community goes on in writing, much of the significant context is set forth in writing. Therefore, the *artifacts of literacy* that you gather there (the various examples of written texts that are used in, produced in, or associated with the classroom community) are likely to be more important to your understanding of the assumed shared values and ways of that community than they were for your study of an informal discourse community.

Through Eric's journal and Tobias's comments, we can see how his physics course was taught, as well as various artifacts associated with its teaching. We learn, for example, that there's a "course handout" that describes various aspects of the course, including the procedures for assessment and grading. Other artifacts that affect the daily <u>how</u> of the course include a calculator, assignment sheets, the blackboard where problems are solved, and the text. The textbook is big (Eric comments on its weight); it has exercises that require working out solutions to problems that are assigned as homework, as well as questions of a "complex, conceptual nature" that aren't used in the course. There are homework assignments and exams (exams that seem to suggest that it's important to understand underlying concepts even though the focus of most of the course work is on working out the solution to problems). There are also (we learn from Tobias's comment about her conversation with the professor), "histograms" that show students the spread of exam grades and that lead them to think that they are being graded on a curve, even though the course handout says they're not. Even this indirect look at the various texts and artifacts named in association with this course indicates a lot about the context that frames Eric's experience.

As this study shows, several sorts of text are particularly important in setting the academic context of a course, and you may want to collect and analyze any or all of them.

- *Course descriptions.* The first of these is the catalog description for the course (which represents the official umbrella under which any specific offering of the course is framed and often the first information that a prospective participant finds about it). Sometimes there is a generic department description of a course, giving more information about the course and where it fits in a sequence (such as a general description of Freshman Writing I that says something about the sorts of writing students are expected to do there and how they relate to the work done in other courses in a sequence, such as Freshman Writing II). There's also the syllabus for a particular section of a course, which spells out how the more general focus and purpose of a course will be realized in the specific work of a specific classroom community.

  Much of the official information about courses will be available not only in a printed catalog but also on a college and/or department website, and often individual faculty will maintain course websites as well. Websites are playing an increasingly important role in framing the work that goes on within colleges and universities and within departments, as well as within the immediate communities of particular courses and classrooms. They constitute significant literacy artifacts that you may want to consider, as a researcher, for these contexts.

- *Required and recommended readings.* Such texts typically constitute a significant portion of the shared knowledge to be developed in a course. Seeing the larger framework they offer for the <u>what</u> of the course can help you, as a researcher, to understand more of what's going on in the specific classroom conversations in which students participate through speaking and writing. They may also suggest possible topics of interest for you to pursue in extending your library research.

- *Course assignments.* These frame many of the conversations that participants will be involved in. All assignments work to connect the formal <u>what</u> of the shared knowledge that the course represents to the specific <u>what</u> of the spoken and written conversations of participants, and they represent much of the <u>how</u> through which a larger, ongoing conversation is carried out. Looking at course assignments—at how they're framed, at what they focus on and what they call for, at how they're sequenced, and at how they're assessed—can help you, as a researcher, to see more about the ways in which participants' contributions to those conversations (including your own) are framed and the context in which those contributions will be evaluated.

Course assignments contribute a lot to Eric's understanding of the course and his response to it. Eric doesn't merely complete his homework and exam assignments, but uses them to analyze what is expected of him and valued in this course. Looking at the kinds of work that you are expected to do when completing assignments for your academic discourse community will give you a similar understanding of what is valued in that class (Look at Vanessa Ortega's study at the end of Part III to see what she discovered by analyzing her music assignments.)

RESEARCH MEMO 7.3	Examine the written materials associated with the course you are focusing on, including course descriptions in the catalog and syllabus, course readings, and course assignments, or choose one type to study closely. As you examine each artifact, make note of the significant details that contribute to your picture of the shared knowledge, shared purposes, and shared ways of this academic discourse community, what is valued there, and what shapes your own position in and response to it. What might each contribute to your further exploration of your guiding question? You'll want to quote from these materials in this response and you may want to draw from them when you prepare your final report. (To carry out a detailed analysis of one assignment and your response to it, turn to the exploratory essay at the end of this chapter.)

If there are other objects and artifacts that are important in this classroom setting (computers, pictures, laboratory equipment, etc.), you'll want to examine them in the same way.

The work you do for a particular written assignment for a course is situated within the framework of the larger assignment sequence, the textbook or course readings, the immediate framing created by the syllabus and the larger framing created by the catalog. You might try to create a vertical map of these elements from top to bottom, showing the what, why, and how that you find at each level and how they interconnect. Does the information you get at any level tell you anything useful in relationship to your initial research questions or guide you to new questions?

Once you've considered the various literacy artifacts that can tell you about the what, why, and how of your academic discourse community, decide which ones give the most useful picture of that community in relationship to the questions you want to explore. Write an extended response in which you discuss what that artifact or those artifacts show you in relationship to those questions, pointing to the details that you find most convincing. |

REFLECTING BACK ON PERSONAL EXPERIENCES AS A STUDENT

From a personal perspective, Eric tries to make sense of how this physics course works for him as a student in several ways:

- Reflecting on the larger understanding he's gotten of the <u>what</u>, <u>why</u>, and <u>how</u> of the academic discipline the course introduces—of the big picture of this academic discourse community. Eric feels that he has gained only a limited perspective on the discipline: "Simply by intuition, I know physics, and more generally science, to involve creativity and finesse; but this man makes it into a craft, like cooking, where if someone follows the recipe, he or she will do well" (p. 353). He hasn't gotten to see any of the creative thinking that physicists might do.

- Comparing the <u>how</u> of the course to other courses to see what he values as a learner. Eric compares what goes on in his physics course to what he's used to from his courses in literature and the humanities, either explicitly or implicitly: "I still get the feeling that unlike a humanities course, here the professor is the keeper of the information, the one who knows all the answers. This does little to propagate discussion or dissent" (p. 354).

- Considering what sort of community the introductory courses in this discipline seem to offer. Eric might be very interested in the work that physicists do as they work, usually collaboratively, to explore ways of understanding the physical universe, but what he's found in the entry hall to that academic community is a different sort of discourse community—one where there's really only one voice, that of the teacher (and the textbook), one way to proceed, and where "this already hard subject matter is made even harder and more frustrating by the pedagogy itself" (p. 361).

- Assessing his own capacity to do work in this discipline, in the way in which it is most typically structured (and ways of altering or adding to those structures). In the process of his participant-observation, Eric has learned that he's not "too dumb" to learn physics. He's figured out some strategies for doing the work of the course, and he's also gained a critical perspective about how teaching and learning may work more effectively for him and for others like him. If he wanted to continue in physics, he might take what he has learned from this experience to try to alter his future experiences. Knowing that he needs to have a chance to talk and write about what he's learning, he might try to form a study group and/or an e-mail discussion group. Knowing that it matters to him to have a sense of the big picture, he might ask his professor for other readings that would give more of that picture. He might also try to talk to students in upper level courses and visit a laboratory section to see if some of the talk and creativity and community that he misses so much in this introductory course is present later—to see if there's something worth waiting for from the perspective of what he values. And since many professors are trying more hands-on ways of teaching introductory physics, he might find another class with a different orientation.

■ Reflecting on the underlying shared values of a course and a discipline in relationship to his own values as a learner and thinker. One big issue that has emerged for Eric is his own dislike of what he characterizes as an unnecessarily competitive classroom environment. While other students might thrive on competition, Eric feels that it hinders his own learning. He could use that concern as a focus of his further explorations—learning more about how physicists work and the extent to which competitive versus cooperative values underlie that work. On the other hand, Eric's inquiry might reaffirm his sense that things he most values as a learner are represented in his study of the humanities and confirm his understanding that he has chosen the direction that will give him the most satisfaction.

How are you making sense of your own position in the academic discourse community you are studying?

REFLECTIVE INQUIRY

Reflect on what you're learning thus far about your own personal positioning in the course you're focusing on for your study of an academic discourse community. Draw on the strategies that Eric uses to reflect on his own positioning in the study of physics in relationship to his introductory course to reflect on your position in relationship to the course and the field you are researching and to write your own, informal "____ Experiment."

■ Reflect on the larger understandings you've gotten so far of the <u>what</u>, <u>why</u>, and <u>how</u> of the academic discipline the course introduces—of the big picture of this academic discourse community.

■ Compare the <u>how</u> of the course to other courses you've taken to see what you value as a learner.

■ Consider what sort of community the introductory courses in this discipline seem to offer you.

■ Assess your own capacity to do work in this discipline, in the way in which it is most typically structured (and possible ways in which you can alter how you work with those structures).

■ Reflect on the underlying shared values of a course and a discipline in relationship to your own values as a learner and thinker.

What understandings do you come to about the fit between your purposes, interests, values and those that are represented in the course and (possibly) in the discipline? If you're preparing to write a library research paper, how do these understandings guide you as you decide on the topic and question you'll pursue?

Matt, who imagined the scale of insiderness, didn't find much open discussion or communication among students in his history class either, but he did get a bigger picture of the field and of how the work of the classroom relates to it:

> The classroom provides the facts of what is already known. The field of history takes that knowledge a step further. It involves reading the works of others, considering where there could be new knowledge to be discovered or where there is incorrect information, and writing in order to formulate new ideas. This can change how the world sees the past and make us understand the present.

And he found that even without much classroom community, the required research papers gave him a chance to find out a little bit of what doing history is like.

> From doing these papers I gained knowledge on how the academic community of historians functions and communicates through written works. I, myself, even became a small part of this process of researching, thinking, and writing these papers. My papers may not have equaled that of a professional, but I understand how new knowledge can be attained and shared when it comes to history or any subject for that matter. It comes with time and effort.

In Matt's experience, unlike Eric's, it's "how much interest and time given to the course [that] determines how much of an insider you are." What is your experience?

WRITING IN ACADEMIC GENRES: THE PERSUASIVE ESSAY

A common academic genre is the *persuasive essay*, one where you try to persuade your readers to think about something in a particular way. In writing a persuasive essay about the work of the course you are studying, you'll want to decide on the audience you'll write for (your professor, your classmates, your parents, other students who might take this course) and the position on a particular assignment or your work in response to it that you want them to hold. Then you'll decide what points you want to make and how you'll use the evidence from your analysis to persuade them to hold this view. What would be most convincing in showing whatever you want to show about this course and the work you're doing for it?

As with all exploratory essays, you'll probably want to discuss the genre of the persuasive essay and the expectations that others in your writing community have for this genre.

EVALUATING A COURSE ASSIGNMENT

Look at one written assignment (either an informal homework assignment or one for a test or essay) that you've completed for the academic course you are studying and make a case persuading your reader of the value or the lack of value of this assignment in relationship to your own goals and or those of the course.

You'll want to describe the assignment you are analyzing:

- What was the prompt for this assignment?
- What was its purpose?
- What kinds of questions were asked?
- What did you have to do to complete it in a satisfactory way or to receive a high grade?
- Were there criteria or rubrics for what should be included in the assignment and how it would be evaluated?

You might also ask yourself: What does this assignment show about what's valued in this course and in this discipline? About the kinds of work students are expected to do and how? What does this assignment tell you about the kinds of work people in this field do (if you think it does relate to what people do in this field)?

Then look at your own response to the assignment:

- How did you approach this assignment?
- What strategies and insider understanding did you use to complete your work?
- Did you feel as if the work of the course up to that point had prepared you for it? (How did you do on this assignment?)
- Did you receive feedback that helped you to see the ways in which you had met the goals of the assignment or, if you didn't, what you should do differently with the next assignment?
- Do you feel as if the assignment and your performance on it represented fairly the knowledge you've gained from the class?
- Did the grade or comments you received for the assignment tell you anything about what is valued in this class?
- Can you make any comments about your level of insider/outsiderness to this class in light of the responses you received on this assignment?

When you've examined both the assignment and your response to it, decide what evidence you'll use to support the points you want to make to persuade your readers about whether or not this assignment is a valuable and appropriate one for the course and/or for your own learning.

If you're following research strand B and working toward producing a library research paper, you might use your analysis of an assignment to guide you in that work. Does your interest in this assignment suggest more about the sorts of questions you might pursue and how you might go about them? Does the sort of work you were asked to do in this assignment prepare you for reading the sorts of books and articles that will be relevant to the question you might pursue? Does this assignment tell you about the ways of the discipline and what's valued there that suggests a direction for your own research?

8

Analyzing Classroom Conversations

Chapter 8 focuses on academic courses, specifically, how they are shaped by disciplines, and what student participants bring to them. We'll read the work of another researcher, Mike Rose, who has studied some of the characteristics of introductory courses and how connections are made or not made between the shared knowledge of a discipline and the prior knowledge and expectations of learners entering those disciplines.

As you continue your study of an academic discourse community, you'll look more closely at an actual classroom moment in the discipline—a typical conversation. You'll see how the shared knowledge, purposes, and ways of the discipline are represented in the various materials you're analyzing for the course you're focusing on. We'll also consider how you can reposition yourself to become more of an insider to the conversations of the classroom and the discipline it represents.

If you are following Research Strand A, the Research Memos in this chapter will contribute directly to your final study. If you are following Research Strand B, Chapter 8 will help you see how the topic you're exploring can be located within the larger interests, concerns, and perspectives of an area of study, and how you'll want to direct your study to place it (and yourself) within a larger conversation in your field of interest.

We'll address the following questions:

- What can we see in the classroom moments that connect learners with the shared knowledge of the disciplines they are studying? What do learners bring to such moments?

- What assumed shared understandings of academic discourse communities are reflected in moments like these and the courses they represent?

- How can you find a space in the work of introductory courses that lets you make connections between your own prior knowledge and experience and the larger field of knowledge represented by the discipline? What strategies can you draw on to reposition yourself as a learner and to place yourself in the conversation invited by this discipline, even as you take on a critical perspective?

We saw in the last chapter that one of Eric's complaints as a newcomer to physics was that he wasn't able to get "the big picture" of physics as a field through this introductory course. Eric's worry about getting the big picture is one students often feel as they begin to study a new academic discipline. They're still partly outsiders to the new community and often find it hard, in the day-to-day conversations of the classroom, to see the shared <u>what</u>, <u>why</u>, and <u>how</u> that connects the pieces of what's done there. It's a concern that other researchers who have looked at the experiences of first-year college students have identified as well.

Remember Mike Rose, whose memoir of moving between a vocational and an academic track in high school was included at the end of Part I? With the help of some supportive teachers, Rose gradually became an insider to academic work and went on to teach at UCLA and do research in composition studies. In *Lives on the Boundary*, Rose describes what the insider world of academic settings looks like to outsiders: students who suddenly find that they don't fully understand what's going on in a new academic setting that they've entered. As a teacher, Rose tried to understand what his students were experiencing and find ways to help them with all of their studies. As a researcher, Rose kept records of the conversations he had with students, analyzed the materials of the courses they were taking, observed some of their classes, and collected the writing they produced. Much of his study takes the form of reflective inquiry of the sort you've been doing; he brings together many different moments in his own experience as a teacher to discover more about the big picture of what's involved for students who are trying to become insiders to the academic work of their courses.

OBSERVING A CLASSROOM MOMENT

Rose begins a chapter on the academic experiences of a number of UCLA students by imagining a typical moment in a lecture hall for an Introductory Sociology course.

> The students are taking their seats in the large auditorium, moving in two streams down the main aisles, entering from a side exit to capture seats in the front. You're a few minutes late and find a seat somewhere in the middle. There are a couple of hundred students around you and in front of you, a hundred or so behind. A youngish man walks onto the stage and lays a folder and a book on the podium. There are track lights above him, and in back of him there's a system of huge blackboards that rise and descend on rollers in the wall. The man begins talking. He raises his voice and taps the podium and sweeps his hand through the air. Occasionally, he'll turn to the moving boards and write out a phrase or someone's name or a reference to a section of the textbook. You begin writing these things down. He has a beard and smiles now and then and seems wrapped up in what he's talking about.
>
> This is Introductory Sociology. It's one of the courses students can elect to fulfill their general education requirements. The catalogue said that Introductory

Sociology would deal with "the characteristics of social life" and "the processes of social interaction." It also said that the course would cover the "tools of socio-logical investigation," but that came last and was kind of general and didn't seem too important. You're curious about what it is that makes people tick and curious, as well, about the causes of social problems, so a course on social interaction sounded interesting. You filled Sociology 1 in on some cards and sent them out and eventually got other cards back that told you you were enrolled.

"These are the social facts that are reflected in the interpretations we make of them," says the man on the stage and then extends his open hand toward the audience. "Now, this is not the place to rehearse the arguments between Kantian idealists and Lockean realists, but . . . " You're still writing down, ". . . reflected in the interpretations we make of them . . . ," and he continues: "But let us stop for a moment and consider what it means to say 'social fact.' What is a fact? And in considering this question, we are drawn into hermeneutics." He turns to write that last word on the board, and as he writes you copy it down in your notes. He refers the class to the textbook, to a "controlling metaphor" and to "microanalyses"—and as you're writing this down, you hear him stressing "constructivist interpretations" and reading a quotation from somebody and concluding that "in the ambiguity lies the richness."

People are taking notes and you are taking notes. You are taking notes on a lecture you don't understand. You get a phrase, a sentence, then the next loses you. It's as though you're hearing a conversation in a crowd or from another room—out of phase, muted. The man on the stage concludes his lecture and everyone rustles and you close your notebook and prepare to leave. You feel a little strange. Maybe tomorrow this stuff will clear up. Maybe by tomorrow this will be easier. But by the time you're in the hallway, you don't think it will be easier at all.

Rose first captures the situation—the setting, the movement and placement of the participants in that setting, and then some typical examples of the discourse of the setting. This course, like many introductory courses, is offered in the *speech genre* of the *academic lecture*, one in which students' participation in the conversation is typically limited to taking notes and perhaps asking questions. The way Rose has portrayed this setting suggests a great deal about what will go on there, but it also suggests something about the issues Rose will explore in this chapter.

Juliette, who is doing library research on the topic of women in science, is guided by her question about women's representation in scientific fields as she carries out her own observations of her introductory biology course.

Class itself is a lecture in a large auditorium. Brian is a great speaker, and he is eloquent in explaining the ideas in each lecture. After he makes each point, he stops and asks for questions from the class, and these are abundant. He is endlessly patient. The class is about 75 students, and it is evenly divided between men and women, supporting my hypothesis that the gender divide between males and females in science is narrowing. Furthermore, my T.A. (teaching assistant for my lab) is a woman, and my Bio 111 T.A. was also.

RESEARCH MEMO 8.1	Look back at the details of Rose's description of the setting for this introductory lecture. Then observe the classroom you've chosen to study, recording as many details of that setting as possible.

- How is the actual classroom structured?
- How many students are in the class?
- Where do students typically sit?
- What does your professor do during class?

Think about the connections between the larger questions that have led you to focus on this particular discourse community or the topic you've chosen for a research paper and what you observe in this setting. Then use a description of a typical moment in this classroom setting, as Rose does, to characterize this academic discourse community.

Rose is particularly interested not only in the <u>how</u> of this typical example of classroom discourse, but in the <u>what</u>. He pays particular attention to the words that are said—the key concepts and significant terms that insiders to the discipline and to the academic world know and use. And he imagines what learners who are not yet insiders might make of such a conversation.

What do you make of this classroom conversation? What does it include and what does it seem to mean from the perspective of Rose's imaginary student? If you haven't taken a sociology course, you may have only a somewhat vague sense of what sociologists might mean by "the processes of social interaction," or the "tools of sociological investigation." And the references to Kantian idealists and Lockean realists may go right by you if you haven't studied philosophy.

Rose probably wants his readers (many of them teachers themselves) to feel a little uncomfortable with these references, a little uncertain about what's meant by terms like "hermeneutics," "controlling metaphor," "constructivist interpretations" in this context. He wants them to imagine how their students might feel when confronted by terms and references that they're assumed to know but don't. If being a literate insider to a community involves knowing <u>what</u>'s talked about and <u>why</u> people talk about it, as well as <u>how</u> to talk about it in the usual ways for this setting, then not being clear about the meanings of terms can leave even the most educated readers feeling somewhat illiterate— somewhat uncertain about whether they can fully make sense of what they're reading or hearing.

Rose has recreated the typical moment in a typical sociology class from his own observations and from his conversations with students about many such classes. But we can also look at a transcript of an actual classroom exchange to see how it connects learners and the discipline.

Here's a moment in an introductory sociology class captured by Sophia, a student researcher.

The subject we are covering at this moment is religion. . . . For the introduction of this chapter, the professor asked a question to the class. The question was, "How does sociology talk about the belief system?" Later, she mentioned two major sociological perspectives, functional theory and conflict theory, relating to this topic. Several hands went up rapidly and students were enthusiastic to answer that question. There were interesting but different answers.

> STUDENT 1: I think that religion supports the functional theory. It provides for spiritual needs.
>
> STUDENT 2: Gives hope to people. That might be good for society.
>
> STUDENT 3: The religion keeps the community tight.
>
> STUDENT 4: Marx is right. All contributions of churches go to pastors. They teach people to contribute because that is part of their reverence to God, but the church's pastors were the most rich in town.
>
> STUDENT 5: I don't like the statement that religion makes people live in peace, because if we study history, many wars were caused by different religions.

While students were making comments, other students listened to them carefully and they tried to look at the face of the students who were speaking. The professor also listened to them carefully, and she had eye contact with the student who is making the comment. Then she repeated their main points and mentioned whether she agreed or disagreed. Later, she related students' thoughts to the different social perspectives.

We can see that at this class session, midway through the semester, many students are contributing to the <u>what</u> of the conversation, to the developing shared knowledge in this classroom (even though this class is taught in large lecture format). Sophia has captured both the content of the exchange and the ways in which one student's contribution adds to another, building what Sophia calls "an exciting debate." We'll see what Sophia says about some of the content of that debate below.

RESEARCH MEMO 8.2

To better understand what goes on in your academic setting, record and analyze a moment of classroom discourse. Tape record a class session (with permission) and transcribe a small portion, or take detailed notes in your observation notebook in which you try to capture as much as possible of what's said and by whom.

You'll want to locate this classroom moment and create the shared knowledge outsiders would need to understand what's going on (what the course is, what the discussion is about, who the participants are, how this classroom speech event is structured—as a lecture, a discussion, group work, combination, etc., and how people are sitting as they take part in it).   *(continued)*

(continued)

You'll want to see <u>what</u> is being talked about and how it links to a larger area of shared knowledge of the discipline/of the course. What assumed shared knowledge lies behind this classroom moment and what is being added, built on here?

You'll want to look at <u>how</u> these things are being talked about. Who gets to introduce topics—students, teacher, and/or particular students? How do people take turns? In what ways are students' comments responded to?

You'll want to figure out <u>why</u> these things are being talked about, and why they're talked about in these ways. What seem to be the larger purposes of the discipline? Of the course? The immediate purposes of the teacher? Of the students? And how does what's going on in this moment seem to meet/not meet those purposes?

Look at and gloss your notes or transcript, thinking your way through these questions, and seeing if you can connect what you're observing here with the larger questions you have about the class/the course/the field. Try to characterize this classroom and your own role in it or your response to it as insider, outsider, or somewhere in-between. Then, as you write up your analysis, pull out the elements of what, why, and how that contribute to what you want to show about it (quoting examples from your transcript or notes).

DRAWING ON A READING

What Learners Bring

The learners who enter the lecture hall for Introductory Sociology bring prior understandings and experiences that may help them to make sense of the conversation that's going on there. But unlike small private conversations, where, if people are talking about a particular music group, someone is likely to turn to you to ask if you've heard them or to tell you what their music is like in terms that will be familiar to you, large classroom conversations don't always make connections between the prior knowledge of individual participants and the shared knowledge of the classroom in explicit ways.

Rose is interested in learners, particularly those who haven't come from mainstream backgrounds, and in how they're *positioned*—in whether they're put into the position of being not prepared enough for their college courses, or too "dumb" for courses in certain disciplines like physics, for example, and how that happens. In his own experience, concerned teachers helped him reposition himself academically after he spent much of his high school time in a vocational track. He knows that the ways in which learners are positioned in academic settings often have little to do with their academic ability, and that these positions can be changed as learners start to think in insider ways about their studies.

Rose's focus is on students who have sought help through UCLA's tutoring center. These are good students who have been admitted to a major university but who nevertheless are getting lost in one or another of their courses, and he offers a sampling of their experiences with different courses in different academic disciplines. The experience of feeling like an outsider in a course is familiar to most students in one or another area of their education, whether or not they seek help from a tutoring center. Rose wants to understand why the experience of miscommunication within in the larger conversations of academic courses is so common. He also questions whether this concern should be addressed only through "remedial" structures like a tutoring center, so he calls this chapter "The Politics of Remediation." We'll come back to the implications of that title later in this chapter.

As you read about Andrea, James, Marita, Denise, and Lucia, see what you can learn about their experiences, expectations and understandings. Try to identify the kinds of things they know and that they need to know about how to place themselves in the academic conversations of the courses they're entering, and what they need to understand about the shared knowledge and shared purposes that underlie such conversations.

Throughout this chapter, Rose continues to use the sorts of terms and references that his students have encountered in courses, without offering explanations or definitions. Each of the fields his students are struggling with has its own <u>what</u>, and outsiders to that field may struggle too. As you read, you may want to gloss the text or keep a list of the terms you're uncertain about—and you may want to work through your lists with classmates who are enrolled in some of the courses Rose discusses. But having his readers understand what outsiderness feels like—even for strong, literate students—is part of Rose's point, and in this case you can get that point, even without getting some of the specific references.

Our purpose in reading Rose's account is to facilitate your own inquiry into these very matters, within your own experience of one of your own academic discourse communities. So you'll also want to read Rose's text while considering your own data, seeing where each helps to shed light on the other. We'll draw on Rose's chapter to expand our thinking about learners and what they bring, and then about the nature of the conversations that go on in the academic discourse communities they are entering.

Read and gloss the rest of Rose's chapter. Look in particular for places where Rose's discussion gives you a picture of what these students bring to their courses and what's involved for each of these students as they try to gain:

READING RESPONSE

- Shared knowledge of the discipline and of what's assumed to be general academic knowledge.

- Shared purpose: a sense of what the field is trying to focus on, to understand, and why.

- A shared sense of how to participate in the field's conversations, to do what insiders ("A" students, more advanced students) do.

(continued)

(*continued*)
Then focus on one of the learners whose experience with a course particularly interests you. Please select some quotations that resonate for you from your glossing of this reading and write about what they show you about these aspects of the learner's academic experience. You may also want to recall a similar aspect of your own experience, relate these experiences, or reframe them from a broader perspective.

The Politics of Remediation

Mike Rose

1   The huge lecture halls, the distance from the professor, the streams of students you don't know. One of the tasks facing all freshmen is to figure out ways to counter this loneliness. Some will eventually feel the loneliness as passage, as the rending of the familiar that is part of coming of age. The solitude of vast libraries and unfamiliar corridors will transform into college folklore, the bittersweet tales told about leaving home, about the crises of becoming adult. But a much deeper sense of Isolation comes if the loneliness you feel is rooted in the books and lectures that surround you, in the very language of the place. You are finally sitting in the lecture hall you have been preparing to sit in for years. You have been the good student, perhaps even the star—you are to be the engineer, the lawyer, the doctor. Your parents have knocked themselves out for you. And you can't get what some man is saying in an *introductory* course. You're not what you thought you were. The alien voice of the lecturer is telling you that something central to your being is, after all, a wish spun in the night, a ruse, the mist and vapor of sleep.

I had seen Andrea before, but this time she was limping. Her backpack was stretched with books. Her collar and pleats were pressed, and there was a perfect white ribbon in her hair. She had been secretary of her high school and a gymnast, belonged to the Biology Club, and worked on the annual. Her father was a bell captain at a hotel in Beverly Hills; her mother a seamstress. They immigrated when Andrea was five, and when they were alone at home, they spoke Japanese. Andrea was fluently bilingual. She graduated fifteenth in a class of five hundred. She came to UCLA with good grades, strong letters, and an interest in science. She had not been eating well since she'd been here. The doctors told her she was making herself anemic. A week before, she had passed out while she was driving and hit a tree on a sidewalk near her home. Her backpack must have weighed twenty pounds.

All colleges have their killer courses, courses meant to screen students from science or engineering or those departments in arts and humanities that aren't desperate for enrollments. At UCLA the most infamous killer course is Chemistry 11-A, General Chemistry. The course is difficult for lots of reasons, but the primary one is that it requires students not just to understand and remember individual facts, formulas, and operations but to use them to solve problems, to recognize what kind of problem a particular teaser is and to combine and recombine facts, formulas, and operations to solve it. Andrea failed the midterm. Her tutor explained that she didn't seem to have much experience solving chemistry problems. Andrea would sit before her book for hours evening after evening, highlighting long stretches of text with a yellow marker, sketching the structure of benzene and butadiene, writing down Avogadro's law and Dalton's law, repeating to herself the differences between ionic and covalent bonds. The midterm exam hit her like a blind punch. It didn't require her to dump her memory. It gave her a short list of problems and asked her to solve them.

Andrea felt tremendous pressure to succeed, to continue to be all things to all people. She was speaking so softly I had to lean toward her. She said she was scared. Her cheek was still bruised from the accident. She missed a week of school then, and as she spoke, I had the sudden, chilling recognition that further injuries could save her, that deliverance could come in the form of another crash. I began talking to her about counseling, how helpful it can be to have someone to talk to, how I'd done it myself, how hard the sciences are for so many of us, how we all need someone to lean on. She looked up at me, and said in a voice drifting back somewhere toward childhood, "You know, I wish you had known me in high school."

5   James had a different reaction to failure.

He sat in my office and repeated that he was doing okay, that he'd been studying hard and would pull his grades up on his finals. "I've got my study skills perfected, and I am punctual about visiting the library." He paused and looked at his legs, placed his two hands palms down on his thighs, and then he pressed. "I will make it. My confidence was down before." James was on academic probation; he needed to pass all his courses or he would be what they called STD: subject to dismissal. "I've got the right attitude now. I took a motivation course over the break, and that helped me improve my study skills and get my priorities straight." He was looking right at me as he said all this: handsome, muscular, preppy. Dressed for success. Mechanical successfulness. I'm okay, you're okay. Jay Gatsby would have noted his poise and elocution. I sat there quietly listening, trying to decide what to do with his forced jock talk. I drifted a little, trying to conjure up the leader of James' "motivation seminar," the person delivering to him a few techniques and big promises: a way to skim a page or manage his time. James listened desperately and paid his money and went off with a positive attitude and his study skills perfected, emboldened with a set of gimmicks, holding a dream together with gum and string.

James's tutor suggested that he come see me because he was getting somewhere between a C and a D in his composition course and seemed increasingly unable to concentrate. His responses to the tutor's questions were getting vague and distracted. I asked James for his paper and could quickly see that he had spent time on it; it was typed and had been proofread. I read further and understood the C–; his essay missed the mark of the assignment, which required James to critically analyze a passage from John Berger's *Ways of Seeing*. What he did instead was summarize. This was something I had seen with students who lacked experience writing papers that required them to take an idea carefully apart. They approach the task in terms they can handle, retell the material to you, summarize it, demonstrate that, yes, they can understand the stuff, and here it is. Sometimes it is very hard to get them to see that summary is not adequate, for it had been adequate so many times before. What you have to do, then, is model step by step the kind of critical approach the paper requires. And that was what I started to do with James.

I asked him what he thought Berger's reason was for writing *Ways of Seeing*, and he gave me a pretty good answer. I asked another question, and for a brief while it seemed that he was with me. But then he stopped and said, "I should have gotten better than a C–. I think I deserve way higher than that." There it was. A brand. I said that I knew the grade was a disappointment, but if he'd stick with me he'd do better. He didn't say much more. He looked away. I had tacitly agreed with his teacher, so we were past discussing the paper: We were discussing his identity and his future. I work hard, he's really saying to me. I go to class. I read the book. I write the paper. Can't you see. I'm not a C–. Don't tell me I'm a C–. He was looking straight ahead past me at the wall. His hands were still on his legs.

* * *

When I was in the Teacher Corps, I saw daily the effects of background on schooling. Kids came into the schools with hand-me-down skirts and pants, they didn't have lunch money, they were failing. The connections between neighborhood and classroom were striking. This was true, though in different ways, with the veterans. The Tutorial Center also served low-income white and low- and middle-income minority students, but because the kind of students who make it to a place like UCLA enter with a long history of success and, to varying degrees, have removed superficial indicators of their lineage, it's harder, at first glance, to see how profoundly a single assignment or a whole academic career can be affected by background and social circumstance—by interactions of class, race, and gender. But as I settled into Campbell Hall, I saw illustrations continually, ones that complicated easy judgment and expectation.

10   Sometimes issues of economics and race were brought up by the students themselves. Such issues were also raised by the existence of the Ethnic Studies Centers, the perennial posters in the hallways, or the lobbying of older, politically active students, and they emerged in some of the students' classes. There was wide variation in the students' responses. Some had grown up watching their parents deal with insult, had heard slurs in their schools about skin color and family and language. A young woman writes in her placement exam for Freshman English:

> I could not go into the restroom, the cafeteria, or any place of the high school area alone, without having some girl following me and calling me names or pushing me around. Some of their favorite names for me were "wetback," "beaner," or "illegal alien." I did not pay much attention to the name calling, but when they started pulling my hair, pushing me, or throwing beans at me, I reacted.

Students like her were drawn to issues of race, read the walls of Campbell with understanding, saw connections between the messages on green paper and the hurt in their own past. They had been sensitized to exclusion as they were growing up.

But there were those who came to Campbell Hall with a different past and a different outlook. Some of those who grew up with the protections of middle-class life knew of the wrongs done to their people, but slavery and Nisei internment and agricultural camps seemed distant to them, something heard in their grandmothers' stories—a hazy film playing in an incomprehensible past. Their own coming of age had been shaped by their parents' hard-won assimilation, the irony of that achievement being an erasure of history for the children of the assimilated. These students had passed through a variety of social and religious clubs and organizations in which they saw people of their race exercise power. They felt at the center of things themselves, optimistic, forward-looking, the force of their own personal history leading them to expect an uncomplicated blending into campus life. I think that many of them were ambivalent about Campbell Hall—it was good to have the services, but they felt strange about being marked as different.

"Why are we reading this junk? This is just junk!" Denise was tapping the page and looking at me, then off across the room, then back at me. Underneath the light strikes of her finger was a passage her history professor had excerpted from the Lincoln-Douglas debates:

15   . . . there is a physical difference between the white and black races which I believe will forever forbid the two races living together on terms of social and political equality. And inasmuch as they cannot so live, while they do remain together there must be the position of superior and inferior, and I as much as any other man am in favor of having the superior position assigned to the white race.

"Yeah," I said, "Abraham Lincoln. Pretty upsetting, isn't it? Why do you think the professor gave it to the class?" "Well," she said, still angry, "that's not the point. The point is, why do we have to read stuff like this?" The week before, Denise and I had the following exchange. She had to write a paper for her composition class. It was built on an excerpt from Henry Roth's immigrant novel, *Call It Sleep*, and the assignment required her to write about the hardships current immigrants face. Our discussion worked its way around to attitudes, so I suggested to Denise that she write on the things she'd heard said about Hispanic immigrants in Southern California. She looked at me as though I'd whispered something obscene in her ear. "No!" she said emphatically, pulling back her head, "that's rude." "Rude," I said. "Explain to me what's—" She cut in. "You don't want to put that in a paper. That doesn't belong." Some things were better left unsaid. Decent people, Denise had learned, just don't say them. There is a life to lead, and it will be a good life. Put the stuff your grandmother lived and your father saw behind you. It belongs in the past. It need not be dredged up if we're to move on. And, in fact, Denise could not dredge it up—the flow of her writing stopped cold by an ugly historical text that was both confusing and painful for her to see.

* * *

The counselor's office was always dusky, the sun blocked by thick trees outside the windows. There was an oversize easy chair by his desk. In it sat Marita, thin, head down, hands in her lap, her shiny hair covering her face. The counselor spoke her name, and she looked up, her eyes red in the half-light. The counselor explained that the graduate student who taught her English had accused Marita of plagiarism and had turned her paper over to the director of Freshman English. He asked her to continue, to tell me the story herself.

Marita had been at UCLA for about three weeks. This was her first writing assignment. The class had read a discussion of creativity by Jacob Bronowski and were supposed to write papers agreeing or disagreeing with his discussion. What, Marita wondered, would she say? "What is the insight with which the scientist tries to see into nature?" asked Bronowski. Marita wasn't a scientist, and she didn't consider herself to be a particularly creative person, like an artist or an actress. Her father had always been absolute about the expression of opinion, especially with his daughters: "Don't talk unless you know." "All science is the search for unity in hidden likenesses," asserted Bronowski. "The world is full of fools who speak in ignorance," Marita's father would say, and Marita grew up cautious and reticent. Her thoughts on creativity seemed obvious or, worse yet, silly next to this man Bronowski. What did it mean anyway when he said: "We remake nature by the act of discovery, in the poem or in the theorem"? She wanted to do well on the assignment, so she went to the little library by her house and looked in the encyclopedia. She found an entry on creativity and used some selections from it that had to do with mathematicians and scientists. On the bottom of the last page of her paper, she listed the encyclopedia and her English composition textbook as her references. What had she done wrong? "They're saying I cheated. I didn't cheat." She paused and thought. "You're supposed to use other people, and I did, and I put the name of the book I used on the back of my paper."

20   The counselor handed me the paper. It was clear by the third sentence that the writing was not all hers. She had incorporated stretches of old encyclopedia prose into her paper and had quoted only some of it. I couldn't know if she had lifted directly or paraphrased the rest, but it was formal and dated and sprinkled with high-cultural references, just not what you'd find in freshman writing. I imagined that it had pleased her previous teachers that she cared enough about her work to go find sources, to rely on experts. Marita had come from a tough school in Compton—an area to the southeast of where I'd grown up—and her conscientiousness and diligence, her commitment to the academic way, must have been a great joy to those who taught her. She shifted, hoisting herself back up from the recesses of the counselor's chair. "Are they going to dismiss me? Are they going to kick me out of school?"

Marita was adrift in a set of conventions she didn't fully understand; she offended without knowing why. Virtually all the writing academics do is built on the writing of others. Every argument procedes from the texts of others. Marita was only partially initiated to how this works: She was still unsure as to how to weave quotations in with her own prose, how to mark the difference, how to cite whom she used, how to strike the proper balance between her writing and someone else's—how, in short, to position herself in an academic discussion.

I told Marita that I would talk with her teacher and that I was sure we could work something out, maybe another chance to write the paper. I excused myself and walked slowly back to my office, half lost in thought, reading here and there in the Bronowski excerpt. It was typical fare for Freshman English anthologies, the sort of essay you'd originally find in places like *The New Yorker*. Bronowski, the eminent scientist, looking back on his career, weaving poetry in with cybernetics, quoting *Faust* in German, allusive, learned, reflective.

The people who put together those freshman anthologies are drawn to this sort of thing: It's in the tradition of the English essay and reflects rich learning and polished style. But it's easy to forget how difficult these essays can be and how developed a taste they require. When I was at Loyola, someone recommended I buy Jacques Barzun's *The Energies of Art*, a collection of "fifteen striking essays on art and culture." I remember starting one essay and stopping, adrift, two or three pages later. Then another, but no go. The words arose from a depth of knowledge and a developed perception and a wealth of received ways to talk about art and a seemingly endless reserve of allusions. I felt like a janitor at a gallery opening, silent, intimidated, little flecks of knowledge—Bagehot, Stendhal, baroque ideology—sticking to the fiber of my broom.

Marita's assignment assumed a number of things: an ability to slip into Bronowski's discussion, a reserve of personal experiences that the writer herself would perceive as creative, a knowledge of and facility with—confidence with, really—the kinds of stylistic moves you'd find in those *New Yorker* essays. And it did *not* assume that someone, by family culture, by gender, would be reluctant to engage the reading on its own terms. Marita was being asked to write in a cognitive and social vacuum. I'm sure the other students in her class had a rough time of it as well. Many competent adult writers would too. But the solution Marita used marked her as an outsider and almost tripped the legal switches of the university.

* * *

25   At twenty-eight, Lucia was beginning her second quarter at UCLA. There weren't many people here like her. She was older, had a family, had transferred in from a community college. She represented a population that historically hadn't gained much entrance to places like this: the returning student, the single, working mother. She had a network of neighbors and relatives that provided child care. On this day, though, the cousin on tap had an appointment at Immigration, so Lucia brought her baby with her to her psychology tutorial. Her tutor had taken ill that morning, so rather than turn her away, the receptionist brought her in to me, for I had spoken with her before. Lucia held her baby through most of our session, the baby facing her, Lucia's leg moving rhythmically, continually—a soothing movement that rocked him into sleep.

Upon entrance to UCLA, Lucia declared a psychology major. She had completed all her preliminary requirements at her community college and now faced that same series of upper-division courses that I took when I abandoned graduate study in English some years before: Physiological Psychology, Learning, Perception . . . all that. She was currently enrolled in Abnormal Psychology, "the study of the dynamics and prevention of abnormal behavior." Her professor had begun the course with an intellectual curve ball. He required the class to read excerpts from Thomas Szasz's controversial *The Myth of Mental Illness*, a book that debunks the very notions underlying the traditional psychological study of abnormal behavior, a book that was proving very difficult for Lucia.

My previous encounter with Lucia had convinced me that she was an able student. She was conscientious about her studies—recopied notes, visited professors—and she enjoyed writing: she wrote poems in an old copy book and read popular novels, both in Spanish and English. But Szasz—Szasz was throwing her. She couldn't get through the twelve-and-a-half pages of introduction. I asked her to read some passages out loud and explain them to me as best she could. And as Lucia read and talked, it became clear to me that while she could, with some doing, pick her way through Szasz's sophisticated prose, certain elements of his argument, particular assumptions and allusions, were foreign to her—or, more precisely, a frame of mind or tradition or set of assumptions that was represented by a single word, phrase, or allusion was either unknown to her or clashed dramatically with frames of mind and traditions of her own.

Here are the first few lines of Szasz's introduction:

> Psychiatry is conventionally defined as a medical specialty concerned with the diagnosis and treatment of mental diseases. I submit that this definition, which is still widely accepted, places psychiatry in the company of alchemy and astrology and commits it to the category of pseudoscience. The reason for this is that there is no such thing as "mental illness."

One powerful reason Lucia had decided to major in psychology was that she wanted to help people like her brother, who had a psychotic break in his teens and had been in and out of hospitals since. She had lived with mental illness, had seen that look in her brother's eyes, felt drawn to help people whose mind had betrayed them. The assertion that there was no such thing as mental illness, that it was a myth, seemed incomprehensible to her. She had trouble even entertaining it as a hypothesis, and thus couldn't play out its resonances and implications in the pages that followed. Szasz's bold claim was a bone sticking in her assumptive craw.

30   Here's another passage alongside which she had placed a question mark:

> The conceptual scaffolding of medicine, however, rests on the principles of physics and chemistry, as indeed it should, for it has been, and continues to be, the task of medicine to study and if necessary to alter, the physiochemical structure and function of the human body. Yet the fact remains that human sign-using behavior does not lend itself to exploration and understanding in these terms. We thus remain shackled to the wrong conceptual framework and terminology.

To understand this passage, you need to have some orientation to the "semiotic" tenet that every human action potentially carries some kind of message, that everything we do can be read as a sign of more than itself. This has become an accepted notion in high-powered liberal studies, an inclination to see every action and object as a kind of language that requires interpretation. The notion and its implications—the conversation within which the phrase "sign-using" situates you—was foreign to Lucia. So it was difficult for her to see why Szasz was claiming that medicine was the "wrong conceptual framework" with which to study abnormal behavior.

Here's a third passage:

> Man thus creates a heavenly father and an imaginary replica of the protected childhood situation to replace the real or longed-for father and family. The differences between traditional religious doctrine, modern political historicism, and psychoanalytic orthodoxy thus lie mainly in the character of the "protectors": they are, respectively, God and the priests, the totalitarian leader and his apologists, and Freud and the psychoanalysts.

While Freud criticized revealed religion for the patent infantilism that it is, he ignored the social characteristics of closed societies and the psychological characteristics of their loyal supporters. He thus failed to see the religious character of the movement he himself was creating.

35   Lucia's working-class Catholicism made it difficult for her to go along with, to intellectually toy with, the comparison of Freud to God, but there was another problem here too, not unlike the problem she had with the "sign-using" passage. It is a standard move in liberal studies to find religious analogues to nonreligious behaviors, structures, and institutions. Lucia could certainly "decode" and rephrase a sentence like: "He thus failed to see the religious character of the movement he himself was creating," but she didn't have the background to appreciate what happens to Freud and psychoanalysis the moment Szasz makes his comparison, wasn't familiar with the wealth of conclusions that would follow from the analogy.

And so it went with other key passages. Students like Lucia are often thought to be poor readers or to have impoverished vocabularies (though Lucia speaks two languages); I've even heard students like her referred to as culturally illiterate (though she has absorbed two cultural heritages). It's true there were words Lucia didn't know (*alchemy, orthodoxy*) and sentences that took us two or three passes to untangle. But it seemed more fruitful to see Lucia's difficulties in understanding Szasz as having to do with her belief system and with her lack of familiarity with certain ongoing discussions in humanities and social science—with frames of mind, predispositions, and background knowledge. To help Lucia with her reading, then, I explained five or six central discussions that go on in liberal studies: the semiotic discussion, the sacred-profane discussion, the medical vs. social model discussion. While I did this, I was encouraging her to talk through opinions of her own that ran counter to these discussions. That was how she improved her reading of Szasz. The material the professor assigned that followed the introduction built systematically off it, so once Lucia was situated in that introduction, she had a framework to guide her through the long passages that followed, all of which elaborated those first twelve pages.

The baby pulled his face out of his mother's chest, yawned, squirmed, and turned to fix on me, wide-eyed. Lucia started packing up her books with a free hand. I had missed lunch. "Let's go," I said. "I'll walk out with you." Her movement distressed the baby, so Lucia soothed him with soft coos and clicks, stood up, and shifted him to her hip. We left Campbell Hall and headed southeast, me toward a sandwich, Lucia toward the buses that ran up and down Hilgard on UCLA's east boundary. It was a beautiful California day, and the jacarandas were in full purple bloom. Lucia talked about her baby's little discoveries, about a cousin who worried her, about her growing familiarity with this sprawling campus. "I'm beginning to know where things are," she said, pursing her lips. "You know, the other day some guy stopped me and asked *me* where Murphy Hall was . . . and I could tell him." She looked straight at me: "It felt pretty good!" We walked on like this, her dress hiked up where the baby rode her hip, her books in a bag slung over her shoulder, and I began to think about how many pieces had to fall into place each day in order for her to be a student: The baby couldn't wake up sick, no colic or rashes, the cousin or a neighbor had to be available to watch him, the three buses she took from East L.A. had to be on time—no accidents or breakdowns or strikes—for travel alone took up almost three hours of her school day. Only if all these pieces dropped in smooth alignment could her full attention shift to the complex and allusive prose of Thomas Szasz. "Man thus creates a heavenly father and an imaginary replica of the protected childhood situation to replace the real or longed-for father and family."

* * *

Remember Andrea? She was the distressed young woman who was failing chemistry. Andrea could memorize facts and formulas but not use them to solve problems—and her inability was representative of a whole class of difficulties experienced by freshmen. What young people come to define as intellectual competence—what it means to know things and use them—is shaped by their schooling. And what many students experience year after year is the exchange of one body of facts for another—an inert transmission, the delivery and redelivery of segmented and self-contained dates and formulas—and thus it is no surprise that they develop a restricted sense of how intellectual work is conducted. They are given Ancient History one year and American History the next, and once they've displayed knowledge of the Fertile Crescent and cuneiform and Assyrian military campaigns, there is little need for them to remember the material, little further opportunity to incorporate it, little reason to use these textbook facts to engage historical problems. Next year it will be American History: a new textbook, new dates and documents and campaigns, new tests—but the same rewards, and the same reasons to forget. John Dewey saw the difficulty long ago: "Only in education, never in the life of the farmer, sailor, merchant, physician, or laboratory experimenter, does knowledge mean primarily a store of information aloof from doing."

Students like Andrea are caught in a terrible bind. They come to the university with limited experience in applying knowledge, puzzling over solutions, solving problems. Many of the lower-division courses they encounter—their "general education" or "breadth" requirements—will involve little writing or speaking or application, will rely on so-called objective tests that, with limited exception, stress the recall of material rather than the reasoned elaboration of it. But the gatekeeper courses—the courses that determine entrance to a major—they up the intellectual ante. Courses like Andrea's bête noire, Chemistry 11-A, are placed like land mines in the uneven terrain of the freshman year. The special nature of their demands is not made the focus of attention that it should be; that is, the courses are not taught explicitly and self-consciously as courses on how to think as a chemist or a psychologist or a literary critic. And there are few opportunities for students to develop such ability before they enroll in those courses. The faculty, for the most part, do not provide freshmen with instruction on how to use knowledge creatively—and then penalize them when they cannot do so.

* * *

40   It is not unusual for students to come to the university with conceptualizations of disciplines that are out of sync with academic reality. Like the note taker in the lecture

hall who opened this chapter, a lot of entering freshmen assume that sociology is something akin to social work, an applied study of social problems rather than an attempt to abstract a theory about social interaction and organization. Likewise, some think psychology will be a discussion of human motivation and counseling, what it is that makes people do what they do—and some coverage of ways to change what they do. It comes as a surprise that their textbook has only one chapter on personality and psychotherapy—and a half dozen pages on Freud. The rest is animal studies, computer models of thought, lots of neurophysiology. If they like to read novels, and they elect a literature course, they'll expect to talk about characters and motive and plot, but instead they're asked to situate the novel amid the historical forces that shaped it, to examine rhetorical and stylistic devices and search the prose for things that mean more than they seem to mean. Political science should be politics and government and current events—nuclear treaties, trade sanctions, the Iran-Contra scandal—but instead it's Marx and Weber and political economy and organizational and decision-making models. And so goes the litany of misdirection. This dissonance between the academy's and the students' definitions of disciplines makes it hard for students to get their bearings with material: to know what's important, to see how the pieces fit together, to follow an argument, to have a sense of what can be passed over lightly. Thus I would see notebooks that were filled—in frantic script—with everything the professor said or that were scant and fragmented, records of information without coherence.

* * *

The discourse of academics is marked by terms and expressions that represent an elaborate set of shared concepts and orientations: alienation, authoritarian personality, the social construction of the self, determinism, hegemony, equilibrium, intentionality, recursion, reinforcement, and so on. This language weaves through so many lectures and textbooks, is integral to so many learned discussions, that it's easy to forget what a foreign language it can be. Freshmen are often puzzled by the talk they hear in their classrooms, but what's important to note here is that their problem is not simply one of limited vocabulary. If we see the problem as knowing or not knowing a list of words, as some quick-fix remedies suggest, then we'll force glossaries on students and miss the complexity of the issue. Take, for example, *authoritarian personality*. The average university freshman will know what *personality* means and can figure out *authoritarian*; the difficulty will come from a lack of familiarity with the conceptual resonances that *authoritarian personality* has acquired in the discussions of sociologists and psychologists and political scientists. Discussion . . . you could almost define a university education as an initiation into a variety of powerful ongoing discussions, an initiation that can occur only through the repeated use of a new language in the company of others. More than anything, this was the opportunity people like Father Albertson, my Shakespeare teacher at Loyola, provided to me. The more comfortable and skillful students become with this kind of influential talk, the more they will be included in further conversations and given access to further conceptual tools and resources—the acquisition of which virtually defines them as members of an intellectual community.

Each of the learners Rose studies brings different prior experience and understandings, but collectively, they bring a lot of prior educational experience. That experience may have given them an introduction to a particular discipline such as history or chemistry. It has taught them some necessary skills—learning facts, formulas and operations (Andrea), summarizing what they've read (James), drawing on secondary sources (Marita)—though they may not always know when these are appropriate responses and when other sorts of responses are required. They bring life experience and a personal history that may give them a perspective on the issues being explored in their courses but not always the stance from which the explorations are taking place (Denise). They bring value systems that may correspond with or conflict with the values and ways of seeing the world represented in their courses (Lucia). Finally, they bring experience with grading systems that have made them see themselves and their learning in terms of the grades they receive (James).

Learners bring experience and understandings that can contribute to but can also complicate their positions in specific academic discourse communities. As we've seen, the same sorts of discourse competence underlie our participation in conversations in all communities, but that competence is realized in very different ways in different communities. In entering new communities we always have to learn new ways if we want to become insiders.

The Ways of Academic Discourse Communities

What does Rose tell us about the new ways students he's studied need to learn in order to become insiders in their academic courses?

- Marita needs to know how to position herself in an academic discussion, to draw on what she reads while creating her own argument, and to bring the words of other writers into her own texts smoothly and appropriately (engaging in the sorts of conversations with texts that you've been doing with the readings in this book).

- James needs to be able not only to summarize what he reads but to analyze it and evaluate it—to engage in what's often termed *critical analysis* (skills you've been developing in analyzing how both written texts and the spoken texts of conversations work).

- Andrea needs not only to memorize facts and formulas but to know when and how to use them to solve problems.

- Denise needs to be able to step out of the framework of her own beliefs and values to see that different values shape ways of seeing the world (the sort of perspective you gain from studying different cultural settings).

- Finally, Lucia, in order to read the work of the psychologist Thomas Szasz, who challenges some of the shared beliefs and values of psychology, needs specific background knowledge from psychology. But she also needs an introduction to what Rose calls "frames of mind" and "predispositions, " and she needs to see how to deal with academic arguments that conflict with the understanding of the world that she's gained from her personal experience.

Embedded in Rose's discussion of the problems facing all of these students, but Lucia in particular, are several elements of <u>what</u> is talked about that are shared in most academic conversations. These elements are:

- their key concepts and terms (such as "sign-using" in the text Lucia is reading);
- their "frames of mind, traditions, and background knowledge," such as a long-standing debate about a "medical vs. social" model for explaining mental illness;
- an understanding not only of particular theories (like that of Freud) but of the place of theory in academic knowledge.

Each of these elements is relevant to your own study, whether it's a field study of an academic discourse community or a library report on a topic that insiders to such a community have studied. We'll look at each element in turn.

Key Concepts and Terms

Any entry-level course will attempt to build an understanding of a discipline's *key concepts*—the critical terms it uses in making sense of the aspect of the world being studied. These concepts might be seen as the field's vocabulary, but they are more than that. They're really tools for thinking. For the study that's been at the center of this book, for example, you've been developing a working concept of the term *discourse community*, not by memorizing a precise definition, but by working with a loose sense of the term and seeing how it applies to different settings—seeing how it can be used to help further an understanding of what's involved in communication in different settings. Because they are immediately present in the notes you take in the classroom, the key concepts and terms of a course are a good place to begin as you look at the way the <u>what</u> of the discipline is represented in the immediate situation of your classroom.

These key concepts and terms are likely to be ones you're expected to use and apply on exams and in the assignments that you complete for the course. For example, Dann writes about the terms that represent shared knowledge in his Music 101 class—the terms he draws on as he completes an assignment to write a review of a performance. He writes: "In my review, I use such terms as "crescendo" and "recitative" that may be unfamiliar to an outsider to our community." And he says of that assignment:

> I found that the concert review helped me better understand my knowledge in music and my understanding of what was being taught in the classroom. I also

found that the shared knowledge in this academic discourse community was incredibly important, especially when writing about a specific musical piece. It is my belief that the review was a major part of the course, finally forcing us, as students, to go out into the real world and apply what we learned, while using our knowledge to push our learning even further.

What he might once have seen as just the vocabulary of the course, with some definitions to be memorized, has become a set of *working concepts* for Dann—concepts that shape what he is now able to observe in music. As he uses the concepts to write his review, the concepts help him understand what he's heard, while applying them to what he's heard gives him a deeper understanding of the concepts. All academic learning tends to work this way, so that people who have spent many years studying and researching in fields like composition studies or music are still furthering their understanding of such key concepts as *discourse community* or *recitative*.

Frames of Mind, Traditions, and Shared Values

Shared knowledge in a discipline involves more than its key concepts and terms. As Rose points out when discussing Lucia's difficulties with reading the work of Thomas Szasz in psychology, most disciplines are shaped as well by "frames of mind and traditions." These are harder to pin down because they're more like the sorts of background understandings and implicit beliefs and values that informal discourse communities share. The professors at UCLA aren't consciously trying to keep these frames of mind hidden from their students—the frames of mind are just so deeply assumed that they're hard to be aware of. Most often these hidden understandings come into view only when some people in the field begin to offer a competing perspective. As Rose points out, Szasz's work offers just such a perspective in psychology. Szasz argues that traditional psychology, in its understanding of abnormal behavior, draws on a frame of mind that comes from psychiatry's position within the field of medicine. It draws on a framework of understanding (what Szasz calls "conceptual scaffolding") that comes out of the sciences rather than the social sciences. So it relies too much on a model of medical intervention and not enough on understanding the ways that people make sense of their lives.

Because such traditions and frames of mind are the sort of knowledge that insiders don't usually discuss explicitly, unless they want to critique them from a different perspective as Szasz is doing, they can be particularly hard for newcomers to identify. But as a researcher, you'll want to begin to look for the shared values and beliefs and ways of seeing the world that underlie work in the academic discourse community you are studying, and also to notice (as Eric did) ways in which what seems to be valued in your particular class may be different from what may be generally valued in the field.

Here's what another student researcher, Agnes, has found about the beliefs and values that frame her introductory course in cultural anthropology.

> Section 2 of Anthropology 103 consists of a very diverse group of undergraduate students, who originate from all parts of the globe. Even the professor is not American. Each one has a different background, set of values and beliefs. In order to be able to fully comprehend ethnology [the comparative study of different cultures], one has to set aside private ideologies in order not to be culture bound, and try to see other cultures and practices in their own context, from a wider "holistic perspective." This course helps to accomplish this task.
>
> As Mike Rose found in his studies, many students have a difficult time grasping certain ideas because they undermine and contradict their personal beliefs, values and experiences (culture bound). Religion plays an important role. For a deep believer of Catholicism, polygamy is immoral and is a sin, but in many of the world's societies it is thought of as a way of life. It is also the outcome of adaptation. In the Trobriand Islands, the wealth of a man is measured by how many pigs he possesses. Women are the only ones that can take care of the pigs; therefore it is essential for him to marry many wives so that they can tend the herds. To change this one element of polygamy would destroy their whole value and economic system. Such examples make everyone realize that their cultures are not the only ones in the world, are not better, nor more primitive, but have to be studied in their own unique context. A student is "trained at" looking at the world through various perspectives.

Theories

Much of the shared knowledge of a discipline involves various theories. A theory is an attempt to explain why some aspect of the world works as it does, and disciplines are often described in terms of what it is that they're trying to explain. Rose describes sociology, for example, as "an attempt to abstract a theory about social interaction and organization" (p. 387). Introductory sociology, then, is intended to introduce ways of thinking about this aspect of the world that have been developed by the field's major theorists. But, as Rose points out, students often bring other expectations about the purpose for such study—that it might have to do with immediate interventions to social problems or the applied study of these problems.

In fact, a lot of academic study has the purpose of developing theories that will explain what's observed in the world or carrying out more observations or experiments that will help to prove, disprove, or refine a theory. Most of what's studied in first-semester introductory physics is a theory of how the physical universe works in terms of concepts like force and motion and gravity. That theory was first put forth by Sir Isaac Newton in the seventeenth century—it has been added to (with Einstein's theory of relativity for example), but it's still the best explanation physicists have for why the physical world that we can immediately observe works as it does. Similarly psychology offers various theories of human behavior, including the behaviorist theory of Skinner (that people are conditioned to behave in particular ways in response to particular stimuli, as are other animals) and Maslow's humanistic theory (that human behavior is motivated by both lower-order needs like hunger and higher-order needs like knowledge and beauty). Included in the shared knowledge of most introductory courses are the theories that have developed in a field and the methods that have been used to gather evidence that supports or alters those theories.

Theories themselves are important conceptual tools. They allow us to organize our experience of the world and our observations about it, to see how many different instances might fit together, to make new and more systematic observations that might help to confirm or alter the theory. We tend to associate major theories with the people who articulated them most clearly: Newton with a theory of gravity, Freud with a theory of the human unconscious, Chomsky with a linguistic theory of how language is structured and how the human mind may be structured to process language.

Here's what Sophia has to say about the theories that were being discussed in the classroom moment she captured and that provide the underpinnings of her sociology course.

> The functionalist and conflict theories are different sociological perspectives based on problems of human society. In general, the functionalist perspective in sociology asks how society carries out the functions necessary to maintain social order, feed masses of people, defend against attackers, produce the next generation, and so on. It is concerned with the large-scale structures of society. On the other hand, conflict theory emphasizes the role of conflict and power (this is the theory that Marx supported). In every chapter we find the definition of functionalist theory and conflict theory of each problem. In that way we see the problems in a different perspective and we expand our point of view. In this case, the functionalist perspective on religion is that this institution is functional for the society. It brings hope to people and makes the society organized. On the other hand, conflict theory declares that religion exists in favor of upper social classes, keeping them in the highest level with honor. It says that religion makes the lower class less powerful. In other words, religion divides society into the highest class and the lowest class.

It's clear both what Sophia says here, as well as from the moment from her class's conversation we saw earlier, that her sociology course is organized to highlight two conflicting theories that try to explain why social institutions take the forms that they do. These theories are drawn from the observation of many facts about the ways in which society works, and each offers a way of explaining what has been observed.

One of the best ways to see what's insider knowledge in a setting is to see what's unfamiliar to an outsider. Exchange your class notes, the conversation you recorded, a reading, a journal article and/or a course assignment with one or two of your classmates, asking them to read and gloss for everything that seems to represent insider knowledge. Then, drawing on the outsider's glosses, analyze your text for

Key Terms and Concepts: Look at the words, terms, and concepts that your classmate has underlined in your notebook or other text. How did you come to understand these words, terms, or concepts? Why are these terms important to the shared knowledge of the course and the discipline? Do you think you have a good working sense of those concepts and terms? If you're analyzing your response to a course assignment, do you think that understanding is reflected in the ways you used the terms, explained them, gave examples for them, and/or connected them to other concepts and terms and to other aspects of the shared knowledge of the course?

Frames of Mind, Traditions, and Values: Looking back through your class notes, classroom conversation, your text and readings, and through your assignments, what do you find to be the traditions and frames of mind, the shared beliefs, values, and purposes, of the academic discipline that the course represents? Be specific in identifying words and phrases that point to those traditions and values.

Theories: Looking back at these materials, do you find reference to particular theories that are significant within the discipline? Do these theories serve as organizing principles for exploring perspectives on the aspect of the world that the discipline studies (as they do in the sociology course Sophia researched)? Do you find them useful in providing ways of seeing how insiders look at whatever part of the world they focus on?

If you're following Research Strand B, think about any key concepts, frames of mind/traditions, and theories within the field that may be connected to the topic you are studying. How does what you've been learning situate you as you pursue this topic? What background knowledge does it present that you might draw on? As we'll see in Chapter 9, library research depends a great deal on being able to identify key terms and concepts that other researchers are likely to use in their work and that library databases are likely to list.

A Shared *Why* and *How*

In the end, understanding the purpose of study in a discipline can make it easier to develop the sort of conceptual map that allows you to fit in new ideas. Asking why about the disciplines you study—why the insiders to the discipline define the field as they do, ask the questions they ask, use particular methods of inquiry and forms of argument—can help you to see some of the big picture that will let you make sense of the details and begin to fit them into place.

Your understandings of the <u>what</u> and <u>why</u> of an academic discipline are also related to <u>how</u>—to what you've come to see about how conversations in the field are carried out, and what insiders ("A" students, more advanced students, faculty, or professionals in the field) do. Rose points out that part of what makes many college courses difficult for students is that their ways are different from those of precollege schooling. He defines the problem this way:

> What young people come to define as intellectual competence—what it means to know things and use them—is shaped by their schooling. And what many students experience year after year is the exchange of one body of facts for another—an inert transmission, the delivery and redelivery of segmented and self-contained dates and formulas—and thus it is no surprise that they develop a restricted sense of how intellectual work is conducted (p. 386).

As a result of such schooling, Rose suggests, beginning students typically have "limited experience in applying knowledge, puzzling over solutions, solving problems" (p. 386).

While college conversations, like those in other discourse communities, involve particular genres and particular styles, the big <u>how</u> of these conversations has to do with ways of thinking as well as talking and writing—in Rose's terms, "how to think like a chemist, or a psychologist, or a literary critic."

RESEARCH MEMO 8.4

One way to begin to see more about <u>why</u> particular concepts, frames of mind, and theories are important to a discipline and <u>how</u> they are added to is to create a concept map that shows the relationship among these types of shared knowledge. Go back to the classroom conversation you recorded or to a glossed page of your class notes. Choose one key idea, term, or name to begin with. Then, working with a blank page, place that word on the page and try to work outward, placing other key concepts, ideas, and names that appear in the conversation somewhere on that page in a position that lets you make connections between the elements that you feel are related to each other.

Why is each of the elements of shared knowledge you've mapped out important within the academic discourse community you're studying? Pencil in a <u>why</u> for each element on your map. Are you able to see why in most instances? Do you think you're getting the bigger picture of the purposes of studying the world through this discipline? If not, why do you think that big picture is missing?

What does your map, supported by your class notes, class text, and assignments, show you about the ways of thinking of the discipline? How do people in the discipline come to new understandings? Do they speculate, reason, investigate something in a lab or in a field setting? Do they try to pose problems or solve them? What does it mean to think like a _____, like an insider within the discipline you're researching?

If you're following Research Strand B, create a map with the topic you're researching at the center. Then move outward, thinking of all the sorts of knowledge you can draw on that can connect with that topic. Then pencil in connections showing <u>why</u> each area of knowledge might be important to the topic you are researching and *how* people in the discipline most closely related to this topic discover new understandings.

EXPLORING STRATEGIES FOR TAKING A CRITICAL PERSPECTIVE

Rose's purpose as a teacher is to work with students to help them to acquire the new understandings and ways that they need to begin to participate as insiders in their academic courses, and to give them strategies that will help that process. He wants to help them to *reposition* themselves, so that they will no longer feel like outsiders to the academic worlds they enter.

But Rose's purpose as a writer and researcher is a different one. It's to take a critical perspective on the work of academic institutions, asking why they have been doing what they've been doing, whose interests are being served by the current situation, and whose are excluded. In reflecting on his own story and on the stories of different learners, he questions whether colleges and universities have to approach the introductory education they offer in the way they do. He is critical of the fact that they leave much of what should go on to help students enter the conversations of the classroom to tutoring centers and other peripheral locations and that they label such work as remedial. Thus his chapter addresses not just the methods but the *politics* of remediation, questioning the term "remediation" itself and the stance towards learners that it implies.

Rose's chapter invites you to engage in two parallel activities: reflecting, on the one hand, on the ways you can reposition yourself to work within a discourse community you want to join and considering, on the other, what might be wrong with and what might be changed about the ways that community deals with outsiders. Unlike the small, private discourse communities you studied earlier, public discourse communities—those of schools, colleges and universities, the government, the legal system—need to be accessible to all who wish to or have reason to enter them, and the necessary repositioning may need to be taking place on both sides.

Repositioning Yourself as a Learner

Drawing on what we know about conversations, the ways insiders participate in them, and the ways outsiders can begin to enter them, we can begin to name some specific strategies that learners can use to move up on the scale of insiderness in any academic discourse community. This is a good moment to reflect on how you have been using some of those strategies as part of your own repositioning.

One important strategy is to *connect with your own prior knowledge*. What learners bring can work to their advantage if they can see how to draw on it. Here's the reflection of a student researcher on how her job at a veterinary hospital has contributed to her position in a biology course.

> It can sometimes seem on the outside that the small details we learn in biology don't have much significance outside of class. I use my experience to think of how it all fits into the big picture. An example of this from Bio 111 is the small details that we learned about how our genes (DNA) code for protein. There are many

> steps to this process and many details to every step. It seemed like these details might be insignificant and a waste of time to learn. By keeping in mind that there are many genetic diseases that affect the lives of people and animals, I got through the details and was able to see how it all fits into the big picture. **(Jessica)**

Other students discover ways they've drawn on but have adjusted the prior knowledge that they had gained in high school courses to the demands of their new discourse communities. Obioma sees that she has had to adjust in several ways in her college chemistry course. One adjustment is to new terminology.

> When I really feel like an outsider is when I notice that most of the others know what is going on and I don't. I learned naming inorganic compounds in high school. That I would say is the beginning of chemistry. But having taken my high school chemistry in a different country, I was not surprised that I was a complete outsider in that topic. When I learned naming of compounds I was taught how to use prefixes like tetra-four, tri-three, and di-two to name compounds. For ClO, I would name it oxocholorate (I) ion but my professor would call it hypochlorite ion. . . .

Obioma's strategy for connecting her prior knowledge to that of her Chemistry course involves translating the terms and methods she knows into their equivalents in the new setting. She doesn't forget what she already knows, but sees how it relates to what she's learning.

A related strategy is keeping a *glossary*—listing key terms as they come up, checking your mental inventory to see where they fit and to confirm your sense of their meaning. Such a glossary can include key concepts but also names of key people (usually proponents of particular theories), and other references and allusions that recur in lectures, discussions, or texts. You needn't always worry about finding precise definitions or explanations for the items you list, but you might check through periodically to see that you're developing some working understandings.

Another strategy involves moving beyond listing to mapping—using a *concept map* like the one suggested for Research Memo 8.4 to show the relationships between key concepts and references. Once Dann puts a term like "recitative" on a map of key concepts in Music 101, what other terms might he link to it, and what terms might be linked to those? What concepts and what names might Sophia connect on a map to the functionalist and conflict theories she's identified as key organizers of thinking in her sociology course? As your picture of a discipline develops, keep redrawing or filling in your maps of the territory, to help you see and think about the shape of the terrain you're studying.

Still another strategy is to move from completing the immediate task in a course to *thinking about the larger implications*. Obioma came to see a more significant difference in how she needs to approach her work in Chemistry—the same shift that Rose proposes Andrea needs to make.

I very much understand why Andrea did not do well in her midterm exam because in my high school I was just required to know formulas, to know how to state laws like Avogadro's law, Dalton's laws of diffusion, and partial pressure in order to know very well. I never worried about the application of the laws and formulas to solving problems. We were not even required to solve problems and that was why Andrea had problems with her chemistry class. She prepared for her midterm exam the way she used to prepare for exams in high school. She memorized definitions, laws and formulas instead of learning how to do real problems with them. When the exam came, "it didn't require her to dump her memory. It gave her a short list of problems and asked her to solve them"(p. 379). Just as Andrea had to adjust her approach to exam preparation in college in order to do well, so I also had to adjust, in order to feel an insider to my chemistry class.

Reflective writing about the work you're doing (of the sort that you've been doing for many of the inquiries suggested in this book) can also help you to think both about the work of a course and the ways in which you're positioned in relationship to that work. It can give you a place to make connections between your prior experiences and understandings, what you're reading and learning in other courses, and what you're learning in this one.

Extending the conversation, not only through writing but also through talk, offers yet another strategy for repositioning yourself. If you form a *study group*, you can support your learning by resituating classroom talk in more comfortable and informal conversations that are closer to the ones you participate in easily in your familiar, informal discourse communities. *Tutoring* is another way to take an academic conversation out of the classroom and out of written texts and to explore it and expand on it. Because, as Rose points out, tutoring is associated with remediation, students are reluctant to seek it out unless they feel they're in serious trouble with a course. But tutoring also represents the sort of one-to-one conversation about academic work that's often seen as the ideal mode of learning.

Using these strategies to think not only about the <u>what</u> of the discipline, but also the <u>how</u> and the <u>why</u> will help you to keep discovering the understandings that insiders share, so that you keep working towards finding "the big picture" that Eric was seeking.

Finally, *reflecting on your own position* in the course and on the past experiences that contribute to this position can help you become more conscious of what shapes your own participation in this community. Juliette, as she explores the topic of women in science, reflects on her own past experience.

At school a girl may feel unique or different for having a serious interest in science, leading to her leaving it behind in favor of more socially "acceptable" goals. This is how it happened to me—I put more and more of my scholarly energy into the things that came the most easily to me, English, Art, and other languages. I came to think that I wasn't cut out for math and science.

But as she describes her physical position in her current classroom setting, she ends up reflecting on her new position in relation to the subject as well.

> I sit in the front row every single day so it is easier for me to ask questions (I ask <u>a lot</u> of questions) and because I have poor eyesight, so I need to be close to see the chalkboard. There is a camaraderie among those of us who sit in the front couple of rows, we share the insider-ness that comes with being good students, which is not to say that the good students only sit at the front—that's just my experience. Most of these insiders share similar goals: most are biology or other science majors, and some are pre-med. Every one shares a keen interest in the subject.

Seeing how her own experience with science has been affected by her positioning as a female lets Juliette actively work to change that position.

REFLECTIVE INQUIRY

What strategies have you been using to position yourself as an insider to the academic discourse community you are studying? In addition to making connections to your prior knowledge, have you tried the strategies of preparing glossaries, creating maps, engaging in reflective writing, or extending the conversation of the classroom through talk outside of the classroom? Are there other strategies you've found to be effective for becoming more of an insider to this context? <u>Why</u> from the perspective of what's involved in moving from the position of outsider to insider in a discourse community, do you think that these strategies have or haven't worked well for you? Are there others that you might try in the future?

If you're working with Research Strand B, you might also consider the strategies you've used in the past to expand on the knowledge a course offered you? Did you pursue related topics that you'd thought about or had experience with before? Did you seek out other sources of information? How are your past strategies influencing your ways of approaching the research topic you're pursuing?

Placing Your Current Work in a Larger Context

Every conversation exists within a context of conversations that have gone before, and that sense of a conversation's history and of where the present moment is located in relation to that history is something that participants in academic conversations are often particularly conscious of. Knowing something about that context helps you locate yourself and your research as you engage in your current conversations.

This book, for example, exists within a larger academic context, a conversation that's been going on in several fields where language and literacy and composition are studied. The book draws on a number of key concepts highlighting the idea that the ways we talk and write are shaped by the contexts in which we carry out those activities (concepts like *discourse community*). It draws from a critical tradition that has arisen in contrast to older traditions in these fields that tended to focus on language and literacy in the abstract, apart from specific uses in specific contexts. It's also influenced by both a particular theory of language and a particular theory of literacy.

The theory of language is what's termed a *functional theory of language*, one developed by linguist M. A. K. Halliday. This theory focuses on the ways language is used in the world, the functions we perform with it, and the ways in which its grammatical structures work to let us achieve those functions. Halliday says we use language to accomplish three major functions. One function is to name the world and make statements about it (what he calls the *ideational function* and we've been calling the <u>what</u> of any exchange). A second function is to interact with each other and achieve various purposes in those interactions (what he calls the *interpersonal function* and we've been calling the <u>why</u> of any exchange). A third function is to do both of these things in words, in ways that will make sense and seem appropriate to others (what he calls the *textual function* and we've been calling the <u>how</u> of an exchange). Halliday's theory offers a way of thinking about what's common to language use across different settings and within particular settings—a way of thinking that has proved useful for the purpose of studying what readers and writers, speakers, and listeners have to know to shape their language to work in particular ways in particular contexts. Because it focuses on *discourse*—on natural stretches of actual language in real contexts—it can also be termed a discourse theory of language.

The theory of literacy used in this book is one developed by a number of people from different disciplines who share a perspective referred to as New Literacy Studies. It's represented, for example, by the work of anthropologist Brian Street (1995) and linguist James Gee (1989). By studying how literacy works in different contexts, they've come to see literacy as "situated" in specific sociocultural contexts and in the specific *social practices* of communities of people. A *situated theory of literacy* focuses on the ways that people use reading, writing, and oral language in specific social situations for social purposes, rather than seeing literacy as a defined body of knowledge and skills possessed by individuals to be used in the same way in all contexts. It suggests that people don't just learn one set of rules or practices for reading and writing that work for all situations, but that they acquire the literacy practices of a specific setting by participating in that setting and becoming insiders.

Gee's article "Literary, Discourse, and Linguistics" is included in the readings at the end of Part III. It was written as an introduction to an issue of a scholarly journal focusing on the ways people practice literacy in different social contexts. Gee's introduction contributed to some of the early work of shaping a theory for the field of literacy studies. In theorizing that work, Gee *named* the understandings that literacy researchers were beginning to develop together, helping them to see more clearly, and from a new perspective, the common elements in what they were finding.

The theories that make up the shared knowledge of courses can appear to be fixed—existing in a final form and forever associated with the name of a particular theorist—when they've actually arisen out of the ongoing conversations in specific contexts in academic discourse communities. Theories are also *abstract*—but that's because theorists have drawn on many specific examples and instances, *abstracted* what's common to them, and represented those common elements with larger terms and concepts. *Theorizing* is an active process. It's a habit of mind that we engage in informally, all of the time, as individuals observing the world around us. But it's also an ongoing social practice of thinking and using language in particular ways that has arisen in particular discourse communities—especially academic ones—a practice that's recorded finally in the formal texts of those communities.

REFLECTIVE INQUIRY	Think about how the concepts and theories underlying this book may influence your own thinking about writing and reading. This book has focused not only on giving you some guidance as a writer and reader, but on exploring the ways in which people use talk and read and write in different communities and different situations. You came to this book with a lot of prior experience as a writer and reader. Are there ways in which reading this book has reframed what you knew from that experience or given you a new perspective on writing and reading in different contexts and/or on yourself as a writer or reader? Does the brief explanation of some of the theoretical underpinnings of this book (perhaps along with Gee's article), add in any way to your perspective on the work you've been doing?

RESEARCH MEMO 8.5	Your instructor in the field that you've chosen for your academic discourse community study and/or research report is likely to be actively involved in that field's conversations. He or she may be a professor/scholar/researcher who is carrying out current studies and participating in the professional conversations about them that go on at conferences and in academic journals, or a teacher or a graduate student who has participated in similar conversations in graduate seminars and has carried out or is planning his/her own studies of related issues. And those prior conversations have certainly influenced the ways in which your own classroom conversation has been structured.

This is a good moment to interview your instructor (in person or through e-mail) to learn more about the underpinnings of the course you are focusing on. Before the interview, it's a good idea to look once again at the course syllabus, to think about what you've been learning through your analysis of course materials and assignments, and to decide on some particular questions you want to ask.

Your questions might include the following:

- What does your instructor see as the goals of the course?
- Where does he/she locate the focus of the course in relationship to the recent history of the discipline and key issues being raised in it currently?

(continued)

- Do your instructor's own scholarly interests fall within a particular area of the larger discipline?

- Do they draw on a particular theoretical perspective within the discipline, and how is that perspective represented in the materials or the methods of inquiry introduced in the course?

- How does the instructor's perspective on the field influence what he/she has decided to do and have you do, and how, in this course?

If you're following Research Strand B, you can use your interview to help you locate the topic you're focusing on within the larger terrain of the field. Within this field of study, who would be likely to be interested in this topic? From what perspective(s)? How might different researchers, representing different theoretical perspectives, approach this topic? Where would they start in order to find what other researchers/scholars have already learned about the topic? What new understandings might they be trying to discover? And how might they go about carrying out their own studies?

Taking a Critical Perspective

Rose uses the term "critical literacy" to name some of what readers and writers need to be able to do in academic settings: "framing an argument or taking someone else's argument apart, systematically inspecting a document, an issue, or an event, synthesizing different points of view, applying a theory to disparate phenomena" (1990, 188). These are situation-specific literacy practices, and they represent work that's often assigned in academic contexts. In fact, the term "critical" appears frequently in assignments: students are asked to write "critical reviews" of books or performances and "critical analyses" of readings. "Critical," in this sense, refers to a way of thinking about something that generally involves both analyzing and evaluating, seeing whether it fits with a particular framework, whether it's a good example of a performance or whether it contains key elements of a genre. Critical analysis is a common academic genre—combining analysis with critical thinking about what's analyzed and evaluation against the standards of the discipline—a critical analysis of a philosophical argument both analyzes an object of study (the argument) and evaluates it in terms of what makes a good one, as does a critical analysis of a work of art, a performance, a medical experiment.

Vanessa, for example, discusses a "representative text" in the field of music, an article about the performance of Corelli's sonatas for violin. She analyzes the article, showing how it's structured, how the author introduces the topic, how he develops it, the details he includes, and what he leaves out. In effect, she analyzes the author's critical analysis of performances.

> The author wants to reflect on the way of performing these important works for violin; he critiques and criticizes different recordings. He discusses which versions

of the manuscript (i.e. scores) the performers should rely on, which performers give the impression of being more "historically aware," that is, play the pieces as they were supposed to be played in that time and as the composer thought of them. The way the author does this is by referring to specific movements of the sonatas (there are twelve sonatas, each generally with three movements) and analyzing them; he is looking at the way each performer plays it, and what differences there are between the different performances, what changes does each violinist make to each movement, which are the pros and cons of these changes, and which manuscript the violinist is relying on. . . .

But Vanessa also sees that the author is *evaluating* the performances on different recordings, and that one of his criteria for evaluation is that the performers give a performance that's "historically aware." Thus the author's analysis of the recordings is combined with evaluation, in terms of some of the shared values of the field of music. And Vanessa's analysis of the article is combined with evaluation as well. She evaluates the article in terms of what understandings it offers to other performers, because "That's how we get better, by reading critiques about other players and deciding whether to perform one way or another, depending on whether we agree with the article or not." (You can read Vanessa's final report on the academic discourse community of her music course at the end of Part III.)

RESEARCH MEMO 8.6

Look at one of the readings for the course you are focusing on that represents an example of critical analysis or your response to an assignment that seems to call for critical analysis.

- What are the elements in the writer's analysis (whether the writer is you or someone else)?

- What is the writer's purpose with this analysis?

- Where do you find evidence of the writer's evaluation of what's being analyzed?

- What are the criteria that the writer is using for that evaluation and where do those criteria seem to come from?

- As a reader (even as the reader of your own writing) do you find that evaluation convincing?

- Is there anything else you'd want to know that would make it clearer or better supported?

The assignments you and your classmates have completed and the articles you've read in your courses have most likely asked for critical analysis in a variety of specific forms and genres. You might also want to compare what you've found as examples of critical analysis in different fields.

(continued)

- What do you think might be some of the common elements of critical analysis (the <u>how</u> of critical analysis) that appear across contexts and texts?

- What do you find that seems to be specific to a particular context of a course or a field or an assignment?

- As you look back at the assignments or readings you've analyzed, do you have a clearer picture of how the work of critical analysis might be carried out? Do new questions arise for you?

All academic discourse communities ask their participants to engage in critical thinking in these ways, from within the framework of the existing knowledge, assumptions, theories, and values of a discipline. But there is another way of thinking critically about the work of an academic discourse community, and that is to step out of the framework of its insider shared knowledge, purposes, and ways and to look at it from an outsider's perspective—to ask not only "how can I use and apply the ways of thinking that are characteristic of this discipline?" but also "how can I reflect on those ways of thinking, to see what they show me and what they don't?" "How can I take a new, *critical perspective* on a world in which I've been participating, to see how its concepts and theories and expected structures not only frame but may also limit what I can see?" It's this critical perspective that Rose takes when he asks us to consider not only the ways in which learners can be repositioned in relationship to our educational institutions, but also how institutional practices might be changed.

People begin to take a critical perspective on their experiences when they start to ask why things are as they are? Who benefits from the present situation (and who loses)? How could things be different? Much research originates with questions that are potentially critical: Tobias, for example, in asking why more humanities students didn't take science courses, was beginning an inquiry that questioned the standard assumptions of science faculty—the lens through which they had traditionally viewed both their students and their own teaching.

Studies that are more explicitly critical in their perspective often raise questions about the larger society and the implicit values that can be seen in its institutions (values that often conflict with the democratic and egalitarian values we espouse). Such studies may look at who benefits or who loses within the present structures from the perspective of race or ethnicity, social class, or gender. For example, a study included at the end of Part III, Jean Anyon's "Social Class and the Hidden Curriculum of Work," examines the different styles of teaching in five elementary schools that serve children from different social classes, asking how this teaching and learning is preparing children for their further lives and why they're being prepared in different ways.

Gee, in "Literacy, Discourse, and Linguistics," suggests that critical perspectives can only be reached by stepping out of our familiar ways of seeing the world—our familiar discourses. For that reason, he argues in his article that

> "primary discourses, no matter whose they are, can never really be liberating literacies. For a literacy to be liberating, it must contain both the Discourse it is going to critique and a set of meta-elements (language, words, attitudes, values) in terms of which an analysis and criticism can be carried out. . . . (p. 450)

In other words, it's stepping outside of a familiar discourse community and looking back at it from another perspective—that allows you to see and name the values that are represented there and to ask whether what's valued (both explicitly in words and implicitly in practices) is what you want to have valued. Do we, as a society, for example, want to continue to have only certain students become insiders to the world of science (still more often male students for physics and other sciences), or do we want to question our assumptions that the world of science education has to lead to that result?

Juliette, who has stepped out of her old ways of seeing her own position as a woman in a field of science, discovers when interviewing her professor, that he is taking a critical position as well, on the very questions of who is served by our traditional approaches to science teaching and on how to do a better job of reaching all students in introductory science courses.

> The professor's name is Brian White, and he is an excellent teacher. In the university setting, before a professor has received tenure (and usually after as well) he or she will have an area of research within the field, and Brian's area of research is teaching. He studies methods of teaching as it relates to introductory biology classes, and there are opportunities for students to participate in various studies. He also asks for a lot of feedback concerning the class and lab.

But it's her own research, as she moves into the library to look for more information about the position of women in science, that helps to ground her own critical perspective on that topic. As she gathers information about the recent history of women in science and of how those women who did become scientists were seen, she learns of the woman scientist, Rosalind Franklin, who contributed to the discovery of DNA but did not receive the same credit as the male researchers. She quotes a passage from *The Double Helix* by James Watson, who won the Nobel Prize for the discovery:

> I suspect that in the beginning Maurice hoped that Rosy would calm down. Yet mere inspection suggested that she would not easily bend. By choice she did not emphasize her feminine qualities. Though her features were strong, she was not unattractive and might have even been quite stunning had she even taken a mild interest in clothes. That she did not. There was never lipstick to contrast with her

straight black hair, while at the age of thirty-one her dresses showed all the imagination of English blue-stocking adolescents. So it was quite easy to imagine her the product of an unsatisfied mother who unduly stressed the desirability of professional careers that could save bright girls from marriages to dull men. . . . Clearly Rosy had to be put in her place . . . given her belligerent moods, it would be very difficult for Maurice to maintain a dominant position that would allow him to think unhindered about DNA. (pp. 491–492)

Juliette comments on this passage:

These words sound so insulting, even shocking to me. However, I am sure that James Watson meant Rosalind Franklin no ill will. This is just the way people thought at the time. Note the discussion of her physical appearance, as if it were her responsibility to present herself in an appealing way to the men around her. He speculates on her reasons for choosing this work, and speaks easily about her being "put in her place" and her "belligerent moods." The last sentence of the quote sums it up—they don't even consider wanting her input on this project; instead they don't want her upsetting Maurice's "dominant" position.

Juliette's research, in the context of her study of discourse communities, lets her see just how the dominant shared values and assumptions of a society can allow someone like Watson to make the comments he does while meaning "no ill will." She finds that "his comments are very sexist by today's standards. This shows how much shared values have changed over the years." But they have changed only because people began to step outside of the dominant values and critique them.

WRITING IN ACADEMIC GENRES: THE CRITICAL ANALYSIS OF RESEARCH DATA

Any of the data you've analyzed from your classroom discourse community can be reanalyzed from a larger critical perspective when you ask the larger questions:

- How have these criteria been established?
- Whose perspective do these criteria represent?
- What might be some of the larger purposes of work in this field, and how do these criteria serve or not serve that purpose?
- Are there other purposes, besides the ones that have dominated the field, that should also be considered?

APPLYING A CRITICAL PERSPECTIVE

Write an extended research memo (or exploratory essay) which frames your critical analysis by naming the perspective you're drawing on, the questions it leads you to ask, and the criteria it leads you to use as you analyze and evaluate from that perspective.

If you're applying a critical perspective to your analysis of a segment of classroom discourse (or an assignment, a reading, or another aspect of your experience in that classroom community), you might consider also

- the perspectives of participants who are positioned in different ways—in different student positions, in the teacher's position, a perspective from outside of the particular classroom

- who seems to be invited into this conversation or excluded. Or how effective the conversation seem to be in generating the shared knowledge that the course is trying to build. Or Rose's question—how effective is this, as a representative classroom moment or assignment or reading, for providing access for all learners to the ways and the privileges associated with higher education

If you're applying a critical perspective to a whole course, you might also consider

- the purposes of classroom activities and assignments
- whether there is a gap between the named purpose of this activity and what it seems actually to accomplish
- the ways of evaluating students' work
- who is best served by the way in which the work of this class is carried out
- whether the work might be carried out differently to meet the named purposes of the course

If you're applying a critical perspective to your library research, you might also consider

- how this topic has been treated before
- why it hasn't had a more prominent place in your own studies before this time
- why you need to do further research to gain the understandings you are seeking

9

Reporting Research
in Academic Disciplines

Chapter 9 looks at where and how insiders to a field carry on the written conversations that represent their current shared knowledge, purposes, and values. You'll use the library to find an article that interests you and that represents the larger academic discourse community of a discipline. You'll see what you can learn from that article about your own position as a reader in that field and about the styles and genres of the field and of much academic writing.

If you're following Research Strand A, you'll be using that article to provide further data about the ways of insiders to that academic community, about your own positioning in that community, and about the features of genre and style that characterize writing in that community.

If you're following Research Strand B, you'll use the first article you select as a starting point for your further research into the topic or question you've chosen as you discover how insiders have studied a topic and what they've learned.

The work of this chapter will lead to your final report on your study of an academic discourse community (Research Strand A), or a report based on secondary, library (and electronic) research that draws on others' studies (Research Strand B). Examples of published research studies, along with student researchers' reports of both types, are included in the Additional Readings at the end Part III, and additional information on library research and working with sources is included in the Strategies in Part IV.

Chapter 9 explores three questions:

- How can we use our understanding of discourse communities to approach the world of the library and its resources? What resources does the library offer as we look for the written conversations of a field?

- What can we learn about the written conversations of academic discourse communities by looking at articles in journals published in an academic field? How can we approach these conversations as readers, writers, and researchers?

- How can we use what we find in such articles to further our understandings of academic style and academic genres?

As a student in an introductory course, you're beginning to get a sense of some of a discipline's shared knowledge—key concepts, thinkers, theories, and its recent history. But as Eric found of his physics course (Chapter 7), introductory courses don't always offer a clear sense of the current work that people who are working in a field actually do. To discover more about what an academic field looks like beyond the work of an introductory classroom, it's necessary to turn to the conversations being carried on by more established insiders.

Researchers in every academic field depend on sharing knowledge as they build on the work others have done to undertake new inquiry and add to or alter existing understandings. They keep careful written records of what they observe and learn, and they report on new findings or they try out a new perspective on work that others have done in the articles that they write. Articles in academic journals represent the most current conversation that's going on in a field. You can learn about what insiders talk and think about, and how, through the process of finding and reading such an article.

When an academic researcher completes a study, writes a report or a paper about it, and sends it to an academic journal to be considered for publication as an *article* (a very important genre within the academic community), that article then typically enters a *peer review* process. In this process, the paper is sent to interested readers who typically are also writing about similar work. They read the paper and respond in several ways. They look at the <u>what</u>, deciding whether the paper's topic fits the conversation that's being carried out in the particular journal. They consider whether the paper sufficiently reflects the shared knowledge and prior conversations of the field, and they decide whether it contributes something new and interesting to those conversations. If the paper addresses each of these concerns and they think the paper will contribute to the conversation that has been going on in that journal, the readers then consider <u>how</u> the paper is written. They look at whether it needs more explanation or examples, whether it needs to take into account other prior studies that its writer hasn't discussed, and whether anything needs to be altered or clarified to address the particular audience of knowledgeable readers in the field who will make up its audience.

A journal's reviewers typically act as peer reviewers in the sense that we use the term in writing courses. They make suggestions for revision that help the writer clarify his or her meanings and link the new contribution more effectively to the field's ongoing conversations. When you find an article in a scholarly journal that's peer reviewed or *refereed*, you can assume that it represents knowledge that at least some of the field's insiders think is important.

Libraries subscribe to these journals and order books that typically extend the discussions that begin with articles. Thus they are repositories of the written record (or they connect you to the electronic record) of these scholarly conversations and the place where most researchers turn to discover the current state of shared knowledge about a question and how others are pursuing answers.

Why does this matter to you, as a reader and researcher? For one thing, it may interest you to know that your professors are likely to be participating in a process of writing and revision that is a lot like one that you go through. But it's also important to know that the articles you read in most academic journals have already been reviewed and critiqued by other scholars in the field, and that they represent the best judgment of those scholars about what's interesting and valuable. There can of course be a lot of interesting conversation that doesn't make it into these journals, and peer reviewers may sometimes find it hard to see the value of work that challenges the dominant understandings of a field. But academic journals are a major source of current shared knowledge in a field.

APPROACHING THE LIBRARY AS A DISCOURSE COMMUNITY

While libraries serve many academic disciplines, providing the written resources necessary to their conversations, library science is also a discipline itself, and the library can be seen as a secondary discourse setting that has its own language, values, and ways of seeing the world. For newcomers to the setting of an academic library, the level of assumed shared knowledge can be daunting. Many students walk away from the library after their first orientation session and return to the safety and familiarity of their computers, relying on whatever information they can access that way for any research they're required to do.

Like any discourse community, an academic library becomes more familiar as you spend time there and begin to discover its ways. Approaching the library itself as a discourse community, you can try to identify some of the shared <u>what</u>, <u>why</u> and <u>how</u> of insiders (librarians, experienced library users and researchers). Getting comfortable there will take time and experience but can be aided by the use of specific strategies. By approaching the library from the stance of a discourse community researcher, you're likely to feel more empowered as a participant.

Entering the Library with a Purpose

Newcomers to discourse communities enter those communities with a purpose—to make friends, to share an interest, to get and keep a job. Without a shared purpose, you might hang around a bit in a setting where you perceive that a discourse community has formed, but you're not likely to become an insider to that community. The same is true in the setting of the library: you can take a tour or attend an instruction session or read the materials that are usually available to guide users, but if you're not in the library with the shared purpose of carrying out an academic inquiry of some sort, you're not likely to come away with a reliable understanding of what you hear or read.

If you've had library research assignments in the past, you may have seen them more as a set of steps to follow than as a way of pursuing an inquiry. If your inquiry is real, the library research process can seem too inexact to get you where you want to go. Yet most inquiry involves inexact steps, trial and error, and patience with the process, and this is true of library inquiry as well.

When Juliette began her study of an academic discourse community, she quickly focused on the topic of women in science, because it related to her own experience. But she didn't immediately have a very clear idea of how to go about learning more about the topic, or what exactly it was that she wanted to know. Gradually, as she kept defining and redefining the problem in relationship to the information she was finding, she arrived at the specific question that guided her final paper: "Are women underrepresented in the broad field of science, and if so, is it the result of negative societal and peer conditioning?" In her case, the question she was most interested in, while associated with the academic discourse community of biology, was not one that biologists study, and her preliminary reflection on what she had learned directly by studying the materials of her course did not give her the terms and concepts she'd need for her research topic, so she had to keep exploring new territory.

RESEARCH MEMO 9.1	Research Strand A: Your work in Chapters 7 and 8 has been guided by a question about the academic discourse community represented by the course you've chosen to focus on. As you take your research into the library, you'll want to extend your focus. Begin by providing preliminary answers to the questions you'll be asking in this chapter:

- What do insiders to the larger academic discourse community of this field study and how?
- What sorts of questions do they ask, and how do they pursue answers to those questions?
- What topic or question within this field do I want to learn more about and use as an example to learn more about the sorts of research that insiders do?

Research Strand B: If your work in Chapters 7 and 8 has already led you to a topic you want to pursue and a preliminary question or questions about that topic, restate briefly:

- what the topic and questions are,
- why you want to pursue these, and
- what some of the key understandings are that you're bringing to your research.

If you haven't yet decided on a topic and question, do the following:

Look back at your earlier research memos and/or the notebook you have kept for the class you are studying, looking for underlying topics, questions, concepts, or concerns that have particularly interested you. Compile key words that characterize these concepts or ideas, and use these as a starting point. With these areas of interest in mind, consider the following questions:

- What am I interested in finding out more about?
- What themes and ideas seem to be related closely to this topic?
- What in the work I've been doing has prepared me to study this topic?

Do this for two or three topics that people are likely to have studied in the academic discipline you're focusing on or that you've wondered about in relation to that community Then decide on the topic and the preliminary question that you'll pursue. Your question may shift as you get to know more about your topic.

Seeing the Shared <u>What</u>, <u>Why</u>, and <u>How</u> of the Library

Libraries are complex, and the tools used to access all of the written material (both print and electronic) that they contain are changing all of the time. People learn to use a library by going there with something they want or need to find out and by trying things out; they talk to friends; they may read a library manual and/or go to a presentation by a librarian; they may call on an expert (a reference librarian) to help them figure out more about how to proceed, or they may access guides to using library resources through the Internet. They'll probably do all of these things at different times.

The field of library science also functions as its own academic discourse community. Technology has altered how the information in libraries is stored and used, so now insider-users must not only know about call numbers, catalogs, and indexes, but also about electronic searches and databases. If you keep a glossary of the key terms and concepts you encounter as you work with your library project, you can map out some of the terrain of library research for yourself or with your research group.

What do library insiders know? They know a lot about the <u>what</u> of library resources and of the process of searching for information using those resources. The <u>what</u> includes the sorts of materials that are available and the ways in which those materials are named. These include

- Larger categories of resources: The largest categories are books, periodicals, and reference materials. These are likely to be housed in specific physical locations (making a map can be a useful way to think about the sorts of resources a library contains).

- Categories within categories: different types of reference materials, for example, including those, like encyclopedias, that offer specific information about topics, and those that offer information about where to get information, like bibliographies and *databases* that contain indexes to resources that are available in the library or on-line, through the Internet.

The <u>how</u> that insiders know includes the ways in which these materials are organized and the ways in which users are expected to be able to access them. The <u>how</u> includes

- A *classification system* that lets users find these materials (most college and university libraries use the Library of Congress system; public libraries are more likely to use the Dewey Decimal system).

- A catalog that lists the library's holdings (almost always an *on-line catalog*, though occasionally a library will still have older holdings catalogued through a card catalog).

- A means of access to *databases* that compile reference information in various academic areas—generally through CD-ROMs or online. (These databases include bibliographies of what has been published and the classification information you need to find it.)

- *Online access* to materials that aren't physically located within the library. Most academic libraries offer easy links to the catalogs of other libraries. Most subscribe to various on-line resources such as *First Search* and *Expanded Academic Index*, databases that index many journals and allow you to search for articles and receive reference information, *abstracts* of the articles (providing a brief summary of their contents), or even the full text of articles. The *Expanded Academic Index* allows you to narrow your request for listings of articles to refereed journals only, and articles with full text only. It also allows you to read full-text articles on the screen and then to print what you find useful or send it to your own e-mail account.

- The services of *reference librarians* whose job is to assist all researchers, whether they're beginners or very experienced, in using the library's resources to find what they need. Knowing that you can and should ask a reference librarian for help at any point in your own search process is a particularly valuable piece of insider knowledge about <u>how</u>.

The <u>why</u> of the world of the library—its purposes and the values that underlie them—are harder to name explicitly because they are in flux. As information technology changes the ways our society thinks about how information is created, managed, and exchanged, the library's purpose is changing as well, with more emphasis on enabling library users to access a vastly expanded world of information in new and ever-changing ways. One advantage to this situation from your perspective is that library insiderness also keeps changing, and someone whose expertise is more than a few years old is likely to need as much help as you do in learning new ways.

As she began to explore the ways of the library, Juliette brought some prior knowledge—like how to use the on-line catalog to find a book—but she had never used any of the databases her library offered, and she wasn't really sure how to work with them to find journal articles. She learned that the most commonly used general database at her school was the *Expanded Academic Index,* that it would allow her to search by subject or by key words, and that she could get citations (the reference information she'd need to find an article in a journal), some abstracts of articles, and even the full text of some articles sent to her by e-mail or for printing on the library's printer. She found that her library gave her access to other databases that she might want to use in the future for more specific topics in her major: *Biological Abstracts,* and the *Science Citation Index* (on CD). She also learned that the library offered a web-based "Information Literacy Tutorial" that included modules on many of the things she'd need to know to carry out her research. Juliette's first exploration suggested to her that while she still felt like an outsider, she could begin to learn her way around.

Many of the elements that you've considered as you've been studying informal discourse communities outside of academic settings and the academic discourse communities of your courses can be relevant to approaching the world of the library as a discourse community and seeing your own insider/outsiderness in relation to what insider library users seem to know.

RESEARCH MEMO 9.2

Prior Knowledge: As in entering any discourse community, you'll find it useful to consider the prior knowledge you bring to it. Take the inventory of library skills included in Strategies for Library Research, and see where you're starting in your movement towards insiderness. Reflect on how you feel about your current library skills, what you feel confident about, where you're uncertain. Are there particular sorts of tasks, at particular libraries, that you can carry out in a routine and comfortable way? As you search for resources for your study, try to expand your library skills. For example, if you already know how to search for an article using a general database like the *Expanded Academic Index,* try using a database that's specific to the field you've chosen and that you haven't used before.

The Setting: If you map out the physical location of various resources in the library, find out what the classification number is for materials in the field you're focusing on, where books with that classification number (in that field) are shelved, where bound periodicals in that field are shelved, and where current periodicals in the field are shelved. As you learn about reference materials, find out which are likely to be most useful for this field and where they are shelved or how you'll access them. When you come to the computer terminals, access the on-line catalog and databases and see what you can discover about how you'd begin to look for something in the field. When you find the location of the reference librarian, ask a question about the best way to find resources related to the field or topic you're focusing on. Then expand your map of the physical setting with a map of the virtual one. Once you've come to the computer terminals, where else do their online resources take you?

Materials: Just as you've analyzed the materials of your course to learn more about that academic discourse community, you can analyze the materials of the library—printed library guide materials, the on-line catalog, (and you can get the help of a reference librarian), to find out what databases and bibliographic resources cover the discipline that's the focus of your study. Find out where and how to get help in using these resources and try them out. (Printed library guides often give such information, CD-rom materials include a guide to their use, and on-line databases offer files of instruction.) What do these materials tell you about the intersection between the discourse community of the academic field you're focusing on and that of the library as it makes the written conversations of that field available for researchers?   *(continued)*

(continued)

Key Terms and Concepts: There are many specialized terms and concepts associated with organizing and accessing library materials. Some will be familiar but you may have a somewhat fuzzy concept of what they refer to, and others may be new to you. As you work in the library, keep a list, as a researcher, of all the discourse-community-specific terms you hear and read. Gloss any library guides you receive, listen for the specific terms of any introductory session you attend, and make note of everything that a complete outsider would have to understand in order to become an insider. At a convenient moment, you may want to discuss your list with other members of your research group or your larger class, sharing your understanding of each term and creating a working glossary.

Using Library Resources to Find the Conversations of a Field

Particularly if you're focusing on an academic discourse community in which you want to continue to study, this is a good time to learn about the resources that insiders to the discipline will use to access information—discipline-specific bibliographies and databases such as *Psychological Abstracts* or the *Publications of the Modern Language Association (PMLA) Bibliography*. If you've chosen to study a classroom discourse community in a field in which you're not so likely to continue to take courses, you can still learn something about the insider knowledge of that discourse community by accessing a journal article through a general academic database such as the *Expanded Academic Index*.

Searching by Subject Headings

To begin to search for information on a subject that interests you, you'll want to know what sorts of subject listings you might be able to find. The Library of Congress (LOC) classification system organizes materials by broad disciplinary areas, assigning a letter of the alphabet to each: H for social sciences, K for law, P for language and literature. Your library will have a quick guide to the big divisions and their call numbers to guide you in finding the location of books and periodicals, which are shelved by the LOC system in academic libraries. But the *Guide to Library of Congress Subject Headings*, usually located in the reference area of the library, is a full subject heading guide that gives you information about specific subject terms and related terms that are used to categorize materials—subject headings that are usually used to organize information in the on-line catalog and in many databases as well as books and periodicals So if you look in that guide for the general subject that you're interested in, you'll find a number of related terms that you can look for as you carry out your search. Juliette did not find a Library of Congress heading for women in science and could not find that heading in her library's catalog (which uses LOC headings). She did find that subject listing in the general database she turned to, the *Expanded Academic Index,* and it gave her a list of 240 titles, 151 in refereed journals.

Searching by Key Words

In addition to searching the catalog and databases for subject listings, you can also conduct a key word search. We've considered the ways in which key terms provide some conceptual tools for thinking within a discipline, and you've mapped out some of the key terms that you have been encountering as part of the shared knowledge of the academic discourse community you're studying. Key terms also play a particularly important role in allowing you to access information in your discipline. The process of finding a journal article in your discipline is often made easier when you draw on the shared knowledge you've already generated and the terms you've begun to use. Most library catalogs, most databases, and web search-engines are set up to allow you to search either by subject categories or by key words. Key word searches look for any item in the catalog or database that contains the key word or words you've chosen, whatever subject heading the book or article is listed under, so they can be a particularly useful way to begin the sort of loose, information-gathering hunt for an interesting article that you're undertaking if you're following Research Strand A. (In this first search effort, you may not find anything precisely on the question or topic you want to explore, but if you're following Research Strand A, you can choose any article from the field that looks interesting to you.)

Juliette also tried a key word search strategy as she searched in the Expanded Academic Index. She started out again with women AND science (AND is used to connect two terms) but that heading brought up over two thousand citations, 410 in refereed publications. She tried women AND biology and found that most of those listings focused on the physical biology of women. She tried women biologists and found only two listings, neither of which looked useful. So she went back to women AND science and skimmed through some of the titles to see what articles under that heading seemed to be about: attracting women to science, losing women scientists from the field, having a critical mass of women to support each other in science, mentoring women scientists, designing a curriculum to produce women scientists, attitudes of high school women towards science. She found that these articles appeared in a wide range of journals, from *Women's Studies Quarterly* to *The Journal of College Science and Math Teaching,* to *Science.* She tried another set of key words, sex AND science, and found an article with that title that talked about Rosalind Franklin, the woman who contributed to the discovery of DNA. She was interested in Franklin's experience, but she also wanted to find something that would help explain her own earlier reluctance to consider science. She kept searching, expanding her original list of brainstormed key terms, adding science anxiety, gender AND education, girls AND science, girls AND schooling, and girls AND self-esteem. Gradually this fuzzy, messy process led her to a list of possible articles and books to follow up on. The citations for some of the articles Juliette found appear with her final paper at the end of this chapter.

Begin your search for an article in the discipline of your academic discourse community study (Research Strand A) or your search for a set of possible sources for your library research paper (Research Strand B). Keep running notes in your observation notebook about what you do with each step of the process. Then sum up what you did, what you found, what you learned about the process that you'll want to remember, and what your questions and concerns are about your search at this point, in your research memo.

Searching by Subject. If you're working within a discipline, consult the *Guide to Library of Congress Subject Headings,* described on page 458, in the reference area of the library. (There is an information guide to the guide at the front of the volume.) Look for the subject headings that come closest to those of the topic or topics that interest you. You'll find it useful to make a copy of the page of headings to draw on as you search for an article.

Return to the lists of words and concepts you may have generated in thinking about the concepts, frames of mind, and theories of your discipline in Chapter 8 and in deciding on a question in the first research memo of this chapter. See if any of those words are represented on the list of subject headings and subheadings related to your topic. Use the closest subheadings to carry out a subject search in your library catalog (for books), and a general database or index, or an appropriate one for your field (drawing on a library guide to the database or information for users that appears on a CD-rom or with an on-line database).

Searching by Key Words. Use the other key terms you've generated to carry out a key word search in a database for journal articles (Strands A and B) and in the catalog for books (Strand B) adding new words as you go along. In your notebook, keep notes on the terms you use as you move through the search, and keep adding to them as you think of new possibilities.

Recording and Collecting Citations and Other Information. When you find possible references/citations, record those that look most interesting to you and that seem to be representative of work done in the field you're studying. Some databases allow you to create a marked citation list as you go along, and to print it out or e-mail it to yourself. If you can't e-mail or print a citation you want, you'll need to copy all of the information you need from the screen. For journal articles, you'll need the name of the journal, the year, volume and issue of the journal, and the page numbers of the article (but you'll need also the name of the author(s) and the title of the article for your final list of references, and it's best to capture that information right away). For books, you'll need the call number for locating the book (but you'll need author(s), title, date and place of publication and publisher for your list of references, and you'll want to capture that information as soon as you decide to use a book).

Journals may make their articles available on line through a database. For these you can get the full text by printing it, e-mailing it to yourself, or copying it to a disk. But you'll find most articles in bound copies in the periodicals section of the library (and the most recent issues in a separate section for current periodicals).

(continued)

Others are available in microfiche/microform (and you can ask your librarian for help in accessing and using them.) To find a bound volume of a journal in the library, you'll need to look in the on-line catalog of your library's holdings to see if the library has the journals and the volumes and where each journal and volume is located (usually by Library of Congress call number or alphabetically by title). If it's in an older bound volume, it will usually be shelved in a bound periodicals section, or, if it's on microfilm/microfiche, in a microform room. If it's very recent, it will most likely be shelved in a separate current periodicals section.

Use Your Searches to Help You Think More About Your Topic or Area of Interest and/or About the Academic Discourse Community of Your Discipline. While you're looking for a specific article, you'll want to find out more about the larger academic field of the discourse community you're studying by seeing what journals publish articles related to the field, and seeing what sorts of articles are published in those journals. If you're using a database that offers abstracts or whole-text articles, look at several abstracts or articles that you think will offer you the most interesting perspective on a topic in the field and/or that suggest other areas to explore. The database may also allow you to view other articles in the same issue, giving you a broader sense of what people are writing about. Note also the names of journals published in the field.

If you look up an article in a bound volume of a journal, take some time to skim the tables of contents for each issue in that volume and in other somewhat recent volumes. See what topics insiders have been writing about. Journals in many fields will include abstracts at the beginning of articles. Reading some of these abstracts will give you even more of an idea of the nature of insider conversations.

If you're searching for books in the library, note the call numbers for possibly useful books and then go to the shelf area with those numbers. See what else is shelved there, browsing through tables of contents, and trying to get a broad sense of the issues that people have explored in this area (and thus some of the <u>what</u> and <u>how</u> of your broader academic discourse community).

From these activities, what picture do you get of what insiders to your academic discourse community are interested in and the ways in which they study those questions of interest?

Finding a Representative Conversation

After you've found some articles to focus on, you'll need to select one to begin working with. Juliette's research interest drew her away from what biologists study toward a broader social question. But student researchers following Research Strand A seek articles that are representative of research in the discipline they've chosen. April, for example, was studying the academic discourse community of Introductory Psychology. She found references in a discipline-specific database, *PsycInfo,* and she chose an article by Carmella Roy and Ruth Russell in the *Journal of the American Academy of Child and Adolescent Psychiatry* (February 2000, v39i2, p. 257) with the title "Case Study: Possible Traumatic Stress Disorder in an Infant with Cancer." In a research memo on why she chose this article, she focuses on her interest in the topic itself: "This article interested me because I know someone who has this disorder. I always associated PTSD with war veterans and adults who were abused as children, so the thought of an infant having it interested me."

From a longer reflection on her process, we can see that, in selecting an article to read for her academic discourse community study, April was also conscious of trying to choose the sort of article that was representative of studies in the field of psychology.

> The article was about a case study done on an infant with Post Traumatic Stress Disorder that these psychiatrists did. Psychologists do a lot of observing and studying people's behaviors. One of the biggest parts of studying in the field of psychology is doing research to find out what causes certain behaviors in humans.
>
> In my psychology class we are required to do a research project where we form a hypothesis, observe people, and record our data. The project is somewhat like the study done in the article because we also have to study people. The hypothesis I chose to research was: Women drive more aggressively than men do. I observed people driving in different settings to try to prove my hypothesis. I gathered the data from my research and wrote my paper.
>
> In my psychology class we discuss studies that have been done on certain illnesses or aspects of psychology such as learning or memory. The case study in the article I chose would be typical of ones we would study in my psychology class. We have studied Post Traumatic Stress Disorder in class, which is why the article caught my eye. I also chose this article because it was a case study, which is the way most articles on psychology are written. This is the way psychologists do most of their research, by observing people. I learned this in my psychology class, and looked for an article that was written in that way.

April makes three important points about the ways in which the article she has chosen represents the work of the academic discourse community she is studying:

- It represents a type of research that psychologists often do—observing people;
- It represents the type of study that she has read about and read articles on in her psychology class;
- It has similarities to the type of study that she has had to carry out as an assignment for the course.

This is a good moment to make your final decision about one article you will work with and to reflect on your process of selection.

RESEARCH MEMO 9.4

What does this article offer you in relationship to:

—your own interest in the specific topic and any prior knowledge you might bring to it;

—the questions and issues you're interested in within the field;

—the ways in which it represents the work of the field;

—any connections it makes to other work you've been doing or might be required to do?

Are there any other factors that affect your choice?

Research Strand B: Why and how do you think that this article will serve as a good entry point for your continued research into your topic?

Carrying Out a Library Research Project (Research Strand B)

If you're combining your study of an academic discourse community with a library research assignment, you'll want to consider how to follow up on the beginning you've made here. Typically such research involves:

—Defining a question. So far you've done that loosely, seeing what match you might make between the articles you found and the interests you have. At this point you'll want to use your reading and your attempt to define a more focused question as complementary processes.

—Carrying out your research. To get a general sense of what's known about a topic, you may want to start with a general source like an encyclopedia. You'll also want to continue to use the library catalog and the databases that are most relevant to your field to search (using subject and key-word searches) for more sources of information and other studies. You'll also want to read and gloss and summarize the materials you find. And you'll want to be sure to record the information that will let you document what you've used appropriately and prepare a list of references or works cited.

—Continuing to focus your question. The processes of finding information and shaping and reshaping your guiding question are likely to be interrelated throughout your research process.

—Determining what you'll want to show in your final report and the evidence you'll draw on in your sources to show it. What have you finally come to understand about the question you've refined from the information you've found, and what will you draw on, from the sources you've used, in your final research report?

Juliette continued her research in these ways, following several related concerns. One focused on the ways in which women scientists were seen and treated in the past. She found a volume of *collected papers* from a 1999 New York Academy of Science Conference that focused on the history and the recent experience of women in science and engineering. Then she followed up on the specific experience of Rosalind Franklin, reading *The Double Helix,* Watson's account of the discovery of DNA, from which she drew the passage we saw in Chapter 8. Another concern was the ways the educational experience of girls affected the likelihood of their choosing scientific careers, and she explored this, beginning with an article written for a general audience in *U.S. News & World Report,* and then looking for work by some of the researchers mentioned in the article.

RESEARCH MEMO 9.5 (RESEARCH STRAND B)	You can use the preliminary work you've done as a basis for more extended library research by: —refining the question you're trying to answer through that research; —expanding on the resources you've found (books and articles) by using other databases and bibliographies and by drawing on the citations/references that appear in sources you've found useful; —seeing how those resources contribute to your understanding of the question you're pursuing and what you can use from them to support the answer you think you're finding; —preparing to write a report in which you present a question or thesis and draw on the evidence of these studies to answer or support it. Prepare one or more progress reports on this continued work.

ENTERING ACADEMIC CONVERSATIONS

As you use an article as a lens to see more clearly the shared knowledge, purposes, and ways valued within a larger academic field, you'll be positioned in a new way both as a reader and as a participant in the field's conversations. Reading a scholarly article gives you another picture of a discipline, with a specific example of what's talked about, how it's talked about, and what the purposes of such conversations might be.

Entering the Conversation as a Reader

Juliette's research question took her away from the specialized journals of the field of biology. But we can see what reading a scholarly article can show you about your own progress towards insiderness in this field by following another biology student. Here's what Jessica found when she read an article on the biology of the immune system in *the Journal of the American Medical Association.*

> The academic discourse community of biology is just one step on my path to entering the larger discourse community of biology. I am just beginning to learn some of the vocabulary that is necessary to enter the larger community. This is to be expected since Bio 111 is only an introductory course to such a broad discipline. Achieving the full vocabulary that belongs to a member of the biology discourse community will be a process that continues throughout my schooling. It was clear to me how far I have to go when I read an article from JAMA [*Journal of the American Medical Association*]. I was also able to see what vocabulary I have learned so far. Take for example part of one sentence from the JAMA article, "The *hydrolyzed peptides* complex in the *cytoplasm* with *transport-associated proteins* that direct the *peptides* to the *endoplasmic reticulum.* (Huston 1997, p. 1808). The words in italics are words I recognize from what I have learned so far in Bio 111. This sentence would have seemed to be in another language just a few months ago.

Looking beyond Bio 111 gives Jessica a sense of both the conversations that go on among researchers in the field of biology and the ways in which the course is preparing her for understanding and eventually participating in those conversations. It also allows her to recapture and to bring into the present conversation, some of her prior knowledge. For example, Jessica discovers that some of what she's heard in her job at a veterinary hospital is more closely related than she first realized to current research in biology: "Since biology is the study of living organisms including animals it makes sense that some of what is discussed in a veterinary hospital would also be discussed in the biology discourse community. What is learned in the study of biology is important to human and animal medicine."

Read and gloss the journal article you've found. Begin by reading the article's abstract (if there is one) to get a sense of what the article is about. Then look at: **READING RESPONSE**

- the introduction—highlighting/underlining the places that tell you what the study is about and the author's purpose,

- the conclusion—highlighting/underlining the places that tell you what was learned,

- the headings in the article, seeing what main topics will be discussed.

Read the article and:

- gloss with one color or symbol the words that seem to be specific to this academic discipline that you understand from general knowledge or from the course you're currently taking,   *(continued)*

(*continued*)

- gloss with another color or symbol the discipline-specific words that you don't understand,
- where there's a whole section you can't follow (a discussion of specific statistical tools if you haven't had statistics, for example) sum up what that section seems to contribute to the whole in the margin, but don't worry about trying to tease out all of its meaning.

What do you discover about your insiderness to the scholarly work of this field, and about the ways in which your course has introduced you to some of that work, from your experience in reading this article? What are you able to read and make sense of now that you couldn't have at the beginning of the semester? What key concepts, frames of mind/traditions, and theories from your course allow you to gain a general sense of the questions this writer raises and how he/she is going about answering them? What general understandings about academic conversations and how they work allow you to make sense of what you've found?

Entering the Conversation as a Writer

When you draw on articles you've discovered through research, you'll often be doing so to answer a question you've been exploring or to support a thesis you want to present. At other times, you may need to present a clear and accurate representation of what the author has presented, preserving the framework of the author's purposes and content and structure. In either case, in writing about the work of other scholars and researchers, you'll need to draw on particular genres or "speech acts" that are common to writing in academic contexts.

A *summary* is a common academic genre that's often used in conjunction with library research to give a clear representation of an article. The common purpose of summarizing an article is to represent the key information in the article in an abbreviated form. How abbreviated usually depends on the specific purpose of the summary. An overview summary or *abstract*, generally written by the author, often appears, as you've seen, at the beginning of an article to give readers a picture of what the article presents. Brief summaries of a number of studies often appear in research papers to provide background knowledge for the reader about other work that's going on in the field. Such brief summaries resituate the work that's being summarized in a new context—framed by the new purpose of the new writer. Longer, stand-alone summaries are more often used in classroom contexts, to show that a reader has fully understood the article or book and can represent its contents to others, and to create shared knowledge for a class where each participant may prepare a summary for others of a significant article or book in the field. You may want to try writing summaries for each of these purposes.

Here's the brief version of April's summary of "Case Study: Possible Post-Traumatic Stress Disorder in an Infant with Cancer" that she included in her final research report on her academic discourse community.

> The article was about an infant who was diagnosed with cancer and underwent many treatments in the hospital. The infant was initially a calm, quiet baby, but started to change after he was admitted to the hospital. He became very irritable and scared. To be diagnosed with Post-Traumatic Stress Disorder there must be a recognizable stressor and symptoms such as the re-experiencing of the trauma (also known as flashbacks), numbing (avoidance), hyper-alertness, sleep disturbances, and exaggerated startle response. The baby was experiencing all of these symptoms as well as some others.

April's summary captures the significant information of the article for a new, nonspecialist audience. But it's framed by her own purpose—to show that her psychology class has helped her take the first steps toward insiderness in the field—and in her longer study she uses this summary in making one of her key points—that she knows what to expect from such articles and knows some of the terminology she needs to read them, because of the work she'd been doing in the course.

You can find another example of a brief summary of a study and how it can be used as a springboard for a new discussion later in this chapter, in the summary of Chafe's research that introduces the topic of academic style.

READING RESPONSE

Create your own summary of an article. Begin by looking through your glossed text and noting the article's structure. What elements are included here? Are there headings to guide you as you move through those elements? Where does the author present a question or thesis, and how does the author structure the paper to address that question or thesis?

Then write a detailed summary of the article's main points. You'll want to think about the <u>what</u>, <u>why</u>, and <u>how</u> of the article you're summarizing, as you move through it and represent it as clearly and accurately as possible. You'll also want to think about the purpose of your own summary, and the likely shared knowledge of those who will read it.

<u>What</u> is the article about? What is being studied and what is the author reporting on here?

<u>Why</u> has the author undertaken this study? What question is the author posing? What is the author trying to discover, explain or understand?

<u>How</u> has the author gone about discovering some answers or gaining some new understandings? What methods has the author used to learn more about the topic and his/her specific question or area of concern within that topic?

<u>What</u> key points does the author present? What evidence does the author examine or use to support those points?   (*continued*)

(*continued*)
        <u>What</u> is the author's conclusion?

        <u>How</u> does this author present this information and how might that mode of presentation be connected to the concerns and purposes of the discipline, and to the likely audience of readers?

        When you've completed a detailed summary, write a second, brief version (3–5 sentences) that you might use in the context of a longer paper.
        A summary should always include full bibliographic information for the article or book being summarized.

A related "speech act" that's used in research papers is a *paraphrase*—a way of representing the ideas of another text in your own terms. Paraphrasing, like quoting, allows you to bring what someone else has said into the conversation you're creating, but without their actual words. April, for example, paraphrases the description she finds of the child who suffered from PTSD in her summary of that article, recasting "a 5-month-old infant in whom a neuroblastoma was diagnosed" as "an infant who was diagnosed with cancer." Some assignments call for longer paraphrases of a text, in which you move carefully through all of the text's main ideas, restating them in your own words, reducing the length of the original text by about a third or a half. Assignments of that type generally have the purpose of making sure that you fully understand what you have read.

Another common genre in academic settings for interacting with the work of others is the essay of *academic argument* (of *thesis and support)* in which you draw on the evidence scholars have found to support a thesis of your own. In this case another author's article provides the supporting evidence you'll use within your own structure and argument, and you'll draw on only the parts of the article that are relevant to your thesis and argument. While the academic argument essay, like the longer summary, is typically a classroom genre of academic writing, assigned in courses but not generally appearing as a distinct genre in the insider publications of a field, it calls on ways of thinking that are represented in those insider genres: being able to state a position or thesis, knowing how to bring in evidence to support that position, being able to use that evidence to counter opposing positions. So its purpose in the immediate academic discourse community of a class is to guide students into the ways of presenting information, making an argument, and using evidence that are characteristic of (and somewhat different for) the various academic disciplines. Of course, like all classroom writing genres, it also serves the purpose of assessment, providing a vehicle through which the writer's understanding and ways of thinking about course materials can be evaluated.

Asking a question and finding evidence that helps you answer it, and presenting a thesis and providing supporting evidence for that thesis are related processes. Generally in writing an academic argument, you engage in a process of inquiry first, find a tentative answer to your question, turn that answer into a *thesis*—into a statement of what you want to prove, and then return to the evidence that helped you answer your question, using it as supporting evidence for your argument. For example, April tells us she thought of PTSD as associated with adults. Having learned something about PTSD in the case of a child, she might have turned her initial surprise (and implicit question) about that into the thesis statement for an argument:

> Although Posttraumatic Stress Disorder has primarily been associated with adult survivors of war or abuse, it needs to be watched for in children as well.

Then she could use the evidence the article presents to make and support several points about the possibility of PTSD in a child.

A line of argument like this may finally be presented in the form of an essay or in the more extended form of a research paper. You can find further suggestions for writing in the essay genre of academic argument in the Strategies section in Part IV.

Entering the Conversation as a Researcher

As a psychology student, April is interested in researching Post-Traumatic Stress Disorder to learn more about why it might appear and what forms it might take in children. As a discourse community researcher, however, her question is different: she wants to know what an article like this can add to her understanding of the sorts of studies insiders to the field of psychology carry out. In her case, the article she's found has extended her understanding of PTSD but at the same time it has confirmed the picture of the <u>what</u>, <u>why</u>, and <u>how</u> of psychology that she had been getting in her introductory course. In her final report on her academic discourse community, she quotes from the course textbook to support that picture.

> Psychology is the "science of behavior and the mind" (Gray, pg. 3). Psychology is used to understand behavior, or why people or animals do certain, observable things. Psychologists do a lot of their research by observing behavior and "often use these data to make inferences about the mind" (Gray, pg. 3)

Your research into the written conversations of insiders to the academic discourse community you're studying, as represented by the journals you found and the journal article you reported on, may have confirmed and extended the understandings you've gained from your current course, as it has for April. It may have given you new understandings and insights, or it may even have offered a picture that conflicts with what you've perceived in your classroom discourse community. But it has provided you with new data for your ongoing inquiry as you consider the ways in which your current course is positioning you as a learner, in relation to a larger field of study.

| RESEARCH MEMO 9.6 | Write a research memo on the insider conversations of a discipline. Consider the following questions: |

- Why did an article you chose interest you as a researcher into the insider ways of this discourse community?

- What new understandings about the nature of scholarly inquiry in your discipline (about what people might study and why and how) have you gained from reading an article from a scholarly journal in that discipline, and how does this compare to some aspect of the work you've been doing in your course?

- What did you learn from this process about the "ways with words" of the discourse community (the academic field) this article represents or of the academic world in general?

- What did you learn from this research activity about yourself as an insider/outsider to the discourse community of a discipline? Is the course that you're in helping you to begin the process of becoming an insider to academic conversations in this field?

EXPLORING STYLE AND GENRE IN ACADEMIC WRITING

As you read an academic article, you're likely to find that the terminology is highly specialized and that, like Jessica, you can make sense of some of it from what you've been learning in your course. But it's not just the specialized terms that make academic articles difficult to read. Researchers who have studied differences between spoken and written language have discovered some significant ways written texts typically differ from spoken ones, even when they address the same topic for the same purpose. Some features of written language arise from how written language is produced by writers and processed by readers. These differences appear even when the same information is being told or written to the same audience.

It's also the case, however, that a particular style can come to dominate both what's said and what's written in a community. In your study of an informal discourse community, you may have found that a distinctive style appeared across different exchanges in different genres, just as Heath found "talking junk" to be a style that showed up in many Trackton exchanges: in stories, in children's playsongs and rhymes, and in the informal conversations that took place on people's porches. In academic settings, the style of much academic writing can carry over into the classroom, despite typical differences in spoken and written language. Understanding more about the features of a typical academic style and about <u>why</u> such features have evolved can help you as a reader in making sense of complex and difficult texts, as a writer in producing texts that make complex ideas accessible to your readers, and as a classroom participant taking part in spoken conversations that are influenced by that style.

We'll begin our inquiry into academic style by looking at a simple spoken text and written text first and then seeing how the features of the written text are concentrated in academic writing.

Seeing Differences in Spoken and Written Language

The linguist Wallace Chafe (1982) studied the ways we present ideas in speaking and writing by analyzing many examples of both spoken and written texts. He found that writing allows ideas to be presented more densely and compactly (Chafe's term for this is *integration*), because the writer has more time to place those ideas in precise relationships to one another, and the reader has time to process that integrated information. In speaking, ideas are typically spread out and added on one at a time as the speaker thinks of them (Chafe's term for this is *fragmentation*). That separation between ideas also helps the listener, who doesn't have time to unpack densely integrated ideas while attending to the flow of speech.

If we look back at Dana's story about his brother smashing up his father's truck, in Chapter 2, we can see that even in these straightforward texts there are differences in how the same ideas are presented. For example, as Dana was telling the story to the class, there were many "ands" and "ahs" and pauses that break his ideas into small units. Dana was presenting each idea that came to his mind one by one, adding on, bit by bit, information about the parking garage.

Writers can write in a style that adds one idea on to another in the ways we typically do in speaking, but more formal writing typically involves greatly expanded units of information that we punctuate as sentences. Writers are likely to subordinate one clause (one group of words with a subject and verb) to another or embed clauses within other clauses instead of adding new ideas in separate clauses strung together with "and." In Dana's written version of his story, we find a more complex sentence structure, as in "Apparently what had happened when my brother Don took the truck out was that he did not pull the emergency brake on all the way when he parked it." This sentence contains many ideas about who did what when. But the difference between this written sentence and Dana's spoken version isn't just that the "ands" and "ahs" have been eliminated. The structure of his sentences (the *syntax*) has become much more complicated. The sentence begins with an introductory element "apparently" that indicates the speaker's perspective on what follows. Then comes a subject ("what had happened when my brother took the truck out"), the verb ("was") and the complement that follows the verb "to be" ("that he did not pull the emergency brake on all the way when he parked it.")

You don't have to have formal knowledge of a lot of grammar to see how complexly these ideas have been interwoven and to see the contrast to a simple subject-verb-complement sentence like "My brother was careless." Chafe refers to this quality of written language, where ideas are packed together in sentences through the use of more complex syntax, as *integration*.

Fragmentation and *integration* define one dimension in which spoken and written language contrast. Another dimension that Chafe identifies is the extent to which the text shows evidence of the speaker's *involvement* with his/her ideas and with the listeners. Some writers also use such features, but often written texts lack them; Chafe calls the absence of involvement features *detachment.* Speakers typically involve their listeners and show their own involvement, as Dana does, in several ways: by using first and second person references. ("You gotta know my father"), by referring to their own thinking ("the thing that I think is hilarious"), by making sure their listeners can follow ("You know?"), and by using words that create emphasis ("It's *totally* disheveled"). They also tend to be fuzzy in their choice of words ("It slams into like . . . a gate thing"). And they often use direct quotes to make an account of an event even more immediate and more involving. Detached writing (or speaking) doesn't use these involvement features.

Academic writing is typically even more syntactically integrated and interpersonally detached for reasons that have to do with the setting. We've already seen that sharing knowledge and ideas is particularly important in academic settings—more important than maintaining interpersonal connections. It makes sense, then, that features that allow more information to be packed into sentences and that reduce the amount of space taken up with interpersonal interaction will be emphasized. And this is what *integration* and *detachment* allow. We'll see how these features show up in an academic context by comparing two texts—April's oral summary of the journal article on the baby with PTSD and the *abstract* that was published with the article.

Here's the oral summary of the article that April gave to her research group:

A baby boy that was born healthy was two weeks old and went into cardiac arrest. He showed traumatic stress disorder. There was recurrent stress and the baby was put into the hospital four times. He was too good a baby to be irritable. He still experienced trauma until he went home at five months. In two weeks he began acting like a normal baby. Now he's four and he's a normal child but he still has some problems. He can't stand for his hands and feet to be touched as a result of nurses holding him down.

Here's the abstract that appeared with the article.

The post-traumatic stress disorder model has been used to describe some children's experience with cancer. This article presents the case of a 5-month-old infant in whom a neuroblastoma was diagnosed at age 2 weeks. His symptoms at the time of the psychiatric consultation were consistent with the criteria for traumatic stress disorder in infants from the ZERO TO THREE: Diagnostic Classification. This case study invites future clinical and research queries about traumatic stress disorder in infants with serious medical illnesses.

April's spoken summary was preceded by introductory comments that placed her as the reader "I found an article about . . . " and was followed by a discussion of how she approached the article as a reader, so she created involvement with her listeners through the larger speech event. But the summary itself is brief and sticks to the point of the article, without any of the involvement features and without the fragmentation that we saw for more informal spoken language. Nevertheless, it's much less complex syntactically than the written abstract, which uses a dense and very detached academic style that's typical of journals in the sciences and of some in the social sciences. There are no first person pronouns in the abstract, for example, so that the writers disappear behind the text: "This article presents . . . " "This case study invites . . . " The *passive voice* also contributes to the quality of detachment: "The posttraumatic stress disorder model *has been used*"; we don't see researchers developing and using a model but a model standing alone, serving as the subject of the sentence.

The writers of this abstract and of the article itself were using a style that's common in this journal and in this discipline. They were probably also affected by specific restrictions on the number of words they could use for their abstract (they used about 80) and they probably had to keep within a defined page limit for the whole article. So a style that packs together as much information as possible into a small space can be explained with two why's—discourse community expectations and the practical concerns of publishing expensive journals.

The writers of such articles have acquired this style by participating in a discourse community that uses it, and probably aren't at all aware of it. Nevertheless, we can identify some features of this style, and being aware of those features can help us to work with the style as readers and to use it or avoid it, as appropriate to our setting, as writers. The following points give more details of how these features work in April's article.

- Formal academic texts often pack as much information as possible into every subject, verb, object slot in the sentence. Just look at the subject of the first sentence—"the post-traumatic stress disorder model." Three words are crammed in before the noun "model," to modify it and give more information about it. And at least one of those words, "post-traumatic," is itself packed with information. To unpack this subject the way a speaker might, we'd need to string together several clauses, something like "people experience trauma, and after the trauma they feel stress, and if they keep feeling stress, their emotional balance can get out of order." But that takes a lot of words, and the phrase "post-traumatic stress disorder," with the abbreviation PTSD, which is used throughout the article, packs all of that information, ultimately, into four letters that refer to a complicated concept that insiders understand.

- Formal written texts often use words that have changed their category from noun to verb to adjective and vice versa. This is one aspect of our grammar that allows a lot of information to be packed together. It means that you can take a noun like "trauma," create an adjective from it, "traumatic," and then put that adjective in front of another noun "disorder"—getting the information associated with two different nouns into a single subject or object slot of a sentence.

A common sort of category change that significantly affects the vocabulary of academic settings is a change from verb to noun by adding "tion," making words like "communication," "acceleration," "magnification," and in this example, "consultation." When you move the verb into the noun slot in this way, you free up the verb slot for new information and can again pack more in. But you also create a formal-sounding style that has come to seem appropriate to the language of ideas.

■ Formal writing also uses different sorts of clauses to bring information together in a sentence, especially "who" or "which" or "that" clauses (*relative clauses*). In the abstract, the second sentence could have been divided in two, reading: "This article presents the case of a 5-month-old infant. The infant was diagnosed as having a neuroblastoma." Instead, we find "*in whom* a neuroblastoma was diagnosed at age two weeks," which saves the repetition of "the infant" and allows a second set of information to be embedded in the first sentence.

These are just a few of the grammatical features that have been studied in written texts, but they'll give you an idea of why and how the style of densely written texts has arisen. If you have trouble with such texts as a reader (and any reader who is an outsider to the academic field of such a text is bound to have trouble at first), you can try the strategy of unpacking the most dense and troublesome sentences, rewording them into a series of shorter ideas that are closer to the way someone would talk.

Formal written texts also tend to use a different vocabulary from spoken ones. That vocabulary is shaped partly by changing one form of speech into another, as we've seen. It's also shaped by the availability of a more formal vocabulary, derived from Latin, for many public and professional contexts and by a concern for expressing precise meanings where shared knowledge can't be confirmed. April glossed the article as she read it, writing the main points of each paragraph to the side and highlighting technical terms she understood (PTSD, startle response, differential diagnosis, and delirium) in pink, and terms she did not fully understand (adverse psychological sequelae, neuroblastoma, laminectomy, and pancytopenia) in orange. Despite her uncertainty about some of these terms, she found that overall "the article's language was not hard for me to understand. It used a lot of medical terms that would be confusing to most. I worked in a hospital for three years, and my mother is in the medical field and uses these terms often, so I understood most of what was written." Because she's used to being around a discourse community that uses technical terms she doesn't fully understand, she doesn't worry so much, as a reader, if she misses specific terms as long as she has an overall understanding of what's being talked about.

April and other student researchers also observe that the language used in their classes is not as formal as the language used in the journal articles they find. The difference between the formal classroom discourse of a lecture and the formal written discourse of an article on the same topic often has to do with involvement features. Professors usually try to make difficult concepts more accessible by talking about them in more informal ways and paying more attention to interpersonal connections. You might want to return to your own analysis of a classroom conversation (Research Memo 8.2) to see whether this is true in your class as well.

Writers too draw on involvement features to try to make more of a connection with their readers. (Even in this book, for example, the personal pronouns "we" and "you" are intended to help make an interpersonal connection.) Speaking directly to the reader, unpacking ideas and sentences, finding ways to create emphasis, and using direct quotations are all ways to make your writing more accessible to your readers and to keep their interest. The most dense style of academic writing may have a function in certain contexts, but many academic readers at all levels of insiderness complain about it, and the more you can do to make your style reader-friendly, the more effective your writing will be for most purposes.

OBSERVATION ACCOUNT

You can begin to look closely at style in academic writing by examining the style of the article you're working with in several ways:

- Take a few sentences that you find to be particularly dense and complex and perhaps hard to understand in the article you read. Unpack these by breaking them apart, making simpler and shorter sentences and trying to represent the ideas in the ways that a speaker might think of them.

- Look at the <u>how</u> of this article from the perspective of style. How would you describe the language used in it? What are some words that the writer or writers use frequently in this study? How would you characterize this style? Once you have described the how of this article, speculate about the <u>why</u>. Why is this kind of language used in this article? Why would the article be written in this style? What sense do you have about how the style of this article meets the expectations of its intended audience?

- Compare spoken and written summaries of the article.

Summarize your article orally for a classmate while that classmate writes down what you say (as April did). Type up the spoken summary and then choose an abstract or one paragraph from the article you're reporting on that's most summary-like. Look at the evidence of integration/fragmentation in each of the two versions. What differences do you find in the sentence structures (the *syntax*) of these two versions? Do they differ in terms of—the packing of a lot of information into each sentence—the formation of nouns from verbs or other changes of grammatical category—the use of <u>who</u>, <u>which,</u> and <u>that</u> clauses? Do they differ in terms of the vocabulary that's used? Do they differ in terms of the presence of involvement features such as the use of personal pronouns (you, we) if any? What other differences do you note?

What would you say about the accessibility of the paragraph from the article for you as a reader? Are there features that help to make it accessible?

Considering Other Aspects of Style in Academic Writing

Different academic discourse communities have tended to develop particular styles that fit with their purposes and their shared ways of seeing and representing the world, and the style of an article in a medical journal is quite different from what you'll find in a composition journal. But there are also some aspects of academic style that are emphasized across most academic discourse communities and that come up frequently in discussions of academic writing. These are qualities of style that you've been drawing on in your own writing, but it's helpful to name them at this point in terms that are typically used in academic contexts.

- *Clarity.* In academic writing, the concept of clarity functions on several levels at once. It involves, in part, your having a clear line of argument or presentation or inquiry that runs through the whole paper, with a structure that's easy for a reader to follow. It means that you'll want to state specific points and ideas clearly in terms that readers will understand. It means that you'll want to give explanations for terms that need them—that might not represent shared knowledge in the particular discourse community you're writing for (perhaps doing so in parenthesis). It may mean that you'll sometimes break very complicated sentences into simpler ones. It always requires that you be sure your own thinking is clear about what you're writing about and what you want to say. Beginning with reflective, informal writing and talking out your ideas with others are good ways to work toward getting your thinking and your writing clear.

- *Focus.* In informal conversation, where people are enjoying hanging out together, the discussion can jump from topic to topic and no one's likely to mind. Some written essays—especially personal and reflective ones—will also weave in a fair amount of digression. But in most academic settings, readers (both students and teachers) have an enormous amount of reading to do and they want that reading to stick to the point. So most of the time, you'll want your writing to have a clear focus and to stick to that focus all the way through. Having a *focusing question, thesis,* or *hypothesis* (a tentative thesis that you'll test out in your discussion) can keep your discussion on track. Keeping a clear focus is also important within paragraphs, which is why traditional writing instruction has often focused on the concept of the *topic sentence*—a sentence that states the main idea of the paragraph.

- *Coherence.* Not only do academic readers want writing to be focused, but they want to be able to see how all of the parts are connected and related, whether within a paragraph or within the whole essay. *Coherence* refers to the quality of connectedness. You can achieve it in an essay, in part, by making clear connections between one section and another—sometimes by using *transitions* like "the first point . . . the second point" or *transitional expressions* like "therefore," "in addition," or "on the other hand" to show how the information in one sentence relates to another. Repetition of words and phrases from one sentence to another or one paragraph to another can also contribute to coherence.

■ *Concreteness.* A lot of academic writing is about abstract ideas and concepts like alienation and determinism and intentionality (to use a few of Rose's examples). To create shared understandings of such concepts, it's almost always necessary to apply them to concrete examples. Likewise, to convince readers about an argument you want to make, or to let them see what has led you to particular conclusions, you need to share with them the details and the evidence that will let them think with you and arrive at those conclusions with you. So as a writer, whether you're writing a research report or a poem, you'll always want to connect your big ideas to details, examples, and evidence.

■ *Readability.* We've seen that what's readable to participants in one discourse community won't necessarily be to others. *Transitions* that contribute to coherence can also help your readers. *Headings* that break up complexly-worded academic studies and tell your reader what to expect in each section will also make such writing more readable. But whatever the discourse community you're writing for, the overall readability of your writing will involve not only the qualities of *clarity, focus,* and *concreteness,* but bringing your reader into the world you're creating through your writing—particularly by providing the insider shared knowledge that's needed to understand what's going on there.

There are also some specific elements of style that help to invite readers into the language as well as the ideas of a text. The involvement features that we've seen associated with spoken texts can also be used in written ones—a writer can address readers directly with "you" and refer to his or her own thinking about the topic (sometimes adding such comments in parentheses), for example, although these features aren't always accepted in some academic writing contexts.

The linguist Deborah Tannen, in her book *Talking Voices* names three other features that invite listeners and readers into a conversation and that contribute to its *aesthetic* or pleasing qualities.

—*Repetition* can include the repetition of sound, of words, of syntactic patterns (like the repetition of the three prepositional phrases in this sentence). Repetition allows readers and listeners to pick up the rhythm and the sense of what has been said and to predict what might follow. It also provides connections across sentences and from one part of a text to another, creating the sense of a coherent whole.

—*Dialogue* involves the direct representation of speech, in the ways you may have used in your memoir and in your report on a discourse community. It brings the reader into a scene directly, through its actual words, rather than indirectly through the writer's reporting on those words. Likewise directly quoting one text within another (something that contributes to the *intertextuality* of most academic writing), brings the reader into the quoted text directly rather than through the indirect report of the new writer. Such quotations, in the ways you've been using them, invite the reader to look at the original writer's words and to think about them along with you.

—*Imagery* includes not only creating visual images, but also giving the sorts of specific details that again create a sense for the reader or listener of being on the scene. If you look back at Rose's opening portrayal of the setting of the Introductory Sociology course, you'll see the ways in which such details allow you to imagine the scene and place yourself within it.

One of the best ways to think about how you want to work with the style of your own writing is to begin to observe the features of style that attract you as a reader, particularly in writing that comes from contexts you'll be writing in.

| **REFLECTIVE INQUIRY** | This is a good moment to think about academic style from a reader's/writer's perspective. Choose a piece of academic writing that you've enjoyed reading, either from the materials in this book or from the readings for another of your courses. What do you appreciate about this piece of writing from a reader's perspective? Can you describe those qualities in the terms often named as desirable for academic writing: clarity, focus, coherence, and concreteness? Can you describe them in terms of the ways in which they involve you and create shared knowledge for you as a reader? Do you find the elements of repetition, dialogue, and imagery that Tannen finds to make both spoken and written texts pleasing to their readers? Is there anything else that you can identify that contributes to your appreciation of this text?

Or choose a piece of your own writing that you've enjoyed writing for any of your academic discourse communities, where you feel that you've achieved a style that seems comfortable to you in addressing that audience for that purpose, and that you feel others might appreciate. Can you see in this piece of writing the qualities of clarity, focus, and coherence? Can you be specific about the way the writing works, and about <u>how</u> you've tried to make it work as you feel it does? Do you find any of the terms from this discussion of style useful in naming what you find, or are there other ways you can name it?

You might also reflect on <u>why</u> you chose to write in this particular academic style for this particular context and whether you think it's important to add this style to your repertoire? What happened when you employed this sort of academic style of writing? Did you start to assume the identity of the community that writes in this style? Why would you want to address your audience in this way? How did you position yourself (in light of your audience and of the larger on-going conversation) when you used academic language in this way? |
|---|---|

Genre in Academic Writing

The article that April is reporting on is written in the genre of a research report, reporting on a particular form of research called a *case study*. The term *case study* means that the study focuses on one case (or on two or three individual cases), rather than many different instances. The authors of this study aren't trying to find patterns across many cases of children with PTSD but to look in detail at the example of one child.

The larger genre of the research report has many different forms, but reports on *primary research* typically include the elements April has found here:

- A *summary* of what other, related studies have found about PTSD in children,

- Some *background information* about how PTSD in children is defined and diagnosed,

- A *detailed account of what's being reported on*—here this includes the experience, treatment, and symptoms of this child's illness (cancer); and the symptoms that led to the diagnosis of this child's problem as PTSD,

- A *discussion of what has been learned* by looking at this case of PTSD, along with unanswered questions to be explored in future research,

- A *reference page* (in this case, in APA style—see the Strategies section for a discussion of citation and reference style).

You'll find similar elements in the research article by Anyon that is included in the Additional Readings for Part III.

In some fields, a great many of the written conversations will be about such *primary research*—about studies that researchers have carried out in laboratories and in field settings, through observations, interviews, or controlled experiments (including field research of the sort you've been doing), as opposed to studies that bring together what others have already learned through *secondary research* (library research). Primary and secondary research are big categories that are used to make a rough division in the ways in which research is carried out. But they're too general to adequately describe the genres scholars work in. In the sciences and social sciences, people often write papers of three types, and you're likely to run into examples of each of these as you look at the journals in a field like:

—*research studies* like the ones we've been reading;

—*reviews of the literature* that bring together what others have shown in their studies, sum up the state of knowledge in the field, highlight areas where there is disagreement, and point to directions for further study; and

—*theoretical papers* that take what's been learned from various studies and try to come up with a larger explanation that can cover these different instances.

The Additional Readings at the end of Part III. include a published research study that reports on primary research in educational contexts—a study by Jean Anyon that looks at schools in different socio-economic areas. An article by Gee offers a theoretical perspective on *literacy* and *discourse* and how these might be defined and applied as working concepts. By looking closely at the <u>how</u> of these articles, you can expand your picture of these genres and how they work.

In other fields—typically the arts and humanities, you'll also find essays that offer new theoretical perspectives and bibliographic essays that review and synthesize what's been written about a topic. But you'll also find articles that focus on the interpretation of a work of art, a piece of music, or a literary work, or that offer critical reviews of a work or of a performance (like the one we saw Vanessa discussing in Chapter 8).

As we saw when we looked at speech genres in discourse communities in Part II, genres arise within the context of a community's ongoing and repeated interactions and take on the shapes that fit the needs of that community. Even the genre of the *research study* will look somewhat different in different fields. Specific features, like the abstract that April finds, may or may not appear in the journals of other fields. Its presence points to the desire of people in the fields of psychology and psychiatry to get key information about a study quickly. A database of abstracts (*Psychology Abstracts*) allows readers to scan quickly for information about all of the recent studies that have been published, and then to follow up on those that are most relevant to their own work. Such a feature assumes a particular position on the part of a reader: The emphasis here is on speed of information retrieval, not on entering the text and following out a process of engaging with the thinking it invites. Disciplines that focus more on bringing the reader into particular ways of seeing the world— like philosophy and literature and the arts—tend less often to highlight the abstract as a dominant feature in their published written conversations.

Once again, genres reflect the shared values and shared purposes of a community, and they change shape or new genres arise as those values and purposes change. *Genre* is a useful concept for naming the repeated ways in which written conversations may be carried out, just as it is a useful concept for naming the repeated patterns like stories and jokes that appear in the spoken conversations of a community. But it's most useful as a way of thinking about and naming the similar repeated patterns that you find, not as a rigid set of names for genre types or a rigid set of rules for producing them. And sometimes you'll make a conscious choice to step outside of the boundaries of a particular genre when you have the freedom to do so. Juliette started to carry out a discourse community study of her biology class. Then she became interested in the topic of women and science and decided to pursue it through secondary research in the library (though she could also have done primary research on this topic by interviewing women scientists, or interviewing young girls about their experiences in science courses). In the end, because her questions focused, in part, on understanding her own experience, she chose to write her final report in a mixed genre, blending what she learned from her observations of the academic discourse community of her biology course, what she learned from her library research, and her reflections on her own experience. She adapted the genres available to her to suit her own purpose and her own inquiry.

Academic writing assignments for courses often draw on particular classroom writing genres (like the longer summary or the argument essay) in essay assignments and essay exams. But the genres that insiders to the field write in are often genres that are represented in the assignments for a course as well (as was true in April's case). For example, music students may be assigned to write concert reviews like those that a professional reviewer might undertake, while sociology students are often asked to write studies of particular settings such as "urban enclaves" in the way that a sociology researcher might do. Looking back at the genres of your course assignments from the perspective you now have on the sorts of writing that professional insiders to the field do, you may be able to see more ways in which the academic discourse community of your classroom provides an entry into the larger academic discourse community of the field.

Here are some ways to learn more about the genres of the discourse community you are studying:

- Take another look at the journal article you have been working with. What elements of this article seem particularly significant to you? Have you come across other articles in your research or class readings that have been formatted, structured, or organized as this one is? What conventions do you think the author of this article followed when writing or revising this article? How would you name the genre of this article? In what settings have you come across this genre before? Will elements of this genre be useful to you as you draft you own study?

- Make a list of the genres your classmates have come across, and list some of the characteristic traits of those genres. What are the similarities between articles written in the same genre? What are the differences between them? What relationship do you find between the genres or examples of a genre your classmates have found and the academic discourse communities they're studying? Does seeing those relationships help you to discover anything more about the relationship between common genres or features of a genre in the academic discourse community you are studying and the shared values and ways of that community?

- Look back again at your assignments for your classroom community. How would you name the genres of those assignments? What are their key features? How do they connect with the genres of scholarly writing that are published in the journals associated with the discipline? What would you say the purpose is of having you write within these genres?

RESEARCH MEMO 9.7

WRITING IN ACADEMIC GENRES

As a participant in an academic discourse community, you'll want to make your own contribution to the conversation, writing to other readers about what you've discovered about that community or about a research interest associated with that community. You may also want to report back orally (whether as an individual or as a research group) in a way that orients those classmates who are outsiders to this academic discourse community to its ways, showing what you need to be interested in and able to do to function effectively in that community and to like the work that goes on there. Sharing this knowledge of the ways of the different discourse communities created in different courses and disciplines will help your classmates to identify some other academic communities they might want to enter through their courses and other research areas they might want to pursue, and to approach those courses and that research with effective strategies for becoming insiders.

Research Strand A: Research Report on an Academic Community

As a researcher, you've explored the shared knowledge, shared purposes and shared ways of an academic discourse community, using many different sources of data. As a writer, you now want to use the academic genre of the field research report to report on what you've found.

Your research report for this unit will be similar to the ethnographic research report you wrote for Part II, with a couple of significant differences. In that ethnographic study, your purpose was to find out what you could about the ways of your community, without pursuing a particular question or determining a focus in advance. Over time, you were able to characterize your discourse community and to use the evidence you'd gathered through your observations, your recording of a conversation, etc., to show that characterization. But, as is typically the case for ethnographic studies, the meanings you found emerged from your familiarity with the community and your position as an insider participant as well as a researcher. Ethnographic studies don't typically begin with a focused question but try to come to as rich an understanding as possible of all aspects of the life of a community or a cultural setting.

For this study of an academic discourse community, you are positioned, at least partially, as an insider to the immediate classroom setting, but you are not yet an insider to the larger field that helps to define that classroom, so you can't fully know all of the shared knowledge and values and ways that shape that academic community. Your research depends not on naming the implicit knowledge that you already share but on analyzing and naming what you see in the new data you've examined. You've begun your study by naming some questions that you wanted to pursue about your academic discourse community, and they've guided your thinking about at least some of what you've found through your research. Here are some final steps you may want to take.

■ *Reflecting on and reshaping your original question, focus, and purpose.* As you prepare to write up your research report, you'll want to return to your guiding questions and reflect on what you've learned about them (and on how your focus may have changed since you began your research—a common experience for researchers). Have you refocused those questions in any way as you've gone along? Have you found evidence that helps you to answer any of those questions, or has your study given you more information about other questions and issues that you hadn't originally thought of? Now that you've completed gathering data and doing various pieces of informal analysis that can contribute to your larger study, what have you found that's most interesting? How do you think you might reframe or revise your original question to ask something that you feel you can answer by looking at the data you've gathered and the analyses you've done? What will you want to show about the course, the way in which it has worked for you as an introduction to an academic discipline or topic, and how it has helped you to understand the <u>what</u>, <u>why</u>, and <u>how</u> of work in that field (or about what you've learned about why it hasn't worked)?

■ *Reading the reports of other academic discourse community researchers.* As you write up this final research report, keep in mind the elements that you've found in the other research studies you've read, including the features of genre that you've identified and the features of style that have made the study clear and accessible and interesting to you as a reader. Several studies by student researchers, focusing on the academic discourse communities of different courses, appear in the readings at the end of this chapter and show some ways in which others have used the research report genre to report on their discoveries about their academic discourse community. What do you find about the <u>what</u>, <u>why</u>, and <u>how</u> of the way in which one of these researchers has reported on his/her study? What elements work for you, as a reader, in helping you to understand the insider ways of this discourse community? Is there anything that you learn from your experience of reading these reports that you want to consider as you write your own?

■ *Planning, drafting, writing, and revising your research report on an academic discourse community.* As you plan, draft, write, and revise your report, think about it once again as a written conversation, one that places you in a community of discourse community researchers. What are other researchers (including those in your classroom) likely to know about the discourse community you're reporting on? What are their expectations of discourse community studies likely to be? What do you want to show them about the particular community you've studied? About the relationship between the sort of work you do for the course and the sort of study scholars do in the field? About your own sense of insiderness based on your experience in the classroom and in reading an article in the field? How does what you've learned connect with what's been shown in other studies of academic settings? What do you want to share with your readers of your own final understandings about the questions that framed your study?

What evidence do you think you'll draw on to show these things? (Read back through your research memos to find evidence you'll draw into this final report.)

In planning your report, you'll want to make a flexible, working outline of the main points you'll make and the key supporting evidence you'll use, and then work from that outline for your first draft. (The informal, working outline is one of the organizing strategies discussed in the Writing Strategies section.)

■ *Working with references and citations.* See discussion for Research Strand B, on page 441.

CHECKLIST FOR REVISING YOUR RESEARCH REPORT	Have you thought about: ■ Audience? Have you imagined a wider audience of readers beyond your class, why this study might be interesting to such readers, and what they'd need to know about your academic discourse community? Have you characterized your academic discourse community in a way that would make sense to such readers? Do you have a *title* that captures your sense of this community and characterizes it for your readers? ■ Introduction? Have you introduced your academic discourse community to that wider audience, brought them into your community and the themes you want to present about it in an interesting and involving way? Have you then given the sort of background information about the course and the field it's in that will give them enough of a picture of it right away so that they can really follow what you say next? ■ Purpose? Have you made a clear statement in your introduction or near the beginning of your report about your purpose for reporting on this community— about what you wanted to learn about it and now want to show about it? What questions/issues can the readers expect to find explored/addressed here? ■ Organization? Have you organized your report in a way that will make it easy for readers to follow? It's a good idea to say something up front about what main topics or themes you'll be addressing. Have you used *headings* that guide your reader through major sections of your study? ■ Examples? Have you given clear examples that support whatever the key points are that you're making about your academic discourse community and your experience of it? Do you quote from your data (catalog description, course materials/artifacts; classroom discourse; library article) to support your points about your academic discourse community and your experience of it as an introduction for you to the work of the field? ■ Connections? Have you made clear and meaningful connections to the other studies you've read in Part III, creating shared knowledge with your readers about what has been learned in other research and how it supports or comple- <div align="right">(continued)</div>

ments your own study or the ways in which your own study expands on, contributes to, alters, or contradicts what others found? Have you quoted from other studies? From other sources (including this book)? Have you included author and page numbers?

- Conclusion? Have you shown what you have learned about this academic discourse community from your study and what your readers should learn from reading this report? This is a good place to name those final, richer understandings that you want people to take away.

Finally, have you used as much as possible from all of your writing in this unit to create the richest, fullest report you can—one that represents your most complete understandings of your own academic discourse community and how it has worked for you in guiding your entry into the study of the larger field? And

- Have you edited?

- Have you attached a page of complete references for the works you've quoted or referred to, including a full citation for your library journal article. (See the guidelines for MLA or APA bibliographic reference style in Part IV, Documenting Sources.)

Research Strand B: Report on Library Research

As a researcher, you've not only explored the shared knowledge, shared purposes, and shared ways of an academic discourse community, but you've carried out your own research into a topic of interest in that community. As a writer, you now want to use the academic genre of the library research report to report on what you've found about that topic. Here are some final steps you will want to take.

- *Reflecting on and reshaping your original question, focus, and purpose.* Now, as you prepare to write up your research report, you'll want to return to your guiding questions and reflect on what you've learned about them (and on how your focus may have changed since you began your research—a common experience for researchers). What were the questions that you originally intended to pursue in your study of an academic discourse community? Have you refocused those questions in any way as you've learned more about what others have studied and the sorts of information available to you? What have you actually learned, and how can the guiding question for your inquiry be reshaped as a guiding question for your report, preparing your readers for what you've discovered? What will you want to show, not only about the topic you've been exploring but about what you've learned about the ways in which research conversations take place in this field?

- *Reading the reports of other researchers.* As you write up this final research report, you'll want keep in mind the elements that you've found in the other research studies you've been reading as you've carried out your library research (as well as those you've read in this book), including the features of genre that you've identified and the features of style that have made the study clear and accessible and interesting to you as a reader. The readings at the end of Part III include Juliette's library research report. What do you find about the <u>what</u>, <u>why</u>, and <u>how</u> of the way in which Juliette, one of your classmates, or another researcher has reported on his/her study? What elements work for you, as a reader, in helping you to understand what the researcher was trying to learn and found? Is there anything that you learn from your experience of reading any other research report that you want to consider as you write your own?

■ *Planning, drafting, writing, and revising your research report on an academic discourse community.* As you plan, draft, write, and revise your report, think about it once again as a written conversation, one that places you in a community of researchers within the field that you've chosen.

☐ What readers are you writing to with this report (a general audience of outsiders to the field, partial insiders like others in your course, or full insiders like scholars in the field)?

☐ What have you learned in your academic discourse community inquiries about what partial insiders or full insiders are likely to know about this topic that outsiders may not?

☐ What sorts of shared knowledge will you have to create for whatever group of readers you've identified?

☐ What do you want to show them about what you've learned?

☐ What new understandings will you want them to gain?

☐ What evidence do you think you'll draw on to show these things? (Read back through your glossed copies of articles, your research notebook, and your Research Memo 9.5, to find evidence you'll draw into this final report.)

Within the genre of the research report there are many variations across disciplines. Have you considered, from your own reading, how articles in your field are typically structured? Are there elements and arrangements you'll want to have in your report in order to place your writing within the conversations of the field?

In planning your report, you'll want to make a flexible, working outline of the main points you'll make and the key supporting evidence you'll use, and then work from that outline for your first draft. (The informal, working outline is one of the organizing strategies discussed in the Writing Strategies section.)

Working with References and Citations

Including a list of references or citations that you've used is an important convention of academic writing. In academic discourse communities, insiders depend on larger, on-going written conversations. They reference the turns that other people have taken in the conversation and cite other sources as they further their own interpretations and understandings. Documentation of other sources, then, provides a way of seeing how any report is placed in the bigger picture of the field's conversations. If you look at the references/citations for a journal article you have drawn on for your study, you'll see that they suggest the company the writer keeps—the people whose work informs his or her own, the titles and topics those people address, and the disciplines they draw on.

Look also at the style of documentation that's used for the references/citations (beginning with whether the section is labeled *References* or *Works Cited.* Can you identify the style as the MLA, or APA (a discussion of these styles, with guidelines and examples, appears in Part IV), or is it different from each of these? The MLA documentation style is typically used in English and foreign languages and literatures, and MLA (or another style, CMS) for other fields situated in the humanities, while APA style is used for many of the social sciences. When you compare the documentation style with that of other articles your classmates have chosen, what differences do you see? Can you speculate about the concerns and priorities of scholars in different fields when you look at differences in citation formats? What seems to be valued in these fields? How can you account for the differences you notice?

Finally, you'll want to choose the appropriate style for your own references/citations of the works you've actually referred to in your study, or a larger bibliography of works you consulted. Determine the style that predominates in your sources or that you know is expected in the discipline you are working in, and consult Documenting Sources in Part IV for an abbreviated guide to two major styles: MLA and APA.

Have you thought about:

- Audience? Have you determined the audience of readers and their likely prior knowledge. Have you explained specialized terms and created the shared background knowledge this audience will need? Do you have a *title* that suggests what will follow? (What are the titles of the articles and chapters in the sources you're using? Is there a typical style of title that seems to be expected in this field?)

- Genre? If you've identified typical characteristics of other studies and reports in the discipline, have you tried to recreate those characteristics in your own writing?

- Abstract? One common element of the genre of the research report in many disciplines is the abstract. If the articles you've been reading have included an abstract, you'll want to write one too, of approximately the same length (typically 80 to 100 words). The abstract provides a brief overview of your study for your readers. But it also can help you to name clearly what you are intending to present in that study.

(continued)

CHECKLIST FOR REVISING YOUR LIBRARY RESEARCH REPORT

(*continued*)

- Introduction? Have you introduced your report in an appropriate way for your audience, helped them understand the background to your question and why it's an interesting and/or significant one? Have you then given the appropriate background information to let your readers follow what you say next? Have you given them an overview of where your report will go and what it will do (an important aspect of longer research reports in many fields)?

- Purpose? Have you made a clear statement in your introduction or near the beginning of your report about your purpose for reporting on this topic or question—about what you wanted to learn about it and now want to show about it?

- Organization? Have you organized your report in a way that will make it easy for readers to follow and that will meet their expectations for such reports, based on their other reading in this field? Have you included an orientation to that organization near the beginning, to guide them as readers? Have you used *headings* that guide your reader through major sections of your study if these are commonly used in reports in your field?

- Evidence? Have you provided clear evidence that supports whatever the key points are that you're making? Do you quote, summarize, and paraphrase what you've learned from other sources to represent what others have found and to bring it into your new written conversation to support your own line of thinking or argument? Have you looked at the ways in which other sources are used in the articles you've read, and have you drawn on them in similar ways (in ways that will be expected by readers in this discipline)? Have you included appropriate in-text citation information, including page numbers?

- Conclusion? Have you shown what you have learned about your question from carrying out this research and what your readers should learn from reading this report? This is a good place to name those final, richer understandings that you want people to take away.

- Have you edited?

- Have you attached a page of complete references for the works you've quoted or referred to in the citation style that's most commonly used in the discipline you're working in?

Consider adding an *afterword* in which you reflect on the following questions:

- What have you learned about the larger academic discourse community of a discipline by researching a topic that insiders to that community have studied and by drawing on the written conversations that go on in the journals and books of that field?

- What have you learned about yourself as a researcher and/or about your interest in continued work on topics like this in an academic discourse community that explores them?

Additional Readings

James Paul Gee, "Literacy, Discourse, and Linguistics"

James Gee is a linguist whose research focuses on the ways in which language and literacy work in social contexts. His newest book is *Power Up: What Video Games Have to Teach Us about Learning and Literacy* (2003). The following article was an introduction to a set of studies by different literacy researchers that appeared in the *Journal of Education* in 1989, and represented his attempt to theorize and frame the specific studies of how people used language and literacy in specific setting that other researchers were looking at. In this article, Gee explores the relationship between literacy, discourses, and social practices. He distinguishes between primary and secondary discourses, and he links discourses to social identities and to people's positions as insiders or outsiders to social roles. He is trying to come up with a new way of explaining and seeing the relationships among all of people's language practices as they participate in particular social settings.

Since this book has drawn on the concepts that Gee begins to name in this article, you're likely to find yourself, as a reader, already *situated* in this way of thinking about discourse and literacy—familiar with these ideas, possessing a working notion of the key concepts, and knowing how they can be applied to specific examples in your own research. Because Gee's purpose in this article is to give shape to a theory of literacy and discourse, the language of the article is abstract—removed from specific examples to emphasize some general elements of a theory that will cover a variety of examples. The high level of abstraction can make such articles difficult to read. But you've already been applying some of the concepts Gee names to specific examples in your own discourse community experience so you're already thinking within the intellectual space in which Gee's discussion is taking place.

Literacy, Discourse, and Linguistics
Introduction

James Paul Gee

1   What I propose in the following papers, in the main, is *a way of talking about* literacy and linguistics. I believe that a new field of study, integrating "psycho" and "socio" approaches to language from a variety of disciplines, is emerging, a field which we might call *literacy studies*. Much of this work, I think (and hope), shares at least some of the assumptions of the following papers. These papers, though written at different times, and for different purposes, are, nonetheless, based on the claim that the focus of literacy studies or applied linguistics should *not* be language, or literacy, but *social practices*. This claim, I believe, has a number of socially important and cognitively interesting consequences.

"Language" is a misleading term; it too often suggests "grammar." It is a truism that a person can know perfectly the grammar of a language and not know how to use that language. It is not just *what* you say, but *how* you say it. If I enter my neighborhood bar and say to my tattooed drinking buddy, as I sit down, "May I have a match please?," my grammar is perfect, but what I have said is wrong nonetheless. It is less often remarked that a person could be able to use a language perfectly and *still* not make sense. It is not just *how* you say it, but what you *are* and *do* when you say it. If I enter my neighborhood bar and say to my drinking buddy, as I sit down, "Gime a match, wouldya?," while placing a napkin on the bar stool to avoid getting my newly pressed designer jeans dirty, I have said the right thing, but my "saying-doing" combination is nonetheless all wrong.

F. Niyi Akinnaso and Cheryl Ajirotutu (1982) present "simulated job interviews" from two welfare mothers in a CETA job training program. The first woman, asked whether she has ever shown initiative in a previous job, responds: "Well, yes, there's this Walgreen's Agency, I worked as a microfilm operator, OK. And it was a snow storm, OK. And it was usually six people workin' in a group . . ." and so forth (p. 34). This woman is simply using the wrong grammar (the wrong "dialect") for this type of (middle-class) interview. It's a perfectly good grammar (dialect), it just won't get you this type of job in this type of society.

The second woman (the authors' "success" case) responds to a similar question by saying: ". . . I was left alone to handle the office. . . . I didn't really have a lot of experience. But I had enough experience to deal with any situations that came up . . . and those that I couldn't handle at the time, if there was someone who had more experience than myself, I asked questions to find out what procedure I would use. If something came up and if I didn't know who to really go to, I would jot it down . . . on a piece of paper, so that I wouldn't forget that if anyone that was more qualified than myself, I could ask them about it and how I would go about solving it. So I feel I'm capable of handling just about any situation, whether it's on my own or under supervision" (p. 34). This woman hasn't got a real problem with her grammar (remember this is *speech,* not *writing*), nor is there any real problem with the *use* to which she puts that grammar, but she is expressing the *wrong values.* She views being left in charge as just another form of supervision, namely, supervision by "other people's" knowledge and expertise. And she fails to characterize her own expertise in the overly optimistic form called for by such interviews. Using this response as an example of "successful training" is only possible because the authors, aware that language is more than grammar (namely, "use"), are unaware that communication is more than language use.

5   At any moment we are using language we must say or write the right thing in the right way while playing the right social role and (appearing) to hold the right values, beliefs, and attitudes. Thus, what is important is not language, and surely not grammar, but *saying (writing)–doing–being–valuing–believing combinations.* These combinations I call "Discourses," with a capital "D" ("discourse" with a little "d," to me, means connected stretches of language that make sense, so "discourse" is part of "Discourse"). Discourses are ways of being in the world; they are forms of life which integrate words, acts, values, beliefs, attitudes, and social identities as well as gestures, glances, body positions, and clothes.

A Discourse is a sort of "identity kit" which comes complete with the appropriate costume and instructions on how to act, talk, and often write, so as to take on a particular role that others will recognize. Being "trained" as a linguist meant that I learned to speak, think, and act like a linguist, and to recognize others when they do so. Some other examples of Discourses: (enacting) being an American or a Russian, a man or a woman, a member of a certain socioeconomic class, a factory worker or a boardroom executive, a doctor or a hospital patient, a teacher, an administrator, or a student, a student of physics or a student of literature, a member of a sewing circle, a club, a street gang, a lunchtime social gathering, or a regular at a local bar. We all have many Discourses.

How does one acquire a Discourse? It turns out that much that is claimed, controversially, to be true of second language acquisition or socially situated cognition (Beebe, 1988; Dulay, Burt, & Krashen, 1982; Grosjean, 1982; Krashen, 1982, 1985a, 1985b; Krashen & Terrell, 1983; Lave, 1988; Rogoff & Lave, 1984) is, in fact, more obviously true of the acquisition of Discourses. Discourses are not mastered by overt instruction (even less so than languages, and hardly anyone ever fluently acquired a second language sitting in a classroom), but by enculturation ("apprenticeship") into social practices through scaffolded and supported interaction with people who have already mastered the Discourse (Cazden, 1988, Heath; 1983). This is how we all acquired our native language and our home-based Discourse. It is how we acquire all later, more public-oriented Discourses. If you have no access to the social practice, you don't get in the Discourse, you don't have it. You cannot overtly teach anyone a Discourse, in a classroom or anywhere else. Discourses are not bodies of knowledge like physics or archeology or linguistics. Therefore, ironically, while you can overtly teach someone *linguistics*, a body of knowledge, you can't teach them *to be a linguist*, that is, to use a Discourse. The most you can do is to let them practice being a linguist with you.

The various Discourses which constitute each of us as persons are changing and often are not fully consistent with each other; there is often conflict and tension between the values, beliefs, attitudes, interactional styles, uses of language, and ways of being in the world which two or more Discourses represent. Thus, there is no real sense in which we humans are consistent or well integrated creatures from a cognitive or social viewpoint, though, in fact, most Discourses assume that we are (and thus we do too, while we are in them).

All of us, through our *primary socialization* early in life in the home and peer group, acquire (at least) one initial Discourse. This initial Discourse, which I call our *primary Discourse,* is the one we first use to make sense of the world and interact with others. Our primary Discourse constitutes our original and home-based sense of identity, and, I believe, it can be seen whenever we are interacting with "intimates" in totally casual (unmonitored) social interaction. We acquire this primary Discourse, not by overt instruction, but by being a member of a primary socializing group (family, clan, peer group). Further, aspects and pieces of the primary Discourse become a "carrier" or "foundation" for Discourses acquired later in life. Primary Discourses differ significantly across various social (cultural, ethnic, regional, and economic) groups in the United States.

10   After our initial socialization in our home community, each of us interacts with various non-home-based social institutions—institutions in the public sphere, beyond

the family and immediate kin and peer group. These may be local stores and churches, schools, community groups, state and national businesses, agencies and organizations, and so forth. Each of these social institutions commands and demands one or more Discourses and we acquire these fluently to the extent that we are given access to these institutions and are allowed apprenticeships within them. Such Discourses I call *secondary Discourses.*

We can also make an important distinction between *dominant Discourses* and *nondominant Discourses.* Dominant Discourses are secondary Discourses the mastery of which, at a particular place and time, brings with it the (potential) acquisition of social "goods" (money, prestige, status, etc.). Nondominant Discourses are secondary Discourses the mastery of which often brings solidarity with a particular social network, but not wider status and social goods in the society at large.

Finally, and yet more importantly, we can always ask about how much *tension or conflict* is present between any two of a person's Discourses (Rosaldo, 1989). We have argued above that some degree of conflict and tension (if only because of the discrete historical origins of particular Discourses) will almost always be present. However, some people experience more overt and direct conflicts between two or more of their Discourses than do others (for example, many women academics feel conflict between certain feminist Discourses and certain standard academic Discourses such as traditional literary criticism). I argue that when such conflict or tension exists, it can deter acquisition of one or the other or both of the conflicting Discourses, or, at least, affect the fluency of a mastered Discourse on certain occasions of use (e.g., in stressful situations such as interviews).

Very often dominant groups in a society apply rather constant "tests" of the fluency of the dominant Discourses in which their power is symbolized. These tests take on two functions: they are tests of "natives" or, at least, "fluent users" of the Discourse, and they are *gates* to exclude "non-natives" (people whose very conflicts with dominant Discourses show they were not, in fact, "born" to them). The sorts of tension and conflict we have mentioned here are particularly acute when they involve tension and conflict between one's primary Discourse and a dominant secondary Discourse.

Discourses, primary and secondary, can be studied, in some ways, like languages. And, in fact, some of what we know about second language acquisition is relevant to them, if only in a metaphorical way. Two Discourses can *interfere* with one another, like two languages; aspects of one Discourse can be *transferred* to another Discourse, as one can transfer a grammatical feature from one language to another. For instance, the primary Discourse of many middle-class homes has been influenced by secondary Discourses like those used in schools and business. This is much less true of the primary Discourse in many lower socio-economic black homes, though this primary Discourse has influenced the secondary Discourse used in black churches.

15   Furthermore, if one has not mastered a particular secondary Discourse which nonetheless one must try to use, several things can happen, things which rather resemble what can happen when one has failed to fluently master a second language. One can fall back on one's primary Discourse, adjusting it in various ways to try to fit it to the needed functions; this response is very common, but almost always socially disastrous. Or one can use another, perhaps related, secondary Discourse. Or one

can use a simplified, or stereotyped version of the required secondary Discourse. These processes are similar to those linguists study under the rubrics of *language contact, pidginization,* and *creolization.*

I believe that any socially useful definition of "literacy" must be couched in terms of the notion of Discourse. Thus, I define "literacy" as *the mastery of or fluent control over a secondary Discourse.* Therefore, literacy is always plural: *literacies* (there are many of them, since there are many secondary Discourses, and we all have some and fail to have others). If we wanted to be rather pedantic and literalistic, then we could define "literacy" as "mastery of or fluent control over secondary Discourses *involving print*" (which is almost all of them in a modern society). But I see no gain from the addition of the phrase "involving print," other than to assuage the feelings of people committed (as I am not) to reading and writing as decontextualized and isolable skills. We can talk about *dominant literacies* and *nondominant literacies* in terms of whether they involve mastery of dominant or nondominant secondary Discourses. We can also talk about a literacy being *liberating* ("powerful") if it can be used as a "meta-language" (a set of meta-words, meta-values, meta-beliefs) for the critique of other literacies and the way they constitute us as persons and situate us in society. Liberating literacies can reconstitute and resituate us.

My definition of "literacy" may seem innocuous, at least to someone already convinced that decontextualized views of print are meaningless. Nonetheless, several "theorems" follow from it, theorems that have rather direct and unsettling consequences.

First theorem: Discourses (and therefore literacies) are not like languages in one very important regard. Someone can speak English, but not fluently. However, someone cannot engage in a Discourse in a less than fully fluent manner. You are either in it or you're not. Discourses are connected with displays of an identity; failing to fully display an identity is tantamount to announcing you don't have that identity, that at best you're a pretender or a beginner. Very often, learners of second languages "fossilize" at a stage of development significantly short of fluency. This can't happen with Discourses. If you've fossilized in the acquisition of a Discourse prior to full "fluency" (and are no longer in the process of apprenticeship), then your very lack of fluency marks you as a *non-member* of the group that controls this Discourse. That is, you don't have the identity or social role which is the basis for the existence of the Discourse in the first place. In fact, the lack of fluency may very well mark you as a *pretender* to the social role instantiated in the Discourse (an *outsider* with pretensions to being an *insider*).

There is, thus, no workable "affirmative action" for Discourses: you can't be let into the game after missing the apprenticeship and be expected to have a fair shot at playing it. Social groups will not, usually, give their social goods—whether these are status or solidarity or both—to those who are not "natives" or "fluent users" (though "mushfake," discussed below, may sometimes provide a way for non-initiates to gain access). While this is an *empirical* claim, I believe it is one vastly supported by the sociolinguistic literature (Milroy, 1980, 1987; Milroy & Milroy, 1985).

20   This theorem (that there are no people who are partially literate or semi-literate, or, in any other way, literate but not fluently so) has one practical consequence: notions like "functional literacy" and "competency-based literacy" are simply

incoherent. As far as literacy goes, there are only "fluent speakers" and "apprentices" (metaphorically speaking, because remember, Discourses are not just ways of talking, but ways of talking, acting, thinking, valuing, etc.).

Second theorem: Primary Discourses, no matter whose they are, can never really be liberating literacies. For a literacy to be liberating it must contain both the Discourse it is going to critique and a set of meta-elements (language, words, attitudes, values) in terms of which an analysis and criticism can be carried out. Primary Discourses are initial and contain only themselves. They can be embedded in later Discourses and critiqued, but they can never serve as a meta-language in terms of which a critique of secondary Discourses can be carried out. Our second theorem is not likely to be very popular. Theorem 2 says that all primary Discourses are limited. "Liberation" ("power"), in the sense I am using the term here, resides in acquiring at least one more Discourse in terms of which our own primary Discourse can be analyzed and critiqued.

This is not to say that primary Discourses do not contain critical attitudes and critical language (indeed, many of them contain implicit and explicit racism and classism). It is to say that they cannot carry out an *authentic* criticism, because they cannot verbalize the words, acts, values, and attitudes they *use,* and they cannot mobilize explicit meta-knowledge. Theorem 2 is quite traditional and conservative—it is the analogue of Socrates's theorem that the unexamined life is not worth living. Interestingly enough, Vygotsky (1987, chapter 6) comes very closely to stating this theorem explicitly.

Other theorems can be deduced from the theory of literacy here developed, but these two should make clear what sorts of consequences the theory has. It should also make it quite clear that the theory is *not* a neutral meta-language in terms of which one can argue for *just any* conclusions about literacy.

Not all Discourses involve writing or reading, though many do. However, all writing and reading is embedded in some Discourse, and that Discourse always involves more than writing and reading (e.g., ways of talking, acting, valuing, and so forth). You cannot teach anyone to write or read outside any Discourse (there is no such thing, unless it is called "moving a pen" or "typing" in the case of writing, or "moving one's lips" or "mouthing words" in the case of reading). Within a Discourse you are always teaching more than writing or reading. When I say "teach" here, I mean "apprentice someone in a master–apprentice relationship in a social practice (Discourse) wherein you scaffold their growing ability to say, do, value, believe, and so forth, within that Discourse, through demonstrating your mastery and supporting theirs even when it barely exists (i.e., you make it look as if they can do what they really can't do)." That is, you do much the same thing middle-class, "super baby" producing parents do when they "do books" with their children.

25   Now, there are many Discourses connected to schools (different ones for different types of school activities and different parts of the curriculum) and other public institutions. These "middle-class mainstream" sorts of Discourses often carry with them power and prestige. It is often felt that good listeners and good readers ought to pay attention to *meaning* and not focus on the petty details of mechanics, "correctness," the superficial features of language. Unfortunately, many middle-class mainstream status-giving Discourses often *do* stress superficial features of language. Why?

Precisely because such superficial features are the *best* test as to whether one was apprenticed in the "right" place, at the "right" time, with the "right" people. Such superficial features are exactly the parts of Discourses most impervious to overt instruction and are only fully mastered when everything else in the Discourse is mastered. Since these Discourses are used as "gates" to ensure that the "right" people get to the "right" places in our society, such superficial features are ideal. A person who writes in a petition or office memo: "If you cancel the show, all the performers would have did all that hard work for nothing" has signaled that he or she isn't the "right sort of person" (was not fully acculturated to the Discourse that supports this identity). That signal stays meaningful long after the content of the memo is forgotten, or even when the content was of no interest in the first place.

Now, one can certainly encourage students to simply "resist" such "superficial features of language." And, indeed, they will get to do so from the bottom of society, where their lack of mastery of such superficialities was meant to place them anyway. But, of course, the problem is that such "superficialities" cannot be taught in a regular classroom in any case; they can't be "picked up" later, outside the full context of an early apprenticeship (at home and at school) in "middle-class-like" school-based ways of doing and being. That is precisely why they work so well as "gates." This is also precisely the tragedy of E. D. Hirsch, Jr.'s much-talked-about book *Cultural Literacy* (1987), which points out that without having mastered an extensive list of trivialities people can be (and often are) excluded from "goods" controlled by dominant groups in the society. Hirsch is wrong in thinking that this can be taught (in a classroom of all places!) apart from the socially situated practices that these groups have incorporated into their homes and daily lives. There is a real contradiction here, and we ignore it at the peril of our students and our own "good faith" (no middle-class "super baby" producing parents ignore it).

Beyond changing the social structure, is there much hope? No, there is not. So we better get on about the process of changing the social structure. Now, whose job is that? I would say, people who have been allotted the job of teaching Discourses, for example, English teachers, language teachers, composition teachers, TESOL teachers, studies-skills teachers. We can pause, also, to remark on the paradox that even though Discourses cannot be overtly taught, and cannot readily be mastered late in the game, the University wants teachers to overtly teach and wants students to demonstrate mastery. Teachers of Discourses take on an impossible job, allow themselves to be evaluated on how well they do it, and accept fairly low status all the while for doing it.

So what can teachers of Discourses do? Well, there happens to be an advantage to failing to master mainstream Discourses, that is, there is an advantage to being socially "maladapted." When we have really mastered anything (e.g., a Discourse), we have little or no conscious awareness of it (indeed, like dancing, Discourses wouldn't work if people were consciously aware of what they were doing while doing it). However, when we come across a situation where we are unable to accommodate or adapt (as many minority students do on being faced, late in the game, with having to acquire mainstream Discourses), we become consciously aware of what we are trying to do or are being called upon to do. Let me give an example that works similarly, that is, the case of classroom second language learning. Almost no one really acquires a second language in a classroom. However, it can happen that exposure to another language, having to translate it into and otherwise relate it to your own language, can cause you to become consciously aware of how your first language works (how it means). This "metaknowledge" can actually make you better able to manipulate your first language.

Vygotsky (1987) says that learning a foreign language "allows the child to understand his native language as a single instantiation of a linguistic system" (p. 222). And here we have a clue. Classroom instruction (in language, composition, study skills, writing, critical thinking, content-based literacy, or whatever) can lead to metaknowledge, to seeing how the Discourses you have already got relate to those you are attempting to acquire, and how the ones you are trying to acquire relate to self and society. Metaknowledge is liberation and power, because it leads to the ability to manipulate, to analyze, to resist while advancing.

REFERENCES

Akinnaso, F. N., and Ajirotutu, C. S. (1982). Performance and ethnic style in job interviews. In J. J. Gumperz (Ed.), *Language and social identity* (pp. 119–144). Cambridge, Eng.: Cambridge University Press.

Beebe, L. M. (Ed.) *Issues in second language acquisition: Multiple perspectives.* New York: Newbury House.

Cazden, C. (1988). *Classroom discourse: The language of teaching and learning.* Portsmouth, NH: Heinemann.

Dulay, H., Burt, M., and Krashen, S. (1982). *Language two.* New York: Oxford University Press.

Grosjean, F. (1986). *Life with two languages.* Cambridge: Harvard University Press.

Heath, S. B. (1983). *Ways with words: Language, life, and work in communities and classrooms.* Cambridge, Eng.: Cambridge University Press.

Hirsch, E. D. (1987). *Cultural literacy: What every American needs to know.* Boston: Houghton Mifflin.

Krashen, S. (1982). *Principles and practice in second language acquisition.* Hayward, CA: Alemany Press.

Krashen, S. (1985a). *The input hypothesis: Issues and implications.* Harlow, U.K.: Longman.

Krashen, S. (1985b). *Inquiries and insights.* Hayward, CA: Alemany Press.

Krashen, S., and Terrell, T. (1983). *The natural approach: Language acquisition in the classroom.* Hayward, CA: Alemany Press.

Lave, J. (1988). *Cognition in practice.* Cambridge, Eng.: Cambridge University Press.

Milroy, J., and Milroy, L. (1985). *Authority in language: Investigating language prescription and standardisation.* London: Routedge and Kegan Paul.

Milroy, L. (1980). *Language and social networks.* Oxford: Basil Blackwell.

Milroy, L. (1987). *Observing and analysing natural language.* Oxford: Basil Blackwell.

Rogoff, B., and Lave, J. (Eds.). *Everyday cognition: Its development in a social context.* Cambridge: Harvard University Press.

Rosaldo, R. (1989). *Culture and truth.* Boston: Beacon.

Vygotsky, L. S. (1987). *The collected works of L. S. Vygotsky, Volume 1: Problems of general psychology. Including the volume thinking and speech* (R. W. Rieber and A. S. Carton, Eds.). New York: Plenum.

1. <u>Reflecting on discourse, literacy, and the context of academic disciplines</u>

   ■ Gee describes Discourse as an "identity kit." What's involved in this identity kit and, from your own experience and research, how would you describe the elements of the identity kit that's needed in a particular setting that you're familiar with?

   ■ Gee distinguishes between our primary discourse and our secondary discourses, but he also suggests that elements from one discourse can be carried over or transferred to another. Have you found examples of such carryover between discourses (transfers of the language appropriate in one setting into another) in your own experience or research?

   ■ Gee goes on to define literacy as "*the mastery or fluent control of a secondary Discourse.*" Why is this definition important for the theorems that follow? If you agree with these theorems, do you then agree with the definition?

   ■ Return to some of the other key points you've glossed as you read this article and try to provide examples—to tie these abstract concepts to the specific and concrete examples you've been finding in your own discourse community observations. How do your examples help you to understand, refine, or question the concept? How do the concepts help you to understand more of what you're seeing in your examples?

   ■ As you contribute your own examples (or do so collaboratively with your research group in the classroom), do you find that the understandings you've come to from your own research fit with the larger theory Gee is presenting, or do you find places where they conflict or remain unexplained?

2. <u>Reading as a writer/researcher</u>

   ■ Gee is writing an abstract and theoretical article that is different from the sort of academic discourse community study or library research report that you may be writing as you read this. Yet many of his paragraphs could help to frame some of the specific ideas you want to present. Look back through the article. Are there are specific paragraphs that connect with what you've been finding and that you might use in this way?

   ■ If you are studying an academic discourse community, do you find that Gee's theorems of literacy apply to what you're observing in your setting? Are insiders to this setting:

     ■ fluent in the discourse, using it to display a particular identity?

     ■ able to take a critical position (from what you've observed) on their own discourse—their own ways of seeing the world?

     Are these theorems or any of the other ideas he discusses useful to you as you consider what's involved in becoming an insider to a particular area of academic study?   (*continued*)

(*continued*)

Gee suggests that stepping back and translating from one discourse or language to another can give you meta-knowledge about that discourse or language, allowing you to see "how the Discourses you have already got relate to those you are attempting to acquire," and make you smarter as you think about how to use, manipulate, or resist different discourses. Have you found that your own research into language, literacy, and discourse communities has provided any of this sort of meta-knowledge? Has your research made you smarter, in any ways you can name, in thinking about the academic discourse communities you're participating in or want to participate in? If so, is that meta-level understanding something you want to bring into your own report?

Jean Anyon, "Social Class and the Hidden Curriculum of Work"

Jean Anyon is a professor of education who has focused her research on urban schools. Her most recent book, *Ghetto Schooling*, was published in 1997. "Social Class and the Hidden Curriculum of Work," published in the *Journal of Education* in 1980, reports on her earlier research on schools in different socio-economic areas. In it, she examines the workings of fifth grade classrooms in five elementary schools within the same city from the perspective of social class, asking what's different about the teaching and learning that goes on in different areas of a city and why. Looking from outside of the insider world of these schools and comparing their ways, Anyon is able to see and name things that the teachers within a school, each trying to offer the best teaching they know within their immediate school world, might not see. Her study is useful to us as we consider the workings of the courses that lead into various disciplines because it offers detailed examples of the different ways of talking, thinking, and working (the different discourses) that students may be learning in different classrooms, not all of which prepare them equally for the ways of advanced academic work. It also offers us an example of a typical research report in the social sciences; it has been widely reprinted in anthologies and research collections, and it is often an assigned reading for courses in sociology and in education.

Social Class and the Hidden Curriculum of Work

Jean Anyon

1   Scholars in political economy and the sociology of knowledge have recently argued that public schools in complex industrial societies like our own make available different types of educational experience and curriculum knowledge to students in

different social classes. Bowles and Gintis (1976), for example, have argued that students from different social class backgrounds are rewarded for classroom behaviors that correspond to personality traits allegedly rewarded in the different occupational strata—the working classes for docility and obedience, the managerial classes for initiative and personal assertiveness. Basil Bernstein (1977), Pierre Bourdieu (Bourdieu and Passeron 1977), and Michael W. Apple (1979), focusing on school knowledge, have argued that knowledge and skills leading to social power and reward (e.g., medical, legal, managerial) are made available to the advantaged social groups but are withheld from the working classes, to whom a more "practical" curriculum is offered (e.g., manual skills, clerical knowledge). While there has been considerable argumentation of these points regarding education in England, France, and North America, there has been little or no attempt to investigate these ideas empirically in elementary or secondary schools and classrooms in this country.[1]

This article offers tentative empirical support (and qualification) of the above arguments by providing illustrative examples of differences in student work in classrooms in contrasting social class communities. The examples were gathered as part of an ethnographical study of curricular, pedagogical and pupil evaluation practices in five elementary schools. The article attempts a theoretical contribution as well, and assesses student work in the light of a theoretical approach to social class analysis. The organization is as follows: the methodology of the ethnographical study is briefly described; a theoretical approach to the definition of social class is offered; income and other characteristics of the parents in each school are provided, and examples from the study that illustrate work tasks and interaction in each school are presented; then the concepts used to define social class are applied to the examples in order to assess the theoretical meaning of classroom events. It will be suggested that there is a "hidden curriculum" in school work that has profound implications for the theory—and consequence—of everyday activity in education.

METHODOLOGY

The methods used to gather data were classroom observation; interviews of students, teachers, principals, and district administrative staff; and assessment of curriculum and other materials in each classroom and school. All classroom events to be discussed here involve the fifth grade in each school. All schools but one departmentalize at the fifth grade level. Except for that school where only one fifth grade teacher could be observed, all the fifth grade teachers (that is, two or three) were observed as the children moved from subject to subject. In all schools the art, music, and gym teachers were also observed and interviewed. All teachers in the study were described as "good" or "excellent" by their principals. All except one new teacher had taught for more than four years. The fifth grade in each school was observed by the investigator for ten three-hour periods between September 15, 1978 and June 20, 1979.

Before providing the occupations, incomes, and other relevant social characteristics of the parents of the children in each school, I will offer a theoretical approach to defining social class.

SOCIAL CLASS

5   One's occupation and income level contribute significantly to one's social class, but they do not define it. Rather, social class is a series of relationships. A person's social class is defined here by the way that person relates to the process in society by which goods, services, and culture are produced.[2] One relates to several aspects of the production process primarily through one's work. One has a relationship to the system of ownership, to other people (at work and in society) and to the content and process of one's own productive activity. One's relationship to all three of these aspects of production determines one's social class; that is, all three relationships are necessary and none is sufficient for determining a person's relation to the process of production in society.

Ownership Relations. In a capitalist society, a person has a relation to the system of private ownership of capital. Capital is usually thought of as being derived from physical property. In this sense capital is property which is used to produce profit, interest, or rent in sufficient quantity so that the result can be used to produce more profit, interest, or rent—that is, more capital. Physical capital may be derived from money, stocks, machines, land, or the labor of workers (whose labor, for instance, may produce products that are sold by others for profit). Capital, however, can also be symbolic. It can be the socially legitimated knowledge of how the production process works, its financial, managerial, technical, or other "secrets." Symbolic capital can also be socially legitimated skills—cognitive (e.g., analytical), linguistic, or technical skills that provide the ability to, say, produce the dominant scientific, artistic, and other culture, or to manage the systems of industrial and cultural production. Skillful application of symbolic capital may yield social and cultural power, and perhaps physical capital as well.

The ownership relation that is definitive for social class is one's relation to physical capital. The first such relationship is that of capitalist. To be a member of the capitalist class in the present-day United States, one must participate in the ownership of the apparatus of production in society. The number of such persons is relatively small: while one person in ten owns some stock, for example, a mere 1.6 percent of the population owns 82.2 percent of *all* stock, and the wealthiest one-fifth owns almost all the rest (see New York Stock Exchange, 1975; Smith and Franklin, 1974; Lampman, 1962).

At the opposite pole of this relationship is the worker. To be in the United States working class a person will not ordinarily own physical capital; to the contrary, his or her work will be wage or salaried labor that is either a *source* of profit (i.e., capital) to others, or that makes it possible for others to *realize* profit. Examples of the latter are *white*-collar clerical workers in industry and distribution (office and sales) as well as the wage and salaried workers in the institutions of social and economic legitimation and service (e.g., in state education and welfare institutions.)[3] According to the criteria to be developed here, the number of persons who presently comprise the working class in the United States is between 50 percent and 60 percent of the population (see also Wright, 1978; Braverman, 1974; Levison, 1974).

In between the defining relationship of capitalist and worker are the middle classes, whose relationship to the process of production is less clear, and whose relationship may indeed exhibit contradictory characteristics. For example, social service employees have a somewhat contradictory relationship to the process of production because, although their income may be at middle-class levels, some characteristics of their work are working-class (e.g., they may have very little control over their work). Analogously, there are persons at the upper income end of the middle class, such as upper-middle-class professionals, who may own quantities of stocks and will therefore share characteristics of the capitalist class. As the next criterion to be discussed makes clear, however, to be a member of the present-day capitalist in the United States, one must also participate in the social *control* of this capital.

10   *Relationships Between People.* The second relationship which contributes to one's social class is the relation one has to authority and control at work and in society.[4] One characteristic of most working-class jobs is that there is no built-in mechanism by which the worker can control the content, process or speed of work. Legitimate decision making is vested in personnel supervisors, in middle or upper management, or, as in an increasing number of white-collar working-class (and most middle-class) jobs, by bureaucratic rule and regulation. For upper-middle-class professional groups there is an increased amount of autonomy regarding work. Moreover, in middle- and upper-middle-class positions there is an increasing chance that one's work would also involve supervising the work of others. A capitalist is defined within these relations of control in an enterprise by having a position which participates in the direct control of the entire enterprise. Capitalists do not directly control workers in physical production and do not directly control ideas in the sphere of cultural production. However, more crucial to control, capitalists make the decisions over how resources are used (e.g., where money is invested) and how profit is allocated.

    Relations Between People and Their Work. The third criterion which contributes to a person's social class is the relationship between that person and his or her own productive activity—the type of activity that constitutes his or her work. A working-class job is often characterized by work that is routine and mechanical and that is a small, fragmented part of a larger process with which workers are not usually acquainted. These working-class jobs are usually blue-collar, manual labor. A few skilled jobs such as plumbing and printing are not mechanical, however, and an increasing number of working-class jobs are *white*-collar. These white-collar jobs, such as clerical work, may involve work that necessitates a measure of planning and decision making, but one still has no built-in control over the content. The work of some middle- and most upper-middle-class managerial and professional groups is likely to involve the need for conceptualization and creativity, with many professional jobs demanding one's full creative capacities. Finally, the work that characterizes the capitalist position is that this work is almost entirely a matter of conceptualization (e.g., planning and laying-out) that has as its object management and control of the enterprise.

    One's social class, then, is a result of the relationships one has, largely through one's work, to physical capital and its power, to other people at work and in society, and to one's own productive activity. Social class is a lived, developing process. It is not an abstract category, and it is not a fixed, inherited position (although one's family background is, of course, important). Social class is perceived as a complex of social relations that one develops as one grows up—as one acquires and develops certain bodies of knowledge, skills, abilities, and traits, and as one has contact and opportunity in the world.[5] In sum, social class describes relationships which we as adults have developed, may attempt to maintain, and in which we participate every working day. These relationships in a real sense define our material ties to the world. An important concern here is whether these relationships are developing in children in schools within particular social class contexts.

THE SAMPLE OF SCHOOLS

With the above discussion as a theoretical backdrop, the social class designation of each of the five schools will be identified, and the income, occupation, and other relevant available social characteristics of the students and their parents will be described. The first three schools are in a medium-sized city district in northern New Jersey, and the other two are in a nearby New Jersey suburb.

The first two schools I will call *Working-class Schools*. Most of the parents have blue-collar jobs. Less than a third of the fathers are skilled, while the majority are in unskilled or semiskilled jobs. During the period of the study (1978–1979) approximately 15 percent of the fathers were unemployed. The large majority (85 percent) of the families are white. The following occupations are typical: platform, storeroom, and stockroom workers; foundrymen, pipe welders, and boilermakers; semiskilled and unskilled assembly-line operatives; gas station attendants, auto mechanics, maintenance workers, and security guards. Less than 30 percent of the women work, some part-time and some full-time, on assembly lines, in storerooms and stockrooms, as waitresses, barmaids, or sales clerks. Of the fifth grade parents, none of the wives of the skilled workers had jobs. Approximately 15 percent of the families in each school are at or below the federal "poverty" level[6]; most of the rest of the family incomes are at or below $12,000, except some of the skilled workers whose incomes are higher. The incomes of the majority of the families in these two schools (i.e., at or below $12,000) are typical of 38.6 percent of the families in the United States (U.S. Bureau of the Census, 1979, p. 2, table A).

15   The third school is called the *Middle-class School,* although because of neighborhood residence patterns, the population is a mixture of several social classes. The parents' occupations can be divided into three groups: a small group of blue-collar "rich," who are skilled, well-paid workers such as printers, carpenters, plumbers, and construction workers. The second group is composed of parents in working-class and middle-class white-collar jobs: women in office jobs, technicians, supervisors in industry, and parents employed by the city (such as firemen, policemen, and several of the school's teachers). The third group is composed of occupations such as personnel directors in local firms, accountants, "middle management," and a few small capitalists (owners of shops in the area). The children of several local doctors attend this school. Most family incomes are between $13,000 and $25,000 with a few higher. This income range is typical of 38.9 percent of the families in the United States (U.S. Bureau of the Census, 1979, p. 2, table A).

The fourth school has a parent population that is at the upper income level of the upper middle class, and is predominantly professional. This school will be called the *Affluent Professional School.* Typical jobs are: cardiologist, interior designer, corporate lawyer or engineer, executive in advertising or television. There are some families who are not as affluent as the majority (e.g., the family of the superintendent of the district's schools, and the one or two families in which the fathers are skilled workers). In addition, a few of the families are more affluent than the majority, and can be classified in the capitalist class (e.g., a partner in a prestigious Wall Street stock brokerage firm). Approximately 90 percent of the children in this school are white. Most family incomes are between $40,000 and $80,000. This income span represents approximately 7 percent of the families in the United States.[7]

In the fifth school the majority of the families belong to the capitalist class. This school will be called the *Executive Elite School* because most of the fathers are top executives, (e.g., presidents and vice presidents) in major U.S.-based multinational corporations—for example, ATT, RCA, City Bank, American Express, U.S. Steel. A sizable group of fathers are top executives in financial firms on Wall Street. There are also a number of fathers who list their occupations as "general counsel" to a particular corporation, and these corporations are also among the large multinationals. Many of the mothers do volunteer work in the Junior League, Junior Fortnightly, or other service groups; some are intricately involved in town politics; and some are themselves in well-paid occupations. There are no minority children in the school. Almost all family incomes are over $100,000 with some in the $500,000 range. The incomes in this school represent less than 1 percent of the families in the United States (see Smith and Franklin, 1974).

Since each of the five schools is only one instance of elementary education in a particular social class context, I will not generalize beyond the sample. However, the examples of school work which follow will suggest characteristics of education in each social setting that appear to have theoretical and social significance and to be worth investigation in a larger number of schools.

SOCIAL CLASS AND SCHOOL WORK

There are obvious similarities among United States schools and classrooms. There are school and classroom rules, teachers who ask questions and attempt to exercise control and who give work and homework. There are textbooks and tests. All of these were found in the five schools. Indeed, there were other curricular similarities as well: all schools and fifth grades used the same math book and series (*Mathematics Around Us,* Scott Foresman, 1978); all fifth grades had at least one boxed set of an individualized reading program available in the room (although the variety and amounts of teaching materials in the classrooms increased as the social class of the school population increased); and, all fifth grade language arts curricula included aspects of grammar, punctuation and capitalization.[8]

20   This section provides examples of work and work-related activities in each school that bear on the categories used to define social class. Thus, examples will be provided concerning students' relation to capital (e.g., as manifest in any symbolic capital that might be acquired through school work); students' relation to persons and types of authority regarding school work; and students' relation to their own productive activity. The section first offers the investigator's interpretation of what school work is for children in each setting, and then presents events and interactions that illustrate that assessment.

The Working-Class Schools. In the two working-class schools, work is following the steps of a procedure. The procedure is usually mechanical, involving rote behavior and very little decision making or choice. The teachers rarely explain why the work is being assigned, how it might connect to other assignments, or what the idea is that lies behind the procedure or gives it coherence and perhaps meaning or significance. Available textbooks are not always used, and the teachers often prepare their own dittoes or put work examples on the board. Most of the rules regarding work are designations of what the children are to do; the rules are steps to follow. These steps are told to the children by the teachers and often written on the board. The children are usually told to copy the steps as notes. These notes are to be studied. Work is often evaluated not according to whether it is right or wrong, but according to whether the children followed the right steps.

The following examples illustrate these points. In math, when two-digit division was introduced, the teacher in one school gave a four-minute lecture on what the terms are called (i.e., which number is the divisor, dividend, quotient, and remainder). The children were told to copy these names in their notebooks. Then the teacher told them the steps to follow to do the problems, saying, "This is how you do them." The teacher listed the steps on the board, and they appeared several days later as a chart hung in the middle of the front wall: "Divide; Multiply; Subtract; Bring Down." The children often did examples of two-digit division. When the teacher went over the examples with them, he told them for each problem what the procedure was, rarely asking them to conceptualize or explain it themselves: "3 into 22 is 7; do your subtraction and one is left over." During the week that two-digit division was introduced (or at any other time), the investigator did not observe any discussion of the idea of grouping involved in division, any use of manipulables, or any attempt to relate two-digit division to any other mathematical process. Nor was there any attempt to relate the steps to an actual or possible thought process of the children. The observer did not hear the terms dividend, quotient, etc., used again. The math teacher in the other working-class school followed similar procedures regarding two-digit division, and at one point her class seemed confused. She said, "You're confusing yourselves. You're tensing up. Remember, when you do this, it's the same steps over and over again—and that's the way division always is." Several weeks later, after a test, a group of her children "still didn't get it," and she made no attempt to explain the concept of dividing things into groups, or to give them manipulables for their own investigation. Rather, she went over the steps with them again and told them that they "needed more practice."

In other areas of math, work is also carrying out often unexplained, fragmented procedures. For example, one of the teachers led the children through a series of steps to make a one-inch grid on their paper *without* telling them that they were making a one-inch grid, or that it would be used to study scale. She said, "Take your ruler. Put it across the top. Make a mark at every number. Then move your ruler down to the bottom. No, put it across the bottom. Now make a mark on top of every number. Now draw a line from . . . ." At this point a girl said that she had a faster way to do it and the teacher said, "No, you don't; you don't even know what I'm making yet. Do it this way, or it's wrong." After they had made the lines up and down and across, the teacher told them she wanted them to make a figure by connecting some dots and to measure that, using the scale of one inch equals one mile. Then they were to cut it out. She said, "Don't cut until I check it."

In both working-class schools, work in language arts is mechanics of punctuation (commas, periods, question marks, exclamation points), capitalization, and the four kinds of sentences. One teacher explained to me, "Simple punctuation is all they'll ever use." Regarding punctuation, either a teacher or a ditto stated the rules for where, for example, to put commas. The investigator heard no classroom discussion of the aural context of punctuation (which, of course, is what gives each mark its meaning). Nor did the investigator hear any statement or inference that placing a punctuation mark could be a decision-making process, depending, for example, on one's intended meaning. Rather, the children were told to follow the rules. Language arts did not involve creative writing. There were several writing assignments throughout the year, but in each instance the children were given a ditto, and they wrote answers to questions on the sheet. For example, they wrote their "autobiography" by answering such questions as "Where were you born?" "What is your favorite animal?" on a sheet entitled, "All About Me."

25   In one of the working-class schools the class had a science period several times a week. On the three occasions observed, the children were not called upon to set up experiments or to give explanations for facts or concepts. Rather, on each occasion the teacher told them in his own words what the book said. The children copied the teacher's sentences from the board. Each day that preceded the day they were to do a science experiment, the teacher told them to copy the directions from the book for the procedure they would carry out the next day, and to study the list at home that night. The day after each experiment, the teacher went over what they had "found" (they did the experiments as a class, and each was actually a class demonstration led by the teacher). Then the teacher wrote what they "found" on the board, and the children copied that in their notebooks. Once or twice a year there are science projects. The project is chosen and assigned by the teacher from a box of three-by-five-inch cards. On the card the teacher has written the question to be answered, the books to use, and how much to write. Explaining the cards to the observer, the teacher said, "It tells them exactly what to do, or they couldn't do it."

Social studies in the working-class schools is also largely mechanical, rote work that was given little explanation or connection to larger contexts. In one school, for example, although there was a book available, social studies work was to copy the teacher's notes from the board. Several times a week for a period of several months, the children copied these notes. The fifth grades in the district were to study U.S. history. The teacher used a booklet she had purchased called "The Fabulous Fifty States." Each day she put information from the booklet in outline form on the board and the children copied it. The type of information did not vary: the name of the state, its abbreviation, state capital, nickname of the state, its main products, main business, and a "Fabulous Fact" (e.g., "Idaho grew 27 billion potatoes in one year. That's enough potatoes for each man, woman and . . ."). As the children finished copying the sentences, the teacher erased them and wrote more. Children would occasionally go to the front to pull down the wall map in order to locate the states they were copying, and the teacher did not dissuade them. But the observer never saw her refer to the map; nor did the observer ever hear her make other than perfunctory remarks concerning the information the children were copying. Occasionally the children colored in a ditto and cut it out to make a stand-up figure (representing, for example, a man roping a cow in the Southwest). These were referred to by the teacher as their social studies "projects."

Rote behavior was often called for in classroom oral work. When going over math and language arts skills sheets, for example, as the teacher asked for the answer to each problem, he fired the questions rapidly, staccato, and the scene reminded the observer of a sergeant drilling recruits: above all, the questions demanded that you stay at attention: "The next one? What do I put here? . . . Here? Give us the next." Or "How many commas in this sentence? Where do I put them . . . The next one?"

The (four) fifth grade teachers observed in the working-class schools attempted to control classroom time and space by making decisions without consulting the children and without explaining the basis for their decisions. The teacher's control thus often seemed capricious. Teachers, for instance, very often ignored the bells to switch classes—deciding among themselves to keep the children after the period was officially over, to continue with the work, or for disciplinary reasons, or so they (the teachers) could stand in the hall and talk. There were no clocks in the rooms in either school, and the children often asked, "What period is this?" "When do we go to gym?" The children had no access to materials. These were handed out by teachers and closely guarded. Things in the room "belonged" to the teacher: "Bob, bring me my garbage can." The teachers continually gave the children orders. Only three times did the investigator hear a teacher in either working-class school preface a directive with an unsarcastic "please," or "let's" or "would you." Instead, the teachers said, "Shut up," "Shut your mouth," "Open your books," "Throw your *gum* away—if you want to rot your teeth, do it on your *own* time." Teachers made every effort to control the movement of the children, and often shouted, "Why are you out of your *seat*??!!" If the children got permission to leave the room they had to take a written pass with the date and time.

The control that the teachers have is less than they would like. It is a result of constant struggle with the children. The children continually resist the teachers' orders and the work itself. They do not directly challenge the teachers' authority or legitimacy, but they make indirect attempts to sabotage and resist the flow of assignments:

30   TEACHER: I will put some problems on the board. You are to divide.

            CHILD: We got to divide?

            TEACHER: Yes.

            SEVERAL CHILDREN: (Groan) Not again. Mr. B, we done this yesterday.

            CHILD: Do we put the date?

35   TEACHER: Yes. I hope we remember we work in silence. You're supposed to do it on white paper. I'll explain it later.

            CHILD: Somebody broke my pencil. (Crash—a child falls out of his chair.)

            CHILD: (repeats) Mr. B., somebody broke my *pencil!*

            CHILD: Are we going to be here all morning?

            (Teacher comes to the observer, shakes his head and grimaces, then smiles.)

The children are successful enough in their struggle against work that there are long periods where they are not asked to do any work, but just to sit and be quiet.[9] Very often the work that the teachers assign is "easy," that is, not demanding, and thus receives less resistance. Sometimes a compromise is reached where, although the teachers insist that the children continue to work, there is a constant murmur of talk. The children will be doing arithmetic examples, copying social studies notes, or doing punctuation or other dittoes, and all the while there is muted but spirited conversation—about somebody's broken arm, an afterschool disturbance of the day before, etc. Sometimes the teachers themselves join in the conversation because, as one teacher explained to me, "It's a relief from the routine."

40   *Middle-Class School.* In the middle-class school, work is getting the right answer. If one accumulates enough right answers one gets a good grade. One must follow the directions in order to get the right answers, but the directions often call for some figuring, some choice, some decision making. For example, the children must often figure out by themselves what the directions ask them to do, and how to get the answer: what do you do first, second, and perhaps third? Answers are usually found in books or by listening to the teacher. Answers are usually words, sentences, numbers, or facts and dates; one writes them on paper, and one should be neat. Answers must be in the right order, and one can not make them up.

The following activities are illustrative. Math involves some choice: one may do two-digit division the long way, or the short way, and there are some math problems that can be done "in your head." When the teacher explains how to do two-digit division, there is recognition that a cognitive process is involved; she gives several ways, and says, "I want to make sure you understand what you're doing—so you get it right"; and, when they go over the homework, she asks the *children* to tell how they did the problem and what answer they got.

In social studies the daily work is to read the assigned pages in the textbook and to answer the teacher's questions. The questions are almost always designed to check on whether the students have read the assignment and understood it; who did so-and-so; what happened after that; when did it happen, where, and sometimes, why did it happen? The answers are in the book and in one's understanding of the book; the teacher's hints when one doesn't know the answer are to "read it again," or to look at the picture or at the rest of the paragraph. One is to search for the answer in the "context," in what is given.

Language arts is "simple grammar, what they need for everyday life." The language arts teacher says, "They should learn to speak properly, to write business letters and thank-you letters, and to understand what nouns and verbs and simple subjects are." Here, as well, the actual work is to choose the right answers, to understand what is given. The teacher often says, "Please read the next sentence and then I'll question you about it." One teacher said in some exasperation to a boy who was fooling around in class, "If you don't know the answers to the questions I ask, then you can't stay in this *class!* (pause) You *never* know the answers to the questions I ask, and it's not fair to me—and certainly not to you!"

Most lessons are based on the textbook. This does not involve a critical perspective on what is given there. For example, a critical perspective in social studies is perceived as dangerous by these teachers because it may lead to controversial topics; the parents might complain. The children, however, are often curious, especially in social studies. Their questions are tolerated, and usually answered perfunctorily. But after a few minutes the teacher will say, "All right, we're not going any farther. Please open your social studies workbook." While the teachers spend a lot of time explaining and expanding on what the textbooks say, there is little attempt to analyze how or why things happen, or to give thought to how pieces of a culture, or, say, a system of numbers or elements of a language fit together or can be analyzed. What has happened in the past, and what exists now may not be equitable or fair, but (shrug) that is the way things are, and one does not confront such matters in school. For example, in social studies after a child is called on to read a passage about the pilgrims, the teacher summarizes the paragraph and then says, "So you can see how strict they were about everything." A child asks, "Why?" "Well, because they felt that if you weren't busy you'd get into trouble." Another child asks, "Is it true that they burned women at the stake?" The teacher says, "Yes, if a woman did anything strange, they hanged them. [sic] What would a woman do, do you think, to make them burn them? [sic] See if you can come up with better answers than my other [social studies] class." Several children offer suggestions, to which the teacher nods but does not comment. Then she says, "OK, good," and calls on the next child to read.

45   Work tasks do not usually request creativity. Serious attention is rarely given in school work to *how* the children develop or express their own feelings and ideas, either linguistically or in graphic form. On the occasions when creativity or self-expression is requested, it is peripheral to the main activity, or it is "enrichment," or "for fun." During a lesson on what similes are, for example, the teacher explains what they are, puts several on the board, gives some other examples herself, and then asks the children if they can "make some up." She calls on three children who give similes, two of which are actually in the book they have open before them. The teacher does not comment on this, and then asks several others to choose similes from the list of phrases in the book. Several do so correctly, and she says, "Oh *good!* You're picking them out! See how *good* we are?" Their homework is to pick out the rest of the similes from the list.

Creativity is not often requested in social studies and science projects, either. Social studies projects, for example, are given with directions to "find information on your topic," and write it up. The children are not supposed to copy, but to "put it in your own words." Although a number of the projects subsequently went beyond the teacher's direction to find information and had quite expressive covers and inside illustrations, the teacher's evaluative comments had to do with the amount of information, whether they had "copied," and if their work was neat.

The style of control of the three fifth grade teachers observed in this school varied from somewhat easygoing to strict, but in contrast to the working-class schools, the teachers' decisions were usually based on external rules and regulations, for example, on criteria that were known or available to the children. Thus, the teachers always honor the bells for changing classes, and they usually evaluate children's work by what is in the textbooks and answer booklets.

There is little excitement in school work for the children, and the assignments are perceived as having little to do with their interests and feelings. As one child said, what you do is "store facts in your head like cold storage—until you need it later for a test, or your job." Thus, doing well is important because there are thought to be *other* likely rewards: a good job, or college.[10]

Affluent Professional School. In the affluent professional school, work is creative activity carried out independently. The students are continually asked to express and apply ideas and concepts. Work involves individual thought and expressiveness, expansion and illustration of ideas, and choice of appropriate method and material. The class is not considered an open classroom, and the principal explained that because of the large number of discipline problems in the fifth grade this year they did not departmentalize. (The teacher who agreed to take part in the study said she is "more structured" this year than she usually is.) The products of work in this class are often written stories, editorials and essays, or representations of ideas in mural, graph, or craft form. The products of work should not be like everybody else's and should show individuality. They should exhibit good design, and (this is important), they must also fit empirical reality. Moreover, one's work should attempt to interpret or "make sense" of reality. The relatively few rules to be followed regarding work are usually criteria for, or limits on, individual activity. One's product is usually evaluated for the quality of its expression and for the appropriateness of its conception to the task. In many cases one's own satisfaction with the product is an important criterion for its evaluation. When right answers are called for, as in commercial materials like SRA (Science Research Associates) and math, it is important that the children decide on an answer as a result of thinking about the idea involved in what they're being asked to do. Teacher's hints are to "think about it some more."

50   The following activities are illustrative. The class takes home a sheet requesting each child's parents to fill in the number of cars they have, the number of television sets, refrigerators, games, or rooms in the house, etc. Each child is to figure the average number of a type of possession owned by the fifth grade. Each child must compile the "data" from all the sheets. A calculator is available in the classroom to do the mechanics of finding the average. Some children decide to send sheets to the fourth grade families for comparison. Their work should be "verified" by a classmate before it is handed in.

Each child and his or her family has made a geoboard. The teacher asks the class to get their geoboards from the side cabinet, to take a handful of rubber bands, and then to listen to what she would like them to do. She says, "I would like you to design a figure and then find the perimeter and area. When you have it, check with your neighbor. After you've done that, please transfer it to graph paper and tomorrow I'll ask you to make up a question about it for someone. When you hand it in, please let me know whose it is, and who verified it. Then I have something else for you to do that's really fun. (pause) Find the average number of chocolate chips in three cookies. I'll give you three cookies, and you'll have to *eat* your way through, I'm afraid!" Then she goes around the room and gives help, suggestions, praise, and admonitions that they are getting noisy. They work sitting, or standing up at their desks, at benches in the back, or on the floor. A child hands the teacher his paper and she comments, "I'm not accepting this paper. Do a better design." To another child she says, "That's fantastic! But you'll never find the area. Why don't you draw a figure inside [the big one] and subtract to get the area?"

The school district requires the fifth grades to study ancient civilizations (in particular, Egypt, Athens, and Sumer). In this classroom, the emphasis is on illustrating and re-creating the culture of the people of ancient times. The following are typical activities: The children made an 8mm film on Egypt, which one of the parents edited. A girl in the class wrote the script, and the class acted it out. They put the sound on themselves. They read stories of those days. They wrote essays and stories depicting the lives of the people and the societal and occupational divisions. They chose from a list of projects, all of which involved graphic representations of ideas: for example, "Make a mural depicting the division of labor in Egyptian Society."

Each child wrote and exchanged a letter in hieroglyphics with a fifth grader in another class, and they also exchanged stories they wrote in cuneiform. They made scroll and singed the edges so it looked authentic. They each chose an occupation and made an Egyptian plaque representing that occupation, simulating the appropriate Egyptian design. They carved their design on a cylinder of wax, pressed the wax into clay, and then baked the clay. Although one girl did not choose an occupation, but carved instead a series of gods and slaves, the teacher said, "That's all right, Amber, it's beautiful." As they were working the teacher said, "Don't cut into your clay until you're satisfied with your design."

Social studies also involves almost daily presentation by the children of some event from the news. The teacher's questions ask the children to expand what they say, to give more details, and to be more specific. Occasionally she adds some remarks to help them see connections between events.

55   The emphasis on expressing and illustrating ideas in social studies is accompanied in language arts by an emphasis on creative writing. Each child wrote a rhebus story for a first grader whom they had interviewed to see what kind of story the child liked best. They wrote editorials on pending decisions by the school board, and audio plays, some of which were read over the school intercom from the office, and one of which was performed in the auditorium. There is no language arts textbook because, the teacher said, "The principal wants us to be creative." There is not much grammar, but there is punctuation. One morning when the observer arrived the class was doing a punctuation ditto. The teacher later apologized for using the ditto. "It's just for review," she said. "I don't teach punctuation that way. We use their language." The ditto had three unambiguous rules for where to put commas in a sentence. As the teacher was going around to help the children with the ditto, she repeated several times, "Where you put commas depends on how you say the sentence; it depends on the situation and what you want to say." Several weeks later the observer saw another punctuation activity. The teacher had printed a five-paragraph story on an oak tag and then cut it into phrases. She read the whole story to the class from the book, then passed out the phrases. The group had to decide how the phrases could best be put together again. (They arranged the phrases on the floor.) The point was not to replicate the story, although that was not irrelevant, but to "decide what you think the best way is." Punctuation marks on cardboard pieces were then handed out and the children discussed, and then decided, what mark was best at each place they thought one was needed. At the end of each paragraph the teacher asked, "Are you satisfied with the way the paragraphs are now? Read it to yourself and see how it sounds." Then she read the original story again, and they compared the two.

Describing her goals in science to the investigator, the teacher said, "We use ESS (Elementary Science Study). It's very good because it gives a hands-on experience—so they can make *sense* out of it. It doesn't matter whether it [what they find] is right or wrong. I bring them together and there's value in discussing their ideas."

The products of work in this class are often highly valued by the children and the teacher. In fact, this was the only school in which the investigator was not allowed to take original pieces of the children's work for her files. If the work was small enough, however, and was on paper, the investigator could duplicate it on the copying machine in the office.

The teacher's attempt to control the class involves constant negotiation. She does not give direct orders unless she is angry because the children have been too noisy. Normally, she tries to get them to foresee the consequences of their actions and to decide accordingly. For example, lining them up to go see a play written by the sixth graders, she says, "I presume you're lined up by someone with whom you want to sit. I hope you're lined up by someone you won't get in trouble with." The following two dialogues illustrate the process of negotiation between student and teacher.

> TEACHER: Tom, you're behind in your SRA this marking period.
>
> 60   TOM: So what!
>
> TEACHER: Well, last time you had a hard time catching up.
>
> TOM: But I have my [music] lesson at 10:00.
>
> TEACHER: Well, that doesn't mean you're going to sit here for twenty minutes.
>
> TOM: Twenty minutes! OK. (He goes to pick out a SRA booklet and chooses one, puts it back, then takes another, and brings it to her.)
>
> 65   TEACHER: OK, this is the one you want, right?
>
> TOM: Yes.
>
> TEACHER: OK, I'll put tomorrow's date on it so you can take it home tonight or finish it tomorrow if you want.
>
> TEACHER: (to a child who is wandering around during reading) Kevin, why don't you do *Reading for Concepts*?
>
> KEVIN: No, I don't like *Reading for Concepts*.
>
> 70   TEACHER: Well, what are you going to do?
>
> KEVIN: (pause) I'm going to work on my DAR. (The DAR had sponsored an essay competition on "Life in the American Colonies.")

One of the few rules governing the children's movement is that no more than three children may be out of the room at once. There is a school rule that anyone can go to the library at any time to get a book. In the fifth grade I observed, they sign their name on the chalkboard and leave. There are no passes. Finally, the children have a fair amount of officially sanctioned say over what happens in the class. For example, they often negotiate what work is to be done. If the teacher wants to move on to the next subject, but the children say they are not ready, they want to work on their present projects some more, she very often lets them do it.

Executive Elite School. In the executive elite school, work is developing one's analytical intellectual powers. Children are continually asked to reason through a problem, to produce intellectual products that are both logically sound and of top academic quality. A primary goal of thought is to conceptualize rules by which elements may fit together in systems, and then to apply these rules in solving a problem. School work helps one to achieve, to excel, to prepare for life.

The following are illustrative. The math teacher teaches area and perimeter by having the children derive formulae for each. First she helps them, through discussion at the board, to arrive at A = W × L as a formula (not *the* formula) for area. After discussing several, she says, "Can anyone make up a formula for perimeter? Can you figure that out yourselves? (pause) Knowing what we know, can we think of a formula?" She works out three children's suggestions at the board, saying to two, "Yes, that's a good one," and then asks the class if they can think of any more. No one volunteers. To prod them, she says, "If you use rules and good reasoning, you get many ways. Chris, can you think up a formula?"

75   She discusses two-digit division with the children as a decision-making process. Presenting a new type of problem to them, she asks, "What's the *first* decision you'd make if presented with this kind of example? What is the first thing you'd *think?* Craig?" Craig says, "To find my first partial quotient." She responds, "Yes, that would be your first decision. How would you do that?" Craig explains, and then the teacher says, "OK, we'll see how that works for you." The class tries his way. Subsequently, she comments on the merits and shortcomings of several other children's decisions. Later, she tells the investigator that her goals in math are to develop their reasoning and mathematical thinking and that, unfortunately, "there's no *time* for manipulables."

While right answers are important in math, they are not "given" by the book or by the teacher, but may be challenged by the children. Going over some problems in late September the teacher says, "Raise your hand if you do not agree." A child says, "I don't agree with 64." The teacher responds, "OK, there's a question about 64. (to class) Please check it. Owen, they're disagreeing with you. Kristen, they're checking yours." The teacher emphasized this repeatedly during September and October with statements like, "Don't be afraid to say if you disagree. In the last [math] class, somebody disagreed, and they were right. Before you disagree, check yours, and if you still think we're wrong, then we'll check it out." By Thanksgiving, the children did not often speak in terms of right and wrong math problems, but of whether they agreed with the answer that had been given.

There are complicated math mimeos with many word problems. Whenever they go over the examples, they discuss how each child has set up the problem. The children must explain it precisely. On one occasion the teacher said, "I'm more—just as interested in *how* you set up the problem as in what answer you find. If you set up a problem in a good way, the answer is *easy* to find."

Social studies work is most often reading and discussion of concepts and independent research. There are only occasional artistic, expressive, or illustrative projects. Ancient Athens and Sumer are, rather, societies to analyze. The following questions are typical of those which guide the children's independent research: "What mistakes did Pericles make after the war?" "What mistakes did the citizens of Athens make?" "What are the elements of a civilization?" "How did Greece build an economic empire?" "Compare the way Athens chose its leaders with the way we choose ours." Occasionally the children are asked to make up sample questions for their social studies tests. On an occasion when the investigator was present the social studies teacher rejected a child's question by saying, "That's just fact. If I asked you that question on a test, you'd complain it was just memory! Good questions ask for concepts."

In social studies—but also in reading, science, and health—the teachers initiate classroom discussions of current social issues and problems. These discussions occurred on every one of the investigator's visits, and a teacher told me, "These children's opinions are important—it's important that they learn to reason things through." The classroom discussions always struck the observer as quite realistic and analytical, dealing with concrete social issues like the following: "Why do workers strike?" "Is that right or wrong?" "Why do we have inflation, and what can be done to stop it?" "Why do companies put chemicals in food when the natural ingredients are available?" etc. Usually the children did not have to be prodded to give their opinions. In fact, their statements and the interchanges between them struck the observer as quite sophisticated conceptually and verbally, and well-informed. Occasionally the teachers would prod with statements such as, "Even if you don't know [the answers], if you think logically about it, you can figure it out." And "I'm asking you [these] questions to help you think this through."

80   Language arts emphasizes language as a complex system, one that should be mastered. The children are asked to diagram sentences of complex grammatical construction, to memorize irregular verb conjugations (he lay, he has lain, etc.), and to use the proper participles, conjunctions, and interjections, in their speech. The teacher (the same one who teaches social studies) told them, "It is not enough to get these right on tests; you must use what you learn [in grammar classes] in your written and oral work. I will grade you on that."

Most writing assignments are either research reports and essays for social studies, or experiment analyses and write-ups for science. There is only an occasional story or other "creative writing" assignment. On the occasion observed by the investigator (the writing of a Halloween story), the points the teacher stressed in preparing the children to write involved the structural aspects of a story rather than the expression of feelings or other ideas. The teacher showed them a filmstrip, "The Seven Parts of a Story," and lectured them on plot development, mood setting, character development, consistency, and the use of a logical or appropriate ending. The stories they subsequently wrote were, in fact, well-structured, but many were also personal and expressive. The teacher's evaluative comments, however, did not refer to the expressiveness or artistry, but were all directed toward whether they had "developed" the story well.

Language arts work also involved a large amount of practice in presentation of the self and in managing situations where the child was expected to be in charge. For example, there was a series of assignments in which each child had to be a "student teacher." The child had to plan a lesson in grammar, outlining, punctuation, or other language arts topic and explain the concept to the class. Each child was to prepare a worksheet or game and a homework assignment as well. After each presentation, the teacher and other children gave a critical appraisal of the "student teacher's" performance. Their criteria were: whether the student spoke clearly; whether the lesson was interesting; whether the student made any mistakes; and whether he or she kept control of the class. On an occasion when a child did not maintain control, the teacher said, "When you're up there, you have authority, and you have to use it. I'll back you up."

The teacher of math and science explained to the observer that she likes the ESS program because "the children can manipulate variables. They generate hypotheses and devise experiments to solve the problem. Then they have to explain what they found."

The executive elite school is the only school where bells do not demarcate the periods of time. The two fifth grade teachers were very strict about changing classes on schedule, however, as specific plans for each session had been made. The teachers attempted to keep tight control over the children during lessons, and the children were sometimes flippant, boisterous, and occasionally rude. However, the children may be brought into line by reminding them that "it is up to you." "You must control yourself," "you are responsible for your work," you must "set your priorities." One teacher told a child, "You are the only driver of your car—and only you can regulate your speed." A new teacher complained to the observer that she had thought "these children" would have more control.

85   While strict attention to the lesson at hand is required, the teachers make relatively little attempt to regulate the movement of the children at other times. For example, except for the kindergartners, the children in this school do not have to wait for the bell to ring in the morning; they may go to their classroom when they arrive at school. Fifth graders often came early to read, to finish work, or to catch up. After the first two months of school the fifth grade teachers did not line the children up to change classes or to go to gym, etc., but, when the children were ready and quiet, they were told they could go—sometimes without the teachers.

In the classroom, the children could get materials when they needed them and took what they needed from closets and from the teacher's desk. They were in charge of the office at lunchtime. During class they did not have to sign out or ask permission to leave the room; they just got up and left. Because of the pressure to get work done, however, they did not leave the room very often. The teachers were very polite to the children, and the investigator heard no sarcasm, no nasty remarks, and few direct orders. The teachers never called the children "honey," or "dear," but always called them by name. The teachers were expected to be available before school, after school, and for part of their lunch time to provide extra help if needed.

DISCUSSION AND CONCLUSION

One could attempt to identify physical, educational, cultural, and interpersonal characteristics of the environment of each school that might contribute to an empirical explanation of the events and interactions. For example, the investigator could introduce evidence to show that the following *increased* as the social class of the community increased (with the most marked differences occurring between the two districts): increased variety and abundance of teaching materials in the classroom; increased time reported spent by the teachers on preparation; higher social class background and more prestigious educational institutions attended by teachers and administrators; more stringent board of education requirements regarding teaching methods; more frequent and demanding administrative evaluation of teachers; increased teacher support services such as in-service workshops; increased parent expenditure for school equipment over and above district or government funding; higher expectations of student ability on the part of parents, teachers, and administrators; higher expectations and demands regarding student achievement on the part of teachers, parents, and administrators; more positive attitudes on the part of the teachers as to the probable occupational futures of the children; an increase in the children's acceptance of classroom assignments; increased intersubjectivity between students and teachers; and increased cultural congruence between school and community.

All of these—and other—factors may contribute to the character and scope of classroom events. However, what is of primary concern here is not the immediate causes of classroom activity (although these are in themselves quite important). Rather, the concern is to reflect on the deeper social meaning, the wider theoretical significance, of what happens in each social setting. In an attempt to assess the theoretical meaning of the differences among the schools, the work tasks and milieu in each will be discussed in light of the concepts used to define social class.

What potential relationships to the system of ownership of symbolic and physical capital, to authority and control, and to their own productive activity are being developed in children in each school? What economically relevant knowledge, skills, and predispositions are being transmitted in each classroom, and for what future relationship to the system of production are they appropriate? It is of course true that a student's future relationship to the process of production in society is determined by the combined effects of circumstances beyond elementary schooling. However, by examining elementary school activity in its social class context in the light of our theoretical perspective on social class, we can see certain potential relationships already developing. Moreover, in this structure of developing relationships lies theoretical—and social—significance.

90   The *working-class* children are developing a potential *conflict* relationship with capital. Their present school work is appropriate preparation for future wage labor that is mechanical and routine. Such work, insofar as it denies the human capacities for creativity and planning, is degrading; moreover, when performed in industry, such work is a source of profit to others. This situation produces industrial conflict over wages, working conditions, and control. However, the children in the working-class schools are not learning to be docile and obedient in the face of present or future degrading conditions or financial exploitation. They are developing abilities and skills of resistance. These methods are highly similar to the "slowdown," subtle sabotage and other modes of indirect resistance carried out by adult workers in the shop, on the department store sales floor, and in some offices.[11] As these types of resistance develop in school, they are highly constrained and limited in their ultimate effectiveness. Just as the children's resistance prevents them from learning socially legitimated knowledge and skills in school and is therefore ultimately debilitating, so is this type of resistance ultimately debilitating in industry. Such resistance in industry does not succeed in producing, nor is it intended to produce, fundamental changes in the relationships of exploitation or control. Thus, the methods of resistance that the working-class children are developing in school are only temporarily, and *potentially,* liberating.

In the *middle-class* school the children are developing somewhat different potential relationships to capital, authority, and work. In this school the work tasks and relationships are appropriate for a future relation to capital that is *bureaucratic*. Their school work is appropriate for white-collar working-class and middle-class jobs in the supportive institutions of United States society. In these jobs one does the paperwork, the technical work, the sales and the social service in the private and state bureaucracies. Such work does not usually demand that one be creative, and one is not often re-warded for critical analysis of the system. One is rewarded, rather, for knowing the an-swers to the questions one is asked, for knowing where or how to find the answers, and for knowing which form, regulation, technique, or procedure is correct. While such work does not usually satisfy human needs for engagement and self-expression, one's salary can be exchanged for objects or activities that attempt to meet these needs.

In the *affluent professional* school the children are developing a potential relation-ship to capital that is instrumental and expressive and involves substantial negotiation. In their schooling these children are acquiring *symbolic capital:* they are being given the opportunity to develop skills of linguistic, artistic, and scientific expression and cre-ative elaboration of ideas into concrete form. These skills are those needed to pro-duce, for example, culture (e.g., artistic, intellectual, and scientific ideas and other "products"). Their schooling is developing in these children skills necessary to become society's successful artists, intellectuals, legal, scientific, and technical experts and other professionals. The developing relation of the children in this school to their work is creative and relatively autonomous. Although they do not have control over which ideas they develop or express, the creative act in itself affirms and utilizes the human potential for conceptualization and design that is in many cases valued as in-trinsically satisfying.

Professional persons in the cultural institutions of society (in, say, academe, pub-lishing, the nonprint media, the arts, and the legal and state bureaucracies) are in an expressive relationship to the system of ownership in society because the ideas and other products of their work are often an important means by which material rela-tionships of society are given ideological (e.g., artistic, intellectual, legal, and scientific) expression. Through the system of laws, for example, the ownership relations of pri-vate property are elaborated and legitimated in legal form; through individualistic and meritocratic theories in psychology and sociology, these individualistic economic rela-tions are provided scientific "rationality" and "sense." The relationship to physical capi-tal of those in society who create what counts as the dominant culture or ideology also involves substantial negotiation. The producers of symbolic capital often do not control the socially available physical capital nor the cultural uses to which it is put. They must therefore negotiate for money for their own projects. However, skillful ap-plication of one's cultural capital may ultimately lead to social (for example, state) power and to financial reward.

The *executive elite* school gives its children something that none of the other schools do: knowledge of and practice in manipulating the socially legitimated tools of analysis of systems. The children are given the opportunity to learn and to utilize the intellectually and socially prestigious grammatical, mathematical, and other vocabular-ies and rules by which elements are arranged. They are given the opportunity to use these skills in the analysis of society and in control situations. Such knowledge and skills are a most important kind of *symbolic capital.* They are necessary for control of a production system. The developing relationship of the children in this school to their work affirms and develops in them the human capacities for analysis and planning and helps to prepare them for work in society that would demand these skills. Their schooling is helping them to develop the abilities necessary for ownership and control of physical capital and the means of production in society.

95   The foregoing analysis of differences in school work in contrasting social class contexts suggests the following conclusion: the "hidden curriculum" of school work is tacit preparation for relating to the process of production in a particular way. Differing curricular, pedagogical, and pupil evaluation practices emphasize different cognitive and behavioral skills in each social setting and thus contribute to the development in the children of certain potential relationships to physical and symbolic capital, to authority, and to the process of work. School experience, in the sample of schools discussed here, differed qualitatively by social class. These differences may not only contribute to the development in the children in each social class of certain types of economically significant relationships and not others, but would thereby help to *reproduce* this system of relations in society. In the contribution to the reproduction of unequal social relations lies a theoretical meaning, and social consequence, of classroom practice.

    The identification of different emphases in classrooms in a sample of contrasting social class contexts implies that further research should be conducted in a large number of schools to investigate the types of work tasks and interactions in each, to see if they differ in the ways discussed here, and to see if similar potential relationships are uncovered. Such research could have as a product the further elucidation of complex but not readily apparent connections between everyday activity in schools and classrooms and the unequal structure of economic relationships in which we work and live.

ENDNOTES

1. But see, in a related vein, Apple and King (1977) and Rist (1973).

2. The definition of social class delineated here is the author's own, but it relies heavily on her interpretation of the work of Eric Olin Wright (1978), Pierre Bourdieu (Bourdieu and Passeron, 1977) and Raymond Williams (1977).

3. For discussion of schools as agencies of social and economic legitimation see Althusser (1971); see also Anyon (1978; 1979).

4. While relationships of control in society will not be discussed here, it can be said that they roughly parallel the relationships of control in the workplace, which will be the focus of this discussion. That is, working-class and many middle-class persons have less control than members of the upper-middle and capitalist classes do, not only over conditions and processes of their work, but over their nonwork lives as well. In addition, it is true that persons from the middle and capitalist classes, rather than workers, are most often those who fill the positions of state and other power in United States society.

5. Occupations may change their relation to the means of production over time, as the expenditure and ownership of capital change, as technology, skills, and the social relations of work change. For example, some jobs which were middle-class, managerial positions in 1900 and which necessitated conceptual laying-out and planning are now working-class and increasingly mechanical: e.g., quality control in industry, clerical work, and computer programming (see Braverman, 1974).

6. The U.S. Bureau of the Census defines "poverty" for a nonfarm family of four as a yearly income of $6,191 a year or less. U.S. Bureau of the Census, *Statistical Abstract of the United States: 1978* (Washington, D.C.: U.S. Government Printing Office, 1978, p. 465, table 754).

7. This figure is an estimate. According to the Bureau of the Census, only 2.6 percent of families in the United States have money income of $50,000 or over. U.S. Bureau of the Census, *Current Population Reports,* series P-60, no. 118, "Money Income in 1977 of Families and Persons in the United States." (Washington, D.C.: U.S. Government Printing Office, 1979, p. 2, table A). For figures on income at these higher levels, see Smith and Franklin (1974).

8. For other similarities alleged to characterize United States classrooms and schools, but which will not be discussed here, see Dreeben (1968), Jackson (1968), and Sarasan (1971).

9. Indeed, strikingly little teaching occurred in either of the working-class schools; this curtailed the amount that the children were taught. Incidentally, it increased the amount of time that had to be spent by the researcher to collect data on teaching style and interaction.

10. A dominant feeling, expressed directly and indirectly by teachers in this school, was boredom with their work. They did, however, in contrast to the working-class schools, almost always carry out lessons during class times.

11. See, for example, discussions in Levison (1974), Aronowitz (1978), and Benson (1978).

REFERENCES

Althusser, L. Ideology and ideological state apparatuses. In L. Althusser, *Lenin and philosophy and other essays.* Ben Brewster, Trans. New York: Monthly Review Press, 1971.

Anyon, J. Elementary social studies textbooks and legitimating knowledge. *Theory and Research in Social Education,* 1978, 6, 40–55.

Anyon, J. Ideology and United States history textbooks. *Harvard Educational Review,* 1979, 49, 361–386.

Apple, M.W. *Ideology and curriculum.* Boston: Routledge and Kegan Paul, 1979.

Apple, M.W., & King, N. What do schools teach? *Curriculum Inquiry,* 1977, 6, 341–358.

Aronowitz, S. Marx, Braverman, and the logic of capital. *The Insurgent Sociologist,* 1978, 8, 126–146.

Benson, S. The clerking sisterhood: rationalization and the work culture of saleswomen in American department stores, 1890–1960. *Radical America,* 1978, 12, 41–55.

Bernstein, B. *Class, codes and control, Vol. 3. Towards a theory of educational transmission.* 2nd ed. London: Routledge and Kegan Paul, 1977.

Bourdieu, P. and Passeron, J. *Reproduction in education, society, and culture.* Beverly Hills, Calif.: Sage, 1977.

Bowles, S. & Gintis, H. *Schooling in capitalist America: educational reform and the contradictions of economic life.* New York: Basic Books, 1976.

Braverman, H. *Labor and monopoly capital: the degradation of work in the twentieth century.* New York: Monthly Review Press, 1974.

Dreeben, R. *On what is learned in school.* Reading, Mass.: Addison-Wesley, 1968.

Jackson, P. *Life in classrooms.* Holt, Rinehart & Winston, 1968.

Lampman, R.J. *The share of top wealth-holders in national wealth, 1922–1956: A study of the National Bureau of Economic Research.* Princeton, N.J.: Princeton University Press, 1962.

Levison, A. *The working-class majority.* New York: Penguin Books, 1974.

New York Stock Exchange. *Census.* New York: New York Stock Exchange, 1975.

Rist, R. C. *The urban school: a factory for failure.* Cambridge, Mass.: MIT Press, 1973.

Sarasan, S. *The culture of school and the problem of change.* Boston: Allyn and Bacon, 1971.

Smith, J.D. and Franklin, S. The concentration of personal wealth, 1922–1969. *American Economic Review,* 1974, 64, 162–167.

U.S. Bureau of the Census. *Current population reports.* Series P-60, no. 118. Money income in 1977 of families and persons in the United States. Washington, D.C.: U.S. Government Printing Office, 1979.

U.S. Bureau of the Census. *Statistical abstract of the United States: 1978.* Washington, D.C.: U.S. Government Printing Office, 1978.

Williams, R. *Marxism and literature.* New York: Oxford University Press, 1977.

Wright, E.O. *Class, crisis and the state.* London: New Left Books, 1978.

---

1. <u>Reflecting on discourse, literacy, and the context of academic disciplines</u>   **READING RESPONSE**

   ■ In the section of this article on social class, Anyon reviews the common understandings about social class that are part of the necessary shared knowledge that underlies her own work. If you've taken courses in economics or sociology, you may find much of what she reviews here to be familiar. The picture she presents of who owns capital in the form of stock, however, has changed since she wrote this article. A much broader segment of the U.S. population now has some stock ownership through retirement plans, confusing the clear definitions she makes here of capitalists and workers. Nevertheless, the class distinctions she's focusing on between those who have the greatest amount of wealth, those who are middle class and those who are lower-end working-class earners remain in place, with the gap between the wealthy and the others getting bigger. The distinctions in social class that guided her choice of schools to research still affect schools in similar ways. As you consider this theoretical discussion of social class or any of the descriptions of specific schools that follow, do you find connections to the experiences represented by Mike Rose in "I Just Want to be Average," or the research of Paul Willis in "The Informal Group?" What is involved, from the inside, in social class identity?

   ■ Of the four types of schools Anyon names—working-class, middle-class, affluent-professional and executive-elite—which most applies to the type of school you yourself attended? As you read the descriptions of what went on in the different schools, does the category of your school fit with the sort of work that goes on in the classrooms as described by Anyon? If not, what do you think might account for the differences?   *(continued)*

(continued)

- In her detailed discussion of the work of the classrooms of these different schools, Anyon describes what that work is, how it's carried out, and whatever the children are told about and why. She also captures some of the typical wording of lessons and instructions in different subject areas. To what extent do you think it's appropriate to consider the different classrooms she studied as different discourse communities? Do you find that the particular ways of talking and working and the values that underlie them within a particular category of classroom outweigh any differences in the subjects being taught? If you take any of the excerpts from conversations that she offers and analyze them as we've analyzed earlier conversations in this book, what do you find? If you were to categorize the discourse of schooling as it's seen in each of these classrooms, would you be most likely to name it first in terms of social class, as Anyon does, or are there other ways in which you might name what you see here?

2. Reading as a writer/researcher

- Anyon frames her article by positioning it within a particular line of research in education focusing on the relationship between schooling and social class, and suggesting what her article will contribute to research on that topic and how. Do her opening two paragraphs provide a clear and sufficient introduction to what follows for you as a reader? Although she's writing to an audience that's probably familiar with the studies she names, does she give enough information about those studies for the purpose of showing where, in the ongoing written conversation, she is placing her own study? For the purpose of informing outsider readers? If you were to write a similar introduction to your own research study, what would you include?

- Anyon includes a brief methodology section, a typical element of both laboratory and field studies in the social sciences and sciences. Using Anyon's model, you may want to draft a brief methodology section for your own report of field research.

- Anyon provides many detailed examples of what she's collected in her observational data for each classroom. Does what she shows provide a convincing portrait of the differences she identifies? Does it provide sufficient evidence to lead to the conclusions she draws?

- As you consider Anyon's conclusion about the different sorts of capital students are acquiring in different schools, you might apply those understandings to what you've been discovering about the academic discourse community of a course you're taking. Are you being placed in a conflict relationship with the knowledge that's being presented there? A bureaucratic relationship? Are you acquiring symbolic capital? Are you gaining the powerful sort of symbolic capital associated with the analysis of systems? How are you and your classmates being positioned in the work you are doing, and is that positioning something you want to consider in your report on this community?

Vanessa Ortega, "Music as a Life-Style"

Vanessa Ortega began her undergraduate career as a prospective physics major at a different university. Although she had long been interested in music and had played the violin as a child, she had stopped when she was still young, and while her interest in music continued, she thought she was too far behind other prospective music students to enter that field. At the time Vanessa carried out the following study of her music theory class, she had just returned to school, was beginning to think seriously about pursuing a music major, and was enrolled in two music courses. She used the opportunity this study provided to think more seriously about what it would mean to be an insider to the field of music, and whether that was a direction she should really pursue. After completing this study, she made her decision, and has become a successful insider to her new field, developing her skill as a violinist to the point where she plays in her university's string quartet and performs frequently at official university functions. The following study shows some of the ways in which she was already beginning to think like an insider to the field of music.

Music as a Life-Style

Vanessa Ortega

1   What is valuable to the insiders of the Music discourse community? To answer this question in a clear way, we have to go through analyzing many aspects of music; what makes the music classes at college different from other classes? Who participates in them? What is the shared knowledge required to be an insider? What is the purpose of it? What are the types of work that professional musicians and students have to do? What are the kinds of questions that students are asked to write about in academic studies?

MUSIC CLASSES AT COLLEGE IN CONTRAST WITH OTHER CLASSES:

My Ear-Training & Sight-Singing and Music Theory classes are unique from my point of view. When I was in college before, all freshman classes were very different; students many times looked bored and distracted, but when classes start getting more focused on the particular field of study (that is in second year) all students are much more interested and seem to enjoy the classes much more. I think this happens because if you are studying Engineering you have to go through the basic cycle of Mathematics, Physics and other courses. These courses are not really ENGINEER-ING courses, but they are required. Eric too, when analyzing a first year physics class, found that "'everyone looks tired' and no one seems particularly excited by the prospect of the five-week introductory physics course that lay ahead. His fellow classmates, as he perceived them, were either 'bored' or 'scared' " (p. 384). Then, in their second year, engineers start the specific courses of the field; for example electric circuits.

On the other hand, in these freshman music classes, everyone seems very interested since the start, and that is probably because, regardless that they are freshman classes, they are directly connected to the field of study. Much of the work we do in class is work that we are going to do throughout our career, work we need to do every day to be successful musicians.

In these classes the participants are both the teacher and all the students. In the theory class, we have to sing individually sometimes, hear intervals and identify them (an interval is the distance between two or more notes), and study from our theory book. In the ear training class, we sing together and individually, and we have to sight-sing (sight-singing is reading music from a score at first sight, and singing it in pitch).

MY OWN EXPERIENCE AS A MUSIC STUDENT:

5   When I was seven, my grandfather decided to go to Italy and he asked me what I wanted him to get me from there. I asked for a violin. That same year I started private lessons with a violinist, but unfortunately these didn't last very long and I stopped playing. I kept on listening to classical music even though I wasn't taking lessons anymore, and I used to enjoy it immensely. In my last year of high-school I took all the savings I had made since I stopped playing (a period of eleven years) and bought myself a new full sized violin. I started taking private lessons again, and at the same time I was starting a physics major at university. I realized that I was way behind people my age on the violin, and thought to myself that the only way of coming back to it was to dedicate my life completely to music and playing, and that is how I became a music major.

This has been a beautiful experience but also a very hard one. My goal is to practice six to eight hours a day, but this is sometimes very hard to achieve because I am a full time student at college and the work that I have to do for my classes takes most of my time.

SHARED KNOWLEDGE:

At the beginning of the semester it is assumed in these classes that everyone is a musician and plays an instrument or sings. This initial shared knowledge is then built upon, step-by-step with the guidance of the teacher and textbooks. We have to read on our own a chapter of the theory book every week, and then it is discussed in class with the help of the teacher, and any questions or comments are then brought up by the students.

TEACHER: What is an inversion?

PETER: To change the places of the notes.

10   TEACHER: Valerie, why don't you read us the definition of inversion from the book.

VALERIE: If the lower note of an interval is raised an octave or the upper note lowered an octave, the new interval formed is called the inversion of the first interval.

TEACHER: So, what would you call this interval (drawing two C major triads in different positions on the board and pointing at one of them) Peter?

PETER: That is ahh . . . an E triad

TEACHER: I see smiles around the room, could one of the people that smiling tell us what it is?

15   VANESSA: It is a C major triad.

TEACHER: yes

BISTRA: But what Peter said is not completely wrong . . .

TEACHER: No, Peter is our renaissance man, and Vanessa is our Baroque woman.

In this excerpt from my class notes, we can see that the teacher is trying to introduce a new topic to the students and is creating some new shared knowledge. He starts by asking a question about the chapter that the students were supposed to read for homework, to introduce the topic. Then, it seems like he wants to start a discussion about the topic so he makes someone read the accurate definition of "inversion" as a starting point for it, and then he gives an exercise for someone to respond to (with the hope that someone makes a mistake so he can clear up completely any doubts about the topic). This way, every week the shared knowledge grows. As we can also see from this excerpt, questions or comments are welcomed by the teacher at almost any time, like that one of Bistra.

TURN-TAKING:

20   The teacher is the one that always introduces the topics, but students always have the opportunity of asking questions, and giving the class the direction they want. When a question is very advanced, it is postponed for later. In these classes everyone participates, because when someone doesn't participate the teacher makes them participate by asking them to do something. Comments are always welcomed. On the previous excerpt from my class notes, we clearly see that at the beginning of the class the teacher introduces the topic, but from then on, the class will take a direction depending on the students' questions and comments.

PURPOSE OF THE CONVERSATIONS:

The larger purpose of the class is to apply ourselves, and to be disciplined. Music requires a lot of dedication and patience. When we have vacation, we still need to practice playing our instrument, and to train our ears, and this never stops because your body forgets how to hear things, and how to play. Your muscles need to train every day to stay in shape. When you study other subjects you can go on vacation, and after not reading at all about the subject, you can come back to school from vacation and start where you left. On the other hand, if a musician doesn't play for a week, it could take him/her a week of hard practice to get back to where he stopped, and no further than that.

It is very important to be patient to be a musician, and to learn how to appreciate the process of studying. It could seem boring, because you have to break things down, make them easy, and then practice very slowly over and over. That's the way musicians practice all their lives, but if you love it then you learn to appreciate it. I think then that the larger purpose of the teacher and the students is to love this process, and become familiar with it.

THE WORK THAT IS REQUIRED IN THESE CLASSES:

For these classes, you are required to do both written and listening assignments. The written assignments are related to all the theory and musical notation that is learnt through the chapter, and the listening assignments are the practice of the theory, to hear and recognize what has been studied in the chapter.

For example, for Chapter 16, "Augmented and diminished triads, and the whole tone scale," there was a written assignment which consisted of writing augmented and diminished triads using the note given as a starting point. This assignment was to:

25   Write the augmented and diminished triads:

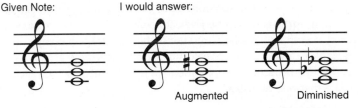

The written assignments are not difficult or challenging at all—any one that reads the chapter can do them and get a good grade. Although they are not hard to do, they are necessary to understanding music and to learning to write music clearly so when you compose performers can understand your music.

Then, there is a listening assignment. The assignment was to recognize major, minor, diminished and augmented triads:

Recognition of Major and minor, diminished and Augmented triads. In each of the following ex. you will hear three triads played in simple position. Place the proper symbol showing the triads in the column in the right.

Triad species

Major triad   M

Minor triad   m

Diminished triad   d

Augmented triad   A

The example is illustrated correctly for you:

M   A   m

_____   _____   _____

_____   _____   _____

_____   _____   _____

_____   _____   _____

This type of assignment, on the other hand is very difficult, and nothing can really guarantee you a good grade. Either you hear it or not. That is the reason all musicians have to do this kind of work over and over throughout their lives. It is really difficult, and it requires continuous work of years to get to hear certain things, and you have to keep on doing this kind work even after you start hearing it.

It is important to look at the type of assignments that are required for music classes to understand what types of people take them. From analyzing these assignments, I can see that classes like these are not often chosen by people of other fields just because musicians have so many advantages over them already; they play an instrument, they have been trying to do listening exercises even before college, and most have sung at some point. It's hard sometimes even for a musician to be in these listening classes at college, now someone that has never had music as a part of their life and has some curiosity for music is going to feel completely lost.

THE KIND OF ACADEMIC RESEARCH THAT IS VALUED IN THIS FIELD

It is very important for musicians to have academic research to rely on when they want to improve their music or their performances.

30   Many of the academic research is then done on topics such as performances, manuscripts, arrangements of pieces, and most common problems of certain instruments in playing and other similar topics. Peter Walls' article "Performing Corelli's violin sonatas, op. 5." is a representative text of academic writing in the field of music. He comments and critiques many recordings of the Corelli violin sonatas, and explains through his paper what pros and cons these recordings have and why. He also includes historical details of the composer and the musical era, and the importance that these pieces have in violin playing. It's important to know how a paper like this would be structured: how the author would introduce the topic, how would he develop it, what details the author should include, and what things he would leave out.

The author introduces the topic by giving us a historical view of Corelli's sonatas for violin. He talks about the importance of this work in the baroque period (early 18th century), what the sonatas brought to baroque and even contemporary music, and how important it was and is for the performer to make these sonatas a part of his/her repertoire.

> The opts sonatas in particular came to be regarded as the hallmark of a performer's musicianship and skill. In the early years of the 18th century to announce that a concert would include 'one of Corelli's Solo's by an extraordinary Hand' (or some such phrase) seems to have been a sure-fire way of attracting an audience. Tartini's advice to Maddalena Lombardini to practice an opts Allegro daily is evidence of the way these works remained at the head of the violinist's canon (Early Music 1).

In this excerpt from the text, the author makes it very clear to the reader that any performance that would include a work by Corelli, would be highly regarded and successful in that period. When the author talks about how Lombardini was told to make one of these works part of her daily practice, he suggests that the works touch upon the most virtuosic aspects of violin playing, and that it is believed that performing such works successfully is a step towards mastering the art of violin playing.

The author wants to reflect on the way of performing these important works for violin; he critiques and criticizes different recordings. He discusses as to which versions of the manuscript (i.e. scores) should the performers rely on, which performers give the impression of being more "historically aware," that is play the pieces as they were supposed to be played in that time and as the composer thought them. The way the author does this is by referring to specific movements of the sonatas (there are twelve sonatas, each generally with three movements) and analyzing them; he is looking at the way each performer plays it, and what differences there are between the different performances, what changes does each violinist make to each movement, which are the pros and cons of these changes, and which manuscripts the violinist is relying on. He also discusses what instruments are supposed to be used for these works, which are appropriate and which the composer had in mind as his "dream instruments". There are many discrepancies as to which are the instruments thought of originally by the composer, and he explains why there are such discrepancies.

The author uses specific recordings as references, and also he talks about the performances of specific violinists. For instance: "Even Kuijken's version of Sonata no. 11 (the only part 2 sonata apart from the Folia variations on his disc) seems tongue-tied alongside the invention of Wallfisch and Huggett—and here I am not just referring to the extraordinary cadential flourish the latter violinist produces in the brief Adagio before the third movement" (Early Music 13). The author here makes reference to the recordings of three violinists and makes a contrast between them. Also, the author mentions other names of people that have arranged the pieces every time a violinist uses his arrangements in a performance.

35   The author concludes by saying which are the best recordings to his judgment, and which failed to captivate the attention of the listener. After talking more or less technically and analyzing, he becomes more informal in his conclusion. And after having studied everything in depth he allows himself to give an honest conclusion about how these recordings make him feel. He can afford this because he has already given the impression that he knows what he is talking about, and backs-up all what he says with his knowledge.

He concludes by asking and answering the question "Which of these recordings give most pleasure?" (Early music 14).

It's very Important for the field that studies like this are written because performers in general (students and any person willing to perfectionate his/her playing) can refer to this type of writings. That's how we get better, by reading critiques about other players. and deciding whether to perform one way or another, depending on whether we agree with the article or not.

After reading. and analyzing this article. I have come to a new view of understanding of my field. I've come to see how important it is for musicians to hear critics of other musician's playing. and their own because after all the goal and dream of many musicians if not all, is to share something that they think is beautiful with other people, and show them why it is beautiful and meaningful to them. And that is also how music progresses through time. The greatest performance of a piece is given; then someone comes and critiques it and although it is so perfect and beautiful, there is always something, a little detail that could make it even better. Other musicians hear it, hear the critiques and give another performance with enhanced beauty. That is why it is so important for musicians to have these writings to rely on.

After reading this in-depth analysis of the academic discourse community, we can conclude that what musicians value has a lot to do with the reaction people get from their music. They need to hear what people think, if people liked their work or not, and it is the only way that they can notice what they have to change in their playing. Although studying an instrument is a very individualistic discipline because it requires the student to spend so many hours alone practicing. When it comes to the time of the performance it becomes an act of community. It becomes an act of sharing with other people. Musicians value immensely the support they get from other people that listen to them.

40   Overall, writing this paper and trying to analyze and understand my own field from very different angles has showed me that this discipline is very different from any other, and that what musicians value is very different from what people in other fields value.

---

1. Reflecting on discourse, literacy, and the context of academic disciplines

READING RESPONSE

   ■ What are some of the differences Vanessa finds between freshman music classes and freshman classes in other fields?

   ■ From reading Vanessa's study, why do you think she gives it the title "Music as a Life-style?" Why does she consider it a lifestyle rather than an interest or a job or a profession?

   ■ Vanessa gives us examples, not only of the sort of work that goes on in her classes, but of academic research in the field. Are you surprised that academic research is important in music? Does Vanessa's discussion of a representative text that she has chosen from a journal give you an idea of the possible directions and purposes of research in this field?

   ■ Vanessa concludes with her more developed understanding of what musicians value. Do you agree with her final statement that those values are very different from those of people in other disciplines? Can you think of any exceptions to her statement?

2. Reading as a writer/researcher

   ■ What do you think Vanessa was trying to learn from her study? How did that affect the things she chose to look at? Do you think she learned what she wanted to?

   ■ If you're an outsider to the field of music, do you find that Vanessa provides enough information, explanations, and examples to help you understand what's involved in the music courses she is taking?

   ■ What specific artifacts does Vanessa use as data for her study? What does each contribute to the understandings she develops about the important shared knowledge, purposes, and ways of this field?   *(continued)*

(continued)

- Vanessa gives an extended, combined summary and analysis of the article she has read, "Performing Corelli's Violin Sonatas," not only summarizing what the author says but considering what his purposes are and why he includes what he does. To what extent does her reading of this study provide you, as an outsider, with an understanding that you might not have gained directly? If you are working with a journal article as one of your pieces of data about your community, do you think you can provide a comparable act of translation for your readers?

Sophia Kang, "An Exciting Debate"

Sophia Kang was born in Korea, moved to Argentina when she was eight, and then to the United States a couple of years before entering college. As a relative newcomer to doing schoolwork in English, she continued to find it easier to read and write papers than to participate in class discussions in most instances. But in her sociology class, she found herself increasingly drawn into the "exciting debate" she found going on there. In the following study she introduces us to the discipline of sociology as she has come to see it through her introductory course. Having lived in several different societies herself, she found that this course, with its emphasis on how people study human societies and human behavior, fully engaged her interest, as you will see in reading her study.

An Exciting Debate

Sophia Kang

1   Sociology is the scientific study of human societies and human behavior in the many groups that make up a society. This is a study to understand the possible futures of people who confront drastic changes, and sociologists continually seek knowledge about what holds societies together and what makes them bend under the impact of major forces. I found out that this course was interesting because here we cover a vast range of social behaviors and problems such as stratification (a society's system for ranking people hierarchically according to various attributes such as wealth, power, and prestige) and social class—if they are inevitable, or if there can be a classless society; inequalities of race and ethnicity—if there must be laws to protect the rights of racially or ethnically in distinct groups; economics and politics—if the institutions like the market and legislatures bring about positive social change; the family—if it is breaking down or simply adapting to new social conditions; and so forth.

CURRENT STUDY IN SOCIOLOGY

The subject that we are covering at this moment is the religion. In our course book, religion is described as following: "Religion has been defined as any set of coherent answers to the dilemmas of human existence that makes the world meaningful. It has also been defined as a system of beliefs and rituals that serves to bind people together into a social group." (W. Komblum, 288)

For the introduction of this chapter, the professor asked a question to the class. The question was "How does sociology talk about the belief system?" Later, she mentioned two major sociological perspectives, functional theory and conflict theory, relating to this topic. Several hands went up rapidly and students were enthusiastic to answer that question. There were interesting but different answers.

STUDENT 1:   "I think that religion supports the functional theory. It provides spiritual needs."

5   STUDENT 2:   "Give hope to people. That might be good for society."

STUDENT 3:   "The religion keeps the community tight."

STUDENT 4:   "Marx is right. All contributions of churches go to pastors. They teach people to contribute because that is part of their reverence to God, but the church's pastors were the most rich in town."

STUDENT 5:   "I don't like the statement that the religion makes people in peace because if we study history, many wars were caused by different religions."

While students were doing comments, other students listened to them carefully and they tried to look at the face of students who are speaking. The professor also listened to them carefully and she had an eye contact with student who is doing comment. Then, she repeated their main points and mentioned if she was agreed or disagreed. Later, she related student's thought to the different social perspectives.

FUNCTIONALIST VS. CONFLICT THEORY

10   The functionalist and conflict theory are different sociological perspectives based on problems of human society. In general, the functionalist perspective in sociology asks how society carries out the functions necessary to maintain social order, feed masses of people, defend against attackers, produce the next generation, and so on. It is concerned primarily with the large-scale structures of society. On the other hand, conflict theory emphasizes the role of conflict and power (this is the theory that Marx supported). In every chapter we find the definition of functional theory and conflict theory of each problem. In that way we see the problems in different perspectives and we expand our point of view. In this case, the functional perspective of religion is that this institution is functional for the society; it brings hope to people and makes the society organized. On the other hand, the conflict theory declares that religion exists in favor of upper social class keeping them in highest level with honor. It says that the religion makes the lower class society less powerful. In other words, religion divides into the highest class and the lowest class. I think that these two perspectives are true. According to the history, the religion always has been for the upper level social class people and they had controlled the groups that were behind them. But today, the religion does not have the same function as those times when the religion was very powerful in one nation. At this moment, most people have their own religion to be consoled of death, misfortune, and every day's problems. Therefore, I think that these days functionalist theory of religion would apply more in our society.

CLASS THOUGHTS AND BEHAVIOR

I agree with Eric in "Introductory Physics: The Eric 'Experiment'." He said, "The best classes I had were classes in which I was constantly engaged, constantly questioning and pushing the limits of the subject and myself." (S. Tobias, p. 358) This class becomes more interesting when students start to bring up their opinions that are in contrast to other student's opinions. That is one of the reasons that Sociology is one of my best classes. Students in this sociology class never agree with each other. Since this class is more than a hundred students, it is expected that the answers may vary. However, there are always students who are alert in participating in class and doing comments on the problem. Sometimes students make comments, argue and even behave inappropriately toward each other because of their opinion differences. For instance, once we were talking about divorce in the United States. The professor asked to the students if divorce caused more problems than it solved or if divorce brings benefit and happiness to the family. Obviously, there were two answers. When a student supported the statement that divorce caused more problems than it solved, a student who was opposed to that idea became furious and tried to stop her classmate's explication and, since it didn't work (because he didn't let her speak by increasing his voice), she just left the classroom irritated. The class was surprised at her reaction and just laughed it off. Her behavior was exaggerated and it was unnecessary to react that way. She could act with fortitude and after her classmate's comment; she could add her thought in a proper way.

Mostly, students who participate in class are known very well both by the professor and among the students. I have observed carefully these students and they are the leaders of a large group that forms to chat just before the class. In that way, I think that they become more confident about themselves in participating in class.

In general, when the class starts, the class gets silent and shows respect to each other, even though sometimes some students irritate for other student's opinion. Students raise their hands before doing comments and wait until the professor points him/her to speak. Generally, the speech acts of students show respect to the professor and to the entire class. Also professor speaks politely and with respect. Even though sometimes students argue about a certain complicated social problem, the professor brings all pieces together and finally concludes the topic in a sociologist's terms.

NORMS AND DISCIPLINES

There are certain rules and disciplines in this class as other college classes. Before the class starts, the professor passes out the attendance sheet in which each student has to find their name and sign next to it. There are three attendance sheets going around the classroom but we need to sign in it only once. In every class, the professor gives us handouts, graphs and summaries of each topic. It is necessary to take them before the class starts because once the class begins she puts away those papers for students who are late. The reason that she is doing that is because she wants to concentrate on her class. If she has to give papers to every student who is coming late, she would stop speaking in every moment and it would cause her and her students to be confused. The other rule for this class is being responsible. Students who were absent in class, they are responsible to copy notes from other class-mates and also go to the professor's office to pick up the handouts. In addition, they are required to complete and hand in the required assignment as well as students who are present in the class.

STUDENTS' BACKGROUND

15   Most students in this class are from different backgrounds and circumstances. I think that the half of the class is freshman (young students) and there are some students who are older. Also, there are students from different states such as New Hampshire, Georgia, Illinois and Florida, and different countries such as Chile, Italy, Korea, China, Vietnam, Haiti and Mexico. Those different backgrounds and ages make the class more interesting. Different experiences from many students allow other students to understand better the topics such as Immigration, Family, and Culture. For example, in culture chapter, each student from different countries explained their typical cultures, such as bowing for Asian students, and their values and beliefs, and how those habits and thoughts have changed when they immigrated to the United States.

OTHER WAYS OF LEARNING SOCIOLOGY

This sociology class is mostly lecture and discussion but occasionally professor brings a video that relates to the topic that we are covering. Those videos are briefly shown to the class and then we have a discussion about it. I believe that videos are one of the important ways to teach. Since we are living in a world where technology is advanced and visual communication is developed, videos are the evidence of what the students are learning. For instance, when we were covering religion, the professor prepared a video about the Japanese oldest religion named "Shinto." The video explained and showed rituals, ceremonies, and constructions that Japanese made for their religion. After watching this video, I had a better understanding on this topic than just reading from the textbook.

During the semester, it is also required to do two museum reports. The museum that is necessary to go is Harvard Peabody Museum. In this museum there is an exposition of African Indians (Bushman) and Central and South American Indians (Mayas, Aztecs, Incas). The purpose of these museum reports is to analyze and compare the differences and similarities between Indians' societies and post-industrial societies (post-industrial society is a higher stage than industrial society where in post-industrial society the technology is very advanced and there is high level of social classes, low birth rate, etc. For instance a typical type of post-industrial society is the United States). We read the plaques, see the pictures and dioramas and watch the videos to answer the questions on the sheet. It has required a lot of effort and time because this museum is next to Harvard Yard (where there is not many places to park) and it takes a minimum of 2 hours to finish one museum report.

OUTSIDER TO INSIDER

Mike Rose wrote about the following problem in his essay: "The huge lecture halls, the distance from the professor, the streams of students you don't know. One of the tasks facing all freshmen is to figure out ways to counter this loneliness."

(M. Rose, p. 378) During the first week of class, I felt that I was an outsider of this class, since I was in a new classroom with new classmates, a new professor, and I also had to adapt to her teaching style. But for the most part, I had to understand and learn new terms and vocabularies that are used in sociology. At this moment, I am comfortable in my sociology class since I have a fine relationship with the professor and some classmates. Furthermore, I have been extremely interested in this field because the study of sociology has improved my perspectives of human behavior in society by learning different points of view represented in the history of sociology.

This Sociology class is taught by professor's lecture but it is also by student's participation. Therefore, students' experiences and opinions are extremely important in this course. I believe that students who participate in this "debate" are the most insiders in the class. For them, this class is an "exciting debate".

BIBLIOGRAPHY

1. "Introductory Physics: The Eric 'Experiment'" by Sheila Tobias. *Exploring Literacy* pp. 136–141.

2. "The Politics of Remediation" by Mike Rose. *Exploring Literacy* pp. 145–154.

3. "Sociology—The Central Questions" by William Kornblum. Harcourt Brace & Company, Florida. 1998.

READING RESPONSE

1. Reflecting on discourse, literacy, and the context of academic disciplines

- Sophia considers two competing theories in the field of sociology: functionalist theory and conflict theory. To what extent does understanding and being able to explain the theoretical underpinnings of this area of study seem to help her to understand how sociologists think and the sorts of problems they try to explore?

- Sophia provides an example of the discourse of the classroom, under the heading "Current Study in Sociology," and then goes on to typical classroom interactions under the heading "Class Thoughts and Behavior." From reading her example and her discussion, what do you think is significant about this style of classroom discourse for engaging students' interest in the field of sociology?

- From Sophia's study, would you say that she is on her way to becoming an insider in this discipline? If insiders know not only what to talk about but how to talk about it and why—if they have, in addition to shared knowledge, shared ways and shared purposes—do you find evidence that Sophia is being introduced to all of these elements? Do you think that, unlike Eric in Tobias's study, she does feel that she is getting "the big picture"? Has this class positioned her differently from the ways that students sitting in the back of the lecture hall that Rose described seem to be positioned with relationship to the what, why, and how of sociology as a field? When Sophia makes a

(continued)

connection to Rose, what does she herself see as having moved her from being an outsider to becoming more of an insider in this class?

- Sophia suggests, under the heading "Students' Background," that it is an advantage in a course like this that students come from different backgrounds and cultures, from around the U.S. and all over the world. Why does she find this difference to contribute to her experience of the course? Do you find that students' backgrounds contribute in a similar way in the course you are focusing on for your own study?

2. Reading as a writer/researcher

- What do you think Sophia was trying to learn from her study? How did that affect the things she chose to look at? Do you think she learned what she wanted to?

- Sophia frames her study with a definition of sociology and a naming of some of the key areas that are studied in the field. Do you find this way of introducing and framing her study to be helpful to you as a reader? Is this a type of beginning that you might consider in writing up your own study? Or would you suggest alternatives in Sophia's case and/or your own?

- Look at how Sophia has structured her study and the headings she has used to organize it and to guide her readers. Do they work effectively to guide you through the study?

Juliette Houlne, "Women in Science and Bio 112"

Juliette Houlne had been out of school for eight years when she decided to take up her studies again at a different university. She had always been somewhat interested in science, but she'd been particularly good at English and languages and, she says, "I always thought that I didn't have the science and math mind." She also felt that, as a girl, she hadn't been encouraged to consider a career in the sciences, even though she'd always had an interest in being a veterinarian. In coming back to school, she decided to start with just one biology course, and she quickly found both that she had changed and that the field had changed. Since writing this paper she has continued with her biology major, with the intention of applying for veterinary school. For this paper, Juliette says, "I chose this topic because I was so inspired by my bio class and my professor, and I was thinking about how my experience in dealing with science was different from what it had ever been before." What she found most difficult about writing it was narrowing down such a huge topic. "I had to remind myself that I couldn't use every single piece of information I found. I had to cull out what was relevant to what I was writing about, and what most related to my personal experience." Juliette's stance for this study has already been discussed in Chapter 8, and her process for carrying out her research for this study was detailed in Chapter 9. Here's the report she produced.

Women in Science and Bio 112

Juliette Houlne

1   Are women underrepresented in the broad field of science, and if so, is it the result of negative societal and peer conditioning?

This is the question I realized I was asking as I began to study my experience and the classroom discourse in my Introductory Biology (Bio 111) class. It came to me as I was reflecting on my reasons for returning to college to seek out a science degree at 28 years old. I never thought too much before about gender differences in different fields of study, other than in a theoretical kind of way.

A great deal has changed for women since I was born, in 1972. That year was the first that women were invited to the annual conference of the New York Academy of Science (NYAS). However, as Gerhard Sonnert of Harvard University wrote, "the organizers took care to invite as participants only women scientists who were also wives and mothers." (1) Also from Sonnert's paper was a quote from Ruth B. Kundsin, author of *Women and Success*. "Finding professional women who wished to participate . . . was more difficult than we had anticipated," (1) she states. In contrast, Sonnert notes that "the difficulty for the 1998 conference organizers was almost the opposite—how to select participants from an abundance of qualified women." (1)

I grew up always thinking that I could do or be whatever I wanted to be, at least I thought I did. I remember my mom always encouraging my ideas and goals. But for some reason, despite excellent performance in school and overall ease learning new subjects, I stubbornly remained convinced of the fact that I couldn't "do" math and science. Why?

BIO 112—SPRING 2001

5   Bio 112 is the second semester class of introductory biology. Whereas the first semester class had many students who were taking it to fulfill a science requirement, this class has a much larger percentage of biology and other science majors. The professor's name is Brian White, and he is an excellent teacher. In the university setting. Before a professor has received tenure (and usually after as well) he or she will have an area of research within the field, and Brian's area of research is teaching. He studies methods of teaching as it relates to introductory biology classes, and there are opportunities for students to participate in various studies. He also asks for a lot of feedback concerning the class and lab.

Class itself is a lecture in a large auditorium. Brian is a great speaker, and he is eloquent in explaining the ideas in each lecture. After he makes each point, he stops and asks for questions from the class, and these are abundant. He is endlessly patient. The class is about 75 students, and it is evenly divided between men and women, supporting my hypothesis that the gender divide between males and females in science is narrowing. Furthermore, my T.A. (teaching assistant for my lab) is a woman, and my Bio 111 T.A. was also.

Lab is held once weekly and consists of exercises that support the weeks' lecture material and make it easier to understand. We usually will have a lab report due as well, which is a written explanation and critical thinking of the previous weeks' lab. There were several field trips that we were able to complete on our own time, including trips to the Harvard Museum of Natural History and the New England Aquarium. These were very fun trips that provided interesting diversions and real world applications of the material.

This class requires a little bit more shared knowledge than Bio 111, which is a prerequisite. Brian makes references to material that we covered in that class frequently, and sometimes he gives a basic review of certain topics to make sure the students are up to speed. There is a certain insider- and outsider-ness that exists between the students who perform very well and those who don't, but to tell the truth I don't really notice the students who may not be doing well because I am not one of them. I sit in the front row every single day so it is easier for me to ask questions (I ask <u>a lot</u> of questions) and because I have poor eyesight, so I need to be close to see the chalkboard. There is a camaraderie among those of us who sit in the front couple of rows, we share the insider-ness that comes with being good students, which is not to say that the good students only sit at the front—that's just my experience.

Most of these insiders share similar goals: most are biology or other science majors, and some are pre-med. Every one shares a keen interest in the subject. When I scrutinize the classroom discourse, I notice the gender equality and the general congenial and positive atmosphere.

WOMEN "IN" SCIENCE—A VERY BRIEF HISTORY

10   Prior to 1960, women were almost unknown as scientists. There were exceptions, Marie Curie for example. She was a Polish-born scientist and chemist, who won one Nobel Prize in Physics, and one in Chemistry for discovering the elements Radium and Polonium. But women like her were few and far between. In the first half of this past century it was expected that women marry and have children, their first duty being taking care of the husband and family. Sometimes women went to college, often secretarial school; but even if they were college graduates they usually did not pursue their own career. Women who did go into scientific careers were met with omnipresent sexism.

Rosalind Franklin is a good example. She was an X-ray crystallographer in England in the 1950s. X-ray crystallography involves taking pictures of microscopic crystal structure using x-ray diffraction. She was an assistant to Maurice Wilkins, one of the scientists who helped the famed scientists James D. Watson and Francis Crick discover the structure of DNA, one of the most important scientific discoveries in hundreds of years. Watson wrote a book called *The Double Helix* (1968) that chronicled his team's race with another researcher to make the discovery.

Here are some actual quotes from his book:

I suspect that in the beginning Maurice hoped that Rosy would calm down. Yet mere inspection suggested that she would not easily bend. By choice she did not emphasize her feminine qualities. Though her features were strong, she was not unattractive and might have even been quite stunning had she even taken a mild interest in clothes. That she did not. There was never lipstick to contrast with her straight black hair, while at the age of thirty-one her dresses showed all the imagination of English blue-stocking adolescents. So it was quite easy to imagine her the product of an unsatisfied mother who unduly stressed the desirability of professional careers that could save bright girls from marriages to dull men. . . . Clearly Rosy had to be put in her place . . . given her belligerent moods, it would be very difficult for Maurice to maintain a dominant position that would allow him to think unhindered about DNA. (17)

These words sound so insulting, even shocking to me. However, I am sure that James Watson meant Rosalind Franklin no ill will. This is just the way people thought at the time. Note the discussion of her physical appearance, as if it were her responsibility to present herself in an appealing way to the men around her. He speculates on her reasons for choosing this work, and speaks easily about her being "put in her place" and her "belligerent moods." The last sentence of the quote sums it up—they don't even consider wanting her input on this project; instead they don't want her upsetting Maurice's "dominant" position.

I would never allow any one to treat me this way, especially in any field of work. It is a given that I demand to be treated with respect at work, home, and school. I think most people would agree with me—his comments are very sexist by today's standards. This shows how much shared knowledge has changed over the years. It is today's shared knowledge for most people that women are treated equally. Many scientists believe that Rosalind Franklin never got the acclaim she deserved for her contribution to this major discovery.

15 Today, women have gained access to every field of scientific study, but not evenly. For example, as is stated in Sonnert's paper, in 1993 female Ph.D.'s in psychology were 40.7%, in biological sciences 28.2%, but in computer and mathematical sciences it was 11.4%, physics and astronomy 5.2% and engineering was a very small 4.3%. Furthermore, within the fields themselves, women are very scarce at the tops of their fields.

According to a study done by Gerald Holton, professor of physics and science history at Harvard University, men and women scientists approach their work and research differently. Men are more likely to take risks that may result in significant discoveries, while women are more apt to practice "good" science, that is, careful and diligent research studies that are less spectacular. Women scientists also publish fewer papers in scientific journals, an average of 2.3 papers per year compared to 2.8 for men. Holton speculates that this contributes to the fact that women are such in the minority in the upper echelons of their fields; publication in these scholarly journals is considered crucial to one's successful career.

DO GIRLS JUST LOSE INTEREST IN SCIENCE AND MATH?

So is there some point in time, some linear demarcation between boys and girls moving forward in studying science? There have been many studies done over the years that show girls and boys having equal aptitude for science and math in the elementary school years. There have also been many studies that show a decline in interest and participation in these same subjects in teenage girls. There is the widely accepted and debated hypothesis that boys receive more attention in school, causing girls to withdraw and suffer lower self-esteem. This hypothesis is discussed in a paper by Amy Saltzman for *U.S. News & World Report:*

> Do schools favor boys? A single numerical assertion—that boys in elementary and middle school call out answers eight times more than girls do—underpins much of the pro-bias case . . . The "8 to 1" ratio originated with Myra and David Sadker, a husband and wife team of education professors at American University in Washington, D.C., regarded as pre-eminent in classroom gender issues. They cite the ratio in articles, interviews, and lectures. When boys call out, report the Sadkers, teachers respond by giving them full attention and making constructive comments, while girls who call out are usually admonished to raise their hands. (3)

However, she goes on to say that the study was flawed, and that studies done since show that while boys may call out more in class, that the attention they get very well may be negative. In my opinion, while this may have been true in the past, I think that it is evening out—there has been so much attention paid to this subject in education, I believe teachers are giving more equal attention.

She also talks about a correlation between girls' decline in self-esteem as they enter high school and a loss of interest in science and math. Although I didn't do extensive enough research and read more articles about this particular aspect, on a personal level this was very true for me.

MY EXPERIENCE WITH SCIENCE, AND MY VERY UN-SCIENTIFIC ANALYSIS

20   I was a smart kid, learning to read when I was three, and I loved to learn. Inasmuch as I loved school, socially I was awkward and shy. When I was five, the first profession I decided I wanted to be "when I grew up" was a veterinarian. I had a high level of empathy for animals, and I had no reason to think there was anything that would keep me from achieving my goal.

As I went through elementary school, junior high school, and then went on to a college preparatory high school, my goal was put aside. I had difficult complications in my family life, and my self-esteem suffered. I didn't see it at the time, but now I believe that it is difficult for teenage girls in our society to accept themselves: we are constantly bombarded with media images of beautiful, sexy, perfectly thin women as the norm, which can cause us to focus on physical appearance more than academics. I am sure that it has never been easy to be in high school, but I think it must be especially confusing now.

There is also the aspect of peer and familial influence. Some families are very traditional and will value marriage and family above other goals for their daughters' future. Others may encourage their daughters' goals, but at school a girl may feel unique or different for having a serious interest in science, leading to her leaving it behind in favor of more socially "acceptable" goals. This is how it happened to me—I put more and more of my scholarly energy into the things that came the most easily to me, English, Art, and other languages. I came to think that I wasn't cut out for math and science.

After high school I went to college briefly but I had no idea what I wanted to pursue, so I left after three semesters. I worked in different fields, mostly arts related, but I continued to work with animals, something I had started to do in junior high school. I worked alongside vets and thought, "I can do that." Eventually, burned out on several fields that each could have become lucrative careers, had I not become bored and restless, I re-thought *why* I had written off science-based careers, and I realized there was no good reason. Science as a broad discipline interested me—I read books, magazines, and journals, and watched various TV programs that dealt with many different scientific ideas and fields. I decided to return to school and try again, and though it's only my second semester back, it's going so well.

What changed? Is it just me? Or are the fields more inviting and accessible to women now? I think it's both.

CONCLUSION

25   This topic and the questions I have asked are much larger than something that can be answered in a ten page paper. There are thousands of books and magazine articles that have been written about the subject of gender inequality in education, and what I've said only touches on the subject.

I can offer some answers, however, but only as they relate to me. I believe that as I've gotten older and more mature, and wiser, society has slowly been changing as well in regards to this issue. Seeing more and more women doing what I always wanted to do, and realizing that it is not a unattainable goal, sent me on my current path. I am sure that this is something I will continue to consider as I go forward in my education and face bigger challenges.

WORKS CITED

Saltzman, Amy. "Schooled in failure? Fact or myth—teachers favor boys; girls respond by withdrawing." *U.S. News & World Report* Nov. 7, 1994.

Selby, Cecily Cannan. *Women in Science and Engineering: Choices for Success.* (Collected Papers from the New York Academy of Science Conference 1999.) New York: New York Academy of Sciences. 1999.

Watson, James D. *The Double Helix.* New York: Atheneum, 1968.

1. <u>Reflecting on discourse, literacy, and the context of academic disciplines</u>

   ■ Juliette raises an interesting question about gender representation in particular discipines. What does she discover about the representation and experiences of women in the sciences? What did Watson's description of Rosalind Franklin in *The Double Helix* show about the ways in which women were expected to talk and act, even in the science laboratory, until recently? Why do you think it was particularly difficult for women to become insiders to scientific communities (and still is in some disciplines)?

   ■ Juliette takes us briefly into her Bio 112 class, viewing it through the lens of her question about the representation of women. Is there anything else in what she says about that class that suggests why she might have begun to feel like an insider there? How does her experience there seem to compare to Eric's in his physics class in the Tobias study?

2. <u>Reading as a writer/researcher</u>

   ■ What do you think Juliette was trying to learn from her study? How did that affect the things she chose to look at? Do you think she learned what she wanted to?

   ■ Juliette's paper doesn't fall into the conventional genres of the library paper or the field research report. Instead, she combines elements of both genres with a memoir-like account of her own experience. As a reader, how effective do you find her movement from observations to library research to recollection and reflection to be? Do these blurred genres seem appropriate for her pursuit of her question? Do they help to engage you as a reader in her exploration? Might they influence what you decide to include in your own report?

   ■ Look at the structure of Juliette's paper and the ways in which she has moved through the different topics she addresses, ending with her personal reflection. Why do you think she has chosen to place her personal reflection at the end rather than the beginning? Do you find this structure effective for you as a reader? Do you think it meets Juliette's purposes?

PART

IV

Strategies for Reading, Writing, and Research

S trategies are techniques, tools, and practices you can use in college reading, writing, and research projects. Some of the strategies presented in this section are linked to specific projects or assignments; most of them can be applied to many different reading and writing situations. Part IV includes sections detailing strategies for the following:

Reading

Writing

Editing

Responding to Peers

Assessing Yourself

Preparing a Portfolio

Presenting and Reporting to a Group

Conducting Field Research

Conducting Library Research

Documenting Sources

READING

Reading in the context of college coursework involves two simultaneous conversations, one that goes on between you as a reader and the writer of the text, and another that situates your reading within an ongoing classroom exchange and within a larger set of readings. Approaching such reading with some conscious strategies can help you read effectively for the purposes set in your classroom context.

Reflecting Before You Read

As you turn to any unfamiliar text, you are entering a new conversation—the one that the author invites with readers. But when you're reading for a classroom context, you typically bring some prior knowledge related to the reading that you can draw on as you read. To become more aware of what you bring as prior knowledge and how you can evoke that prior knowledge when you start a new reading, reflect in writing before you begin:

- Look at the title and think about what it suggests in relationship to the themes of the course for which you're reading. Glance quickly through the pages to get some sense of what this reading is about, and then reflect on the background knowledge you bring to this topic.

- Consider the genre of the reading. Is it a memoir, a piece of fiction, a research study? How does the genre influence what you expect to find?

- Look at the way the text is structured and organized and the topics it appears to cover. If there are headings, look through them and note what each section addresses. If there are no headings, skim the reading, looking quickly at the opening sentences of various paragraphs. What does this quick look tell you about what you might find here?

- Think about your prior knowledge in relationship to <u>what</u> you see in this first look at a reading. What do you bring to your reading of this text from your prior experience? What do you bring from your studies in this course? What do you expect that this reading might contribute to what you know?

- Think also about your purposes for reading (<u>why</u>) in the context of the course, as well about the writer's possible purposes for writing. What do the purposes of reading in this context lead you to expect to find?

- Think about how those purposes will affect <u>how</u> you read. For example, you might read quickly to get information, or you might read more slowly and carefully to get a fuller understanding of the writer's argument or perspective or to participate in the experience the writer is creating. Will your reading be participatory, analytical, or evaluative (see Chapter 1), or a combination?

In reading, you become an effective participant by being sensitive to context, versatile in trying out different ways for different contexts, aware of what you bring from prior contexts or prior experience in this context, and conscious of the possibilities and strategies you can draw on as you shift contexts and purposes.

Glossing

Here are some ways of glossing a text that will help you reconstruct what you've found in the text, make connections, and build larger understandings. Together, these ways of glossing will support your participatory, analytical, and evaluative readings, and you may find that you rely more on particular ways of glossing, depending on your own purposes with a reading.

- Think about the framework of understanding you bring to the text and note in the margin the places where you find connections with what you already know from experience or reading.

- Note the main point the writer is making in each paragraph. This is useful when reading long and complicated texts and it provides you with a map of a text that will make referring back to a specific section quick and easy.

- Circle or underline key terms that the writer is using. Writers typically name key ideas and concepts that they develop and use through the details and examples of their texts. Marking those key terms, ideas, and concepts and creating a glossary can help you to understand the concepts the writer is presenting and to draw those concepts into your future thinking and writing.

- Jot down examples in the margins, either from your own experiences or from class discussions or readings, that support or dispute a point a writer is making. By providing your own examples, or those contributed by others in your class, you'll be able to more fully understand and remember a point a writer makes.

- Pose questions. If you come across a section of text that you don't understand or don't agree with, make note of this in the margin. You can later return to such questions to speculate about them. In many cases, you'll find that these questions offer great subjects for journal entries and/or more formal papers.

- Use checks (or any other mark) to signify sections that you would like to explore more fully in journal entries.

- Use another kind of mark to indicate passages that resonate for you and that you might like to quote in an essay or journal entry. If you are writing an essay about gender and language, for example, and come across a section of text that comments on just that, you may want to section off potential quotations, so that when you go back to write your essay, you will have some material to work with.

- Talk back to the writer in the margins, expressing your thoughts about what the writer says.

12 / HUNGER OF MEMORY

many from lower-class homes, to use their family language as the language of school. (Such is the goal its supporters announce.) I hear them and am forced to say no: It is not possible for a child—any child—ever to use his family's language in school. Not to understand this is to misunderstand the public uses of schooling and to trivialize the nature of intimate life—a family's 'language.'

R's / *THESIS*

Memory teaches me what I know of these matters; the boy reminds the adult. I was a bilingual child, a certain kind—socially disadvantaged—the son of working-class parents, both Mexican immigrants.

TWO POINTS

LIKE ROSE

In the early years of my boyhood, my parents coped very well in America. My father had steady work. My mother managed at home. They were nobody's victims. Optimism and ambition led them to a house (our home) many blocks from the Mexican south side of town. We lived among *gringos* and only a block from the biggest, whitest houses. It never occurred to my parents that they couldn't live wherever they chose. Nor was the Sacramento of the fifties bent on teaching them a contrary lesson. My mother and father were more annoyed than intimidated by those two or three neighbors who tried initially to make us unwelcome. ('Keep your brats away from my sidewalk!') But despite all they achieved, perhaps because they had so much to achieve, any deep feeling of ease, the confidence of 'belonging' in public was withheld from them both. They regarded the people at work, the faces in crowds, as very distant from us. They were the others, *los gringos*. That term was interchangeable in their speech with another, even more telling, *los americanos.*   → *IMPLICATION: "WE ARE NOT AMERICANOS."*

SETTING THE STAGE FOR LATER SELF-CONSCIOUSNESS

AS IF IT WOULD THESE DAYS

I grew up in a house where the only regular guests were my relations. For one day, enormous families of relatives would

■ Make reference to other texts you have worked with. By bringing what you've found in another text to an essay you are presently reading, you'll broaden your understanding of common points both writers make and you'll begin to find ways of representing one in terms of the other and reframing both.

■ Frame your reading for a particular context and purpose by asking questions that emerge from that context and noting places in the

JAKE WARK
ARIA / 13

visit and there would be so many people that the noise and the bodies would spill out to the backyard and front porch. Then, for weeks, no one came by. (It was usually a salesman who rang the doorbell.) Our house stood apart. A gaudy yellow in a row of white bungalows. We were the people with the noisy dog. The people who raised pigeons and chickens. We were the foreigners on the block. A few neighbors smiled and waved. We waved back. But no one in the family knew the names of the old couple who lived next door; until I was seven years old, I did not know the names of the kids who lived across the street.

FRAGMENTS (RECOLLECTIONS)

In public, my father and mother spoke a hesitant, accented, not always grammatical English. And they would have to strain—their bodies tense—to catch the sense of what was rapidly said by *los gringos*. At home they spoke Spanish. The language of their Mexican past sounded in counterpoint to the English of public society. The words would come quickly, with ease. Conveyed through those sounds was the pleasing, soothing, consoling reminder of being at home.

INTERRUP-TION; REINFORCES POINT

During those years when I was first conscious of hearing, my mother and father addressed me only in Spanish; in Spanish I learned to reply. By contrast, *English (inglés)*, rarely heard in the house, was the language I came to associate with *gringos*. I learned my first words of English overhearing my parents speak to strangers. At five years of age, I knew just enough English for my mother to trust me on errands to stores one block away. No more. *REINFORCES POINT*

I was a listening child, careful to hear the very different sounds of Spanish and English. Wide-eyed with hearing, I'd listen to *sounds more than words*. First, there were English (gringo) sounds. So many words were still unknown that when

CONSISTENT THEME

⭐ *THEME OF SOUNDS*

text that relate to that context. Within the context of this book, with its focus on discourse communities, you're likely to pay more attention to what writers say about their experiences in different discourse communities. You might note more about their experiences in the discourse communities of their homes or schools, for example, than you might if you were reading these essays for a different course.

Using a Double-Entry Notebook

One effective way of working closely with readings, as a supplement (or alternative) to glossing, is to use a *double-entry notebook* (or *dialogue journal*) format: a format with two columns, in which you keep a list of key quotations or moments from the text in one column, and your thoughts about the quotations (connections, questions, speculations, exploration of meanings) and about the larger text (connections across parts, ideas for your own memoir) in the other.

There are several advantages to using a double entry format.

■ It allows you to keep track of quotations that you found significant so that you have them to draw on easily when you're writing about that reading.

■ It guides you to move back and forth between the text and your own thinking.

■ It also allows you to observe and learn about your own thinking as a reader—the kinds of connections you make, the questions you ask, the ways in which you "make meaning" as you think about the things you read. Engaging not only in the process of thinking and meaning-making, but in reflecting on that process, can lead you to meta-level understandings about your own thinking, learning, and processes of discovery.

You can begin to use the double-entry format by looking back through your glossings of a text to find a few places that particularly capture your interest or that seem significant to what the writer is saying or to your classroom discussions. For each of these places, select a small portion of that section to draw on as a quotation, and copy that quotation (with page number) to start your notebook entry. Working with the quotation, explore why you think it's interesting or important. How does it contribute to the meanings the writer is trying to express in the immediate context of the surrounding paragraph(s)? In the larger text? Are there questions that it raises or answers for you? Connections it makes for you to other readings, class discussions, or experiences?

The double-entry notebook is also good for taking notes in the classroom. Drawing a line down the middle of your page, you can take class notes on one side, and keep track of connections, thoughts, questions on the other. It's also useful for making observations of a setting, as discussed under field research strategies.

Here's an example of a double-entry notebook response to Barbara Mellix's "From Outside, In" (from Chapter 2) with quotations from her memoir in the left column and the student writer's response to those quotations on the right. Note how Dina has used the response column to make connections to other readings, restate her understanding of Mellix's experience, speculate about what it means to Mellix, ask questions, and comment on similarities in her own experience and on her experience as a reader of this text.

"We would mock our relatives the moment we were out of their hearing. . . . Our relatives had made us feel 'country,' and this was our way of regaining pride in ourselves while getting a little revenge in the bargain" (p. 61).

"I was extremely conscious that this was an occasion for proper English. . . . It did not matter that Toby had not spoken grammatically correct English. He was white and could speak as he wished. I had something to prove. Toby did not" (p. 61).

"My sentences were short, rigid, perfunctory, like the letters my mother wrote to relatives. . . . The language was not ours. It was something from outside us, something we used for special occasions" (p. 62).

"Slowly and imperceptibly I had ceased seeing a sharp distinction between myself and others" (p. 63).

"The voice here is stronger, more confident, appropriating terms like 'physically damaging,' 'wounds them further,' 'insensitive,' 'disease'—terms I couldn't have imagined using when writing about my own experience" (p. 65).

"I was free to move about in the language of 'others' so long as I was speaking of others. I was unaware that I was transforming into my best classroom language my own thoughts and feelings about people whose experience and ways of speaking were in many ways similar to mine" (p. 65).

Like Rodriguez's family, Mellix also cherished her home language by making fun of the outside, foreign language of more distant communities. The relatives are rigid in their communication in proper English like Rodriguez's parents were in speaking English, and feel free and comfortable communicating in their private language, whether it's Spanish or "Black English."

Mellix has to prove that she is not inferior and can speak proper English just as well. Therefore she puts it on display at the appropriate occasion like her church clothes, although she feels uncomfortable in them.

Mellix always saw writing as very artificial. She learned from her mother to write a personal, rigid letter and later even used this skill in her business letters for an insurance company, the most empty and meaningless kind of communication to her personally.

Although she got used to speaking proper English after living in the city so much, she still couldn't master free-flowing writing in their language. Writing seemed like it had to be formal and proper for much longer than speaking for Mellix. It was the "others" language at its most extreme. This language being something "from outside" made it hard to find her personal voice in writing, but as the title suggests, it eventually trickled "in" and became part of her, shaping who she is, in all of her discourse communities.

Is she afraid to sound pretentious or to exaggerate? To make her own experience sound more important than it really is or should be (perhaps with relation to other people's)? I often feel that way when I have to write about my own experience rather than describe someone else's.

It is amazing that she now has the ability to analyze her own writing, having come so far from writing in a language of "others," and can see and note these things now. She manages a true meta-level understanding of what moved her then and now. But on the other hand, being conscious and critical of her early writing, she forces her readers (and perhaps herself) to be conscious and critical of her current writing, and it unavoidably makes me, for one, see certain parts in her current writing as a little pretentious (specifically, the middle of page 65 and the last paragraph).

Creating a Glossary of Terms/Working Concepts

When a reading introduces a significant amount of new information or new ways of thinking about something, along with new vocabulary, it can be useful to create a glossary of the terms you encounter (with page numbers so you can refer back to them in the text). Build a list as you go along.

- Look back over the list to see which words represent key concepts—for the ideas the writer is presenting and that relate to the ongoing conversation of your course.
- Group related terms, and try to name those groupings.
- Use your list to create an outline or map of the key ideas of this text. Which concepts and terms seem most important, and which represent additional supporting ideas?

Your glossary may suggest places that you'll want to look at more closely as you reread.

If you maintain a running glossary through the readings of a course, you're likely to find that most of the new terms you've listed at the beginning become old and familiar as you go along, that others drop by the wayside as less significant to the overall meanings of the course material, but that some new ones are also being added.

Reading Within a Genre

Genres take shape as people develop forms for writing (or speaking) that are used over and over again. As a reader, you can use your experience of genres to guide you as you encounter new examples, looking for common elements of the genre to help you make sense of what you're finding.

For example, in reading a *memoir*, you might look for:

- the past experiences the writer is bringing into the present;
- ways the writer has introduced and represented these experiences;
- the interpretation or understanding of these experiences that the writer offers.

In reading an *ethnographic report*, you might look for:

- the information the writer gives about the setting being studied;
- the larger questions the writer is trying to answer and how they relate to the way the writer has approached the study;
- a discussion of the methods that were used for the study—how data were collected and analyzed;
- a discussion of the cultural meanings and the shared values that emerge, with examples from the data studied;
- connections between what the writer has found and what other researchers have found.

Reading within a genre can also guide you as a writer within that genre, as discussed below.

WRITING

When writing for a course, writers typically draw on strategies they might use across contexts, but apply those strategies in particular ways. As you explore the following strategies, consider how to make them work within the specific context of the work you are doing and the conversations you are trying to create with your readers.

Generating Ideas

All writers need to generate ideas to write about, to come up with possibilities for the topic and focus of their writing and the things they'll include. Here are some examples of such strategies.

- *Listing.* Begin by making an open-ended list of possible topics to explore. For a memoir, your list might include a number of moments in your own experience within particular discourse communities that you would feel comfortable sharing in the classroom—past experiences with friends, with family, in school. Likewise, as you choose a discourse community to study, or a topic to pursue in a research paper, you can begin by listing many possibilities. You needn't make your list at one sitting; you're likely to have more ideas if you allow time to think about it for a day or two.

- *Responding to a focused prompt.* A way to generate ideas is to start with a beginning phrase that connects to what you'll be writing about. For stories and memoirs, for example, write as many sentences as you can think of to complete the line: "I remember." With fifteen minutes or so of quiet time, most writers find that a number of rich and powerful memories come to mind. To work toward a memoir of your experience in a discourse community, focus your "I remember . . ." lines on moments of speaking and hearing words spoken.

  I remember hearing my grandmother say . . .

  I remember my father's words as . . .

  I remember the kid in the cafeteria shouting . . .

  I remember the way I felt the first time I heard someone say . . .

  For a discourse community study, your prompt might focus on recalling what people talk about or particular ways in which people talk, including the words that you say or hear people say in particular settings.

  In *(setting)*, we talk about . . .

  we say . . .

For a study of an academic discourse community or of a research topic that would be pursued within that community, your prompt might be a list of questions starting with "What . . .?"; "Why . . .?"; "How?"; "When?"; or the phrase "I wonder . . .", as in "I wonder whether children ever suffer post-traumatic stress disorder," or "I wonder why more women don't go into science."

- *Creating a timeline.* In writing about anything where events have occurred over time, it can be helpful to create a timeline.

  For memoirs, you may want to create a timeline of events in your life. Locating everything that seems significant somewhere in time can help you think of other events that came before and after and can suggest important moments.

  For research reports, you may find that placing historical events or pieces of literature on a timeline can help you see significant relationships that you might want to explore.

- *Mapping.* Creating a map in which you put a key idea at the center of a page, and move out in all directions as other, related ideas occur to you, allows you to generate ideas as a list would do but also to show how some of these ideas are related. For a memoir, a map with "me at twelve" at the center, and moving out to all of the associations you can make with yourself at that age can help you recall more of your experiences and what shaped those experiences at that point in your life. Likewise, if you make a map in which you place yourself in the center of a field of discourse communities, and move out to name all of those in which you currently participate, you're likely to generate more ideas for the focus of your study. A different sort of map—one in which you trace your movements through a day, marking all of the places where you pause to interact with others, can also help you to see the possibilities for communities to explore. For a research study, placing a topic of interest at the center, and moving out from it to some of the things you already know about the topic, or want to know, can help you define some of the possibilities of your research.

- *Freewriting.* Still another way to do free and exploratory thinking that can lead to ideas for writing is simply to write freely for ten or fifteen minutes about whatever comes to mind, just keeping your pen moving all of the time so that you're getting words down on paper. You might also try *focused freewriting*, where you focus your attention on a specific topic or question but still write freely about that topic to see where your pen takes you in the time allotted. If you pause after ten or fifteen minutes to reread what you've written and to look for a central idea that you want to pursue, write for another ten or fifteen minutes working from that idea, and repeat this several times, you'll find you've generated a lot of material to work with as you begin to shape a draft of an essay.

■ *Rereading assigned texts, glossings, double-entry notebook responses, and informal writings.* One of the most typical ways of generating ideas for writing is to look back at what you've been reading and writing. If you look back to see what has resonated for you, intrigued you, or puzzled you in what others have written and imagine yourself extending the conversation, you're likely to find much that you want to say. Try picking out some quotations that interest you and seeing what sorts of connections or tensions they create when you place them in relationship to one another, writing freely about whatever ideas or questions occur for you as you do this. Likewise, if you look back through a set of your own informal writings, highlighting things you've already thought about that now seem worth considering some more, you're likely to find some of the pieces that you'd like to bring together in a formal paper. In this case, write freely to extend what you've already written, to make connections among different ideas, and to discover new thoughts you'd like to add.

As you make choices about the topic you'll write about and some of what you want to include in an essay or report on that topic, you'll also want to consider the context. What are the purposes for this type of writing in this setting and how do they match with your own purposes in pursuing this topic? Who will be reading what you write, and how can you address those readers' likely interests and concerns? What stance do you want to take toward your topic (objective, critical, ironic) and how do you want to position yourself as a writer (do you want to approach it from a personal perspective or from a more distanced and formal one)? Thinking about these questions is also part of the process of generating ideas for your writing.

Planning, Drafting, and Shaping

The processes of planning a piece of writing, drafting portions of it, and working to give it an overall shape are typically interwoven, though writers might work in different ways for different contexts and purposes. While some writers might sketch out a preliminary plan for a course paper and then just write through it until they've reached the end (and still others admit to sitting down at the computer without any plan at all, just hoping for inspiration), most writers move back and forth between planning and drafting, stepping back periodically to think about the overall shape of what they're producing. In turn, their sense of shape or form helps them discover places where they need to generate more ideas and draft new sections to fill in what they've already written, and to revise their preliminary plan to fit with what they're learning as they write. It's moving back and forth in this often messy process that helps them emerge with a full draft in which everything fits together in a way that will be satisfying to both the writer and possible readers. Again there are some specific strategies that can help with this process.

■ *Planning, drafting, and shaping within a genre.* In most instances, whether you're writing within an academic setting or a nonacademic one, you'll be writing in a particular genre that's common within that setting—a personal letter, a business memo, or one of the many types of academic essays and reports. Reading other examples of that genre, seeing what people write within it and how, can help you to develop your initial ideas into a fuller piece of writing. It can give you a sense of the elements you want to include, of what you want to do with each of those elements, and of some of the possible ways in which you might want to arrange them. Once you've identified key elements of a memoir or an ethnographic report or an argument essay, you'll be able to expand your thinking about each element as you draft. Suggestions for common genres of academic essays with typical key elements appear at the end of most chapters.

- *Planning and organizing from informal writing.* When you're writing a longer paper or report that draws on a lot of informal writing—reading responses, research notes and memos, and responses to reflective inquiries, for example—you already have a lot of draft material, but you also have a lot of material to organize.

    For planning and organizing longer essays and reports, begin by asking yourself:

    ☐ What are some of the significant things that I've learned through my informal writing?

    ☐ What, in the data I've gathered and analyzed and/or the texts that I've read, has helped me to see these things?

    ☐ What do I want to show my readers about the focus of this paper or report?

    Then look back through all of your research notes, responses to informal inquiries, and journal and essay responses that are relevant to this final paper. Highlight and gloss places in your own writing that seem to give strong evidence of something you want to show about the topic, places where you've come to some new insight, places where you've found points of contact with the work of other researchers—anything that you think you might want to draw into your final paper.

    Finally, see where you can draw these pieces into your plan or how you can adapt your plan to encompass these pieces. Making an outline, with points that you can finally use as headings, can help you organize this to guide your writing of a draft.

- *Planning and organizing with an outline.* When you've been thinking about a topic for a while and already have a clear sense of what you'll write about, or if you have only a limited writing time and need to organize your thinking quickly, you might want to jot down an *informal outline* to work from. Here's an informal outline that Karen might have used for the memoir in Chapter 3.

```
childhood
    me and Melanie
    two different families
    how each contributed to my identity
        Black
            music—gospel and rap
            hair—corn rows
        White
            music—hymns and "Good Ship Lollipop"
            hair—curls
early teens
    others see Whiteness
    friends argue for Blackness
high school
    racial divisions and categories
    awareness of racism
    double consciousness
    racial categories not necessary, socially constructed
now
    questioning categories
    studying these issues
    trying to move beyond these limitations
```

We know, however, from what Karen wrote afterwards about her writing process, that she didn't work this way at all. Instead, she started in the middle with the experiences of her early teen and high school years, and moved out in both directions, back to her earlier childhood and forward to what she's learning in college. Writers often discover what they want to include by beginning with something they know they want to write about and then seeing what to add from there. In that case, outlining might be a useful strategy, not as part of the initial planning and drafting process, but to guide a revision process. In any case, if you begin with some sort of outline, you should revisit it frequently, adapting it as your own text develops.

A *formal outline* can feel more rigid and harder to adapt, but it is useful in creating a clear structure. It allows you to see exactly how the points you're making in each paragraph line up, letting you find more easily whether you've presented a clear line of argument and whether you've provided supporting evidence for all of your points. In the following formal outline for the essay "Alone Among the Others" which appears on page 166, Jake Wark included brief versions of the quotations he planned to use. Working back and forth between the readings and his outline, he sometimes decided what point he wanted to make and then looked back to his glossed text for words that would support that point, and he sometimes found words in the text that suggested a new point that he could make.

I. The role of social outsider provides an author with experience that can engage a reader.

    A. Cisneros, Rodriguez, Mellix show self-doubt, alienation, aloneness.

    B. Each finds strength and courage.

    C. Each succeeds in finding identity through language that had made them different.

II. Cisneros suggests that her outsider role led her to be a writer.

    A. As a child, she was an outsider because of gender.

        1. She was "only daughter"(p. 2).

        2. She had a "solitary childhood"(p. 3).

        3. Her "best friend . . . never materialized"(p. 3).

    B. In college, she was different from her classmates socio-economically.

        1. It was the "first time I felt 'other'"(p. 4).

    C. She dropped imitations, embraced difference and found her voice.

        1. She found "the voice I'd been suppressing"(p. 4).

III. Rodriguez was also an outsider as a child.

    A. He was an outsider as a Latino and son of immigrants.

        1. He felt alone among peers "who were white, many the children of doctors and lawyers"(p. 28).

        2. He thought even the "house stood apart"(p. 29).

        3. His family used phrases *los gringos," "los Americanos."*(p. 29).

    B. Spanish reinforced separateness

        1. He felt "separateness from *los otros.*"(p. 30).

        2. He felt like "a foreigner"(p. 31).

    C. Rodriguez left role of insider in family to become insider to larger public world.

IV. Mellix's identity also shaped by language.

    A. Her issue was when to speak public language.

        1. She was taught that "ordinary, everyday speech" (p. 60) was inferior.

        2. She felt foolish speaking "proper" English "because we were ashamed to be our true selves"(p. 62).

        3. She couldn't use "proper" language with intimates "for no good reason" (p. 62).

4. She decided, "the language was not ours" (p. 62).

B. She saw standard English and her variation as "two distinctly different languages" (p. 60).

   1. She studied it like a foreign language, "memorizing phrases" (p. 63).

   2. She saw her writing as "mechanical" (p. 63).

   3. She felt "restricted by the language" (p. 62).

C. In college she began to make the language her own.

   1. She gave up her shame about her background, like Cisneros.

   2. She exposed herself to feel comfortable with the language, like Rodriguez.

   3. She imagined herself "part of the culture of that language" (p. 67).

V. All three went through similar steps.

   A. All were insiders in family, then outsiders.

   B. All found identities by stepping beyond limits defined by others.

   C. All took a risk to move into larger culture.

   D. All solidified individuality.

■ *Planning, drafting, and shaping your writing with a chart.* When you're placing several readings, studies, observations or examples against each other, you may find that the outline format is too linear to let you see relationships clearly. You may find it more useful to plan your writing using a chart that lets you see a number of different points of connection across your different examples. Start by listing the texts or studies you're discussing in columns across the top of your chart. Then list possible points of connection or comparison down the right side. This will give you a grid that you can fill in with the details from each text that address each point. It will help you develop your thinking about each of those points, and it can then guide your writing as well. Here's a format you might use. Look also in Chapter 5 at the chart a student writer used to guide her comparison of her own discourse community with those Heath studied—Roadville and Trackton (p. 239).

	Text or situation 1	Text or situation 2	Text or situation 3
1st point of comparison			
2nd point of comparison			
3rd point of comparison			
Etc.			

An alternative organizer for planning your comparison of two things is a Venn diagram. Here you would put points of difference in the outer portions of the two circles and points of similarity in the overlapping middle section.

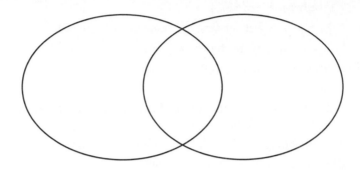

- *Planning, drafting, and shaping your writing about one or more readings.* Within the genre of an academic essay, assignments often call for working with readings. After reviewing your glossings of those readings to generate ideas to write about, you can work with the points in the text that you see as most significant to the topic you've decided on, creating a preliminary plan for the order in which you'll address them as you draw your readers towards the larger point you want to show them. Or you might want to draft a discussion about particular points in a text, deciding when and how to draw the words of the text into your own discussion, and moving from some of this drafting to planning how different parts of your discussion best fit together. Specific suggestions for working with quotations in your text appear below.

Working with Quotations

Many of the conversations that take place in the academic world draw on what others have written and said. As a participant in conversations that draw from written texts, you'll be pointing to those texts, sometimes summarizing what they say, and often quoting from them as you speak and write. Some reasons for drawing quotations from others texts into your own include the following:

- to illustrate or give an accurate representation of a writer's ideas;
- to open up a discussion about the writer's ideas (to invite your own readers to explore your understanding of the writer's point with you);
- to use the writer's words to support your own point;
- to give evidence for your interpretation of the writer's words.

There are "appropriate" ways of introducing and punctuating quotations in academic writing that are part of the discourse style of academic settings. One expectation is that quotations will be introduced and not just dropped into the new text you're creating—that you will make clear connections for your readers between what you've been saying and the quoted text. While the *formatting of quotations* is a technical concern that you might review as you edit your paper, *introducing quotations* and working them into your text effectively is an important part of your drafting process.

Here are some examples of ways in which writers have introduced quotations that they've used from Mellix's essay. Each writer suggests what will be found in the quotation and then explains briefly the meaning or significance of the quotations chosen.

Example 1

Block quotation: In this example, the writer has included a longer quotation of several sentences, and therefore has set it in a block, apart from the main text. Quotations of more than four lines of text should be indented in this way, with no quotation marks.

> Some of the distinct discourse communities Mellix describes within her memoir titled, "From Outside, In," would be for one her home:
>
> > I was at home, alone with my family, and my daughter understood that this way of speaking was appropriate in that context. She knew, as a matter of fact, that it was almost inevitable; when I get angry at home, I speak some of my finest, most cherished black English. Had I been speaking to my daughter in this manner in certain other environments, she would have been shocked and probably worried that I had taken leave of my propriety (p. 60).
>
> Here Mellix describes her home to be a place where she can be loose and free without criticism. However she explains that in another setting or environment she may not be so loose with her language. For example, she would be more posed and proper, expecting criticism if she spoke otherwise. **(Erin)**

Erin introduces this quotation with a sentence that lets her reader know what to expect from it: that it will show us Mellix's description of the discourse community of her home. She follows the quotation by restating in her own words the meaning she's drawing from it: Mellix's home is a place where "she can be loose and free." Then she goes on to connect this idea to others that follow in Mellix's essay. Thus, the quotation serves to give an accurate representation of Mellix's ideas and to provide evidence that supports Erin's larger point: that Mellix uses different discourses in different settings. It also lets us, as readers, form our own interpretation of Mellix's words in a way that brings us into this conversation, exploring these ideas along with Erin.

Example 2

Brief quotation embedded in a longer paragraph: In this example, the writer has selected fewer words to quote and has omitted some words in the middle (indicated by the ellipses—three spaced periods—between "important" and "Now").

> At home, she speaks "Black English." Mellix was with her ten year old daughter, who sat close to her complaining of boredom and sighing around. Mellix said, "Looka here, Allie, you to old for this kinda carryin' on. I done

> told you this is important . . . Now git on outa here and leave me off be-
> fore I put my foot all the way down" (p. 60). Her daughter understood that
> this way of speaking was appropriate when they are at home, and will be in-
> appropriate if spoken in certain other environments. **(Lawrence)**

Lawrence makes that point that Mellix speaks "Black English" at home, and he uses this quotation to give his readers an example, using the clause, "Mellix said," to introduce it. (In an earlier version, Lawrence referred to Mellix as "Barbara"; here he follows the convention that published writers are referred to by their last names in academic and other public writing—even if you know them personally, or feel as if you do.)

Example 3

Quotations embedded within a sentence: In this example, the writer has embedded quotations from the reading within a longer sentence of her own, placing them within parentheses.

> I think it's pretty interesting to see how one language can change so much
> with the same people. I mean, Mellix describes how she and her family con-
> sciously change the way they speak depending on who they're with: family
> from the city ("My mother's face took on a strained expression when she
> spoke. I could see that she was being careful to say just the right words in
> just the right way. Her voice sounded thick, muffled" [p. 60]), White people ("I
> was extremely conscious that this was an occasion for proper English. I had
> taken out my English and put it on as I did my church clothes, and I felt as if I
> was wearing my Sunday best in the middle of the week." [p. 61]), or each
> other ("'Superior!'" my sister mocked. 'You mean I'm acting "biggidy"?' My
> sisters and brothers sniggered, then joined in teasing me." [p. 61]) **(Deni)**

Deni begins with a larger generalization about people changing their language in different settings, goes on to list a number of the specific changes that Mellix shows her readers, and gives examples, in parenthesis, of those changes.

There are also specific discourse community conventions for how to *punctuate quotations*, and how to show where you're working the writer's words into your own text. Notice these also in the responses above.

Punctuation for quotations:

- Commas and periods go <u>inside</u> quotation marks when the quotation isn't followed by citation information such as a page number:

  > Mellix speaks for all writers when she says, "Writing and rewriting, prac-
  > ticing, experimenting, I came to comprehend more fully the generative
  > power of language."

- Semicolons and colons go <u>outside</u> quotation marks:

  > Looking back on a paper she wrote in college, Mellix thinks, "I would start
  > my paper with a quotation that caught my interest"; she would see other
  > possibilities besides the ones her teacher suggested.

> At times, Mellix felt a "new fragmentation that spoke to [her] in many voices": the voices of her family, the places she had worked, and her college classes.

■ Exclamation points and question marks go <u>inside</u> the quotation marks if they're part of the quotation. If they're not part of the quotation but part of your larger sentence they go outside:

> As Mellix compares pieces of writing that she did in different parts of the semester, she asks "What caused these differences?"

> Why was Mellix "free to move about in the language of 'others' so long as [she] was speaking *of* others"?

[Note that brackets have been used in the sentence to allow the new writer to change Mellix's sentence slightly, replacing "I" with "she," to fit the new sentence.]

■ Citation information goes in parentheses after the quotation marks but before the punctuation at the end of a clause or sentence. If you're writing a paper that draws from only one reading, you only need to provide a page number for in-text citations. More information about citations can be found below under Documenting Sources.

> Mellix, in describing her writing of this essay as "trying to bring order out of chaos" (p. 60), confirms the writing process is often a messy.

> Mellix concludes: "I write and continually give birth to myself" (p. 67).

Working quotations into your own text.

■ Use brackets [ ] for things you add to a quotation to make a sentence work smoothly in your text: Mellix tells us that when she "started writing this paper [she was] trying to bring order out of chaos."

■ Use an ellipsis (. . .) if you leave information out of a quotation: "The letters I wrote for the company . . . were . . . an indication of my growing mastery of English."

■ For a quotation within a quotation, use single quotation marks:

> Mellix tells us how her sister would respond to her own proper language: "'Superior!' my sister mocked."

■ If you are using a quotation that has an error, add [sic] after the error to show that it was the quotation's error and not your own.

Another use of quotation marks in writing is to indicate that a word you're using is not really your own, to distance yourself somewhat from the term, or to call attention to it.

> Mellix talks of "proper" English as if other varieties of English are "improper"; however, her examples show that what she really means is "inappropriate."

For including source information for quotations, see Documenting Sources.

Rereading and Revising

The word "revision" means "reseeing." It often takes stepping away from what you've written, trying on the perspectives of other readers, and stepping into the role of reader yourself, to allow you to resee your first version of a piece of writing—to see it with new eyes and to find in it new possibilities. Several specific strategies can help you with this process:

- *Glossing and outlining.* Although outlining has often been considered to be a strategy to use before writing, many writers discover what they have to say through their actual writing. For these writers, outlining works most effectively as a step toward revision, after they've written a first draft. Try glossing your draft, noting main ideas in the margin of your text. Then create an outline that represents what you have written, showing which ideas are most important and which are subordinate. The outline will let you see what's out of place or out of balance, so that you can make adjustments to create a more clearly ordered text. (If you outline prematurely or hold to an early outline too rigidly, you may leave out important ideas that come up as you write but don't fit into your preconceived plan.)

- *Rereading your draft from the perspective of a reader.* Step back and reread your draft from these three perspectives:
  - Participatory: Ask "Does this work to get me interested and to keep me involved in the conversation? Can I follow everything clearly as a reader?"
  - Analytical: once you've glossed your draft paragraph by paragraph, you can analyze <u>what</u> you've said, <u>why</u>, and <u>how</u>, seeing how the whole draft works and why it works as it does.
  - Evaluative: Ask "Does what I've said make sense? Have I included everything I need to include, given enough background and created enough shared knowledge, provided enough details and examples to illustrate my point? Is the overall ordering of what I've included effective, and have I made clear connections from one part to another? Is the style appropriate to the purpose and the setting?"

- *Trying out new structures.* Once you've created a structure within a draft, you can try variations on that structure. If you look at a set of texts within a genre—memoirs, ethnographies, research reports—you'll find that although there are similar elements within different examples of one type of writing, there are also some significant variations in how these pieces are structured—in how they begin and the order in which those key elements are represented. Follow the example of another text and try out a structure that is significantly different from the one you've created in your draft. Once you've compared your two versions, you can choose the one you find to be most effective, or you can create a third version that draws from both. (Two versions of a memoir by Dina appear at the end of Part I.)

- *Creating and using a checklist.* Whenever you're writing within a common genre, it's a good idea to generate, with classmates or on your own, a checklist of the elements you want to be sure to include—the elements that readers of that genre will commonly expect to find. To decide what should be on your checklist, you'll want to look at the assignment sheet that guides the writing you're doing to see what's expected. You'll also want to look at other examples of this sort of writing—particularly among your course readings, to see what other writers have included.

    A checklist of key elements does not necessarily define the order in which you have to include particular elements. Both Heath and Spradley and Mann, for example, address all of the elements on the following checklist in their studies (in their larger books if not completely in the selections included in this book) but they present them in very different patterns of organization and style.

    Here's an example of a checklist with elements that might be included in many sorts of reports:

    ☐ A title
    ☐ An introduction with necessary background information
    ☐ A statement of purpose—a question or hypothesis that you're going to explore or thesis you're going to set out to prove and the main points or topics you intend to address
    ☐ A clear pattern of organization (possibly with headings)
    ☐ A discussion of the methods you used in your study
    ☐ Examples that support the main points you're making
    ☐ Connections to other research
    ☐ A conclusion that reaffirms new understandings
    ☐ An edited, proofread, and spell-checked text, with numbered pages
    ☐ References

- *Drawing on the responses of readers.* It's helpful to get responses from various readers—from other writers in your classroom writing response groups (discussed below), from other readers who will be interested in your topic or interested in helping you (friends, family), and as well as from an instructor. A checklist can guide these responses, or you might want to ask your own questions, to get the feedback you want as a writer.

- *Rereading for key understandings and elements.* Once you've had feedback from readers, have looked closely at the ways in which other writers have crafted their texts, and have experimented with some new forms, you have a new perspective from which to resee your paper and to prepare a final version. As you do so, think about what's most central to the understanding you want to convey in this piece of writing. And try to see, from a reader's perspective, whether you've met the reader's likely expectations and provided everything that you'd want your reader to take away from what you've written.

Suggestion for revising within specific genres can be found in Chapters 3, 6, and 9.

EDITING

In editing your final, formal writing, you'll want to read through it carefully:

- to make sure that the sentences are smooth, that the connections and transitions between sections are clear, and that no necessary information is missing.

- to watch for any place where what you've written deviates from the forms expected in Standard Written English.

Many varieties, styles, and forms are appropriate to different contexts. But when something from one setting gets carried over to another, or when a mixed form is produced that isn't conventional in any setting, most listeners and readers notice that something isn't quite right, most editors will make changes, and most teachers will mark what's not conventional in Standard Written English as an error. At the same time, most writers will find some patterns of variation from conventional forms—variations in punctuation, in grammar, in word choice—that are repeated in their texts.

Researchers have asked professionals which "errors" bother them the most. The ones that respondents are most bothered by are those that most show a writer to be an outsider to the formal world of educated, English-speaking professionals. Not surprisingly, the things that bother them most are the insider forms carried over from other varieties of English: different verb forms ("brung" instead of "brought"; "we was" for "we were"; "he don't" for "he doesn't"); double negatives (such as "can't hardly," "nobody don't go"), and using the objective pronoun form as a subject ("Him and me went to the game"). At the next level of concern are the conventions associated with written English—spelling, punctuation (particularly of sentences) along with some features of grammar, like subject-verb agreement. Then come finer points of grammar and punctuation.

Finding Mixed Varieties, Styles, and Forms in Your Writing

The best long-term strategy for dealing with mixed and unconventional forms is to see where they've been marked in your own writing, watching for patterns that appear. Here are several types of mixed and unconventional forms to watch out for.

- *Mixed forms related to learning English as a second language or to writing in standard English as a second dialect.* Typical patterns of variation for such writers might include the following:

☐ omitting articles (a, an, the) where they're typically used in English or inserting them where they usually don't appear. (But not all formal dialects of English agree on the use of articles in some places. The British say "He's in hospital" while Americans say "He's in the hospital.")

☐ omitting the plural 's': (Those two boy[s] go downtown).

☐ omitting the 's' on the third person singular present tense form of the verb: (That boy walk[s] downtown right now).

☐ omitting the 'ed" ending on the past tense of the verb. (That boy walk[ed] downtown yesterday.)

■ *Mixed forms related to moving from spoken language to written text.* Many errors have to do with how words and sentences are conventionally represented in written language and these conventions change slowly over time, so editors will disagree about some smaller points of using commas, for example. But here are some serious concerns to watch out for involving sentence punctuation:

☐ punctuating two sentences as if they're one. (This unconventional form is referred to as a run-on if there is no period between sentences, a comma fault/comma splice if a comma is used in place of a period.)

> Example: Mellix used her "cherished Black English" at home however she switched to "proper English" at school.

> Correct with a period to separate two sentences, with a semicolon to separate two closely-linked main clauses representing two ideas, or with a comma and a conjunction

> [at home. However, she . . .] or

> [at home; however, she . . .] or

> [at home, but she . . .]

☐ punctuating a fragment as a sentence. (A sentence requires both a subject and a main verb. In the fragment below, *being* is a participle form and it doesn't have a subject.)

> Example: Mellix varied her language frequently. *Being* careful that she always paid attention to what was appropriate.

> Correct by attaching the fragment (Being . . .) to the previous sentence with a comma [frequently, *being* careful]

> Or make it into a complete sentence by adding a subject and using a main form of the verb: [frequently. *She was* careful to pay attention . . .]

Writers may sometimes intentionally vary the conventional pattern of punctuation, as Rodriguez does when he uses fragmented phrases to capture the experience of his intimate family language. (*We are family members. Related. Special to one another.*) But those variations are effective in part because they play against the convention that's in the background of most written texts.

- *Variation in verb tense and voice.* Two common concerns are the following:
  - ☐ keeping a consistent tense in narration. The tense we choose often has to do with how we think about what we're telling or writing, particularly in narration. It's common in speaking to narrate the events in the present tense, as if they're happening right in front of the audience—to replay them for listeners. We can see an example of this in Dana's spoken narrative in Chapter 2: he begins his story in the past tense but then switches into the present as he brings his listeners into the action of the truck traveling down the ramp. The convention for appropriate written style would keep the whole narrative in the past tense, as Dana does in his written version. (But you can try putting some moments in the present tense, as Karen does at the beginning and end of her memoir in Chapter 3, as long as the pattern for where you're using present and where you're using past is clearly determined and makes sense for your narrative.)
  - ☐ writing about the work of other writers in the present tense. Another convention for written style is that if you are writing about a written text, even if the writer wrote it years ago, you use the present tense. For example, "Rodriguez describes his experience in moving from a private to a public identity." This convention may have arisen because we resee the text in the present moment when we're writing about it or discussing it.
- *Mixed styles or styles that don't match the context.* Frequently writers find themselves doing several things:
  - ☐ using words that are too informal for the more public and formal context that's assumed for writing in academic settings, for example, "What Rodriguez says about bilingual education is *garbage*" instead of something like "Rodriguez's position on bilingual education is not fully supported by the evidence of his own experience."
  - ☐ trying out a more formal or specialized vocabulary or more complex sentence structures and having the use of the word be slightly off the mark or not appropriate for the context, or the sentence structure be somewhat tangled. All writers have examples like this. Amy Tan gives us an example from an early draft of one of her stories, a sentence that she thought at the time was "wittily crafted."

    That was my mental quandary in its nascent state.

    And here's an example that Karen found when she looked back through some old papers she'd done in high school to find mixed and unconventional forms in her own work. This is from the draft of a paper on Amy Tan's book, *The Joy Luck Club* about how hard it was for Chinese-American daughters to understand their Chinese mothers' experiences, where Karen was trying out new vocabulary words. The new words, which are somewhat awkwardly inserted into her sentences, are italicized here.

> To finally fully understand their mothers' experiences and put to use their morals and lessons, they first needed to experience *a prototype or similar situation* to what their mothers had gone through. Until each daughter *regressed back* in their mothers' footsteps and experienced something of *much less magnification, but of similarity* to what their mothers had gone through, then and only then did the bond start to grow, being that it was the differences in culture and cultural barriers began to diminish.

■ *Using clichés that represent common ways of thinking.* We're always drawing familiar ways of talking and thinking into our own, but writers also try to work towards shaping their own specific meanings with language that more precisely represents those meanings. Here's a sentence that Mellix finds to be clichéd when she looks back at her own freshman writing. (The clichéd phrases are italicized.)

> My *excitement was* soon *dampened,* however, by what seemed like *a small voice in the back of my head,* saying that I should be careful with my *long awaited opportunity.*

■ *Overusing features that distance you as a writer from what you're saying.* Writers have often been taught not to use "I" in formal writing, and it's true that in much academic writing, the person doing the thinking disappears. (You can see an example of this in the abstract of the article April reports on in Chapter 9.) To avoid saying "I", writers then draw on the passive voice to create sentences where the actor doesn't have to be named or create other convoluted structures. But in many cases, particularly where you're writing about your own observations, a first-person pronoun and an active form of the verb are more appropriate in academic writing. Here are some examples that highlight such distancing features from the work of another writer, Bryan, as he writes about his own experience with language variation:

Example I

Version I: "After 18 years of being exposed to standard writing practice and grammatical procedure, variation in writing *is* something that is hard to really merge into as a writer."

Revised version: "After eighteen years of being exposed to standard writing practice and a focus on grammatical procedure, I find it hard to work with the idea of variation as a writer."

In this case, Bryan is writing about himself, so he is the appropriate actor/subject in the sentence. It's "I" that is described by the modifying clause that opens the sentence—an "I" who has had eighteen years of standard writing instruction. The revised sentence also eliminates the problem of a dangling modifier, where a modifying element doesn't actually modify the noun it's closest to. In this case, it's the person, represented by *I,* who has spent 18 years being exposed to standard writing practice, not, as in the first sentence, *variation.* If a sentence begins with a clause that has the "ing" form of the verb acting as a modifier (giving some information about someone or something), then that someone or something needs to be the subject of the sentence. Here, reworking the sentence so that *I* replaces *variation* eliminates a grammatical problem, while making the sentence clearer and easier to understand.

Example 2

Version 1: "This class is the first time ever that a sense of freedom seems ever present from within to venture into new projects . . ."

Revised version: "This class is the first time that I've felt free, from within, to venture into new projects . . ."

Again the sentence becomes clearer when Bryan puts himself back in as the subject of the *that* clause, changing "a sense of freedom" to "I've felt free."

Example 3

Version 1: "Although excitement is brewing from strong within me on this great chance to grow as a writer, hesitation fights back and the result is a constant power struggle. After years of developing bad habits and being limited to a standard way of writing, it is quite a formidable challenge to experiment with new writing procedures. Ultimately I fear the wrath of the red ink."

Revised version: "I'm now in a constant power struggle between my excitement at having a chance to grow as a writer and my hesitation at having to try something new. After years of developing bad habits and being limited to a standard way of writing, I find that it's a formidable challenge for me to experiment with new writing procedures. Ultimately I fear the wrath of the red ink."

In the revised version, Bryan has used "I" as the subject of both the first and second sentences so that they build directly to the closing sentence. Sentence 3 is very powerful, both because Bryan has already placed himself as its subject—as the person who is doing the fearing—and because the "wrath of the red ink" is such an effective way to say what many writers have learned to fear about writing.

In the revised version, Bryan also corrects another dangling modifier in the second sentence, where "developing bad habits" doesn't apply to the subject of the main clause "it," but to the writer, "I."

Example 4:

Version 1: "Over the years, bad habits were developed."

Revised version: "Over the years, I developed bad habits."

As he worked on the sentences in Example 3, Bryan tried a version using the passive voice of the verb. Here he used what would have been the object in an active sentence, *bad habits*, as the subject of the sentence and combined it with a passive form of the verb (using a form of *to be* plus the past participle—*were developed*). In the revised version, he used "I" as his subject and changed the passive verb form *were developed* into an active form, *developed*.

Editing advice to avoid excessive use of distancing features:

- make sure your sentences show clearly who or what is acting,
- make modifiers with "ing" connect clearly to the noun they modify,
- don't hide the actor in a sentence by using a passive form of the verb where an active one, with the actor as the subject, makes sense.

Examples like these point to the writer's discourse competence—taking risks and trying out new words and sentence structures that seem appropriate to the new setting. If you never produce such an example, you're probably not taking enough risks as a writer, and you really can't improve your writing for new contexts without taking those risks. But if you sense that you're trying something new, reread carefully to make sure that you've been as clear as possible and ask others to read what you've written to see whether you've made it work.

There are enough common variations to fill chapters of this book, and a handbook or style manual will give you explanations for more of them. Such guides point to the conventions of communities that use a formal and complex level of discourse in standard written English, and you'll keep acquiring their finer and finer points for years—as long as you write for such a community. What you need is a strategy for dealing with the mixed and unconventional forms that are bound to occur as you keep trying out what might be appropriate to a setting.

The simplest overall editing strategy is the following:

- look for patterns in the unconventional forms that show up in your writing (a number of sentence fragments, a number of times that "verb tense" is noted by a reader, the repeated misspelling of the same word or the confusion of sound-alikes like "their," "they're," and "there" that aren't caught by spellcheckers);
- keep a list of the unconventional, mixed or overly-distanced forms that show up most frequently in your writing;
- check your list when you're editing drafts of a formal paper and when you're proofreading your final copy, to remind yourself of what to watch out for in particular.

Your list will change over time, but you'll probably always have a list. Most writers do (at least in their heads).

Editing for Style

Beyond editing for any mixed forms and styles in your writing, you may also want to edit your sentences for other aspects of style, considering these points from the perspective of a reader.

- *Clarity.* Does each sentence make its point as clearly as possible?
- *Connectedness.* Does each sentence connect clearly to what comes before and after? Where you've used a pronoun, will a reader be able to tell exactly what earlier word the pronoun refers to?
- *Transitions.* Are there clear transitions (such as "in addition," "however," "on the other hand") that show the relationship between your ideas and whether a sentence or paragraph is adding to, qualifying, or presenting a contrast to what has gone before?
- *Aesthetic qualities.* If you read your sentences aloud, do you find that they flow easily? Do you find the qualities of effective repetition, imagery, and dialogue (drawing in the spoken or written words of others) discussed in Chapter 9 (pp. 433–434)?

    Rodriguez uses all three. He creates rhythm by repeating the same form of the verb three times within a sentence: "Conveyed through those sounds was the *pleasing, soothing, consoling* reminder of being at home."

    He presents strong images: "Quickly I turned to see my mother's face *dissolve in a watery blur behind the pebbled glass door.*"

    He repeats the words spoken to him in the classroom: "The nun would persist, 'Richard, stand up. Don't look at the floor. Speak up.' "

    These features help to bring his readers into the moments he is creating.

- *The style of the community for which you're reading and writing.* Are the texts you're reading personal or impersonal, informal and even colloquial or formal? Do they present ideas in relatively straightforward ways, in simple or compound sentences, or do they have much more complex and information-packed sentences? Do they use vocabulary that addresses a general audience of readers, or do they use the more specialized vocabulary of a particular field or a particular discourse community? Find an example that you have enjoyed reading, and look for some of these features. Read aloud from it. Then read aloud from your own text. Does the flow of reading one carry into the other? If not, can you reshape some sentences in your own text to make them more similar to the ones you've read?

Other important features of style in writing are related to the fact that we most often need to assume, as writers, that we are writing for readers outside of our immediate, most familiar discourse communities, who don't already share a lot of what goes on in our heads. Writers who address broader audiences need to build that shared knowledge, explicitly, through:

- *elaboration*—offering explanations, details, examples

  Rodriguez, for example, offers repeated examples of the Spanish words that helped to define his world: *los gringos, los otros, ingles,* while he explains the significance of those words to his experience of the world: "Like those whose lives are bound by a barrio, I was reminded by Spanish of my separateness from *los otros, los gringos* in power."

- *naming*—finding a key term to cover many different examples of an experience or observation

  Rodriguez uses the term *public identity* to name the identity he began to assume when he began to use the English of the public society. The naming of *private* and *public* offers a theme that he can explore throughout his memoir, and that ties different moments of his experience together in a coherent way.

- *stating and restating*

  As Rodriguez explores and adds to his understandings of his experience, he restates and expands on his meanings:

  "What I needed to learn in school was that I had the right—and the obligation—to speak the public language of *los gringos.*"

  "What [my teachers] understood was that I needed to speak a public language."

  "Because I wrongly imagined that English was intrinsically a public language and Spanish an intrinsically private one, I easily noticed the difference between the classroom language and the language of home."

You'll develop many of these features of style, in ways appropriate for the discourse communities you're writing for, over time as you keep reading and writing for these communities. But pausing at some moments in your editing to look for these features can make you more aware of what contributes to the styles you want to achieve.

Proofreading

Your final proofreading is aimed at catching typos, missing words, spelling errors that haven't been picked up by a spell-checker, at checking punctuation and capitalization, and at looking for any other surface errors. Effective proofreading strategies include the following:

- *reading aloud.* Reading each sentence aloud allows you to hear places where words are missing, a sentence is garbled, etc.
- *reading line-by-line.* Cover up your paper with a blank sheet, which you'll move down the page line by line. This slows down your eyes and

helps you move your attention from the larger meanings of what you've written to the surface details of each line. If you note on the sheet the actual errors that you find and correct, you'll have a working list of things to watch for in future proofreading. You'll also want to note things you're uncertain about, to get further information from an instructor, a classmate, or from a style manual.

RESPONDING TO PEERS

Response groups can help writers at all stages of the process. Reader responses do several things:

- help writers to work out what they want to say, and why, and how;
- help them to see whether they've accomplished their intentions;
- give them a reader's perspective so they can see whether they've met the needs of an audience;
- give feedback that can guide revision; and
- help them to edit and proofread.

In peer response, writers working on similar tasks work together in shared problem solving about each others' texts. Such feedback and problem solving helps the writer, but giving feedback also helps the other writers in the group: they get to see how other writers have handled the issues associated with a particular writing task, experience other possibilities besides the ones they explored for carrying out that task in that context, and talk about writing in a way that helps them become better readers of their own work. The purpose of peer writing groups is to give you helpful, working responses, not just traditional teacher responses.

Peer response is particularly useful when you've completed a draft of a piece of writing, and are considering what you might want to do in a revision. You can structure your peer writing responses in various ways:

- the writer reads aloud and listeners make notes on what they hear;
- the writer reads aloud while listener/readers follow along on their own copies of the writer's draft; or
- writers and readers pass drafts around, read each others' work silently, and write responses to what they read (in the classroom or at home).

Sometimes, particularly for early drafts, it can be helpful for writers to get general feedback from listener-readers about what they found interesting or confusing, what drew them in, or what they wanted to know more about. For later drafts and revisions it's often more helpful to work with a guiding set of questions—ones that take into account the genre of writing as well as the writer's interests and purposes and that represent the shared knowledge that writers have developed about what makes an effective piece of writing in that genre, for a particular purpose and context. Here are some specific peer re-sponse strategies.

Reading and Listening

Share your first drafts by reading them aloud to other members of your group. (You should read them aloud two times.)

As listeners/readers, your role is participatory.

■ Listen the first time, to get a sense of the whole. Follow along as the writer reads, as if you were listening to an oral story. Imagine yourself in a con-versation with the writer. You're not concerned here with how the words appear on the page, and that's part of why it's important to listen to the words rather than read them, so you're not distracted by those features.

■ Reading aloud and hearing others read also allows you to hear and be-come familiar with each others' voices as they carry into writing. What do you hear the writer saying to you? Do you follow everything the writer says or do you get lost anywhere? Do you find yourself needing more information at any point? Are there spots where you want to jump in and say "huh?", "I'm not sure what you mean"?

■ During a second reading, make notes about whatever strikes you as interesting and of the specific places where you're especially drawn in as a listener.

■ After the second reading, write down a brief version of <u>what</u> you heard the writer telling about and <u>why</u> you think these points might have been significant to the writer, along with any questions you have about the <u>what</u> and the <u>why</u>. Your purpose is to say what you heard and what you think the writer's purposes and meanings are. Any comments you make or questions you ask should be positive and en-couraging, but also clarifying.

■ Each member of the group should then read his/her responses back to the writer. The writer can explain, answer questions, continue the dis-cussion of any points he or she chooses, and ask questions back.

If you participate in the conversation the writer has invited, you'll find it natural, as respondents, to do all of these things:

■ restate what you think the writer has said in your own words;

■ pick up the writer's ideas, discuss them, and expand on them; and

■ ask questions, ask for more information at the points where you don't fully understand.

Your discussion should go on until group members understand what the writer has said or why the writer has included something and/or until the writer feels the group has a sufficient shared understanding of the exploratory essay.

Peer Response Within a Genre

Read for the general expectations associated with the genre. For memoirs, discourse community reports, or research reports, you can create a list of key elements and questions about them, based on the guidelines at the end of Chapters 3, 6, and 9.

Here is an example of questions you might ask when responding to draft essays where the writer has explored a question/thesis/theme about a reading.

- Has the writer found an interesting and productive question to explore?

- Has the writer presented a clear focus and maintained that focus from beginning to end?

- Has the writer elaborated wherever possible, giving sufficient information, details, evidence, explanations, commentary about significance, to fill gaps for you as a reader and to make explicit the understandings and meanings you should take away from this essay?

- Has the writer's essay added something more to your own understanding of an aspect of the reading? Where and how does the essay do this most strongly?

Peer Editing

Editors help writers work with a final text, not to have them significantly resee it or make major alterations or additions, but to work at the level of sentences and paragraphs, to make the text itself as clear as possible. (It is often helpful to work with peer editors who haven't already worked with your text in a writing response group, so that they can see it with fresh eyes.) Read and mark each others' texts for:

- clarity of information and of references to assumed shared knowledge from the larger world and to the shared knowledge that's already been created within the text. (If two boys are named in one section, a later "he" may not be sufficient to make it clear which boy is being referred to later.)

- smooth connections and transitions from one part to another.

- a consistent voice and style, without jarring shifts from informal to formal levels of discourse or between standard written English and other varieties of English (although a writer may choose to draw on another variety in a consistent way).

- use of appropriate discourse conventions for academic writing in standard written English (such as referring to published writers by their last names, underlining book titles, using quotation marks for titles of short stories or poems, naming a person or object or concept again rather than just using a pronoun in each new paragraph).

- use of conventional spelling, punctuation.

When all peer editors have marked the text, each writer should review the markings and discuss them with the editors, to come to an understanding of why each thing was marked. (The writer may, of course, disagree with the editors, but should take into consideration each of their concerns.)

Drawing on the feedback of peer editors, make final changes to your text. Then proofread a last time before turning in the final copy.

If there is a pattern of a particular unconventional form, the writer should add this to his/her personal editing checklist.

You might also want to do peer editing directly in a document on a word processor. Microsoft Word allows a writer to make changes to another's text on the computer, tracking those changes in a different color. By attaching a Word document to an e-mail, you can send a draft back and forth with a writing partner. By using the editing and turning on the track changes functions, you can highlight the sentence-level changes you would make to a writing partner's text, and your partner will be able to see and accept or reject those changes in preparing a final document.

Peer Proofreading

Here our task is to act as proofreaders of each other's final printed text, to catch any remaining surface glitches—typos, punctuation, capitalization, left-out words, etc. At this point, you want to try not to read for meaning, because that will distract you from the proofreading task. Move slowly, line by line, through the text. Using a pencil, mark corrections that you're sure of. Put a question mark by anything you're uncertain of, and note your question on a separate piece of paper, along with the page and paragraph number of the spot you're uncertain about.

When you've finished, discuss the spots you questioned with the writer and with other members of your group. The writer should finally decide how to handle such spots in his/her text. (It's generally okay to make corrections in pencil or ink on a final print copy you've prepared—much more important, in terms of the shared values of most communities that rely a lot on writing, than having an unmarked but incorrect printed text.) You may want to try to answer some of the questions that came up by consulting a handbook or style manual.

Responding to Peer Response as a Writer

As a writer you'll want to respond to the peer response you receive in two ways:

- listen or read with the purpose of revising your own work. Take notes on comments that are made orally, or read any written responses carefully, and make your own notes on points that you find helpful and want to consider as you work on another draft of your work.

- listen or read with the purpose of giving feedback on the feedback you've received. Let your peer readers know how you might follow up on something they've said, or why you don't think that a particular comment fits with the direction you now want to go in, or what you find you did draw on after you've completed a revision.

ASSESSING YOURSELF

As you move back and forth between the roles of writer and reader, you'll become better able to assess your own writing, in terms of both what you're trying to accomplish and the norms of the classroom community you're writing for. For assessing your own writing, read both analytically and evaluatively, seeing what is in the writing and how well it works for the purposes set by you and the assignment. Revising checklists, like those shown under the rereading and revising section of Writing Strategies above, offer a good starting point for essays and reports.

Assessing Essays and Reports

- Reread the assignment and see whether you've done what it calls for.
- Recall the common assumptions for all essays and reports in the context you're writing for.
- Generate your own list of elements to address.

For example, here is the assignment for an exploratory essay on Mellix's essay, from Chapter 2.

EXPLORATORY ESSAY 1	Drawing on a theme or question or understanding that has emerged from your informal writing and sharing responses, write a more extended response in which you draw from Mellix's memoir and show how it supports or leads to that theme or understanding or responds to that question. Your purpose here is to give more formal shape to the ideas that you were exploring earlier, to take a reader into consideration as you present them, guiding the reader through your ideas and the supporting evidence from Mellix's memoir in a way that shows the reader "this is what I've come to understand and why."

Here are some typical expectations that would follow from this assignment, in the form of a *rubric*: a template for considering the key elements in an assignment and the expectations of a particular writing context. Creating such a template from an assignment can guide your efforts as a writer, to decide how to represent your ideas to your readers, and it can also help you, as a reader of your own writing, to assess whether you've met the terms of the assignment.

1. A clear statement of a theme or question that you're going to explore
2. A focus on that theme and a clear line of argument in support of that theme or question

3. Evidence from Mellix's text, supported by appropriate quotations used to illustrate or give an accurate restatement of a writer's ideas; to open up a discussion about the writer's ideas (to invite your own readers to explore your understanding of the writer's point with you); and/or to use the writer's words to support your own point

4. A conclusion that sums up or restates what you've come to understand and why

5. Effective introduction, explanation of quotations

6. Use of conventions for punctuating quotations, with page numbers

Assessing Your Own Developing Writing Process

It's useful to pause periodically to reflect on your work as a reader and writer, to consider for yourself the ways in which you're working, the things you feel most confident about, and what you're still working to develop as you write in new academic settings. Here are some topics you might consider:

1. Your engagement as a reader and writer (glossing and rereading, working closely with texts to understand what the writer is saying and why, creating a thoughtful dialogue with readings, making connections across readings, integrating references to other texts into your own in meaningful ways).

2. The relationship between your writing and your thinking (Do you push your own thinking, try out new ideas, in both response papers and drafts? Are you writing longer response papers? Do you read comments on returned papers and think about questions/issues they raise? Do you discover new understandings, new connections, new meanings as you write? Do you try to see a subject from different perspectives?)

3. The richness and detail of your writing (Do you elaborate on ideas, giving details and explanations that help the reader see what you've seen about a text or about the world? Do you make generalizations supported by specific evidence—from reading or experience?)

4. Developing larger meanings (Are you conscious of drawing out the significance of what you're writing about, answering the reader's implied "so what?", seeing and stating what might be the meaning of what you observed, why it might be important to pay attention?)

5. Building a relationship with a reader (Do you take a reader's perspective as you reread your own writing? Do you orient readers in an introduction, making it clear what the focus of this essay, this exploration, will be? Do you let the reader know what you're writing about and include enough background information so that any moderately informed reader who picked up your paper could make sense of it? Do you offer

guidance to a reader through clear structure? Do you share with readers what you've learned through the writing in a conclusion? Do you use the feedback you receive from other readers to resee or revise your essay?)

6. Revision (Do you do substantive revisions of early drafts, genuinely re-seeing what you've written before from the perspective of what you know later from class discussions, from seeing examples of other essays? Do you refine what you've written by taking the perspective of a reader? Do you resee/rewrite sentences?)

7. Editing (Do you proofread your papers before handing them in? Do you use a spell-checker, a dictionary? Do you check for problem areas such as punctuation, particularly where there is something that has been pointed out on earlier essays. Do you reread writing that has been returned to you and ask questions when you don't understand something that has been marked?)

8. The relationship between the focus of the course readings/inquiries and your own writing (Has the study of discourse communities, for example, contributed any understandings to the way you look at what you bring to your writing and what you are now trying to do as a writer?)

Assessing Your Own Writing Skills

You may find it helpful, periodically, to step back from working within a particular piece of writing to assess what you've accomplished with that piece— the writing skills demonstrated there and in your writing overall. The following checklist identifies many of the writing skills that are typically expected in freshmen courses.

Writing Skills Checklist

1. <u>Working with other readings in your own writing</u>

   introducing readings appropriately (including information about author and title)

   presenting a clear understanding of what you've read, in your own words

   engaging with the ideas of the texts

   drawing on the words of other texts to support your discussion (quoting)

   introducing quotations effectively

   explaining their significance for the point you're making

   using appropriate punctuation for in-text citations

2. <u>Providing orientation, focus, organization, conclusion in essays</u>

   introducing an essay in a way that:

   > creates shared knowledge for your reader and engages your reader's interest and attention

   > sets forth the question or idea you'll be exploring in the paper (thesis)

   > suggests how you'll go about exploring the question/idea (typical of report writing)

   maintaining a clear focus on your central idea, so that each part clearly relates to it

   organizing an essay so that a reader can follow its movement clearly, can gloss its key points easily (and using organizing strategies like charts and outlines)

   concluding an essay in a way that's consistent with the question or idea you set out to explore

3. <u>Making generalizations and supporting them with evidence</u>

   providing examples and quotations to support the main points you are making

   working from larger generalizations to details, examples, quotations that offer support

   working from the evidence of texts or observations to make larger generalizations

4. <u>Elaborating</u>

   giving full background information where needed (not assuming too much insider knowledge on the part of the reader)

   giving full explanations, discussion, details

   being explicit in naming, defining, putting ideas into words

5. <u>Working toward ideas, meanings, significance, new perspectives, new understandings</u>

   seeing and reseeing an idea or question you're pursuing, by writing about it from multiple angles, both informally and formally

   pushing towards new understandings, deeper meanings throughout an essay

   discussing the significance of the points you make and the examples you include

   working to enlarge your perspective, take on new perspectives (seeing insider/outsider perspectives, writer/reader perspectives, local culture/wider culture perspectives)

   exploring relationships and complex connections (between your own experience and those of others, among multiple readings, across multiple settings) shaping conclusions that represent the new understandings you've gained, the larger understandings a reader might take away, the significance of what you've learned

6. <u>Revising</u>

substantially reorganizing and rearranging elements of essays as you work through different drafts, trying out new structures and forms, making additions

reworking for overall organization and movement

reworking for style, smoothness, clarity

using responses from readers to add, expand, clarify, restructure

7. <u>Editing</u>

rereading carefully for:

clarity of each sentence in relation to what's gone before

conventions of academic written texts (for what needs to be stated explicitly, for background information that needs to be included, for citation information, adding reference/citations page if required)

proofreading (after spell-checking) to find homonym problems (their/they're/there) and missing words, to check punctuation

PREPARING A PORTFOLIO

Writing classes often call for work to be presented in a final portfolio, in which the writer selects work to include and/or determines the arrangement of pieces and which should be highlighted in a final assessment. The most important strategy for working with a portfolio is to keep, in an organized way, all of the writing you do over a semester—from in-class free-writes, to observation notes, to drafts and revised versions of essays and reports. Portfolios are useful for both a writer and an instructor, because they show how writing is developing over time and they offer multiple examples of the important skills, such as those listed on the writing checklist above.

Selecting and Organizing Your Writing

Before you submit a portfolio, you will need to organize it in a way that makes sense to you and your instructor. Possible organizational strategies include the following:

- putting all of the pieces you have written in the order in which you have written them;

- dividing them into sections, such as "texts I feel are strong" and "those that could use more work";

- dividing the portfolio into sections for formal and informal writing;
- selecting a number of pieces that you most want to highlight.

For a research portfolio, you'll want to include all of the materials that didn't make it into your final report, as well as those that did. Typically researchers gather a lot of instances of whatever they're observing through observation notes, transcriptions, etc., while they're trying to understand whatever they're investigating, but they choose just some examples to report on, to illustrate what they've found. Nevertheless your research materials—your observation notes, your full transcripts and analyses of taperecorded interviews, conversations, your journal responses and/or research memos—provide rich evidence of the research you've done and of how your thinking has developed along the way. Or you may want to group them by levels of your own work with them—with one section for raw data, observation notes, or transcripts, a section for analyses, a section for reflections on what you were discovering. Your research portfolio should give a full picture of what you've done to achieve the understandings represented in your final report.

Whatever format you use, provide a guide or a table of contents, so that the reader of your portfolio knows what to find where. You may also want to include further comments on any of the work you've included—new understandings you came to later about an earlier analysis, an explanation of any problems you encountered. You may also want to extend some aspect of the work you've done—perhaps adding to a journal response or to an analytical essay.

PRESENTING AND REPORTING TO A GROUP

Preparing an Individual Oral Report

As you think about reporting back to your classmates about what you have learned while working on your own memoir, discourse community study, research report, or any other assignment, reconsider the term *shared knowledge*. As you present your work to the class, you will be building on the shared knowledge of this academic discourse community. Whenever you prepare a report, you should think about the following questions:

- What understandings have you come to that you think are important for other members of this classroom community to consider?
- What ideas could you discuss that would build upon the shared knowledge already created in this community and key concepts represented there? What new shared knowledge will you need to build?
- What about the work you have done has been significant to you?
- What specific examples, drawn from your work, will best show the understandings you want to share?

Once you have decided what understandings, ideas, or information you want to present, you should:

■ make some notes or an outline to follow while giving your presentation,

■ identify all of the important points you want to cover, and

■ follow this list or outline loosely as you give your presentation.

Before you give your presentation, go over in your mind what it is you want to say, and be sure that you are comfortable enough to relay your ideas in a calm and articulate way.

Preparing a Group Oral Report and/or a Written Overview of Work Members of a Group Have Done

To give an oral report or write a group overview, you will first want to:

■ survey and synthesize the work you have done individually

■ make a chart or use a mapping technique to visually arrange and connect ideas or points that emerge from each of your essays or studies and to review what it is individual group members have been working on

■ look for connections

  □ Are there any common themes present in all of your work?

  □ Are there similarities among the pieces you have written?

  □ Are there any differences that seem particularly important?

■ decide <u>what</u> aspects of your work you will highlight in your report or overview

  □ What are the important themes, ideas, points that emerge from viewing your work collectively?

  □ What are the most interesting examples, moments, details to support and highlight these points and to engage the interest of your listeners?

■ consider <u>how</u> you'll shape your presentation

  □ Will you focus on each participant's work individually, highlighting common themes and significant differences, or will you present the overarching themes and ideas, moving back and forth among the individual reports to provide examples and support?

  □ How much time or space will you give each project under either pattern of organization?

  □ If you'll organize the presentation around group members' individual work, what order will you place them in?

  □ How will you structure your presentation to get and hold your listeners' interest?

    ☐ Who will give an introduction or overview and who'll present specific points and examples, so that everyone has a role?

■ consider the <u>why</u> of this task as you think of ways to organize it

    ☐ Why do you think you are being asked to prepare this presentation?

    ☐ What ways of presenting seem to follow from this why?

    ☐ Why is what you've discovered, collectively, likely to be meaningful and significant to this audience, and how can you present what you've learned to build on others' shared knowledge, offer them new understandings, and show the significance of what's been learned?

These strategies can be adapted to report on different types of work. In reporting on memoirs, your group might find:

■ thematic connections among memoirs,

■ powerful moments from individual memoirs that address the common theme,

■ the ways in which the moments illustrate the theme.

In reporting on discourse community studies, members might address the following four elements:

■ connections among studies—by types of participants (male friends, female friends, coed friends), by setting (family/primary discourse communities, workplaces or gyms/secondary discourse communities), by the use of specific genres such as stories, by roles within the community and patterns of interaction (whether someone has most of the speaking rights or those rights are shared), or by the ways in which the communities draw on the wider culture (on music, sports, religion);

■ the most interesting moment or example from the writer's study;

■ how that moment works to represent something that's characteristic of the writer's discourse community;

■ what this study contributes to a larger understanding about discourse communities or discourse communities of this type.

In reporting on library research, groups might organize by related topics, exploring:

■ relationships among the individual research papers and how each might contribute to a larger topic,

■ the contributions each paper makes to the topic,

■ some of the specific evidence each paper offers as a contribution to the topic,

■ what understandings can be gained by seeing this larger topic in this multi-faceted way.

CONDUCTING FIELD RESEARCH

Field research involves moving out of the library and collecting data from the world around you. While there are particular types of data that will be specific to the study that you are doing (discussed in Parts II and III), there are several useful strategies for all field research.

Keeping an Observation Notebook

One of the best ways to take observation notes for any field research, including an ethnographic study, is with the double-entry notebook format explained under reading strategies.

When you keep an observation notebook in a double-entry format, you'll use it in the same way.

- In one column, you'll keep your detailed observation notes, recording what you observe about the setting and the people in it and about what they say and do there in as much detail as possible.

- In the second column, you'll want to add your own reflections on what you're seeing and hearing. You might reflect on the <u>how</u> and particularly on the <u>why</u> of a particular action or interaction. You might note that the action or interaction seems to reflect some aspect of the larger concerns and values of this group of people. You might reflect on connections between the ways in which people dress or act or some aspect of the setting and how they talk. You might make connections between what you're observing and what has been observed by other researchers whose studies you have read or are reading—Heath, or Spradley and Mann, for example, and the other researchers in your class.

- Make an entry for each period of observation, noting date, time, place, participants and any other aspects of the context that you think might be important.

- Review your entries and reflections periodically to look for emerging themes and questions and to guide you in your further observations.

Taping and Transcribing Conversations and Discussions

While an observation notebook can help you gather and make sense of a lot of observational data, audiotaping conversations, class discussions, or any other spoken exchanges allows you to look more closely at what goes on and how. Here are some general guidelines for taping:

- Decide on where and when you will be doing the taping, making sure that the participants you seek will be present;

- Ask the participants for permission to record the conversation or class. (It's unethical to record someone's words and to play them or transcribe them for others to hear or read without permission.) Most people don't mind participating if they know you're looking at the way that conversations are structured as part of a school research project and that they don't have to be identified by name if they don't want to be. While verbal permission is sufficient for an informal project, your class may decide to use a common written permission form. A typical format would be:

> I understand that [name] has recorded a conversation in which I was a participant as part of a research project for [course], and I give him/her permission to use that recording and a transcript of it for that project.
>
> Signed, _____.

■ Make sure the tape recorder is working properly. (Test it before you begin.)

■ As soon as possible after taping the conversation, jot down supporting notes about who was present, what was talked about, and anything else that you think might be significant. You'll find it easier to locate segments of the conversation that you want to return to if you sketch it out roughly before you listen to the whole thing, and then fill in your sketch as you do listen.

Videotaping allows you to capture nonverbal elements of a conversation, gestures, positions, etc., but it's much more intrusive.

Interviewing

Many studies draw on interviews of people in a setting. (An example is Willis's study of the informal group formed by working class British school boys on page 292.) In the context of the studies suggested in this book, you might want to extend your memoir by interviewing others who would have participated in the moments you've told about, getting their perspectives and understandings. In your study of a discourse community, you might want to replay your taped conversation for those who participated in it, and then interview them about what they think about what was going on and why. In your study of an academic discourse community, you're likely to want to interview your professor and/or your classmates from the class you've focused on, students from other sections of the course, or advanced students who are becoming real insiders to the field the course introduces. Or you might want to extend your work with your memoir by interviewing other participants in the events you have told about, seeing how their perspective adds to your own.

Here are some general suggestions for good interviews:

■ generate a list of questions in advance. Think about:

  ☐ the focus of your inquiry—the key themes and ideas that are emerging that this interview can help you to understand;

- what you think you already know about the areas you'll cover in this interview—what you want to confirm, what you want to learn more about, and what else you need to know;

- why you've chosen to interview this person, and what you hope to add to your understanding with the sort of information he/she is likely to be able to provide;

- whether you'll want the interviewee to look at something with you (such as the transcript from a conversation) or expand on what's said in a document you already have (such as a course syllabus). If so bring any relevant materials or documents with you.

- decide whether to tape the interview and transcribe it later, or to take detailed notes. If you tape, jotting down some notes as well will allow you to move back through the tape to find the sections you think are most significant.

- draw on your questions but be flexible in following up on any new ideas that emerge from the responses of the interviewee. Sometimes the most interesting ideas relate to things you haven't thought to ask a question about.

- ask your interviewee if you can contact him/her later about anything that's unclear to you or that you'd like to have more information about as you work with your notes or transcript.

Once you've transcribed your interview data or reviewed your notes, gloss your data, looking for key themes that fit with or add on to or alter the picture you had already developed.

Carrying Out a Survey

In some instances you might want to find out what a number of people think about a particular issue. For example, one student researcher, James, after observing that flirting was a common act in the discourse community formed by his college friends, decided to see what other students on campus thought about flirting. He designed a brief questionnaire and distributed it to students in the cafeteria and in other public gathering places on campus.

In planning a survey, think about:

- respondents. Who will be the most useful respondents for your purposes and where and how can you contact them?

- the process for the survey. Formal surveys that require a lot of thought from participants often involve the mailing of questionnaires but such mailings often have a low response rate. For a smaller or informal survey, you might want to distribute something that can be filled out on the spot (as James did with his campus survey) or to structure your survey so that you ask the questions and record or check off respondents' answers.

- demographic information. Decide which sorts of information about the respondents will be significant to your study. Do men and women have the same responses about flirting? Does age or academic status (freshmen versus seniors) matter? Do different cultural groups have different opinions about flirting or define flirting in different ways?

- the actual questions. Create questions that will get at the issues you want to explore. Try out your questions with a few people in advance, to see if you need to refine them to get the quality of response you need.

- the way you'll analyze your data and present your results. For informal surveys, you probably won't use any complex statistical methods of analysis, but you will want to pull out whatever seems significant in your data and present your results in a way that will be easy for readers to follow. You might find tables and graphs to be useful forms of display.

Keeping a Folder of Documents, Artifacts, and Related Materials

Researchers who are studying some aspect of the world directly, rather than through the library, nevertheless gather a variety of materials found in the setting they are studying. The term *artifacts* represents virtually anything that might be gathered—eating utensils, examples of art, clothing, as well as written texts. In your studies of discourse communities, the artifacts you gather will most likely be written texts—examples of the sorts of writing your friends or family do that give you a picture of their literacy practices; banking forms, restaurant menus, or other artifacts that represent shared knowledge in a workplace setting; course materials, assignments, and a syllabus for a course you are studying. But you might also want to reproduce a photograph that people refer to in a conversation, or to capture the lyrics from a song they're listening to.

As you move through your study, think about the materials that will contribute to your understanding of the shared knowledge, purposes, and ways of this discourse community and collect those in one place. Then look at them together, to see how they complement each other, what they add to the picture you've been developing from the other data you've been gathering, and what individual pieces you might want to analyze more closely in terms of what, why, and how in relationship to this discourse community context.

CONDUCTING LIBRARY RESEARCH

All research involves building on the inquiries and discoveries of prior researchers, and those who undertake field research also draw on library research to discover what others have learned that's related to the focus of their study. Researchers interested in the ethnography of communication, for example, will turn to the library to learn what other ethnographers have discovered about the communicative ways of communities, the methods they've used for their studies, the theory that helps them interpret what they're finding.

Library research (some of which takes place, not within the walls of the library itself, but by accessing electronically the resources the library makes available) is often referred to as secondary research because it draws on the research that others have done, and undergraduate research paper assignments often focus on discovering something about a topic by looking at prior research, rather than by conducting primary research in the field or in a lab. Many useful strategies for carrying out library research are imbedded in the suggestions for research memos in Part III of this book. This section provides an overview of strategies that you might want to use for any research paper, noting where a strategy is described more fully in a particular chapter.

Deciding on a Topic

Often broad topics for research papers are set in courses, but within those broad topics you generally have some choice about the specific topic you'll pursue. One starting strategy is to begin by brainstorming many possible topics and then sorting and selecting from them.

Finding a good topic typically depends on a mixture of three elements:

- your own interests and prior knowledge. Why are you interested in this topic? How did you come up with this idea? What prior knowledge do you bring to it? What do you hope to learn by pursuing it? How do you feel it will contribute to knowledge you might want to draw on in the future?

- the shared knowledge, understandings, and concerns set by the disciplinary and/or course context. Where does this topic fit into the areas of concern addressed in this field and in the course for which you're carrying out this research? What key concepts from your work thus far might help you explore this topic? What is your own research on this topic likely to contribute to the shared knowledge of the classroom?

- the extent to which the topic has been of interest to other researchers and thus the availability of resources about this topic. What do course readings suggest about the sorts of writing people do in this field and the kinds of materials that might be available? Once you start to look for materials, how much possibly relevant material do you find? How can you reshape your topic to reflect what you're actually finding to be available? (If you look at Juliette's research process in Chapter 9, you'll see how she worked with what she was finding to shape the way she addressed the topic of women in science in her final study.)

One concern for student researchers is working with a topic that is too broad. As you work with your topic and discover what resources are available, you'll want to keep focusing and narrowing it as much as possible. For example, the topic of "women and science," the starting point for Juliette Houlne's study, was very broad and led her in many different directions. Gradually she focused it on two specific issues of interest to her—attitudes to women scientists in the past, and the educational experiences of young girls that affect their self-esteem in this area of study.

Finding Information

Finding Information in the Library

■ Begin by taking an inventory of your current state of insider knowledge about the library.

Check off the elements that apply before you begin to work in the library, and recheck the list afterwards.

	Have you ever	At your college or university
1. visited a research library	____	____
2. used a library for research	____	____
3. used an electronic catalog of library holdings	____	____
4. looked up a book in the electronic catalog and found it in the stacks	____	____
5. used a guide to periodical literature (hard copy or electronic)	____	____
6. used an electronic database to access periodical literature	____	____
7. found a citation in an electronic database for periodical literature and then found the journal and the article	____	____
8. used a discipline-specific database (e.g., *Psychology Abstracts*)	____	____

	Have you ever	At your college or university
9. used key terms/key words to search an electronic database	____	____
10. used the electronic catalog to find out whether the library carries a specific journal	____	____
11. asked a reference librarian for help	____	____

As you search for research materials, try to expand your library skills. For example, if you already know how to search for an article using a general database like the *Expanded Academic Index,* try using a database that's specific to the field you've chosen and that you haven't used before.

■ Use library resources (and Internet resources discussed below) to build a working bibliography. Your working bibliography includes possible sources that you think might be useful to you. As you look at and sift through these sources, you'll eliminate some, and you probably won't use everything from your working bibliography in writing your final paper. You'll want to look for sources that are fairly recent, and that are reliable, as discussed below. If you use a database that offers abstracts, you'll be able to decide quickly whether a source provides relevant information for the question you're trying to answer. For a course research project, you'll probably decide to exclude materials that aren't available in your own library; however, most libraries belong to a larger consortium of libraries, and you can often arrange to get materials that your own library doesn't own or have direct access to.

■ Find possible sources of information in course texts and materials. One often overlooked source of information on many academic topics is material you've received in the course for which you're doing the research, or related courses. Most course texts include bibliographies, and articles will have a list of references or works cited. Look through the course materials you've received to see if any are closely related to the topic you've decided to research. If so, look to see what resources the writer or writers have drawn on, and seek out the ones that look most valuable through your own library and its databases. Generally, writers in a field will know and draw on some of the best-known and most respected studies in their own work, or they will critique other studies that they find less valuable. Your professor may also be able to guide you to other possible sources.

- Find possible resources through the library catalog and databases. See Chapter 9, and particularly Research Memos 9.1, 9.2, and 9.3, on carrying out your library research using these sources.

- Record information. You'll need to have bibliographic information for every source that you use in your paper, and as you sift through possible sources, you should record all of the necessary documentation information (see *Documenting Sources* below) for all of the sources you find potentially useful. You can keep bibliographic information on notecards (which can then be alphabetized when you prepare your bibliography), on electronic card file systems, or in a research notebook. Most journal articles have the necessary documentation information on the first page, so it will be available if you photocopy the article. For chapters in books, you'll need to record information about the book's publisher, place, and date of publication from the title page and the back of the title page. Decide also about how you'll take notes and what you'll find in these materials—using notecards, glossing, keeping a double-entry notebook are all good strategies.

- Evaluate the reliability and usefulness of your sources. If you've drawn from peer-reviewed scholarly journals, you'll know that what you find represents what was considered to be a substantial contribution to thinking on the topic at the time the article was written. (See discussion of the peer-review process for journals in Chapter 9.) Books in a college or research library have also been selected because they represent a perspective that faculty, research librarians, and other researchers who contribute to these selections consider to be important (even if they disagree with it). Articles with more recent dates will reflect the most current thinking, but many classic studies with earlier dates will continue to inform current thinking in the field, as is the case with Heath's study, *Ways with Words,* published in 1983. Reference materials, such as encyclopedia entries, have been carefully selected and are reliable. More general versus academic sources, such as popular news magazines or news articles, may reflect a variety of views—not all of which have been well-researched, and if you use such sources, check what they tell you against your other, more scholarly sources.

Finding Information Using Websites and Other Internet Resources

The Internet provides on-line access to libraries and their resources. But it also offers other sources of information through webpages and through discussion groups.

- *Find information.* Using *browser* software such as *Internet Explorer* or *Netscape Communicator,* you can enter the addresses (known as URL's) for sites that you know (such as your library). Using a *search engine* provided with these browsers or another such as Yahoo (http://www.yahoo.com) or AltaVista (http://www.altavista.com), you can enter keywords related to your topic, and the search engine will search the database it has created from the materials available on the Internet. Yahoo also connects with a webcrawler, Google, that is programmed to scan all text on the web to find the words you've entered.

When you begin to use a search engine, go to the link provided on the home page that gives you information and tips about how to use it effectively. Use the same key word strategies that you'd use in library research. Most on-line resources use similar syntax—ways to put combinations of words together. Searching for *discourse* AND *communities* on Yahoo will bring up all sites on which both of the terms appear, separately or together (over 181,000 webpages). Searching for "discourse communities" with the quotation marks to indicate that the two words should be kept together as a unit brings up all sites in which the combined term appears (over 21,000 webpages). Many of these webpages are associated with writing courses and have been created by instructors to provide course information and assignments, some are from university catalogs, and some are from book publishers. You'll see in the following examples that the search results give the title for the webpage on which the words appear, a few surrounding words that offer some sense of the context, and web addresses (URL's) for both the particular page and the larger site on which that page appears; edu at the end of the URL designates an educational institution, and com a commercial one.

> <u>Bedford Books—The Bedford Bibliography: Curriculum Development</u>. Fifteen essays examine the textual construction of professions, the dynamics of professional **discourse communities,** and the operational force of texts . . . http://www.bedfordstmartins.com/ bb/curr11.html. More results from: www.bedfordstmartins.com.
>
> <u>Master of Arts in Rhetoric: Intercultural Rhetoric</u>. At and across the borders of linguistic difference, or at the tacit borders of disciplinary and **discourse communities?** How do our literate practices, social purposes, and cultural patterns . . . http://english.cmu.edu/degrees/ marhetoric/intercultural.html. More results from: english.cmu.edu.

A search engine like Yahoo will search not only for websites and webpages, but also for news sites, and for research documents. If you want to search for material on discourse communities, you'll find that the term appears not only on many webpages, but in many research documents, typically in academic journals like the ones indexed in the library's electronic databases. The term rarely appears in news articles however, suggesting that it's primarily a term that is used within academic communities.

Your search may also point to postings from electronic discussions— newsgroups, web-based forums, and electronic mailing lists (often referred to as listservs), where people can contribute to ongoing conversations in an area. For most college research projects, you probably won't want to have to follow an extended conversation about a topic, but at some point you might want to subscribe (add your name to the mailing list via e-mail) to a group that's likely to talk about that topic. For example, the topic of discourse communities comes up frequently in electronic conversations at **saussure.linguistlist.org**. Electronic discussion groups form another sort of discourse community—one made up of people who share an interest in a topic—a medical concern, dog breeding, assessment in schools—and such on-line communities have also been studied by academic researchers.

■ *Record information.* When you've found a website that's useful, be sure to record the web address/URL, either writing it down or copying and pasting it into a word-processing document for research notes on your computer. It's also possible to copy and paste information from the site to your own document of research notes, particularly where you think you might want to quote it directly. But be very careful not to copy the original text into your own without quoting directly. The same web-crawler resources that can track down the words you're using in your search can track down a sequence of words from your paper making it a simple matter for professors to uncover plagiarism.

One important issue to consider in using Internet sources for academic research is documentation—what information you need to capture in order to be able to give a reference for a webpage or a newsgroup conversation. For a webpage you'll need to include:

—the author's name (if known)

—the title of the work or the page

—the full http address (http://www._____)

—the date of your visit to that page

For newsgroup and e-mail citations:

—the author's name

—the subject line from the posting

—the address of the listserv or newslist (personal e-mail can just be listed as "personal e-mail" without the actual address)

—the date

To return easily to a site you've found, you can save the site with the bookmark function on your browser.

■ *Evaluate information.* Material accessed through research libraries and their databases has generally been reviewed through the peer review processes of academic publishers and academic journals; even where data or interpretations of data conflict, these materials represent information and ways of seeing that information that people in the field find valuable. Information posted on webpages or offered through electronic discussions has not been reviewed in this way. Ways of evaluating the information you find include seeing who's responsible for a website, seeing what you know about the qualifications of the company or organization or person responsible for the information presented there, considering whether there's any obvious self-interest—on the part of a company for example—in a recommendation or a position that's given, seeing whether the site includes ratings or recommendations from other readers, and seeing how the information on the site fits with what you've learned from other sources.

Gathering, Organizing, and Synthesizing Information

A common concern in doing library research is how to manage the information you gather, both practically and intellectually. To start with, you'll want to:

- Organize your information as you gather it. Keep a folder of articles you've photocopied, notes you've taken, printouts you've made. Have a folder on your computer desktop with any working files that relate to your paper. As you begin to think about what you'll draw on to answer your research question, create a guide for yourself to what's where.

- Read back through the materials you've gathered, glossing information that you're likely to draw on by summarizing or paraphrasing it (see Chapter 9, pp. 422–424) or through direct quotation.

- Begin to explore ways to synthesize the information you've gathered, to bring different pieces together and place them in relationship to one another. At this stage a visual organizer like the web or the chart described under Writing Strategies, is very useful in helping you connect ideas and compare what different sources have to say about your topic. As you begin to discover connections and relationships, you'll want to create a working outline that lets you see how your own report will build, where you'll address particular points, and where you'll bring in the evidence of the information you've gathered.

Research writing, while it typically brings together a significant amount of information from a variety of sources, nevertheless relies on the sorts of strategies you use for all of your writing.

Working with Sources and Avoiding Plagiarism

One of the norms of writing in all academic and most public discourse communities is that you must tell your readers when you've used words, ideas, or information from another source, if what you've used isn't general knowledge or a common expression. A major purpose of the conversations that go on, in both speaking and writing, in these communities is to create and share knowledge about the world, and the intellectual work that is carried on, whether by individuals or groups, always involves building on the understandings of others and placing new ideas in relationship to what has come before. Therefore, readers want to know not only what was said earlier, but who said it and where, and to be able to go back and find the source of information that a writer has used—very often to examine that source and see what further understandings are offered there. Because of the nature of the work of academic communities, accurate citation and documentation of sources is a significant shared value, and violating the rules not only marks you as an outsider, but may evoke the sorts of outraged responses that members of any discourse community are likely to exhibit when someone violates the rules associated with one of their core values. (That's why university codes for student behavior stress this issue as an aspect of academic honesty, and the penalties for violating the rules are often severe.) For further suggestions for avoiding plagiarism, go to the web site: http://www.lib.duke.edu/libguide/plagiarism.htm.

Most student writers who don't cite and document sources accurately aren't intentionally violating the insider rules, but just aren't sure of all of the nuances of working appropriately with other sources. Here are three simple rules to follow:

- Use quotation marks around the exact words that you quote from a source (or use a block indented form for quotations longer than four lines).

- Give the source for whatever you quote, paraphrase, or summarize.

- When you paraphrase (giving a detailed version in your own words) or summarize (giving a brief version in your own words) something you've read, step away from your original source and think of how else to word the information you find there. Changing the sentence structure around may help. For example, here are a few sentences from Heath's introduction to storytelling in Roadville, and two ways of restating that information.

Original Version

> Stories recount an actual event either witnessed by others or previously told in the presence of others and declared by them 'a good story.' Roadville residents recognize the purpose of the stories is to make people laugh by making fun of either the storyteller or a close friend in sharing an event and the particular actions of individuals within that event. However, stories 'told on' someone other than the storyteller are never told unless the central character or someone who is clearly designated his representative is present (149).

Too Closely Paraphrased Version

Here the writer has made small changes but keeps much of the wording and the sentence structure of the original, as you can see in the bolded words. In most cases the writer hasn't copied the words exactly but has turned them around a little to try to avoid plagiarizing—"Residents of Roadville" replaces "Roadville residents." But most of the words and the structure of ideas from one sentence to the next haven't been changed.

> As Heath tells us, in **Roadville,** people tell stories to **recount actual events** that **others have witnessed** or heard told and that have been **declared to be a good story. Residents of Roadville** understand that

stories have **the purpose of making people laugh by making fun of either the storyteller or the storyteller's friend** when telling about an event and the **ways individuals acted within that event**. But stories aren't ever **told on someone other than the storyteller** unless the **central character** or a **representative** of that person **is present** (149).

Acceptably Paraphrased Version

Here the writer has kept Heath's key points but has moved farther in the direction of representing the points in new language. A few key ideas are still captured with Heath's words, but there are only two phrases that have been drawn directly from Heath: **make people laugh** and **make fun**—ideas that it's hard to represent accurately in other words. More significantly, the writer has provided a new summarizing phrase in the first sentence, "have their own purposes," and has reordered some of Heath's points, while keeping the sense of the original.

> As Heath tells us, people in **Roadville** have their own purposes for story-telling. They use stories to **make people laugh,** and to **make fun** of themselves or their close friends by describing their actions in whatever **events** are talked about. They always focus on events that have actually happened and that others have already found to be **a good story.** But they never tell stories about people who aren't **present** themselves or **represented** by a friend or family member (149).

Brief Summary

Here the writer has reduced Heath's version to one sentence and put the name of the source into the end of the sentence citation.

> In the community of Roadville, stories are told to make people laugh, making fun of the storyteller or others who are present, but not of those who aren't there (Heath, 149).

Note that source information is given for the summary and paraphrase as well as the quotation.

Synthesis

A synthesis of material from different sources often brings together several brief summaries and places them in relationship to one another. For example, in the notes to her chapter on "Oral Traditions," Heath synthesizes the research done by others on the structure of stories as follows:

> Roadville's stories as coached by adults make especially apparent the story-grammars or story-schemata children learn in those situations in which adults ask them to tell about an experience. . . . This naturally-occurring request for story-recall bears many similarities to the recall tasks experimental psychologists have given children and adults in laboratory settings. There children are read or told a story and then asked to recall the narrative. Researchers have then derived models of story structures from these recalls. For example, Rumelhart's (1975)

proposal of a story grammar, as developed in the research of Mandler and Johnson 1977, Stein 1978, and Stein and Glenn, 1979, includes a setting episode, initial
development, reaction, and outcome in the structure of children's recall of fantasy
stories. Botvin and Sutton-Smith 1977 applies Propp's (1968) structural analysis
of fairy tales to children's fantasy narratives and sketches a developmental pattern
of plot and form complexity (see also Sutton-Smith, Botvin, and Mahoney 1976).
Applebee 1978 analyzes the plot-structure, content, and evolution of the stories
of children aged two to five years. The stories of Roadville children from a very
early age fit, with two exceptions, the characteristics of story-grammars based on
story-recall in laboratory experiments. First, as Roadville children grow older,
their plots do not develop the complexity described for children of their age by
Botvin and Sutton-Smith 1977 and Sutton-Smith 1980b. Their plots are bound by
both chronology and the "real" experience as conceived by an adult coaching the
narrative. Second, Roadville children rarely tell fanciful stories. (1983, p. 382)

Notice how Heath begins by making a connection between the naturally
occurring stories in Roadville and the stories that children have been asked to
recall in laboratory settings, then brings together and summarizes what was
learned about story structures by different researchers, and then returns to
state the relevance of this research to what she's learned about the structure of
Roadville children's stories.

A real danger when using electronically available materials is that you'll
inadvertently copy sections from a text that you've downloaded into your own
paper, without adequately paraphrasing what you've found. Be extra careful
not to copy and paste anything but what you want to use as an exact quotation,
and put quotation marks around it.

When you're drawing directly from a source, whether through quotation,
summary, or paraphrase, you will always want to cite that source. But what if
you're drawing on information that the readers you're writing for are likely to
know? Whether you need a citation depends a great deal on what is shared
knowledge in the community you're writing for. For example, if you have
been reading and discussing Heath's study of Roadville and Trackton in the
classroom, and you write about that study in an essay, you'll need to give
source information (in this case, a page number) for places where you draw directly from the text by quoting or paraphrasing. But in the same classroom, the
fact that people in Roadville tell stories to make people laugh, or that the person
is supposed to be present, is likely to be common knowledge. In that case, you
might write a summary sentence about what Heath found about storytelling in
Roadville without having to give a specific page number. On the other hand, if
you were writing about Heath for another academic community, one where participants didn't share a deep knowledge of Heath's study, you'd need to point
to that study if you mentioned its major points at all. For example,

In some communities, people use stories to make fun of themselves and to point out
their own failings; in others, they may use stories to make fun of others and to
reassert their own power (Heath, 1983).

In deciding what's commonly shared knowledge that you don't need to document, you'll want to consider the discourse community you're writing for.

DOCUMENTING SOURCES

One of the most important conventions for written conversations is giving appropriate credit for ideas and words that you draw from other writers. All academic discourse communities have the shared assumption that other writers' work must be credited and the source of those words and ideas must be documented. But different segments of the academic world have different expectations for exactly how, technically, this should be done, both within a text and in the reference/works cited section that appears at the end of a paper. There are several major styles that are used in different disciplines including:

- MLA (Modern Language Association) style. This style is typically used in the humanities, and is the style normally expected in English courses.
- APA (American Psychological Association) style. This style is typically used in the social sciences and education and is generally expected in courses in those areas.

Because this book focuses primarily on readings and research drawn from the humanities and social sciences, the following brief discussion of citation and documentation information will focus on these two styles. (More detailed information about these documentation styles can be found in most handbooks and style manuals.)

Other styles are typically used in other disciplines, for example: CMS (Chicago Manual of Style) in history and other areas of arts and sciences; and CBE (Council of Biology Editors) style, in many of the natural sciences. All of these styles are supplemented with guidelines for citing online sources from the Internet through COS (Columbia Online Style).

The several styles offer the same basic information but in different formats, with different details about the order of information and about capitalization, punctuation, line-spacing, etc. They have different rules for citations that appear within the text in parentheses. They even differ as to how to label the reference page: APA style uses the heading "References"; MLA style uses the heading "Works Cited." These two terms are used for works the writer has actually referred to or quoted in the text of a paper. A "Bibliography" includes a wider range of materials on the topic.

For a research report, you'll need to decide with your professor about the style that you will follow. If the choice of style is up to the individual writer, you may want to choose the style of the disciplines you're likely to take the most courses in—to begin to practice a style that you'll be using a lot. If you expect to be doing a lot of work in another disciplinary area or are accustomed to using another documentation style, you may want to ask a course instructor if you can continue to work in that style. The most important concern is that you be consistent in following the style you've selected.

The documentation style you choose will govern both what you include in in-text citations where you give source information within your text, and what you include in your list of works cited/references. The purpose of a list of works cited is to allow readers to go back to the sources you've referred to for further information if something you've cited interests them. Including such a list in a research report is one of the necessary elements of the genre—one that's expected in all academic discourse communities that use variations on the research report genre.

MLA Style (Used in the Humanities)

In-Text Citations

Insert source information in your text, immediately after the quoted, paraphrased, or summarized information before the end punctuation of a sentence or clause. For a longer quotation in block format, put citation information outside of the end punctuation.

- If you are discussing only one text, or if you've included the author's name in your introduction to the quotation, summary, or paraphrase, use a page number in parentheses before end punctuation. (If you've used a block quotation, put the page number in parentheses outside of the end punctuation.)

     Example for a paper wholly about Heath's "Oral Traditions," where you've included her name and the title in your introduction.

    > "In Roadville, in telling a story, an individual shows that he belongs to the group. He knows about either himself or the story, and he understands the norms which were broken by the story's central characters" (211).

     Example for a paper in which the writer has referenced Heath in the introduction to a quotation or paraphrase.

    > Heath points out some of the conventions of storytelling in Roadville: "a major requirement of a 'good story' [is that] it must be factual, and any exaggeration or hyperbole must be so qualified as to let the audience know the story-teller does not accept such descriptions as literally true" (213).

- If you are making a general reference to a source as a whole, you don't need a page number.

    > Heath describes the typical features of storytelling in two communities, Roadville and Trackton.

- If you are writing a paper that draws on several sources, and you haven't included the author's name in your introduction to the quotation, summary, or paraphrase, include both author and page number in parentheses before the end punctuation.

"The form, occasions, content, and functions of . . . stories differ greatly" (Heath 228). The same is true of shared rituals in other settings, such as ordering a drink in a bar (Spradley and Mann).

Note that the first sentence makes a specific reference to a particular place in Heath's text. The second sentence gives a general reference, to an overall idea in Spradley and Mann's study that is supported throughout the text. Therefore it doesn't include a specific page number.

■ If you are using more than one work by the same author, include a brief form of the title in your citation.

"The patterns of interaction surrounding the actual telling of a story vary considerably from Roadville to Trackton" (Heath, "Oral Traditions" 228).

List of Works Cited

Your list of works cited should include every source you've referred to in your paper and should follow the last page of your text.

Use the title "Works Cited."

Use a hanging indent for each entry, in which the first line of an entry starts at the left margin and following lines are indented five spaces.

Arrange your entries in alphabetical order by the last name of the author. If you have more than one work by an author, arrange them alphabetically by title.

Double space.

■ Books

Give last and first name of author and any middle name or initial followed by a period.

Give title, underlined, and capitalize main words, followed by a period.

Give publication information, beginning with the city of publication, followed by a colon, then the publisher's name, followed by a comma, and then the year of publication with a period. For "university press" in the publisher's name, you may use the abbreviation UP.

□ One author

Heath, Shirley Brice. <u>Ways with Words.</u> Cambridge UK: Cambridge UP, 1983.

□ Two or three authors

Spradley, James, and Brenda Mann. <u>The Cocktail Waitress: Woman's Work in a Man's World.</u> New York: Wiley, 1975.

□ For four or more authors, give the first author, followed by *et al* (Latin for "and others").

□ If no author is given, alphabetize by the first main word of the title.

☐ If the book is an edited collection, use the same format as above but include ed. or eds. (for more than one editor) after the editor's name(s).

■ Articles and book chapters

Give last and first name of author and any middle name or initial followed by a period.

Give title of article or chapter in quotation marks and capitalize main words, followed by a period inside the quotation marks.

Give the title of the book or journal, underlined and followed by a period.

If the book is an edited collection by someone other than the author of the article, use ed. followed by the editor's first and last name.

Give publication information for books, beginning with the city of publication, followed by a colon, then the publisher's name, followed by a comma, and then the year of publication with a period.

For articles, give the volume and issue number, year of publication, and page numbers.

☐ Selection from a book by the author

Heath, Shirley Brice. "Oral Traditions." <u>Ways with Words</u>. Cambridge UK: Cambridge UP, 1983.

☐ Article in a journal

Mellix, Barbara. "From Outside, In." <u>The Georgia Review</u> 41.2 (1987): 258–67.

☐ Unpublished writing

Karen Thornton. "Memoir." Unpublished Essay. UMass/Boston, 1999.

For more than one author, list names in the same ways as suggested under books.

■ Field Resources

☐ Interviews

Juliette Houlne. Personal Interview. 20 April, 2002.

☐ Conversations (not specified in MLA)

Conversation of 6 November, 2000. Taped and transcribed by Pebely Vargas.

☐ Observations (not specified in MLA)

Vargas, Pebely. Observations of Cafeteria Conversations. November 1–22, 2001.

☐ Lectures

White, Brian. Lecture in Biology 111. UMass/Boston. 17 April, 2001.

■ Online sources

For on-line sources, try to supply as much information as possible in a format that's comparable to that used for a print source.

Include author, title, and other publication information.

Give the date the material was posted.

Give the URL or Internet address.

Give the date that you accessed the source.

Give any page information provided.

(Columbia online style information can be found at http://www.columbia.edu/cu/cup/cgos/basic.html)

- E-mail

    Anderson, Kevin. E-mail exchange with ____. September 28, 2001.

More detailed information on MLA documentation style can be found in most handbooks and style manuals and on the Web at http://www.mla.org/set_stl.htm, or at http://www.wisc.edu/writing/Handbook/Documentation.html

APA Style (Used in the Social Sciences)

In-Text Citations

APA style emphasizes the date of publication, which is always included in the text when a source is mentioned. Insert the date of publication in parentheses after the author's name or immediately after the quoted, paraphrased, or summarized information before the end punctuation of a sentence or clause. Use p. before a page number. For a longer quotation in block format, put citation information outside of the end punctuation.

- If you don't use the author's name in introducing your quotation, summary or paraphrase, include name, date, and page in parentheses before the end punctuation.

    "In telling a story, an individual shows that he belongs to the group: he knows about either himself or the story, and he understands the norms which were broken by the story's central characters" (Heath, 1983, p. 211).

- If you use the author's name in the introduction to a quotation or paraphrase, put the date in parentheses immediately after the name.

    Heath (1983) points out some of the conventions of storytelling in Roadville: "a major requirement of a 'good story' [is that] it must be factual, and any exaggeration or hyperbole must be so qualified as to let the audience know the story-teller does not accept such descriptions as literally true" (p. 213).

- If you are making a general reference to a source as a whole, you don't need a page number, but you do need the date.

    Heath (1983) describes the typical features of storytelling in two communities, Roadville and Trackton.

- If you are writing a paper that draws on several sources, and you haven't included the author's name in your introduction to the quotation, summary or paraphrase, include author, date, and page number in parentheses before end punctuation.

> "The form, occasions, content, and functions of . . . stories differ greatly" (Heath, 1983, p. 228). The same is true of shared rituals in other settings, such as ordering a drink in a bar (Spradley & Mann, 1975).

Note that the first sentence makes a specific reference to a particular place in Heath's text. The second sentence gives a general reference, to an overall idea in Spradley and Mann's study that is supported throughout the text. Therefore it doesn't include a specific page number. Note also that the ampersand (&) is used in place of "and" when listing two authors within parentheses.

- If you are using more than one work by the same author, written in the same year, add *a*, *b*, etc. to the dates.

> "The patterns of interaction surrounding the actual telling of a story vary considerably from Roadville to Trackton" (Heath, 1983a, p. 228).

- If you cite a work more than once within a paragraph, you don't need to repeat the date if the reference is clear.
- For webpages, cite the URL in parentheses.

Reference List

Your list of references should include every source you've referred to in your paper on a separate page following the last page of your text.

Use the heading "References" (without quotation marks). Center the heading.

Use a hanging indent for each entry, in which the first line of an entry starts at the left margin and following lines are indented five spaces.

Arrange your entries in alphabetical order by the last name of the author. If you have more than one work by an author, arrange them by date of publication.

Double space the references.

- Books

  Give last name of author, then initials.

  Give date in parentheses, followed by a period.

  Give title, underlined, with only the first word (and the first word after a colon) capitalized, followed by a period.

  Give publication information, beginning with the city of publication, followed by a colon, then the publisher's name, followed by a period.

  □ One author

> Heath, S. B. (1983). <u>Ways with words.</u> Cambridge UK: Cambridge University Press.

☐ Two or more authors

> Spradley, J., & Mann, B. (1975) <u>The cocktail waitress: Woman's work in a man's world.</u> New York: Wiley.

☐ Give names of all authors, no matter how many there are.

☐ If no author is given, alphabetize by the first main word of the title.

☐ If the book is an edited collection, use the same format as above but include ed. or eds. (for more than one editor) after the editor's name(s).

■ Articles and book selections

Give last and first name of author and any middle name or initial followed by a period.

Give the date in parentheses.

Give the title of the article or chapter and capitalize only the first word (and proper names), followed by a period. Do not use quotation marks.

Give the title of the book or journal, underlined and followed by a period. Capitalize the title of a journal. Capitalize only the first word of a book title.

If the book is an edited collection by someone other than the author of the article, use ed. followed by the editor's first and last name.

Give publication information for books, beginning with the city of publication, followed by a colon, then the publisher's name, followed by a period.

For articles, give the volume number and page numbers.

☐ Selection from a book by the author

> Heath, S. B. (1983). Oral traditions. <u>Ways with words</u>. Cambridge UK: Cambridge University Press.

☐ Article in a journal

> Mellix, B. (1987). From Outside, In. <u>The Georgia Review</u>, 41, 258–67.

☐ Unpublished writing

> Karen Thornton. "Memoir." Unpublished Essay. UMass/Boston, 1999.

For more than one author, list names in the same ways as suggested under books.

■ Field Resources

☐ Interviews

> Cite the interview only in the text, not in the references. (J. Houlne, personal interview, April 20, 2002.)

☐ Conversations, observations, and other unpublished raw data. Include topic in brackets.

> Vargas, P. (2000). [Transcript of cafeteria conversation]. Unpublished raw data.
>
> Vargas, P. (2000). [Observations of cafeteria conversations]. Unpublished raw data.
>
> Houlne, J. (2001). [Transcript of Biology 111 by Brian White]. Unpublished raw data.

■ Online sources

For on-line sources, try to supply as much information as possible in a format that's comparable to that used for a print source.

Include author, title, and other publication information.

Give the date the material was posted.

Give the URL or Internet address.

Give the date that you accessed the source.

Give any page information provided.

(Columbia online style information can be found at http://www.columbia.edu/cu/cup/cgos/basic.html)

☐ E-mail. Include citation only in the text, as personal communication.

> (Anderson, K., personal communication, September 28, 2001).

More detailed information on APA documentation style can be found in most handbooks and style manuals and on the Web at http://www.apa.org and at http://www.wisc.edu/writing/Handbook/Documentation.html.

For information on other styles, consult a style manual that contains them or one of the following webpages at a site maintained by the University of Wisconsin Writing Center:

For CMS (the Chicago Manual of Style), used by some fields in the arts and sciences, such as history, go to http://www.wisc.edu/writing/Handbook/DocChicago.html.

For CBE (Council of Biology Editors), used in the natural sciences, go to http://www.wisc.edu/writing/Handbook/DocCBE.html.

abstract   A concise summary or overview of a paper. Abstracts are typically included at the beginning of scholarly articles in the social sciences and sciences.

academic article   A genre of writing through which scholars share knowledge in the journals of their field.

academic essay   An essay in one of the genres that is typically used in academic settings.

academic lecture   A speech genre, common in academic settings, in which one speaker presents information and ideas to listeners in an extended turn.

academic literacy   The uses of reading and writing that are typical in academic contexts.

academic style   A style, typical of much academic writing, which focuses more on the presentation of knowledge than on interpersonal engagement, and which is often characterized by densely-packed information and highly integrated syntax.

analysis   A type of critical thinking that involves identifying the parts of something (an object, an argument, a text), and seeing how the parts work together in relationship to each other and to the whole.

analytical reading   A way of reading that involves stepping back from a text to see how it works and why it works that way.

appropriateness   The adjustment of language style to particular settings and purposes.

artifacts of literacy   Objects, such as books and newspapers, associated with literacy use; any object (such as a poster) that includes writing.

assumed shared knowledge   The prior knowledge that a writer or speaker expects readers or listeners to bring to a particular moment of reading or listening.

character   A person portrayed in a work of literature or other creative medium. A concept used in literary analysis to address how people are portrayed and why they are portrayed as they are.

citation   The acknowledgement of someone else's work in one's own spoken or written text.

clarity   Clear, accessible thought and expression in writing or speaking.

classification system (Library of Congress)   A method of classifying knowledge systematically by fields, subfields, and authors that is used to organize print and recorded materials in the U.S. national library and in most academic libraries.

coherence   The quality in writing or speaking of having all parts connect clearly to a whole. Coherence is typically achieved through the repetition of nouns and the use of pronouns and through the use of transitional expressions that show how one sentence or paragraph relates to another. (The overall thematic and structural unity of a larger spoken or written text.)

collected papers   A genre of academic book that brings together a set of articles or essays that have been published elsewhere by one writer on different topics or by different writers on a common topic.

competence   A speaker's or writer's underlying knowledge of the grammatical system of a language.

concept map   A visual representation of the key terms and ideas in an area of study.

concreteness   The quality in writing or speaking of being definite, detailed and specific.

context   The environment or surroundings of a particular text or event. May include the textual context—the surrounding sentences and paragraphs; the situational context—the setting, participants, etc.; and the cultural context—the larger understandings and knowledge that participants share.

conventions   A set of shared understandings within a group about the customary ways of doing things. Standard American Written English represents a set of conventions for representing, in writing, the written language as it is used for public purposes in the United States.

conversational data   Conversations captured through audio-recording or detailed note-taking for the purpose of study and analysis.

critical analysis   Analyzing and evaluating an event, object, or text, often from a particular perspective or in relation to particular criteria.

critical perspective   An evaluative perspective from which one judges something in relationship to particular criteria.

cultural expectations/norms   The shared assumptions within a group about how any behavior or activity will be carried out.

culture   The shared beliefs, values, and practices of a group.

culture of a setting   The shared ways of frequent participants in a setting, even when they don't otherwise form a coherent cultural group.

database   A systematically arranged collection of data, structured so that it can be automatically retrieved or manipulated by computer. Library reference materials include databases of scholarship within various fields that can typically be retrieved by author, subject, or key word.

detachment   A quality of much formal written style that eliminates most evidence of personal stance and interpersonal connection; the opposite of involvement in speaking and writing.

dialogue   In speaking and writing, the inclusion of the actual words of another speaker or text; an interaction between the writer's words and the words of others.

discipline   An academic field, subject, or area of study.

discourse   Language as used by speakers and writers in actual communicative contexts; the shared language of a setting or a field.

discourse community   A community of people, small or large, who share interests, purposes, beliefs, values, *and* ways of talking or writing about them.

discourse competence   The knowledge of how to use language in ways that are appropriate to particular discourse settings; the ability to function in insider ways within a discourse community and to adapt to new discourse settings.

discourse style   The characteristic ways of using language for particular purposes within a particular discourse context.

documentation   Providing a source or reference for information, ideas, or quotations.

documentation style   A set of conventions for providing information about the sources of information, ideas or quotations. Different disciplines use different documentation styles such as the MLA and APA styles presented in Part IV.

elaborating   Providing extended discussion and detail in speaking or writing.

ethnographic report   A genre of academic writing presenting the results of small studies that use ethnographic methods.

ethnography   An extended study of the life and culture of a group of people, using field research methods that include observing the group's actions and behaviors, studying the objects and artifacts that are important to their lives, and recording their interactions, stories, and traditions.

ethnography of communication   A study that focuses on the communicative behavior of a group and the relationship between its ways of communicating and other aspects of the group's culture.

evaluative reading   A way of reading that involves not only stepping back from a text to see how it works and why, but also judging how well it works in relationship to a particular purpose or concern.

explicitness   Being detailed and direct in speaking and writing; providing background and stating meanings clearly rather than leaving them implicit.

exploratory essay   A semi-formal genre of academic writing in which the emphasis is on exploring and giving shape to ideas rather than presenting them in a final, tightly-structured form.

focus   In writing, having a clear direction, emphasis, or area of concern.

formal writing   Writing that follows the conventions for language, style and genre that are appropriate to a particular setting and purpose and that is intended for public or semi-public (such as school) rather than private purposes.

fragmentation   The quality (characteristic of speaking) of adding ideas one at a time rather than integrating them in more syntactically complex sentences.

frames of mind, traditions, and values   The ways of thinking about and viewing particular areas of knowledge that are characteristic of academic fields; the shared knowledge, beliefs, and values of academic discourse communities.

framing   Defining how something will be viewed, the lens or perspective from which it will be approached.

functional theory of language/discourse theory of language   A theory of grammar that explains how language works in relationship to the functions it serves in human communication and the ways it allows for extended interaction. The best-known functional theory of language is that of M. A. K. Halliday. *See* ideational function; interpersonal function; textual function.

genre   A type of spoken or written text (or other representation) involving characteristic form, style, and/or subject matter that arises when speech or writing is used repeatedly within similar situations for similar purposes.

glossary   A list of key terms and their meanings, drawn from a particular context (such as a book or a course).

glossing   The act of marking up a written text; recording the reader's interactions with the text.

ideational function (what)   The use of language to present ideas, state propositions, create and maintain shared knowledge; what is talked or written about.

identity kit   The various discourses or ways of using language that an individual can use to realize particular identities (to take on the role of professor, chemistry major, or soccer player) in particular settings.

imagery   In writing, a representation of ideas, experiences, or events through either literal images such as sensory details or figurative images such as metaphors.

immediate situation   An aspect of context that includes the time and place of a conversation or speech act and the participants who are directly involved in it.

informal writing   Writing that is not intended for formal public purposes and that does not have to address the conventions for genre, form, and style that are associated with formal writing; informal genres include early essay drafts, journal responses, and research memos.

integration   The use of complex sentences and other syntactic features in writing that bring a lot of information together rather than adding it gradually; the opposite of fragmentation.

interpersonal function (why)   The use of language to maintain an interpersonal relationship in speaking and writing, to create and maintain individual and/or shared purposes.

interpretation   An explanation or determination of the meaning or significance of something.

intertextuality   The relationship between texts or the reference in one text to another, either directly or indirectly.

involvement   The use of features, such as the first and second person pronouns (you and I), that reflect an interpersonal interaction between speakers and listeners or writers and readers; the opposite of detachment.

key word searches   A way of accessing information through library databases by searching on words and combinations of words that are closely associated with the topic.

language variation   How a particular language varies in regular ways among the people who use it, whether geographical (variation in how English is spoken in different parts of the United States) or social (variation in how English is spoken within different social settings and circumstances within the same region).

literacy functions   The purposes for which people use reading and writing.

literacy practices   The typical ways in which people use reading and writing.

memoir   A genre of formal writing in which the writer recounts past experience from a present perspective.

meta-level understanding   Going beyond the process of gaining new understandings to perceive how you do so and how these understandings are related to others. Going beyond thinking or using language in particular ways to understand how and why you do so.

naming   An aspect of critical thinking that involves identifying and giving a name to what you observe.

observation account   A genre of informal writing in academic settings for reporting in detail on what you observe but without the requirement of a formal report structure.

on-line catalog   The record of a library's holdings that is accessible on-line, through a computer terminal.

paraphrase   A restatement of someone else's ideas in the speaker's or writer's own words.

participant's stance   Taking the perspective of an insider participant in a setting.

participatory reading   A way of reading that involves stepping into a text and participating with the flow of what the writer has written.

patterns of unconventional and mixed forms   The regular patterns of forms of language that would not be used by insiders to a setting but that appear when speakers and writers are moving from one language setting to another and are hypothesizing about the appropriate forms for the new setting.

peer response   A genre of communication in the writing classroom in which students respond, through speaking or writing, to each others' written texts; peer review of writing.

performance   (1) A speaker's or writer's actual production of language at a given moment as opposed to the speaker's underlying knowledge of the grammatical system of the language (or discourse requirements of a setting). (2) The display of physical or verbal behaviors to gain the attention of others in a setting.

personal framework of understanding   The structure of prior knowledge, present understandings, and new ideas that each individual creates and recreates in the process of learning.

point of view   The perspective from which events are narrated. A concept used in literary analysis to describe the ways the reader is presented with the materials of the story—whether from the perspective of a particular character or through a narrator who is not limited to individual characters' perspectives.

positioning/being positioned   The way in which someone (a reader, a learner) is placed in relationship to a text or experience, such as being positioned as someone who is competent, who brings knowledge, authority and the ability to think along with the ideas and events being presented.

primary discourse   The language and ways of using language that are acquired first, in one's home and family.

primary research   Research that involves the direct investigation of a subject through field study (as in anthropology), controlled study (as in psychology), the study of primary textual materials (as in history or literature), or experiment (as in the sciences).

primary sources   Original texts, interviews, and other original, uninterpreted data that are used in primary research.

readability   A quality of written texts that concerns the extent to which they are easily accessible (and pleasing) to readers.

reader-response theory   A theory of reading that considers what readers bring to a text and the ways in which meaning is created in a transaction between reader and text.

reading as conversation   A concept of reading as a communicative interaction that takes place between a writer and a reader.

reading response   A genre of informal writing in which a reader explores his/her response to a written text.

recalling, representing, relating, reframing   Four ways in which readers might respond to a written text: by recalling and making connections to their own experiences; representing and restating what the writer has said; finding relationships to different experiences or different texts; or generating a larger theme or idea that can encompass several experiences or texts.

refereed journal   A scholarly journal for which peers in the relevant field review articles that are submitted, selecting only those they consider to be of high quality and to make a significant contribution to the field.

reference librarian   A librarian whose role is to guide users in accessing the library's materials.

reflective inquiry   A type of inquiry that involves reviewing and reflecting on what one has experienced or read.

research memo   A genre of informal writing that presents preliminary understandings gained from a particular research activity.

researcher's stance   Taking the perspective of a researcher who stands outside of a particular situation to observe what goes on there.

resituating texts   Using what was said in a text to explore new purposes and understandings that may be different from the original purposes and understandings of the writer.

review   A genre of speech or writing that involves a critical examination of something; a consideration of its quality.

rituals   Repeated patterns of words and/or actions performed by insiders to a setting.

search strategies   The different ways in which a library or Internet user works systematically to access information.

secondary discourses   The languages, styles of language, and ways of using language that are acquired or learned as people move out from their homes into a variety of other settings.

secondary research   Research that draws on the prior research of others.

secondary sources   Materials that present the interpretations and analyses that others have made of original data and materials.

setting   The location of a conversation, an event, or a piece of literature in time and space. A con-
cept used in literary analysis to consider the geographical and physical location, the cultural context, and the time in which the action takes place.

shared knowledge (<u>what</u>)   The information and ideas possessed by insiders to a setting or created by participants in a spoken or written conversation.

shared purpose (<u>why</u>)   The common intentions and goals negotiated by insiders to a setting or participants in a spoken or written conversation.

shared way to proceed (<u>how</u>)   The common assumptions and expectations for genres, styles, and other aspects of how communication should be carried out that are held by insiders to a setting or participants in a conversation.

situated literacy   A theoretical position arguing that literacy isn't the same in all settings but is practiced in different ways appropriate to different situations.

situation (<u>who</u>, <u>where</u>, <u>when</u>)   The setting and circumstances in which conversations take place and which help to shape spoken and written texts.

social practices   The practices and behaviors that are shared within a social group.

speech act   A way of using words to have particular effects and to accomplish particular purposes. Particular speech acts are characteristically used in particular settings.

speech event   A sequence of exchanges or speech acts that take place within one encounter. Such exchange sequences (such as those involved in ordering food) follow similar patterns in similar settings.

speech genre   A characteristic form and style of speech activity such as a joke or a story that is used to accomplish particular purposes within a setting.

style   The characteristic features of language used within a particular setting for particular purposes by a particular group.

style-shifting   Using different styles of language (such as a casual style or a more formal style) for different settings and purposes.

subculture   A separate, small group within a larger culture.

subject searches   A way of searching for information in libraries or on the Internet which involves looking in conventional subject categories.

summary   An account of the essence of an original passage or text; a shortened version that gives the main points.

syllabus   A written genre in academic courses that provides an overview of the course, its goals, the work required, and the means of evaluation, along with other useful information for the course participants.

syntax   The ways the words of a language are combined in phrases and sentences.

synthesis   A type of critical thinking in which material from different sources and from one's own or others' prior knowledge is brought together.

text   Any set of utterances, spoken or written, that can be represented in writing.

textual function (how)   The function of language that allows speakers to attend to and structure discourse and to carry out the ideational and interpersonal functions simultaneously in a discourse context.

theoretical paper   A genre of scholarly article in which the writer sets forth or discusses a theory or theories that are relevant to the field and that provide a larger explanation of individual examples and instances that have been observed.

theory   A set of ideas and principles that are set forth in an attempt to explain what might be behind a number of individual examples and instances of a phenomenon.

varieties of English   The different dialects, codes, and styles that are used by English speakers in different contexts.

versatility   The quality of being able to adapt one's ways of using language (among other characteristics) in ways appropriate to different settings.

voice/voices   In writing, a writer's distinctive way of writing as realized in particular contexts.

wider culture   The cultural knowledge that is shared among many members of the larger society, including the popular culture represented in music, movies, magazines, and television programs.

working concept   An idea or principle that is developed by seeing how it might apply to different examples and circumstances as opposed to learning a fixed definition.

writing as a process   The idea, developed from studying the practices of writers, that writing involves many different activities from generating ideas to editing final texts and that this process may be carried out differently in relationship to different purposes and contexts.

writing as conversation   A concept of writing as a communicative interaction that takes place between a writer and a reader.

BIBLIOGRAPHY

Anyon, Jean. "Social Class and the Hidden Curriculum of Work." *Journal of Education* 162 (Winter, 1980), 67–92.

Avicolli, Tommi. "He Defies You Still. The Memoirs of a Sissy." *Radical Teacher* 24 (1985): 4–5.

Bambara, Toni Cade. "The Lesson." *Gorilla, My Love.* New York: Random House, 1972.

Chafe, Wallace. "Integration and Involvement in Speaking, Writing, and Oral Literature." *Spoken and Written Language: Exploring Orality and Literacy.* Ed. Deborah Tannen. Norwood, NJ: Ablex, 1982.

Cisneros, Sandra. "Ghosts and Visions: Writing from Obsession." *The Americas Review* 15.1 (Spring 1987): 69–73.

Corrente, Richard. "The Dragon Court World." English 101, UMass/Boston 2001.

Dillard, Annie. *An American Childhood.* New York: Harper and Row, 1987.

Eggers, Dave. *A Heartbreaking Work of Staggering Genius.* New York: Vintage Books. 95–103.

Gangemi, Bryan. "The Birth of a New Writer." English 101, UMass/Boston, 2001.

Gee, James Paul. "Literacy, Discourse, and Linguistics." *Journal of Education* 171 (Winter, 1989), 5–10.

Halliday, M.A.K. *Language as Social Semiotic. The Social Interpretation of Language and Meaning.* London, Edward Arnold, 1978.

Heath, Shirley Brice. "Oral Traditions." *Ways with Words.* Cambridge, UK: Cambridge University Press, 1983. 149–57, 174–84, 184–89.

———. *Ways with Words. Language, Life and Work in Communities and Classrooms.* Cambridge, UK: Cambridge University Press, 1983.

hooks, bell. "Talking Back." *Talking Back.* Boston: South End Press, 1989.

Houlne, Juliette. "Women in Science, and Bio 112." English 101, UMass/Boston, 2000

Hymes, Dell. *Directions in Sociolinguistics: The Ethnography of Communication.* New York: Holt, Rinehart and Winston, 1972.

Jean, James. "Memoirs of an Indivisible Man." English 101, UMass/Boston, 2001.

Kang, Sophia. "An Exciting Debate." English 101, UMass/Boston, 2000.

Mellix, Barbara. "From Outside, In." In *Negotiating Academic Literacies.* Eds. Ruth Spack and Vivian Zamel. Mahwah, NJ: Lawrence Erlbaum, 1998. 61–70.

Moffat, Michael. *Coming of Age in New Jersey. College and American Culture.* New Brunswick NJ: Rutgers University Press, 1989.

O'Connor, Flannery. "The Catholic Novelist in the Protestant South." *Collected Works.* New York: Library of America, 1988. 853–54.

———. "Fiction is a Subject with History." *Collected Works.* New York: Library of America, 1988. 849–52.

———. "The Regional Writer." *Collected Works.* New York: Library of America, 1988. 843–48.

———. "The River." *The Complete Stories.* New York: Farrar, Straus and Giroux, 1972. 157–174.

Ortega, Vanessa. "Music as Lifestyle." English 101, UMass/Boston, 1999.

Rodriguez, Richard. "Aria. A Memoir of a Bilingual Childhood." *Hunger of Memory.* New York: Bantam, 1983. 12–28.

———. *Hunger of Memory.* New York: Bantam, 1983.

Rose, Mike. "I Just Wanna Be Average." *Lives on the Boundary.* New York: Penguin, 1990. 24–31.

———."The Politics of Remediation." *Lives on the Boundary.* New York: Penguin, 1990. 167–68, 174–99.

———. *Lives on the Boundary.* New York: Penguin, 1990.

Shillue, Edie. "Good Craic." *Peace Comes Dropping Slow.* Amherst: UMass Press, 2003.

Smith, Sean. "Language Memoir." English 101, UMass/Boston, 1999.

Spradley, James and Brenda Mann. "How to Ask for a Drink." *The Cocktail Waitress: Woman's Work in a Man's World.* New York: Wiley, 1975.

Street, Brian. *Social Literacies: Critical Approaches to Literacy Development, Ethnography, and Education.* New York: Longman, 1995.

Tan, Amy. "Mother Tongue." In *Across Cultures.* Eds. S. Gillespie and R. Singleton. Allyn & Bacon, 1993. 178–83.

Tannen, Deborah. *Talking Voices: Repetition, Dialogue, and Imagery in Conversational Discourse.* Cambridge, UK: Cambridge University Press, 1989.

Tobias, Sheila. "Introductory Physics: The 'Eric' Experiment." *They're Not Dumb, They're Different.* Tucson, Arizona: Research Corporation, 1990. 19–32.

Tsirelson, Dina. "Memoir." English 101, UMass/Boston, 2001.

Vargas, Pebely. "DSP Continues." English 101, UMass/Boston, 2000.

Wark, Jake. "Alone Among the Others." English 101, UMass/Boston, 2001.

———. "Means and Motives." English 101, UMass/Boston 2001.

Willis, Paul. "The Informal Group." *Learning to Labor.* New York: Columbia University Press, 1981. 22–30.

CREDITS

INDEX

Note: Entries in **boldface** indicate the pages on which the work itself appears.